Date Due

Aug '91

SEP 2 1	1991		
NOV 2 6	1991		
FEB 2 2	1992		
FEB 2 4	1993		
MAR 1 7	1993		
MAR 23/95			
ILL-NH-BA			
MAR 2 1 '95			
FEB 2 4	1996		
APR 1 1	1997		
NOV 2 6	1997		
FEB 2 0	2003		

ERRATUM

The captions on two of the maps have been transposed. The map on page xi shows the Prefectures today. The map on page xii shows the Provinces up to 1871.

THE JAPANESE ACHIEVEMENT

Other works by Hugh Cortazzi include

Isles of Gold: Antique Maps of Japan (1983)

Dr Willis in Japan 1862–1877: British Medical Pioneer (1985)

Victorians in Japan: In and around the Treaty Ports (1987)

Edited
Mary Crawford Fraser: A Diplomat's Wife in Japan: Sketches at the Turn of the Century (1982)

Mitford's Japan: The Memoirs and Recollections, 1866–1906, of Algernon Bertram Mitford, the First Lord Redesdale (1985)

With George Webb
Kipling's Japan: Collected Writings (1988)

Translated
Genji Keita: The Lucky One and Other Humorous Stories (1980)

SIDGWICK & JACKSON GREAT CIVILIZATIONS SERIES

THE JAPANESE ACHIEVEMENT

HUGH CORTAZZI

SIDGWICK AND JACKSON
LONDON

ST. MARTIN'S PRESS
NEW YORK

Copyright © 1990 by Hugh Cortazzi

First published in Great Britain in 1990
For Sidgwick & Jackson Ltd,
1 Tavistock Chambers, Bloomsbury Way, London WC1A2SG

First published in the United States of America in 1990

ISBN 0-283-99647-1 (Sidgwick and Jackson)
ISBN 0 312 04237 X (St Martin's Press)

Library of Congress Cataloging-in-Publication Data
Cortazzi, Hugh.

The Japanese achievement; a short history of Japan and its culture/Hugh
Cortazzi.
P.   cm. (Sidgwick & Jackson great civilization series)

Includes Bibliographical references.

1. Japan Civilization.   I. Title.   II. Series.

952 dc20   89 70071 CIP

Printed and bound in Great Britain by
Butler & Tanner Ltd, Frome and London
for Sidgwick & Jackson Limited

Contents

List of Illustrations

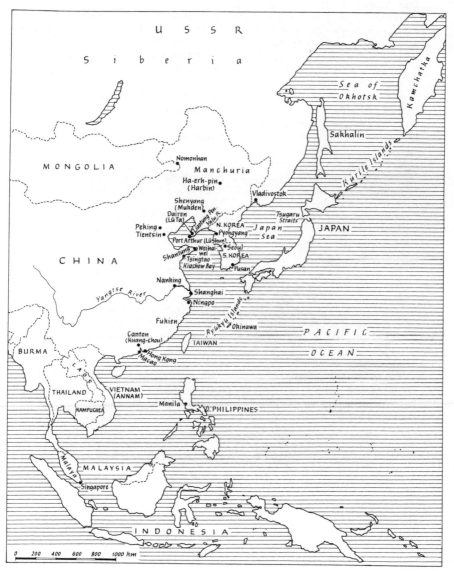

General map of Asia

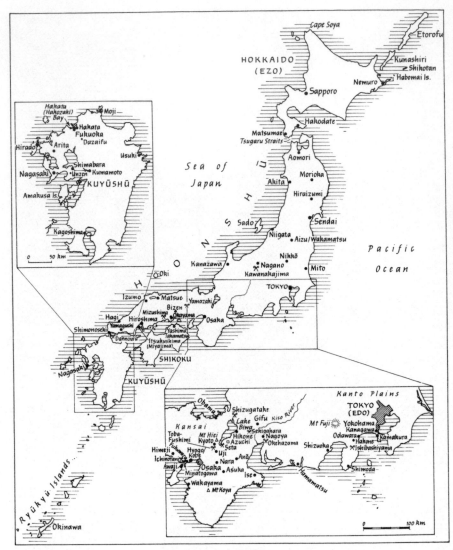

Cape Soya
Etorofu
HOKKAIDO
(EZO)
Kunashiri
Shikotan
Nemuro
Habomai Is.
Sapporo
Hakodate
Matsumae
Tsugaru Straits
Aomori
Morioka
Akita
Hiraizumi
Sea of
Japan
Sado
Niigata
Sendai
Aizu/Wakamatsu
Pacific
Ocean
Nikkō
Kanazawa
Nagano
Mito
Oki
Kawanakajima
Izumo
Matsue
TOKYO
Yamazaki
Bizen
Mizushima
Okayama
Hagi
Hiroshima
Osaka
Shimonoseki
Yamaguchi
Yashima
Dannoura
Takamatsu
Itsukushima
(Miyajima)
Nagasaki
SHIKOKU
KUYŪSHŪ

Hakata
(Hakozaki)
Bay
Moji
Hakata
Fukuoka
Dazaifu
Hirado
Arita
Usuki
Shimabara
Nagasaki
Unzen
Kumamoto
KUYŪSHŪ
Amakusa Is.
Kagoshima
0   50 km

Ryūkyū Islands
Okinawa

Kanto Plains
Obama
Shizugatake
Kiso River
TOKYO
(EDO)
Kansai
Lake
Gifu
Mt Fuji
Yokohama
Toba-
Fukushimi
Biwa
Sekigahara
Kanagawa
Mt Hiei
Hikone
Nagoya
Odawara
Hakone
Kamakura
Kyoto
Azuchi
Okehazama
Ishibashiyama
Himeji
Seta
Shizuoka
Ichinotani
Hyogo/
Kobe
Uji
Anō
Awaji
Nara
Ise
Hamamatsu
Minatogawa
Osaka
Asuka
Shimoda
Wakayama
△ Mt Koya
0   100 km

General map of Japan

Map showing Japanese provinces today (up to 1871)

Map showing Japanese prefectures today

Preface

When I was asked to write this book, I hesitated before agreeing. I am not a professional scholar or Japanologist. There is a wealth of material available about Japanese civilization in English and other foreign languages, and I wondered whether there was scope for yet another book. Had not the late Sir George Sansom in his book *Japan: A Short Cultural History*, first published in 1931, said it all so well? And there are excellent books about Japan, its history and culture by later able scholars such as Professors Donald Keene, Edward Seidensticker, Edward Reischauer, W. G. Beasley and the late Richard Storry. But perhaps there might be room for another book which summarized the history of Japan and its culture from the earliest times to the present day and tried to give equal weight to the classical and the modern.

One problem for anyone who tries in a single short volume to describe the civilization of another country, particularly one which covers such a wide range as Japan, is how to select the relevant facts and examples. I have tried to be as objective as possible, but some subjective and sweeping judgements have been unavoidable.

In the history of any country there are few definite turning-points. The division into periods which I have adopted generally follows historical convention. I have tried to make each chapter stand on its own, but periods inevitably overlap.

I should like to stress my debt to the many outstanding scholars who have written about Japanese history and culture. I am particularly indebted to the writings of the late Sir George Sansom, to the works of Donald Keene and to the books of all those scholars whose works I have consulted. I have tried to list under Suggestions for Further Reading the main works in English which I have consulted in preparing this history. I have also, of course, made use of works in Japanese, but as this book is intended for English readers I have not listed these.

Acknowledgements

I should like to thank in particular Dr Carmen Blacker and Dr Michael Loewe of Cambridge University, who have kindly read the typescript and made numerous helpful suggestions. Any errors which may have crept in are, however, entirely my responsibility.

I must also express my gratitude for much help, especially over copying the typescripts, to Mrs Margaret O'Malley, my secretary.

I should also like to extend my thanks to the following authors and Publishers for permission to quote/reproduce:
R. H. Brower and E. Miner, *Japanese Court Poetry*, London, The Cresset Press, 1961; Dorothy Britten, *A Haiku Journey: Bashō's Narrow Road to a Far Province*,

Tokyo, Kodansha International, 1980; Kaneko Mitsuharu, *Shijun* ('Poet') translated by A. R. Davies, University of Sydney East Asian Series, 1988; Donald Keene, *Anthology of Japanese Literature*, London, Allen & Unwin, 1986 and *Modern Japanese Literature from 1868 to the Present Day*, Rutland, Vt, and Tokyo, Tuttle, 1963; Lewis Mackenzie, *The Autumn Wind*, London, John Murray, 1957; Ivan Morris, *The Pillow Book of Sei Shonagon* and *The World of the Shining Prince*, London, Oxford University Press, 1964; Professor Yuasa Noriyuki, *The Narrow Road to the Deep North*, London, Penguin, 1966; P. G. O'Neil, *A Guide to Nō*, Tokyo and Kyoto, Hinoki Shōten, 1954 and 'A *Michiyuki* Passage from the *Taikeiki*', University of London, *Bulletin of the School of Oriental and African Studies*, Vol. XXXVI, 1973; Kato Shūichi, *A History of Japanese Literature; the First Thousand Years*, London, Macmillan and Paul Norbury, Vol. I, 1979; Arthur Waley, *The Nō Plays of Japan*, London, Allen & Unwin, 1921.

Special thanks are due to the Fuji Art Museum/Taplow court, the Japan Tourist Office, and Nihon Keizai Shimbun for the use of a photograph of a painting by Higashiyama Kaii, and the Nihon Mingeikan for the Munakata Shiko and Hamada Shoji photographs.

Introduction

The Japanese achievement in the arts, in literature and in social and economic development has been such that Japan must be counted among the great civilizations of the world.

The aim of this book is to relate briefly the history of Japanese culture (political, economic, social, literary and artistic) from the beginning of recorded time to the present day so that a fair assessment of the Japanese achievement can be made. This is a formidable task because of the range of facts which should be covered and because of the wealth of material available. This book does not pretend to be a piece of original research or to present any definitive interpretations. It is not intended to be yet another attempt at analysing Japanese character and society, but tries rather to explain the background to modern Japan. It will have filled a useful purpose if it introduces readers to the nature of Japanese culture and induces them to delve more widely in the many excellent books in English about Japan, its history and culture. Hopefully, it may also encourage the study of the Japanese language in its modern and classical forms.

Japanese civilization has been called by some observers imitative and derivative. On this basis they have argued that Japanese culture cannot be considered as being in the same class as that of ancient Greece, Rome or China. Such a judgement is not justified by the facts. The civilization of Japan is living and dynamic, and it is wrong to compare it with dead civilizations. In fact all modern civilizations owe much to classical and extraneous influences. The cultures of western Europe derive largely from Greece and Rome. That of North America has had even wider sources of inspiration.

Japan learned much from China and something from Korea and India. Japan has also been deeply influenced by the West. Japan has imitated, absorbed and adapted a great deal from abroad, but a Japanese dimension has always been added, and much has been improved and perfected in the process.

Japanese civilization like other cultures has gone through periods of relative stagnation, followed by revivals as the creative abilities of Japanese people have been reinvigorated. The river has never dried up but has flowed on ever changing. The banks have been widened as new streams have been added. Sometimes the waters have been clear and sparkling; at other times they have been muddy and turbulent.

One of the most significant elements in Japan's contribution to world civilization has been the Japanese sense of beauty and aesthetics. Major elements in the past were community with nature, restraint and harmony. Effect in literature and art has often been achieved by suggestion and outline rather than by explicit statements which leave little to the imagination. Japanese art has also reflected nature in its asymmetry, its curves and its abrupt changes. But Japanese art has not eschewed brilliant colours. The Japanese have produced many miniature masterpieces but, as in nature, grandeur can equally be found.

Japanese painting, whether in the Chinese style or in Japanese traditional forms, including magnificent and unforgettable screens, stands comparison with the greatest western painting, but it requires an eye attuned to different aesthetic standards. The Japanese print has made an outstanding contribution to Japanese and to western art.

The sculpture of Japan has been primarily Buddhist in inspiration. As early as the seventh and eighth centuries Japanese sculptors were producing statues which were not only technically superb but very beautiful and moving. Portraits, especially of Buddhist monks, developed in parallel with the carving and casting of Buddhist images, and many incomparable pieces have survived. The art of sculpture began to decline from about the fifteenth century, perhaps because religious inspiration was less powerful, but sculpture has remained a major art form in Japan.

Japanese ceramics are regarded by some critics as being inferior to Chinese; but even if Japanese artist craftsmen never made masterpieces to compare with those of the best T'ang and Sung pieces, ceramics are a living art in Japan, and over the ages Japanese potters have produced works of the finest quality and design which have every right to be regarded as great works of art. Japanese ceramics have been an inspiration to many in western countries and have been much imitated.

In its design of Buddhist temples, palaces and domestic buildings, Japanese architecture was initially inspired by Chinese models, but *Shintō* shrines had been built in accordance with indigenous, native traditions, and Chinese-inspired architecture soon took on a Japanese character which ensured that it harmonized with the Japanese landscape and climate. Although its forms remained relatively static for many centuries, it achieved a perfection of design adapted to the Japanese environment and aesthetic sense. The Japanese art of landscape gardening also had Chinese origins, but the great gardens of modern Japan, large and small, mirror the Japanese feel for nature and harmony.

The decorative arts, such as lacquer and metalwork, have achieved very high standards of craftsmanship and design in Japan and have been justly admired in the West.

Japanese literature was relatively unknown outside Japan until translations began to appear in the twentieth century. Since the Second World War, innumerable Japanese literary works, including novels, plays and poetry, have appeared in English translations. These have greatly enhanced the reputation and popularity of Japanese authors in the West. Japanese literature was a living force as early as the eighth century and reached one of its greatest apogees in the court literature of the Heian period in the eleventh century. Japanese poetry does not have the same range as that of the greatest western poets, but it has much charm and sensibility and deserves to be better known. Japanese novelists have shown that they can stand comparison with the giants of western fiction. Japanese dramas may not be easy to understand without a deep knowledge of the Japanese language, but Japanese actors in performances of traditional Japanese dramas can have a major impact on western audiences.

Buddhism took root in Japan and managed to coexist with the indigenous cults which came to be called *Shintō* (literally, 'the way of the gods'). Japanese Buddhism has been a major force for good and has been an inspiration to Japanese artists, sculptors and writers. Confucian thought imported from China has been of vital importance for Japanese ethics. But Japan has not produced any great or original philosophy. Nor has Japan contributed much so far to basic scientific discoveries, although Japanese scientists and engineers have been outstandingly successful in developing and applying technology imported from the West.

To the westerner, Japanese society, with its comparative homogeneity and discipline, may seem to discourage individuality, personality and originality. It has, however, achieved a high degree of harmony which has helped to ensure peaceful co-operative communities. Japanese traditions, ethical attitudes and conscious efforts by those in authority in Japan have also ensured that Japanese people have achieved very high standards of education.

In the field of government the Japanese managed to establish a relatively unified state as early as the seventh century. When the early structure, based loosely on Chinese models, broke down, forms of Japanese feudalism under a series of military oligarchies were developed. In the fifteenth and sixteenth centuries regional warlords caused a period of horrific civil strife. Semi-independent warlords were eventually suppressed, and between 1600 and 1868 Japan was governed by a tightly controlled feudal-style autocracy which all but closed Japan to contacts with the outside world. Japan's greatest political achievement was the way in which it modernized its society and structure in the final decades of the nineteenth century. Sadly this led on to a phase of imperialism which ended in her total defeat in 1945. The revival of Japan in the post-war era, the drafting of a new democratic constitution with a commitment to peace and the establishment of a modern parliamentary democracy (Japanese style) are major developments which hopefully can be made to last.

The most striking Japanese achievement for many people in the West today has been the country's economic growth and seemingly miraculous success. Until the reopening of Japan to the West in the second half of the nineteenth century, Japan was basically an agricultural society. An industrial revolution was, however, speedily accomplished, and Japanese industry was developed in support of Japanese military ambitions. At the end of the war in 1945 Japan's industry was in ruins, and her people were on the verge of starvation. Although her recovery would not have been possible without American aid and special procurements, Japan's subsequent economic successes have been largely due to the determination, application and ability of Japanese management and workers with assistance from the country's educated and dedicated bureaucracy.

The greatest blots on the Japanese record have been the ruthless, selfish and frequently treacherous behaviour of Japanese warlords and their minions throughout the centuries of feudalism; the cruel persecution of the Christians in the seventeenth century; the greed, ambition, self-deception and self-righteousness of the Japanese military in their depredations in Korea, China and South-East Asia; and their barbarous treatment of prisoners of war. But in judging these actions we should bear in mind that there are blots on the history of every country and that the Japanese people themselves also suffered greatly under the militarists. We should beware of ascribing the qualities of one group to the Japanese people as a whole and should remember the artistic, literary and human achievements of Japanese people over the last fifteen hundred years.

Note on Orthography and Pronunciation

Japanese words have been reproduced throughout in the Hepburn system of romanization (*romaji*). Long vowels have been marked, except where these appear as the first letter of a word that is capitalized. The long vowels in well-known place names such as Tokyo and Kyoto are not marked.

Japanese names are given throughout in the Japanese order; that is, surnames are shown first, and given names appear second. Where historical figures had more than one name, the name by which they are most commonly known is used.

The Wade–Giles system has generally been used for Chinese place and personal names, as the names in this spelling are still those best known outside China. But the Pinyin, or modern, Chinese spelling has where appropriate been added in brackets.

Japanese words should be pronounced without any stresses.

I

Origins

The Setting

Japan, as we know it today, consists of four main islands from Hokkaidō in the north, through the main island of Honshū, with Shikoku lying on its southern flank, to Kyūshū in the south. Off the coasts of the main islands there are numerous smaller islands which are inhabited by people of Japanese origin or race. The most important of these are the Ryūkyū (or Loo-Choo) Islands to the south of Kyūshū, including the main island of Okinawa. Four islands or groups of islands off the north-east of Hokkaidō in the Kurile chain (Etorofu, Kunashiri, Shikotan and Habomai), which the Japanese claim to be part of Japan, have been under Soviet occupation since 1945. The territory of Japan today accordingly stretches from latitude 45° 33′ north at the northern tip of Cape Soya to below 25° south on the southernmost island in the Ryūkyū chain, that is, just above the tropic of Cancer. The Japanese islands form an arc from the cool and temperate north of Hokkaidō to the semi-tropical islands in the southern Ryūkyū Islands.

The Japanese islands come under the influence of the Asian continental system, but this is tempered by a warm current (the *Kuroshio*, literally 'black tide') which splits and flows up the west and east coasts of Japan. Winters in Hokkaidō are severe, and heavy snows fall along the western side of the main mountain ranges in Honshū. On the eastern side of the mountains, winters tend to be cold but dry and sunny. Summers are hot and humid, especially in central and southern Japan, with a distinct rainy season in June and July. The Japanese islands, especially Kyūshū, Shikoku and Honshū, also lie in the path of many typhoons spawned in areas to the south.

Some 75 per cent is mountainous. The mountains are steep and sharp. They resulted from volcanic eruptions. Off the eastern seaboard there is a deep sub-marine trench. The huge and sudden differences of height and depth cause great stresses and strains which result in numerous earthquakes. These have often caused severe damage and destruction. There are few natural plains. The largest is the Kantō plain in the area round the modern city of Tokyo. Another relatively flat area lies in what is called the Kansai in the Osaka area. Rivers are generally short and fast running. Flooding has been a serious problem, especially in the rainy season or when the winter snows melt. The climate is suitable for wet rice cultivation, although it has only been economic in Hokkaidō with the development of modern strains. But the hilly character of the land has meant that terracing has been essential for rice cultivation, and allocation of water supplies has been a key factor in the development of Japanese agriculture.

In the Pleistocene era (perhaps some 150,000 years ago) the Japanese islands were connected to the mainland of Asia by land bridges, and what is now the

1

Japan Sea was once a huge lake. For this reason the flora and fauna of Japan and the Asian continent are similar. However, following the end of the Ice Ages there was a rise in temperatures; sea levels rose, and the land bridges were severed. A distinct difference between the flora and fauna of northern Honshū and Hokkaidō was noted in the second half of the nineteenth century by Thomas Wright Blakiston (1832–91), a British resident of Hakodate. The divide has since been termed the Blakiston line.

The Japanese islands have only limited mineral resources, most of which are no longer economic to mine. Coal, which was found in workable quantities in Hokkaidō and Kyūshū, was of low calorific value. Copper, gold and silver as well as iron ore were also mined, and small quantities of oil have been tapped, especially in what is now the Niigata area.

The People

Hominids or prehistoric man came to the area perhaps some 200,000 years ago. It is not clear whether these were the ancestors of the present inhabitants of Japan or whether the Japanese today are descended from later migrations. Probably the latter is correct. The Japanese race is generally considered to be of Ural-Altaic stock. They are Mongoloid, but with some admixture from the south, from south China, South-East Asia or Polynesia. The Japanese were not, however, the only indigenous inhabitants of the Japanese islands. The Ainu, who now represent a tiny minority of the inhabitants of Hokkaidō and have almost disappeared as a separate race, are of an entirely different racial origin from the Japanese, being more hairy and less yellow-skinned.

The Ainu have sometimes been considered Caucasoid or Australoid, but recent studies suggest racial ties with some of the Uralic populations of Siberia. They were dominant at least in northern Honshū until the development of the Japanese state some twelve to thirteen hundred years ago. There may indeed have been groups of people similar to the Ainu as far south as Kyūshū, where apparently some fifteen hundred years ago they posed a threat to the increasing Japanese race. In Kyūshū such tribes were known as *kumaso*. Hokkaidō was known until the second half of the nineteenth century as Ezo or Ezochi, the territory of the Ezo or barbarians.

Language

The genetic origins of the Japanese language have not been clearly established. It is quite different from the language of the Ainu, but has syntactical resemblances to Korean. It also has some similarities to Altaic languages. There seem in addition to have been Malayo-Polynesian influences on Japanese vocabulary. (One feature of Japanese, which is found in Polynesian languages, is the formation of some plurals by repetition; for example, *hito* = man, *hitobito* = men.) However, the only really kindred language is that spoken in the Ryūkyū Islands, which can be regarded as a derivative of Japanese with an admixture of Chinese.

Japanese is polysyllabic and agglutinative, almost without stress and tones, and is thus totally different to Chinese, which is monosyllabic, tonal and without inflexions. In vocabulary and even in structure Japanese was enriched and changed when writing was introduced from China in the fifth century (see Chapter II). The language has been again transformed by the adoption of innumerable western words, primarily of English origin. It is impossible to speak of 'pure Japanese'.

The Stone Age: the Jōmon Era

Towards the end of the Pleistocene period (that is, the Ice Age), wide coastal shelves were exposed. Archaeologists believe that some early Stone Age men lived in these areas. Some chipped stone tools, found in Japan, have been ascribed to dates before 10,000 BC, but little is known about these very early times in Japan. However, evidence has been found of an early Stone Age culture which began to develop in Japan after about 10,000 BC. Some two thousand shell mounds or kitchen middens have been found, particularly around Tokyo Bay and rivers in the Kantō plain, from which archaeologists have been able to reconstruct some idea of how the Japanese of this period lived. Warm coastal currents made natural breeding grounds for shellfish, and these provided a good source of food. Stone Age men in Japan also caught fish and hunted and ate wild animals, including birds, deer, wild boar and bears. In addition, they ate nuts and wild berries; but they did not, at least in the early periods, grow any crops.

Stone Age men in Japan lived in small communities in pit houses of square shape and simple construction. Five or six posts were used to provide props for a shelter; an open centre was left for a fireplace. They used tools of stone and bone. They probably wore simple clothes made of mulberry bark and primitive ornaments made of stones or bones. From these developed the *magatama* or curved jewels which became important symbols later in Japan. They also made wicker baskets. But the making of pottery was the distinctive feature of Japanese Stone Age culture after about 10,000 BC. Pots were used for both the storage and the preparation of food. These pots, known as *jōmon* ('rope-pattern pots'), were made by rolling a twisted coil or cord over the surface of the pot when it was half dried. Jōmon has become the name of the period. Archaeologists distinguish a number of phases of Jōmon. The initial and early phases lasted from 10,000 to 3,500 BC, the middle period to about 2,000 or 2,500 BC and the late and final periods to about 300 BC.

In addition to making pots for cooking and storage, the Jōmon people made numerous pottery figurines. The first of these were flat and two dimensional, but in later periods larger and more fully formed images were made. The figurines were mostly of females with large breasts and stomachs. This and the fact that stone phalluses have also been found suggests that they were intended as fertility symbols. The figurines, which should not be confused with the *haniwa* of a later period, have rarely been found in an unbroken state; this would seem to imply that they were made to be broken in some kind of ceremony. They may have been intended as substitutes for living people, from whom evil could be transferred. Certainly the life of the Jōmon people seems to have been a hard one, and broken bones were commonplace. In the late Jōmon period stone circles were built, especially in northern Japan, apparently for burial and fertility rites. The

3

most notable of these circles is at Oyu in Akita prefecture, where numerous stones were formed into two concentric circles in a sun-dial pattern around a standing pillar. It seems probable that a form of shamanism developed and that the Jōmon people felt a fear of the dead and their spirits.

The population increased as the climate warmed up following the Ice Age, and was concentrated in the coastal belt. Settlements were later established in the foothills of the mountains, but a deterioration in the climate forced the population back to the coastal areas, and the population decreased to less than half the peak reached in the middle period. In the final period, rice cultivation seems to have been introduced from the continent of Asia into Kyūshū, where rice was first raised in dry seed beds or swamps. However, the Jōmon culture was essentially a primitive one based on hunting, fishing and gathering.

The Bronze Age: the Yayoi Era

The primitive rice culture which developed in Kyūshū gradually changed into wet rice cultivation and spread to other parts of Japan. The need to share out available water resources forced the creation of village communities; and, as settlements evolved, some form of authority was required. It is not clear to what extent the development of agriculture in Japan was due to methods imported from China or whether it resulted from a wave of Mongoloid immigrants from the Asiatic mainland. But it is clear both from artefacts found in Japan and from early Chinese records that contacts with China grew in significance as the centuries passed, and it is probable that at least a nucleus of immigrants controlled many of the communities. Because of archaeological finds in an area near to Tokyo University at Yayoi-chō, the period has come to be called the Yayoi period.

An important feature of the new culture was the use of bronze and later of iron tools and weapons. Many Chinese bronze mirrors were imported and these led the Japanese to make mirrors of their own, but bronze was also used to make weapons, including double-edged swords, spears and halberds, helmets and bells. The bronze bells known as *dōtaku* are thought to have been developed indigenously, because they are generally unlike Korean or Chinese bells. The *dōtaku* may originally have been intended to be used to make sounds, as early examples had clappers, but later *dōtaku* could hardly have been so used and were probably made for ceremonial purposes. They range in size from about five inches in height to almost four feet. They were open at one end and oval in form, with semi-circular handles. They usually have flanges on the two side seams and have elaborate designs on the outer surface. Designs included various patterns and figures such as people and animals. One *dōtaku* shows scenes of hunting and pounding rice as well as of a raised storehouse. One suggestion is that the bells were offerings to the nature spirits to induce them to bring about better harvests. Another theory is that they were used to cover phallic symbols along the sides of roads; but they have usually been discovered in buried caches, and no firm conclusions about their origin can be reached.

The pottery of the Yayoi period was mainly made on the wheel, and there are fewer types than in the Jōmon period. Styles of decoration are also less varied; techniques used included scraping and incising with a piece of wood, combing and smoothing with a wet cloth. Yayoi pottery was reddish in colour and fairly thin. The various types of pottery of this period are thought to be continental in origin, but Yayoi pottery probably developed naturally from the former Jōmon pottery with some continental influences. A few clay figurines continued to be made, and some human-headed jars have been found. Pottery jars were also used to bury the dead, although in the earlier part of the period bodies had been buried in cist graves formed by a number of thin slabs of stone.

The main sources of information about the nature of Japanese society during this period are Chinese records[1] made in the light of Chinese contacts with Japan (see Chapter II). The *Hou Han Shu* – that is, the history of the Later Han (AD 25–220) – compiled in the fourth and fifth centuries, mentions the land of the 'Wa'. The Chinese character used (倭) means a dwarf and is different from the character with the same reading which the Japanese use (和) to mean 'peace' or 'harmony' and which is used to denote Yamato, the area to the south of the modern Kyoto. Japan was said to consist of a hundred communities. One of these, the Nu (or Na no Agata, near Hakata in Kyūshū), is recorded as having sent tribute to the Han court. The chronicle mentions a country called 'Yamatai', which Japanese historians have endeavoured to identify with Yamato; but it is not possible to prove this, and some historians identify Yamatai with a part of Kyūshū. The *Wei Chih* (*Wei zhi*) – that is, the record the Wei (221–65) – gives a rather fuller account. Between 238 and 247 when the Wei dynasty was dominant in north China, embassies were apparently sent from Japan to the Chinese governor in Korea, resident near the modern city of Seoul. Return visits were made probably to Kyūshū, and the accounts in the chronicle appear to have been made on the basis of reports from these visitors. The chronicle speaks of 'thirty countries' which seem to have been governed by tribal chieftains who had come together under the rule of a queen who lived as a sorceress and priestess and who apparently governed by spiritual power. She is referred to as 'Pimiko', which Japanese have suggested as being the same as *himeko*, a word used for 'princess' or 'sun princess'. The chronicle declares that 'the social customs are not lewd'. Divination was a common practice. Various taboos were observed, and ritual practices, including purification after mourning for the dead, were followed. The society was well ordered, and class distinctions were maintained. Taxes were collected and markets held under the supervision of officials. The queen was said to have been buried under a great mound, and over a hundred male and female attendants 'followed her to the grave'. (The so-called Kofun or 'burial mound' period began in Japan in about the year 300.)

The Iron Age and the Kofun or Burial Mound Era

Archaeology is the only reliable source of information about prehistoric Japan up to about the second century AD. The Chinese chronicles then begin to provide some information of value, but archaeology remains the most reliable source until about the sixth century, when the Chinese language, which had been brought to Japan by scholars from Korea (see Chapter II), ensured that records could be kept. The chronicles produced at that time throw some light on the earlier period, although much of the information is of doubtful reliability, being based on oral tradition.

The Yayoi period was followed by what archaeologists call the Kofun or old tomb period. Various dates are given for this period. It can be said to have begun around 250–300 and lasted into the seventh century, perhaps until about 700. The most striking characteristic of this period, from the archaeological point of view, was the construction of large grave mounds to provide burial places for Japanese chieftains of the time. The fact that huge resources of labour could be made available for such building and digging implies that the agricultural economy, which had developed during the Yayoi period, had made notable progress. An important factor in this had been the increasing use of iron implements. But at least equally significant was the achievement of a tightly organized social system such as that described in the *Wei Chih* chronicle.

Over ten thousand tombs from this period have been discovered. The early tombs were mainly located on hillsides. Later tombs were built in prominent places in the middle of plains, and as suitable sites became less easily available tombs were again located on hillsides. While grave mounds have been found in areas north of the modern Tokyo, the greatest concentrations are in northern Kyūshū and in the Kansai, south of Kyoto. A number of different shapes were used, including round and square mounds, but the type which is regarded as the classical form was the so-called 'keyhole' type (or *zenpōkōen*, meaning 'square front and round back'). This consists of a circular mound with a rectangular projection. The largest tomb of this type is situated near Osaka and dates from the first half of the fifth century. Surrounded by three moats, it covers approximately 39 hectares and is some 821 metres in length. It is thought to be the tomb of the leader known in the earliest Japanese chronicles as the Emperor Nintoku (dates uncertain).

The tombs provide much evidence about the life of the time. The quantity of metal horse trappings, including iron bits, stirrups and nose guards, as well as bronze horse bells and other ornaments, testifies to the important role which horses had come to play in the development of Japanese society. Horses also feature in many of the wall paintings to be found in the corridors leading to the burial chamber.

The most interesting feature of the tombs for the historian are the *haniwa* (literally, clay rings) which were found on the surface and around the great tombs. *Haniwa*, which can be nearly five feet tall, were made in various forms. The most common are cylinders, but they also include numerous reproductions of animals, buildings and human figures. They were made of a reddish clay also used for ordinary household pots. They were fired at low temperatures. Clay was applied to form human features and to represent clothing and other ornaments, although eyes and mouths were usually indicated by cutting through to the interior of the pot, which was hollow. The cylinders and the figures were half embedded into the earth, presumably for stability and to mark off the area. *Haniwa* were made by a special group of potters called the Hajibe whose pots are known as *haji* ware.

There has been much debate about the origin of *haniwa*. According to an account given in the *Nihonshoki*, produced in 720 (see page 7), they were intended as substitutes for sacrificial victims, that is, attendants of the dead who were buried alive to keep them company and attend them in the next world. But no evidence

6

has been found in the course of archaeological excavations to justify this theory. It has also been suggested that the origins may have been Chinese, but the methods used to make them and the way they were placed outside tombs in Japan were so unlike the Chinese system of funerary figures that the connection, if any, seems at best remote.

The animals most commonly depicted in *haniwa* are horses which usually look intelligent. Chickens are the next most frequent, followed by deer, wild boar and dogs. The wild boar appear sinister, while the dogs look friendly. The figures are more frequently male than female. Faces are stylized but quite human. Many different kinds of hats, clothing, fans, arms and armour as well as jewellery, including *magatama*, are shown. Many of the faces have been touched up with paint.

Haniwa in the shape of houses provide a rich source of information about the living conditions of the people of the time. Although some *haniwa* suggest that the pit dwellings of an earlier age were still to be found, others indicate a considerable sophistication in building techniques. Many models of two-storey buildings have survived. Elaborate roofs are also shown; some indeed are so fanciful that it is difficult to imagine how they could have been placed in a practical form on a large building. In fact the dwellings of the chieftains seem to have been mainly single-storeyed, with a hipped-gable roof, but more elaborate structures were probably made as palaces and as shrines for the gods. Some of the ancient shrines have hardly changed their appearance over the centuries, but it is not clear how far their original styles were influenced by Buddhist architectural designs imported into Japan from the fifth century.

Haji ware was not the only pottery in use in this period. *Sue* ware was placed inside the tombs and has been termed ceremonial ware. *Sue* ware was introduced from Korea. It is a generally a greyish pottery, but colours vary from brown through a bluish grey to black. It is thin and brittle, and was fired at a high temperature. Glazing techniques did not reach Japan until about the seventh century, but occasionally a salt-like glaze appears on *sue* pots as a result of very high temperatures achieved in the kiln. It was made on a fast wheel. *Shino* ware is also mentioned but does not seem to have been in such extensive use as *haji* and *sue* ware. Glass bowls found in the tomb of the Emperor Ankan (sixth century) were probably imported into Japan, but by that time glass-making was developing in Japan.

Legends and Early Histories

The oral traditions and legends, preserved in the earliest written histories of Japan, help to put some life into the bare facts revealed by archaeology, but in the absence of early contemporary records the accounts which have been preserved have to be treated with reserve. Much would seem to be based on imagination and is clearly mythological. These early histories were the *Kojiki*,[2] or 'Records of Ancient Matters', which was written down in 712, and the *Nihonshoki*,[3] also called the *Nihongi* or 'Chronicles of Japan', which was produced in 720. The two accounts are similar in most material respects, but the *Nihonshoki* takes the story of Japan up to 697, whereas the *Kojiki* concludes its account around the end of the fifth century. There is said to have been an earlier chronicle known as the *Kujiki*, or 'Chronicle of Old Matters', which was allegedly compiled in 620, but this did not survive a fire in 645. The *Kojiki* was edited in the eighteenth century by the Japanese scholar Motoori Norinaga (1730–1801). Motoori was a Japanese nationalist opposed to Chinese ideas and he attempted to turn the text into a nationalist tract which also promoted the native religion which had come to be called Shintō or way of the gods (see page 10).

The myths about the gods, the creation of the Japanese islands and the development of the early Japanese state are confused and frequently inconsequential. They may be summarized as follows. After the creation of numerous gods of no subsequent importance two deities, brother and sister, called Izanagi ('the male who invites') and Izanami ('the female who invites') were given by the other deities a jewelled spear which they thrust down from the bridge of heaven into the brine and created the island of Onogoro. They then went round a pillar together; but as Izanami, the female, spoke first, and this was thought to be unlucky, they did it again with Izanagi in the lead. They then copulated, and Izanami gave birth to the various islands of the Japanese archipelago. They next produced various other gods, but Izanami died in giving birth to the fire god. Izanagi pursued Izanami into Hades and implored her to return with him. While Izanami was consulting with the demons in Hades, Izanagi impatiently bit off one of the teeth of the comb in his hair, lit it and went in to find Izanami. She had turned into an ugly corrupt mass and chased Izanagi away. Izanagi decided to purify himself by bathing in a stream. New deities were born from the articles of clothing which he threw down, and other deities were born from his body. The most important of these, emerging from his left eye, was the sun goddess, Amaterasu-o'mikami-no-Mikoto. From his nostrils the god Susano-ō-no-Mikoto – whom Basil Hall Chamberlain, the scholar who first translated the *Kojiki* into English in 1883, refers to as the 'Impetuous Male Deity' – was created and was charged with the dominion of the sea. Amaterasu and Susano-ō had a violent quarrel, and Susano-ō, having destroyed the banks of his sister's paddy fields (a particularly heinous crime in a primitive agricultural society), broke through the roof of her palace, while Amaterasu was sitting at work weaving with her maidens, and let fall 'a heavenly piebald horse which he had flayed with a backward flaying'. Amaterasu was so shocked by this behaviour that she withdrew into a cave and caused the world to become dark. She could only be lured out by an entertainment including a lewd dance in which one of the female deities pulled out the nipples of her breasts and pushed down her skirt string as far as her private parts. (Chamberlain with typical Victorian prudery translated this and other explicitly sexual references into Latin.) Amaterasu remained in heaven and became the prime deity in the Japanese pantheon with her shrines at Ise.

The bulk of the remaining legends about the time of the gods are concerned with Susano-ō, who was banished from heaven for his misbehaviour towards Amaterasu after being fined a 'thousand tables', that is, trays of offerings, by the other gods. Susano-ō went off to the Izumo area of Japan, where he killed an eight-forked serpent. His grandson was the god O-Kuni-Nushi-no-Mikoto, who came to be regarded as the god of rice. Various legends about the gods of Izumo are followed by an account of how Amaterasu determined to bestow the sovereignty of Japan on one of her children. After three unsuccessful embassies to Izumo to arrange matters, a fourth was successful, and the monarch of Izumo promised to serve the new sovereign if a palace or shrine were built for him – this was the great shrine of Izumo. The story then turned to Kyūshū, where the gods built a palace on Mount Takachiho. One of the gods married his aunt and had four sons, two of whom moved against the chiefs of Kibi and Yamato in Honshū. One of these brothers was called Kamu-Yamato-Ihare-Biko, who was eventually given the title of Emperor Jimmu or Jimmu *Tennō*. According to the *Kojiki*, he was the first 'Emperor' of Japan and allegedly reigned from the year 660 BC. Even if there was such a tribal chieftain, the date is clearly fictitious.

The chronicles thereafter concentrated on the story of the Yamato area, but the subsequent stories of the early 'Emperors' are of limited historical value. No dates are given in the *Kojiki*, and the dating given in the *Nihonshoki* is wholly unreliable, some of the early 'Emperors' allegedly reigning for unbelievably long periods or to impossibly old age. The Emperor Kōan, for instance, was said to have reigned from 392 to 291 BC and to have lived to 123 years old. Dates given for before AD 400 can only be regarded as approximate.

The most memorable legend is that of Prince Yamato-Takeru-no-Mikoto, the son of the Emperor Keikō, the traditional dates of whose reign were 71–130, but who probably lived in the 4th century AD. The Emperor Keikō is reputed to have achieved the feat of marrying his own great-great-granddaughter. Yamato-Takeru, after killing his elder brother in the privy, because he failed to turn up for meals at his father's table, was sent off to Kyūshū to subdue the *kumaso*, the barbarian tribes, but before setting off visited his aunt, the high priestess of the great shrine of Izumo. When he reached the *kumaso* stronghold he found that preparations were being made for a banquet. He then unfastened and combed his hair so that he looked like a girl and dressed in his aunt's robes. The two *kumaso* chiefs were attracted by this 'maiden', and he was asked to sit between them. At the height of the banquet the prince stabbed the elder chieftain through the chest and chasing the younger one out of the room thrust his sword up the chief's backside. Impressed by the prince's bravery, the chief gave him the name of Yamato-Takeru and was then slashed to pieces 'like a ripe melon'. After various other adventures he was sent by his father to the east to subdue the *emishi*, a group of 'barbarians' probably similar to the *kumaso* of Kyūshū. He married the Princess Ototachibana on the way to carry out his mission but died on his way back to the capital, having been deceived by a deity. According to the legend Prince Yamato-Takeru was transformed after his death into a white bird. Despite his blood-thirsty character, Yamato-Takeru came to be regarded as a Japanese romantic hero, because he died in tragic circumstances and because of his alleged love of poetry.

The earliest Japanese state seems to have been established after a struggle for hegemony between various groups, particularly in Kyūshū and on the north-west coast area of Honshū around Izumo. The conflict appears to have been won by the Kyūshū people under a line of chieftains who were given the title of *Tennō*, now translated as Emperor, and who claimed descent from the sun goddess Amaterasu. They managed to conquer the area known as Yamato in the Kansai, perhaps in some form of alliance with the Izumo people. The frequent references to expeditions against the *kumaso* people in Kyūshū and the *emishi* in the east suggest that strife was fairly continuous and that the hegemony of the dominant groups, who made their headquarters in Yamato, was not achieved without great difficulties.

The establishment of Yamato paramountcy does not seem to have been due to outstanding leadership or military prowess. It appears to have been more the consequence of an astute balancing of forces. Significantly the chieftains who became *Tennō* rarely if ever seem to have exercised real power, but depended for their position on their priestly status resulting from their descent from the sun goddess. Effective control lay with the successive families which, by marriage, assassination and plots, had the imperial family in their grasp and used it to further their own ends. Thus began the process of indirect rule which became such a feature of Japanese governments in later centuries.

The histories record that in the time of the Emperor Seimu in the early part of the fourth century governors of the provinces were appointed, presumably in an effort to confirm the authority of the dominant group. Under the next Emperor, Chūai, in the middle of the fourth century further efforts were made to subdue the *kumaso*.

The Structure of Early Japanese Society

There seem to have been three main social groupings. The *uji*, which is usually translated as 'clan', although this term is rather misleading, were not so much a large family group as a collection of families which were bound by various ties of loyalty to a leader of the main family, who came to be known as the *uji-no-kami*. They also 'worshipped' a tutelary deity who somewhat confusingly was known as the *uji-gami* or *uji-kami*. The *uji-no-kami* was both the leader and the chief priest. Significantly the original Japanese word for government, *matsurigoto*, meant 'celebrating' or 'worshipping'.[4] The members of the *uji* were the ruling class. They depended on certain occupational groups which formed hereditary corporations or guilds. These were known as *be* or *tomo* and performed prescribed functions. The *Imibe* or *Imbe* were professional abstainers or performers of rituals. The *Mononobe* were armorers; the *Oribe* were weavers, the *Urabe* diviners, the *Hasebe* and the *Suebe* potters, the *Sakabe* brewers or sake (rice wine) makers, the *Tanabe* rice field workers, the *Kibe* woodcutters and the *Amabe* fishermen. Below these groups were the *yatsuko* (*yakko*) or slaves who acted as servants. Titles (*kabane*) given to the *uji-no-kami* included *miyatsuko* for those closest to the ruling family, *omi* for other grandees and *muraji* for lesser grandees.

The Early Religion: Shintō

The religious practices of the early Japanese, which were entirely indigenous in origin, seem to have been a primitive form of animism, combined with an element of ancestor worship. The *kami*, which for want of a more appropriate word has come to be translated as god or deity, were beings or spirits akin to humans, who lived, made love and died like ordinary mortals. The word *kami* indeed meant 'above', 'head' or 'superior', and the translation of *kami* as 'god' is at best an approximation. The Japanese pantheon is shadowy and confused in comparison with that of ancient Greece and Rome. The account of Izanagi's visit to Hades has been contrasted with the story of Orpheus, but there is no real comparison. Many of the Japanese gods referred to in the *Kojiki* have been forgotten, and most of the popular Japanese shrines today, apart from the great shrines at Ise and Izumo, are dedicated to later gods such as the warrior god Hachiman, who is supposed to be a personification of the legendary Emperor Ojin. Inari, generally regarded as the rice god, was probably originally Ukemochi-no-Kami, who is worshipped with Amaterasu at Ise. Images of Japanese gods were not made, and *kami* were not considered to have a shape of their own. They did, however, reside in vessels or objects, which came to be known as *shintai* or *go-shintai* (literally, 'god body'). The *shintai* of Amaterasu is a mirror which symbolizes one of the items used to entice her out of the cave (see above). Natural features such as mountains, trees and waterfalls could also be *shintai*.

One aspect of early Japanese religion which has been maintained was the emphasis placed on ritual purification after such polluting events as birth, menstruation and death (see, for instance, Izanagi's attempt to purify himself by bathing in a stream after he had visited Hades). Pollution also occurred if crimes such as murder or drawing blood were committed. The Japanese word *kega*, usually translated as 'wound', can also be used to mean defilement. The word *tsumi*, which is now translated as 'sin', meant something concealed and implied shame. There was no real ethical content in early Shintō, and it is doubtful how much there has been in later developments.

One important feature of the early religion, which became a fundamental part of Japanese culture, was the feeling for nature. Nature was both bountiful and beautiful, but natural disasters were frequent. These were thought to be the result of the misbehaviour of man or of the gods, and the gods had to be propitiated. Shrines (*miya* or *jinja*) were built on mountain tops, by waterfalls and in other places of natural beauty. They were and still are generally indicated by a *torii* or gateway. The Chinese characters used for *torii* mean 'bird' and 'to be'. They were almost certainly adopted because of their sounds rather than their meanings and they do not indicate that this symbol had anything to do with birds. The origin of the *torii* is unknown. The basic structure is two columns surmounted by two cross-beams.

Norito or ritual prayers of thanksgiving or supplication, such as for a good harvest, appear to have been in fairly general use, and the most important ceremonies were all connected with agricultural events such as rice planting and tasting the new fruits. Fertility in an agricultural economy was all important. So it is not surprising that phallic symbols were common and phallicism was an important part of the early religion.

Worship, apart from the reading of prayers, involved bowing and making an offering. Offerings, in addition to food and drink, took the form of a wand with a piece of cloth or paper attached. These *gohei*, as they came to be called, became sanctified. Purification was carried out not only by washing but also by the sprinkling of salt and the waving of ceremonial wands by the priests over the heads of the worshippers.

It is not known when the first shrines were built, but the great shrine of Izumo seems to have been one of the earliest. The great shrines at Ise are also of very early design. They are still pulled down every twenty years and rebuilt in exactly the same way as they have been for centuries.

The native cults were only called Shintō after the adoption of Chinese words and modes of thought (see Chapter II). Shintō is the Sinico-Japanese reading of two characters which can also be read as *kami* or 'god' and *michi* or 'way'.

Until the fifth century AD Japan was a primitive agricultural society with at best a rudimentary system of government. Its religious practices amounted to little more than an animist fertility cult without coherent philosophy or ethical system. Its traditions were little more than blood-thirsty and crude myths. It had no written language and no literature, although some poetic songs were preserved in the oral memory of a few. Its buildings were simple wooden structures. Art was limited to the making of unglazed and simple pottery, the modelling of pottery figures and the making of increasingly complex metal items in bronze and iron. The early development of plastic arts of this kind was an augury of future artistic achievements, but Japan before the arrival of Chinese influence and language, as well as of the Buddhist religion, had no real claim to a civilization of its own.

II

The Beginnings of Japanese Civilization: The Impact of China and Buddhism

The arrival in Japan, at the beginning of the fifth century, of the scribe Wani from Korea marked an important turning-point in Japanese history, but it did not lead to a sudden revolution. The development of a written language took two to three centuries. The first Japanese history and the first work which can be regarded as a piece of Japanese literature, the *Kojiki*, was not produced until the beginning of the eighth century. Centuries passed before Chinese ideas were fully adapted to meet Japanese needs. It took many generations before Buddhism became an essential part of Japanese life. Before summarizing the history of these three centuries in which Japan passed from prehistoric semi-chaos to the beginnings of civilized society, three of the most significant influences on Japanese life and history must be briefly described.

The Japanese Language and the Development of Writing in Japan

The Japanese language, which had no indigenous script of its own, is polysyllabic, consisting today of forty-eight basic sounds, which may be defined as being the five vowels and the consonants k, s, t, n, h, m, y, r and w followed by a vowel (although yi, ye and wu are excluded). The single consonant 'n' was added later because the final 'n' in Chinese words, as pronounced by the Japanese, did not exist in ancient Japanese. The consonant 't' is subject to an inflexion, becoming 'd' or 'z'; 's' also can become a 'z'; 'k' can become a 'g', and 'h' a 'b' or a 'p' (hu came to be pronounced as fu), thus adding considerably to the number of different syllables available. The early Japanese vocabulary was limited, and the constructions and inflexions were complicated and imprecise. Ancient Japanese also used more vowels than there are in modern Japanese.

Chinese is monosyllabic and tonal, with more concise constructions; it also had developed a rich vocabulary by the time the Japanese came in contact with the language. Instead of a phonetic script, the Chinese adopted ideograms to express their basic ideas, but to these basic ideograms they attached other ideograms or parts of ideograms to indicate additional meanings and sounds. The characters, as the ideograms came to be called, for tree (木) and for mouth (口) may not be immediately recognizable as pictures of trees and mouths, but it is easy to see how they developed from pictures of a tree and a mouth. Two trees together (林) mean a wood. 'To say' can be depicted by a mouth with lines above it (言). More complicated characters were constructed by putting two ideograms or parts of ideograms together. The key part is called the radical and usually denotes the general theme; thus almost all trees have the tree character as their radical. The

13

other part of the character may indicate the sound to be used in reading the character, that is, it may be a phonetic element.

When Buddhism was brought to China probably in the first century AD, the Chinese had to find ways of writing Buddhist names for which they had no appropriate characters. They had no alternative but to use some of their characters phonetically, that is, to represent a sound rather than an idea. This was an important factor when Chinese characters came to be used to record Japanese names and words.

At first records were kept in Chinese; indeed, Chinese continued for centuries to be the language of scholarship in Japan. But, as Chinese and Japanese constructions are so different and as Chinese was not a living language in Japan, Chinese prose came in due course to be read in a Japanese word order with some Japanese words added or implied. The Japanese word order in such cases was indicated by diacritic marks. This method of reading Chinese classical texts, which the Japanese termed *kanbun* (literally, 'Han writing'), was called *kundoku*. Some Chinese texts are indeed still read in this way in Japan.

The Japanese found that their indigenous vocabulary was inadequate to express many ideas. They accordingly adopted many Chinese words and expressions. These were mainly compounds of two or more Chinese characters read together as one idea. The word usually translated as 'Analects', the title of the famous and basic Confucian text, is written with two characters which may be translated as argument and speech: 論　語 . The Japanese did not attempt to read these two characters in polysyllabic Japanese mainly because there was no suitable Japanese word or words for 'Analects'. Instead they gave the two characters the sounds which they thought approximated to Chinese of their time. The Japanese reading thus became 'Rongo'. (Lun Yü is the Wade-Giles reading of these characters Lun-yu in pinyin).

Unfortunately the ways of reading Chinese characters in Japanese are frequently more complicated than this example suggests. Because Chinese was imported into Japan over a lengthy period, the so-called Chinese pronunciation, which is now generally far removed from modern Chinese pronunciation, varied considerably. One style of 'Chinese' reading, or *on*, was the Go-on, which was supposed to be based on the pronunciation used in the province of Wu. Another and more generally used style was the Kan-on said to be the pronunciation in Shensi or Kansu province. There were also a few Tō-in readings which were supposed to be pronunciations of the T'ang dynasty. Thus the character 明 , which is made up of the character 日 , meaning sun or day, and 月 , meaning the moon, and which has the general connotation of 'light' or 'bright', is read *myō* in Go-on, *mei* in Kan-on, and *ming* in Tō-in. Chinese characters were also used to convey indigenous Japanese words; this method of reading a character is called the *kun* reading. The various *kun* readings of 明 include *'akarui, akiraka, a(keru), a(ku), akari* and *aka(su)*.

No hard-and-fast rule, specifying which reading is the correct one in any given context, can be produced, and the reader has to know from experience which reading to use. The character with the largest number of readings in Japanese, *on* and *kun*, is said to be the character 生 , which is radical number 100 and which means to live, to give birth to, to be fresh, and so on. The *on* readings are generally given as *shō* and *sei*. Some seventeen *kun* readings are commonly listed.

The Japanese had considerable difficulty in developing a method of reproducing Japanese names and words or inflexions which did not exist in Chinese. There were many alternative characters which could be used for any one sound, and the writing of many of these was highly complicated, involving the use of many brush strokes to convey a single syllable. Gradually, however, it became customary to use a limited number of simplified characters to denote particular sounds or syllables. One such early system was that used in the first major collection of poems, the *Manyōshū*, or 'The Collection of Ten Thousand Poems', which was compiled in the latter part of the eighth century (see Chapter III). The symbols used were called *kana* and in the case of this collection were termed the *Manyōgana*. The *kana* syllabaries now in use, the *hiragana* and the *katakana*, both developed from simplified Chinese characters. The *hiragana*, which derived from a cursive form of Chinese characters, are reputed to have been developed by the famous Buddhist priest Kōbō Daishi (774–835). The syllable 'a' in *hiragana* is written あ and derived from the character 安 . The *katakana*, which in some cases developed from different Chinese characters, were literally side-*kana* used to explain the reading of a character. They are squarer and derived from the more regular form of writing. They are now generally used for foreign words adopted into Japanese. The *katakana* 'a' is written ア and was derived from the character 阿 . The reader of Japanese handwritten letters in the now rarely used cursive script or *sōsho* also has to be ready to encounter a third and more complicated form of *kana*, the *hentaigana* or *sōgana*, which were nearer the old *Manyōgana*.

The Japanese language has evolved over the centuries. The admixture of Chinese words and phrases and, in later centuries, of western vocabulary and idioms has increased from era to era. It has not, at least over the last 1,000 to 1,200 years, been possible to speak of 'pure Japanese'. However, some words and phrases which existed before Japanese was influenced by Chinese are sometimes called *Yamato-kotoba* or Yamato words. Early Japanese poems were indeed usually written in *Yamato-kotoba*.

In the last 120 years the question of adopting roman script or *romaji* to write Japanese has been discussed from time to time, but the movement has made no real headway. Apart from the fact that it would mean that much of Japanese literature would be available only to the specialist who had studied traditional Japanese ways of writing, romanization would compel the Japanese to adopt still more western words to replace the many homophones which are found in Japanese texts. These resulted from the large number of Chinese compounds introduced into the Japanese language, which, having no tones, could not distinguish meanings by tonal differences. Kenkyūsha's Japanese–English dictionary (fourth edition, 1974) lists ten different words read as *kanjō* and written with different pairs of Chinese characters. Meanings include a wand, a bulwark, a bacillus, an account or bill, feelings, a citation, a tube, annulment and 'on board a warship'. Sometimes in ordinary speech the Japanese find it necessary to explain a word by indicating the character or characters used.

The Japanese adoption of Chinese characters was of major importance for the development of Japanese art. Chinese sayings and Buddhist phrases and sutras, as well as Japanese poems, provided material for artistic writing. Many hanging pictures (*kakemono*) and scrolls (*makimono*) were formed by pieces of calligraphy. The art of writing with the brush, or *fude*, was cultivated by scholars, courtiers

15

and others. *Shūji*, the study of writing with the brush and black Indian ink, was an essential part of Japanese education until the Second World War. It was also directly relevant to the art of painting, both black and white (that is, *sumie*) and in water-colours.

The adoption of Chinese characters designed for a monosyllabic language, and their adaption to express Japanese polysyllabic words, seems and was a very complicated method of writing. But the Chinese system of writing was available. Other forms of writing were unknown to the early Japanese.

Confucianism and Chinese Philosophy

The sage Wani is reputed to have brought with him to Japan in the early years of the fifth century a number of Chinese texts and to have started to teach Chinese philosophy. Over the next three centuries the Chinese classics began to exert an increasing influence on Japan. Japanese scholars, such as Minabuchi no Shōan in the early seventh century and the priest Sōmin (died 653), were sent to China and brought back copies of the Chinese classics. In about 670 some Korean scholars are supposed to have established a Confucian 'university' in Japan. Certainly, when the so-called *ritsuryō* system of government, based on Chinese models (see page 30), was established in Japan shortly after this, a *daigakuryō*, or university for the teaching of the Chinese classics, was set up, and children of families of officials of the fifth rank or higher were encouraged to master what was regarded as the source of all learning. The Japanese gradually became more selective in their attitude to the precepts in the Chinese classics and freely adapted them to suit their own needs.

Confucianism is essentially the philosophy of life which was said to have been taught by K'ung Ch'iu (*c.* 551–478 BC) (Kong Qiu), known to us as Confucius, and to the Japanese as Kōshi, and developed by his followers over the centuries. The most important Confucian text was the 'Analects', a collection of the sayings of the master. Another text in the canon, which was much respected in both China and Japan, was 'The Classic of Filial Piety'. 'The Book of Changes', 'The Book of Songs' (or 'Book of Odes'), 'The Record of Ritual' (or 'Book of Rites'), 'The Book of Documents' (that is, of Chinese history), 'The Spring and Autumn Chronicles', 'The Great Learning' and 'The Doctrine of the Mean' were also studied, as were the teachings of Mencius (Meng-tzu or Mengzi), one of Confucius' disciples. As the number of different texts implies, Confucianism did not consist of any uniform body of doctrines or of a single coherent philosophy. It had ethical elements, it propagated theories of politics and it developed a cosmology. In later centuries in what came to be known as Neo-Confucianism metaphysical theories were formed which tried to reconcile Confucian teachings with Buddhist and Taoist elements.

Confucius claimed that he was primarily concerned with practical and moral questions and that his main wish was to restore the society which he believed had existed in earlier years and which had been based on a harmonious and hierarchical system. He was a conservative and was fundamentally against change. He thought that the ideal society should be achieved not so much by the enforcement of laws as by the example of those in authority. They should be chosen for their intellectual and moral qualities and not by birth. It was incumbent on the ruled to observe the rituals of conduct and respect their rulers who had 'the mandate of heaven'. If the rulers ceased to behave properly and lost the mandate, they could be deposed. Great emphasis was placed on the family and consequently on filial piety. 'The law of filial piety is that one should serve one's parents as one serves heaven.' The supreme virtue, however, was benevolence (仁 , read *jin* in Japanese).

In Confucian philosophy as it developed later, heaven was supreme but impersonal. All ordinary phenomena resulted from the interaction of the negative or female principle (*yin* in Chinese, *in* in Japanese) and the positive or male principle (*yang* in Chinese, *yo* in Japanese). Phenomena which could not be explained by such interaction were considered to be the work of the spirits of the dead, who at least for a time had to be propitiated by offerings. Hence developed Confucian ancestor worship. From this was also derived the cult of divination called in Japanese *onyōdō*. Man, in Confucian philosophy, was naturally inclined to good, and harmony was achieved by adherence to the middle way or mean (the *chūyō*).

Most of the main principles of Japanese ethical behaviour today can be traced in some way to aspects of Confucian teaching, but in the course of time the precepts were Japanized and fused with other indigenous and extraneous elements, giving them their uniquely Japanese quality. The Japanese never accepted some elements of Confucian teaching. In particular they did not endorse the Confucian view of the mandate of heaven; for the Japanese their sovereign, being descended from the sun goddess, naturally had the mandate of heaven. The Japanese also failed to follow the Confucian principles for the selection of wise and virtuous officials. The Chinese system of competitive examinations was not adopted, and entry to the Confucian university in Japan was restricted to families who had achieved high rank in the hierarchy.

The Japanese developed the Confucian emphasis on the family into the concept of the *ie*, literally the house. This came to imply an extended family and was developed to mean any closely knit group. A company, for instance, has some of the aspects of the *ie*. Many Japanese will refer to their company as *uchi no kaisha*, meaning 'our company as if it was their family company'. Thus Japanese 'groupism' can be said to have a Confucian origin.

Confucian emphasis on respect for those set in authority and on obedience to parents can be regarded as the basis of the Japanese regard for hierarchy and seniority. Age is still respected, and seniors (*senpai*) in Japan have a particular relationship with and responsibility for helping their juniors (*kōhai*), who in turn have special obligations to their seniors.

Confucius also stressed the importance of service. The Japanese, finding service to their lords vital to the maintenance and development of an effective and disciplined feudal structure, made loyalty the supreme virtue; indeed, it became in Japan more important than filial piety.

Giri, or moral obligation, is another virtue stressed in Japan which derives from the Confucian concepts of benevolence and paternalism. But it is also related to loyalty. Loyalty, if it is to be maintained, requires an obligation on both sides. The master must look after his servant if he expects loyal service. The Japanese have come to regard this paternal relationship as central to their society. The phrase *oyabun-kobun*, literally 'parent–child relationship', extends to every walk

17

of life from the political faction through the company to today's criminal gangs, the *yakuza*. The recipient of a favour, or *on*, must repay that favour. If he does not he is liable to be accused of being either *on-shirazu* or *giri-shirazu*, which is equivalent to a serious moral failing.

One other principle of conduct in Japan, that of *enryō*, or reserve, probably has its origins in Japanese adaptation of Confucian ethics. It derives from the desirability of not causing trouble or embarrassment to others. This also led to the importance attached to 'face', or appearance, and is the basis of the Japanese preference for vague statements or replies, where a point-blank negative might upset someone and cause embarrassment to the speaker.

The Japanese system of polite formulas and bowing to the appropriate extent, depending on the status or seniority of the other person, derives from the Confucian emphasis on ritual behaviour. Even the Japanese emphasis on *ninjō*, or human feeling, and on *wa*, or harmony, in society can be traced to Confucian ideas, although they have all been given a particular Japanese quality by their adaptation and development to Japanese circumstances over the centuries since Confucianism was first imported into Japan.

The generally low status given to women in Japan after the import of Chinese ideas can also be traced to Confucian attitudes. This contrasts with the role of women in many of the Japanese myths and accounts of Japan's early history in the *Kojiki*, where some Empresses played significant roles. The legendary ancestor of Japan's ruling family was a goddess. Nevertheless women managed to achieve a significant role in the literature of the Heian period (see Chapter IV), especially in the tenth century.

Confucianism never became a religion in Japan, although bi-annual ceremonies in honour of Confucius were held for some centuries. A shrine to Confucius was built in Edo (the modern Tokyo) during the Edo period (see Chapter VIII), and ceremonies to Confucius are still held there from time to time.

Buddhism

Buddhism came to Japan through China and Korea. In China, Buddhism was adapted and developed. Korea was a staging post of historical importance but of no religious or philosophical significance for Japanese Buddhism. The official date for the introduction of Buddhism into Japan is AD 552, but it is probable that Buddhist scriptures and ideas were brought to Japan by travellers from Korea some years earlier.

Buddhism originated from the life and teaching of Siddhartha Gautama, who was born about 446 BC. He was the son of King Suddhodana of the Sakya clan in what is now Nepal. At the age of twenty-nine he renounced the luxurious life which he led as a prince and spent six years in ascetic practices seeking to find answers to the problems of human existence. While seated under a *bo* tree at Buddhagaya he achieved enlightenment. He thus became a Buddha, meaning one who has awakened to the truth. Thereafter, until his death at the age of eighty, he travelled through central India, explaining what he had learned and experienced. He was given the honorary name of Sakyamuni (the silent sage or holy one from the Sakya clan). In Japanese the name became Shaka, and he is thus referred to as Shaka-sama (sama is a more polite form of san, used as a title to indicate Mr, Mrs, etc).

Gautama did not enunciate any specific or clear dogmas, and, in its initial stages at least, Buddhism can hardly be described as a religion. There was no Buddhist doctrine defining God or explaining creation. Gautama never claimed to be god and he considered that it was meaningless to speculate on such questions as whether the world is finite or infinite, whether the body and soul are one or separate and whether there is life after death. He stressed *dharma*, which may be translated as 'true eternal law'. This was valid for all humanity in all ages and transcended all other beliefs.

Life was suffering, Gautama declared, and, in the face of suffering, man was helpless. Suffering occurred because of ever-changing conditions and causes. Nothing was constant; everything was transient. A man's *karma* or life was not complete in itself. It was both a sequel and a prelude. It was conditioned by past lives and in turn affected future lives. Life was the result of a long chain of events and different existences. In each existence a person's deeds and character had their natural and inescapable results. An individual's life was also conditioned by the group in which he lived.

Gautama considered that there was nothing in the world of matter or thought to which the term 'self' could be applied. There was no 'I' which could possess or not possess something or which had a particular quality. Man must not become absorbed in analysing his own conduct or piety. The objective and subjective worlds were one and the same.

To achieve an end to suffering, confusion and illusion, the causes, which lay in blind desire, had to be extinguished. Enlightenment involved understanding of the causes of suffering, of the impermanence of all forms of life and matter and of the non-existence of self. Lust and desire could be eradicated by spiritual discipline and meditation, as well as by the pursuit of a middle way which involved neither suffering nor pleasure. This led ultimately to *nirvana* or the absence of all causes of suffering.

Running through all the teachings of Gautama is a spirit of compassion and kindness as well as a strong wish to help others to find enlightenment. This resulted in a missionary zeal.

Buddhist teachings have been summed up in various categories. There were 'three treasures', namely the Buddha, the law and the order of monks. There were 'five precepts', which were not to kill, not to steal, not to act immorally (that is, not to fornicate), not to lie and not to drink intoxicating liquor. But the basis of Buddhist teaching can be found in the 'four noble truths', which were: all existence is suffering; the cause of suffering is desire; the cause can be prevented; and the way to prevent suffering is through the 'eightfold path'. This consists of right views, right aims, right words (or speech), right action, right living, right efforts, right mind (that is, right understanding of the non-existence of self) and right rapture (that is, the ecstasy of perfect knowledge or enlightenment, leading to *nirvana*). Sir Charles Eliot in his classic work on Japanese Buddhism defines enlightenment as being 'direct intuitive knowledge, superior to reasoning and discussion, and for those who receive it certain and incontrovertible'.[1]

The student of Buddhism will also encounter other categories, such as the 'three baskets' or *Tripitaka*. These were the *Vinaya* or the practical rules for

Buddhist monks, the *Sutras* or the holy books (there are 34 long sutras and 154 medium-length sutras) and the *Abhidharma* or technical expositions of the law. Gautama in his last days emphasized four stages in the spiritual life. These were morality, ecstasy, knowledge and deliverance. Buddhism also recognized 'five aggregates', which consisted of form, sensation, perception, predisposition and practical knowledge. There were 'five admonitions'; these covered prohibitions on eating at the wrong time, dancing and singing, ostentatious dress, sensuousness and covetousness. The Buddhist ethical system was thus wide-ranging, but Buddhism did not offer a comprehensive metaphysical explanation of existence, as in Gautama's view efforts to explain life and the universe were both impossible and pointless.

In Japan, Buddhist teachings were adapted and mixed with Confucian and indigenous ideas to produce a peculiarly Japanese amalgam, which suited the political requirements of an agricultural and warrior society. Significantly, in view of the emphasis on loyalty throughout Japanese history, loyalty is not a virtue which features in Buddhist ethics.

Buddhism permeated Japanese life throughout the centuries until the modern era, but Japan cannot be described as a Buddhist country in the same way as most European countries can be termed Christian. Buddhism in Japan was tolerant and eclectic; it thus had no real difficulty in coexisting with the indigenous cults. Indeed, after some initial clashes between adherents of the two religions, a dual form of Shintō and Buddhism developed which lasted until the Meiji restoration in 1868.

Buddhism was a dominant influence in Japanese literature and art until the nineteenth century. The Buddhist emphasis on the impermanence of life has, for instance, been a major theme for Japanese poets of every age. The underlying motif in novels and histories has frequently been that grandeur and power are here today and gone tomorrow like the cherry blossom, which flowers and falls in a few brief days. In Japanese this is *mujō*. The Japanese emphasis on *aware*, which may be translated as pity or compassion, is a reflection of the Buddhist belief in the inevitability of suffering. Combined with the Buddhist concept of the non-existence of self (in Japanese, *muga*), this provided the basis for the Japanese stress on self-renunciation, including the acceptance of suicide as a valid way of escape from shame, and on the inevitability of cruelty and suffering in man's relations with man.

In Gautama's teachings, as in the teaching of Jesus Christ, there is some lack of precision about the extent to which man can achieve enlightenment or salvation by his own efforts (that is, by works) and how far he is dependent on factors outside his control. In Christianity we speak of 'the grace of God', achieved through faith. In Buddhism the help of the Buddha may be sought and obtained. In Japanese Buddhism the contrast is between *jiriki* (own power) and *tariki* (other power).

Buddhist doctrines had some notable practical effects on Japanese life. The Buddhist injunction against killing applied to all living beings. As a result the Japanese did not generally eat meat. Fish were caught and died; fish could therefore be eaten except by the monks and other strict adherents to Buddhist teachings. Exceptions were also made for wild birds, and a euphemism for a wild boar in the Edo period was a mountain whale (*yama-kujira*). The Buddhist attitude towards death also brought about a change in Japanese burial customs. Cremation generally replaced coffin or tomb burials, and the Kofun period was brought to an end by the spread of Buddhism in Japan.

The Buddhist sects which came to Japan were of the Mahayana or 'greater vehicle' form, in contrast to the Hinayana or 'lesser vehicle'. Mahayana Buddhism developed in the first century AD and consisted of a more complicated series of doctrines than the Hinayana, which was perhaps closer to the teachings of Gautama. Hinayana remains the form of Buddhism generally found in Sri Lanka, Burma and Thailand. Mahayana Buddhism predominated in Tibet, where it became absorbed in tantrism and magic formulas. It was developed in China into a significant religion with many philosophical theories. The Mahayana sects recognized that the ideals of Gautama were unattainable by the majority of people and substituted the ideal of the compassionate Bodhisattva, or aspirant to Buddhahood, who worked for the salvation of all living beings. It assured all human beings that they too could become Buddhas. A Japanese euphemism for death is to say that a person has become a Buddha (*hotoke*). In Mahayana Buddhism the emphasis was placed on the discovery of the Buddha-nature which lies within every human being. Gautama was no longer seen as a human teacher who showed the way to enlightenment; he became a transcendent being.

In Mahayana Buddhism, Shaka was not the only Buddha, and a large Buddhist pantheon was developed. The most important of these deities in Japan, in addition to Shaka, were Dainichi Nyorai (Roshana or Vairocana), Yakushi Nyorai (Bhaishajyaguru), the healing Buddha, and Amida (Amitabha), the Buddha of the western paradise, who saved the souls of men who were too weak or foolish to save themselves and who called on Amida for help. The Japanese pantheon included many Bodhisattvas (Bosatsu in Japanese). The most important of these were Miroku (Maitreya), the Buddha of the future; Kannon (Kuan-yin or Avalokitesvara), the personification of mercy, who later became a goddess, who has a share in Amida's paradise and who is multiform (hence with eleven faces or heads (*jūichimen*) or one thousand hands (*senju*); Monju (Manjusri), the personification of wisdom and intellect, who is generally shown with the sword of knowledge and a book in his hands; and Jizō (Kshitigarbha), who vowed to deliver all creatures from hell and who in Japan is the special protector of dead children. Other Buddhist deities whose images are frequently found in Japanese temples include the Niō ('Two Kings'), the Shitennō (the 'Four Deva Kings') and the Myōō, who are terrible in appearance (the two most commonly represented in images are those of Fudō and Aizen). The Rakan (Arhat) were disciples of Shaka. An image of Binzuru, who, according to legend, offended against the rules of his order of monks and had his entry into *nirvana* indefinitely delayed, may frequently be found sitting outside the main hall of Japanese temples; sick people who touch him may expect his healing powers to cure them. Deities such as Benzaiten or Benten, Emma-O, the king of the underworld, and the Shichifukujin (the seven gods of good luck) have hazier connections with Buddhism.

The multiplicity of the doctrines elaborated in Mahayana Buddhism resulted in the development of numerous sects, which frequently taught very different concepts of Buddhism and how to achieve enlightenment. Buddhist sects in Japan were even more varied in their presentations of their faith than the later Protestant sects in Britain, and some paid even less attention to the teachings of Gautama

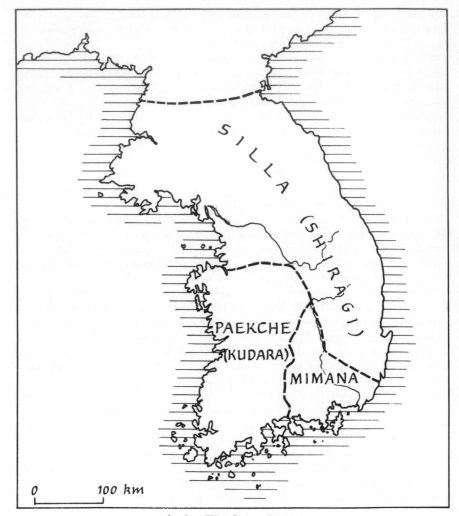

Ancient Kingdoms of Korea

than some Christian sects do to the basic teachings of Jesus Christ. In the first few decades after Buddhism reached Japan it tended to be regarded primarily as another way to gain material advantages or to ward off disease and disaster. The first appeal of Buddhism in Japan was, therefore, as a magic formula.

Relations with Korea and Political and Social Change

In the development of a more centralized form of government, in a Japan which consisted of groups of clans frequently at war with one another, relations with Korea played an important role. The Japanese were tough, courageous and aggressive warriors. According to Japanese legends the Empress Jingū (also known as Jingō), who is alleged to have reigned between the death of her husband the Emperor Chūai and the reign of the Emperor Ojin, her son, having completed the subjugation of the *kumaso* in Kyūshū, then led a Japanese expedition to Korea and defeated the forces of the kingdom of Silla (known to the Japanese as Shiragi). Japanese histories also assert that, under the Emperor Ojin, Japanese troops attacked the Korean kingdom of Paekche (known to the Japanese as Kudara). The Korean kingdoms, which had come under the influence of Chinese civiliz-ation, had developed in both wealth and culture. This attracted the predatory instincts of the Japanese clans, and pirate raids and expeditions to Korea seeking plunder were frequent.

In the fifth century and the first half of the sixth century, Japanese groups exercised control over the small kingdom of Mimana in the south-east corner of the Korean peninsula (in the area round what is now the city of Pusan). Korean politics at this time were dominated by the rivalries between the other southern Korean kingdoms of Silla and Paekche. In 527, when the Japanese enclave in Mimana was under threat from Paekche and Silla, an expedition on its way to defend the Japanese position there had to be diverted to northern Kyūshū to deal with an uprising against Yamato hegemony led by a chieftain called Iwai, who was in league with Silla. Eventually, after Iwai had been defeated, an under-standing was reached with Paekche, which needed Japanese help against Silla. But the alliance with Paekche was undermined by treachery among the Japanese in Mimana, who had become Koreanized. Paekche sent Buddhist gifts to Japan in 552. The Japanese for their part sent a force to Mimana in the same year, but in 554 Silla defeated Paekche and in 562 annexed Mimana. The Japanese were not easily reconciled to the loss of their position in Korea and continued for some time to try to regain their influence there. In 602 Japanese troops were assembled for an attack on Silla, but the prince commanding the Japanese force died. The project was then abandoned. From about this time Japanese policy changed from an aggressive to a defensive stance, and Dazaifu, just south of Hakata/Fukuoka, became the headquarters of the Japanese defence in Kyūshū.

As a result of their involvement in Korea, the Japanese came into contact with Chinese civilization and thought, as well as with Buddhist religion and philosophy. Japanese difficulties in Korea and their ultimate expulsion from the peninsula brought home to Japanese leaders the inadequacy of Japanese power. They were forced to realize, as they had to do a number of times in their history, that military prowess is not enough. They lacked the organization and techniques needed to maintain a dominant position in Korea. They had to recognize that the Chinese civilization with which they came in contact was in every way far ahead of their own primitive culture. Hardly surprisingly, however, the need for revolutionary change was not universally appreciated. There was a powerful conservative clique of clan chieftains who resisted reform and believed that Japan should cleave to its indigenous traditions and gods.

In the middle of the sixth century, when Buddhist influence reached Japan, the ambitious Soga clan, which had formed close ties with the imperial line, saw that the adoption of Buddhist practices and Chinese concepts of government could be used to strengthen their power. Opposed to the Soga were the *Mononobe*, the soldiers, and the *Nakatomi*, the priests to the indigenous cults. They stood for the status quo. Initially Soga no Umako, the leader of the Soga clan, had to be content

23

with a private Buddhist temple in his home, but when a pestilence broke out, his opponents argued that this was due to the jealousy of Japanese gods. His house was then destroyed, and the Buddhist image in his temple was thrown into a canal at Naniwa, part of the modern city of Osaka.

However, in 587 Soga no Umako managed to defeat the *Mononobe* and in 592 he arranged for the succession to go to his niece, who became the Empress Suiko. He also had his nephew by another marriage, Prince Umayado, appointed Regent and Crown Prince. Prince Umayado, who is better known as Shōtoku Taishi (574–622), is generally regarded as the patron saint of Japanese Buddhism. Very little is known about his life, but it seems that he was a serious student of Buddhism and the Chinese classics. During Shōtoku Taishi's regency, Soga no Umako, who had been ruthless in his pursuit of power, was apparently content to exercise his influence behind the scenes.

The first notable event in the regency of Shōtoku Taishi was the establishment in 603 of a system of court ranks. This implied the acceptance of Chinese ideas of government and established a new form of hierarchy in Japanese society.

The second and much more important development was the promulgation in 604 of the so-called 'constitution' of Shōtoku Taishi. This was not a constitution in the sense we use that word and was not what we would consider a legal document. It consisted of a set of seventeen principles and moral exhortations. It was as much Confucian as Buddhist in inspiration. Article I stressed the importance of harmony (*wa*) in human relations. Other articles enjoined obedience and acceptance of hierarchy in society, hard work and good faith. The people were also warned against flattery, envy and anger. The 'constitution' was the first attempt from the centre to establish the basic principles of government and to present written rules of conduct for the guidance of the Japanese people.

In 607 the great temple of Hōryūji (also called Ikarugadera or Wakakusadera), near Nara in the Yamato area, was founded by Shōtoku Taishi. Here Shōtoku Taishi established his residence. It has ever since provided an artistic and religious inspiration to Japanese people.

In the same year (607) an official emissary, Ono no Imoko, was sent to China, where a united Empire had been formed under the short-lived Sui dynasty (589–618). He was not the first Japanese envoy to the Chinese court, but his mission had particular significance, because two members of his mission stayed in China for thirty years and, when they returned to Japan, they were able to make a major contribution to Japanese understanding of Chinese and Buddhist culture. They were Takamuku no Ayabito, a lay student, and Bin, a Buddhist priest. When they returned to Japan, they were given the title of *kuni no hakase* (teacher of the nation). Ono's mission had problems. The opening words of the letter which he carried to the Chinese court suggested that the 'Emperor of the sunrise country' (that is, Japan) was the equal of the 'Emperor of the sunset country' (China). This inevitably caused offence to the Chinese court, and the letter which Ono was supposed to take back to Japan was in the terms normally addressed to a vassal state. Ono, perhaps realizing the trouble this would cause, managed to lose the haughty Chinese message on his way home.

In the period up to 837 some twelve official Japanese embassies were sent to China, but there were also many unofficial travellers, and the official missions generally consisted of many hundreds of Japanese. Owing to the difficulties of

24

sea travel in those days before the development of sturdy and reliable sea-going vessels, the journey to China was a hazardous one.

Following the death of Shōtoku Taishi the feuding around the throne resumed. Prince Naka no Oe,[2] who had been passed over in the succession, joined with the *Nakatomi* in 645 in a plot to eliminate Soga no Iruka, the grandson of Soga no Umako. The leader of the *Nakatomi* at that time was a man of outstanding personality; under the name Fujiwara no Kamatari he established the Fujiwara dominance at the imperial court which was to last through much of the subsequent Nara and Heian periods, that is, from the eighth to the twelfth century.

In the *coup d'état* in which Soga no Iruka was assassinated, the coup leaders represented reform not conservatism. The leaders chose Naniwa, part of modern Osaka, as their capital. They proclaimed a new era, Taika ('great change'), and introduced changes in 646 which have come to be called the Taika reforms. These reforms were introduced gradually over the next half-century up to the beginning of the Nara period in 710. They included the *Taihō* legal code of 701 (ascribed to Fujiwara no Fubito and others). The reforms were inspired by Chinese models, but the prime motive of the new leaders was the strengthening of their own power around the throne. The territorial magnates and clan leaders acquiesced in the changes, because they tended to confirm their own existing powers and strengthened their position in the hierarchy. Where the reforms ran counter to these interests they were either modified in practice or ignored.

One of the most significant elements in the reforms was the official abolition of private title to land. Surveys of population and of land were instituted. Old taxes were abolished and new ones substituted. Naka no Oe, who had become Crown Prince, set an example by surrendering title to his own estates. But the changes were frequently more cosmetic than real. Japanese society was not ready for the egalitarian land tenure system instituted in China after many centuries of experiment, failure and reform. The Japanese had no such experience, and records had hardly begun. Moreover, Japanese rice land, partly because of the hilly nature of much of the Japanese terrain, was less easily divisible on a logical pattern. However, in the relatively primitive agricultural society in Japan at that time, land was unproductive without labour to cultivate it, and concepts of land-ownership were thus hazy. As a result of the practical surveys and censuses which were carried out, the first Japanese estate (*shōen*) maps were produced to allocate land to the producers. This was the so-called *ku-bun-den* (literally, 'mouth-division-rice field') system. Under this a man was supposed to be entitled to two *tan* (one *tan* = approximately 1,000 square metres) and a woman two-thirds of this amount. The new taxes were a land tax (*sō*) paid in rice, a labour tax (*yō*) on individual producers and a produce tax (*chō*) on products other than rice. Unfortunately, because so many people and institutions, such as temples, were able to obtain exemptions, the main burden of the new taxes continued to fall on the farmers who were least able to bear them.

Under the *Taihō* code of 702 a new system of administration was set up. The council of religious practices (the Jingikan), which was responsible for Shintō rites, took precedence over all other offices. This was a radical difference from the Chinese models on which the rest of the organization was based. It also underlines the fact that Buddhism had not yet displaced the local gods. The main council of state was the Dajōkan. This was headed by the chancellor (or *dajōdaijin*).

25

He was supported by the 'minister of the left' (the *sadaijin*), whose deputy was the 'minister of the right' (the *udaijin*). Below them were the 'great councillors' (the *dainagon*), as well as 'middle' and 'junior councillors' (the *chūnagon* and *shōnagon*). The various offices included the Treasury or Okurashō, a name still used for the Japanese Ministry of Finance.

On the surface at least Japan had become a Chinese-style state, but the reality was rather different. Theoretically governors of the provinces were appointed and dismissed by the court; in practice the court depended on the goodwill of the territorial chiefs, who were accordingly left in practical command if not always in nominal charge. Communications in seventh-century Japan were poor. There were very few people who were literate, let alone educated in the Chinese classics, and who understood the Chinese system. Agriculture remained primitive. Trade was very limited, and money was not in general use; such coins as existed came from China. Natural disasters – earthquakes, fires and epidemics – were frequent, and life for most people was short and hard.

However, Japan was changing. An ethical framework of Confucian and Buddhist principles was grafted on to concepts of purity derived from the indigenous cults. Buddhism was spreading into the provinces. In 685 an order was issued that there should be a Buddhist shrine in every 'house', and by 692 there were 545 Buddhist monasteries throughout the land. Buddhism was being accepted because it was the vehicle of a new and obviously superior culture. Its impressive rituals and its profound beliefs inspired the arts, especially architecture, sculpture and painting.

The Arts

Before the establishment of the capital at Nara in 710 there was no fixed Japanese government headquarters. This changed at least whenever there was a new Emperor. One of the main reasons for this was the traditional belief that a place became polluted as a result of death. In the early days it was fairly easy to maintain this practice, as the apparatus of central government was negligible, and buildings, which were of wood, tended to be simple and temporary. But with the adoption of Chinese concepts of government, improvements in the agricultural economy of the country and the progress of Buddhism in Japan, the construction of more permanent and better-appointed buildings (fortifications, palaces and temples) became not only desirable but also possible. Architecture was thus the first art form to be developed in Japan in the sixth and seventh centuries.

Unfortunately, none of the palaces which were built in these centuries have survived, but archaeologists have been able to trace the foundations of a number of the early palaces, and from these it is possible to reconstruct a picture of what they were like. Prince Shōtoku's palace at Ikaruga was begun in 601 near the site where in 607 the Hōryūji was started. This palace was destroyed in 643 and the Tōin or eastern temple of the Hōryūji was built on the site in the eighth century as a memorial to Prince Shōtoku.

A number of other palace sites have been found near Asuka, south of Nara, and the name Asuka has come to be given to this first major period of Japanese art. This is generally regarded as lasting from the introduction of Buddhism in about 552 until the beginning of the Nara period in 710. (Some art historians, however, call the latter part of this period the Hakuhō period.) One of these palaces, the so-called Asuka Itabuki Palace (about 643–5), had extensive areas of stone floors and, as the name implies (Itabuki means shingle roof), presumably had a wood-board and shingle roof instead of the more usual thatch.

The grandest of these early palaces was the Fujiwara palace near Nara which was in use between 694 and 710. This seems to have been built in a Chinese style. It covered a large area, each side being roughly a kilometre in length. The quarters of the sovereign (the *dairi*) were in the centre towards the northern gate. Ministerial offices were built south of this, around a central court which was used for ceremonial purposes. The palace area was surrounded by a wooden palisade and a moat. Beyond this were houses for retainers, artisans and so on, arranged in streets on a grid pattern.

The first large Japanese temple, Hōkōji or Gangōji, but more usually called Asukadera, was started in 588. But none of the original buildings have survived, and Asukadera today provides little idea of what it once was. The Shitennōji in Osaka, which was begun in 593, is now a post-war ferro-concrete building. The Hōryūji, which was founded in 607, alone remains to provide an idea of the grandeur of these early Japanese temples. Unfortunately Hōryūji too could not escape the ravages of fire. The original buildings were burned down and rebuilt after 670. The *kondō* (golden or main hall) from that period was probably the oldest surviving wooden building in the world when it too was consumed in a fire which occurred during repairs in 1949. It has been replaced by a perfect replica. The lecture hall (*kōdō*) was burned down in 925 but rebuilt in the tenth century. The pagoda near the *kondō* in the *saiin* (western temple) is now the oldest original building at Hōryūji.

The architectural style of all these buildings seems to have been similar to that current in China in the sixth century. It had reached Japan through Korea. The *kondō* at Hōryūji has a double roof and massive pillars, but its balanced proportions and the graceful curves of its tiled roof ensure that it does not appear heavy. The five-storey pagoda, surmounted by a tall stupa, provided a model for Japanese pagodas for centuries to come, but it has a more solid appearance than some of the lighter structures of later ages. The whole complex of buildings in the *saiin* and *tōin* (eastern temple), which was built later, make the Hōryūji one of the world's architectural marvels.

The Buddhist priests sought images for their temples, and the art of sculpture began to flourish in Japan. The first Buddhist sculptors in Japan probably came from Korea, but there was clearly already some indigenous talent available. This is demonstrated by some strange carved granite figures discovered near Asuka. One carving of a combined male and female figure dating from the seventh century was made for use as a fountain in a garden. These stone carvings are primitive in appearance, but they have powerful lines and show technical skill.

The oldest surviving Buddhist sculpture in Japan is that of the Asuka Daibutsu or Great Buddha. It was cast in bronze, apparently in 609, by Kuratsukuribe no Tori. It has been extensively repaired over the centuries, but the elongated face, the almond-shaped eyes, the upward-turned crescent-shaped lips and the symmetrically folded clothes are regarded as clear characteristics of the Tori style, which was influenced by the Buddhist art forms of the northern Wei dynasty in

China. These characteristics can also be found in the *Shaka* triad in the *kondō* at the Hōryūji and in the so-called *Guze-Kannon* in the Yumedono (Hall of Dreams) which was built in the tōin at Hōryūji in memory of Prince Shōtoku. (The Yumedono is a marvellous eighth-century octagonal building, sometimes wrongly described as Prince Shōtoku's meditation hall.) There is a simplicity and nobility in these works of sculpture, but in comparison with some of the images of later ages they seem archaic.

The Tori style was not, however, the only type of sculpture practised in the Asuka period. A number of other works in wood, or dry lacquer over wood, have a freer, lighter and more graceful appearance. Examples are the *Kudara Kannon* also in the Hōryūji, the incomparable *Miroku Bosatsu* in the Kōryūji in Kyoto and the wonderful small *Kannon* in the Chūguji, a convent next to the *tōin* of the Hōryūji. It is impossible to avoid superlatives in describing these works, especially the latter two, which by their grace and charm must be counted among the greatest works of sculpture in the world. They are both moving and technically perfect, conveying the calm and peace of the Buddha to all generations. In images such as these, art historians have traced influences back through Korea and China to India and thence via the eastern conquests of Alexander the Great, to ancient Greece.

Japanese painting also had its origins in the seventh century. The wall paintings in the *kondō* at the Hōryūji, which dated from about 710, can now be seen only in accurate reproductions, as the originals were destroyed in the disastrous fire of 1949. They are thought to have been inspired by Indian models, but they are in the syle of T'ang dynasty paintings on Buddhist themes. They were painted in a technique similar to that used in mural paintings in Khotan and in the Ajanta frescoes. The paintings on the walls of the Takamatsuzuka burial mound, found in the Asuka area in 1972, were also painted towards the end of the seventh century and were based on Chinese models. The depictions on the walls of male and female figures were finely executed, and the colour has been well preserved. The ceiling is dotted with small pieces of gold leaf, which are joined by reddish lines to represent groups of stars.

Progress was also made in the seventh century in other art forms. The *tamamushi no zushi* ('portable shrine'), preserved in the Hōryūji, has panels painted with lacquer and lead colours mixed in oil (*mitsuda-e*). The panels were also ornamented with Buddhist images embossed on gilt bronze foil. Small Buddhist images, finely executed, were cast in gilt bronze. Bronze coffin fittings, as well as mirrors, have also survived from this period. Ornamental tiles of various types were manufactured for use on temples and palaces, and Buddhist images were stamped in relief on brick tiles (*senbutsu*).

Early Japanese art owed much to Chinese influence and inspiration, but by the seventh century the Japanese genius for selection and adaptation had been demonstrated, and the flowering of an individual Japanese civilization had begun.

III

The Establishment of the First Capital City: The Nara Period (710–84)

The eighth century in Japan, when the capital was for most of the period at Nara, saw the growth of Buddhism, the flourishing of the arts, especially sculpture and architecture, and the first flowering of Japanese poetry. Administration and agriculture were developed, but the collection of adequate revenue to support an unproductive court and priesthood produced economic problems. Life was more secure, but disease and natural disaster meant that life for the majority of the approximately 6 million people of Japan at that time was hard and brief.

Political Developments

The city of Nara, then called Heijōkyō, was originally built between 708 and 712, and the capital was established there in 710 during the reign of the Empress Gemmei (661–721; reigned 707–15). It was modelled on the T'ang dynasty (618–907) capital of Ch'ang-an (Sian), on a rectangular grid pattern. It was nearly 5 kilometres by $4\frac{1}{2}$ kilometres. The temples of Saidaiji, Tōshōdaiji and Yakushiji lay on the west side of the city, with Kōfukuji, Gangoji and Daianji on the east side. Tōdaiji and Shin-Yakushiji lay outside the boundaries of the city. Heijōkyō had no outer wall or moat, neither being considered necessary, because of the relatively peaceful state of the country at this period.

The political history of the Nara era is essentially the story of relations between, on the one hand, the titular sovereign and his or her court, family and advisers, who were drawn primarily from the Fujiwara family, and on the other, the increasingly powerful Buddhist hierarchy.

Few Japanese titular sovereigns made any memorable individual contributions to the development of Japanese civilization and institutions or emerge in the pages of history as outstanding personalities. But two eighth-century sovereigns were at least of symbolic importance for the future development of Japan, although their own personal contributions may have been marginal. The Emperor Shōmu (701–56; reigned 724–49) did much to promote Buddhism in Japan. In 741 he ordered the establishment of temples in every province (the so-called *kokubunji*). He was also instrumental in the building of the great temple of Tōdaiji, as well as in making grants of land to Buddhist temples. The arts flourished, and government expenditure increased. Shōmu abdicated in 749 to become a Buddhist monk (he was the first Japanese Emperor to do so). He was succeeded by his daughter, who took the name of Kōken. She came under the influence of her cousin, Fujiwara no Nakamaro (also known as Oshikatsu), who persuaded her to abdicate in 758 to make way for the Emperor Junnin, but the ex-Empress retained much of the real power. A Buddhist priest, known as Dōkyō, won her favour. A quarrel ensued with Nakamaro, who was defeated and killed. Junnin was then deposed and banished to the island of Awaji in the inland sea, where he died (he was probably strangled). In 764 Kōken gave up being a nun and once again became the titular sovereign of Japan, taking the name of Shōtoku. Dōkyō was appointed chief minister and was given the title of Hō-ō (a title now used for the Pope). He took up residence in the palace, and his behaviour became increasingly autocratic. In 769 he overreached himself. He claimed that the (Shintō) god Hachiman (sometimes described as the god of war), whose main shrine is at Usa in Kyūshū, thought that Dōkyō should become Emperor. The Empress decided to send her own messenger to consult the god. The reply, as relayed to the Empress, was that, as Dōkyō was not of imperial lineage, he could not become Emperor. Dōkyō was furious, and the messenger was exiled for bringing back a 'false' message; but when the Empress sickened and died in 770, Dōkyō was banished.

After their experience with the Empress Kōken/Shōtoku and other female rulers in the seventh and eighth centuries, who had been under priestly control, a consensus seems to have emerged that there should be no more female sovereigns in Japan. At any rate there were none until the Tokugawa era, when the sovereigns, confined in Kyoto, had only a ceremonial role.

The power of the Buddhist hierarchy had grown so greatly in the seventh and eighth centuries that a reaction in favour of Japan's indigenous cults was inevitable. As a result, Shintō shrines, as well as Buddhist temples, thrived, and traditional ceremonies, such as the national purification and harvest rituals, were revived. Another result of the reaction was the production in 712 of the *Kojiki* and in 720 of the *Nihongi*.

The *Taihō* legal code, completed in 701 (see page 25), has not survived and is only known through ninth- and tenth-century commentaries which took account of revisions made in the intervening period. There were four categories of laws. The *ritsu* formed a penal code, the *ryō* a civil and administrative code, while the *kyaku* and *shiki* were regulations covering the enforcement and interpretation of the basic codes. The *Taihō* code was revised in 718, but the revised or *Yōrō* code, as it came to be called, was not enforced until 757.

One of the more important administrative developments in the Nara period was the attempt to expand the power of the court over the provinces (*kuni*). By the beginning of the ninth century there were sixty-six provinces, including five 'home' provinces known as *kinai*. The other provinces were organized in groups which came to be called *dō*. Some of these names are still used today, for example Tokaidō (literally, 'eastern sea road'), which now means the main route between Kyoto and modern Tokyo. A governor (*kokushi*) was appointed by the court. He was nominally responsible for all legal, civil, military, judicial and religious matters in his province, but in reality his powers were limited by the strength of the local clan chiefs. Their control over the land and its cultivators made the appointment of effective governors difficult, although by the eighth century the influence of many of the clans had been reduced by the lack of a tradition of primogeniture and the consequent break-up of big estates. None the less the governors found their real powers circumscribed. Their salaries were low, and corruption was rife. Annual inspections and rules to prevent governors handing over to their successors until they had been cleared by the inspectors seem to have been generally ineffective.

Many of the provincial governor's tasks were carried out by the lieutenant-governors of the districts into which each province was divided. The districts were called *gun*, and the lieutenant-governors were entitled *gunshi*. They were in theory appointed for life and were almost invariably local chiefs. There were eventually 592 *gun*. These were subdivided into an average of twenty *go*, which are sometimes described as townships, but which were generally collections of households spread over a fairly wide area. *Go* were in their turn divided into groups of five households (termed *goningumi*) under a headman who was responsible for law and order, taxes and so on. (This principle of collective responsibility remained an important feature of Japanese life up to the twentieth century.) It has been estimated that the average *go* consisted of about nine hundred people. On this basis a *gunshi* probably controlled some 20,000 people.

One of the tasks which fell to provincial governors was the supply of men for military service. Many of those conscripted were in fact used as labourers on the construction of temples and palaces in the capital, and military service was thus a form of corvée. The palace guards, who had a largely ornamental role, were selected on the basis of social status. The only real soldiers were those employed on garrison duties either in Kyūshū or in the northern provinces where the *emishi* remained a threat. The Nara period was one of comparative tranquillity, and soldiering was not highly regarded in Japan at this time.

The government in Nara needed better communications to ensure closer control of the provinces and to bring in supplies and taxes for the capital. Tracks were improved and bridges built. In this task the government had the help of the Buddhist priest Gyōgi (670–749), who was later given the posthumous title of *Bosatsu*. He has been called Japan's first civil engineer. He is also reputed to have produced the first map of Japan.

The main aim of the central government was to get increased revenue from the provinces, in order to provide for the large number of unproductive people at court and for the growing number of monks and nuns in the temples and monasteries in the capital. Constant efforts, which were to be repeated over the centuries, were accordingly made to squeeze the maximum out of the farmers and to bring more land under cultivation. In 722 orders were issued to the provincial governors that one million *chō*, equivalent to about $2\frac{1}{2}$ million hectares and almost equal to the amount of land already being cultivated, was to be turned into farmland. The governors were to make the necessary iron tools available and to provide rations for the workmen involved. Temples such as the Tōdaiji in Nara helped with the supply of tools, but iron for essential tools such as spades and hoes was not yet easily available; and the task of building terraces and irrigation canals needed for rice growing in a country as mountainous as Japan was particularly arduous and time-consuming. To encourage those involved to ever greater efforts, exemptions from tax on the new land brought into cultivation, and uninterrupted tenure for up to three generations, were granted. This meant that the government's hope of doubling the amount of land for allocation under the *ku-bun-den* system was largely nullified, and the tax on old land had to become ever more onerous. As a result many farmers neglected their original allocations of land and concentrated on the new fields, which were exempt from

31

tax. As an incentive to maintain cultivation of taxable land, the government provided advances of seed rice, but the high rates of interest charged, up to 35 per cent, merely increased the farmers' burden. The land allocation system, which was never universally applied in Japan, broke down, and many cultivators fled from controlled land and sought the protection of powerful local chiefs and monasteries. Thus began the slow process which led in the twelfth century to the development of Japanese-style feudalism.

The economic problems must not, however, be exaggerated. The great temples of Nara were built and endowed. The court became the centre for an increasingly cultivated aristocracy. Civil disturbances were relatively infrequent, and there were signs of increased prosperity. One indication of this was the growing use of money in the eighth century. In 708 copper was discovered in the Chichibu mountains to the west of the Kantō plain. A mint was established to produce copper and silver coins. In 712 the price of rice was fixed by edict at one *mon* (copper cash) for six *shō* (one *shō* equals 1.8 litres). Salaries of officials also began to be expressed partly in monetary terms as well as in quantities of rice. Gold coins were first produced in 760, following the discovery of gold in northern Japan. The authorities had difficulties in fixing the exchange rate between copper, silver and gold, and counterfeiting grew. Huge quantities of copper were required to produce bells and images for the Nara temples. For instance, the great bell of the Tōdaiji, which was cast in 732, weighed just under 50 thousand kilograms (49 tons); the Daibutsu of Tōdaiji (see page 34) required ten times as much copper.

Eighth-Century Buddhism

Buddhism brought Chinese civilization to Japan. In the Nara period it was still the religion of the élite around the sovereign and had not yet achieved popular appeal. Even at the court it was seen more as a form of magic than a way of life. The Buddhist sutras came to be read as a piece of ritual rather than as a means to study Buddhist philosophy and ethics. Regular readings of the Buddhist sutras, which derived from Sanscrit originals, were prescribed but, as few of the monks understood the contents of the scriptures, and in view of the vast quantity of holy books, the practice of 'skipping' (*tendoku*) evolved. The sutras were covered by the reading of a few phrases at the beginning, in the middle and at the end of the book. In this way numerous sutras could be read comparatively quickly. Sutras which became popular in Japan included the *Hannyakyō* (*Prajñāpāramitā*), which taught that all things are empty, the *Kegonkyō* (*Avtamsaka*), which taught the altruistic way of the Bodhisattva, the *Hokkekyō* (*Saddharmapundarīka*), commonly known as the Lotus Sutra, which taught that Buddhist practices would lead to perfection and that there was one eternal Buddha, and the Pure Land Sutras, which advocated belief in the saving powers of Amida Buddha.

Many of those who became monks or nuns did so, not so much to achieve personal salvation, but as a form of self-sacrifice on behalf of others. The inspiration was thus not so much Buddhist as the traditional virtue of loyalty to a superior or as a result of filial piety. But elements of Buddhist thinking were permeating Japanese life. Cremation replaced tomb burial. The growing abhorrence of taking life led to exile being used more often than execution as a form of punishment. An element of compassion for the sufferings of others also began to be shown by the authorities at the court.

During the Nara period there were six main sects or schools active in Japan. Monks frequently studied a number of differing doctrines. Buddhist teaching was rarely exclusive in its approach, and in Japan Buddhism responded to Japanese mood and tradition by being particularly eclectic.

The imperial family still asserted their divine origins, and the sovereigns, although they were now mostly supporters of Buddhism and increasingly frequently became monks or nuns on abdication, spoke of themselves as 'manifest gods'. (The Emperor Shōmu exceptionally styled himself as the servant or slave of the three Buddhist treasures when in 749 he addressed the eternal universal Buddha of the Tōdaiji.) The court worshipped the traditional Japanese gods as well as the Buddhist deities, and the great Kasuga shrine was established in a central site in the essentially Buddhist capital of Nara.

As a result of a typically Japanese compromise, Shintō gods were often treated as if they were manifestations of the Buddha. This syncretism is known as *honji-suijaku* or Shinbutsu-konkō. Later a system of dual Shintō or Ryōbu-Shintō was developed by the Shingon sect (see page 52), in which the deities of the Ise shrine (Amaterasu-O-Mikami and Toyoukehime) were identified with Dainichi-Nyorai (Roshana/Mahavairocana). This syncretism led to temples having Shintō shrines in their precincts and vice versa.

It is not clear who was responsible for developing Japanese forms of religious syncretism. It almost certainly evolved over a long period, but Gyōgi Bosatsu is often claimed as the originator. According to one story he was sent with a Buddhist relic to the shrine of the sun goddess at Ise, in about 742, to seek Amaterasu's agreement to the casting of the great image of Dainichi-Nyorai (Roshana/Mahavairocana), which became the *Daibutsu* of the Tōdaiji (see page 34). After seven days and seven nights of prayer the goddess is said to have indicated her welcome for the project. This was recorded in elliptical terms in the extraordinary medium of Chinese verse. The Emperor is later said to have had a confirmatory dream in which the sun and the Buddha were declared to be the same.

Another event, showing the development of Japanese religious syncretism, is said to have occurred in 749, shortly after the accession that year of the Empress Kōken. Hachiman, whose main shrine is at Usa in Kyūshū, was reported to have declared his wish to visit Nara to support the construction of the Daibutsu. A large retinue was sent to Usa to escort the symbol (*shintai*) of the god to Nara. The symbol was then placed in a shrine built within the precincts of the Tōdaiji, and five thousand Buddhist monks prayed and chanted sutras in his honour. Dances were also performed, and the god was given a 'cap' marking the conferment on him of the highest court rank. In 793 Hachiman was officially designated a Bodhisattva.

Four of the so-called Nara sects had in fact been introduced into Japan before 700. These were Jōjitsu and Sanron in 625, Hossō in 654 and Kusha in 658. Jōjitsu was soon absorbed by Sanron, which means 'the three treatises'. It was a Mahayana sect, which asserted an extreme form of idealistic philosophy, arguing that all phenomena are unreal. The Hossō sect took the line that consciousness was the only reality. The Kusha sect, on the other hand, which followed the Hinayana form of Buddhism, took a realistic approach to phenomena. All four sects, in their different ways, sought to understand the nature of the universe, but their metaphysical approach had little appeal to the pragmatic mind of the Japanese and had no influence outside the monasteries in Nara. Of these sects only the Hossō has any followers in Japan today. The Hōryūji, Yakushiji and Kōfukuji in Nara all follow the Hossō school. The patron of the southern branch at the Gangōji in Nara was at one time Gyōgi Bosatsu.

The Ritsu sect was brought to Nara in 754 by the Chinese priest Ganjin. He had been invited to come to Japan as early as 733 and made six attempts to make the journey. When he eventually reached Japan in 753 he was aged sixty-six and blind. He took up residence in the Tōdaiji where the imperial messenger Kibi no Mabi, who is reputed to have invented *katakana*, passed on to him the imperial authority to perform ordination rites. The Ritsu sect's prime concern was with monastic discipline and ensuring that ordinations were carried out correctly. A special ordination platform (*kaidan*) was built, and four hundred novices, including the Empress dowager, were ordained by Ganjin in a solemn ceremony. At the same time forty monks, whose original ordination was not considered to have been performed properly, were re-ordained. Two other *kaidan* were then established, one in Kyūshū and one in northern Japan, for the performance of ordinations. Ganjin later moved to the Tōshōdaiji in Nara, where another *kaidan* was built. He died there in 763 at the age of seventy-seven.

The sixth Nara sect was the Kegon. This was based on the *Kegon* (*Avatamsaka*) *Sutra*, which in addition to teaching the altruistic way of the Bodhisattva argued that Shaka (Sakyamuni) was a manifestation of Dainichi-Nyorai (Roshana/Mahavairocana), the universal Buddha. Dainichi-Nyorai was portrayed as living on a lotus flower with a thousand petals. Each petal on which a Shaka sat was thought to represent a universe in which there were a myriad world, each with its own Buddha. It was suggested that this pattern reflected the hierarchy of the state in Japan. In 749 the Emperor Shōmu decreed that the *Kegon Sutra* was to be regarded as the authoritative Buddhist book. Tōdaiji was also called Kegondaiji, and the provincial temples (*kokubunji*) which were established following an order in 741 were placed under the supervision of the Tōdaiji. The provincial convents were at the same time placed under the supervision of the Hokkeji in Nara.

The outstanding Buddhist event of the Nara period was the establishment of the Daibutsu of the Tōdaiji. In 735, following a serious epidemic probably of smallpox, plans were made to set up a vast image of Dainichi-Nyorai, but disturbances in western Japan led to delays, and the first attempt in 744 to cast the image failed. In 747 a new attempt was made, and under the supervision of one Kamimaro, who was of Korean ancestry, the image was completed in 749. A great hall, some 86 metres in length, 50 metres wide and 46 metres high, was built to house the image. The Great Buddha or Daibutsu was dedicated in 752 in a magnificent ceremony, during which the eyes of the image were touched as a symbol of life. The figure is just over 16 metres high and weighs some 560,000 kilograms (or 550 tons). After gold was found in 749, gold leaf was used to cover the surface of the image. The hall was burned down in the twelfth century, and the present building is only two-thirds the original size. The image has had several repairs and is not now, even if it once was, an outstanding work of art, but the image and the hall are none the less impressive.

Art

The Nara period (710–84) roughly corresponds with the dates (725–94) for the era which art historians call Tempyō. This was an epoch when Buddhist sculpture reached its highest point. Vast temple complexes were built, primarily in and around Nara. Contacts with China and Korea expanded, and the arts were boosted by the demands of an increasingly prosperous court and growing priesthood.

The great Nara temples such as Yakushiji, Tōdaiji, Kōfukuji and Tōshōdaiji required the services of many skilled carpenters and hordes of labourers. The task of finding, cutting down and transporting the huge cedar trees for the main columns and beams of the temples was a major operation at a time when roads were mere tracks and there were no cranes or other modern equipment. The building of the huge hall of the Daibutsu at the Tōdaiji was a colossal engineering feat. The foundations had to be firm and the buildings strong to withstand earthquakes and typhoons. Expert potters were required to make tiles, while carvers, painters and other craftsmen had to be trained and employed on the internal decoration of the temples.

Unfortunately few of the original buildings from the Nara period have survived earthquake, fire and civil war, but many buildings rebuilt in later periods give some idea of the Nara of the eighth century. Of the original buildings still surviving one of the finest is the three-storey pagoda of the Yakushiji (it appears to be a six-storey pagoda because of the roofs over the outer corridors). It has a lightness and graceful balance which give it a unique beauty. The Sangatsudō (also called Hokkedō) of the Tōdaiji is relatively small, but its classic simplicity gives a feeling of serenity. Another fine eighth-century building is the main hall of the Shinyakushiji. The scale is modest and the pitch of the roof low, expressing a sense of reticence. The kondō of the Tōshōdaiji, with its portico of eight massive columns and jutting-out eaves, underlines the solidity and simplicity of Nara-period temple architecture. The kōdō (lecture hall) of the Tōshōdaiji, originally a palace building in Nara, is another memorable building of the period.

One building which has come to symbolize the architecture of the Nara period is the Shōsōin. This was built to house the personal treasures of the Emperor Shōmu, which were dedicated to the Buddha of the Tōdaiji by his widow in 756. It was built on forty pillars over two and a half metres above the ground. It had no windows and was made in what is called the azekura system whereby beams cross each other and project outwards at right angles. The logs were made to swell in damp weather and contract in the dry winter climate of Japan. This ensured ventilation when it was needed but prevented humidity from affecting the contents. This system provided a solidity to the building and ensured that internal pillars and walls were not needed. As the building is formed from two separate log buildings, the interior is divided into three sections. Long, narrow and imposing, the Shōsōin has inspired modern Japanese architects.

The Shōsōin contains a unique and unparalleled collection of treasures. Many of these were gifts or imports from China and central Asia; some may even have come from as far away as Persia and even Greece. But there were also many objects made in Japan. The treasures include weapons, utensils in metal, lacquer, glass and pottery, musical instruments, mirrors and textile items, as well as numerous manuscripts.

One of the finest collections of Nara-period sculpture is in the museum of the Kōfukuji. The Ashura with three faces and six arms is supposed to be a wrathful and fierce deity, but the faces are beautiful, and the slender body gives this statue great charm. The realism and humanity of the statue are enhanced by the use of a dry lacquer technique over wood. The Sangatsudō, which forms part of the Tōdaiji, is crowded with statues, mainly of deities of Indian origin. The main image is a Kannon, about five metres high, in dry lacquer, surrounded by guardians in the same medium. In addition, there are dry clay statues of four other deities. The Kannon is masculine and powerful; it has a sparkling silver crown, approximately seventy centimetres in diameter, and ornamented with filigree and gems of many kinds. The four guardian kings in dry clay in the Kaidanin of the Tōdaiji are outstanding examples of this form of image. They are life size, and each stands on a diminutive demon, in differing poses suggesting vitality and power. The central figure in the Shinyakushiji is a large wooden figure of Yakushi Nyorai. He is surrounded by images of the twelve divine generals in unbaked clay. Each figure is different in pose, gesture and feature and almost frighteningly realistic. A number of portrait sculptures have also survived from the Nara period. One of the most memorable is of the blind priest Ganjin in the Tōshōdaiji.

Little painting from the Nara period has survived. In a small painting of Kichijōten, preserved in the Yakushiji, embroidered and flowing drapery are depicted with a grace and delicacy which confirm the inspiration and ability of Nara-period artists. An illustrated sutra preserved in Rendaiji in Kyoto shows a mastery of colour and design.

Casting in bronze made great progress. Apart from statues and bells, one of the finest surviving relics of the period is the bronze lantern which stands before the Daibutsuden of the Tōdaiji. It has delicate tracery and includes a number of fine embossed images.

Literature

Japanese literature had its origins in the Nara period. The *Kojiki* was completed in 712 and can be counted as the first piece of literature in Japanese. Even if the myths which are recorded in it seem crude and often inconsequential, the stories and especially the poems in the *Kojiki* have a certain charm and are of real historical interest and importance. The writing of the *Kojiki* with Chinese characters often used phonetically was a considerable feat.

The *Nihongi* or *Nihonshoki* and its sequels such as the *Shokunihongi*, which records events from 697 to 791, being written in Chinese, cannot be counted as Japanese literature. Nor can the *Kaifūsō*, the first collection of poems in Chinese by Japanese poets, which was completed in 751. But these works underline the central role of Chinese education in Japan at this period. Chinese was the language of government and scholarship in much the same way as Latin was in medieval Europe.

The *Fūdoki*, which were gazetteers covering the natural resources and traditions of the provinces, were early compilations in Japanese. Only five of any length have survived, and only one of these, the *Izumo Fūdoki*, compiled in 733, is in its original form. Its account of the *Taika* reform is the sole contemporary account of how the reforms were carried out in the provinces.

The *norito*,[1] which were Shintō prayers or incantations used in ceremonies, probably in many cases date from pre-Nara times. They have literary qualities, but they were not committed to writing until the Engi period (901–23).

The great Japanese literary work of the Nara period was the compilation in about 760 of the *Manyōshū*. The title means literally the collection of ten thousand (or myriad) leaves. In fact it contains some 4,500 poems, divided into twenty books. The poems were written in Chinese characters, largely but not invariably used phonetically, in a way roughly similar to that used in the *Kojiki*, but the use of Chinese characters had become somewhat more consistent, and the characters written in this way in the *Manyōshū* have come to be called *Manyōgana*. Even so some readings remain obscure, and scholars have had difficulty in reconstructing a modern *kana* text. Some of the poems in the *Manyōshū* were accompanied by prefaces and notes in Chinese, indicating that to some at the court writing poems in Japanese was regarded as verging on the vulgar. The *Manyōshū* was the first of the great Japanese collections of poems and in the view of many critics the greatest of them all, not least because of the freshness of the sentiments expressed. It seems to have been an anthology of other earlier anthologies, which have since been lost. A production of this kind in the Dark Ages of eighth-century Europe would have been unimaginable.

Most of the poems in the collection were written by a limited number of educated people at the court in Nara. Some, however, predate the Nara period. A few reflect traditional songs. *Azuma-uta* are, for instance, songs from the eastern part of the country. The themes covered are fairly limited. The American scholars Brower and Miner identify four basic themes: 'beauty, "tragedy" (perhaps better irony), cause and effect, and time'.[2] They also note the naivety of many of the poems. A favourite theme in the *Manyōshū* and in later collections is the Buddhist concept of the impermanence of life, shown, for instance, in the fading of flowers and the falling blossoms. Many poems show the delicacy of feeling for human relationships which has characterized Japanese poetry through the ages. The depiction tends to be impressionistic, and there is a rich use of imaginative imagery. The Japanese have come to associate the word *makoto*, which may be translated as 'sincerity', with the poems in the *Manyōshū*.

The absence of stress in Japanese means that there is no exact equivalent in Japanese poetry to the rhythms found in western verse. The limited number of word endings (all Japanese words end in a vowel sound, except for a few imported Chinese words which end in 'n') leaves no scope for rhyme, which is not found in Japanese poetry. The music of poetry in Japanese has to be achieved by the careful selection of mellifluous words and by such techniques as alliteration.

The majority of the poems in the *Manyōshū* (some 90 per cent), and almost all poems in later imperial collections, were brief single-stanza poems called in Japanese *tanka* (literally, short poems) or *waka* (Japanese poems) or simply *uta* (songs). A *tanka* consists of 31 syllables set out in five lines of 5, 7, 5, 7 and 7 syllables. (*Haiku*, which were developed in the seventeenth century, are even shorter, consisting of only 17 syllables set out in three lines of 5, 7 and 5 syllables.) The *Manyōshū* also includes some sixty poems with an additional 7 syllables in a combination of 5, 7, 7, 5, 7 and 7 syllables. These are called *sedōka*, but they are not found in later collections and are not generally considered to be among the more successful poems. There are also some 260 longer poems called *choka* or *nagauta* (literally, long poems) of up to 150 lines, usually of 5 and 7 syllables. These include what are called *hanka* or 'envoys', a form of supplementary or summary verse. *Chōka* are almost unique to the *Manyōshū*. There are no epic poems or ballads in Japanese.

Japanese poetry from the earliest times used a number of conventions. Later these became highly stylized, but in the *Manyōshū* their use is not as meretricious as it became in later anthologies. One of these conventions is the *makura kotoba* (literally, 'pillow word'). These are adjectives or adjectival phrases, usually forming one line of five syllables, applied to particular nouns or names. They have been compared with Homer's use of phrases such as 'swift-footed' whenever he mentioned Achilles[3] or 'rosy-fingered' when referring to dawn. Brower and Miner[4] prefer to call them amplification phrases which became part of a stylized imagery. They give as one example the phrase *shirotae no* meaning 'white hempen' or 'white linen' as the conventional epithet applying to the word *sode* meaning sleeve. Another example is *chihayaburu* meaning 'mighty' before the word *kami* or god.

Another convention, which began in the *Manyōshū*, but which became more important in later anthologies and indeed tended to replace *makura kotoba*, was the use of *kakekotoba* or 'pivot words'. These are words which can be used in two different senses and may be described as a kind of punning device. They were used in a semi-humorous way in the linked verses called *renga* which developed from about the twelfth century. They were also used in later ages in prose fiction and in dramas. *Kakekotoba* complicate the problems of translating Japanese poems into English.

Some of the poets represented in the *Manyōshū*, such as Kakinomoto no Hitomaro (*fl.* 680–700), Yamanoue no Okura (?660–733) and Yamabe no Akahito (*died* 756), are regarded as among Japan's greatest poets. One of the main compilers seems to have been Otomo no Yakamochi (718–85). Poems by him and by his father Otomo no Tabito (665–731) feature largely in the *Manyōshū*, but there are also many anonymous poems in the anthology.

It is difficult to convey in roman script and in translation the visual and melodic appeal of Japanese poetry, but the following examples of *tanka* from the *Manyōshū* may help to give some idea, at least, of the sentiment of Japanese poets of this time.

By Kakinomoto no Hitomaro:[5]

Ame no umi ni	In the ocean of the sky
Kumo no nami tachi	Course the undulating waves of cloud,
Tsuki no fune	Rising by the moon-boat
Hoshi no hayashi ni	As it seems to disappear in rowing
Kogikakuru miyu.	Through the forest of the stars.

By Otomo no Yakamochi:[6]

Uraura ni	The lark soars
Tereru harubi ni	Into the spring air that shines
Hibari agari	So gloriously —
Kokoro kanashi mo	But I am left behind alone,
Hitori shi omoeba.	And burdened with my thoughts.

By Yamabe no Akahito:[7]

Masurao wa	The noble warriors
Mikari ni tatashi	Set forth upon the royal hunt,
Otomera wa	While the ladies
Akamo susobiku	Trail their scarlet skirts
Kiyoki hamabi o.	Along the clean-swept beach.

And Yamabe no Akahito's famous poem about Mount Fuji (one of the many in Japanese literature):[8]

Tago no ura yu	Emerging from behind
Uchiidete mireba	The barrier shadow cast by Tago's shore,
Mashiro ni zo	I am startled by
Fuji no Takane ni	The lofty cone of Fuji whitely dazzling
Yuki wa furikeru.	Underneath its newly fallen snow.

Finally an anonymous poem with irregular numbers of syllables in the third and fourth lines:[9]

Niwakusa ni	A passing shower
Murasame furite	Has fallen on the garden grass
Korogi no naku	And I hear the voice
Koe kikeba	Of the crickets singing
Akizuki ni keri.	Autumn is here.

IV

The Civilization of the Court:
The Heian Period (784–1185)[1]

During the Heian period of four centuries, Japanese culture of great refinement and sensibility, independent of and distinct from that of China, developed. Chinese influence remained significant, however, especially in the first century of this period. The civilization of the Heian court was created by a small hereditary aristocracy, who were largely divorced from the agricultural economy which provided the economic basis for their existence. At the court an aesthetic cult of beauty in nature and art was cultivated. The courtiers abhorred violent and coarse behaviour. A unique society was created, for which there are few parallels. It existed at a time when Europe was just emerging from the Dark Ages.

Buddhism grew in importance and popularity under the leadership of some outstanding teachers, but the indigenous cult survived and developed in association with Buddhism.

In the provinces, while more land was brought under cultivation, land available for allocation to farmers and providing revenue for the court was increasingly displaced by estates owing allegiance to local chiefs. Gradually a feudal structure evolved as central rule weakened and law and order declined. At the same time a military caste developed, and the foundations of the regimes of subsequent centuries were laid.

The New Capital

In 784 the Emperor Kammu (734–806), who had become Emperor in 781, decided to move the capital away from Nara. The decision was probably due primarily to a desire to escape from the strong priestly influences which were at work in Nara. A site at Nagaoka near the present city of Kyoto was chosen, and a palace for the Emperor was built. In 793, however, instructions were suddenly given for the capital to be moved to another site nearby. The move took place in the following year. The new capital came to be called Heiankyō or 'the capital of peace and tranquillity', and this became the modern city of Kyoto (this name, which simply means 'capital city', was adopted in the twelfth century). One factor in this further move appears to have been fears arising from an incident that occurred in 785. Fujiwara no Tanetsugu, a favourite of the Emperor Kammu and an advocate of the move to Nagaoka, was assassinated by Prince Sawara, the Emperor's half-brother, who considered that he had a better claim to the throne than Kammu. The Prince was banished to the island of Awaji in the Inland Sea, but died or was murdered on the way. A number of calamities which followed

40

this event were ascribed to his vengeful spirit, and in an attempt to pacify his ghost he was eventually named posthumously in 799 as the Emperor Sudo.

Heiankyō was laid out on the lines of the T'ang dynasty capital of Ch'ang-an. Like Nara it was rectangular in shape, about five kilometres by four and a half kilometres. It was divided symmetrically by broad avenues and oriented to the points of the compass. The blocks between the avenues were criss-crossed by narrow streets. Tree-lined canals ran beside the main thoroughfares, and the whole city was surrounded by a moat. Suzaku Oji, a street some 82 metres wide, divided the city. At its southern end was a huge gateway, the Rashōmon, where beggars, vagabonds and criminals congregated. This gate provided the only thoroughfare into the city. Suzaku Oji and Rashōmon no longer exist, and almost all of the early buildings have been lost as a result of fire, earthquake and war. But the city has much the same lay-out today as it had in Heian times, and a number of buildings such as the Imperial Palace, last reconstructed in 1856, give some idea of what the old city probably looked like. In the northern part of the city, the Imperial Palace occupied a large enclosure with fourteen gates. Among the many buildings in the palace enclosure were the *daigokuden* or great hall of state, the *shishinden*, a ceremonial pavilion, and the *seiryōden*, which contained the Emperor's living apartments. The palace buildings are said to have been of unparalleled splendour. The senior members of the aristocracy had their residences in the vicinity of the palace. Government offices and the university were also situated in the neighbourhood. The city was bounded on the east by the Kamo river and on the west by the Katsura river. It lay in a basin surrounded by mountains, although it was relatively open to the south.

Prior to the establishment of the capital, the area had been settled by the Hata and Kamo clans. The Hata, who 'donated' the land for the new capital, had been instrumental in building temples in the area. Kōryūji temple, for instance, is said to have been constructed in 622 to house a Buddhist statue. Rokkakudō was supposed to have been put up on the orders of Prince Shōtoku to provide shelter for a statue of Kannon who had appeared to the Prince in a dream. Kiyomizu temple was built in Heian times, but the site seems to have been regarded as sacred when the capital was established. Some of the capital's famous Shintō shrines also date back to a period before the city was founded. The Fushimi Inari and Matsuo shrines were family shrines of the Hata clan, while the Shimo-Kamo shrine was the ancestral shrine of the Kamo family. The Yasaka or Gion shrine, dedicated to Susano-ō no Mikoto, also predates the move to Heiankyō. The Komponchūdō, part of what became the temple of Enryakuji on Mount Hiei, which lies to the north-east (a malignant direction) of the capital, was put up to protect the capital from evil influences. The first temples to be built in the new capital were the Tōji (eastern temple) and the Saiji (western temple) to the east and west of Rashōmon.

Relations with China

During the ninth century Chinese learning was dominant. Official documents continued to be written in Chinese. Japanese students went to study in China. Orthodox Confucian studies were maintained at the university, but the commentaries on the classics, which were prescribed for study, were mostly those of the Han period and not those current in China in the eighth and ninth centuries. The Chinese language was essentially a dead language as far as the Japanese were concerned, and Japanese scholars preferred to emphasize the practical aspects of Confucian teaching rather than the ethical and philosophical aspects. 'The Classic of Filial Piety' was much studied, while the 'Analects' tended to be neglected.

The Japanese were attracted by Chinese astrology and geomancy. In particular they studied the *onyōdō* or the way of the *yin* and the *yang*, the negative and positive principles which, operating on the five elements (fire, water, wood, metal and earth), were thought to cause all phenomena. A bureau, the Onyōryō, was established to advise on the application of the *onyō* principles to everyday events. Bureau staff were the experts on divination, including such matters as auspicious days and directions as well as how to deal with evil spirits.

Many scholarly works, including histories, encyclopaedias and various treatises on such diverse subjects as ceremonial and aspects of administration, were produced in Chinese during the ninth and early tenth centuries. Chinese poetry, especially the works of Po Chü-i (772–846)(Bo Juyi), were studied and copied. The gentlemen of the court were expected to be able to write Chinese verse in much the same way as educated gentlemen in England in the eighteenth century might write Latin and Greek verse. The Emperor Saga (786–842; reigned 809–23), in particular, liked to be accompanied on excursions by men capable of turning out an appropriate Chinese poem to suit the occasion. The court also enjoyed 'winding water banquets', in which courtiers sat beside an artificial stream, drank sake (rice wine) from a cup as it floated by and recited an appropriate verse before they let the cup pass on. One of the main anthologies of Chinese verse during this period was the *Ryōunshū*, produced in 814, but Chinese poetry written by Japanese is not of any literary significance.

Official missions to China were maintained in the early part of the ninth century, but the journeys were dangerous and consequently unpopular. In 803 Fujiwara Kadonomaro was appointed Ambassador to the Chinese court. His mission set off in May of that year, but all of their four ships were damaged in storms, and some members of the mission were drowned. They set off again the following year, but only two of the four vessels reached China and these arrived separately in different places. The Ambassador eventually reached Ch'ang-an (Chang an) in 805, the last year of the T'ang (Tang) Emperor Te-Tsung (De Zong). Following the death of the Chinese Emperor, Kadonomaro set out for home and managed to reach the island of Tsushima, but the second vessel was lost. In 833 envoys were sent to China primarily to acquire books, pictures and luxury items such as perfumes. However, the mission had great difficulties and had to be aborted. The mission leader, Fujiwara Tsunetsugu, again sailed for China in 838. He had major problems in returning to Japan and had to come back via Korea in 839. Thereafter no more official missions were sent to China.

A trade mission was, however, sent in 874–5 to buy incense, perfumes and medicines, and as there was a demand in Japan for Chinese goods – especially scrolls, images and paintings – other trading vessels went to China. Korean traders from the kingdom of Silla were also involved in the trade with China. The Japanese did not seem to be worried about any possible invasion from Korea or even piratical attacks. Sir George Sansom notes that a proposal to exclude Koreans from Japan was not approved, because it was the 'kingly attitude' to treat refugees and castaways with compassion.[2]

Japanese monks continued to go to China to study aspects of Buddhism, and Chinese monks visited Japan. Thus despite the cessation of official missions fairly close cultural relations were maintained. Better ships began to be built in China and Korea, so that travel between China and Japan became somewhat less hazardous.

In 894 a decision was made to send a further official mission to China, and the famous scholar of Chinese classics, Sugawara no Michizane (845–903), was chosen to lead the mission. Michizane had been appointed professor at the university in 877 and from 886 to 890 he was governor of Sanuki province (the modern Kagawa prefecture in Shikoku). On his return to the capital he was promoted to high office by the Emperor Uda (reigned 887–97), who wanted a counterbalance to the growing power of the Fujiwara. Despite his interest in the Chinese classics Michizane had no desire to go to China. He probably saw the appointment as a way of getting rid of him or at least rendering him impotent. Accordingly he argued strongly against the despatch of any further missions to China, emphasizing that conditions in China were unstable. His recommendation was accepted, and in 899 Michizane was appointed 'minister of the right' (udaijin); but his patron, the Emperor Uda, had abdicated in 897, and his successor, the Emperor Daigo (885–930; reigned 897–930), was more favourable to the Fujiwara. In 901 Michizane was accused of plotting against the throne and exiled to an appointment at Dazaifu, the government headquarters in Kyūshū, where he died two years later after writing various poems lamenting his fate and protesting his innocence. Following his death a number of misfortunes were ascribed to his vengeful spirit. He was posthumously pardoned and promoted to the highest court rank. Shrines were dedicated to him in Kyoto (the Kitano Tenjin), in Dazaifu and elsewhere. He has come to be venerated as the god of scholarship and calligraphy; Japanese students, facing examinations, still pray to him for success in their ordeals.

Following the fall of the T'ang dynasty in 907, official relations lapsed. However, Chinese vessels continued to visit Japan during the early part of the Sung (Song) dynasty (960–1279); and although Japanese subjects were forbidden to leave the country, an exception was made for some monks and scholars. In 984, for instance, the Japanese monk Chōnen was given gold by the court to enable him to visit India and China, where he received a friendly reception from the Chinese Emperor. Chinese monks visiting Japan were well received, but there do not seem to have been any significant numbers of Chinese or Korean residents in Japan at this period.

The Ascendancy of the Fujiwara

Throughout much of the Heian period the Fujiwara family were dominant at the court, and the age is sometimes called the Fujiwara period. During most of the ninth century there were some Emperors who were not wholly beholden to the Fujiwara. But by the tenth century the position of the Fujiwara family seemed assured. In the eleventh century, however, their power began to decline, and by the twelfth century they had been largely usurped by other families.

The Fujiwara family produced many leaders of outstanding ability. They had the good sense to realize that any attempt to usurp the throne would jeopardize their position and that they could exercise effective power without having the nominal title of Emperor. They did not, however, shun the trappings and splendour of power, and their palaces were often grander than those of the Emperors they nominally served. The Fujiwara ensured their control over the imperial house by a series of carefully engineered marriages. They fathered a succession of nubile daughters who became imperial consorts. This meant that the leading Fujiwara was often father-in-law of the Emperor and grandfather of the Crown Prince. When the supply of eligible Fujiwara girls ceased, as it did towards the end of the period, Fujiwara family power declined.

In the ninth century the T'ang administrative offices, which the Japanese had adopted, ceased to carry with them real power and became largely titular. The post of chancellor, *dajōdaijin*, was left vacant during much of the eighth century and the first half of the ninth century. The functions of the Dajōkan or grand council of state were taken over in the ninth century by the *kurōdo-dokoro* or bureau of archivists or chamberlains. The *kurōdo-dokoro* was established in 810 by the Emperor Saga (786–842; reigned 809–63), who wanted a private office of men he could trust to handle the most important affairs of state. The impetus for the establishment of the bureau was the plot to replace the Emperor Saga by his elder brother the ex-Emperor Heizei (774–824; reigned 806–9). The leader of the plot was Fujiwara no Kusuko, daughter of Fujiwara no Tanetsugu and a favourite of Heizei. The plot was discovered, and Kusuko poisoned herself. The *kurōdo-dokoro* later expanded to take over the issuing of imperial edicts and the conduct of the affairs of the palace, including the regulation of ceremonies and even the food and clothing worn by the Emperor. Appointment as *kurōdo* or chamberlain grew in importance, and the Fujiwara took care to ensure that, whenever this was possible, their nominees were chosen.

The Kusuko incident also led to the establishment, on the orders of the Emperor Saga, of the *kebiishi* (imperial police) to maintain order in the capital. The *kebiishiichō*, whose head was entitled *bettō*, assumed wide-ranging powers to arrest, try and punish offenders not only in the capital but also in the provinces.

Another office established around the beginning of the ninth century was that of the *kageyushi* (audit officers). Their task initially was to ensure that provincial governors in particular did not misappropriate taxes for their own use, but the scope of their authority was gradually expanded into other areas.

Not all Emperors in the Heian period abdicated, but out of thirty-three Emperors between the accession of the Emperor Kammu in 781 and the abdication of the Emperor Go-Toba in 1198, nineteen abdicated and one, the Emperor Antoku, was deposed in 1180. During the height of Fujiwara power many Emperors were minors, who abdicated or were forced to abdicate when they were still young. This practice necessitated the appointment of regents (*sesshō*). *Sesshō* were originally appointed from among members of the imperial family, but in 866 Fujiwara no Yoshifusa, who had placed his grandson the Emperor Seiwa (850–81; reigned 858–76) on the throne, had himself appointed *sesshō*. The Fujiwara were not, however, generally satisfied with the powers that this office gave them. In 887 the office of *kanpaku* was created and filled by Fujiwara no Mototsune, who had already occupied the post of *sesshō* during the minority of the Emperor Yōzei (868–949; reigned 877–84). The *kanpaku* was supposed to assist an adult Emperor in carrying out his duties, but he was in practice a kind of dictator. The Emperor Uda, who exceptionally was not the son of a Fujiwara daughter, resented Mototsune's high-handed behaviour, but was unable to remove him. However, following Mototsune's death, the Emperor Uda managed to prevent another *kanpaku* being appointed, and it looked for a time as though the growing Fujiwara hold on power had been broken. But the Fujiwara out-manoeuvred Sugawara no Michizane and others surrounding the Emperor Uda and his successor the Emperor Daigo. In 899 Fujiwara no Tokihira was appointed to the key post of 'minister of the left' (*sadaijin*). Tokihira did not assume the post of *kanpaku*, but he was *de facto* ruler of the country. Tokihira's brother, Tadahira, however, took the title of *kanpaku* in 941, and the post was thereafter filled by members of the Fujiwara family with only a few breaks up to 1180. In later periods the post was filled by members of the five branch families of the Fujiwara (the so-called *gosekke* – the Konoe, Kujō, Nijō, Ichijō and Takatsukasa).

The Fujiwara exercised their control of affairs through their family administrative office, the Fujiwara *mandokoro*, which became virtually the main organ of government. It included a *kumonjo*, which dealt with documents, and a *kurōdo-dokoro* (secretariat).

The apogee of Fujiwara power was reached in the time of Fujiwara no Michinaga (966–1028). He was one of the younger sons of Fujiwara no Kaneie, who was *dajōdaijin*, *sesshō* and *kanpaku*. On the death of his father and elder brothers Michinaga became head of the Fujiwara family and became 'minister of the right' (*udaijin*) and examiner of imperial documents (*nairan*). He had his nephew and rival, Fujiwara no Korechika, banished in 996 and until his death in 1028 he was all powerful. Four of his daughters married Emperors, two Emperors were his nephews, and three were his grandsons. In 1016 he became *sesshō* for his grandson Go-Ichijō and in 1017 *dajōdaijin*, but he never took the formal title of *kanpaku*, although after his nominal retirement on grounds of ill health in 1019 he was known as the *Midō-kanpaku* (*Midō* being the name of his residence). He was an accomplished poet, was a student of Buddhism (he built the magnificent temple of Hōjōji, which alas no longer exists) and enjoyed music and splendour. Recognizing the growing power of the provincial clans, he allied himself with the Seiwa branch of the Minamoto family.

The survival of the Fujiwara hegemony for so long, despite their lack of any effective military force under their direct control, demonstrates that loyalty to a leader and his family was more important in Japan than any question of principle. Sansom summed up the Fujiwara hegemony in these words:

> Their general aim and purpose was to increase the wealth of their family. This they might have achieved by administrative competence; but the refinement of intrigue, the weighing and balancing of character and motive, the constant interplay of personality, the game of skill with living pieces, is to a certain temperament a more fascinating exercise of talent than is called for by passing laws and supervising a herd of civil servants. It requires a delicacy of perception, a sensitiveness to fine shades of behaviour, and a superb confidence, which, when used for deliberate ends, can be a source of aesthetic pleasure, of epicurian delight.[3]

The Period of 'Cloister' Government

In 1068 the Emperor Go-Sanjō (1034–73; reigned 1068–73) succeeded to the throne. His mother was not a Fujiwara. While he was Crown Prince during the rule of his half brother, Go-Reizei (reigned 1046–68), he had quarrelled with the then regent, Fujiwara no Yorimichi, who accused him of plotting against Go-Reizei. When Go-Sanjō succeeded, he was determined to break the power of the Fujiwara and he surrounded himself with officials who were not members of the Fujiwara family. In 1073 he abdicated in favour of his son, who became the Emperor Shirakawa (1053–1129; reigned 1073–87) and arranged for the succession to pass in turn to two other sons by a consort from the Minamoto family. Go-Sanjō died soon after his abdication, but he had intended to continue his rule from his retirement and was known as Go-Sanjō In (*In* meaning 'cloister'). When the Emperor Shirakawa abdicated he established his own form of 'cloister' government. With the title of *Hō-ō* he controlled affairs under his three successors, the Emperors Horikawa, Toba and Sutoku, until his death in 1129. At times there was more than one retired Emperor active and commanding revenue for their courts. This peculiarly Japanese system of government came to be termed *insei* (from *in* = cloister and *sei* = government). The Emperors who abdicated did so in order to free themselves from the burdensome ceremonial which accompanied the imperial office. The practice, known as *inkyō* (literally, 'sheltered life'), was later adopted by other office holders.

The Emperor Go-Shirakawa (1127–92; reigned 1155–8) was 'cloistered' Emperor during the reigns of the Emperors Nijō, Rokujō, Takakura and Antoku and part of the reign of Go-Toba, but the power of the cloistered Emperors had by then been destroyed as result of the military conflict known as the *Hōgen no Ran* (1156). This arose from jealousy between the regent Fujiwara no Tadamichi (1097–1164) and his younger brother Yorinaga (1120–56). Tadamichi supported the then reigning Emperor Go-Shirakawa, who also had the backing of the two leading military figures of the time. They were Minamoto no Yoshitomo and Taira no Kiyomori (the subsequent struggle for power between the Minamoto and the Taira dominated the next thirty years). Yorinaga sided with the retired Emperor Sutoku, who had the backing of Minamoto no Tameyoshi, the father of Minamoto no Yoshitomo. Yorinaga was killed, Tameyoshi executed and the Emperor Sutoku exiled. Go-Shirakawa had in theory won, but the power now lay with the military leaders.

Law and Order

During the four centuries of intrigues and power broking which marked the political life of the capital during the Heian period, the central government's hold on the provinces and tax revenues from public land were declining. The life at court was increasingly divorced from the realities outside the capital, and even in the capital law and order began to break down.

During the Nara period the *emishi* or Ainu inhabitants of northern Honshu in the area of the province of Mutsu had made frequent raids on Japanese settlers further south, and the government had had to establish frontier posts to protect the farmers. In 789 Ki no Kosami and his ill-prepared force were beaten by the *emishi* in a pitched battle. In 791 supplies and weapons were requisitioned, and Sakanoue no Tamuramaro (758–811) was ordered to subdue the *emishi*. In 797 Tamuramaro, who became a legendary figure in Japanese history, was named *Seii-tai-shōgun* ('barbarian-quelling generalissimo'). He pushed the frontier north-wards, establishing new military posts in what is now Iwate prefecture. In the course of this campaign his forces were generally successful in suppressing the *emishi*, but the northern provinces remained for much of the Heian period frontier areas, where the life of the settlers was tough and dangerous. Disturbances continued for centuries, but a good deal of intermarriage took place, and eventu-ally the northern provinces were assimilated.

In 1050 Abe Yoritoki, the commander-in-chief in the province of Mutsu, assumed a semi-independent role. Minamoto no Yoriyoshi (995–1048) was appointed governor and commander-in-chief of the province and ordered to suppress the Abe family. The war against the Abe, in which Yoriyoshi was assisted by his son, Yoshiie (1041–1108), lasted some nine years from 1055 to 1063. Yoshiie was again employed in the north-east some twenty years later against the Kiyowara family who had served in the campaign against the Abe, but had later misused their position. They too were defeated after fighting which lasted from 1083 to 1087.

One of the military strongholds in what is now Iwate prefecture was at Hiraizumi. It was here that Fujiwara no Kiyohira (1056–1128), who had assisted Yoshiie in the war against the Kiyowara, settled with his followers in 1094. He and his successors developed Hiraizumi as the main centre of power in the north-east. He built the famous and splendid temple of Chūsonji, whose main hall, the gold-decorated Konjikidō, remains as a memorial to past glories.

Although the north-east continued to be the main area of disorder throughout the Heian period, there were disturbances in other areas from time to time. In 940 Taira no Masakado, who had quarrelled with other members of his family in the Kantō area, attacked the government headquarters first in the province of Hitachi and then in other provinces in the Kantō. He appointed new governors and went so far as to declare himself 'New Emperor', while attempting to turn the Kantō into an autonomous state, independent of the central government in Heiankyō. Masakado was killed by forces under the leadership of Fujiwara no Hidesato in 940. His army was dispersed, and the leaders were captured and executed.

At roughly the same time an ex-governor of the province of Iyo in Shikoku (the modern Ehime prefecture), Fujiwara no Sumitomo, had joined a band of brigands who carried out acts of piracy on the Inland Sea. He invaded Sanuki province (Kagawa prefecture) and then moved into Awa (Tokushima prefecture). Sumitomo was attacked by a large fleet sent by the court and forced to flee to Kyūshū. He returned to Iyo in 941 and was eventually captured and killed.

Even in the capital, life was far from secure. The *kebiishi* became increasingly dependent on the Taira and Minamoto military families for the forces which they required. Appointments to it were made on the basis of pedigree not ability. The Emperor Toba in 1107 declared that the appropriate qualifications for the head of the *kebiishi* were 'good family, good sense, knowledge of precedent, good looks, high court rank, and wealth'. Following Buddhist precepts, the Heian court was reluctant to apply the death penalty, and amnesties for criminals were frequent. In 1040 robbers even broke into the imperial palace and stole some of the Emperor's clothes.

Turbulent monks from the temples on Hieizan not only attacked the branch temple of Onjōji (Miidera) on the shore of Lake Biwa, but engaged in fights with monks from the Kōfukuji in Nara. These monastic quarrels were usually about land and had nothing to do with matters of doctrine. In 989 the monks of Hieizan refused to accept an Imperial nominee as abbot and put up a violent resistance. During the regency of Fujiwara no Yorimichi (1027–74) they sent down three thousand armed monks into the capital to threaten the regent in his palace. The imperial guards were powerless to deal with these turbulent priests, and the help of the Taira and the Minamoto had to be sought. From 1080 onwards armed bands of monks frequently invaded the streets of the capital, where they besieged and tried to blackmail the Fujiwara leaders and even the Emperor himself. The Emperor Shirakawa (1053–1129), a fervent Buddhist, declared that there were three things he could not control; these were the flooding of the Kamo river, the hazards of gambling and the monks of Hieizan.

The growth of the military families was not solely the result of the increase in lawlessness. An important factor was a fatal lack of interest or concern in the capital for developments in the provinces. Governors of the provinces were appointed from the court aristocracy, but these posts were increasingly regarded as titular sinecures, and many governors never took up their posts or even visited their provinces. Instead they found substitutes or even mythical nominees, while they enjoyed the salaries of their office. These were measured in quantities of rice and other products from taxes on public land, but, as the area of public land diminished, salaries became increasingly inadequate to meet the demands of the court aristocracy. Towards the end of the Heian period, therefore, the palaces in the capital became dilapidated. Those lower-ranking aristocrats who did take up provincial posts tended to regard their time away from the capital as a form of exile. In their writings they sometimes sound like the characters in a Chekhov play. The authoress of the *Sarashina nikki*, written in the early part of the eleventh century, begins her story with these words: 'I was brought up in a part of the country so remote that it lies beyond the end of the Great East Road [the Tōkaidō]. What an uncouth creature I must have been in those days!'[4] She prays fervently that things may be so arranged to enable them to go to the capital. Even Mount Fuji, which has become one of the symbols of Japan, was practically unknown to the people in the capital. The Lady Sarashina saw it on her journey to the capital and described her impressions in these words: 'There is no mountain like it in the world. It has a most unusual shape and seems to have been painted deep blue; its thick cover of melting snow gives the impression that the mountain is wearing a white jacket over a dress of deep violet.'

The practice of granting exemptions from taxes to land brought under cultivation had begun in the Nara period. In Heian times the trend intensified, while at the same time holders of public land, to ensure an element of safety for themselves and their families, increasingly commended their land to local chiefs. From about 850 allotments of land under the *ku-bun-den* system became infrequent and after 902 ceased altogether. The number of *shōen* or exempt estates continued to grow throughout the period. Some of the first such exempt estates had been granted to the large Buddhist temples. The Fujiwara also controlled many *shōen* and wherever an opportunity occurred they took more land under their control. The Emperors themselves took advantage of the *shōen* system to make grants of land to their many offspring who had to be found the means of livelihood. These were the future military families, such as the Minamoto and the Taira. The cloistered Emperors in their time too grabbed what *shōen* they could get hold of. The process which led to the impoverishment of the court and reduced still further their power to control events was a gradual one. Various attempts were made to arrest the trend, but most of the edicts issued to this end by the court were in practice little more than empty gestures. In 902 the Emperor Daigo, for instance, issued orders designed to stop the process by which public lands were taken out of the system of taxation, but these were largely ignored. In 985 a further attempt was made without real success to assert the imperial rights over public land. In 1056 yet another move was made to prevent the formation of new *shōen*. A public record office (*kirokujo*) was set up during the reign of the Emperor Go-Sanjō (reigned 1068–72) to keep a register of land and to enquire into titles. This caused some alarm to the Fujiwara and some of the large temples, but the main result was the development of a system of written exemptions rather than any increase in public land.

By the latter half of the eleventh century the court had lost the bulk of its revenue, most of its power and much of its prestige. The provinces were developing into semi-independent fiefdoms. Violent feuds had become endemic, and the country was in danger of falling into anarchy. The development of a centralized system under strong military leadership eventually led to the re-establishment of order. The revolution, when it came, was not a popular uprising. The position of the farmers was little changed; they merely provided the wherewithal for the military caste rather than the court aristocracy. The differences between freemen and serfs tended to disappear. The new military leaders were themselves scions of the court aristocracy, and there was no question of any kind of democratic movement.

Religion in the Heian Period

The Nara Buddhist sects had developed a magnificent ceremonial, but had failed to produce doctrines which could be understood by an intelligent layman. At the beginning of the ninth century two new sects were introduced from China. These were Tendai and Shingon. They had a wider appeal, although Buddhism in the first half of the Heian period, before the Pure Land (Jōdo) movement had become popular, was primarily a religion for the élite. The two sects were promoted by two of the most impressive personalities in the history of Japanese Buddhism – Saichō or Dengyō Daishi, the founder of the Tendai sect in Japan, and Kūkai or Kōbō Daishi, the founder of the Shingon sect.

Saichō (767–822) was born in Omi province (Shiga prefecture) near the modern city of Kyoto. He began to study Buddhism at the age of twelve and after he had been ordained there in 785 he decided to leave Nara, whose rituals he found empty. He set up a hermitage on Mount Hiei, north-east of Kyoto, where he practised meditation. He soon attracted a following, and the Emperor Kammu, who was also critical of the Nara priesthood, showed interest in Saichō's teachings. In 802 Saichō was given permission to study the teachings of the T'ien Tai sect in China. He left with an official mission to the Chinese court in 804. He returned after a nine-month stay, during which he visited Mount T'ien Tai (Tian dei) and studied the doctrines of the sect. He also received some instruction from a master of esoteric Buddhism. On his return to Japan he established the monastery of Enryakuji on Mount Hiei and sought official recognition of the Tendai sect. The Emperor Kammu granted this on the understanding that esoteric teachings would be incorporated in the doctrines of the sect in Japan. He did this because he believed that esoteric rituals performed by Saichō had helped his recovery from a serious illness. The main exponent in Japan of esoteric doctrines was Kūkai, and for some years Saichō and Kūkai were on good terms, but they eventually parted company in 816, when Kūkai claimed that his teachings were the only true ones and refused to return a disciple of Saichō who had defected to Shingon. Saichō next sought permission to establish an independent ordination platform (kaidan) on Mount Hiei, separate from the officially approved kaidan in Nara. In the face of the fierce opposition of the Nara priests permission was at first refused, and it was only granted after Saichō's death in 822. Saichō also wanted his disciples to study for twelve years on Mount Hiei and then go out to preach Buddhism throughout the nation. He was thus claiming that his doctrines were of universal application. The Tendai sect was, however, generally eclectic in its approach.

The doctrines of Tendai are not easily defined. The most important text used by Tendai is the Lotus Sutra (the Hokkekyō). The fundamental doctrine of the sect is the belief that all things, being impermanent, have no separate and independent identity. The absolute is inherent in all phenomena. Ultimate reality cannot be explained in terms of existence and non-existence. 'Everything is real'; 'each thing is identical with all things'; and 'one's ignorant unenlightened state is identical with the state of Buddhahood'. In other words, every being has an element of the Buddha in it, and Buddhahood is attainable by all living beings who achieve enlightenment, which comes from wisdom, good works and intuition. Meditation is an essential means to enlightenment, and adherents are enjoined to meditate on a specific Buddha or Bodhisattva such as Amida or Kannon. The Lotus Sutra exhorted aspirants to 'enter the abode of the Tathagata, put on the robe of the Tathagata and sit in the seat of the Tathagata. And what is the abode of the Tathagata? It is to abide in charity to all beings. What is his robe? It is sublime forbearance. And what is his seat? It is to enter into the emptiness of all things.' Tathagata is rendered in Japanese as Nyorai, which may be defined as 'he who has come as his predecessors came' or as a person who has attained Buddhahood.

Saichō's work was carried on by a number of distinguished successors. Ennin (794–864) went to China in 839 and studied there for nine years. He was a master of esoteric Buddhism and ensured its role in Tendai practices. Enchin (814–91) went to China in 853 and returned in 858. He too had a thorough knowledge of esoteric Buddhism and like Ennin was popular at the court. The followers of Ennin and Enchin, however, followed separate ways, and in 993 the Enchin group established a separate branch of Tendai at the Onjōji (Miidera) on the shores of

Lake Biwa. Quarrels between Enryakuji and Onjōji led to frequent violence in subsequent years.

Kūkai (774–835) or Kōbō Daishi, who introduced the Shingon sect into Japan, has become a legendary figure. He was born in the province of Sanuki (Kagawa prefecture) on the island of Shikoku. The temple of Zentsūji marks his birthplace. Zentsūji is the seventy-fifth of the eighty-eight Shikoku temples which form the Shikoku pilgrimage (henro). Most of the temples on the pilgrimage belong to the Shingon sect and are believed to mark places visited by Kōbō Daishi in the wanderings he undertook after he had withdrawn from the university at Nara, where he had studied the Chinese classics, but had found such studies unrewarding. In 804 he joined the official mission to China on which Saichō also sailed, but in another ship. In Ch'ang-an, the T'ang capital, he studied esoteric Buddhism. He returned to Japan in 806 and in 809 became abbot of a temple on Mount Takao, outside Heiankyō, which is now known as Jingoji. In 819 he established a religious centre on Mount Koya, south of Nara in what is now Wakayama prefecture. In 823 he was allocated by the Emperor Saga (reigned 809–23) the temple of the Tōji at the southern entrance to the capital, and this became the headquarters of the Shingon sect in Japan.

Kōbō Daishi spent most of the last three years of his life on Mount Koya in ascetic practices. He was known not only as a preacher, but also as a sculptor, poet, calligrapher and lexicographer. He is reputed to have developed the *hiragana* syllabary and composed the poem which came, under the name 'Iro Ha', to be thought of as the Japanese 'alphabet'. The poem, of forty-seven syllables, using all the syllables in use in Japanese except the final consonant 'n', expresses the Buddhist view of the transience of human existence. The poem is read in modern pronunciation:

> *Iro wa nioedo chirinuru wo*
> *Waga yo tare zo tsune naran(u)*
> *Ui no okuyama kyō koete*
> *Asaki yume miji ei mo sezu.*

This may be translated as:

> The colours blossom, scatter, and fall.
> In this world of ours, who lasts forever?
> Today let us cross over the remote mountains of life's illusions,
> And dream no more shallow dreams nor succumb to drunkenness.[5]

The doctrines of the Shingon sect, because of their esoteric character, are even more difficult to explain briefly and to comprehend than those of the Tendai sect. Shingon, with its emphasis on mysticism, incantations, ritual and magical spells, cannot be properly explained in words. Sir Charles Eliot has said that the main idea of Shingon is cosmotheism, which is not quite the same as pantheism:

> The whole universe is regarded as the body of the Supreme Buddha *Vairocana* [in Japanese, Dainichi-Nyorai or Roshana-Butsu], being composed of the six elements earth, water, fire, air, ether, and consciousness. These elements play

a prominent part in *Shingon* symbolism and are represented not only by various letters and colours but by a peculiar form of monument often found in cemeteries and called *Sotoba* [a modified form of the *stupa*]. . . . All thoughts, words, and actions, called the three mysteries, are the thoughts, words, and actions of *Vairocana*; he is present in a grain of dust or in a word, and the object of the elaborate mystic ritual is to make us feel that our thoughts, words, and actions derive all their meaning and force from the fact that they are his. . . . *Shingon* has two doctrines, the apparent or *Kengyō*, and the secret or *Mitsukyō*: the former can be studied in literature, the latter is taught only orally and to the initiated.[6]

Shingon, like Tendai, believed that man has the Buddha nature in him and that by proper ritual processes this Buddha element in ourselves can be felt to be identified with the great cosmic Buddha *Vairocana*. Kōbō Daishi defined ten stages in the process of enlightenment. In the tenth and last stage, which is Shingon itself, enlightenment is achieved through the two *mandaras*.

The word *mandara* comes from the Sanscrit word *mandala*, meaning 'a circle or assemblage of persons in a limited space and thence a picture, round or more often quadrangular, divided into several compartments in which are arranged a number, often very considerable, of deities'.[7] The two *mandaras*, representing the two aspects of the cosmic life, consist of two elements – the diamond (*kongōkai*) and the womb (*taizōkai*). 'Diamond is explained as having the two qualities of hardness and utility', where hardness implies eternal and indestructible truth, utility and wisdom. The womb emphasizes the element of living, growth and change. The *kongōkai* can be said to represent the action of wisdom and the *taizōkai* that of reason. Kōbō Daishi held that faith comes through the grace (*kaji*) of the Buddha.

Shingon developed its own pantheon. The Myō-ō are peculiar to Shingon. Though awful in appearance they are in practice benevolent, as they protect their worshippers by frightening away evil spirits and destroying passion and ignorance. Fudo, the most important of the Myō-ō, represents the fierce side of *Vairocana*, when he demonstrates his hatred of wrong-doing. From *Vairocana*, the eternal Buddha, emanate all other Buddhas, and he is conceived as being surrounded by four such emanations. On the west is Amida, the Buddha of the western paradise. One rite peculiar to Shingon is that of *kanjō*, which involves sprinkling with water and has been described as a form of baptism, but it was reserved for those who had made progress in their religion, not for novices.

Shingon, like other Buddhist sects in Japan, had its schisms, the two major divisions being the old and the new. In 1980 there were forty-seven sub-sects of Shingon.

Both Tendai and Shingon were tolerant of the indigenous cult and contributed to the development of Ryōbu-Shintō. Dainichi was, for instance, neatly aligned with the sun goddess, Amaterasu, although the goddess's principal shrine at Ise was always carefully insulated against Buddhist influences which might pollute its purity. Buddhist priests, wishing to make a pilgrimage to Ise, were supposed to wear wigs to disguise their shaven heads, which demonstrated their status as monks. Kōbō Daishi is often regarded as one of the great developers of Ryōbu-Shintō, while Saichō for his part honoured the mountain gods of Hieizan. Even

the most devoted Buddhist Emperors continued to perform Shintō ceremonies. The Fujiwara, despite their adherence to Buddhism, supported their
family shrine, the Kasuga shrine at Nara, as well as other shrines associated
with their family. Shintō shrines throughout the country were maintained and
improved. At this time the main religion of the country was the indigenous cult,
as Buddhism had yet to become a really popular religion. But shrines had temples
within their boundaries, and temples had shrines. Buddhist priests were often put
in charge of Shintō shrines in their compounds. Despite the schismatic tendencies
of Japanese Buddhist sects, religious questions rarely aroused bitter antagonisms
in Japan. The Japanese preferred to look for compromise and accommodation
rather than to emphasize principles. For instance, Buddhism in Japan found no
difficulty in accepting Shintō reverence for ancestors. Buddhism in Japan, like
Shintō, was never monotheistic, and Shintō gods were easily assimilated into the
Buddhist pantheon. This amalgamation of the two faiths provided the basis for
the development of both Tendai and Shingon hermits who lived in the mountains
and frequented the sacred places of Shintō, making them sacred to Buddhists
as well. These became the *yamabushi* or mountain priests and the *shūgenya* who
practised austerities. The Japanese in the Heian period were deeply imbued with
the feelings inspired by Shintō, with its 'joyful acceptance of the natural world
and gratitude for its bounty, coupled with a horror of illness and death, which
are regarded as the source of all pollution'.[8] The only doctrines which were
proscribed in Japan were those which were thought to promote subversive
movements against the state.

An important factor in the Japanese attitude towards life in the Heian period
and the basis for the pessimism current at this time was the general belief among
Buddhists that this was the age of the 'latter days of the law' (the *mappō*). This
was based on statements such as in the Lotus Sutra about 'the last five hundred
years when the true law shall be in a state of decay'. There was no clear definition
of when this period would begin, but most seemed to think that it had already
started. This belief, together with the breakdown of law and order, the weakness
of the court, the despotism of the new military caste and the decadence and
quarrelsomeness of the clergy, provided the basis for the development of 'Pure
Land' Buddhism (*Jōdoshū*). One of the pioneers of 'Pure Land' was the priest
Kūya (903–72), who travelled through Japan urging the people to invoke the
name of Amida Buddha to ward off evil. Such invocation was called the *nenbutsu*,
and Kūya led groups chanting the *nenbutsu* to the accompaniment of bells, drums
and ecstatic dancing. Another early advocate of the *nenbutsu* was the Tendai monk
Genshin (942–1017), who in 985 wrote the *Ojōyōshū* (the 'Essentials of Pure Land
Rebirth'). He believed that mankind must trust in the saving powers of Amida.
As man refrains from evil he is drawn to the realm of peace and tranquillity
through his devotion to Amida and thus escapes from the *karma* of rebirth.
Another Tendai monk, Ryōnin (1072–1132), favoured the *yūzū* (or circulating
nenbutsu), whereby the merit gained from invoking Amida was transferred to all
sentient beings and the *nenbutsu* of one believer procured salvation for others.
The advocates of the *nenbutsu* insisted that salvation came through faith and that
we have to rely on the strength of Amida (*tariki* = other power). Amidism was
not a totally new faith. Historians have traced it back to the days of Shōtoku
Taishi. A *nenbutsuin* was established at the Tōdaiji in Nara in 939, and almost all

the Buddhist sects felt obliged to incorporate at least an element of Amidism in their teaching. Amidism, however, really developed as a popular faith in the Kamakura period with the preaching of Genkū, better known as Hōnen Shōnin (1133–1212), who founded the Jōdo or Pure Land sect of Buddhism in Japan.

Religion for most people in Japan in the Heian period was more a matter of magic and ritual than of ethics and philosophy, although the Buddhist doctrine of *karma* and reincarnation had spread quite widely, and the people at court at least thought that their lives were guided by their destinies (*sukuse*) which arose from their past lives and would condition their future existences. This was *inga* or cause and effect. Divination was regarded as an important government function. Belief in evil spirits was general, and, as Ivan Morris says, 'the world of Heian was heavily populated with goblins, demons, spirits and other supernatural beings' such as the long-nosed *tengu*, foxes and ghosts.[9] Exorcism was a common practice, illness being ascribed to evil spirits or possession. Primitive shamanist practices, including spells and incantations, were frequently invoked. Taboos, requiring avoidance of various activities as well as purifications, arising from Shintō beliefs, were an everyday matter for the aristocrats at the court, but the Japanese bath had not yet become a daily ritual. Indeed, in Heian times 'bathing, at best a rather perfunctory process, could take place only once in five days – and then only if the day was auspicious'.[10]

The Court and Aristocratic Society

Heian civilization centred around the court at Heiankyō. It was created and sustained by a few thousand aristocrats. It existed at a time when Europe was just emerging from the Dark Ages and when Chinese civilization under the Sung dynasty (960–1127) had reached new heights of brilliance in art, literature and philosophy.

In the tenth and eleventh centuries a unique and original culture of exquisite refinement, great aesthetic sensibility and discriminating taste was created in Japan. It was not a philosophically profound culture; it had deep-seated superstitions, and its thought processes were sentimental rather than rational. While members of the court enjoyed splendour and brilliance in their costumes and rituals, their lives were far from luxurious. Simplicity, purity and frugality marked their existence. They pursued with intensity the cult of beauty which, as the late Ivan Morris remarked in his outstanding account of Heian civilization *The World of the Shining Prince*, 'helped to produce a society of great elegance and charm which, despite its many lacunae and fatal weaknesses, will always occupy an important place in the world's cultural history'.[11]

One of these arts was that of making love. It would seem from the literature of the time that assignations and seduction were a major element in the lives of the aristocrats in the capital. But there was nothing coarse or overtly erotic in Heian literature; love was a matter for sentiment, an occasion for charming verses and for the melancholy and sadness of parting:

54

Artistic sensibility was more highly valued than ethical goodness. Despite the influence of Buddhism, Heian society was on the whole governed by style rather than by any moral principles and good looks tended to take the place of virtue. The word *yoki* ('good') [the aristocrats regarded themselves as *yoki hito*; literally, 'the good people'] referred primarily to birth, but it also applied to a person's beauty or to his aesthetic sensibility; the one implication it lacked was that of ethical profundity.[12]

Some historians regard Heian civilization as effete, effeminate and amoral. Japanese nationalists prefer the 'manliness' of the Kamakura period with its military virtues. Marxists consider Heian culture irrelevant and regret their inability to discover signs of a class struggle. Puritans, such as James Murdoch, condemn Heian society in vituperative terms as thoroughly immoral, but they judge by standards which are inapposite. Murdoch described the Heian court as 'an ever-pullulating brood of greedy, needy, frivolous dilettanti – as often as not foully licentious, utterly effeminate, incapable of any worthy achievement, but withal the polished exponents of high breeding and correct "form"'.[13] The more discriminating student will discover in Heian culture some of the finest achievements of Japanese civilization.

We are fortunate in being able, through the mirror of contemporary diaries and novels written by women at the court, as well as from the colourful picture scrolls produced towards the end of the period, to gain a fairly accurate picture of what the court life of the time was like.

The aristocratic families of Heiankyō lived in mansions built in the *shinden* style. (The word *shinden* means 'the master's quarters'.) The *shinden* or main hall was constructed in the centre of a plot of land. It faced south and was rectangular in shape. The sloping roof with wide eaves was usually covered with cypress bark. To the sides and to the north galleries stretched to other pavillions, the northern pavilion being the quarters of the principal wife. On the south side there would be a landscape garden including a lake, with a small island covered with pines, and a stream. Around the whole would be a white wall with a covered entrance for ox-drawn carriages. The pavilions were simple in the extreme and consisted of one room which could, however, be divided by screens. The floors were of bare wood raised about a foot above the ground to allow air to circulate and limit rising damp. Cushions and individual straw mats would be laid directly on the floor, and there was practically no furniture. A *chōdai* (curtain platform) about four-fifths of a metre square formed a kind of bedchamber. The ladies of the household spent most of their lives in seclusion behind their *kichō*, which was a portable screen a little over a metre and a half long, with opaque hangings to protect them from prying eyes. Their love life seems to have begun and ended in semi-obscurity; as a result they were not always quite certain who their lovers were. The pavilions were cool in summer but icy cold in winter. Charcoal braziers were few and inadequate, and the pavilions were drafty. Many layers of clothing were accordingly worn, with much attention paid to the selection of appropriate colours and designs.

Their food was simple, consisting primarily of rice, seaweed, radishes, fruit and nuts. Fish was not generally available in the capital in those days, when even short journeys took many hours (the ox-carriages in which the ladies travelled in great discomfort rumbled slowly over the rough paths at a rate which rarely exceeded 3 kilometres an hour). No meat was eaten except for game, such as quail and pheasant. The main vegetables were sweet potatoes, eggplant (aubergine), carrots, onions and garlic. Tea was introduced into Japan from China in the ninth century, but in those days it was primarily used for medicinal purposes. Sake (rice wine) or water were practically the only drinks available. Sake, weaker in alcoholic strength than it is today, was intoxicating because of the lack of fat in the diet (we read of many drunken courtiers). There were two main meals at about ten in the morning and four in the afternoon, but there was little sense of time in the Heian period.

Much of the life of the ladies of the court was boring in the extreme, while they waited behind their screens in the hope of amatory encounters. The men usually had some nominal office, which might require their occasional presence, but they seem to have reserved their energies for their nocturnal excursions – the *yobai* (literally, 'night crawl'). Marriages were, of course, generally arranged for political and dynastic reasons, but these too involved three visits by night to the bride's house. A 'marriage ceremony' took place after the third nightly visit, when the bridegroom would meet the bride's parents officially. The bride generally remained for some time at her parents' home and often had her first child there; but, if she were the principal wife, she would move to her husband's home when he became head of the family. Many ladies were, however, only the second wife or concubine; their lives were much less secure. All aristocratic love affairs were supposed to be conducted with decorum and sensitivity. In the 'Tale of Genji' (Genji Monogatari) the greatest novel of the time and one of the world's outstanding novels of all ages, the Emperor is recorded as having rebuked Prince Genji for the way in which he conducted his affairs, emphasizing that all women should be treated fairly and not humiliated or given cause for resentment. Great importance was attached to the way in which emotions of love were expressed. Refinement and aesthetic sensibility were very important. A night-time visitor was expected to send a beautifully written letter and appropriate poem to his beloved the next day. This would be accompanied by a seasonal emblem, such as a flowering branch of a plum tree. The lady would in turn reply quickly with an equally appropriate verse.

The gentlemen and ladies of the court much enjoyed the numerous ceremonies, Shintō and Buddhist, which marked many days in the year in Heiankyō. These involved colourful costumes, chanting, music and formal dances. The members of the court judged these events on the basis of their estimate of the aesthetic aspects, including the correct and appropriate balance of colours of the costumes and the ability of the dancers and musicians. Sei Shōnagon commented in *Makura no Sōshi* ('The Pillow Book'):

> Nothing annoys me so much as someone who arrives at a ceremony in a shabby, poorly decorated carriage. It is not so bad if the person has come to hear a sermon with the aim of clearing himself of sin; but even then a very inelegant carriage is bound to make a bad effect. At the Kamo Festival, of course, such negligence is quite inexcusable. Yet there are people who actually attend the ceremony in carriages where plain white robes have been hung up instead of the proper blinds.[14]

The ladies especially looked forward to occasional excursions to temples in the vicinity of the capital. The courtiers had a deep appreciation of the beauties of nature. As Ivan Morris explains, the capital was

situated in beautiful country, encircled on three sides by thickly forested hills and mountains, often delicately wreathed with trails of mist; in the autumn evenings one could hear the deer's cry in the distance and the desolate call of the wild geese overhead; the landscape abounded in streams and waterfalls and lakes; and into its green slopes and valleys the countless shrines and monasteries blended as if they too had become a part of nature.[15]

On these excursions they could give vent to their melancholy and sense of pathos (*mono no aware*) and their resignation in the transience of life and beauty. However, as Ivan Morris put it, 'here was no turbulent, romantic emotion, lending itself to wild expressions of melancholy or grief. Rather it was a restrained and elegant form of sensibility, a quiet feeling of resignation.'[16] *Mono no aware wo shiru*, literally 'to understand the pathos of things', came to signify good taste.

The courtiers had many pastimes. Much time was spent in poetry competitions (*uta-awase*), painting contests (*e-awase*) and producing perfumes. Great importance was attached to calligraphy and to the sensitive performance of music. One courtly sport was *kemari*, a kind of football, where the objective was to prevent the ball falling to the ground.

The 'plebs' were hardly mentioned, except for comments on the uncouth language and behaviour of servants or carriage drivers. Military men were regarded with particular contempt as near-barbarians.

It was indeed an artificial and limited world, but for the privileged it was a life of aesthetic refinement. The court of Louis XIV had some similarities, but it was far and away grander and more luxurious, while sensibilities were, if Molière is to be believed, even more contrived than in Heiankyō in the tenth and eleventh centuries.

Literature

In the Heian period some of the finest works of Japanese literature were produced. Most men were supposed to study and write in Chinese; women were not expected to know or be able to write in Chinese. Instead they wrote largely in the *kana* syllabary. Much of the prose literature of the period written in Japanese and known as *kana-bungaku* was composed by women. Both men and women, however, wrote poetry in Japanese, and some of the best short poems in the Japanese language were produced in this age.

In the ninth century almost all literature in Japan was composed in Chinese and it had little literary merit. But the traditions of the *Manyōshū* poets were maintained, and in 905 the first of a series of imperial collections of poetry was produced. This was the *Kokinshū* or more correctly *Kokinwakashū*, that is, a collection of poems ancient and modern. It consists of 1,111 poems, selected from verses produced since the *Manyōshū* appeared in 759. It contains only five *chōka* (long poems) and four *sedōka*. All the rest are in *tanka* form. It is divided into twenty 'books'. The first six are devoted to poems about the four seasons. Books eleven to fifteen consist of love poems, and book sixteen contains poems about sorrow. The collection was made by Ki no Tsurayuki (872?–945), his cousin Ki no Tomonori and two other poets. Ki no Tsurayuki, in his *kana* preface to the collection (there was another preface written in Chinese by one of his collaborators), set out in an elegant style his view of the nature of Japanese poetry:

> The poetry of Japan has its roots in the human heart and flourishes in the countless leaves of words. Because human beings possess interests of so many kinds, it is in poetry that they give expression to the meditations of their hearts in terms of the sights appearing before their eyes and the sounds coming to their ears. Hearing the warbler sing among the blossoms and the frog in his fresh waters – is there any living being not given to song? It is poetry which, without exertion, moves heaven and earth, stirs the feelings of gods and spirits invisible to the eye, softens the relations between men and women, calms the hearts of fierce warriors.[17]

Ki no Tsurayuki also listed in the following words some of the themes of the poets represented in the collection:

> when they looked at the scattered blossoms of a spring morning; when they listened of an autumn evening to the falling of the leaves; when they sighed over the snow and waves reflected with each passing year by their looking glasses; when they were startled into thoughts on the brevity of life by seeing the dew on the grass or the foam on the water; when, yesterday all proud and splendid, they have fallen from fortune into loneliness; or when, having been dearly loved, are neglected.[18]

In his preface Ki no Tsurayuki discussed poems by six writers who have come to be called the six poetic sages or *rokkasen*. These were Sōjō (Bishop) Henjō, Ariwara no Narihira, Bunya no Yasuhide, the priest Kisen, Ono no Komachi and Otomo no Kuronushi. Of these, Ariwara no Narihira and Ono no Komachi have become legendary figures in Japan. Ariwara no Narihira (825–80) had a reputation as a famous lover. The *Ise monogatari* ('The Tales of Ise') has been attributed to him, but even if he did not write the stories in it, he is the main character in most of the tales and composed more than a third of the poems in it. Ono no Komachi was a famous beauty who lived in the middle of the ninth century and is reputed to have had many lovers. According to one of the many legends about her, she became possessed in old age by the vengeful spirit of one of her lovers who died in a snowstorm, waiting for her to accept his suit.

In comparison with the *Manyōshū* some critics have found the range of the *Kokinshū* poets limited and lacking the fresh innocence of the former collection. Others assert that the Kokinshū does not have the profundity of the *Shinkokinshū* (the new collection of poems ancient and modern) produced in the Kamakura period and point to an element of artificiality and an enjoyment of witty conceits. But it has also been argued that it is more original and more responsive to life.[19] Certainly many of the poems in the collection have become almost household items among educated Japanese. The following examples may help to give a feel for the poetry of the Kokinshū:[20]

An anonymous poet:

Haru tateba	Like the ice which melts
Kiyuru kōri no	When spring begins
Nokori naku	Not leaving a trace behind,
Kimi ga kokoro mo	May your heart melt towards me!
Ware ni tokenamu.	

Ono no Komachi (mid-ninth century):

Iro miede	A thing which fades
Utsurou mono wa	With no outward sign –
Yo no naka no	Is the flower
Hito no kokoro no	Of the heart of man
Hana ni zo arikeru.	In this world!

Ono no Komachi:

Hana no iro wa	The flowers withered,
Utsurinikeri na	Their colour faded away,
Itazura ni	While meaninglessly
Waga mi yo ni furu	I spent my days in the world
Naga seshi ma ni.	And the long rains were falling.

Sōjō Henjō (815–890):

Waga yado wa	The weeds grow so thick
Michi mo naki made	You cannot even see the path
Arenikeri	That leads to my house:
Tsurenaki hito wo	It happened while I waited
Matsu to seshi ma ni.	For someone who would not come.

Finally perhaps the most famous poem by Ariwara no Narihira, which is also an example of a *Kokinshū* type of conceit:

Yo no naka ni	If in this world
Taete sakura no	The cherry blossoms
Nakari seba	Were to die out,
Haru no kokoro wa	Our hearts in springtime
Nodoke kara mashi.	Could enjoy peace.

There were a total of twenty-one imperial collections or anthologies of Japanese poems in later years. The second, the *Gosenshū*, for instance, was produced in 951, and there were five others before the *Shinkokinshū*, which was commissioned by the ex-Emperor Go-Toba in 1201. Poems are notoriously difficult to translate into foreign languages, and Japanese literature of the Heian period is better known abroad through the many prose works, novels, chronicles and stories, all called in Japanese *monogatari*, and diaries which have appeared in English translations.

One of the earliest of the *monogatari* was the *Taketori monogatari*.[21] This was produced between 850 and 950. It is a Japanese fairy tale with Buddhist and Taoist overtones. It is simple in style and is not a work of great literary merit.

The *Ise monogatari*,[22] which has been attributed to Ariwara no Narihira, dates from the middle of the ninth century. It is the oldest of the *uta-monogatari*, which are stories built around one or more short poems. It greatly influenced later *monogatari* in the same genre. Another famous *uta-monogatari* was the *Yamato monogatari* of about 952. Both works are more appreciated by the student of Japanese poetry than by the general reader.

The *Ochikubo monogatari*, ('Tale of the Lower Room')[23] was probably composed around 960 or 970. It recounts the miseries and the revenge of a girl who was persecuted by her stepmother, being forced to live in a room on a lower level (hence the title). The story has similarities to that of Cinderella. The characters are well depicted and the dialogue lively.

The *Utsubo monogatari* ('Tale of the Hollow Tree'), which was also produced in the latter part of the tenth century, is the story of a Japanese nobleman and his family. He is shipwrecked on his way to China and finds himself on the shores of a strange land, where he has a series of adventures and learns to play the *koto*, a seventeen-stringed instrument of the zither variety, which he brings back to Japan. The novel also recounts the loves and intrigues of members of the nobleman's family.

The outstanding novel of the Heian period and of all Japanese literature is the *Genji monogatari* ('Tale of Genji'), generally believed to be by Murasaki Shikibu or the Lady Murasaki, a lady at the court. It was written early in the eleventh century. It recounts the life and loves of a prince, who is given the name of Hikaru ('Shining') Genji (or Minamoto), and after his death, the less successful loves of a young man, who is described to the world as being Hikaru Genji's son. The novel, which covers events over almost three-quarters of a century, is a complex one. It includes many hundreds of different characters. These are delineated with skill and understanding of human psychology. The episodes are carefully unravelled with a consistent mastery of the art of story-telling. Anyone interested in Japanese culture and in world literature should read one of the two readily available English versions of the tale. The first version in English was completed by the late Arthur Waley in 1935.[24] It is a fine piece of writing which can best be described as a brilliant and imaginative recreation, but as a translation it leaves something to be desired. It is very free; much has been left out, and Waley has amplified and improved the text in parts. The other version is the excellent translation made by Professor Edward Seidensticker and published in 1976.[25] This makes a very readable and enjoyable book. (Japanese, unless they have made a special study of Heian literature, can only read the original text if they have a good commentary and explanations. Most prefer to read the text in one of the good modern Japanese versions.) The work runs to over a million words and a thousand pages in translation. This makes it considerably longer than Tolstoy's *War and Peace*; but, as the episodes generally stand on their own, the novel can be read at a leisurely pace.

There are thought to have been some thirty 'novels' which predate the 'Tale of Genji' and some sixty others in the Heian period, but most of these have not survived and are known only through their titles. Among the successors to the 'Tale of Genji' the best known is the *Sagoromo monogatari*, which was written probably in the years between 1070 and 1090. Its hero, who is a handsome aristocrat and who eventually becomes Emperor, is given to periods of melancholy but also enjoys bouts of philandering.

These novels are primarily concerned with the life at the court and provide little information about the ordinary people of Japan. There was, however, one work, the *Konjaku monogatari*,[26] which throws some light on popular legends of the time. It consists of about a thousand short tales in thirty-one volumes (three volumes have been lost). It has been ascribed to a nobleman, Minamoto no Takakuni (1004–77), who is said to have transcribed the stories from the mouths of passers-by, but more probably the collection dates from about 1120. It includes stories from India and China as well as Japan. Many of the stories are based on Buddhist themes. The title *Konjaku* has a meaning roughly equivalent to 'once upon a time' and reflects the opening words of each story. Many of the stories are told in a down-to-earth style and deal with actions rather than feelings. They are not confined to the doings of courtiers. The *Uji shūi monogatari*, which was probably produced at the beginning of the Kamakura period, contains 197 stories. About half of these are similar to stories in the *Konjaku monagatari*. Douglas Mills has commented that the stories include accounts of 'humorous and even salty or grotesque incidents about the everyday life of the people, high and low alike. Its characters range from great men and eminent divines to confidence tricksters.'[27]

During the latter part of the Heian period another form of prose narrative, the *rekishi-monogatari* (historical story), began to be written. These were attempts to describe what happened at particular times to famous people. Most of the authors of these 'chronicles', which are generally fairly accurate in their content and tended to concentrate on personalities, are unknown.

One of the most famous of the Heian *rekishi-monogatari* was the *Eiga monogatari* ('Tale of Flowering Fortunes'), which was written in the eleventh century. It covers a period of almost 200 years from the reign of the Emperor Uda (reigned 887–97) to that of the Emperor Horikawa (reigned 1087–1107). The first and longer part focusses on the life of Fujiwara no Michinaga, which represented the pinnacle of Fujiwara power. The second part covers the declining fortunes of the family. The *Okagami* ('The Great Mirror'),[28] which was produced at the end of the eleventh century or early in the twelfth century, covers much of the same ground as the *Eiga monogatari*, but its approach is different. It is more critical of the Fujiwara than its predecessor.

More important as sources for a picture of life in the Heian period, particularly for court life, are the diaries which have been preserved from the tenth and eleventh centuries.

The *Tosa nikki* ('Tosa Diary'),[29] describes the return journey to the capital in 934–85 of the governor of the province of Tosa in southern Shikoku. It is attributed to Ki no Tsurayuki (872?–945), one of the compilers of the *Kokinshū*, but the writer pretends to be a woman, perhaps because it was written in *kana* and men at that time were supposed to write in Chinese. The diary starts with an account of preparations for the voyage and of the farewell parties at which everybody apparently got drunk and the entertainment was boisterous. His young daughter had just died, and he was deeply grieved. They travelled in a rowing boat with a small cabin. The sea was rough, and they were frightened of being drowned. They also feared attacks by pirates. The diary is studded with numerous poems.

The *Sarashina nikki*[30] is another record of travel of about a century later. This was written by the daughter of one Sugawara no Takasue. It is, however, more an account of her emotions and the exchanges of poems which she had during her life than a record of events.

The *Kagerō nikki*[31] is a memoir of a lady who is known as the mother of Fujiwara no Michitsuna and was a secondary wife to Fujiwara no Kaneie (929–90). It covers the years 954–74. Her story is one of great unhappiness, as her marriage brought only frustration and bitterness.

Murasaki Shikibu also produced a diary and a set of poetic memoirs.[32] The diary gives an interesting picture of life at the court.

Izumi Shikibu was an outstanding Japanese poet who flourished around 1000. She was married twice, but between her two marriages she was the mistress of two imperial princes, who were brothers and who both died young. She was particularly grieved by the death of Prince Atsumichi (981–1007), the younger brother, and recorded her feelings of sorrow in over one hundred poems. The so-called *Izumi shikibu nikki*[33] recounts her love for Prince Atsumichi in the third person and in fictional form.

The most fascinating account of life at the Heian court is contained in the *Makura no sōshi* ('Pillow Book') of Sei Shōnagon. This is more a collection of jottings than a diary. Her anecdotes, descriptions and lists of likes and dislikes reveal her tastes and prejudices as well as her mordant wit and humour. Sei Shōnagon was the daughter of Kiyohara no Motosuke, a scholar and poet. She was probably born in about 965. In the early 990s she became a lady in waiting to the Empress Sadako, consort of the Emperor Ichijō. Murasaki Shikibu, who had perhaps suffered from the gossip of the court ladies and probably regarded Sei Shōnagon as a rival, described her as 'the very picture of conceit and arrogance', but the fact that she had aroused the jealousy of other ladies should not deter the reader from a book which is one of the most amusing in the Japanese language.[34] The following excerpts from Ivan Morris's translation give some of the flavour of the work:

Small children and babies ought to be plump. So ought provincial governors and others who have gone ahead in the world; for if they are lean and desiccated, one suspects them of being ill-tempered. . . .

A lover's visit is the most delightful thing in the world. But when the man is a mere acquaintance, or has come for a casual chat, what a nuisance it can be! He enters the lady's room, where numerous other women are ensconced behind the blinds chatting to each other, and gives no sign that his visit will be brief.

Graceful things for her include:

A slim handsome young nobleman in a court cloak. A pretty girl casually dressed in a trouser skirt, over which she wears only a loosely sewn coat.... A letter written on fine green paper is attached to a budding willow branch.... One day by the balustrade before a set of thin head-blinds I saw a pretty cat with a red collar and a white name-tag. He looked very elegant as he walked along, pulling his anchor cord and biting it.

Unsuitable things include:

A woman with ugly hair wearing a robe of white damask.... Ugly handwriting on red paper.... Snow on the houses of common people. This is especially regrettable when the moonlight shines down on it.... A handsome man with an ugly wife.... Officers on duty should abstain from visiting the women's quarters; the same applies to Chamberlains of the Fifth Rank.

Charming things include:

Through a partition one hears a lady's hushed voice, followed by the youthful voice of someone answering her and the rustling of clothes as she approaches. It must be time for the lady's meal; for then comes the sound of chopsticks and spoons, and then the clatter made by the handle of a jug as it falls on its side....

Hateful things include:

It is hateful when a well-bred young man who is visiting a woman of lower rank calls out her name in such a way as to make everyone realize that he is on familiar terms with her. However well he may know her name, he should slur it slightly as though he had forgotten it.

Art in the Heian Period

The art and architecture of the Heian period depended for patronage on the court at Heiankyō or on the large Buddhist temples around the capital and in Nara. There was great progress in all the arts, and many masterpieces date from this time. Some art historians refer to the period from 794 to 894 when Japanese culture was under strong Chinese influence as the Kōnin era, although the Kōnin period in fact only ran from 810 to 823. The ninth century is also thought of in art terms as an extension of the Tempyō or Nara era. The rest of the Heian period is then referred to as the Fujiwara era when Japanese art developed on more independent lines.

The religious architecture of the early Heian period is hardly distinguishable from that of Nara times. The buildings were basically simple in construction with graceful lines, but the large number of religious buildings, which the newly imported Tendai and Shingon sects required, led to improvements in technique and refinements in construction. The Japanese became, as they have remained, master carpenters, who understood the nature and grain of the woods they used.

Without modern systems of transport and cranes and without mathematical surveying technology they nevertheless managed to put up some of the finest wooden buildings the world has ever seen. Most Heian buildings have alas been destroyed by war and fire, but it is clear from those that have survived that they were well built and capable of surviving the earthquakes and typhoons which have so often devastated Japan.

One of the finest temples which remains from the early Heian period is the Shingon temple of Murōji in the mountains to the east of Nara. The relatively small five-storey pagoda with widely overhanging shingle roofs was built in about 800. The main hall or *kondō*, which dates from the early ninth century, has five bays and an elegant curved roof covered in shingle bark. (The Shingon sect later developed its own form of pagoda, the *tahōtō*, or 'pagoda of the treasures', which is closer to the Indian form of *stupa* than the normal Japanese pagoda. Between the two roofs of the *tahōtō* there is a round semi-dome roof surrounding a round central tower.) The five-storey pagoda of the Daigoji at Kyoto, completed in about 951, is much heavier with its ponderous tiled roofs than that at Murōji. The three-storey pagoda of the Jōruriji, on the border between Kyoto and Nara prefectures, which dates from the second half of the twelfth century, is much more delicate with its shingle roofs. Painted in red lacquer, it is reflected in the temple pond and looks across to the simple and low late-Heian-period *hondō* (main hall), which houses nine fine wooden statues of Amida covered in gold leaf. The Amidadō of the Hōkaiji to the south of Kyoto is a simple square building with an elegant pyramid-shaped roof of shingle. It was built in about 1098, but the veranda and intermediary roof are said to date from the early thirteenth century. Another late Heian building, reconstructed in the seventeenth century, is the simple and beautiful *hondō* of the Sanzenin temple at Ohara to the north of Kyoto.

But the most sublime of all the Heian buildings which have survived is the Byōdōin at Uji between Kyoto and Nara. This was originally part of the private palace of Fujiwara no Yorimichi (990–1074), the eldest son of Fujiwara no Michinaga, and thus gives some idea of what the finest Heian palaces might have looked like if they had survived. The Byōdōin consists of a central Amida hall with two bronze phoenixes on the two ends of the central ridge. Galleries on either side lead to two smaller halls at each end, surmounted by elegant small towers like miniature two-storeyed pagodas. The building faces a pond in which its symmetrical and beautiful shape is reflected. Beyond the wall of the garden is the Uji river. The whole complex is designed to represent the western paradise of Amida.

Shintō shrines were not neglected in the wave of temple building. The famous Itsukushima shrine at Miyajima in the Inland Sea near Hiroshima probably dates from the sixth century. But the elegant fan shape of the shrine, which is built over the sea shore in such a way that at high tide the shrine appears to be floating on the water, dates from 1149–69. The shrine was reconstructed on these lines on the orders of Taira no Kiyomori (see Chapter V). The graceful shape of the shingle roofs is a reminder that Shintō and Buddhist architecture evolved on parallel lines. The reflection in the water of the shrine, with its red lacquered balustrade and pillars with the imposing torii out to sea, makes Miyajima one of Japan's three most famous beauty spots. It is an unforgetable experience to visit

Miyajima at festival time, when, under the full moon and a high tide, traditional dances are performed to the eerie music of the Heian period.

The main secular style of architecture was the *shinden-zukuri* used in palaces (see page 55). An important part of any Heian palace was its garden. The traditional Japanese garden involving small hills, water, shrubs, pines and bamboo had its origin in the Heian period. In about 800 in Heiankyō a large lake and island park in the Chinese manner was built to the south of the Imperial Palace. It was called the Shinsenen, or Garden of the Divine Spring. Today all that remains of this imperial park is a small pond off a quiet back street in Kyoto. The Emperor Saga (786–842) in 823 retired to his estate to the north-west of Kyoto, the Saga-no-in. Here he had a park with a lake on which his courtiers enjoyed boating parties. Today the remains of the Saga-no-in lake are the Osawa pond with its two small islands. On its bank stand the buildings of Daikakuji temple, which incorporated the Saga-no-in. The bottom of the pond was covered with small stones packed together with clay – a feature of later Japanese gardens. There was also a waterfall, another 'must' in a traditional Japanese garden.

Many of the gardens of Kyoto, such as those at Sanzenin and the Byōdōin, have features which originated in the Heian period, but no authentic Heian-period garden has survived. An attempt to recreate a Heian-style garden was made in the Meiji period, when the Heian shrine was built in 1895. The garden may not be authentic but it is nevertheless beautiful. Views and features unfold in an elegant way, and the stepping stones and pavilions have been set out in a pleasing and tasteful fashion.

Heian-period sculpture has been compared unfavourably by some critics with the superb images produced in the Nara era. The grounds for this criticism are that Heian statues seem to lack the vitality and fresh naturalism of the earlier period and that many Heian-period works are mannered and contrived. This may be true of some of the works produced, but many impressive and moving Buddhist images have been preserved and have a rightful place among Japan's national treasures.

Some significant technical developments were made in sculpture during Heian times. The single-piece construction (*ichiboku-zukuri*) which prevailed in the ninth century was followed by the 'split-and-fit' technique known as *warihagi*. In this the torso is split vertically, both sides are hollowed out and the two shells fitted together again. In mid-Heian times this gave way to a method of sculpture in which blocks or panels were put together and glued. The outer form was carved, and the pieces were then dismantled and hollowed out into thin shells before being put together again, to be covered with cloth and gold lacquer or painted. This technique was called *yosegi*.

The Shingon sect was the main source of inspiration for sculpture in the ninth century, which is often referred to as the Jōgan period after the era which lasted from 859 to 876. The Shingon temples trained their own monks in sculpture. William Watson has commented that 'In *Shingon* sculpture a coldness and some gloom have dispersed the warmth of Nara feeling. . . . Even the angry deities of *Shingon* rage in a spiritual dimension, their aspect more ferocious but their impact much less direct than that of comparable statues of the previous century.'[35] But we should not be put off by such comments. Some of the finest examples of early

Heian sculpture of the Shingon school are to be seen in the main hall (*kondō*) at Murōji and in the lecture hall (*kōdō*) of the Tōji (also called the Kyō-ōgokuji) in Kyoto. The central figure in the Murōji hall is a monumental and austere figure of Shaka. In the latter twenty-one statues stand in a mandala-like grouping with the five manifestations of the Buddha in the centre.

With the growing popularity of the cult of Amida there developed a softer, more ethereal type of sculpture. Images of Amida were produced in large numbers by *daibusshi* (great Buddha masters). The outstanding of these was Jōchō (died 1057), who flourished in the first half of the eleventh century and used the *yosegi* technique. His most famous work was the gold-covered image of Amida in the main hall of the Byōdōin at Uji. The shell of the figure is exceptionally thin. Jōchō also designed the group of fifty-two Bodhisattvas on the walls of the hall. The lightness and delicate charm of these figures provide a contrast to the calm passivity of the main seated image of Amida on his elaborate lotus throne surrounded by a finely carved nimbus and baldachin. The Amida of the Hōkaiji, also a national treasure, seems heavy in comparison. The Amida trinity in the Sanzenin at Ohara, north of Kyoto, where Amida is attended by Kannon and Seishi-Bosatsu in a kneeling position as if welcoming him to paradise, is, however, radiant and deeply moving. The nine seated figures of Amida covered in gold leaf at the Jōruriji, all with different features, seem to have been looking out from time immemorial to the pagoda across the tranquil pond which they face.

Some examples of portrait sculpture have survived. A fine eleventh-century carving of the priest Rōben, the first abbot of the Tōdaiji, is preserved in the Kaidanin at Nara. Unfortunately it is only shown once a year.

Painting in the Nara period and in earlier times had been in the Chinese tradition and had been largely derivative. In the Heian era Japanese painting developed independently and began to be a significant element in Japanese art and culture.

The Shingon sect inspired the painting of *mandaras*, incorporating images of the Roshana Buddha (Dainichi-Nyorai). These frequently came to be regarded as sacred paintings with magical powers. Inevitably many of these have faded or been damaged by the ravages of time, but from the surviving examples we can appreciate the balance and detail of their composition as well as the skilful use which Buddhist painters made of colour. The images of Buddha depicted in these paintings are inevitably stylized but none the less impressive.

Japanese monks, in reproducing the sutras, frequently illuminated their copies with religious paintings. These were often not only both highly decorative but also technically proficient. They also included in the background stylized Chinese landscapes. Manuscripts were produced on different-coloured papers, and gold and silver paints were much used. These illuminated manuscripts were the forerunners of the scroll paintings or *emaki* of the later Heian period.

It is a simple step from illuminating a manuscript with landscapes and figures to representing the substance of a sutra in a series of pictures. The arts of painting and of calligraphy were indeed synonymous in the Heian period and have at the very least been closely connected ever since. Some of the finest early calligraphy consisted of copies of the sutras, but from the earliest times Confucian mottoes and Chinese poems were also subjects for Japanese calligraphers. It is difficult for us, brought up on a relatively simple alphabet, to grasp the power of a fine piece of calligraphy, done with the brush in jet-black ink. Japanese calligraphy depends for its effect as much on its visual impact as on the meaning of the characters depicted. The balance of thick and thin lines, the movement indicated by the brush strokes and the force shown by the intensity of the ink are among the factors which can make a piece of calligraphy into a work of art. Extracts from popular sutras, such as the Lotus Sutra, were sometimes reproduced on the fans which the court ladies used. This helped to popularize the sutras, but calligraphy needed no boosting. The men at court studied the Chinese classics and learned the art of writing a beautiful hand, while the ladies as they studied the composition of Japanese poems realized that the writing of a good poem depended not only on choosing apposite and rhythmical words but also on transcribing the chosen words in a delicate and elegant manner on the right kind of paper. The art of making fine paper by hand was developed to meet the demands of the court. Numerous kinds of paper with delicate shades of colours and designs were produced.

The earliest secular paintings of the Heian period were formal paintings often on screens in the Chinese style called *kara-e* (*Kara* is the Japanese reading for the character used to designate T'ang). Kudara no Kawanari (783–853) is reputed to have been a master of such painting at the early Heian court, but none of his paintings have survived. *Yamato-e* or Japanese-style paintings were for more informal occasions. They were softer and more feminine in style. The earliest exponents of this style of painting were the members of the Kose group of painters, who belonged to the court painting studio, founded in 886. None of the works of the original Kose group are unfortunately extant. The main schools of *yamato-e* were the so-called Kasuga and Tosa schools. *Kara-e* and *yamato-e* had much in common, and *yamato-e* copied many of the themes of the paintings on screens (*byōbu*) in the Chinese style.

The novels and diaries of the middle Heian period were justly popular among the ladies and gentlemen of the court, but in the days before works could be easily reproduced by wood-block printing there was an understandable demand for simple pictorial representations of the themes and incidents in these works. Thus developed the art of the *emaki* or picture scroll. *Emaki* began to be popular towards the end of the Heian period in the early twelfth century. Their themes appealed to the exponents of the *yamato* style.

Emaki vary in width up to about half a metre and can be as long as 24 metres, although most are between 9 and 12 metres. They were rolled up into cylinders, and a set might consist of anything up to forty-eight rolls or even more. They unfold from right to left as in a Japanese book and need to be viewed on a flat surface. *Emaki*, which were the product not of one single artist but of a group of painters, are a very suitable way of reproducing a narrative pictorially.

The 'Tale of Genji' inspired many scrolls. The oldest and finest examples are to be found in the Tokugawa art museum in Nagoya and in the Gotō art museum in Tokyo. These date from the early twelfth century, but only some twenty of the fifty-four chapters of the 'Tale of Genji' are represented in the surviving portions. Originally there were probably ten scrolls. The scenes chosen for illustration generally depict not so much the actions of the novel as the moments of contemplation before or after the action. The figures tend to have sterotyped and indistinguishable features. An interesting technique used is what has been called the 'blown-off roof' style, whereby roofs of buildings are left out so that the viewer can have a clear view as from above of the characters involved. Colours are used lavishly to reflect the moods of the moment depicted. The result is exquisitely decorative.

Emaki were also used as a vehicle to spread Buddhist teaching. One twelfth-century example was the Jigokuzōshi, or 'Scrolls of Hell'. The Shigisan Engi emaki, or Legends of Mount Shigi, in three scrolls, relates miracles performed by the priest Myōren. The Chōjū giga, or 'Scrolls of Frolicking Animals and Humans', has no accompanying text. Done in black and white, it satirizes the failings of monks and priests. It is traditionally attributed to Toba Sōjō, a monk of the Tendai school, and belongs to the Kōzanji temple in Kyoto. It is a national treasure which is vibrant with life and humour.

Most of the other surviving emaki strictly belong to the Kamakura period. Famous Heian-period novels such as the Ise monogatari and the Sagoromo monaga-tari, as well as the Makura no sōshi and diaries such as the Murasaki Shikibu nikki, were turned into colourful emaki. So too were the later tales of battles and the heroic deeds of the wars such as the Heiji monogatari emaki.

During the early Heian period the decorative arts in Japan were largely influenced and inspired by imports from China. But as the period progressed, individual Japanese styles and techniques developed.

In ceramics the Japanese still produced mainly rough practical earthenware and never approached the perfection of Chinese ceramics, which were so much admired at the Heian court. Suemono, which were a form of hard-fired stoneware, developed some individual features, but few vessels other than those which had been buried have survived from the Heian period. Kilns at Bizen, Settsu, Sanuki, Mino and Owari are known to have existed from Heian times.

Bronze was no longer used in Heian times for the casting of large Buddhist images, but it was still used to make bells and religious reliquaries, as well as small Buddhist images. Some of these reliquaries have been recovered from the ceremonial burial places of various sutras. Metal fittings of exquisite workmanship were produced for such items as writing boxes (suzuri-bako) used by the court aristocrats. Bronze was also used to produce mirrors. Many of these were decorated with delicate motifs of flowers, birds and landscapes.

The art of sword-making developed as the warrior class grew in size and importance. It was of such importance that it was given a religious significance by the performance of Shintō ceremonies at sword smithies. By the end of the tenth century blades of a very high quality were being made by Japanese swordsmiths, and sword blades began to be signed by the master-craftsman making them. Chinese merchants were apparently so impressed that they came to Japan to buy Japanese swords. The Japanese also developed their own form of armour, in which narrow iron plates are bound together with coloured cords to protect vital parts of the body. Breastplates were, however, made of solid metal. Some of these early suits are preserved in famous Shintō shrines. The Itsukushima shrine at Miyajima, for instance, preserves the armour donated to it by the great warrior Taira no Kiyomori, while the Kasuga shrine at Nara has armour from the Fujiwara family.

The Japanese had used lacquer to embellish buildings and shrines for many centuries, but it was only at the beginning of the tenth century that the Japanese lacquer craftsmen evolved the technique of *maki-e* (sprinkle painting). This involves the sprinkling of gold and silver powder over lacquer, before it has had time to dry, on previously drawn designs. The surface is then covered with black lacquer and later polished until the motif reappears. Finally a further coating of lacquer is applied. Mother-of-pearl was also used in the decoration of many pieces of lacquer in the Heian period. Fortunately a number of fine lacquer items have survived. Among these are sutra boxes, altar tables, saddles, cosmetic boxes, writing boxes and small trunks. The oldest surviving cosmetic box in the Tokyo National Museum has a black lacquer background with gold lacquer and mother-of-pearl inlay. The motif is of cartwheels in water.

Music and dancing had existed from the earliest times in Japan. The forty-five musical instruments imported from Asia and preserved in the Shosoin at Nara testify to Japanese enthusiasm for the new music imported from China and Korea. Music and dancing were also features of early Buddhist rites and Shintō ceremonies in Japan. But Japanese music and dance, as they have come down to us today, really began in the Heian period, when the old forms of music called *gigaku* largely fell into disuse.

Court music, called *gagaku*, was based on Chinese models. *Gagaku* uses two basic heptatonic (seven-tone) modes, called *ryō* and *ritsu*. Both developed from original pentatonic (five-tone) scales. The *ryō* and *ritsu* modes are each subdivided into three subscales, according to the tonic position. The *ritsu* mode, which harmonized with the ancient Japanese scale, formed the basis of later Japanese music, which has a five-tone scale. This is the scale used for the Japanese National Anthem. The pentatonic scale sounds strange to western ears and makes the appreication of Japanese music difficult for the average foreigner, (although it has recently been suggested that if speeded up *gagaku* pieces can sound like rollicking tunes). Sir Francis Piggott declared of Japanese music: 'Much of the charm of the music, all its individuality nearly, depends on its graceful and delicate phrasing.'[36]

Musical instruments used in court music include: various drums, such as the *kakko* and *san-no-tsuzumi*, which were side-drums, as well as the *taiko* and *shōko*, which were kinds of kettle drums; stringed instruments, such as the *biwa* or lute, and two types of *koto*, a thirteen-stringed semi-cylindrical plucked zither; and various simple wind instruments, such as the *hichiriki*, a kind of Japanese oboe, and a number of different types of flute such as the *kagura-bue* and *koma-bue*.

Chinese, Indian and Korean music, as well as Japanese compositions, was played at the court. The orchestra of the 'left', in red court costumes, played Chinese and Indian as well as Japanese music, while the orchestra of the 'right', in green, blue or yellow costumes, depending on court rank, was responsible for playing Korean music and the obsolete *gigaku*.

Gagaku is usually played by a small Japanese orchestra of about sixteen players. It may also be played as an accompaniment to *bugaku*, which are formal court dances, but the stringed instruments are in this case omitted from the orchestra. A *gagakuryō* or court music office was established as early as the eighth century. In the tenth century this became the court music school or *gakusho*. *Bugaku* developed greatly from the time of the Emperor Ichijō (968–1011) and was, as we know from the 'Tale of Genji', performed with feeling and enjoyment by the courtiers. For instance, at the Festival of the Autumn Leaves, Prince Genji is said to have danced with Tō no Chūjō before the Emperor at the Suzaku-in palace:

> As Genji danced, the rays of the setting sun fell on his body, and at that moment the music swelled up in a crescendo. It was a brilliant climax. Familiar though the dance was to the onlookers, they felt that never before had there been such loveliness of movement and expression; and the accompanying song seemed as melodious as the music of the Kavalinka birds in Buddha's Paradise. Moved beyond words by the beauty of the performance, the Emperor burst into tears.[37]

More than a hundred different Heian *bugaku* have been preserved, and many are still performed by court musicians on special occasions in Japan today. Masks were used in performances of *bugaku*, and twenty-four different types have survived. Many of these masks are impressive works of art.

But music was not only performed by orchestras. The ladies and gentlemen of the court prided themselves on their musical abilities, and there were many impromptu concerts or solo performances by the courtiers in their palaces. Emperors and Empresses, as well as their courtiers, played on flutes and stringed instruments. There are numerous references to music in both the 'Tale of Genji' and in Sei Shōnagon's 'Pillow Book'.

Japanese songs can be said to date back to prehistoric times. Amaterasu was induced to come out of her cave to view a dance called the *kagura* which was accompanied by singing. *Kagura-uta* or songs, which were performed at Shintō ceremonies, were developed in the Heian period. *Kagura* songs consist of two parts – the *moto* or rise and the *sue* or fall, which are independent verses in *tanka* form. Singers were accompanied by stringed and wind instruments. Chanting was also an essential part of many Buddhist services; and as Murasaki Shikibu noted in her diary: 'Evil influences were warded off with the ceaseless chanting of loud spells.'[38] In addition, there were traditional folk songs and drinking songs.

V

Military Rule Established: The Kamakura Period (1185–1333)

Under the Kamakura Shōguns a Japanese form of feudalism was developed and a military caste of samurai formed. With the enforcement of law and order economic conditions improved. The first and only serious attempt before 1945 to invade Japan was made by the Mongols, but their forces were dispersed by typhoons. Popular forms of Buddhism spread, and Zen Buddhism, which came to be regarded as the religion of the samurai, began to flourish. In the arts sculpture found new inspiration. Painting developed, and the new Zen temples were built in a modified style of architecture. In literature there was a renewed flowering of poetry; military epics in prose became popular.

Rivalry between the Taira and the Minamoto: the Genpei Wars

The *Hōgen no ran* or *Hōgen* disturbances in 1156 demonstrated that power had moved from the court to the military landowning class. But, although the Minamoto had taken a hard knock and the Taira were in the stronger position, neither family were yet dominant.

Following the defeat of Fujiwara no Yorinaga in the *Hōgen no ran*, Minamoto no Tameyoshi (1095–1156), the head of the Minamoto family (the so-called Seiwa Genji), who had supported Yorinaga and the ex-Emperor Sutoku (1119–64; reigned 1123–42), was condemned to death. His son, Minamoto no Yoshitomo (1123–60), who had sided with Taira no Kiyomori in support of the Emperor Go-Shirakawa (1127–92; reigned 1155–8), was ordered to kill his father. Yoshitomo understandably refused this task, which was undertaken by a Minamoto retainer who then committed suicide in expiation. Fifty of the ex-Emperor Sutoku's supporters were also executed; this was the first time in 350 years that capital punishment had been applied to members of the court.

These measures had been proposed by the monk Shinzei (Fujiwara no Michinori), who allied himself to Taira no Kiyomori and won the favour of the Emperor Nijō (1143–65; reigned 1158–65), who had acceded to the throne following the abdication of Go-Shirakawa. Go-Shirakawa retained the support of Fujiwara no Nobuyori and of Minamoto no Yoshitomo, who bore a grudge against his former ally Kiyomori. The Taira and the Minamoto were now in different camps, and the struggle for power had begun.

The first trial of strength took place in 1160 in what came to be called the *Heiji* uprising. This occurred when Kiyomori and his family were on a pilgrimage. The Emperor Nijō was forced to appoint Fujiwara no Nobuyori chancellor (*dajōdaijin*), and Shinzei was captured and killed. On his return to the capital

Kiyomori took up a defensive position. The Emperor Nijō, disguised as a lady in waiting, was smuggled out to Kiyomori, who then attacked Yoshitomo in the palace. Yoshitomo was forced to flee and was eventually killed with two of his sons. One son, Yoritomo (1147–99), managed to escape through snowstorms to the east, where the Minamoto had their base. His younger brothers Noriyori (1156–93) and Yoshitsune (1159–89), who were still mere youths, were spared. Thus ended the *Heiji* uprising; Kiyomori was now supreme.

Taira no Kiyomori (1118–81), who dominated the court for over twenty years from 1160 until his death, became a legendary figure in Japanese history as a symbol of pride. He has been depicted as obstinate, determined, quick tempered and generally ruthless, but he was reputed to have had a gentler side and to have recognized the importance of the arts. He thought of himself as a Buddhist, but he also believed in the native gods and gave particular support to his family shrine of Itsukushima at Miyajima, near the modern Hiroshima. He attached importance to the traditional and figurehead role of the Emperor and adopted the Fujiwara practice of dominating the court by arranging marriages of his daughters into the imperial house and that of the Fujiwara regents. He was content to let the Fujiwara continue to fill most of the nominal posts at court, although in 1167 he did briefly fill the post of chancellor (*dajōdaijin*), resigning it in 1168 when be became ill and took the tonsure.

Kiyomori's pride and the arrogant behaviour of members of the Taira family inevitably aroused deep resentment, and various plots were hatched against him. The ex-Emperor Go-Shirakawa, generally described as a devious character, who was said by a contemporary 'not to know black from white', was frequently at the heart of these intrigues. In 1177 a Fujiwara-led plot, the so-called *Shishigatani* affair, which was known to Go-Shirakawa, was discovered, and the perpetrators, including a priest, were executed. In 1177 and 1178 the monks of Hieizan, who were at odds with Go-Shirakawa, caused disturbances in the capital. Kiyomori refused to intervene to protect the court, as he regarded himself as a friend of Myōun, the abbot of Enryakuji, who was opposed to Go-Shirakawa. Go-Shirakawa then provoked Kiyomori by confiscating some property which had belonged to Shigemori, Kiyomori's favourite son, who had just died. In 1179 Kiyomori, who had been living at his headquarters at Fukuwara, near Hyogo, marched on the capital, and Go-Shirakawa was placed in strict confinement for a time. In 1180 the Emperor Takakura abdicated in favour of his baby son and the grandson of Kiyomori, the Emperor Antoku (1178–85; reigned 1180–84). This marked the beginning of the civil wars, which came to be called the *Genpei* wars (*Gen* and *Hei* are the Sino-Japanese readings of the characters for Minamoto and Taira).

The first encounters in 1180 resulted from a plot by Minamoto no Yorimasa (1104–80), who had been a comrade of Yoshitomo, but who had kept aloof in the *Heiji* uprising, to support Prince Mochihito (1151–80), a son of Go-Shirakawa, in a claim for the throne. Kiyomori again marched on the capital. The conspirators fled to Uji; Yorimasa, who had been wounded, committed suicide at the Byōdōin, and Prince Mochihito was captured and killed. The Nara temples of Tōdaiji and Kōfukuji, whose monks had joined in the uprising, were burned. Meanwhile Yoritomo, who had been with his Taira-appointed guardian, Hōjō Tokimasa (1138–1215), in Izu, collected a small body of men and attempted to move westwards, but his force was stopped at Ishibashiyama. Kiyomori then moved the Emperor and the ex-Emperors temporarily to his headquarters at Fukuwara, while the situation in the capital deteriorated. Kiyomori was now seriously ill. His fever was said to have been so great that he radiated a great heat. This was supposed to come from hell − 'so deep was his guilt'.[1] He died early in 1181, and the leadership of the Taira passed to his son Munemori (1147–85), who had little of his father's abilities.

During the next few years the Minamoto gradually increased their strength and pushed back the Taira, although they suffered defeats as well as victories. The Minamoto were not a united force. Yoritomo was supported by his half brothers Noriyori and Yoshitsune. Another Minamoto force was led by Yosh-inaka (1154–84, known as Kiso Yoshinaka, as he was brought up on the Kiso river), Yoritomo's cousin. A third group was led by Yukiie (died 1186), his uncle. Yoshinaka, after defeating a Taira force in Echizen, reached the capital and pursued the Taira to the west, but his force was defeated at Mizushima on the borders of Bizen and Bitchu (Okayama prefecture). He was jealous of Yoritomo and plotted with Yukiie to destroy Yoritomo's forces. However, Yukiie warned the devious ex-Emperor Go-Shirakawa, who passed on the warning to Yoritomo. Yoshinaka was then defeated by Noriyori and Yoshitsune in legendary battles at the long bridge of Seta and the bridge of Uji in March 1184.

The Taira, who controlled the Inland Sea, had despatched the Emperor Antoku to Kyūshū, where a temporary court was set up at Dazaifu, but local revolts forced the court to move to Yashima (now Takamatsu) on the northern coast of Shikoku. Their forces then moved back to the mainland and established a seem-ingly impregnable position in a defile. However, Yoshitsune managed to bring a small force of warriors to a position overlooking the defile, and in March 1184 the Taira forces were defeated in what has come to be called the battle of Ichinotani. They retired to Yashima. In March 1185 Yoshitsune effected a landing in Shikoku and moved on Yashima. The Taira put to sea with the Emperor Antoku and his mother Kenreimonin. Yoshitsune, who was joined by Kajiwara Kagetoki with a number of ships, pursued the Taira down the Inland Sea. At the sea battle of Dannoura on 25 April 1185 the Taira were annihilated. The Emperor Antoku was drowned, and the sword of state, one of the imperial regalia, was lost, although his mother was saved and spent her remaining years at the Jakkōin convent in the village of Ohara outside Kyoto.

The Minamoto had triumphed, but Yoritomo did not yet feel secure. He was particularly jealous of his younger brother Yoshitsune and was suspicious of Yukiie. His jealousy and suspicions were fed by his spy, Kajiwara no Kagetoki. Yoshitsune, after his victory at Dannoura, travelled to Kamakura to see his brother, but was refused permission to enter the city. He returned to Kyoto, where he joined his uncle Yukiie. Go-Shirakawa was intriguing once again and commisioned Yoshitsune and Yukiie to move against Yoritomo, but they were unable to gather adequate support. Yoshitsune, accompanied by his faithful and legendary follower Musashibō Benkei and his mistress, Shizuka Gozen, were forced to flee. Yukiie was captured and killed in June 1186, and soon afterwards Shizuka Gozen was captured. In the spring of 1187 Yoshitsune, together with Benkei, disguised as itinerant *yamabushi* monks, accompanied by his wife and family, dressed as children, managed to escape to the province of Mutsu in northern Japan. There he was protected by Fujiwara no Hidehira, Yoritomo's only serious rival, aged ninety. In the spring of 1188, however, Fujiwara no Yasuhira, who had succeeded his father in Mutsu, yielded to pressure from Yoritomo and turned on Yoshitsune, who after killing his family committed suicide. Yoshitsune's head was then sent to Kamakura. But Yoritomo did not trust Yasuhira, and in 1189 Yasuhira was forced to flee to Ezo, the modern Hokkaidō, where he was murdered.

At last Yoritomo was supreme, but he continued to harbour suspicions against his other half brother, Noriyori, against whom charges were trumped up in 1193, and who was then killed. Yoritomo also still had his problems with the court in Kyoto, which he visited in 1190. His power could not be challenged, but he wanted the title of *Seii-tai-shōgun* and was forced to wait for this until 1192 after the death of the ex-Emperor Go-Shirakawa. In 1196 Yoritomo's nominee at court, Fujiwara no Kanezane, was removed as a result of intrigues. Yoritomo intended to reassert his position with the court, but before he could do so he died in 1199 as a result of a fall from a horse. However, he had already achieved a good deal of progress in consolidating the warriors' position and in establishing the beginnings of a centralized military regime. He was determined to keep this untainted by the atmosphere of the court. He had accordingly chosen as his headquarters the small town of Kamakura in the eastern provinces where the main Minamoto lands were and where the family shrine to the god Hachiman was situated. Emphasizing the character of the regime, the Kamakura government came to be called, from about 1190, the *bakufu*. This means literally 'tent government' but it was originally used to describe the headquarters of an army in the field.

Stories from the *Genpei* wars and of the escape and death of Yoshitsune have become a part of Japanese folklore and have been the subject of many traditional Japanese dramas. Japanese nationalist historians are inclined to emphasize the undoubted courage and the loyalty displayed on occasions during the fighting, but the many examples of double-dealing, jealousy, anger, rapacity, greed and cruelty which marked these years cannot be overlooked. It would also be wrong to try to see any kind of ideological conflict in these wars. The Taira and the Minamoto both sought power for the military landholding class and the ending of the power of the court, but they could not agree on a share-out. While the Taira and the Minamoto were the dominant families, other military families who became famous in later centuries, such as the Hōjō, the Chiba and the Ashikaga, were extending their power also.

Yoshitsune is a typically Japanese tragic and romantic hero. He was a brave, charismatic and aggressive military leader. Yoritomo, on the other hand, was a more important figure in Japanese history than either Yoshitsune or Kiyomori. He was a firm but cautious and careful schemer, endowed with remarkable foresight and self-control. He was not a reformer or in any sense an idealist. He was a ruler rather than a military leader. In character he was neither noble nor moral; he was cold, often inhuman and ruthless. Despite this he was one of the greatest figures in the history of Japan.

The Shōgunate, the Hōjō Regents and the Court

Yoritomo had two sons, both of whom in due course became shōgun. But his elder son Yoriie (1182–1204) was only seventeen when Yoritomo died. He was an unstable young man, and a council of regency was established under the chairmanship of Hōjō Tokimasa, who was the father of Masako, Yoritomo's forceful wife, who came to be known as the Ama shōgun (*ama* means nun). Yoriie, who became ill in 1203, was deposed after a plot against the Hōjō had been exposed, and was killed in 1204. His successor was his younger brother Sanetomo (1192–1219), who became shōgun at the age of eleven. He was attracted by what he knew of life at the court in Kyoto and preferred poetry to military pursuits. He was married to a Fujiwara and established friendly relations with the ex-Emperor Go-Toba. Hōjō Tokimasa, who had become *shikken* (regent for a shōgun) plotted to depose Sanetomo. The plot was foiled by the shōgun's mother, Masako, and her brother, Hōjō Yoshitoki, who took over as *shikken*. Sanetomo was, however, powerless and was eventually assassinated in Kamakura in 1219. Thus ended the Minamoto line of shōguns.

But the shōgunate was kept in being by the Hōjō regents, and the post was filled by scions of the Fujiwara or the imperial family. None of these were allowed to gain real power. If they tried to do so, they were deposed, and the shōguns became puppets under the control of the Hōjō regents. Especially in the first half of the twelfth century, the Hōjō produced a series of able rulers, but their prestige and ability began to decline as the century wore to its end. They had to deal with continuing problems with the court. The frugality and discipline of the early days of the shōgunate were not maintained, and a liking for luxury led to a decline in the standards of probity and efficiency within the administration in Kamakura. The efforts needed to meet the Mongol attempts to invade Japan led to a serious drain on the limited resources of the country and strained the loyalty of the military landholders most directly involved. The taxes which the shōgunate was able to collect were inadequate for the various needs of the government, especially as in the thirteenth century Japan encountered a series of natural disasters, which affected the economy. Like the Emperors, many of the Hōjō regents took the tonsure and resigned the nominal position of *shikken*, but continued to control events from their monastic 'courts'. At times therefore there was an Emperor and one or more ex-Emperors, enjoying the privileges of 'cloister government', an imperial regent (*sesshō*), a 'dictator' (*kanpaku*), a titular shōgun and a titular regent to the shōgun (*shikken*), with the real power being exercised by a retired *shikken*. This was indirect rule developed to an extreme degree, but it seems to have worked at least for a time.

Despite the fact that the centre of real power had shifted to Kamakura and the court's wealth and prestige had been undermined, the Kamakura *bakufu* had a series of disputes and difficulties with the court. The prestige of the imperial institution meant that the Hōjō regents felt that they must at least go through the motions of consulting the court on major issues, such as the Mongol threats. This inevitably gave the court the illusion that, if only they could find an effective way of using their prestige against the *bakufu*, they could topple the Hōjō, whom they hated as usurpers of their privileges.

The Emperor Go-Toba (1180–1239), who had abdicated in 1198 in favour of his son, the Emperor Tsuchimikado, repeatedly intrigued against the *bakufu*. In 1221 his intrigues led to what came to be called the *Jōkyū* disturbances, when Go-Toba publicly called for the removal of the regent Hōjō Yoshitoki. Yoshitoki sent a large force to Kyoto and speedily quelled the supporters of Go-Toba, who was exiled for the rest of his days to the remote Oki Islands in the Sea of Japan. Two other ex-Emperors, Tsuchimikado and Juntoku, were also exiled, and the *bakufu* confiscated the property of Go-Toba's supporters, using this to reward their own vassals. The *bakufu* thereafter kept two senior officials, called *tandai* in Kyoto, together with a military force, to ensure that the court was properly supervised and prevented from causing further disorders. They ensured that Emperors and regents (*sesshō*) were appointed only with their approval and that ex-Emperors behaved themselves. Interestingly they favoured the system of cloistered government, even going so far as to appoint one cloistered Emperor, Go-Takakura, who had never been Emperor. But despite the presence of their forces in Kyoto the *bakufu* had great difficulty in maintaining law and order in the city and dealing with the monks of Hieizan and Kōfukuji (in Nara), who continued to be an obstreperous and violent nuisance.

The Emperor Go-Saga (1220–72; reigned 1242–6) was subservient to the *bakufu*, but the rivalry between his two sons, the Emperor Go-Fukakusa and his successor, the Emperor Kameyama, led to a dispute which in the fourteenth century resulted in the creation of dual northern and southern courts (the so-called *Nanbokuchō jidai*). The *bakufu* tried to keep the peace by alternating the succession between the senior and junior lines descended from the two brothers, but neither line accepted this arrangement as fair, and there was constant friction over property. The dispute came to a head in the time of the Emperor Go-Daigo (1288–1339; reigned 1318–39), in whose time the Kamakura shōgunate was ended. Go-Daigo determined to restore the imperial power. His first plot in 1324 failed, as did his second in 1331 in what came to be called the *Genkō* incident. He was forced to flee to Nara when the shōgunate appointed the Emperor Kōgon to succeed him. In 1332 he was captured and exiled to the Oki Islands, from which, however, he escaped in 1333 to join his son and Kusunoki Masashige, who became a legendary figure symbolizing indomitable courage in the face of overwhelming odds and devoted loyalty to the Emperor. Ashikaga Takauji (1305–58), who had been sent by the Kamakura *bakufu* to suppress the rebellion, changed sides and took Kyoto in Go-Daigo's name. Go-Daigo then inaugurated what came to be called the Kenmu restoration, while an army under Nitta Yoshisada (1301–38), which had marched on Kamakura, destroyed the remnants of the Hōjō and set fire to the city.

Kamakura is reputed to have been founded in the seventh century by Fujiwara no Kamatari (614–69), the first of the great Fujiwara leaders. He is said to have come to the Kantō plain on a pilgrimage and to have stopped one night at a fishing village, where he had a dream in which the god Hachiman ordered him to bury his *kama* (a broad knife) on a nearby hill. The Hachiman shrine was founded in 1063 near the seashore by Minamoto no Yoriyoshi in honour of the Minamoto family deity, the god of war. It was moved to its present site by Yoritomo in 1180, and it was only in his time that Kamakura became an important centre. The city lies in a sheltered valley by the sea, guarded by seven mountain passes. When the *bakufu* had its capital at Kamakura, the broad avenue which runs from the Hachiman shrine towards the sea was bordered by the residences of the main vassals and officials. The shōgun's own residence lay on the west side of the shrine. Traders were confined to an area near the harbour which was developed to facilitate trade with Sung China.

In the middle of the thirteenth century Kamakura may have had a population of some 50,000. According to contemporary accounts most of these people were poor, and the town was dirty and full of refuse. The great temples of Kamakura were mainly established during the thirteenth century. The famous Zen (see pages 86–88) temple of Kenchōji was founded in 1253, and Engakuji was founded in 1282. The Great Buddha of Kamakura was successfully cast in bronze in 1252 after many unsuccessful attempts. It was originally housed in a large hall, but the building was wrecked by storms and eventually demolished by a tidal wave in 1495. The image is of Amida Buddha and exemplifies the popularity of the Amidist sects in Kamakura times (see page 85). During the Kamakura period the city housed many monks. In addition to prayer, preaching, meditation and political manoeuvring, they found time to help with the sick and did something to alleviate the periodic famines of the thirteenth century in Japan. After the destruction wrought by Nitta Yoshisada in 1333 the city was rebuilt and remained the main centre for the Kantō until Edo became the capital of the Tokugawa shōgunate in 1603.

Institutions and Law

Yoritomo established in 1180 the *samuraidokoro* (the board with responsibility for controlling and disciplining the warriors). In 1184 he set up a *kumonjo* (office of public documents); this was later absorbed by the *mandokoro* (administrative board). In the same year the *monchūjo* (board of inquiry) was created as a court to review claims and lawsuits. These three offices formed the key institutions of the new central government established in Kamakura and were retained under the Hōjō regents. The council of regency was superseded by the appointment of a *shikken* (single regent), but a council of state was created to work under the regent. Its deliberations were regarded as secret, and its decisions were a collective responsibility. Unanimity or consensus was demanded, a practice which still prevails in many businesses in Japan today. The members of the council had to swear in the name of the Buddhist and Shintō deities that they would 'give judgement without fear or favour in accordance with reason'.

Important though these new organs were for the running of the *bakufu*, the shōgunate's main need was an apparatus in the provinces which could ensure obedience to Kamakura and the collection of the taxes or rents which the regime needed to survive. These objectives were achieved, initially at least, by the appointment of key supporters, who were confirmed in their estates, accorded the status of *gokenin* or *kenin* (literally, 'house-men', that is, vassals) and given special privileges at Kamakura. The samurai came below the *kenin* in status. They were mounted warriors who had a number of attendants. The foot soldiers came next and were called *zusa*. The regime survived because it provided a stable framework of mutual loyalties. It failed when this framework broke down.

To control the provinces *shugo* or *sō-tsuibushi* (constables) were appointed by the *bakufu* to ensure that their authority was upheld. They did not supersede the governors of the Heian period, but in practice the real power lay in their hands. They were responsible for drafting men for the imperial guard, suppressing uprisings and arresting violent criminals, but they naturally assumed many other duties on behalf of the Kamakura regime. The *bakufu* also needed to exercise direct control of many public and private domains, which as a result of the *Genpei* wars had come into their possession. For this purpose *jitō* (stewards) were appointed. They were allocated for their own use one-eleventh of the land placed under their direct control. One of the duties of the stewards was to levy the *hyōrōmai* (commissariat tax) which the *bakufu* demanded to cover the costs of the wars. This was levied at a rate of about one-fiftieth of the yield on *all* land, including the many estates or *shōen* which had hitherto been exempt from tax. The establishment of this tax came as a shock to the many privileged holders of *shōen* and aroused much resentment against the *bakufu*. The court managed to delay for a time the application of the levy, but when it was universally applied it greatly strengthened the position of the stewards, who took on new powers and obligations. Many stewards were engaged on such tasks as bringing waste land under cultivation or supervising the building of roads and bridges as well as the organization and operation of post stations. This led to a rivalry between the constables and the stewards; the constables generally won and went on to become local magnates or 'feudal barons'.

The system of land tenure and government in the provinces was an illogical hotchpotch of old and new, as the old rules continued to operate alongside the new. For each parcel of land there were various rights, known as *shiki*, which differed accoring to the historical circumstances of the land in question. This complicated the administration of land tenure and taxation and was the basis of much dispute, but the *bakufu*, at least initially, did its best to enforce impartial judgements; and, except in the frequent periods of natural disaster, agricultural production improved.

In 1232, in the time of the regent Hōjō Yasutoki, a formulary or list of practical rules was adopted. This came to be called the *Jōei shikimoku*, after the Jōei era, during which it was promulgated. This was not so much a legal code as a collection of maxims and practical rules. It consisted of fifty-one articles. It enjoined loyalty and filial piety, but it also covered such matters as religious observances, the functions and duties of officers in the provinces, tenure of fiefs and the punishment to be given for various criminal offences. It was designed for the guidance and discipline of the military caste and was applied only to the vassals, or *kenin*, of the *bakufu*. The rest of the population remained subject to the old *Taihō* code, but in practice the new rules tended to be applied throughout the country. It naturally upheld the rights of the territorial magnates, but it also provided some protection for tenants against unauthorized exactions and injustice. The *bakufu* recognized that the economy of the country depended on the cultivator and that there were limits to how far he could be squeezed. There was, therefore, an element of expediency in the new rules. Sir George Sansom quotes the letter which the regent Yasutoki sent to Hōjō Shigetoki, then *tandai* in Kyoto, to explain the document: 'In deciding upon the procedure to adopt we were influenced by a desire for impartial verdicts without discrimination between high and low.... We have written this Formulary in such a way that even the most

Top left, Dōtaku (bell-shaped bronze) — Middle Yayoi period. Tokyo National Museum.
op centre, Haniwa terracotta figurine of a man — Kofun period (6th–7th century). Tokyo National Museum.
Top right, Haniwa terracotta figurine of a woman — Kofun period (6th–7th century). Tokyo National Museum.

Bottom left, Haniwa terracotta house — Kofun period (4th–5th century). Tokyo National Museum.
Bottom right, Haniwa terracotta hawk — Kofun period (6th–7th century). Tokyo National Museum.

Above, Wall painting from Takamatsuzuka tomb, south of Nara — Kofun period (6th—7th century).
Left, Bronze statue of Buddha (Shaka Nyorai) — Asuka period (552—645). Kanimanji temple, Kyoto.
Opposite page, Wood statue of Miroku Bosatsu — Asuka period (552—645). Kōryūji temple, Kyoto.

Left, Wood statue of Jikokuten — one of the four guardian kings (8th century). Tōshōdaiji temple, Nara.

Opposite page, Wood statue (probably originally gilden and now looking like black lacquer) of Nyoirin Kannon (7th century). Chūguji convent of the Hōryūji temple, Nara.

Right, Clay statue of Bazara (head only) (mid-8th century). Shinyakushiji temple, Nara.

Right, Five-storey pagoda —
originally constructed in 607.
Reconstructed with the
original timbers after the
Second World War. Hōryūji
temple, Nara.
Below, Octagonal pavilion,
the Yumedono (7th century).
Hōryūji temple, Nara.
Overleaf, The Hō-ōdō
(Phoenix Hall) of the Byōdō
in temple at Uji between
Kyoto and Nara.

illiterate fellows can understand its meaning. The old laws are like complicated Chinese characters; the new laws are like the simple syllabary [*kana*].'[2] Various supplements were issued later, but the formulary remained, with amendments and additions, as the basis of feudal justice until the nineteenth century.

The formulary was a historically significant and influential document, which underlines the fact that military rule brought real benefits to Japan at that time. Indeed, if it had not been for the development of a military caste and the system of government established by Yoritomo the Japanese would almost certainly have been overwhelmed by the Mongol invasions, and the history of Japan would have been very different.

Trade with China and the Mongol Invasions

Although there had been no official relations with the Chinese court since 894, intercourse with the mainland did not come to a complete stop. An occasional Chinese ship called at Kyūshū ports to trade, and Japanese monks continued to make periodic visits to China to study. In the twelfth century Taira no Kiyomori recognized that there were benefits to be obtained from trade with China and built port facilities in Hyōgo bay. He exchanged gifts with the Sung court (his gifts were treated as tribute), while the court exchanged 'private' letters with the Sung court. After the establishment of the shōgunate at Kamakura trade with China was expanded, mainly in Chinese vessels, as the Japanese had not yet made much progress in shipbuilding. For this trade ports were also developed in Kyūshū.

The main Japanese imports from China were silk, brocades, perfumes, incense, sandalwood, porcelain and copper coins, as well as tea. Japanese exports consisted mainly of gold, mercury, fans, lacquer ware, screens, timber and swords. These lists show not only the extent of Japanese interest in Chinese luxuries but also the development of Japanese arts and crafts. The inclusion of swords among Japanese exports underlines the progress made by the Japanese in metalwork. Even though Chinese artists under the Sung dynasty had produced many great works of art, the Chinese were sufficiently impressed by Japanese art to import screens and fans as well as lacquer. The list of Japanese exports confirms that, despite the emphasis on warlike pursuits, the arts of peace were flourishing. The import of copper coins shows that internal trade in Japan was developing. Money and credit indeed began to displace the barter arrangements which had developed after the ending of the minting of coins in Japan in the tenth century.

From about 1230 northern China came under the domination of the Mongols. In 1259 Kublai Khan was proclaimed Emperor of China and in 1264 he established his capital at Peking (Beijing). Southern China and the Korean peninsula soon succumbed to the Mongols, and Kublai Khan determined to add Japan to his conquests. In 1266 two envoys sent to demand Japanese surrender failed to reach Japan to deliver their message, but a further mission in 1268 got as far as Dazaifu. Their letters were sent to Kamakura and forwarded from there to Kyoto, where the Emperor was aggrieved to find himself described as 'the king of a little country'. The court prepared a weak draft reply, which was rejected by the *bakufu*, who ordered the Mongol envoys to return to China. Steps were immediately taken to strengthen the defences in Kyūshū, while the court spent its time in religious services praying for the safety of the land. A further Mongol envoy, who arrived in 1272 with an ultimatum, was expelled, and the Japanese awaited the now inevitable invasion. This came in November 1274. The invasion force, consisted, according to some estimates, of about 15,000 Mongols and 8,000 Koreans with 7,000 Korean sailors. After capturing the islands of Iki and Tsushima, a landing was made near Hakata. The Japanese fought hard against the superior weapons of the Mongols, but failed to eject the Mongol force. However, as a storm was approaching, the Koreans urged the Mongols to re-embark. Their advice was accepted, and in the storm some two hundred vessels and 13,000 soldiers were apparently lost.

Kublai Khan, refusing to accept defeat, sent further envoys in 1275 demanding that the king of Japan do homage to him at Peking. The envoys were summarily executed at Kamakura, and further strenuous efforts were made to strengthen the defences in Kyūshū. A stone wall was constructed along Hakozaki bay by forced labour, and all available men in Kyūshū were mobilized to repel the Mongol invasion when it came. The expedition sent in 1281 consisted of a much stronger force than in 1274. Two Mongol fleets from Korea and south China, consisting of some 4,400 vessels, were to bring some 140,000 soldiers to Japan. The fleet from Korea arrived first and, after recapturing Iki and Tsushima, a landing was again made near Hakata. The Japanese, with the help of the wall they had built, managed during weeks of severe fighting that summer to prevent the Mongols achieving a firm foothold. The arrival of the second fleet from south China gave the Mongols the forces they needed to launch new attacks. These might have overwhelmed the defenders. Once again, however, the Japanese were saved by a storm. The typhoon, which struck on 16 August 1281, destroyed most of the Mongol fleet and forced a Mongol withdrawal. It is reckoned that about half the Mongol force was either killed or drowned in the storm. The winds which saved Japan came to be called the *kamikaze* or divine wind.

Kublai Khan, until his death in 1294, never gave up his desire to chastise the Japanese, and fresh plans to invade Japan were made, but each time they had to be called off so that he could deal with other threats to his regime. The Japanese could not, therefore, relax their defence effort for many years. The necessary expenditure involved in strengthening the Kyūshū defences was a serious burden on *bakufu* finances, and the number of men tied up in the defence forces led to a decline in agricultural production, particularly in Kyūshū. The war yielded neither lands nor booty which could be used to reward those involved in the fighting. The shōgunate was faced with demands for recompense not only from the clans most directly involved but also from the monasteries, which claimed that the victory was due to their prayers. The *bakufu's* inability to meet these demands by confiscating lands to allocate or by enforcing increased taxes on private and public estates led to disaffection among the vassals concerned. Many feudal lords, whose expenditure was increasing, found themselves forced to raise money by mortgaging or selling their property. Attempts to alleviate the consequent distress by *tokusei* (acts of grace), such as in 1297, in practice only exacerbated the problem. The development of credit helped to create a merchant class who also managed to benefit from the inflationary price rises which occurred. But the consequent insolvency of the shōgunate proved to be one of the main causes of the downfall of the Hōjō.

The Samurai and their Code: Life in Kamakura Times

The samurai formed the officer class in the military structure developed under the Kamakura shōgunate. Some were also yeomen farmers. The term *samurai* comes from a word meaning to serve. This derivation underlines the basic duty of the samurai which was to give loyal service to his feudal lord. The Chinese character used for samurai had a Sino-Japanese reading of *shi* – hence the terms *bushi* (where *bu* means 'military' or 'fierce') and *bushidō* or the way (that is, code) of the warrior. In fact, the word *bushidō* is of comparatively modern origin, and its precepts were adopted and adapted over many centuries. The basic elements were developed in Kamakura times, but the summary which follows represents the code as it became in later periods, not as it was in medieval Japan.

The warriors of medieval Japan have sometimes been compared with the European knights who fought in the crusades, and *bushidō* with the code of chivalry. Some similarities may be found, but the differences are more significant. The samurai generally fought for their feudal lords. Although they worshipped the *kami*, while also considering themselves to be believers in a form of Buddhism, they did not fight for a religious cause. Their wives were expected to display courage and devoted loyalty to their husband's lord even to the extent of sacrificing their own children to save him, but the samurai would have found the attitudes of medieval European knights towards their lady-loves incomprehensible. There was no element of romantic love about the samurai; indeed, their spartan upbringing, perhaps as pages to a feudal lord or in a monastery, encouraged homosexual practices, although they would also marry for the sake of family alliances and would beget children to continue the family name. They were usually monogamous, although they could have secondary wives. The European and Japanese warriors had, however, at least one aim in common; they sought glory and honour as well as booty. They were both capable of behaving with ruthless cruelty and greed in war, and cases of treachery and deceit can be found in the annals both of Japan and of the crusades. But the European knight and the samurai were also capable of acts of courage and self-sacrifice.

The warriors' code in Japan had three main sources, Confucian, Buddhist and Shintō. Its ethical elements were largely of Confucian origin where the emphasis was placed on the hierarchical relationship involving loyalty and obligation between master and servant or in the Japanese case between lord and vassal. This relationship was essentially a family one and was not contractual as it essentially was in Europe. Sir George Sansom has commented: 'In Japan the samurai owed absolute and unconditional duty to his lord, without claim to recompense and irrespective of other claims upon his service and even upon his life.'[3] Other Confucian elements included the requirement to work for justice and to show compassion and benevolence towards the oppressed. The samurai was supposed to abhor underhand dealings and to speak the truth. He was trained to endure hardships and to exercise self-control and patience. He must not display his emotions. He should adhere to the correct rules of etiquette and politeness. He was expected to despise money and commerical transactions. The preservation of his honour was of paramount importance, and he must endeavour by all means to avoid disgrace and shame.

Through his Buddhist faith the warrior recognized the impermanence of life.

81

Professor Nitobe Inazo, who romanticized and idealized the creed of the samurai, said that the samurai should have 'a calm trust in Fate, a quiet submission to the inevitable, that stoic composure in the sight of danger or calamity, that disdain of life and friendliness with death;.[4]

From Shintō he was supposed to have learned patriotism and loyalty, although there was in Kamakura times, at least until the Mongol attempts to invade Japan, no real concept of nationality, and loyalty was a Confucian concept. The samurai also learned from Shintō that his country was the sacred abode of the gods and that the Emperor was at least the spiritual guardian of the land.

The samurai's sense of honour lay behind his determination to revenge insults. It was also the basis for his acceptance of the institution of ritual suicide to avoid the dishonour of execution or an ignoble death. Ritual suicide involved cutting open the belly with a dagger or short sword, the head then being cut off with a sword by a loyal friend or retainer. This rite was called *seppuku* or more vulgarly *harakiri*. A. B. Mitford, later Lord Redesdale, has given a vivid account in the *Tales of Old Japan*, first published in 1871, of a ritual suicide which he witnessed in 1868. Suicide was not condemned as wrong by the Buddhist sects in Japan.

One of the first attempts at producing a written code for the warriors was the *kakun* (family instructions) of Hōjō Shigetoki (1198–1261).[5] This emphasized the moral duty of the samurai. 'A good heart and the faith of a warrior are like the two wheels of a carriage.' He was to perform his duty, even at the cost of his life and that of his family, 'holding to the good, not yielding to the strong'. A warrior must never surrender, but must die fighting. One consequence of this belief was that prisoners could generally expect neither respect nor compassion. When the Mongols invaded Japan, all prisoners were slaughtered.

The samurai, being human, did not always adhere to the warriors' code; and the oath of loyalty which they had to swear to their lord did not prevent many from changing sides in battle and being accepted as vassals by the victor despite their treachery to their original lord. Nor were all samurai always courageous; the cowardly samurai, indeed, became a comic character in Japanese farces in the subsequent Muromachi period.

In the early days of the Kamakura shōgunate the warriors, who were for the most part illiterate, generally lived a simple and frugal life. While the shōgun's residence was built in the Kyoto *shindenzukuri* style, the houses of the warriors, or the *buke-yashiki*, were built in a more austere form, called *bukezukuri*. The warriors' houses were modest in size and unpretentious. Their grounds had to provide space for stables as well as outbuildings to accommodate vassals, foot soldiers and servants. The senior retainers also needed open spaces where archery, horsemanship and fencing could be practised. In some places outside the main centres of population the residences of the samurai were fortified with fences, walls and ditches. The entrance was through a gate surmounted by a turret (*yagura*). These were the forerunners of the castles (*shiro*) of later centuries.

Living conditions were spartan. The only heating came from small charcoal braziers or the kitchen fire. The primitive oil lamps gave little light. *Tatami*, the Japanese rush mat which nowadays covers the whole floor in Japanese-style rooms, did not come into general use until the fifteenth century, and floors were of either plain wood or beaten earth. The staple food of the samurai was rice supplemented with vegetables and game from the hunting which was an important pastime in times of peace. Sugar was a luxury which was used mainly as a medicine. Soya sauce which adds spice to Japanese food did not become popular until the fourteenth century.

The life of the farmers was still more primitive. They rose with the sun and went to rest when the sun went down. Their life, except in the winter months in the northern part of Japan, was one of unremitting toil. Taxes in rice, other produce or labour were onerous, and a farmer might find that he had to yield in taxes or other imposts up to two-thirds of his harvest. As yields in those days were probably about a quarter of what they are today, it is hardly surprising that for the farmer rice was a luxury, their staple food being wheat and millet. The famines which followed a series of droughts in the latter part of the fourteenth century led to the growing of *soba* (buckwheat) as an alternative crop. The primitive nature of the roads, the general lack of bridges and the number of robbers wandering the country made travel very difficult and prevented the movement of most grains from one part of the country to other parts to alleviate famines, although coastal shipping was beginning to develop with the growth of trade. The farmers did not have family names in those days. This was the origin of the Japanese word for peasant – *hyakusho* or 'man with a hundred names', that is, someone who having no family name was referred to by various assorted nicknames.

In times of peace the samurai wore simple clothes, his only distinguishing mark being his headgear, an *eboshi*, triangular in shape and made of black stiff cloth. Only the very rich and members of the court wore silk. In battle the samurai donned his armour. His breastplate was made of leather or lacquered steel and was joined by thongs to separate sections covering his sides and back. Jointed sections were used to protect the shoulders and to provide a kind of protective skirt. He had a steel helmet with 'wings' to deflect sword cuts and a vizor to guard his face. He usually carried one or two swords, together with a bow and a quiver for his arrows, and would have a dagger in his belt. A samurai did not carry a shield (*tate*), but a servant would sometimes have one and would use it to protect his master while, for instance, he fitted an arrow to his bow. The samurai had to be a master horseman. The foot soldiers (*ashigaru*), who began to be recruited in the latter part of the fourteenth century, were of lesser status and had more primitive equipment. Like the farmers they generally went barefoot or wore simple straw sandals. Men as well as women used make up, and it was thought fitting that the samurai should go into battle clean and perfumed.

Discipline on the field of battle was rudimentary, and the samurai had little or no training in fighting in formation. Indeed, their preference was for single combat, and battles would often commence by one of the leading samurai challenging a leading figure on the other side to a duel which would begin on horseback. In the absence of distinguishing uniforms the feudal lords developed heraldic emblems or *mon*, which they displayed on banners and the curtains which enclosed their camps.

There were few amenities at this time, but in the Kamakura period the Japanese developed their liking for the bath. Two types of bath became popular. These were the hot bath (*yu*) and the steam bath (*furo*). Such baths were mainly found in large temples and the houses of the wealthy. Medicine consisted largely of charms and incantations to exorcise evil spirits, although in the towns there were practitioners who had some knowledge of Chinese medicine and herbs. Crafts developed with the relative peace which marked much of the thirteenth century. Carpenters were much in demand, not only to build new temples, shrines and houses, but also to repair the damage caused by fire, natural disasters and war.

Religion

The samurai and still more the ordinary people found the fine rituals and esoteric teachings of the Tendai and Shingon sect incomprehensible and unsatisfying. They craved for a simpler answer to their fears and longings. The general pessimism brought about by the series of natural disasters which marked the thirteenth century in Japan, and by the destruction wrought by civil war, was enhanced by the general Buddhist belief that these were 'the latter days of the law' (mappo – see page 53).

In this atmosphere it was natural that the Japanese people should look for help from their traditional gods, the kami, and that Shintō shrines should enjoy a revival of interest. But Shintō had little more to offer in the way of philosophy than a belief in ritual purity and affinity with nature. It had no clear teaching about the meaning of life or about life after death and it had no general ethical dogmas. Its festivals and its rituals nevertheless played an important part in the lives of the farmers, the samurai and the court.

There was also a revival of interest in Confucian teaching in this period. Chinese monks, who came to Japan in the latter years of the Sung dynasty, brought with them new commentaries on Confucian doctrines, especially those by the Chinese philosopher Chu Hsi (Zhu XI) (1130–1200). The samurai eagerly sought out Chinese treatises on the art of war. The philosophy of Lao-tzu (Laozi) (Taoism) aroused the curiosity of literate Japanese. Confucian and Taoist thought influenced not only the code of the warriors but also Zen Buddhism as it developed in Japan (see pages 86–88).

The philosophical approach of Chu Hsi, who was the father of Neo-Confucianism, cannot be summarized in a few brief sentences. But his teachings included the idea that enlightenment can be achieved by the use of reason and is not dependent on intuition. He believed that a man seeking enlightenment must make a profound study of 'all things under heaven'. He regarded the universe as a duality of 'law' and 'matter' and he advocated a process of synthesis in coming to conclusions. His ideas were much in vogue in Japan in the Edo period (see Chapter VIII).

Taoism is supposed to represent the philosophy of Lao-tsu, who, if he ever existed, may have lived in the fifth or sixth century BC in China and is reputed to be the author of the Tao Te Ching (Daode jing). The Tao is an ancient Chinese term used to mean the great reality of the universe or what we might call the absolute. Taoist mystics believed that the Tao could not be comprehended by reason and study, but only by a rejection of human values in a search for eternal truth. Taoism developed as a religion in the second century AD, when leaders emerged who promised a cure for all ills and the elixir of eternal life in return for monetary contributions. Taoists advocated inaction and placidity, as well as regulated breathing, discipline and diet, including the consumption of substances to prolong life, as aids to achieve immortality.

Amidism, or the particular worship of the Amida Buddha, had begun to spread in late Heian times, but it was Hōnen Shōnin (*shōnin* means holy man; he was also called Genkū)(1133–1212) who established Amidism as a sect separate from Tendai (although the Pure Land sect, Jōdoshū, which regards him as its founder, was not recognized as a separate sect until much later). Hōnen, who had been a monk on Mount Hiei, believed that, because of human frailty, it was impossible for the vast majority of people to achieve Buddhahood. They must rely on outside help (*tariki*). This meant that they should put all their trust in Amida Buddha. He declared that all can enter into the Pure Land 'merely by invoking his name, Amida, with complete faith'. Just before his death he wrote 'The way of final salvation . . . is nothing else but the mere repetition of the *Namu Amida Butsu*, without any doubt as to His mercy, whereby a man can be born again in the Land of Perfect Bliss. The mere repetition, together with an ardent faith, takes in all the practical details. . . .'[6] Hōnen offended the monks of Hieizan by his teaching and despite support from the Emperor Go-Toba he was exiled in 1207 and not allowed to return to Kyoto until shortly before his death. Some critics of the Pure Land teaching have argued that it allowed its believers to commit evil and still achieve salvation by a simple recitation of the *nenbutsu*. But Hōnen also stressed the need for right conduct, which in his view went with right faith. If faith was not pure, Amida could not save those who invoked his name.

Hōnen was essentially a simple and gentle character; he was neither a philosopher nor a forceful preacher, but he had many followers who propounded his teaching with variations. The most important of these was Shinran Shōnin (1173–1262), the founder of Jōdo Shinshū (the True Pure Land sect), more usually known simply as Shinshū, whose main headquarters are now in the great temples of the Nishi-Honganji and Higashi-Honganji in Kyoto (*nishi* means west, and *higashi* means east). Shinran too was a monk on Hieizan and studied with Hōnen. But he declined to follow the monastic rules and married the daughter of the regent Fujiwara no Kanezane. He was also exiled in 1207 and following Hōnen's return to Kyoto in 1211 he set out on a missionary trip to north-eastern Japan. Shinran believed that faith and morality, which he referred to as *shintai* and *zokutai*, were needed for salvation. *Shintai* was the real truth, that is, salvation in the next world through the grace of Amida. *Zokutai* was common truth or morality, that is, man's duty as a member of the social order. He sought to break down the division between the clergy and the laity by encouraging a married priesthood, but it was his simplification of the *nenbutsu* to a single declaration, made with faith, which has come to characterize Shinshū. His trust in Amida Buddha was such that he believed that Amida could save even the wicked. He declared: 'If one has faith in the original vow [of Amida], there is no necessity for any other good deed, for no good deed can surpass the act of adoration (*nenbutsu*); there is no need to fear committing an evil action, for no evil action can stand in the way of the original vow of Amida.' Not surprisingly such teaching had an instant appeal for many warriors.

Another important disciple of Hōnen was Ippen Shōnin (1239–89), who helped to popularize Amidism among the common people. He travelled round the country chanting the *nenbutsu* and dancing.

The proponents of the Amida *nenbutsu* were generally tolerant and compassionate in their teaching. Nichiren Shōnin (also called Risshō Daishi)(1222–82), the founder of the Nichiren sect of Buddhism, on the other hand, was a polemical and intolerant preacher who established a form of Mahayana Buddhism peculiar to Japan. He was more like an Old Testament prophet than a revivalist preacher; he has also been compared to Savonarola (1452–98), who denounced the profligacy and corruption of medieval Florence. He was totally uncompromising towards anyone who disagreed with him, but he was renowned for his devotion to his disciples. He was a Japanese nationalist before the concept of nationalism was recognized in Japan. He asserted in the *Risshō ankokuron*, written in 1260, that the form of Buddhism which he preached was the only true one and should be accepted as such by the state. He believed that heretics should be killed.

Nichiren's attacks on other sects were violent. He called Kōbō Daishi 'the greatest liar in Japan' and condemned the *nenbutsu* as 'a hellish practice'. His denunciations aroused so much anger that he was exiled in 1261 to the Izu peninsula. He was allowed to return to Kamakura in 1263. In 1271 he prophesied the Mongol invasions of Japan. He was condemned to death as a conspirator, but he was saved by a 'miraculous' thunderbolt, which allegedly broke the executioner's sword into three pieces as it was about to fall and sever Nichiren's outstretched neck. He was then exiled to the island of Sado, where he wrote in 1272 the *Kaimokushō* ('The Eye Opener'). In this he declared that he would be the pillar, the eyes and the great vessel of Japan. After his return to Kamakura in 1274 he retired to Minobu on the slopes of Mount Fuji, where he spent his remaining days in the establishment of the Nichiren sect which he declared was the one universal Buddhism.

The essence of Nichiren's teaching was that the Lotus Sutra (the *Saddharma pundarika-sutra* or the *Hokkekyō* in Japanese) could alone bring salvation. According to Nichiren, the sutra taught that the three bodies of the Buddha, namely transformation, bliss and the law, were essentially one. Nichiren identified himself with the Bodhisattva of Superb Action (*Visishtacaritra* or *Jōgyō* in Japanese) who had preached the law after the death of Sakyamuni and had devoted himself to the spread of Buddhism. Belief in the sutra was to be affirmed by calling on its help in the words *Namu Myōhō-Rengekyō*, which may be translated as 'reverence for the scripture of the Lotus of the Good Law'. In this respect his teaching had some similarity with that of the *nenbutsu* sects. There were many mystical elements in Nichiren's teachings, but 'what he recommended to ordinary believers was by no means abstract and difficult but concrete, plain, and even matter of fact: a practical moral life, supported by the utterance of a formula, the worship of a symbol [a *mandara*] and combined with an active protest against tenets of other schools'.[7] 'Nichiren was perhaps the most remarkable figure, as his sect was the most exceptional development, in the religious history of Japan.'[8]

The Nichiren sect in common with other Buddhist sects in Japan has suffered from numerous schisms. One modern sect of political importance which derived from the teaching of Nichiren is Sōka Gakkai, or the 'value-creating society'. This was founded in 1930 by Makiguchi Tsunesaburō, as an independent lay organization of the Nichiren Shōshū sect of Buddhism.

The third new form of Buddhism to be promoted in the Kamakura period was Zen. Zen had its origins in various forms of meditation practised in India.

Meditation was a significant element in Hinayana and Mahayana Buddhism, but the Zen form of meditation was developed in China, where it was called Ch'an, which is the Chinese reading of the character read as Zen in Japanese. In China it took on Taoist and other mystical elements. 'The *Mahayana* concept of void and *nirvana* were explained in terms of the Original Nothing (*pen-wu*) (ben wu) of *Taoism* and the famous Middle Way was equated with the Chinese concept of the Mean (*wu-wei*, 'non-action'); and the Absolute, as understood in enlightenment (*sambodhi*), was compared with the Great One (T'ai-yi) (*taiyi*).'[9] The solitary hermit was revered by Taoists and by early adherents of Zen.

The first Chinese patriarch of Zen was Bodhidharma (*c.* 470–534), known as Daruma in Japan, who appears to have been of southern Indian origin. He is reputed to have told the Liang Emperor Wu (502–50) that his good works in building temples were futile. According to one legend he crossed the Yangtse river on a reed and he is often thus depicted in Zen paintings. He is said to have spent nine years sitting in meditation. As a result of squatting immobile for so long he apparently lost the use of his legs; hence the Daruma dolls in Japan which are made so that they cannot fall over. According to another legend, the staring eyes which are a characteristic of depictions of Daruma were the result of his having torn off his eyelids in fury with himself for falling asleep when he was meditating. Allegedly he threw his eyelids into the ground, and from these 'seeds' the first tea bushes grew. Tea, especially in the Japanese form of powdered green tea, is an effective stimulant and antidote to sleep.

Zen concepts first reached Japan during the Nara period, but they did not become popular until the end of the twelfth century. Eisai, also called Zenkō Kokushi (1141–1215), seems to have been the first Buddhist priest to establish Zen as a separate sect in Japan. He visited China twice to study Buddhism and brought back the teachings of the Rinzai form of Zen. He was appointed abbot of the Kenninji in Kyoto by the second Minamoto shōgun, Yoriie (1182–1204). Here he also had to maintain Shingon rituals, and the Rinzai form of Zen has ever since been more willing to compromise with other Buddhist sects than, for instance, the Sōdō or Sōtō form which was brought to Japan by Dōgen (1200–53), one of Eisai's contemporaries. These two are still the main forms of Zen to be found in Japan.

Zen denies the validity of logic in relation to religious beliefs. The philosophy of Zen cannot be summarized in any straightforward way or communicated in words. Its essence lies in an attempt to achieve enlightenment, or *satori*, by some sudden experience or flash of inspiration. The student of Zen aimed to comprehend the real nature of the universe by 'comtemplative vacuity', by intuition as well as by recognition of the Buddha in oneself and of the non-existence of the individual ego, or *muga*. The believer had to establish total control of his body, its instincts and desires and had to purge himself of all illusions. The total rejection of logic and the emphasis on non-self as well as on calmness and self-reliance had a particular appeal to the warriors, who had to be prepared to die on the field of battle.

There were a number of aids to enlightenment. Among these were the *kōan*, of which there are reputed to be some 1,700 (although there were many fewer basic ones). These were essentially illogical propositions, which were prescribed as themes on which the aspirant must meditate during periods of *zazen* (Zen meditation). According to the Zen scholar Suzuki Daisetsu a *kōan* 'has a most definite objective, the arousing of doubt and pushing it to its furthest limits'.[10] Suzuki gives as an example of an early *kōan* the following question put by the sixth patriarch: 'When your mind is not dwelling on the dualism of good and evil, what is your original face before you were born?' The patriarch Hakuin used to produce one of his hands and demand of his disciples to hear the sound of it; by this he struck at the logical or scientific basis of everyday experience.[11] Another and more complicated *kōan* was ascribed to the Chinese monk Nan-ch'üan (Nan Quan) (748–834). One day when some monks were quarrelling over possession of a kitten, he picked the kitten up and asked: 'If any among you can tell me why I should not kill this cat, I will spare its life.' Since none of the monks spoke, he dashed the kitten to the ground and killed it. Later the monk Chao-chou (Zhao Zhou; known in Japan as Jōshū), returning to the monastery after a day away, was asked what he could have said if he had been there. Jōshū did not reply. Instead he removed his straw sandals, placed them on his head and went out. Nan-ch'üan then declared that this action would have saved the kitten. Jōshū's action simply expressed the void which is the only answer to any problem.[12] When Jōshū was asked about the significance of Bodhidharma's coming east, which is proverbially the same as asking about the principle of Buddhism, he replied: 'The cypress-tree in the courtyard.'

Another aid to enlightenment was the stick, which the Zen master uses freely to ensure that the novice does not lose his concentration while meditating and in the hope that the sudden pain of the blow may cause a flash of intuition which will lead to enlightenment. A similar effect may be achieved by the sudden yell of 'Katsu!' which the Zen master uses to shock the aspirant for enlightenment while he is meditating.

The appeal of a contemplative sect such as Zen to an active military caste lay in its rejection of logic and preference for intuition over reasoning. The principles of Zen were summed up in China at an early date in the following lines:

> A special transmission outside the scriptures,
> No dependence on the written word,
> Direct pointing at the soul of man,
> Seeing one's nature and attaining Buddhahood.

Zen has had a profound influence on Japanese culture. Its austerity inspired the frequent Japanese preference for restraint and understatement as well as for suggestion rather than full description in poetry and painting. The Zen identification with nature also lies behind much of the Japanese worship of beauty in nature. Its rejection of logical argument is reflected in Japanese preference for pragmatic rather than rational answers to problems. Zen influence has been so pervasive that often when we think of some characteristic as being peculiarly Japanese it can in fact be traced to Zen.

Literary Developments

In the Heian period, writing in Chinese – that is, entirely in Chinese characters (*kanji*) – was the official language of government and scholars and remained distinct from writing largely using words of Japanese native origin, recorded mainly in *kana*. In the Kamakura period, writing which combined Chinese characters and the Japanese syllabary, known as *kanamajiri*, became the main vehicle for literature, and it remains to this day the primary way of writing the Japanese language. The change was naturally a gradual one, and many works were still written in Chinese. The development of *kanamajiri* coincided with the growth of the military caste and the growing popularity of travelling story-tellers who recited accounts of the heroic deeds of the civil wars which led up to the establishment of the Kamakura *bakufu*. The Japanese language has evolved and changed greatly since Kamakura times, with the addition of many new words which were invented or imported from foreign countries. The grammatical forms of the written style of the period are also no longer in use. The reading of the literature of the Kamakura period, therefore, presents difficulties to modern Japanese who have not made a special study of it, but in style and vocabulary it is easier for them to understand than much of the literature of the Heian period.

The court in Kyoto continued throughout the period to be the main cultural centre, but the deeds and the code of the warriors, as well as developments in Buddhism, had a significant influence on literature.

The spirit of the age was reflected in the *Shinkokinshū* or *Shinkokinwakashū*. This was completed in 1205 on the orders of the Emperor Gotoba (1180–1239). It was the eighth of the twenty-one imperial anthologies and is ranked by many critics at least on a par with the *Kokinshū*. It was compiled by Fujiwara no Teika (or Fujiwara no Sadaie; 1162–1241) and four other courtier poets. It consists of twenty books and 1,981 *waka*. Gotoba carefully supervised the compilation of the anthology, and this led to strained relations with Fujiwara no Teika, who disagreed with many of his sovereign's decisions. The arrangement of poems in the anthology generally reflected that of the *Kokinshū*. The first six books cover the seasons, spring and autumn having two books each. Books eleven to fifteen were devoted to love poems. The last two books were devoted to Shintō and Buddhist poems.

Fujiwara no Teika was a talented poet who became the poetic mentor of the third Minamoto shōgun, Minamoto no Sanetomo (1192–1219). He urged Sanetomo to imitate the poets of the *Manyōshū* 'when the hearts of men were unsophisticated'. This implied that he should concentrate on showing *makoto* or 'sincerity' and should eschew poetical conceits. Sanetomo was also urged to avoid vulgar words and phrases. For his part, Gotoba sought to achieve a 'lofty' or elevated tone (*taketakakiyo*).

Teika's ideal was that of *yōen*, which may be translated as 'ethereal beauty', and *ushin*, which implies 'conviction of feeling'. But the word which has come to symbolize the poetry of the *Shinkokinshū* is probably *yūgen*, which implies 'mystery and depth'. It was the ideal of Fujiwara no Shunzei, who was one of the great nature poets of the period. Natural phenomena, such as the moon, cherry blossom, autumn colours, rain and snow, were thought to symbolize universal human feelings and aesthetic sensibilities. The dominant theme throughout the *Shinkokinshū* is that of sadness, melancholy and loneliness, and these came to be represented by the Japanese word *sabi*, whose meanings include 'loneliness' and 'rust'.

Images were deployed with renewed artistry and polish, and the best *waka* in the collection are evocative of particular moments and scenes. They reflect a limited range of feeling and inevitably if only because of their brevity they lack philosophical and psychological depth. Poetic techniques were perfected, but the attachment to poetic conventions and the conservatism of Japanese poetic judgements inevitably led to some artificiality, and the emphasis on decorum to an element of pedantry. The rules, indeed, became so rigid that in due course they killed much of the spontaneity which had maintained the vitality of the Japanese poetic genius.

Perhaps the greatest poet of the Kamakura period and one of Japan's outstanding poets was the priest Saigyō (1118–90). Born in Kyoto of samurai stock, he became a priest of the Shingon sect at the age of twenty-two. He spent many years at the Shingon headquarters on Mount Koya, but he was also an inveterate traveller. During his journeys he visited the shrines at Miyajima and Ise; he also toured Shikoku and journeyed in the northern provinces as far as Aomori. Saigyō had a deep feeling for nature, and his best poems are simple and evocative. His cultivation of melancholy and of *sabi* reflects the poetic ideals of his time. The sadness of many of his poems responds to the Buddhist sentiments of a period when the world was disordered and natural disasters were frequent. Saigyō was a lyrical poet of real sincerity, but his laments on his sufferings and those of the world around him sometimes verge on the sentimental. Two hundred and sixty-two poems by Saigyō were included in imperial anthologies, 94 in the *Shinkokinshū*. His own personal collection the *Sankashū* contains 1,569 poems.

The poems in the *Shinkokinshū* as in the other imperial collections used only words of Japanese origin, that is, *yamato kotoba*. *Kangō*, that is, words borrowed from Chinese and given Sino-Japanese reading, were avoided by Japanese poets until much later times. Japanese poetry owed little if anything to Chinese cultural influences. The following brief poems are a few examples of typical poems in the *Shinkokinshū*.[14]

The first by Saigyō is one of his most famous:

Kokoro naki	Even to someone
Mi ni mo aware wa	Free of passions [that is, a priest] this sadness
Shirarekeri	Would be apparent:
Shigi tatsu sawa no	Evening in autumn over
Aki no yūgure.	A marsh where a snipe rises.

Another poem by Saigyō:

Furuhata no	In a tree standing
Soba no tatsu ki ni	Beside a desolate field,
Iru hato no	The voice of a dove
Tomo yobu koe no	Calling to its companions —
Sugoki yūgure.	Lonely, terrible evening.

A peom by Fujiwara no Teika:

Miwataseba	In this wide landscape
Hana mo momiji mo	I see no cherry blossoms
Nakarikeri	And no crimson leaves —

| Ura no tomoya no | Evening in autumn over |
| Aki no yūgure | A straw-thatched hut by the bay. |

A poem by the priest Jakuren (died 1202):[15]

Murasame no	The hanging raindrops
Tsuyu mo mada hinu	Have not dried from the needles
Maki no ha ni	Of the fir forest
Kiri tachinoboru	Before the evening mist
Aki no yūgure.	Of autumn rises.

Another poem by Jakuren with the same final line:[16]

Sabishisa wa	Loneliness –
Sono iro to shi mo	The essential colour of a beauty
Nakarikeri	Not to be defined:
Maki tatsu yama no	Over the dark evergreens, the dusk
Aki no yūgure.	That gathers on far autumn hills.

A poem by Shunzei:[17]

Yū sareba	As evening falls,
Nobe no akikaze	From along the moors the autumn wind
Mi ni shimite	Blows chill into the heart,
Uzura naku nari	And the quails raise their plaintive cry
Fukukusa no sato.	In the deep grass of secluded Fukukusa.

Another poem by Shunzei makes skilful use of onomatopoeia:

Katsu kōri	Now here frozen over,
Katsu wa kudakuru	Now there just fleeing from the grip of ice,
Yamagawa no	The stream between the hills
Iwama ni musebu	Is choked within its rocky channel
Akatsuki no koe.	And sobs its suffering in the winter dawn.

The 'Tales' or *monogatari* of the Heian period did not cease when the *bakufu* was established. The *Tsutsumi Chūnagon monogatari*, for instance, is a collection of ten stories arising from incidents at the court during the latter part of the Heian period and the early part of the Kamakura period. The earliest story probably dates from the middle of the eleventh century, and the last may be as late of 1385. As in earlier *monogatari* the episodes consist of prose introductions to exchanges of poems.[18]

Of much greater literary importance was the development of the *Gunki-monogatari*. These were stories of war and were designed for a much wider audience than was ever achieved by the novels of the court. The greatest of these was the *Heike monogatari*, which tells the story of the Taira family from their defeat of the Minamoto in 1160 to their own defeat by the Minamoto in 1185 at the battle Dannoura. The main character in the first part of the story is Taira no

Kiyomori; the second part is dominated by Minamoto no Yoshinaka and the third by Minamoto no Yoshitsune. None of the three main characters emerges as a conventional hero. Kiyomori appears as arrogant and cruel, Yoshinaka as boorish and Yoshitsune as short and pale. The main theme is the vanity and illusory nature of power. The Buddhist sentiments which dominate the story reflect the attitude of the chanters or *biwa-hōshi*, who were Buddhist priests who travelled around the country reciting this and other texts to wayside audiences to an accompaniment on the lute or *biwa*. Many of them were blind men who learned the story by heart and elaborated on it as they moved from place to place. The prose texts on which these recitations were based thus took on a poetic quality, often with alternating lines of five and seven syllables. The stories of battles and of heroic deeds, which provide the substance of the *Heike monogatari* and other 'war tales' of the time, recounted in this way give these stories an epic quality.

The first few lines of the *Heike monogatari* are among the most memorable in Japanese literature and are known to any educated Japanese. Even for someone who does not fully understand the Buddhist sentiments and can read the lines only in a romanized version, the sounds used create an impression of the vanity of human existence:

Gion shōja no kane no koe, shōgyō mujō no hibiki ari. Shara sōjū no hana no iro, jōsha hissui no kotowari wo arawasu. Ogoreru hito mo hisashikarazu. Tada haru no yo no yume no gotoshi. Takeki mono mo tsui ni horobinu. Hitoe ni kaze no mae no hokori ni onaji.

The sound of the bell of *Jetavana*[19] echoes the impermanence of all things. The hue of the flowers of the teak-tree declares that they who flourish must be brought low. Yea, the proud ones are but for a moment, like an evening dream in springtime. The mighty are destroyed at the last, they are but as the dust before the wind.[20]

The *Heike monogatari* has been preserved in many varied texts and mixed styles. The author cannot be firmly determined. It has been ascribed to one Yukinaga, but whoever the author or authors were, he or they were clearly well informed not only about the events of the time but also about the life of the samurai in those times. Some of the accounts of famous battles such as the sea battle of Dannoura contain evocative descriptions, and the *Heike monogatari* must be counted among the greatest works in the Japanese language. The *Hōgen monogatari* and the *Heiji monogatari* covered the period before the *Heike* begins; neither has the same force and impact.

Another classic of the Kamakura period, which every educated Japanese knows, is the *Hōjōki* ('The Ten Foot Square Hut')[21] by Kamo no Chōmei (1156?–1216). This is a Japanese *zuihitsu*, meaning 'jottings', which describes briefly the author's retirement to a simple country retreat. His hopes of becoming a priest at the Kamo shrine at Kyoto having been thwarted, he became a Buddhist priest in 1204 and retired to a mountain hermitage. Like the author of the *Heike monogatari* he begins his 'jottings' with a Buddhist lament on the vanity of human endeavours. The opening sentences of the *Hōjōki* have a poetic and sonorous quality:

Yuku gawa no nagare wa taezu shite, shikamo moto no mizu ni arazu. Yodomi ni ukabu utakata wa, katsu kie katsu musubite, hisashiku todomaru koto nashi. Yo no naka ni aru hito to sumika to mata kaku no gotoshi.

The flow of the river is ceaseless and its water is never the same. The bubbles that float in the pools, now vanishing, now forming, are not of long duration: so in the world are man and his dwellings.[22]

Kamo no Chōmei described the disasters which engulfed his world. These included the great fire of 1177, which destroyed much of the capital, a whirlwind of 1180, the temporary move of the capital in the same year, the famine of 1181 and the great earthquake of 1185. He noted that 'those who are powerful are filled with greed; and those who have no protectors are despised. Possessions bring many worries; in poverty there is sorrow. He who asks another's help becomes his slave; he who nurtures others is fettered by affection.' He sought peace by escaping from the world. In his simple hut he was able to enjoy the seasons in a way which typified the sentiments of his time:

In the spring I see waves of wisteria like purple clouds, bright in the west. In the summer I hear the cuckoo call, promising to guide me on the road to death. In the autumn the voice of the evening insects fills my ears with a sound of lamentation for this cracked husk of a world. In winter I look with deep emotion on the snow, piling up and melting away like sins and hindrances to salvation.

He declared: 'My greatest joy is a quiet nap; my only desire for this life is to see the beauties of the seasons.'

Art

The wars which marked the beginning of the Kamakura period, and the growth of a military caste, trained to fight rather than to appreciate beautiful things, might have turned Japan into an artistic desert. But the new Buddhist sects, the continuing cultural influence of the court and contacts with Sung China all ensured further artistic development. In fact many Japanese art forms were revitalized under the new regime. The Kamakura period is considered by many critics as the last of the great ages of Japanese sculpture. The period also saw further developments in painting, metalwork, pottery, lacquer and architecture.

Kamakura sculpture evolved from that of the Heian period, and there was no sudden change. The main developments were a new realism, renewed vitality and an emphasis on decorative elements. Realism was enhanced by the use of crystal to depict eyes and by ornaments, including crowns, made of metal and jewels. Robes were depicted with long flowing sleeves and pleated skirts with

93

lavish decorations. The medium was generally painted wood or lacquer and gold leaf over wood.

The greatest sculptor of the period is reputed to have been Unkei (died 1223). His Dainichi-Nyorai in the Enjōji in Nara, which dates from 1176, is vivid in style, but conveys a feeling of great tranquillity. Following the destruction of the Todaiji he worked on the restoration of the temple and produced statues of the two guardians (Niō). These depict in realistic manner the anger and violence attributed to these two deities. He later moved to Kyoto, where he worked at the Tōji. From there he went to the Kantō, where the invigorating atmosphere of the military capital inspired in him a heroic if rougher style, which in turn appealed to the warriors and was easily appreciated by the average person. Among his works in the Kantō area is the Amida triad at Jōrakuji in Kanagawa prefecture. This was done in lacquer and gold leaf over wood in 1189.

Unkei had six sons who all became sculptors. Unfortunately few of their works survive. One of the most famous works that has been preserved is that of a Senju Kannon ('thousand-armed Kannon') by Tankei, which forms the central sculpture in the Sanjāsangendō in Kyoto. In lacquer and gold leaf over wood it is an impressive work. A statue in painted wood by another son, called Kōshō, of the priest Kūya in the Rokuharamitsuji in Kyoto is a striking example of the portrait sculpture which developed during the Kamakura period. The Sung style of sculpture, which involved both artifice and delicacy of treatment, was favoured by Jōkei I and Jōkei II. Under Sung influence late Kamakura sculptors tended to produce figures with fleshy faces and bodies and deeply carved robes.

Another great sculptor of the period was Kaikei (late twelfth to early thirteenth centuries). Although he was of the same school of sculpture as Unkei, he developed an independent style, which came to be known as the Annami style after his Buddhist name of An Amida Butsu. He added to the realism which marked his early period elegance and what critics have termed 'intellectual beauty'. Most of his statues were relatively small, being not more than about one metre in height. He was particularly famed for his statues of Amida. Among other works by Kaikei which have been preserved, the statue executed in painted wood in the Tōdaiji at Nara of the god Hachiman, in the form of a Buddhist priest, is particularly striking. Another memorable work by him is the Kujaku-Myōō (Myōō on a peacock), in the Kongōbuji on Mount Koya.

One of the most significant developments in sculpture during the Kamakura period was the increasing popularity of portraiture, especially of Buddhist patriarchs but also of lay figures. Striking examples include the seated figure, in painted wood, of the priest Eison by Zenshun, in the Saidaiji at Nara, and the figure of Hōjō Tokiyori, also in painted wood, in the Kenchōji at Kamakura. Many of these portrait sculptures, which were executed with great realism, convey in a vivid way the character of the men portrayed. The realism used in portraiture led the sculptors of the period to give human qualities to their images of Buddhist deities.

Portraits of priests and warriors were also an important part of the painting of the Kamakura period. Particularly famous is a painting of Yoritomo belonging to the Jingoji in Kyoto. The new Buddhist sects, particularly the Amidists, inspired various Buddhist paintings. Paintings of court scenes continued to be produced by the Tosa and Kasuga schools, which coalesced and formed the *yamato-e* school, that is, the school of Japanese-style painting in contrast to the Chinese style which developed in line with the spread of Zen Buddhism. The painting of *emaki*, or picture scrolls, continued to be popular, and some of the finest painting in this genre were produced in the Kamakura period. One outstanding example is the *Kitano tenjin emaki*, consisting of nine scrolls illustrating the life of Sugawara Michizane (see page 43), to whom the shrine was dedicated. Famous battles were commemorated in such *emaki* as the *Heiji monogatari emaki* in three scrolls.

The growth of the warrior class naturally gave an impetus to sword making. The Emperor Gotoba took a personal interest in this art and summoned the twelve most famous swordsmiths to Kyoto to work there for a month in the year. The greatest Japanese swordsmith was probably Masamune of Sagami (1264–1343). The making of armour was also encouraged by the warrior class, and the Myōchin school of armour makers was established in Kamakura. *O-yoroi* was a form of grand body armour developed in this period. This style of armour is marked by wing-like projections on each side of the helmet, by flat shoulder pieces and by lavish decoration. The art of casting remained popular, and bronze mirrors and lanterns from the Kamakura period are much prized.

Art pottery began to be produced at Seto near Nagoya by Katō Tōshirō (Shirozaemon Kagemasa), who studied ceramic art in China at the beginning of the thirteenth century. In the kiln which he established on his return he produced glazed stonewares with light brown and mottled black glazes; these have come to be called *ko-Seto* or old Seto wares. Tōshirō II produced wares with a yellow glaze, and these are termed *ki-Seto* or yellow Seto. Seto wares, which were fired at very high temperatures, were often decorated with incised and stylized floral patterns. Seto has remained ever since a centre of the pottery industry; indeed, the word *setomono* is used in Japan to denote pottery. Among other famous kiln sites in the area are Shino and Oribe.

Lacquer wares continued to be produced in Kyoto, but some of the gold lacquer artists moved to Kamakura, where the traditions of fine craftsmanship were maintained. In the thirteenth century a new style of lacquer called *Kamakura-bori* was developed under the influence of Sung lacquer. *Kamakura-bori* with its red colour and incised patterns is still made in Kamakura. It remains distinct from other styles of Japanese lacquer and retains a certain Chinese character.

Chinese architectural styles of the Sung dynasty called *karayō* also influenced the building of temples of the Zen sect. This style was later amalgamated with the native (*wayō*) and the Hindu (*tenjikuyō*) styles to form a hybrid type of architecture. The *wayō* style was generally a simple one with broad proportions and little decoration. The hybrid style which evolved was more elaborate than earlier Japanese styles and involved columns on footing stones, fan raftering, upward-curving roofs, panelled doors and arched windows. The Zen sect also had their own arrangement for temple buildings. These were built on a rectangular plan south to north. At the south entrance there was a main gate (*sōmon*). Behind this was a pond with a stone bridge. Then came the Buddha hall (*Butsuden*) and behind this the preaching hall (*hattō*) and finally the residential quarters called *hōjō* and *kuri*. On the east and west sides there would be a belfry, a library to house the sutras, bath-house and toilet.

VI

Civil Wars and the Rise of the Warlords:
The Muromachi or Ashikaga Period
(1333–1573)

The first Ashikaga shōgun, Takauji, was not in fact appointed shōgun until 1338, but as the Kamakura *bakufu* was destroyed in 1333 the Ashikaga shōgunate can be regarded as beginning in 1333. It can be said to have ended in 1568 when Oda Nobunaga entered Kyoto, although the Ashikaga shōgunate was not officially terminated until the deposition in 1573 of Ashikaga Yoshiaki, the fifteenth Ashikaga shōgun. Muromachi was the name of the area in Kyoto where the shōgun's palace and administrative headquarters were located from 1378. From 1336 to 1392 were the years of the Southern and Northern Courts or *nanbokuchō*. The century from 1467 to 1568 is referred to as the *sengoku* (country at war) period.

These centuries were ones of almost constant civil war. Lands were won and lost; families prospered and were then cast down. Kyoto was frequently devastated by marauding bands. It was a time of changing fortunes, of loyalty and of treachery, of heroism and of cruelty. Much blood was spilt, and men died in battle or were assassinated, but the numbers involved in the numerous battles and skirmishes were exaggerated by the early chronicles. Life went on. Indeed, despite or perhaps because of the wars in which the fighting men needed supplies the farmers, who generally ceased to be serfs, grew in importance. As the peasants' plots became smaller and as productivity improved, food supplies increased. Trade with China developed. Towns grew up around temples and the seats of feudal magnates. The arts fourished under the patronage of the Ashikaga shōguns and the Zen monastries. In literature the Nō theatre was created. The story of the fighting makes dreary reading, but the contribution of the Muromachi period to Japanese civilization was significant.

The Period of the Southern and Northern Courts (*nanbokuchō*)

The Emperor Go-Daigo (1288–1339), who had come to the throne in 1318 at, by medieval Japanese standards, the late age of thirty, was not content to remain the puppet of the Kamakura *bakufu* and had been banished to the Oki Islands in the Japan Sea in 1331. Go-Daigo's son, Prince Morinaga, continued to resist and was assisted by Kusonoki Masashige and other warriors. In 1333 Go-Daigo managed to escape from his island confinement and, on his return to Kyoto in 1333, with the support of Ashikaga Takauji inaugurated the Kenmu restoration. Go-Daigo, who tried to re-establish the power of the throne, failed to appreciate his dependance on the support of the military. He alienated many powerful warriors by his arbitrary behaviour and failure to make the sort of awards of domains which his supporters thought were their due. His treasury was empty, but he had at his disposal the estates of the Hōjō and could have used these to satisfy at least some claimants. Instead he contemplated a return to the pre-feudal land tenure system of the *Taihō* codes. The office of awards which he established was slow and inefficient. The officials controlling the awards were appointed because of their connections; they were inexperienced and corrupt. Promises were broken, and loyalties soon became strained. Go–Daigo was reputed to be a scholar, but he lacked wisdom. He had learned nothing from his banishment and did not recognize that the old system had become largely irrelevant. He compounded his folly by planning an extravagant new palace and demanded that all estates should contribute one–twentieth of their income towards the costs of the buildings.

Ashikaga Takauji had taken over the functions and premises at Rokuhara of the former garrison of the Hōjō regents in Kyoto. He was not yet shōgun, but he was the most powerful of the warlords. Only Prince Morinaga had the power and prestige to challenge him. In 1334 Takauji, who feared an attack by Morinaga, arranged for the Prince to be arrested and confined. The Prince was taken to Kamakura, where in 1335 he was killed on the orders of Ashikaga Tadayoshi, Takauji's brother. Go–Daigo pretended he knew nothing of plots against Takauji and did nothing to save his son, but he continued to intrigue in his own devious way to re–establish the imperial power. In 1335 Takauji left Kyoto without the Emperior's permission to assist his brother Tadayoshi who had been driven out of Kamakura. Kamakura was recaptured, and Takauji refused to return to Kyoto, where he felt unsafe. In November 1335 Go–Daigo ordered the destruction of the Ashikaga family, and Nitta Yoshisada, who had quarrelled with Takauji, was placed in command of the imperial forces. Eventually after a series of reverses, in which Nitta had had the upper hand, a decisive engagement took place at Minatogawa in July 1336 between the supporters of Go–Daigo and the Ashikaga brothers. The supporters of Go–Daigo were defeated after a heroic fight by the 'loyalist' hero Kusonoki Masashige, who was killed in the battle, but Nitta Yoshisada was not eliminated until 1338. Go–Daigo had surrendered in 1336 and been forced to give up the imperial regalia (it was later claimed that the regalia were not the real ones) to the Emperor Kōmyō, whose accession was declared in September 1336. Takauji determined to rule from Kyoto in accordance with the Jōel forumulary (*Jōei shikimoku*), although this was supplemented by the so-called *Kenmu shikimoku* of seventeen articules. The new regime began with the appointment of Go–Daigo's son as Crown Prince, thus confirming the system of alternation between senior and junior imperial lines. But Go–Daigo was determined to fight on. In January 1337 he managed to escape from Kyoto and took refuge at Yoshino in the mountains south of Nara. Here he was joined by a number of ministers and court officials and had the support of warriors who felt no loyalty to the Ashikaga. Thus began the period of the Southern and Northern Courts (*nanbokuchō*).

In the following decades neither the Northern, nor the Southern Court and their supporters were able to achieve a decisive victory. This was partly because jealousies and self-seeking caused a number of important warlords to change sides at crucial times. For much of the time the Northern Court was the stronger, but

Kyoto was taken from their control for brief periods, and the Northern Emperor had to flee from the supporters of the Southern Court. Neither court had an irrefutable claim to greater legitimacy than the other. Possession of the authentic regalia was claimed by the Southern Court, and this was supposed to give it a superior status, but this was a dubious claim.

When an agreement was finally reached in 1392 to end the schism (previous attempts to reach agreement had foundered), the Southern Emperor was Go-Kameyama, and the Northern was Go-Komatsu. The understanding was that the lines would once again alternate, but when Go-Komatsu abdicated in 1412 he did so in favour of his son. The agreement had in fact been shown to be worthless in 1392, when the proposed ceremonial transfer of the regalia and formal abdication of Go-Kameyama were abrogated by the then Ashikaga shōgun Yoshimitsu.

The first Ashikaga shōgun, Takauji (1305–58), spent most of his life fighting. Cruel and calculating, he had moments of Buddhist repentance. Apart from the conflict with the Southern Court, Takauji had to deal with quarrels among his own supporters. He was at first able to depend on his brother Tadayoshi, who dealt with civil administration. In 1350, however, the long-standing jealousy between Tadayoshi and Takauji's military deputy, Kō no Moronao, led Tadayoshi to offer his services to the Southern Court. In 1351 Tadayoshi managed to occupy Kyoto after defeating the forces of his brother and Kō no Moronao. A reconciliation was then effected at Moronao's expense (he was forced to take the tonsure and was later murdered). The quarrel between the two brothers, however, smouldered on; in 1352 Tadayoshi died suddenly, and it was rumoured that he had been poisoned. When Takauji died he was succeeded by his second son Yoshiakira (1330–68), who was shōgun from 1359 to 1368. On Yoshiakira's death his son Yoshimitsu (1358–1408) was nominated as the third Ashikaga shōgun at the age of ten. During his early years the power fell to Hosokawa Yoriyuki, who served as *kanrei* (shōgun's deputy) between 1368 and 1379. The post of *kanrei* was then held alternately by members of the Shiba, Hatakeyama and Hosokawa families. There was also a *kanrei* in the Kantō; this post was held between 1349 and 1439 by members of the Ashikaga family with the post of deputy being filled by members of the Uesugi family. The Kantō *kanrei* caused much trouble to the shōguns. Hosokawa Yoriyuki was a stern and generally upright warrior under whose leadership the Northern Court began to achieve more of an upper hand in the civil war with the Southern Court, thus paving the way for the eventual agreement of 1392.

The supporters of the Southern Court described themselves as 'loyalists'. After the death of Kusonoki Masashige the leading 'loyalist' was Kitabatake Chikafusa (1293–1354). He came from a line of court officials and despised the military leaders, whom he regarded as upstarts, but he became a formidable fighter in his time. He set up his base in the north-eastern province of Hitachi (now part of Ibaragi prefecture) in the first years of the Southern Court and challenged the power of the Northern Court in the Kantō region; but he was forced to withdraw in 1343 and died eleven years later at Anō, to which the Southern Court had moved. He is remembered primarily for his work, the *Jinnō shōtōki*.[1] The aim of this work, which began with the words 'Great Japan is the land of the gods', was to show the divine descent of the imperial line and the legitimacy of the Southern

Court. Chikafusa was well versed in Confucian and Buddhist teachings, but his line of thought was primarily Shintō.

There was no real ideological element in the conflict between the two courts. It was for all practical purposes a struggle for power and wealth in the form of land.

The Ashikaga Shōguns

The first two Ashikaga shōguns, Takauji and Yoshiakira, had little time for anything except warfare. The third shōgun, Yoshimitsu, did much to consolidate the power of the shōgunate. In 1391 he defeated the Yamana, who were posing a threat to his regime. In 1394 he had himself appointed chancellor (*dajōdaijin*), but in 1395 he took the tonsure and had his son Yoshimochi appointed shōgun. However, he retained the real power in his own hands. He built a fine palace for himself at Kitayama in the north-western part of Kyoto, where in 1408 he entertained the Emperor Go-Kameyama in great state. The Kitayama Palace included the famous Kinkakuji (the Golden Pavilion). Yoshimitsu was a patron of the arts and supported the Nō theatre troupes of actors. He also endeavoured to develop trade with China. He died in 1408 after a pilgrimage to Ise. Ambitious, cruel and vain, Yoshimitsu was nevertheless one of the great figures of the Muromachi era.

Yoshimochi (1386–1428) and his son Yoshikazu (shōgun from 1423 to 1425) were both heavy drinkers and made no great impact on the Japanese scene. The next shōgun, Yoshinori (1394–1441), was Yoshimochi's younger brother. When he assumed the office of shōgun in 1428 he had already taken the tonsure. However, he never allowed Buddhist sentiments of compassion to influence his behaviour, although he was severely puritanical in his attitude towards the sexual peccadillos of the court nobility. His ruthlessness and cruelty earned him many enemies, and he was murdered by one of them, Akamatsu Mitsuzuka, at a banquet to which he had been invited.

The only other Ashikaga shōgun of any real historical importance was Yoshimasa (1436–90), the eighth shōgun. As a political leader he was weak and ineffectual. The power of the shōgunate was for practical purposes destroyed by the Onin war (1467–77), and Yoshimasa abdicated in favour of his son Yoshihisa in 1464, retiring to the Higashiyama district of Kyoto, where he built the villa and temple known as Ginkakuji (Silver Pavilion). Yoshimasa's fame came from his patronage of the arts, especially of painting, the tea ceremony and the Nō drama.

After Yoshimasa's death the shōgunate was dominated by the Hosokawa family, and the Ashikaga shōguns between 1490 and 1550 were puppets who were generally appointed or deposed at the will of the Hosokawa.

The Court

The military despised the court, which had ceased to have any real power or resources, and many did their best to humiliate the Emperor. The arrogant and rough Kō no Moronao is reputed to have asked: 'What is the use of a King? ... And why should we bow to him? If for some reason a King is needed, let us have one made of wood or metal, and let all the live Kings be banished.' A drunken warrior called Dōki saw the cloistered Emperor (the *In*) passing by with his retinue. Being rebuked for insolence he shouted out: 'What is this *'In'* you talk about? If it is an *inu* [a dog] I'll shoot it!'[2] He and those with him then charged the cloistered Emperor's carriage and shot arrows at it. The harness was cut, and the oxen ran away, while the cloistered Emperor burst into tears. Dōki was arrested and executed, but more for disciplinary reasons than out of respect for the throne.

The third shōgun, Yoshimitsu (1358–1408), enjoyed making court officials perform menial functions and treated the Emperor with familiarity. He induced the court to appoint his mother as Empress dowager and may have hoped that his favourite son would become Emperor, but the boy died shortly after his coming-of-age ceremony in 1408.

The poverty of the court was such in the fifteenth century that during the Onin war the body of the Emperor Go-Tsuchimikado remained unburied for want of the means to hold a proper funeral, while accession ceremonies had to be delayed sometimes for years for similar reasons.

The Onin War

The Onin war (1467–77) resulted from a quarrel between two warlords, Hosokawa Katsumoto and Yamana Sōzen. Both warlords brought their armed men into the capital, and much of the initial fighting took place within the city. The shōgun Yoshimasa was induced to declare his support for Hosokawa, but his wife Tomiko and Yoshimasa's brother, Yoshimi, gave their backing to Yamana, who also obtained the assistance of the Ouchi family. After five months of incessant fighting, burning and looting the capital city lay in ruins. In 1469 the war became essentially a struggle between the forces supporting Yoshimasa and those backing Yoshimi. At one stage Yamana found a pretender to the throne and seems to have considered setting up another Southern Court, but nothing came of this. In 1473 Hosokawa Katsumoto and Yamana Sōzen both died. The war, however, continued in and around Kyoto as well as in the provinces until 1477 when the Ouchi submitted to Yoshimasa and withdrew their forces. The only result of this futile and sanguinary struggle was the destruction of the capital and much loss of life and property.

The Country at War (*sengoku*)

After the breakdown of the discipline imposed by the Kamakura *bakufu* Japanese society underwent fundamental changes. The constables (*shugo*) appointed by the Ashikaga were granted or seized autocratic powers and established themselves as semi-autonomous rulers in the provinces under their control. The *hanzei* ('half taxes') which Takauji had instituted as a temporary measure and had allowed the constables to keep as a matter of expediency became a permanent imposition. But in the state of near anarchy and constant warfare which prevailed during the Ashikaga period such authority as existed depended on the force at the disposal of the constable or his deputy.

The serfs of the Heian period had mostly been emancipated and become small farmers. To protect themselves the farmers frequently banded together with holders of small estates who were called *ji-samurai* or *kokujin*, which may be thought of as a Japanese equivalent of gentlemen-farmers and yeoman-farmers. They had acquired their land as a result of the break-up of estates at a time when primogeniture did not prevail. The groupings formed by the farmers and small landowners, termed *ikki*, endeavoured to enforce their rights against extortion and oppression. Some of these revolts have been termed peasant uprisings or *tsuchi-ikki*. The first large-scale rising seems to have occurred in 1428 when concerted attacks were made on money-lenders. Some of these risings were suppressed by force; in other cases compromises were reached and concessions made. The shōgunate for its part increasingly resorted to edicts remitting debts. The first of these *tokusei* was issued in 1441 following violent demonstrations in the capital. But these edicts could not be enforced and were largely meaningless gestures.

These risings can be seen as part of the process of ferment and change which led to a radical alteration in the structure of medieval society in Japan. Insecurity in the countryside resulting in the theft of land and crops, together with the heavy burden of taxation, led many peasant farmers, who had little left to lose, to take up arms and join the wandering bands of marauders. Families were forced to recognize that they could only live on their land if they commended it to the strongest son as leader, and the old practice of splitting estates on the death of the holder generally ceased. Farmers had always had to co-operate in local communities to ensure fair shares of water resources. Co-operation in medieval times was essential for survival, and village councils were formed to represent the interests of the villagers.

A different form of *ikki* was that formed by the Ikkō sect of Amidism. This sect was established by Rennyō (1415–99), who was in the line of succession to Shinran (1173–1262) and was abbot of the sect's main Kyoto temple, the Honganji. His unorthodox and anti-monastic utterances provoked the monks of Enryakuji to burn his house. He escaped and became a travelling preacher, attracting many adherents from among the farmers. The sect became particularly influential in Echizen (now Fukui prefecture) and in Kaga (now part of Ishikawa prefecture). In 1486 they forced out the constable in Kaga and took charge of the province after defeating a force sent against them from Echizen. The Ikkō sect continued to rule Kaga until 1576 when they were defeated by the new military rulers of Japan.

During the *sengoku* period and earlier the warlords tried to strengthen their position by strict house laws which emphasized the vital importance of the survival of the family and its property and which imposed severe punishment for any step which might benefit a rival family. The traditional Japanese doctrine of joint responsibility of members of a family for the actions of any one of its

101

members (*enza*) was even more strictly enforced than ever before.

During the century following the end of the Onin war many of the families of the old warlords were destroyed or eclipsed, and new families rose to power. The fittest survived and the strong prospered while the weaker went under. The process has been termed by some Japanese historians *gekokujō* or 'the low oppress the high'. But in fact it was a matter of naked force triumphing, and there was no ideological element in the changes which took place.

Some of the struggles of the warlords have become legendary, such as that between Uesugi Kenshin (1530–78), who controlled Echigo province (now Niigata prefecture), and Takeda Shingen (1521–73), who held sway in Kai (now Yamanashi prefecture). Takeda Shingen, having seized control of Shinano province (now part of Nagano prefecture), came into conflict with Uesugi Kenshin, and the battle which their armies fought at Kawanakajima in 1561 is one of the more famous in Japanese history. Both daimyō had ambitions to control the whole country but died before they could achieve their aim.

The ethical system of the samurai which had been worked out by the Minamoto and the Hōjō and which later came to be called *bushidō* remained an ideal but in practice it was largely ignored. Survival dictated that loyalty was due only to the strong who were capable of providing protection as well as loot.

Medieval warfare in Japan was constant, but most battles were on a limited scale involving relatively small armies. Many were little more than skirmishes in which single combats on horseback prevailed. Foot soldiers (*ashigaru*) only came into their own in battles such as those which marked the Onin war and took place in urban areas. There were no firearms in Japan until the first Portuguese arrived in 1542 at the small island of Tanegashima.[3] The muskets which the three Portuguese adventurers carried were soon copied in large numbers, and the introduction of firearms brought about gradual changes in Japanese warfare.

Economic and Social Developments

Despite the almost continuous civil wars during the Ashikaga shōgunate and despite the natural disasters which regularly devastated Japanese crops, agricultural production increased to such an extent that surpluses became available for use in internal trade. The increase was brought about more by bringing new land under cultivation than by improvements in productivity. The average size of holdings had declined as a result of the splitting of family estates between children during the Heian period, and consequently more intensive farming, using human and animal manure, became essential. Better and more efficient farm implements became available following improvements in metalworking. Double cropping of land spread from the Kansai to the Kantō area. Barley began to be grown as a second crop in many areas from the thirteenth century onwards, while *champa*-type rice, imported from Indo-China, was grown in increasing quantities. Although this was of a lower quality to types of rice grown hitherto in Japan, it provided increased yields, as it was more resistant to cold and matured more quickly. More vegetables were planted, especially in areas near the developing towns. The growing of tea, which was encouraged by the Zen monasteries, became popular especially in Yamashiro province near Kyoto (tea is still grown in large quantities around Uji between Kyoto and Nara). Hemp for clothing and mulberries to provide food for the silkworms and thus to meet the increasing demand for silk fibre became important crops in appropriate areas. Fresh fruit was not in those days a part of the average Japanese diet, but plums, persimmons and melons began to be grown to meet a demand for variety and something sweet, as sugar which later came in increasing quantities from the Ryūkyū Islands was still a scarce commodity.

There was no real industry in Japan in the Muromachi period. But the warriors needed weapons and armour in increasing quantities, and this gave a boost to the swordsmiths and metalworkers. There was accordingly a growing demand for ores of all kinds. Feudal lords with exploitable resources of minerals did all they could to develop mining techniques. There was not much iron ore, and Japanese metalworkers had to rely on iron sands. Copper had been available in Japan from the Nara period. Mining of gold and silver was developed both as a source of funds for the warlords and in the second half of the sixteenth century to meet the demands for decoration and for coinage. In about 1530 skilled smelters were brought to Japan from China and Korea, and methods improved.

Skilled artisans were much in demand, and crafts were given a boost. Silk weavers were brought in from Ming China and introduced Chinese techniques for the making of brocade silk. Thus began the famous Kyoto brocade silk industry producing *Nishijin-ori*. Craftsmen from Korea taught the Japanese how to make cotton cloth. Paper-making was developed, especially in the provinces of Mino and Echizen. The pottery industry in the Seto area also contined to grow, but the Japanese pottery industry remained small and relatively primitive until the latter part of the sixteeth century when many Korean potters were brought to Japan.

Minting of coins had ceased in Japan in the tenth century, and barter had tended to replace monetary transactions in trade in the late Heian period. Peasants paid their taxes in kind or in labour, but money was increasingly used in the Kamakura period. Copper coins in large quantities were imported from China;[4] and, despite the interruption in the import of coins as a result of the attempted Mongol invasions of Japan in the thirteenth century, the use of money increased as internal trade grew. A number of coins privately minted in Japan or China also began to circulate in Japan. Many of these were of lower quality, and the practice of *erizeni* (selecting good coins) developed. Various edicts were issued by the shōgunate and by individual daimyō as well as important temples to try to prevent such selection but without avail.   .

The growing use of money coincided with the development of markets. These generally started in towns or settlements which sprang up either at the gates of large and famous temples or around the strongholds or castles of the daimyō.[5] Many of these markets were held on fixed days of the month, such as the 4th, 14th and 24th.[6] In the early days the *shōen* had been largely self-sufficient, and there had been no surplus for trade; but the bigger units which developed round the headquarters of the larger feudal lords needed a wider selection of products, including salt, fish and certain metals, which could only be provided by markets for which specialized merchants supplied goods for sale.

In the course of time trading arrangements became more sophisticated, and a form of wholesale trade was developed. Such merchants, who became commission agents and were known as *tonya* or *toiya*, began to develop a primitive form of banking and even futures trading. The merchants who lent seeds or tools to the cultivators or money to the warriors charged high rates of interest, and these inevitably led to anger against them in times of distress. Such central and local authorities as were able to exercise power in the anarchic state of many parts of the country tried generally unsuccessfully to deal with the discontent by issuing periodic 'acts of grace' (*tokusei*), but these were usually ineffective as the merchants then withdrew the facilities they had offered hitherto, and the farmers and warriors were left in the lurch.

Members of the various trades and crafts frequently banded together to defend their interests and to maintain a monopoly in their own trade. These guilds were called *za*, which means literally a 'seat'. The term probably derived from the fact that members of a guild occupied a specific spot in a market.[7] The guilds frequently sought the protection of shrines, temples or noble families. The pawnbrokers in Kyoto, for instance, looked to Enryakuji on Mount Hiei, while the fishmongers had the noble Saionji family as their patron. The *za* had some similarities to the merchant guilds of medieval Europe; but, although they enjoyed certain tax exemptions and developed their own monopolies, they did not establish a country-wide network, and their political power was strictly limited.

An improvement in communications was a crucial element in the development of internal trade. River and coastal traffic improved despite the ever-present fear of pirates who remained particularly active in the Inland Sea. Where boats could not be used to carry goods and to enable bodies of fighting men to reach their campaigning areas, tracks were turned into primitive roads, and, especially in the eastern part of Japan, post-stations were established. Communications were, however, hampered by the many barriers (*sekisho*) which continued to harry merchants and other travellers. The numerous imposts levied on goods in transit greatly inflated the prices of items from other parts of the country sold in local markets. Nevertheless the number of travellers increased as pilgrimages to famous shrines and temples grew in popularity.

Kyoto was devastated by the Onin war (1467–77), but it recovered amazingly quickly. New buildings were speedily put up, and the citizens of the capital showed great resilience. Wooden buildings are consumed by fire but are easily rebuilt. The residents of each district formed their own association (*machishū*) which regulated affairs in their area and joined together to contribute to festivals such as that of the Gion shrine.

New towns developed around ports and other centres. Otsu near Kyoto on Lake Biwa and the ports of Obama and Tsuruga on the Japan Sea coast date from the Muromachi period. Hakata in Kyūshū, Sakai (part of modern Osaka) and Hyōgo (now incorporated in Kobe) also developed greatly during this period. Uji-Yamada became a prosperous town as pilgrimages to the shrines of the sun goddess at Ise grew in popularity. Castle towns such as those at Yamaguchi in western Honshū, Sumpu (the modern Shizuoka), Odawara on the Kantō side of the Hakone mountain range and Kagoshima in the province of Satsuma in southern Kyūshū all developed in this period.

The population of Japan was probably around 10 million in the thirteenth century. It had risen by the beginning of the seventeenth century to perhaps 18 million, but these are very rough estimates.[8]

Relations with China, Korea and the Ryūkyū Islands

Following the failure of the Mongol attempts to invade Japan in the thirteenth century, contacts with China and Korea were cut until 1342 when on Takauji's orders a ship was chartered by merchants in Hakata to reopen trade with China. Takauji's decision seems to have been prompted by the Zen priest Musō Kokushi, the abbot of the Tenryūji, a temple at Arashiyama near Kyoto, which had been founded by Takauji. The building funds had run out, and it was hoped that the voyage would bring profits which would benefit the temple. The ship was accordingly called the *Tenryūjibune* (*fune* or *bune* means a ship).

When the Ming dynasty came to power in China in 1368 the first Ming Emperor, Hung-wu (Hong wu), wanted to expand the number of tributary states, and a message was sent to Kyūshū, where Prince Korenaga was in control. He was at first reluctant to respond, but in 1371 he sent a mission to China consisting largely of Buddhist monks. The Chinese in their turn sent a group of monks to Japan. But in 1376 Hung-wu refused to receive a Japanese envoy, and relations were not resumed until 1401, when the shōgun Yoshimitsu sent a mission to China with presents and a letter which was sufficiently humble to be acceptable to a Ming Emperor. The mission was well received, and the Ming court recognized Yoshimitsu as 'King of Japan'. An agreement with the Chinese authorities for an exchange of missions once every ten years was concluded. This also gave the *bakufu* a monopoly on trade with China. The first mission under the terms of this agreement was sent in 1404. After the mission's credentials had been examined at Ningpo (Ningbo) it went on to Peking (Beijing) to deliver the Japanese gifts. As the Chinese regarded the mission as one bearing tribute, all local expenses were met by the Chinese. The limit of one mission every ten years and other restrictions, such as on the numbers of ships involved and passengers carried, were ignored. But the Chinese demanded that the Japanese authorities take steps to suppress the Japanese pirates, called *wakō*, who were harassing Chinese shipping. Yoshimitsu agreed, and some stern measures were taken which kept piracy in check at least for a time. Five further missions were despatched up to 1410. The Japanese sent horses, swords, armour, copper, gold, lacquer, screens, fans and sulphur. In return they obtained silver and copper coins, brocades, silk, jade, pearls, porcelain, incense, books and drugs. Zen temples participated in this trade, and Zen monks handled the diplomatic correspondence. Yoshimitsu's motives were mixed. He was attracted by Zen and interested in its Chinese origins. He was also flattered by the terms in which he was addressed by the Chinese. But above all he recognized the commercial benefits to Japan and to his own finances from this trade.

Yoshimitsu's successor, Yoshimochi, reversed his father's policy on trade with China and rejected overtures from Yung-le (Yong le), the second Ming Emperor. However, following an approach from Hsüan-te (Xuan de), the third Ming Emperor, trade was resumed in 1432 during the shōgunate of Yoshinori. Trade increased until about 1450 when it declined for a time, but after the Onin war the Hosokawa and the Ouchi families competed to expand trade with China. Their rivalry led in 1523 to a serious clash in Ningpo as a result of which the Ming authorities shut Ningpo to trade with Japan. Although some trade continued for a time it seems to have come to a halt in 1548.

Trade also developed with Korea during the Muromachi period. Items imported included pottery, copper coins, cotton and textiles, while Japanese exports included sulphur and copper. The Koreans tried without success to ban the export of coins. The Japanese sent ships to the Ryūkyū Islands, where goods from what is now Indonesia and Malaysia could be purchased and sold on to China and Korea. The Ryūkyū Islands, which were not yet under either Japanese or Chinese control, were unified under their own king in the early part of the fifteenth century. Envoys were sent to both Ming China and the *bakufu* through the Shimazu family in southern Kyūshū.

Religious Developments

Intellectual and cultural life in the Muromachi period was deeply effected by Zen, and Zen priests exercised considerable political influence. Musō Kokushi, also known as Musō Soseki (1275–1351), was closely associated with Takauji. He had studied Shingon as well as Zen and introduced elements of esoteric Buddhism into the so-called Gozan (or 'five temples') form of the Rinzai school of Zen whose main temple was that of Nanzenji in Kyoto. He was at times abbot of Nanzenji and of Tenryūji. He converted the Kyoto temple of Saihōji, better known as Kokedera or the 'moss temple', to Zen and was regarded as one of the originators of the Zen style of landscape gardens. He was also instrumental in establishing Zen temples throughout many of the sixty-six provinces under the name Ankokuji (that is, 'temples of a peaceful country', a rather ironic name in the circumstances of the time).

The great monasteries of Daitokuji and Myōshinji in Kyoto were also founded in the Muromachi period. Like the Gozan temples, they too followed the Rinzai school of Zen, but kept themselves apart from the Gozan. Instead they developed close contacts with the townspeople in Kyoto.

Zen was of particular significance for the development of Japanese culture, but the other Buddhist sects continued to be influential. Great temples, such as Tōdaiji and Kōfukuji in Nara, as well as Kyoto temples like Tōji and Enryakuji and the temples on Koyasan, retained their prestige despite the reduction in their wealth caused by the decline of the *shōen* system. The Nichiren sect obtained many samurai adherents especially in the Kantō, and the Ikkō sect of Jōdoshū took over the province of Kaga between 1486 and 1576.

Shintō rites and ceremonies were maintained, and syncretic forms such as Ryōbu-Shintō continued to develop. Sannō Ichijitsu Shintō sought to harmonize the teachings of the Tendai sect with the cult of the shrines on Mount Hiei. This was based on the belief that Shintō deities correspond to manifestations of the Buddha. Such beliefs were frequently reflected in art and literature, for example in Nō plays.

Literature

The *Gunki monogatari* of the Kamakura period remained popular in the Muromachi period. One major new work in this genre was the *Taiheiki* (literally 'The Chronicle of the Great Peace', which probably reflected more a pious wish than a piece of irony). It is of unknown authorship. It covers the conflicts between the Northern and Southern Courts in the years between 1318 and 1367 and consists of forty volumes. Like the *Heike monogatari* it was recited by itinerant priest storytellers, but while the emphasis in the *Heike monogatari* was primarily Buddhist, the tone of the *Taiheiki* is more Confucian, and there are many references to Chinese classics. The first part covers the Emperor Go-Daigo's plots against the Kamakura shōgunate up to the Kenmu restoration. The second part deals with the rebellion of Ashikaga Takauji and ends with the death of Go-Daigo. The third part covers the period up to the appointment of Hosokawa Yoriyuki as deputy to the shōgun. The *Taiheiki* begins by favouring Go-Daigo, but ends by praising the rule of the Ashikaga shōguns. Much of the work is devoted to detailed descriptions of battles, but it lacks the colour of the *Heike monogatari*.

The style adopted by the reciters of the *Taiheiki* was often poetic. In particular, some of the *michiyuki* (literally, 'going along the road' or recitatives covering journeys) in five- or seven-syllable lines have become famous. *Michiyuki* also feature in dramatic works of this and later periods. The elegant language used, the many allusions and the numerous plays on words make them difficult to translate. One of the best-known *michiyuki* in the *Taiheiki* describes the journey of Toshimoto no Ason back to the Kantō:[9]

Rakka no yuki ni / fumimayō	When he trod with uncertain foot
Katano no haru no / sakuragari	The spring snow of fallen blossom
momiji no nishiki o / kite kaeru	While seeking the cherry at Katano
Arashiyama no / aki no kure	Or returned at dusk on an autumn day
hitoyo o akasu / hodo dani mo	From the slopes of Mount Arashi
tabine to nareba / monouki ni	Clothed in maple leaf brocade,
on'ai no chigiri / asakaranu	A single night spent away from home
waga furusato no / tsuma-ko oba	Brought melancholy enough.
yukue mo shirazu / omoioki	Now, as he leaves on this sudden journey
toshi hisashiku mo / suminareshi	While his thoughts linger on
kokonoe no / teito oba	In his native place with his wife and child
ima wo kagiri to / kaerimite	Whose fate he will not know
omowanu tabi / idetamō	Though closely tied to them by bonds of love;
kokoro no uchi zo / aware naru.	And as he looks back for his last sight
	Of the ninefold imperial capital
	Where he has lived for so many years
	What sadness fills his heart.

Another tale which became popular in the Muromachi period and which provided material for Nō plays and other dramatic performances was the *Soga monogatari*. This was a story of revenge. Two brothers after a wait of eighteen years found an opportunity during a hunt near Mount Fuji in 1193 in the time of Minamoto no Yoritomo to kill Kudō Suketsune, who had had their father murdered. The elder Soga brother was killed in the fighting which followed the killing of Suketsune. The younger brother Gorō was captured and brought before Yoritomo. Although there was understanding and sympathy for the motives for his revenge he was executed. The earliest version of the story was written in *kanbun* in the first half of the fourteenth century. There were other versions in *kanamajiri*.[10]

A much more important prose work of the period is the *Tsurezuregusa*, which was written in about 1331–3 and which is regarded as a landmark in Japanese literature. The *Tsurezuregusa* is a series of miscellaneous jottings of the genre which the Japanese call *zuihitsu* and of which the most famous example in earlier times was the *Makura no sōshi* of Sei Shonogon. The *Tsurezuregusa* was written by Yoshida Kenkō (*c.* 1283–*c.* 1352). He was a middle-ranking courtier who became a monk in 1324. It consists of 243 separate fragments. In a short preface Yoshida Kenkō said that he jotted 'down at random whatever nonsensical thoughts have entered my head'. These jottings include many anecdotes and cover a wide variety of topics including women, sake, cooking, flowers, birds and martial arts. He also reflects on the transience of life and worldly things; this was the Buddhist *mujōkan* or feeling of impermanence. The jottings are disconnected and sometimes contradictory, but they have much charm and throw an interesting light on contemporary life and attitudes.

The *Tsurezuregusa*[11] encapsulates many typically Japanese aesthetic ideals. One of these is summed up in the following famous passage:

Are we to look at cherry blossoms only in full bloom, the moon only when it is cloudless? To long for the moon while looking on the rain, to lower the blinds and be unaware of the passing of the spring – these are even more deeply moving.

The Japanese preference for simplicity and the intellectual's love of books are exemplified by the following:

Things which seem in poor taste: too many brushes in an ink-box; too many Buddhas in a family temple; too many stones and plants in a garden; too many children in a house; too many words on meeting someone; too many meritorious deeds recorded in a petition. Things which are not offensive, no matter how numerous; books in a book cart, rubbish in a rubbish heap.

Kenkō too saw beauty in irregularity and lack of completeness:

In everything, no matter what it may be, uniformity is undesirable. Leaving something incomplete makes it interesting, and gives one the feeling that there is room for growth.

This was a sentiment which was followed in such Japanese arts as the tea ceremony (see page 119).

Yoshida Kenkō's aristocratic feelings for nature and tranquillity are reflected in words such as these:

Towards the end of spring, on a lovely, mild day, I strolled by a stately-looking mansion set on a large property with ancient trees. A cherry tree was shedding blossoms in the garden. It was impossible to pass without stopping, and I went in. The shutters on the south side were all lowered and the place looked deserted, but I could see then, through an opening in the bamboo blinds over double doors that faced east and had been left attractively ajar, a handsome young man of about twenty, at his ease but maintaining an elegant composure. He was reading a book he held open before him on a desk. I wonder who he was. I should like to visit him and ask.

Kenkō had few illusions about the world or himself:

We cannot trust in anything. The foolish man places great trust in things, and this sometimes leads to bitterness and anger. If you have power, do not trust it; powerful men are the first to fall. You may have many possessions, but they are not to be depended on; they are easily lost in a moment. Nor should you trust in your learning if you have any. . . . You may have virtue, but you must not rely on it. . . . Do not trust in the favour of your lord. . . . You cannot depend on your servants either; they will disobey you and run away. Nor should you trust in another person's kind feelings; they will certainly change. Do not rely on promises; it is rare for people to be sincere.

Poems in the *tanka* form continued to be written by courtiers and warriors, but composition became stereotyped, and artifice became more important than true sentiment. There was thus little new and memorable in the poetry of the Muromachi period. But here was one noteworthy development. This was the vogue for *renga* or linked verses. In *renga*, which became a popular pastime, groups of versifiers would get together. One person would write the first three lines (5, 7 and 5 syllables), the *kami no ku* or *hokku* of a *tanka*; another would write the last two lines (7 and 7 syllables), the *shimo no ku*. These last two lines would then provide a lead into a second poem which would be begun by a third member of the party and so on. One theme led to a second and then to a third, etc. The norm was one hundred stanzas, although some were as long as one thousand stanzas. The composition of *renga* became a test of ingenuity as well as providing an opportunity for the versifiers to demonstrate their acquaintance with the works of former poets and with classical allusions. The game, which began among the courtiers, spread to monks, warriors and merchants. *Renga* composed by these 'lower classes' were called *chika* ('underground') *renga*. One famous anthology of *renga* was the *Tsukubashū*, which was compiled in 1356–7 by Nijō Yoshimoto (1320–88) and by the priest Gusai, also known as Kyōsai (?1284–1378). This was in twenty volumes. The themes followed the lines of the earlier imperial anthologies. Cherry blossom and autumn leaves were inevitable favourites.

A famous example of a hundred-stanza *renga* is the *Minase sangin hyakuin* composed by three poets, Sōgi (1421–1502), Shōhaku (1443–1527) and Sōchō

(1448–1532), when they met at the village of Minase between Kyoto and Osaka in 1488. The first six verses of the sequence[12] show the way in which a 'progression' of themes is achieved so that in this brief space we move from spring to autumn:[13]

Snow yet remaining   Sōgi.
The mountain slopes are misty –
An evening in spring.

Far away the water flows   Shōhaku.
Past the plum scented village.

In the river breeze   Sōchō.
The willow trees are clustered.
Spring is appearing.

The sound of a boat being poled   Sōgi.
Clear in the clear morning light.

The moon! does it still   Shōhaku.
Over fog-enshrouded field
Linger in the sky?

Meadows carpeted in frost –   Sōchō.
Autumn has drawn to a close.

As *renga* became increasingly popular the language grew more colloquial and themes from everyday life began to replace the aristocratic preference for poetic subjects such as nature, love and parting. Popular *renga* came to be called *haikai renga* and are the forerunners of *senryū*, humorous verses in the *haiku* form (5, 7 and 5 syllables) (see page 165). Some of these *haikai renga* were humorous, and some of the themes were lewd. Sometimes *haikai* versifiers parodied famous *tanka*. The Muromachi period also saw the spread of *kouta*, which were popular songs on themes such as love and sex.

Theatre: Nō, *Kyogen* and *Kowaka*

One of the most significant artistic and literary innovations of the Muromachi period was the development of the Nō theatre. The word *nō* literally means 'ability, talent or performance'. The Nō theatre developed from primitive dancing, miming, juggling and acrobatics, which had become an element in local shrine and other festivals. In Heian times there had been two traditional forms; these were the *dengaku*, literally rice field music, and the *sarugaku*, literally monkey music. In fact the word *sarugaku* was probably a corruption of *sangaku*, which was a Chinese term used to describe variety acts including those by acrobats, jugglers and conjurors. By the thirteenth century *sarugaku* performances incorporated humorous dialogues as well as dancing and music. The players established their own guilds (*za*), and towards the middle of the fourteenth century *sarugaku* troupes had begun to perform in a serious as well as a comic strain. This was the basis of the Nō theatre as we know it today; serious pieces – that is, Nō plays – are performed interspersed with *kyōgen* (literally, 'mad words'), which are comic, farcical and satirical interludes. The term *sarugaku* or *sarugaku no Nō* continued to be used until the nineteenth century. The term *sarugaku* has now been largely dropped in favour of the term Nō.

Nō plays are not strictly dramas in the western sense. They consist primarily of song, recitative, and dance and the dramatic elements are of relatively minor importance. Nō plays do not generally attempt to tell a story in a dramatic way. Rather, as Professor P. J. O'Neill puts it, they try 'to recapture the mood of a moment and to represent it in an aesthetically satisfying way by a blend of words, music and dance'.[14] Nō plays eschew realism and achieve much of their effect by symbolic actions or *mono mane*, which may be translated as miming. Props are few and very simple, but costumes used are elaborate and gorgeous. Masks (*men*) worn by some of the players are of wood; many old masks are works of art involving fine and imaginative carving. The dancing (*mai*) consists of highly stylized and slow movements and includes gentle rhythmic tapping of feet. The musical accompaniment to Nō provides a background to the performance and is meaningless on its own. Three main instruments are used; these are a flute and two or three types of drum. From about 1420 a chorus which sang during dances or mime to explain the action played a part in many Nō plays.

The players in Nō are divided into three groups. These are the *shite*, who provide the lead part and may wear masks, the *waki*, who play the secondary parts, act as a foil for the *shite* and never wear masks, and the *kyōgen* group, who act in *kyōgen* farces, fulfil minor roles such as boatmen and servants in Nō plays, sometimes wear masks and in two-act Nō plays tell the story of the play in the interval between the acts.

More than two thousand Nō plays were written, and the texts of over 800 survive, but only about 240 are still performed. Most of these date from the fifteenth century. Nō plays are divided into five groups. The first group consists of 'congratulatory' pieces in which the lead part is generally taken by a 'god'. In the second group the lead part is generally taken by a warrior of the Minamoto or Taira clan, who appears as a ghost. In the third group the lead part is that of a beautiful young woman, and the emphasis is on elegance; these plays are generally static. Plays in the fourth group are numerous and more dramatic than those in other groups; mad men and women often feature in these pieces. In the fifth group the lead part is normally a 'god' or a devil, and the tempo is faster than in plays in the other groups. All plays are supposed to consist of an introduction, a development section about three times as long as the introduction and a climax of about the same length as the introduction. There is an element of ritual in many Nō plays. For instance, in 'ghost' plays the implication is that the 'ghost' can be redeemed through the play.

The texts, or *utaibon*, are partly in prose described as *kotoba* (literally, words) and partly in verse, or *utai*. The prose parts are in what is called *sōrōbun*, because the final verbs all have the ending *sōrō*. This has an impressive sound, as the voice of the speaker falls on the last syllable, but it does lead to monotony. The verse passages are fitted to regular beats or *hyōshi*. Pivot words or *kenyōgen* are frequently

111

used, and there are many allusions in the texts to poems which would be well known to educated viewers. The themes were generally taken from legends or stories of heroic deeds which had become legendary. The plays were not so much new compositions as new compilations.

In the Muromachi period the Nō were generally staged at temples and shrines. Special performances were also given in dry river beds. Some Nō competitions were arranged by the shōgun or by noblemen to collect subscriptions, for example for the repair of a temple, a shrine or a bridge. Especially in later centuries Nō were also staged in private houses. Nō theatres today follow a strict pattern. A bridge or corridor leads from the dressing room at the left with three pines along the side to a square stage jutting out into the auditorium. The musicians are at the back, and the chorus is on the side of the stage opposite to the entrance. The stage has a traditional Japanese sloping roof of wood bark. Steps lead down to the audience from the centre of the stage. The unpainted wood of the stage and its pillars has the simplicity of the best traditional Japanese architecture and craftsmanship.

The actors, who were all men, belonged to troupes, who developed their own traditions. They were outcasts from society. Five main schools were formed. Four of these, the Komparu, Hōshō, Kanze and Kongō, date from the Muromachi period. The fifth, the Kita school, dates from the seventeenth century.

The outstanding figures in the development of the Nō in the Muromachi period were Kanami (1333–84) and his son Zeami (1363–1443). Kanami, the founder of the Kanze school, made the popular *sarugaku* into an art form acceptable to the aristocratic and samurai élite when he performed the play *Okina* before the shōgun Ashikaga Yoshimitsu in 1374. But it was his son Zeami (also known as Seami or Kanze Motokiyo) who really established the Nō as the classical theatre of Japan. Zeami was only eleven years old when his father performed before Yoshimitsu and he had a small part with his father. He was a pretty boy, and Yoshimitsu was attracted by him. Zeami was taken into the shōgun's household, and the Nō quickly became popular in Kyoto.

Zeami's success did not depend only on a homosexual relationship with the shōgun; he was an artistic genius, and the Nō would not have developed into the classical theatre of Japan without his inspiration and dedication to the art. He is reputed to have written about ninety plays, although many of these were probably rewrites or adaptations of older plays. He also wrote about his art and established the aesthetic criteria for the Kanze school. The *Fūshi kadenshō*, written in seven parts between 1400 and 1418, summarizes his views on the Nō. In this work he emphasized the *hana* (literally, 'flower'); by this he meant the fresh appeal of a fine actor to his audience. The actor must be responsive to the audience and at the same time he must convey to them by his inspired performance the feelings implicit in the theme of the play in which he is acting. Even more important in his view, however, was *yūgen*, the word which has come to typify the artistic sentiment of the Muromachi period and which means anything from grace and elegance to mystery. Zeami was probably the greatest figure in the history of the Nō.[15]

One of the most famous Nō plays is *Hagoromo* by Zeami. There are four characters in the play. The *shite* is an angel, and the *waki* is a fisherman who is accompanied by two other fishermen. They are walking on the beach at Matsubara on Miho bay (now part of Shizuoka prefecture) opposite Mount Fuji when one of them finds a beautiful robe hanging from a pine tree. When he prepares to take this home with him an angel appears and explains that it is a robe of feathers which has come from heaven. This makes the fisherman all the more eager to have the robe, but when the angel tells him that without the robe she can never return to heaven the fisherman agrees to return it if the angel will dance for him first. The angel reproves him for his refusal to give up the robe before she dances. The fisherman is ashamed and hands over the robe. The angel then puts it on and before ascending to heaven performs a dance of joy.

The following chorus from *Hagoromo* gives some idea of the poetry to be found in Nō plays.[16]

> Now upon earth trail the long mists of Spring;
> Who knows but in the valleys of the moon
> The heavenly moon-tree puts her blossom on?
> The blossoms of her crown win back their glory:
> It is the sign of Spring.
> Not heaven is here, but beauty of the wind and sky.
> Blow, blow, you wind, and build
> Cloud walls across the sky, lest the vision leave us
> Of a maid divine!
> This tint of springtime in the woods,
> This colour on the headland,
> Snow on the mountain,
> Moonlight on the clear shore –
> Which fairest? Nay, each peerless
> At the dawn of a Spring day.
> Waves lapping, wind in the pine-trees whispering
> Along the quiet shore. Say you, what cause
> Has Heaven to be estranged
> From us Earth-men; are we not children of the Gods,
> Within, without the jewelled temple wall,
> Born where no cloud dares dim the waiting moon,
> Land of Sunrise?

Among other famous Nō plays are *Sotoba Komachi*, based on the life of the famous poetess Ono no Komachi, *Funa Benkei*, *Hashi Benkei* and *Ataka*, based on the legends which grew up about the relationship between Minamoto no Yoshitsune and his retainer Musashibō Benkei.

An example of a 'ghost' play is *Atsumori* by Zeami. This had its origin in the death at the battle of Ichinotani of Taira no Atsumori, who was killed by the warrior Kumagae no Naozane. Naozane's sense of remorse at having killed Atsumori leads him to become a monk. In the play he revisits the scene of the battle, where he meets a man who turns out to be the 'ghost' of Atsumori.

Ukai ('The Cormorant Fishers') recounts how two priests meet the 'ghost' of an old cormorant fisherman who had been drowned in the river for having broken the Buddhist rule against taking life by acting as a cormorant fisherman. The priests promise to pray for his soul, and he shows them how cormorants are used to catch fish in the river.

Yuya by Zeami is a single-act play which 'deals with the reluctance of Taira no Munemori to allow Yuya, his mistress, to return to her home to see her dying mother because he wants her company at the flower viewing'. There are many famous *michiyuki* passages in Nō plays. One of the most charming is the following from *Yuya*:[17]

Chorus:	He calls to the groom to bring the ox-cart
	And urges Yuya to leave at once
	What she now regards
	As a very Burning House of sorrows.
	But her heart is heavy,
	Like the lumbering carriage
	Which the oxen drag with faltering tread,
	As, powerless to oppose,
	She goes to view the flowers.

The scene gradually changes as they go to the Kiyomizu-dera on Higashi-yama, the 'Eastern Hill' [in Kyoto].

Yuya:	Now that we come to the pure waters
	On our way to the temple of that name,
Chorus (for Yuya):	The sounds of the rushing river
	Echo amid the mountain cherries
	On Otowa-no-yama.
Yuya:	The road we travel is the road to the east,
	But we go no further than the Eastern Hill.
	Beyond, far beyond,
	Is where I long to be.

She gazes into the far distance and begins to weep.

Chorus (for Yuya):	Rain before spring
	And blossom comes early;
	No rain past autumn
	And leaves fall late.
	Over the hills stand other hills,
	Hills without end.
Yuya:	The hills turn white with drifting cloud,
	Then green again as it passes.
Chorus (for Yuya):	So those who are merry and those who are sad
	Give the world the face it wears.

The Nō is not an easy art form to appreciate without an understanding of the language and the background. The slowness of the movements, the symbolism and the musical accompaniment which is primarily designed to convey the atmosphere can seem boring to the uninitiated.

Attempts have been made to compare the Nō with classical Greek tragedy, but the differences are greater than the similarities. It makes more sense to regard the Nō as a peculiarly Japanese art form with its own special characteristics rather than to try to force comparisons with entirely different traditions. Although there are many Nō plays written in the seventeenth and eithteenth centuries, Nō ceased to evolve some four centuries ago, and modern Nō performances can be regarded as a fairly accurate representation of what the Nō was like in the Muromachi period.

Kyōgen, which still provide a little light relief between the serious, sad and nostalgic Nō plays, are examples of popular Japanese humour. The aim of most *kyōgen* is to make fun of someone who is in a position of authority such as a daimyō, a samurai, a priest, a headman or even a devil. The humour is simple, and the satire is superficial and obvious. The discomfiture of the butt is sometimes cruel. Dr Richard N. McKinnon sums up the art in the following words:

> The mountain priest whose occult powers are useless in the presence of the measured antics of a crab; the daimyō who learns from a monkey; the master who is bested by his resourceful servant; the husband in mortal fear of his wife; the fox which traps the trapper – this is the stuff from which the *kyōgen*, classical Japanese comedy, is shaped. Wonderfully funny, irresistible, effervescent, impudent and irreverent, but also thoughtful and poignant, daring in its treatment of material, a marvel in its art of pantomime, warm and compassionate, in its commentary on the human condition.[18]

The *kowaka* was also developed in the Muromachi period and seems to have been almost equally appreciated by the samurai. Today it survives only in the village of Oe in Fukuoka prefecture in Kyūshū. The *kowaka* has similarities to Nō both in the themes covered and in presentation; but mime, dialogue and dance are lacking in *kowaka*. James T. Araki notes that the performances in Oe village are 'staged by three men who are garbed in the ceremonial attire of the seventeenth century samurai and recite the *kowaka* text in a highly stylized vocal fashion, utilizing various modes of speech and melodic intonation. Neither masks nor costumes are used for portraying characters. The players stand abreast of one another throughout most of the performance, maintaining a rigid, erect posture with arms outstretched.[19] *Kowaka* seems to have been founded as an art form in the fifteenth century by Momonoi Naoaki.

The Arts

Ink paintings in the so-called *suiboku* (literally, water and black ink – also referred to as *sumie*, that is, charcoal ink paintings) by Chinese Zen artists of the Sung (Song) and Yūan (Yuan) dynasties were imported into Japan and copied by Japanese artists. These paintings were simple and direct in their appeal to the imagination – frequently more sketches than detailed paintings. The favourite themes of these artists were Buddhist and Taoist sages as well as landscapes, birds and flowers. The Zen artist had an intuitive feeling for the hidden beauty in nature. His was not a representational form of art, but rather an emotional response to the natural phenomena we see around us. Among the many Chinese masters studied by Japanese Zen artistis were works by Mu-ch'i (Mu qi) (Mokkei in the Japanese reading of the name) of the Southern Sung dynasty and Yen Hui (Yan hui) (Ganki).

Japanese Zen artists, some of whom went to China to study directly under

Chinese masters, began to produce paintings from the late fourteenth century in the *suiboku* style. Minchō (1352–1432), who was influenced by Chinese masters, including Ganki, and who was a priest of the Tōfukuji in Kyoto, was known for his paintings of Buddhist and Taoist figures. A striking portrait of the aged priest Shōichi Kokushi preserved by the Tōtukuji depicts the priest sitting in a high chair. Themes from nature were popular with other Japanese Zen artists. In the first half of the fifteenth century Jōsetsu and Shūbun became famous for their landscape sketches, but the greatest *suiboku* painter of the fifteenth century was probably Sesshū (1420–1506). He visited China in 1467 in the hope that he could learn something from Chinese masters. On his return to Japan in 1469 he travelled widely before settling in Yamaguchi in western Honshū away from the capital which was being devasted by the Onin war. The great majority of Sesshū's works were landscapes, and many of these were executed in a style called *shin* from the caligraphic style *shinshō*, which was used to describe characters written in an accurate or angular form, as compared with *gyōshō* (rounded characters) and *sōshō* (cursive style, the so-called 'grass writing'). In Sesshū's *shin*-style paintings angles in the bold strokes with which he depicted landscapes tended to be exaggerated. But Sesshū also executed works in the *gyō* style. In these broad brush strokes and curving or wavy lines replaced the angular strokes of the *shin* style, and the scene became blurred. Sometimes he preferred the cursive style. Japanese paintings in this style are referred to as *hatsuboku* (splashed-ink) or *haboku* (broken-ink). In this style images appear misty and hazy, and the appeal is primarily to the imagination.

Other famous artists in the *suiboku* Zen style during the fifteenth century included Jasoku and a trio named Nō-ami, Gei-ami and Sō-ami, who while they did work for Zen temples were, as their names imply, followers of Amidist sects. The outstanding artist in *suiboku* style in the sixteenth century was probably Sesson. The Zen artists not only produced hanging pictures (*kakemono*) and scrolls (*emaki*); they were also employed in decorating screens and sliding doors.

In the Muromachi period one of Japan's greatest schools of painting – the Kanō school – was established. This was essentially an adaptation of the Tosa style of painting which had developed in Heian times, but it combined elements derived from Chinese painting of the Sung dynasty and from the Japanese Zen painters. The founder of the school was Kanō Masanobu (1434–1530), who studied in Kyoto possibly with Shūbun or, another painter in the same style, Sōtan. Masanobu was a layman and not a monk like the Zen painters with whom he studied. His paintings appealed to the warrior class by their directness and clarity; less was left to the imagination, and he did not follow the mystical approach of his Buddhist mentors. Masanobu's son, Kanō Motonobu (1476–1559), established the pre-eminence of the Kanō school. He developed the decorative elements and use of striking colours which became such important features of painting in the subsequent Momoyama period. He was a member of the Nichiren sect of Buddhism, but spent much time decorating the fortified monastery of the Amidist Honganji temple at Ishiyama (the modern Osaka). This temple was destroyed by Toyotomi Hideyoshi (see page 123), and much of Motonobu's work has thus disappeared. But some of his landscape paintings have been preserved in Dairen-in of the Daitokuji and in the Reiun-in of the Myōshinji in Kyoto. Motonobu was an expert painter of large-scale screens. He had help from his brother and from his sons, who included the famous painter Naonobu (also known as Shōei), and his grandson Eitoku, who became one of the great exponents of the Kanō school in the Momoyama period.

In the Muromachi period the art of sculpture found little new inspiration. The emphasis was on portraits rather than images of Buddhas. Some fine portrait carvings of important priests of the Zen sect were produced. There are also some interesting and striking portraits of the Ashikaga shōguns in the Tōji-in in Kyoto.

Inevitably in a world dominated by the military caste a great deal of effort was put into the production of swords and items of armour. Some of these were presented to temples or shrines and have been preserved. Significant progress was also made in the decoration of pieces of lacquer using gold designs; many of these were created by artists such as Kanō Motonobu and the three Amis. Some of the finest pieces were writing desks (*bundai*) and ink-stone boxes (*suzuri-bako*).

Zen temples continued to be built in the *karayō* style, which was a Japanese adaptation of certain Chinese designs. One notable aspect of the *karayō* style was the upward slant given to the eaves of roofs, which were frequently covered in bark from the *hinoki* tree. In the rebuilding of the Kōfukuji temple at Nara, however, a conscious effort was made to go back to the original styles of the Nara period.

The two greatest examples of the domestic architecture of the Muromachi period are the Kyoto temples of Kinkakuji, built for Yoshimitsu, and Ginkakuji, where Yoshimasa sought peace from the internecine strife of his time. The architecture of the Kinkakuji is in part a throw-back to the *shinden-zukuri* of the Heian period. The architecture of the Ginkakuji, on the other hand, marks a new departure which was to be fully developed in the Momoyama and Edo periods. This was the style called *shōin-zukuri*. One characteristic of this style was a room on a slightly higher level called the *jōdan-no ma* in which an alcove, called a *toko-no-ma*, was a main feature. The *toko-no-ma* came to be used to display a hanging scroll with a vase of flowers or an incense burner placed on the ledge below the scroll. (The *toko-no-ma* became an essential feature in every traditional-style Japanese room of any size.) The shelf or ledge nearby would be on two levels and was called a *chigaidana*. Rooms were divided by sliding screens on which scenes might be painted. The front, as well as the right and left of the room, could also be opened to the garden if the screens were removed. The building was generally designed to form an integral part of the garden.

In the Muromachi period the feudal lords built various kinds of fortifications to provide some protection for their lands. These tended intitially to be on the tops or slopes of hills and were generally of a temporary nature; they also began to fortify their headquarters in the growing towns. From these forts, with their watch-towers (*yagura*), the Japanese castles of the subsequent Momoyama and Edo periods developed.

The Japanese had had gardens from early times. In the Nara period wild flowers and flowering shrubs and trees were planted to form gardens, and there are references to gardens in poems in the *Manyōshū*. Gardens with artificial lakes formed an important feature of the *shinden-zukuri*-style palaces and residences of the nobles of the Heian period. Gardens of this type were also built in the Kamakura period, but no complete Japanese garden built before Muromachi times has survived. Muromachi gardens were much influenced by Zen. There were two main types of Muromachi garden: these were the *kaiyū-shiki* and the *kare-sansui* or *hira-sansui*. The *kaiyū-shiki* gardens were 'stroll gardens', that is, gardens designed to be viewed from different angles by the owner or his visitors strolling around the garden. *Kare-sansui* means 'dry mountain water'; the implication is that mountains and rivers were shown symbolically by rocks and sand. *Hira-sansui* means 'flat mountain water'. *Kare-sansui* and *hira-sansui* gardens were basically the same.

One of the oldest Muromachi *kaiyū-shiki* gardens is that of Tenryūji at Arashi-yama outside Kyoto. It was designed by Musō Kokushi, and the temple was built on the orders of the first Ashikaga shōgun Takauji. The garden incorporates a pond with a small island reached by a stone bridge. The garden is at the foot of a hill which provides a backdrop. As in so many other Japanese gardens great skill has been used in the finding and placing of rocks selected for their shapes and colours and of shrubs and trees planted with artifice to give an impression of harmony and natural beauty. Another famous garden designed by Musō Kokushi is that of Saihōji (also known as Kokedera or the moss temple) on the outskirts of Kyoto. This is also a *kaiyū-shiki* garden centring on a small lake (Ogon-chi or Golden Pond). The lake contains some tiny wooded islands; more than twenty different types of moss cover the ground under the surrounding evergreen trees.[20] The gardens of Kinkakuji and Ginkakuji are also of the *kaiyū-shiki* type, but are very different in atmosphere. The garden of Kinkakuji (the Temple of the Golden Pavilion) is dominated by the pavilion, which juts out into the waters of the pond. The pavilion was destroyed by a disastrous fire after the Second World War, but it has been rebuilt in an exact replica and is regilded from time to time. The garden of the Ginkakuji (Silver Pavilion) seems more restrained, as the pavilion is not quite such a dominating feature of the garden, but its wonderful proportions add greatly to the natural beauty of one of the loveliest gardens of the Muromachi period.

Zen influence in the *kaiyū-shiki* gardens is reflected by the emphasis on nature and communing with nature. In the *kare-sansui* gardens the inspiration is almost wholly from Zen. In these gardens the emphasis is on meditation, and the rocks and sand which form the main features of these gardens are intended to inspire thought which hopefully will lead to enlightenment. A *kare-sansui* garden is not intended to be explained; its appeal is to the feelings rather than to the intellect. Its contemplation should be a mystical experience. The garden has to be viewed from the veranda of the temple before which the garden has been built.

The most famous *kare-sansui* garden of the Muromachi period and probably of all periods is that of Ryōanji on the outskirts of Kyoto. In a rectangle, some 31 metres by 15 metres, in front of the temple veranda are fifteen carefully selected rocks, set in a harmonious but irregular way among white sand, bounded by a low wall some 2 metres high. Behind this lies a wood which provides a backdrop. There are no flowers, trees, grass or water in the garden, but the rocks suggest small islands in a stretch of water which might be a stream, a lake or a sea. Inevitably any verbal description is inadequate, and the reader who has never experienced a Zen garden may wonder what there is to rave about in a collection of rocks and sand, but the garden is very beautiful to any viewer able to set aside western prejudices about the nature of gardens and to absorb the atmosphere, which should be one of peace and tranquility.[21] Ryōanji also has a *kaiyū-shiki* garden outside the temple wall; this is particularly beautiful in spring and autumn.

Another outstanding *kare-sansui* garden of the latter part of the Muromachi period is that of the Daisen-in of the Daitokuji in Kyoto. This is quite different in style. In the Daisen-in the garden is layed out on two sides of the temple with walls of baked earth on the outer side of the garden. Carefully selected rocks are used to suggest a waterfall and a mountain stream; flat rocks are used to symbolize bridges, and water is indicated by a stretch of white sand. Moss and shrubs, particularly camelias, are used to add an element of natural beauty to the harmonious arrangement of rocks and sand.

Tea had become a popular drink in Japan after tea plants had been imported into Japan from China in the Kamakura period. But the tea ceremony or *cha-no-yu*, as it is called in Japanese (literally, 'hot water of tea'), did not develop until Muromachi times when tea utensils were also imported from China. At first the Japanese enjoyed tea contests (*tōcha*) when members of the artistocracy judged teas rather as they had judged perfumes in Heian times. These contests were also occasions for the imbibing of large quantities of sake as well as of tea. But for the priests of the Zen sect tea had a spiritual meaning and was seen as an aid to meditation.

One of the founders of the tea cermony as it has come down to us today was the priest Murata Shukō or Jukō (1422–1502), who had studied under the priest Ikkyū and who became curator of Chinese art for the shōgun Yoshimasa. He made tea using Chinese utensils, and the guests assembled in a small room of four and a half mats (that is, *tatami*). This is called *yojōhan* in Japanese and is equivalent to 2.73 square metres. This size became a standard measurement for Japanese tea rooms or *chashitsu*. The measurement is said to be that of the cell of the Indian Buddhist teacher Vimilakîrti, known in Japanese by the name Yuima. Utensils were greatly prized. Simplicity, restrained glazes and irregularity were regarded as important elements in fine tea bowls. The tea which came to be used in the tea ceremony was powdered green tea, which was placed by means of a small bamboo spoon into the tea bowl. On to this hot or near-boiling water was ladelled from an iron pot and then whisked up into a fine green froth. *Usucha* was a thin mixture, while *koicha* was a thicker mixture. Today *usucha* or *o-usu*, as it is sometimes referred to, is used in most tea ceremonies. Every movement in making the tea, drinking it and admiring the tea bowls and other utemsils has to be done ceremoniously and in accordance with fixed and preordained rules; but the ceremony as we know it today and the different schools of tea did not develop fully until considerably later, after the time of the great tea-master of the Momoyama period Sen no Rikyū (1522–91) (see page 125).

The Japanese cult of flower arrangement goes back to the earliest times after the import of Buddhism from China. Indeed, the offering of flowers before Buddhist images is said to have been a ritual brought back by Ono no Imoko after he returned to Japan from his mission to China in 607. The first Japanese school of flower arrangement, the Ikenobō school, claims him as its founder. Flowers were arranged in Buddhist temples in what was considered to be a natural way. The style called *tatebana* (standing flowers) involved the use of three flowers; the main stem was supposed to be one and a half times the height of the vase and was placed in the centre; the other two flowers were arranged symmetrically on the left and right sides of the vase. From this comparatively simple method of arranging flowers the *rikka* style (the 'Chinese' reading of the characters for tatebana) was developed in the Muromachi period. In 1462 one Sengyō or Senkei is said to have arranged some flowers in a gold vase in an asymmetrical way depicting in symbolic fashion the mythical Buddhist Mount Sumeru and thus the universe. Sengyō can be regarded as the first great master of the *rikka* style and of the Ikenobō school. *Rikka* flourished especially in the subsequent Momoyama period when the Japanese art of flower arrangement became firmly established.

The cult of tea and the import into Japan of Chinese ceramics of the Sung dynasty, particularly celadons (called in Japanese *seiji*) and black wares (known in Japanese as *tenmoku*), encouraged the development of pottery in Japan. Tea utensils began to be made in Japan after the potter Tōshiro had been to China to study Sung ceramics and on his return had established a kiln at Seto (near the modern city of Nagoya). In addition to Seto wares, pottery was produced at Shino, also near the modern city of Nagoya, at Shigaraki near Kyoto, at Bizen in what is now Okayama prefecture and at Karatsu on the north of Kyūshū. Shino wares were rough pieces covered with a thick white glaze which was crackled in the firing. Shigaraki wares, on the other hand, were hard, heavy and glazed with a deep yellowy red, although some pots had a light blue glaze. Bizen wares were dark brown in colour and unglazed. Karatsu wares of this period were attempts at imitation of Korean wares, which were much appreciated by the *chajin* or connoisseurs of tea. Although some fine pots were made in Japan in the Muromachi period, Japanese pottery had not yet reached the standards of technical perfection which it achieved in subsequent centuries.

VII

The Momoyama Period (1573–1616)[1] and First Contacts With The West

As a result of the efforts of three outstanding military rulers (Oda Nobunaga, Toyotomi Hideyoshi and Tokugawa Ieyasu) Japan had become a unified feudal state by the end of the sixteenth century. According to one analogy Oda Nobunaga mixed the dough, Toyotomi Hideyoshi baked the cake, but Tokugawa Ieyasu ate it. Another metaphor is that Nobunaga quarried the stones for New Japan, Hideyoshi rough-hewed them, and Ieyasu set them finally in their place. All three were very different personalities, but they were all equally determined, vigorous, ambitious and ruthless. They each made their own way up to a position of dominance and were thus self-made men. The differences in their characters has been summed up in the following way. If the cuckoo (*hototogisu*) would not sing Nobunaga would have killed it, Hideyoshi would have made it sing, while Ieyasu would have waited until it did sing. They liked colour and ornamentation. Momoyama art is thus highly decorative, with a great deal of gold leaf; it is saved from vulgarity by the vitality and imagination of its artists. The Momoyama period coincided with the Elizabethan period in England. In terms of energy and spirit of adventure the two eras had a certain similarity, but the differences are greater than the similarities.

The arrival of the Portuguese, the Spaniards and later the Dutch and the English in the Far East led to the introduction of firearms, the development of trade and the arrival of Catholic missionaries. Western ideas and techniques began to influence attitudes in Japan. There were upwards of 600,000 professed Catholics in Japan at the height of missionary activity. The fortitude of the many Christian martyrs during the persecutions, which began with Hideyoshi, and the survival of Christian practices in remote parts of Kyushū and the neighbouring islands throughout two centuries of isolation and persecution shows that the 'Christian century'[2] was a significant episode in Japanese history.

Oda Nobunaga (1534–82)

The anarchy which prevailed in Japan in the middle of the sixteenth century provided opportunities for the ambitious and strong to win lands and fame at the expense of their neighbours or of those weakened by strife and natural disaster. Many of the feudal lords were tempted in these days to try to gain hegemony over their rivals, but those with large domains had to devote most of their attention to defending what they had and were under close observation from their neighbours and rivals. Perhaps it was this that gave an opportunity to the determined and daring minor chieftain Oda Nobunaga, who came from a minor

121

feudal family in the province of Owari, now part of Aichi prefecture in central Japan, to try his hand at winning a dominant position. In 1559 he gained control of Owari and in 1560 at the battle of Okehazama he defeated the Imagawa family who controlled parts of what is now Shizuoka prefecture. One of the Imagawa vassals was Matsudaira Motoyasu, who entered into an agreement with Oda Nobunaga. Motoyasu later took the name of Tokugawa Ieyasu. Nobunaga then turned westwards and in 1567 he seized what became Gifu castle. Thereafter he marched on Kyoto and established Ashikaga Yoshiaki as shōgun, but he was not prepared to allow Yoshiaki to exercise real power and following plots by Yoshiaki against him Nobunaga deposed the shōgun in 1573, thus bringing the Ashikaga shōgunate to an end.

In the meantime, in a series of complex campaigns against his rivals Nobunaga had strengthened his position. He was also opposed by the militant monks of Hieizan, and in October 1571 his forces destroyed the great temples on the mountain and massacred some three thousand monks. The temples were later restored under Nobunaga's successors, but the political and military power of Hieizan was destroyed for ever. Nobunaga also had to contend with militant opposition from the armed leagues (*ikkō ikki*) who were followers of the Jōdo Shinshū sect of Buddhism centring on the Ishiyama Honganji in Osaka. He overcame them as well as other feudal lords, such as the Takeda, who threatened his position in eastern Japan. (Takeda Shingen, the famous warrior leader, died in 1573.) Among the lands which came into Nobunaga's hands were domains in northern Omi, now Shiga prefecture; these he granted to one Kinoshita Tōkichirō, better known as Toyotomi Hideyoshi (1537–98).

In 1576 Nobunaga began to build his castle at Azuchi overlooking Lake Biwa. Nobunaga conceived of this as a symbol of his wealth and power. Accordingly he spared no effort to make the castle overwhelming in its magnificence. Painters such as Kanō Eitoku (1543–90) were employed to decorate the screens which filled the castle. This was completed in 1579 after unprecedented efforts involving vast gangs of forced labour and compulsory contributions from Nobunaga's vassals and other feudal chiefs. A town with a population estimated as being about five thousand people in 1582 grew up below the castle. There was a free market in the town, and every effort was made to attract money, trade and artisans to Azuchi.

But Nobunaga's position was not yet secure. The exiled shōgun Yoshiaki managed to secure the support of the Mōri, who then controlled what is now Hiroshima prefecture in the west, and of the Uesugi in the north-east. Much of the rest of Nobunaga's life was spent in dealing with these threats. Uesugi Kenshin's death in 1578 was followed by the surrender of the Ishiyama Honganji in Osaka and the final defeat in 1580 of the Jōdo Shinshu followers who held out in Kaga (now Ishikawa prefecture) (see page 101). Other enemies remained, but before he could tackle the remaining threats Nobunaga was assassinated by one of his own generals, Akechi Mitsuhide (died 1582). On his way to join his forces in western Japan, Nobunaga stopped at the Honnōji temple in Kyoto. Here he was surprised by Mitsuhide's forces. Nobunaga is said to have put up a valiant resistance and ultimately to have disembowelled himself while the temple was consumed in flames.

Nobunaga tried to break the local trade monopolies and to promote the use of money instead of barter. He also encouraged internal trade by the building of roads and the reduction of barriers. In Echizen (now Fukui prefecture) Shibata Katsuie (1522?–83), the general he appointed to run the conquered domains, began to carry out policies, adopted more generally under Hideyoshi, to separate the agricultural and military classes, to confiscate weapons from the farmers (the so-called *katana-gari* or sword hunt) and to establish a land survey.

Nobunaga was primarily a warrior. He was a tough and courageous fighter, who took every advantage of the opportunities which came his way. He made good use of the firearms whose use the Japanese had learned from the Portuguese, and he recognized the importance of ensuring discipline among his forces, although it is questionable whether he had exceptional military talent. As a man he seems to have been totally ruthless and exceptionally cruel even in an age when cruelty was commonplace, but he remains one of the outstanding figures of his time if only because of his energy and determination.

Toyotomi Hideyoshi (1537–98)

Toyotomi Hideyoshi, who was first known as Kinoshita Tōkichirō, came from a family of foot soldiers in the service of Nobunaga's father. In 1558 he joined the army of Nobunaga, who quickly took a liking to him and called him 'Saru' (Monkey). Hideyoshi proved himself an able military leader and master of siegecraft. In 1577 he gained possession by a strategem of the castle now known as Himeji. In 1582 he took the castle of Takamatsu in Bitchu (now part of Okayama prefecture) by flooding the area of the castle.

When he learned of the murder of Nobunaga, he came to an arrangement with the Mōri family with whom he was fighting on behalf of Nobunaga and marched his forces back towards Kyoto. At the battle of Yamazaki he defeated Akechi Mitsuhide. In 1583 he defeated Shibata Katsuie at the battle of Shizugatake, made himself master of the Hokuriku area and after dealing with other opponents began to build the great castle of Osaka. Ieyasu meanwhile was occupied in the north-east and made no attempt to challenge Hideyoshi; a breach between the two men in 1584 was healed in 1585. In the same year Hideyoshi had himself appointed *kanpaku* (regent) by the Emperor.

But he was not yet supreme throughout Japan. In Kyūshū, Shimazu Yoshihisa (1533–97) refused to acknowledge his authority; he is reputed to have commented on hearing of Hideyoshi's appointment as regent: 'His Majesty must have made a hasty choice!' Hideyoshi collected a huge army, said to have consisted of up to 200,000 men, and in 1587 forced his way south into Satsuma. At a point north of the Sendai river the Satsuma forces were routed, but Hideyoshi was persuaded to allow the Shimazu to retain their fief. He returned in triumph to Kyoto, where he celebrated his victory with a magnificent outdoor tea ceremony at the Kitano shrine. In 1588 he invited the Emperor Go-Yōzei (reigned 1586–1611) to his new residence, the Jūrakutei, where all the feudal lords pledged their loyalty to the Emperor and the regent. Hideyoshi took the opportunity to impress those present by a display of his wealth and by distributing gold to his followers.

Hideyoshi faced one further challenge. The Hōjō, who were linked by marriage with Ieyasu, barred the way to the Kantō by the commanding position of their castle at Odawara at the foot of the Hakone mountain range. Ieyasu sided with Hideyoshi, who mounted a siege against the Hōjō stronghold. Eventually after a long siege, during which the besiegers enjoyed the company of their wives and mistresses, Odawara castle capitulated on 12 August 1590.

Hideyoshi persuaded Ieyasu to accept domains in the Kantō in place of his former fiefs further west. Ieyasu thus gained the stronghold of Edo, the modern Tokyo, in the centre of the Kantō plain. He rewarded his other supporters with confiscated land elsewhere. The careful shuffling of fiefs, known as *kunigae* (province change), ensured that the daimyō who were transferred had to build up a new following and were not in a position to threaten Hideyoshi.

Hideyoshi extended to the whole country the measures which Shibata Katsuie had begun to adopt in Echizen. From 1588 the *katana-gari* was pursued ruthlessly in order to prevent possible uprisings and to distinguish clearly between the farmers and the soldiers or samurai. In 1590 a population census was proclaimed; this was a further step designed to ensure that the farmer was tied to his land. At the same time Hideyoshi ordered the destruction of many feudal strongholds.

Hideyoshi continued Nobunaga's policies designed to encourage trade and he developed the coinage. He appointed a commissioner (*shoshidai*) to keep order in the metropolitan area of Kyoto, but always kept the real power in his own hands. Hideyoshi proved an able administrator, although he operated more by improvisation and *ad hoc* rules than by any comprehensive system of law.

Following his appointment as regent in 1585 Hideyoshi had himself appointed chancellor (*dajōdaijin*) in 1586. He resigned as regent in 1592 in favour of his nephew Hidetsugu (1568–95) and took the title of a retired regent, *taiko*, a title by which he is still generally known in Japan. In the same year he began to build a castle and residence at Fushimi in Kyoto; this came to be called Momoyama-jō.

Invasion of Korea

In April 1592 Hideyoshi issued orders for the invasion of Korea. A striking force of over 150,000 men, with reserves of some 75,000, was mobilized, and elaborate commissariat plans were prepared. The first contingent of some 18,000 men, commanded by Konishi Yukinaga, reached Pusan towards the end of May 1592. Further contingents followed. The Korean authorities were weak and incompetent, and the Japanese armies sweeping northwards captured Seoul on 12 June 1592. Pyongyang (now the capital of North Korea) then fell to the Japanese. The Korean king, who had escaped to the north of the Yalu river, appealed for Chinese help against the Japanese invaders. The Japanese forces came under increasing pressure as a result of action by the Korean navy under Admiral Yi and by the guerrilla forces which sprang up behind their lines in opposition to attempts to impose a Japanese-style feudal system in occupied territory. Katō Kiyomasa, one of Hidyoshi's outstanding generals, did, however, manage to enter briefly into Manchuria in the winter of 1592–3, and the first Chinese forces sent to Korea to oppose the Japanese were annihilated. But the Japanese position in Korea could not be sustained. The Japanese were forced to evacuate first Pyongyang and then in May 1593 Seoul. Negotiations for a settlement were started but dragged on while Hideyoshi demanded the surrender to Japan of the southern provinces of Korea and resumption of trade with China. In December 1596 a Chinese embassy arrived in Kyoto to invest Hideyoshi as King of Japan, but Hideyoshi was furious when he learned the patronizing terms of the Chinese message, and negotiations were broken off. Hideyoshi threatened another attack in Korea, and a new force of 100,000 men was sent there in 1597. Although the Chinese were at first defeated, they renewed their attack on the Japanese forces, and most of the latter were withdrawn except for a rearguard of some 60,000 men mostly from Satsuma. These were finally brought back to Japan after the death of Hideyoshi in September 1598. Thus ended Hideyoshi's abortive efforts at expansion on the Asian mainland.

Hideyoshi's motives for the invasion have been the subject of much historical debate. He may have concluded that the only way of ensuring that the large military forces which had grown up in Japan during a century or more of civil strife did not further endanger peace was to occupy them in fighting outside Japan. In his later years he had begun to show signs of mental instability and megalomania. His successes in Japan indeed seem to have gone to his head, and his grandiose ideas of continental conquests seem to have been conceived without any clear idea of this size of the task he was undertaking. By 1592 Hideyoshi was in his fifties and despite the successes and reverses of his forces in Korea he never led them in person, but accepted that he should command from Japan. He failed to recognize the importance of naval power, and the absence of an effective Japanese navy was one of the causes of the ultimate defeat of the Japanese invasion attempt.

One important result of this episode for the history of Japanese culture was the arrival in Japan of a large number of Korean artisans, especially potters, who settled in places famous in the subsequent history of Japanese pottery such as Hagi (Yamaguchi prefecture), Karatsu and Satsuma in Kyūshū.

Hideyoshi had been desolated by the death of his son Tsurumatsu in 1591 and had despaired of having a direct heir. However, in 1593 his favourite concubine, Yodogimi, presented him with a son, Hideyori, on whom he doted. Following the birth of his son he grew increasingly jealous of his nephew Hidetsugu to whom he had transferred the Jūrakutei as well as the office of regent. Hidetsugu seems to have interfered with some of Hideyoshi's decisions and by his depraved conduct and blood lust he attracted many enemies. In 1595 Hideyoshi had him banished to Koya-san, where he was ordered to commit suicide. Hideyoshi then pursued Hidetsugu's family and retainers, including his women and children, with ruthless cruelty and exterminated everyone directly connected with his nephew.

In his later years Hideyoshi became increasingly subject to fits of temper and wanton cruelty. In 1591 he ordered the famous tea master Sen no Rikyū to commit suicide. Hideyoshi's reasons for this order are obscure, but according to one theory Rikyū had refused to give his daughter to Hideyoshi.

In a desperate attempt to ensure that his son Hideyori should succeed to his power when he died, Hideyoshi created in the summer of 1598 a council of five elders, the go-tairō, who were made to swear allegiance to Hideyori. One of these elders was Tokugawa Ieyasu, who was also appointed guardian to Hideyori.

Hideyoshi died on 18 September 1598. All his precautions proved vain, and power was seized by Ieyasu.

Hideyoshi was undoubtedly a remarkable man. He took decisions quickly and never faltered in his pursuit of power, but, as he showed in the siege of Odawara, he also knew how to exercise patience. He recognized the importance of careful planning not only in the attack but also in ensuring adequate supplies. He seemed untiring. He was shrewd and generally a good judge of men. He was passionate, frank and informal, but he was also ostentatious, and his tastes would have been regarded by the aesthetes of Yoshimasa's circle as vulgar. In his early years he was, by the standards of his time, relatively humane, but in his later years his affections and jealousies, combined with bouts of wild rage, led to horrifying excesses.

Tokugawa Ieyasu (1543–1616)

Tokugawa Ieyasu was the son of Matsudaira Hirotada, a petty feudal chief of Okazaki (Aichi prefecture). His father made an alliance with the Imagawa, his neighbours to the east, who controlled Suruga province (now part of Shizuoka prefecture). As a guarantee of loyalty to his Imagawa allies, his son, Ieyasu, aged four, was sent in 1547 as a hostage to the Imagawa headquarters at Sumpu (the modern Shizuoka city). In 1560 Nobunaga had defeated the Imagawa at the battle of Okehazama, and in 1561 Ieyasu joined forces with Nobunaga. By so doing he gradually expanded his domains into what had been Imagawa territory. Ieyasu was careful not to offend Nobunaga; in 1579 in order to demonstrate his continuing loyalty he had his first wife, who was an Imagawa, put to death and caused his first son to commit suicide, as Nobunaga suspected them of colluding with his enemies.

By the time of Nobunaga's death in 1582, Ieyasu was in a strong position in eastern Japan. His relations with Toyotomi Hideyoshi were at first chequered, but both recognized the desirability of working together. Ieyasu accordingly sent a son to be adopted by Hideyoshi and married Hideyoshi's sister aged forty-three. After the fall of Odawara in 1590 the alliance with Hideyoshi led to Ieyasu being given the five provinces in the Kantō plain. Ieyasu managed to avoid any major involvement in Hideyoshi's invasion of Korea, although he had to spend eighteen months at the campaign headquarters in Kyūshū.

When Hideyoshi died in 1598 Ieyasu was the strongest of the daimyō, having a fief of 2.5 million *koku*,[3] more than twice that of any of the other daimyō. Ieyasu was determined to preserve the unity achieved by Hideyoshi, but he had many enemies among the other feudal chiefs. One of these was Ishida Mitsunari (1560–1600), who gained the support of a number of other daimyō including the Mōri in western Honshū and the Shimazu in Kyūshū. On 20 October 1600 at the battle of Sekigahara, perhaps the most significant of all civil war battles in Japan, Ieyasu routed his opponents with the help of Kobayakawa Hideaki and other supporters of Ishida Mitsunari, who changed sides in the middle of the battle. Mitsunari was later captured and executed.

The Mōri leader, Mōri Terumoto, and other opponents of Ieyasu decided to make their submission in the hope of keeping their domains. Ieyasu accepted their submission and undertook a major redistribution of fiefs. These were divided into *fudai* fiefs – that is, the fiefs of daimyō who were related to the Tokugawa or who had been consistently loyal – and the *tozama* (literally, 'outer') fiefs of the daimyō whose loyalty had only been won by force of arms. Ieyasu ordered many *kunigae* (changes of provinces); thus the Hosokawa were moved to Kumamoto in Kyūshū and the Mōri westwards to Nagato (also called Chōshū) in what is now Yamaguchi prefecture. The *fudai* daimyō, many of whom adopted the name of Matsudaira, were placed in strategic spots throughout Japan in order to ensure the security of the realm. Some ninety fiefs were totally confiscated. The smallest size of fief was 10,000 *koku* and the largest, other than those of the Tokugawa, was that of the Maeda in Kaga province (now Ishikawa prefecture), amounting to 1.19 million *koku*.

In 1603 Ieyasu's supremacy was confirmed by his appointment as shōgun. He was, however, careful in exercising his powers at this time not to challenge directly the position of the young Hideyori and his mother Yodogimi who were allowed to keep the stronghold of Osaka castle. The Nijō castle, whose construction in Kyoto had been started by Nobunaga, was completed.[4] It was assigned for the use of the *shoshidai* (the shōgun's deputy). Ieyasu spent much of his time at Sunpu, while his son Hidetada, to whom he ceded the post of shōgun in 1605, occupied Edo, which became the Shōgun's headquarters. Ieyasu, however, kept his hands on the reins of power up to his death in 1616.

Ieyasu realized that his regime would not be wholly secure while Hideyori remained in his Osaka stronghold as an alternative focus for discontent. Accordingly from about 1611 he began to put pressure on Hideyori. In 1614 he took advantage of an alleged plot against him to launch an attack on Osaka castle. The first campaign led to the destruction of the outer moats. The siege was resumed in May 1615, but the castle, which was stoutly defended by supporters of Hideyori including many *rōnin* (masterless samurai), did not fall until 4 June 1615 after Hideyori and his mother Yodogimi had committed suicide.

Ieyasu was now supreme. He set out his rules for the Tokugawa government in the *buke-shōhattō* (laws for military houses). These were more a code of conduct than a set of laws. The first of thirteen articles called for the study of civil and military arts, while the second article prohibited licentious behaviour. Another article provided for the reporting of all repairs to castles and prohibited the building of new castles, while a further article demanded that all marriages of daimyō had to be properly authorized. Dress had to be appropriate for the daimyō's rank, and samurai were enjoined to live frugally. These rules were elaborated in the so-called Legacy of Ieyasu. The following article from the Legacy epitomizes the austerity of his philosophy of life: 'Avoid things that you like and turn your attention to unpleasant duties'.

Ieyasu's remains were first interred at Kunōsan, not far from the modern city of Shizuoka. In the following year they were transferred to Nikkō, north-east of Tokyo, where the magnificently decorated Tōshōgū shrine was dedicated to his memory. He was canonized as a manifestation of the Buddha, the posthumous title of *Tōshō Daigongen* – or, to use the more popular term, *Gongen-sama* – being given to him.

Ieyasu's contribution to the establishment of Japanese feudalism, unity and internal peace was considerable. He had a fair modicum of luck, but his success was also the result of his shrewdness and patience. He was primarily a soldier, although he was more of a scholar than some of his contemporaries. He was a practical ruler rather than an administrator or political philosopher. He had much native cunning and was unscrupulous if by such behaviour he could gain the advantage. He was undoubtedly a great leader, though he was neither virtuous nor likeable and he lacked compassion.

Momoyama Art

Nobunaga, Hideyoshi and Ieyasu sought to demonstrate their power and wealth by the splendour of their residences and castles. They demanded that walls ceilings and screens should be covered by the painters they employed. They liked conventional Japanese nature themes such as pine trees and willows, as well as cherry and plum trees in blossom and the autumn maple. Other popular subjects included depictions of characters from Chinese legends. Brilliant colours and gold leaf were preferred in contrast to the back and white and restrained painting of the Muromachi period. The most popular school of painting was that of the Kanō family of artists.

Kanō Eitoku (1543–90) served Nobunaga and Hideyoshi. He used large brushes, and his style was vigorous and striking. He had to cover huge spaces and had no time to spend on details. He depicted pines and other types of trees on a vast scale (up to about seven metres) and life-size men. Many of his paintings were destroyed when Osaka castle was burned in 1615, but a number have survived. The Imperial Household has a fine pair of large screens depicting a couple of fabulous lions on a gold-leaf background.

Kanō Sanraku (1559–1635), who was an attendant on Hideyoshi, was adopted into the Kanō family. His style was similar to that of Eitoku. A striking painting of trees, flowers and tigers by Sanraku is in the Tenkyūin, a sub-temple of Myōshinji in Kyoto.

Another famous painter of the Momoyama period was Hasegawa Tōhaku (1539–1610), who painted some of the superb screen paintings preserved in the Chishakuin temple in Kyoto. Kaihō Yūshō (1553–1615) studied with the Kanō school and produced black-and-white as well as colour paintings on gold backgrounds. A pair of screens in the Imperial Household collection depicts fishing nets hung out to dry, set off by a group of rushes.

The Momoyama leaders also wanted gorgeous buildings to impress their potential rivals. This was the greatest period in the building of Japanese castles. Unfortunately Nobunaga's huge fortress at Azuchi has not survived, and the present Osaka castle is a replica. Hideyoshi's castle at Fushimi-Momoyama near Kyoto was destroyed during the time of the third Tokugawa shōgun, Iemitsu, but some of its buildings and contents were transferred to the Nishi-Honganji temple in Kyoto. One of these, the Hiunkaku pavilion,[5] is a wonderful building which, as its name ('the pavilion of the flying clouds') suggests, seems to float in the air. Other fine rooms transferred from Fushimi, including the *jōdan-no-ma*, are in the *shōin-tsukuri* style, which had begun to be used in the Muromachi period. In the Momoyama period such buildings became more gorgeous with painted ceilings as well as vast painted walls and screens. The friezes (*ranma*) above the sliding screens were also elaborately carved. Another characteristic of this form of architecture was the spacious open gallery or veranda facing the garden.

The art of garden construction was encouraged by Hideyoshi. Perhaps the finest example of a Momoyama garden is that of the Sanbōin sub-temple of Daigoji to the south of the city of Kyoto. This was laid out on Hideyoshi's orders and is one of the loveliest of Kyoto gardens with its rocks, pond, stone bridges and abundant shrubs. It was intended to be viewed from the main reception hall, itself a beautiful example of Momoyama architecture.

Three of the *karamon* (Chinese-style gates) from Fushimi castle were moved to other sites in Kyoto. The most elaborate of these has been preserved by the Nishighonganji. It has a beautifully curved roof covered in *hinoki* wood bark. Over the lintel there is a large carved peacock, decorated in bright colours and gold leaf, while on the side beams there are carved tigers in bamboo thickets. On the door panels various lions are carved. Another of these gates was transferred to the Nijō castle in Kyoto. The Nijō castle is a palace built in the *shōin-tsukuri* style. It contains many beautiful paintings from the beginning of the seventeenth century.

The finest surviving castle from the Momoyama period is Himeji-jō (*jō* means castle). Other castles which have not been destroyed and replaced by ferro-concrete replicas include those at Matsumoto in Nagano, Matsue in Shimane and Matsuyama in Ehime prefecture. Among the striking features of Japanese castles are the massive walls made of hewn rocks put together without mortar, the wide moats, the massive gateways, the carefully planned access routes providing plenty of opportunities for the defenders to ambush parties which might get beyond the gates, the watch-towers (*yagura*) and finally the colossal keeps (*tenshūkaku*).

Industrial arts such as metalwork and lacquer were boosted by the demand for ornamental items. Beautifully designed ornamental door and sword furniture, as well as highly decorated armour, was produced by a growing number of metalworkers primarily in and around Kyoto. Gold lacquer bowls and trays were used at banquets, and lacquer writing boxes (*suzuri-bako*) were sought by scholars and poets. Tea bowls were also needed for the tea cermonies which were popular among the daimyō at this period. Hideyoshi's extravagant taste – he had a tea room which had walls and ceiling all in gold leaf – was hardly in keeping with the refined approach of the earlier Zen masters. But Hideyoshi recognized that the Kyoto potter Chōjiro was a master craftsman and allowed him to use the character *raku* ('enjoyment') on the tea bowls which he made with clay found near Hideyoshi's Jūrakutei palace. Thus began the famous Kyoto *raku-yaki* style of pottery.

Traders and Missionaries: Japan's 'Christian Century' (1543–1640)

Japanese demand for Chinese goods, in particular for silks, grew as the country was unified under Nobunaga, Hideyoshi and Ieyasu and as Japan became more prosperous. But the depradations of the *wakō* (Japanese pirates) caused the Ming court in China to impose a ban on trade with Japan. The arrival of the Portuguese in the Far East provided a means for the resumption of trade with China through the base which they opened at Macao in about 1555, partly at least to enable them to pursue the potentially profitable trade with Japan. The missionaries came with the Portuguese traders and largely met the costs of the mission from their share in the profits from the trade. The history of Japan's 'Christian century' is, therefore, bound up with the development of Japan's foreign trade in this period.

Fernao Mendes Pinto[6] claimed to be the first European to visit Japan, but he seems to have been an expert liar, and his stories have to be regarded with scepticism. In fact the first Portuguese to reach Japan came in 1542 or more likely in 1543. Antonio Peixoto, Francisco Zeimoto and Antonio da Mota were sailing on a junk bound for the Chinese port of Ningpo with a largely Chinese crew in September 1543 when their ship was blown off course to the island of Tanegashima off southern Kyūshū. There, despite language problems, they were well received, and the Japanese showed particular interest in the muskets which the Portuguese were carrying. The Japanese soon managed to make copies. In the following year Portuguese traders apparently reached the province of Bungo in Kyūshū (now Oita prefecture), and a regular trade began to deveop. At first the Portuguese did not use any fixed Japanese port, although Hirado attracted Portuguese ships at least until 1571, when the first Portuguese ship went to the little fishing port of Nagasaki; this soon became the main harbour used by the Portuguese ships.

Portuguese ships were carracks (called in Portuguese *nao*). They were tall and black in colour; the Japanese accordingly referred to them as *kurofune* (black ships). In the sixteenth century the voyage from Lisbon to the Far East was slow and hazardous, and a ship to Japan took two or three years to accomplish the trip. Ships usually left Lisbon in the spring, rounding the Cape of Good Hope in the middle of the year. They reached the Portuguese settlement of Goa in India in about September. The voyage was resumed the following spring, and the ship might reach Macao in July or August after calling at the Portuguese settlement at Malacca on the way. The journey to Japan was not usually made until the following July when the 'great ship', which had taken on board Chinese silks and other Chinese goods, left with the south-west monsoon for Japan. Nagasaki might be reached in two to four weeks.

The Portuguese ships faced many hazards. The Portuguese were pioneers in the production of maps and charts, but their knowledge of the geography of the Far East in the sixteenth century was very limited, and their maps were vague and inaccurate. Portuguese navigators accordingly had to rely on detailed accounts of previous voyages to guide them. These accounts (*roteiros* or *rutters*) included descriptions of coastlines as well as notes on prevailing winds, depths and shallows. Other dangers included storms, pirates and disease. Later when Dutch ships began to operate in the Far East and Portugal was at war with Holland, Portuguese ships were liable to be intercepted by Dutch privateers. The 'Fidalgos', as the Portuguese merchant adventurers were called, were determined men, and the profit from a voyage to Japan was such that many were ready to accept the risks and make the voyage. It has been suggested that the generally austere and aristocratic Portuguese who commanded these expeditions had something in common with Japanese samurai.

In December 1547 the Portuguese captain Jorge Alvares met at Malacca the Jesuit priest Francis Xavier (later canonized and known at St Francis Xavier). Jorge Alvares was accompanied by a Japanese refugee, Yajirō, and two other Japanese. Yajirō studied Portuguese and was accepted into the Catholic Church in 1548. Xavier determined to go to Japan to preach the gospel. On 15 August 1549 Xavier, accompanied by two other Jesuits and by Yajirō as interpreter, reached Kagoshima in southern Kyūshū. Some weeks after their arrival they were given a friendly reception by the daimyō of Satsuma, Shimazu Tadahisa, who hoped that his welcome for the missionaries would lead to the arrival of Portuguese merchants. Xavier's first efforts at making conversions caused difficulties with local Buddhist monks, who saw him as a rival. In September 1550 he left Kagoshima and made his way first to Hirado in north-western Kyūshū, then on to Yamaguchi in western Honshu and finally to Kyoto. Xavier hoped to meet 'the king of Japan' in Kyoto, but he arrived in the middle of winter and found the capital devastated by war. He was forced to retrace his steps to Yamaguchi, where he managed to make some five hundred converts. In September 1551 Xavier, who had moved on to Bungo in Kyūshū, received letters urging him to return to India. He left Japan and never returned.

Xavier's mission, however, continued. The Jesuit missionaries, who came to Japan in very small numbers in the next few years, worked hard to convert not only the local peasants in the areas which Xavier had visited but also the samurai and the daimyō. They recognized that if they were to make a real impact in Japan they had to win the support of Japanese leaders. They faced many difficulties. Not the least of these was language. There were no really appropriate Japanese equivalents for Christian theological terms. Even the word for God presented problems. *Kami*, which is translated as 'god', means essentially 'superior being' or 'spirit'. When Xavier equated God with Dainichi, one of the manifestations of the Buddha, this inevitably caused confusion and misunderstanding. The missionaries' condemnation of Buddhism as idolatry aroused the fury of Buddhist monks of all sects. Their denunciation of the indigenous gods was also provocative in view of the flexibility of the Buddhists towards the worship of the Shintō *kami*. Their attacks on sodomy angered the samurai, who like the Spartans, had homosexual as well as heterosexual relationships.

In 1560 Father Gaspar Vilela, one of the six Jesuits then in Japan, managed to obtain an interview in Kyoto with the shōgun, Ashikaga Yoshiteru, who was persuaded to order that the missionaries should be well treated. Vilela managed to make a number of converts in and around the capital with the help of Brother Lorenzo, his blind Japanese assistant, but following disturbances in the capital he had to move to the port of Sakai (now part of Osaka), returning to the capital only in 1563.

In 1564 Vilela was joined by two other fathers; one of these was Luis Frois, who was to remain in Japan until his death in 1587 and whose letters give a vivid picture of Japan as seen by a Jesuit priest in the late sixteenth century. Vilela and Frois had to leave Kyoto once again for Sakai in 1565, following the issue of an edict from the Emperor ordering the expulsion of all missionaries.

Among the converts made by Vilela was one Takayama, a daimyō of Settsu province (now part of Osaka and Kyoto prefectures). Takayama took the given name of Dario but became known as Takayama Ukon (*ukon* being an honorary rank in the imperial bodyguard). With the assistance of Ukon's elder brother Frois managed in the summer of 1569 to have an interview with Nobunaga, while the latter was supervising the construction of the Nijo castle. Nobunaga, determined to destroy the power of the Buddhist monks who had caused him so much trouble, responded favourably to Frois's approach; and following an inter-view with the new shōgun, Yoshiaki, he was granted a licence to preach. This aroused the fury of the Buddhist monks, who pressed Nobunaga to have the licence rescinded. At a second interview with Nobunaga an argument developed with a Buddhist monk who was acting as a kind of secretary to Nobunaga and who threatened to cut off Brother Lorenzo's head to see if he had a soul. The monk was restrained by Hideyoshi, who was present. The missionaries were allowed to continue their work in and around the capital. By 1579 there were reported to be about 15,000 Christians in central Japan.

In 1581 at Azuchi castle Nobunaga received the commanding figure of Ales-sandro Valignano, the Jesuit Vicar General. Valignano reported in 1582 that there were some 150,000 Christians and 200 churches in Japan. Some of the converts may have been following the prevailing fashion (the wearing of items of Por-tuguese clothing had become fashionable in Kyoto). Others may have simply followed the example of their masters, but many seem to have been faithful and ardent converts. Converts were from all classes, although the Jesuits made little or no headway among the merchants, perhaps because of their attacks on usury. The numbers are a tribute to the success of the Jesuit fathers, who made strenuous efforts to learn Japanese and to adapt to local customs. (Many became experts in the tea ceremony, cha-no-yu.) Even in 1580 there were probably not more than twenty fathers with about thirty Japanese helpers.

Shortly before the death of Nobunaga in 1582 and the assumption of power by Hideyoshi, Valignano decided as a means of gaining support in Europe for the Jesuit mission in Japan to take a group of four young Japanese of high birth to Europe. He accompanied the four boys as far as Goa. They eventually reached Lisbon in 1585. King Philip II of Spain welcomed them to Madrid. Pope Gregory XIII arranged for them to ride to the Vatican in Japanese costume; after they had kissed his foot he embraced them. As a result of the tour the Jesuits were granted a monopoly of mission work in Japan and an annual subsidy. After an absence of eight years the four young men returned to Japan in 1590. During their absence the position of the Christian community in Japan had deteriorated. Two prominent Christian daimyō had died, and persecution of Christians had begun.

Nobunaga's dislike of the militant Buddhist monks made him seem favourable to Christianity, but there was never any likelihood that he would be converted. Hideyoshi showed no interest in religion, but he gave permission for a church to be established in the vicinity of the castle which he was having built at Osaka. He also gave a friendly welcome to the Jesuit Vice-Provincial Gaspar Coelho in 1586. Coelho in an attempt to gain Hideyoshi's support for the Christians offered to ask the Portuguese authorities to help with a campaign against China which Hideyoshi was then contemplating. He also seems to have promised to secure the co-operation of Christian daimyō in Kyūshū against the Shimazu. These injudicious offers probably aroused Hideyoshi's suspicions by suggesting that the church had temporal as well as spiritual power and ambitions.

However, in 1587 the prospects for the church in Japan seemed good. On his way back from his Kyūshū campaign against the Shimazu, Hideyoshi visited a small Portuguese ship at Hirado and had a friendly talk with Coelho on 24 July 1587. Then Hideyoshi did a sudden volte-face. On the following day Takayama Ukon was ordered either to give up his Christian faith or to be deprived of his fief; Ukon had no hesitation in choosing the latter. At the same time Hideyoshi sent a message to Coelho accusing the missionaries of treasonable actions. He demanded to know why they used force to make conversions, why they destroyed Buddhist temples and Shintō shrines, why they killed and ate useful animals such as horses and why Portuguese merchants dealt in slaves. Coelho's replies to these questions were ignored, and Hideyoshi ordered the missionaries to leave Japan within twenty days. Coelho's protest that this was impossible as there was no available Portuguese ship was accepted, but the missionaries were commanded to collect in Hirado, while the port of Nagasaki, which had been placed under Jesuit jurisdiction in 1580 by the local daimyō, was returned to Japanese control. Hideyoshi then seems to have lost interest, as he took no steps to enforce the expulsion order and showed himself keen to continue the Portuguese trade.

Historians have speculated about the reasons for Hideyoshi's decision to expel the missionaries. But it is probable that the basic reason was his feeling that the church, by its claim to represent God, who was superior to all temporal rulers, was in the long run a potential threat to his rule. Why then did he not enforce the order? Perhaps at this stage he was content to give the Jesuits a warning; he was not yet as capricious and unpredictable as he became in his final years.

The Jesuits were able to continue their work so long as they behaved with circumspection, but their position was insecure. So when Valignano returned to Japan in July 1590 with the four young Christian samurai he determined to try to regularize matters and he made his way cautiously to Kyoto. In March 1591 Hideyoshi was induced to receive him in his capacity as ambassador from the Portuguese Viceroy in India. The audience, at which the four young Japanese performed on musical instruments which they had brought back from Europe, went well; and although the expulsion decree was not formally rescinded, the missionaries felt optimistic about their future.

But another threat soon became apparent. The Spanish authorities in Manila were anxious to join in the profitable trade with Japan, and Spanish Dominican and Franciscan friars were jealous of the monopoly granted by Pope Gregory XIII to the Jesuits in Japan. Hideyoshi, in his growing megalomania, had begun to cast covetous eyes at the Philippines. In 1591 he sent a message to Manila demanding an oath of submission from the governor. After various abortive efforts to develop contacts between Japan and the Philippines a mission of four Franciscan friars reached Japan from Manila in 1593. Hideyoshi was prevailed upon to permit them to visit Kyoto and even granted them the site of a former Buddhist temple, where they built a church and a small leper hospital. There, much to the alarm of the Jesuits, the Franciscans flouted Hideyoshi's earlier decrees against Christianity.

During the first half of the 1590s the church prospered, and by about 1595 the Jesuits estimated that there were some 300,000 Christians in Japan, of whom perhaps 60,000 had been baptized since the expulsion edict of 1587. But in October 1596 there occurred an incident which was to have fatal consequences for the Christian community in Japan.

A Spanish galleon, the *San Felipe*, foundered off Shikoku, while on a voyage from Manila to Mexico. The rich cargo on board was seized, and the protests of the Spanish captain and the Spanish missionaries in Kyoto were ignored. It is possible, although this has not been proved and the story may have been an invention of some Jesuit supporters, that the Spanish captain may have threatened that, to quote Sir George Sansom, 'the long arm of the King of Spain would soon reach Japan, where the Christians would rise in his favour'.[7] Hideyoshi may also have been concerned by evidence of the growing number of Christian conversions in Japan including those of a number of important people. At any rate his suspicions and fury were aroused by this incident, and in January 1597 he ordered the execution of seven Franciscans and nineteen Japanese followers in Kyoto. After torture and mutilation they were taken to Nagasaki, where they were crucified upside-down like common criminals.

The death of these twenty-six martyrs was followed by other measures against the Christians. An order was issued that all Jesuits should be expelled from Japan, except for a small number to serve the religious needs of the Portuguese merchants in Nagasaki. However, no Jesuits were martyred or tortured at this time, and many of the 125 Jesuits then in Japan evaded the expulsion order by going into hiding. Hideyoshi appears to have been mainly concerned to teach the Spaniards a lesson. Shortly before he died he gave a friendly reception to Father Joao Rodrigues, who had mastered the Japanese language and had previously acted as an interpreter for him. The Jesuits hoped that once again under Hideyoshi's successors their position might be retrieved.

The problems posed by the missionaries were not at first in the forefront of Ieyasu's mind. When Valignano arrived on his third visit to Japan in 1598 he was cautiously optimistic. Father Joao Rodrigues became the confidant of Ieyasu, and letters patent were granted allowing the fathers to use churches in Nagasaki, Kyoto and Osaka. The number of Christians increased in the early years of the seventeenth century, and optimism seemed justified. But the Jesuits lost ground as a result of the redistribution of fiefs following the battle of Sekigahara; some of the Christian daimyō in Kyūshū were replaced, and this meant that the Jesuits lost the crucial support of local daimyō. Spanish rivalry also continued to be a problem. The Spanish friar Jeronimo de Castro slipped back into Japan; when he was caught and brought before Ieyasu, he was agreeably surprised by his welcome. Ieyasu saw in the friar an opportunity to develop trade with Manila; this would strengthen his hand with the Portuguese merchants and missionaries, whom he tolerated primarily in order to keep going the profitable trade they brought with them.

In 1600 a new and significant development occurred. The Dutch ship *Liefde* was stranded off the Usuki peninsula in the province of Bungo (now Oita prefecture) in Kyūshū. The pilot was an Englishman from Gillingham in Kent, William Adams, who became known in Japan as Anjin-san.[8] Adams was brought before Ieyasu, who decided that the Englishman could be useful to him. Adams was forbidden to leave Japan, given an estate and employed in building small ocean-going ships. In due course he replaced Joao Rodrigues as Ieyasu's foreign interpreter and adviser. The Dutch sent merchants to Japan in 1609 and the British in 1613; trading posts, called 'factories' were established at Hirado in Kyūshū. The arrival of the Protestant Dutch and English further complicated the position of the Portuguese and the Jesuits. The newcomers, who had been brought up to hate papists, did their best to poison Japanese opinion against the Catholics.

In the early years of the seventeenth century Japanese trading ships also presented a threat to what had hitherto for all practical purposes been a Portuguese trading monopoly. Japanese ships permitted to take part in foreign trade (in order to distinguish them from the unauthorized Japanese pirate vessels) had to carry an official licence issued by the *bakufu*. These ships were called *go-shūin-sen*, or 'august red-seal ships'. They played an important trading role until 1635 when Japanese were prohibited from going abroad.[9] The most popular destination of Japanese ship-owners was Indo-China, especially Annam. The Philippines also attracted many Japanese traders. Japanese merchant colonies were established in Annam, and a prosperous trade developed. In the Philippines the Japanese were particularly interested in buying Chinese silks, hides and ceramics which had been exported there from China.

The Japanese seamen who went on these voyages had the pugnacity of the *wakō* pirates before them, and inevitably quarrels and friction occurred in the foreign ports which they frequented. In 1608 they caused serious trouble in Macao. Andre Pessao, who was acting governor because he was captain of the next Portuguese voyage to Japan, attacked the Japanese trouble-makers, many of whom were killed in the mêlée. However, some fifty who surrendered were spared and eventually returned to Japan. They had been forced to sign an affidavit absolving the Portuguese from blame for the death of their comrades, but when they got home they declared that this had been obtained under duress and they complained against Pessao to Ieyasu. Ieyasu at first hesitated to take action against Pessao's ship which had by then arrived at Nagasaki, but at this point another Spanish galleon, the *San Francisco*, was wrecked not far from Edo, the modern Tokyo. It was under the command of the governor of the Philippines, Don Rodrigo de Vivero y Velasco. Don Rodrigo was enchanted by Japan and, when he was brought before Ieyasu and was asked if the Spaniards could provide the bulk of the silk which the Japanese wanted, he replied enthusiastically that the Spaniards would gladly send two or three ships a year to Japan. Ieyasu was encouraged by this response and then gave his permission for an attack on Pessao's ship, the *Madre de Deus*. As it was leaving Nagasaki in early January 1610 a chance shot led to a gunpowder fire, and the ship sank. The destruction of the *Madre de Deus* caused a short break in the Portuguese trade, and suspicions against the Jesuits increased. The trade resumed in 1612 when the Portuguese ship *Sao Felipe e Santiago* reached Nagasaki, but the Portuguese trade had received a blow which was eventually to prove fatal.

It was becoming clear to the Japanese that they could do without the Portuguese trade. They reckoned that they could play the Spaniards off against the Portuguese and the Protestant Dutch and English off against the Iberian Catholics. The Dutch and then the English, moreover, fanned Japanese suspicions that the Christian missionaries were the fore-runners of Iberian colonization and attempts to dominate the Far East. These suspicions were enhanced by the arrogance of Sebastian Vizcaino, who in 1611–13 obtained Japanese permission to survey the east coast of Japan in order that Spanish galleons bound for Mexico from the Philippines might use Japanese ports if they were blown off course. Ieyasu was further irritated against the Christians by intrigues involving the Christian daimyō family of Arima in Kyūshū and by the discovery that some of his own household were Christians. Ieyasu was also warned by his advisers that Christian doctrine enjoined the faithful to obey their spiritual leaders rather than their temporal lords.

On 27 January 1614 an edict proscribing Christianity in Japan was promulgated.

This marked the beginning of a persecution which ensured that for more than two and a half centuries Christianity could not be lawfully practised in Japan. Takayama Ukon was exiled to the Philippines, and the missionaries were interned near Nagasaki until ships could fetch them away. Some seventy Jesuits sailed for Macao in November 1614, but some thirty-seven missionaries and about a hundred Japanese assistants went underground to cater for the Christian community.

In the next two decades following the issue of this decree the Christian community suffered persecutions of increasing severity, although at first the edicts against the Christians were not very effectively enforced by some of the daimyō in Kyūshū, who sympathized with their Christian followers. The position of the Christian communities was, however, made more precarious by the discovery of seven priests and numerous Christian samurai among the defenders of Osaka castle, which fell in 1615. The ambivalence of the Portuguese was a further complicating factor. The Portuguese merchants, who above all wanted to maintain the trade with Japan, gave at least tacit support to the anti-Christian measures of the *bakufu*, while the Dutch and the English collaborated with the authorities in the hope that this would enable them to eliminate their trading rivals. At the same time Portuguese ships continued to smuggle missionaries into Japan despite the fact that Ieyasu's successor, the shōgun Hidetada, issued an order in 1616 limiting foreign trade to the ports of Nagasaki and Hirado. From 1619 onwards the hunt for missionaries and their followers was pursued with increasing vigour.

In 1621 an English ship intercepted a Japanese junk off Formosa, and two Spaniards were found hiding in the cargo. They were taken to Hirado and eventually confessed that they were friars (one Augustinian, the other Dominican). Hidetada condemned to death the two priests as well as the crew of the ship and all Christian prisoners in the gaols of Suzuta and Nagasaki. In all fifty-one Christians were martyred at Nagasaki on 10 September 1622. In December 1623 Iemitsu, who had succeeded his father Hidetada as shōgun early in 1623, had fifty Christians burned at the stake in Edo to mark his assumption of office. Among the martyrs was the Jesuit Girolamo de Angelis, who had looked after small Christian communities in northern Japan and was the first European to visit the island of Ezo, the modern Hokkaidō.

Under Iemitsu the persecutions were intensified, and tortures intended to obtain apostasy were refined. Tortures included suspension head downwards in a pit and immersion in the boiling sulphurous waters of the Unzen hot springs in the neighbourhood of Nagasaki. Japanese were forbidden to travel abroad under pain of death. All Japanese were forced to register at Buddhist temples, and the rite of trampling on a religious picture, the so-called *fumi-e*, was instituted. In 1635 an artificial island, Deshima, was built in Nagasaki bay to provide secure accommodation for the remaining merchants, and all the children of mixed marriages were deported from Japan. Despite these stringent regulations and the ferocity of the continuing Japanese persecutions, five missionaries managed to enter Japan in 1637, but they were almost immediately captured.

The final tragedy occurred in 1637–8. The peasants in the Shimabara peninsula in Kyūshū and on the Amakusa Islands, many of whom were still Christians, in 1637 rose against the tyrannous extortions of the local daiymō. Some 20,000 men together with 17,000 women and children took refuge in an abandoned castle on the Shimabara peninsula. They were not all Christians, but many were and these included some Christian *rōnin* (masterless samurai). The defenders put up a stout resistance to the besieging *bakufu* troops, who were helped by a Dutch ship which joined in the bombardment. Eventually on 12 April 1638 the castle fell, and the defenders were massacred.

The Japanese authorities who had been jolted by the peasant uprising determined to put an end to the Portuguese trade, and the Portuguese ships which came in 1639 had to depart without unloading their cargo. In 1640 a mission from Macao, which came without any cargoes to plead for the resumption of the trade, was arrested, and sixty-one members of the mission and crew were executed. Thirteen crew members were spared so that they could bring back the sad tidings to Macao. Some months later the Dutch factory at Hirado was ordered to move to Nagasaki. Japan had turned its back on the world, and the period of seclusion (*sakoku*) which was to last for over two centuries had begun.

Priests continued to try to enter Japan and were martyred, although a small number under torture apostatized and were kept in a prison in Edo, which came to be called the *kirishitan yashiki*. No reliable figures can be given of the number of martyrs, but Professor Boxer has commented that 'even if the number of martyrs who endured to the end was only about two per cent of the total, the figure nevertheless constitutes a truly remarkable record when all the circumstances are considered'.[10]

Despite the harsh punishments and the pressure to conform, Christianity did not entirely die out in Japan. In remote villages in Kyūshū and in the Urakami area on the outskirts of Nagasaki the faith, which was euphemistically known as *onando-buppō* or 'back-room Buddhism', was kept alive for over two centuries. Children were baptized and catechisms taught; inevitably some superstitions crept in, but when the Urakami Christians were discovered in 1865 there was no doubt that they were true followers of the doctrines which their ancestors had learned from the Jesuit missionaries. It has been estimated that in 1865 there were some twenty thousand of these 'hidden Christians' in Japan.

Nanban Art[11]

The Jesuits may have seemed intolerant in their attitude to other religions in Japan and many of them, including Valignano, did not care for Japanese food. But they realized that if they were to make any progress in Japan they must adapt themselves to a culture which they recognized had many fine qualities. They worked hard to learn Japanese, and several works were produced by the Jesuits on the Japanese language; in particular Father Joao Rodrigues's lengthy treatise of 480 pages entitled *Arte da Lingua de Iapan*, produced at Nagasaki in 1608, was the first attempt to make a systematic analysis of the Japanese language. It was more than just a grammar, as it contained comments on pronunciation and on dialect. The Jesuits also reported in detail on the country as they saw it, and their records provided valuable material for the historian.

The Jesuits set up their own seminaries or boarding schools where Japanese could study European arts, including painting and music, as well as science and Latin. At the college for Jesuit studies, which was moved to Nagasaki from Funai in the province of Bungo (now Oita prefecture), astronomy was taught, as it was thought that this argued for the existence of God as the creator of the universe. The Portuguese also introduced Japanese students to western methods of surveying and navigation. Abraham Ortelius's *Theatrum Orbis Terrarum* showed the Japanese the position of Japan in world geography.

The Jesuits operated their own printing press in Japan between 1590 and 1614. The press was used principally to produce books for Japanese students at Jesuit seminaries. Most of these were books on religious themes in Latin and in Japanese written in Roman script. One literary work, produced in 1593, was a romanized Japanese version of Aesop's Fables; an abbreviated version of the *Heike monogatari*, written in colloquial Japanese and romanized, was bound together with the fables.

The Japanese, with their penchant for fashionable crazes, tried out Portuguese dress. They also adopted Portuguese dishes. *Kasutera*, for instance, is still made in Nagasaki; it is a sponge cake, which was said to have originated in Castile. The word *tempura*, a Japanese dish in which fish and vegetables are dipped in a batter made of eggs, flour and water and deep fried, was probably derived from the Portuguese *tempero*, meaning 'cooking'.[12] Other words of Portuguese derivation still in use in Japan include *tabako* (tobacco), *pan* (bread) and *botan* (button).

The Jesuits, in particular Giovanni Nicolo who arrived in Japan in 1583, taught talented Japanese pupils how to paint in the western style. Most of the paintings he and they produced were of a religious character, but some were of a secular nature. Japanese painters learned how to use oils, but generally used their traditional paints and combined the clarity of the Kanō school with western techniques. Western people were usually shown with some Japanese features, the eyes in pariicular being given an oriental slant.[13]

Metal or pottery items with a foreign or Christian motif were also produced at this period. Tea bowls, lacquer objects and sword furniture with such motifs have been found and are much prized by connoisseurs.

The Portuguese merchants and missionaries were also popular subjects for Japanese artists at this time. Such artists had neither studied nor been directly influenced by foreign methods. They depicted the strange-looking foreigners in accordance with Japanese traditional methods. Thus their paintings continued to ignore the western rules of perspective. The finest examples of this form of *nanban* art are the various pairs of screen showing the Portuguese *nao* arriving in Japan and disembarking missionaries and merchants.[14] One of the greatest of the exponents of this form of painting was Kanō Naizen (died 1616).

Maps were another subject of interest to contemporary Japanese artists. A number of pairs of screens depicting on one the world in the shape which they had learned from maps imported from Portugal and drawn by Abraham Ortelius and on the other Japan as they imagined it or had observed it.[15]

VIII

Peace and Seclusion: The Edo or Tokugawa Period (1616–1853)[1]

The Edo period, when Japan cut herself off from the rest of the world, apart from a limited trade with China and Holland through the port of Nagasaki, was not an era of intellectual stagnation, as the seclusion policy adopted by the *bakufu* might have implied. The peace which was enforced for over two centuries provided the basis for economic growth, and with greater prosperity and some more leisure the arts and literature found new scope. Indeed, in the Edo period some of Japan's greatest artistic and literary geniuses flourished. New forms of drama, the novel and poetry became popular. Some of Japan's most brilliant painters found opportunities to display their talents, and a new form of popular art, the wood-block print (*ukiyoe*), was developed. Buddhism failed to develop further, but Confucian studies were encouraged, and there was a revival of interest in Shintō.

The political and social system was, however, rigid and inflexible. While more land was brought under cultivation and trade and crafts were greatly developed, the system was unable to adapt to the changes needed to meet external threats or to cope with natural and man-made disasters. The burden of providing for some two million samurai, who had no real function when the country was at peace, and for the extravagances of the shōguns required ever-increasing taxation of the oppressed peasantry. The arrival of the western powers at Japan's door provided the catalyst for change, but the system had by then ceased to be able to cope and had to be replaced.

The Tokugawa System and Life in the Edo Period

Ieyasu and his successors had two main objectives. These were to ensure that their hegemony over the Japanese islands was unchallengable and to provide handsomely for themselves and their followers. The main instrument to achieve these ends was confiscation or escheatment of estates of any daimyō who might seem to be a threat to the Tokugawa. It has been estimated that, after the battle of Sekigahara, Ieyasu had direct control of about one-quarter of the assessed revenue of the land. His successors took over large additional estates. The estates of the Tokugawa and of the *fudai* diamyō well exceeded the total of the estates of the *tozama* daimyō.

One of the main ways in which hegemony was ensured was through the *fudai* daimyō, who were placed in strategic positions throughout the country. The Tokugawa made certain that they knew what was happening throughout Japan by an efficient intelligence system. The censors (*metsuke*) appointed by the *bakufu*

139

had to report regularly on all the daimyō. The loyalty of the daimyō was also confirmed by the *sankin-kōtai* (alternate attendance) system, formalized in 1635 by Iemitsu the third Tokugawa Shōgun. This required the daimyō to establish residences in Edo and to reside there in alternate years or in the case of hereditary vassals in alternate half years. When they returned to their fiefs they were required to leave their women and children in the capital as hostages. One of the functions of the barriers established on the roads outside Edo, such as the barrier by Lake Hakone near Mount Fuji, was to check that women and children were not smuggled out and that arms were not smuggled into the capital. As the daimyō were expected to travel with retinues numbering between 150 and 300 persons along designated routes under the control of the *bakufu*, their journeys were easily supervised. The costs of the journeys and of the daimyō's residences in Edo, together with the expense of providing lavish presents to the shōgun and his minions on each arrival in the capital, was a heavy burden on daimyō revenues and forced many into debt to the money-lenders.

The Tokugawa family was divided into three main houses. These were the daimyō of Owari (Nagoya), of Kii (Wakayama prefecture) and of Mito (Ibaragi prefecture). These families were known as the *go-sanke*. In the eighteenth century three new Tokugawa households were established by the shōgun Yoshimune (1684–1751) to provide a check on the power of the main houses. The new families, called the *go-sankyō*, were granted lesser estates but as they were closer to the main house (the *honke*) they were more likely to be called on to provide a successor if the main line failed.

Society was rigidly divided into four classes. These were the so-called *shi-nō-kō-shō*, or samurai, farmer, artisan and merchant. There was very little mobility between the classes. The samurai were supposed to be the élite. The farmers were in theory highly regarded, as it was recognized that they provided the essentials for life, but their treatment did not reflect the theory. They were squeezed unmercifully. The artisans managed a fair life by organizing themselves in guilds. The samurai regarded the merchants with contempt, but they had to use the services of the merchants to dispose of their rice and to provide them with funds. The merchants developed much profitable business in the growing towns of Japan.

There were various grades of samurai under the daimyō. The *hatamoto* were samurai with revenues of less than 10,000 *koku*. In the middle of the seventeenth century there were about 5,000 *hatamoto*, but efforts were made in later years to reduce these numbers. The *gokenin* were the lowest-ranking of the direct vassals of the Tokugawa, with revenues of less than 260 *koku*; they were primarily employed in minor official or military posts. By 1800 there were reputed to be about 20,000 *gokenin*.

The *rōnin* were samurai who had no liege lord and were therefore unemployed. Many had to seek a living by becoming teachers of military arts. After the storming of Osaka castle the large numbers of *rōnin* who managed to avoid being killed presented a social problem, and there was an abortive *rōnin* rising in 1651; but the numbers declined as their families died out or took up other occupations. The *rōnin* nevertheless remained a problem throughout the Edo period.

The samurai class probably numbered about 2 million in a population which during the Edo period fluctuated around 25 million. Their duties were to serve their lords, and they were trained to regard loyalty to their master as the paramount virtue. They must be prepared to accept death readily if this served his purposes; indeed, until the practice was forbidden in 1663 many senior retainers of a daimyō would commit suicide, *junshi*, when their lord died. *Seppuku* or *harakiri*, both of which mean cutting open the belly, was the correct ritual form of suicide for a samurai, but in practice after the first cut a friend was usually there to ease the agony by cutting off the suicide's head with his sword. The samurai was entitled, under a clause called *kirisute-gomen*, to kill members of the lower classes if he was seriously provoked on a point of honour. He could also try out his sword on condemned criminals. Serious attempts were made to refine the code of the samurai (later called *bushido*), but many samurai in the peaceful times which the Edo authorities achieved were both bored and impoverished. The vendetta, or *kataki-uchi*, which became another popular theme for Japanese drama, was not only a duty; it provided excitement and an opportunity to practise swordsmanship.

The most famous of all Japanese vendettas was one which began in 1701. According to the story books, Asano Naganori, lord of Akō in Harima province (now part of Hyōgo prefecture), was asked to serve as one of the shōgun's representatives, when the envoys from the Emperor in Kyoto arrived to present New Year greetings. He was supposed to receive advice on the correct etiquette to be followed from Kira Yoshinaka, the shōgun's chief of protocol. But Kira, who apparently thought that Asano should have given him a handsome reward for his advice, allegedly behaved arrogantly towards Asano, who was provoked into drawing his sword on Kira within the shōgun's castle. This was a serious offence; Asano was condemned to commit suicide there and then, and his fief was confiscated. Kira escapted without punishment. Forty-seven loyal retainers from Akō, led by Oishi Yoshio, vowed to avenge their lord's death. After two years, during which the forty-seven pretended to pursue a life of dissipation, they mounted a raid on Kira's mansion and killed Kira, who tried to hide from them. They then took Kira's head to the temple of Sengakuji in Edo to present it at the grave of their master. Although in accordance with the code of the samurai the retainers had behaved correctly, they had taken the law into their own hands and had to be punished. They were therefore ordered to commit suicide; this took place in February 1703, and their graves at Sengakuji are one of the tourist sites of Tokyo. In 1706 the great dramatist Chikamatsu Monzaemon wrote a puppet drama about the incident, but the most famous play based on the incident was the *Kanadehon Chushingura* or 'The Treasury of the Loyal Retainers', produced as a *kabuki* play in 1748 by Takeda Izumo and two others.

In the Edo period there were two other social classes. These were the *hinin* (literally, non-humans) and the *eta* (outcasts). The former were beggars who were subject to forced labour and given such tasks as dealing with dead bodies and people with contagious diseases. Some were born into the class and some were condemned to it because of crimes they had committed or because they were too poor for anything else. Travelling pedlars, actors and some craftsmen such as makers of bamboo objects were also regarded as *hinin*. The *eta* were tanners and butchers and performed other tasks generally regarded as unclean.

Criminal 'justice' in the Edo period was arbitrary and excessively harsh. Torture was commonplace and execution a regular form of punishment. Relations and associates were also often made to suffer with the criminal.

The fiefs were largely self-governing, and the *bakufu* did not usually interfere, unless there were reports of serious misgovernment or of activities which might pose a threat to the shōgunate. One frequent problem was that of succession. There was no absolute rule of primogeniture, and succession quarrels, called *o-ie-sōdō*, occurred in many fiefs (and became themes for Japanese dramas). The fiefs which did not belong to the Tokugawa or their immediate vassals were not directly taxed, but the daimyō were expected to make a significant contribution to building works. In the early part of the eighteenth century a special tax (*agemai*) was levied on the daimyō to meet a deficit in the shōgun's finances. This amounted to one per cent of revenues on top of the other compulsory contributions. It was very unpopular and was later withdrawn.

At the centre in Edo the administration was carried out through a hierarchy of officials. At the top, nominally under the shōgun, were the *tairō* (great elders). Under Hideyoshi there had been five *tairō*, but under the Tokugawa the numbers were reduced first to three, then to two and finally to one. The appointment was filled only from time to time and when necessary. The function of the *tairō* was to act as supreme adviser to the shōgun and to provide a regency during the minority of the shōgun. Next came the *rōjū* (*gorōjū*) (elders). They had advisory and administrative functions. These included supervision of the affairs of the shōgun's domains and relations with the imperial court, where the shōgun's representative held the office of *shoshidai*. There were four *rōjū*, who served one at a time for a month. They communicated with the shōgun through the chamberlains (*sobayōnin*).

The *hyōjōsho* was a council to which the *rōjū* and certain commissioners belonged. These were the *machi-bugyō* (city magistrate/administrator), the *jisha-bugyō* (commissioner for shrines and monasteries), the *kanjō-bugyō* (financial controller) and the *ō-metsuke* (chief censor). The *hyōjōsho* also had some judicial responsibilities. Under the *rōjū* were the *wakadoshiyori* (young elders); they were first appointed in 1631. There were usually four to six *wakadoshiyori*, who were responsible for supervising the *hatamoto*, controlling craftsmen and superintending buildings and public works.

Revenues came primarily from assessments on land. The tax was at the high level of 40 per cent of the crop in the case of paddy and an equivalent in cash for other crops. This was increased by the shōgun Yoshimune in 1727 to 50 per cent. The policy of the *bakufu* was to tax the peasants to exhaustion. One of the *rōjū* who was an advocate of harsh measures is reputed to have remarked in the eighteenth century: 'Peasants are like sesame seed. The more you squeeze them the more oil you get.'

Agriculture was the mainstay of the Japanese economy in the Edo period as well as the main source of revenue of the *bakufu*. But the increase in trade and the oppressive regime in the countryside led to a migration from the countryside to the towns. This meant that in order to meet the exorbitant demands of the tax collectors the land had to be made to produce more and more. This was achieved by ever more intensive farming using every bit of human and other manure and improved farm implements. Much effort was put into developing irrigation and building embankments to reduce flooding. New strains of plants were also produced by experimentation.

Farming villages were reorganized following the 'sword hunt', instituted by

Left, Wood statue of Amida Buddha by Jōchō (1053) in the Byōdōin temple at Uji. *Centre,* Wood statue of a Bodhissattva, again by Jōchō, on the wall of the Amida hall in the Byōdōin at Uji.

Gold lacquer over wood statue of Amida Buddha looking over the left shoulder *(Mikaeri-bosatsu)* in the Eikandō, Zenrinji temple, Kyoto (11th century).

Above, Amida Hall of Jōruriji temple, southern part of Kyoto prefecture (12th century).

Below, Nine statues of Amida Buddha (gold lacquer over wood) in the Jōruriji temple, southern part of Kyoto prefecture.

Above, Kondō (main hall) of Daigoji temple — Kamakura period (probably 13th century).
Below, Amida Hall of Hōkaiji temple, southern Kyoto (11th century).

Below, Wood statue of priest Kūya, the 10th-century founder of Rokuharamitsuji temple, Kyoto — Kamakura period (13th century). Rokuharamitsuji temple, Kyoto.
Right, Wood statue of the sculptor Unkei (13th century). Rokuharamitsuji temple, Kyoto.
Bottom right, Wood statue of Raijin — the thunder god (13th century). Rengeōin (Sanjūsangendō), Kyoto.
Bottom left, Wood statue of Basu Sennin — one of the twenty-eight Buddhist spirits (13th century). Rengeōin (Sanjūsangendō), Kyoto.

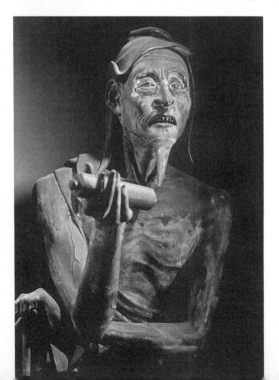

即於佛前受三自歸
於是閻浮提中唯此
長者為優婆塞爾初
獲得供養三寶
爾時又育耶舍朋類
中出家備道各自今
五十長者子聞佛出
世又聞耶舍於佛法
言世聞今者有无上
尊長者子耶舍聰慧
辯了才藝魚人乃能
捨其豪族棄五欲樂
毀形守志而為沙門
我等今者復何顧戀
不出家耶作是念已
共詣佛所未至之間
逢見如來相好殊特

ove, Buddhist sutra with
strations depicting the life
Buddha (8th century).
awa museum of art, Osaka.
ht, Detail of the Tale of
ji scroll (12th century).
ō Museum of Art, Tokyo.

Right, Detail of the Chōjūgiga scroll (13th century). Kōzanji temple, Kyoto.
Below, Landscape painting by Sesson (16th century). Tokyo National Museum.

Left, Garden of the Sanzenin temple, northern Kyoto. Dates from the Heian period (9th – 12th century).
Below, Stone garden of the Zen temple of Ryōanji, Kyoto. Constructed about 1500.

Above, Tea house and garden in the grounds of Ryōanji temple, Kyoto. Much later than the stone garden.
Below, *Chōzubachi* (water basin) at Ryōanji temple, Kyoto.

Hideyoshi, which had ensured that farmers could no longer be fighting men. The family-type relationship between the leading farmers, *honbyakushō*, and their retainers gave way to a division between landowning farmers and tenant cultivators. At the same time village autonomy increased; headmen were chosen and families organized in groups of five, the so-called *goningumi*; this organization provided a basis for mutual help at planting and harvest time as well as in time of trouble. It also helped the tax collectors, who made the group responsible for producing the required revenue. In accordance with Japanese tradition the group could be made to suffer if one of their number committed a criminal act.

The land surveys instituted by Hideyoshi were continued in the Edo period; they were supposed to be conducted once every ten years. They provided a constant source of dispute, as the peasants understandably tried to mislead the surveyors to underestimate the likely crops from land newly brought under cultivation. Land reclamation became increasingly important during the Edo period as the burden of taxation grew.

The life of the peasantry was hard. They were rarely left with adequate rice for their needs and had to make do with substitutes such as millet and buckwheat, supplemented with vegetables and *miso*, made from fermented soya beans. Natural disasters were frequent. Earthquakes destroyed embankments, typhoons caused flooding, fires destroyed villages and granaries, insects and plant diseases decimated crops, and climatic variations such as cold summers or dry rainy seasons caused poor harvests resulting in localized or more general famine conditions. Nevertheless there were improvements in the rural standard of life if only because of the enforced peace and the demand from the growing cities for vegetables, fruit and other agricultural byproducts. Cotton was produced in increasing quantities from the sixteenth century, and the demand for silk led to widespread sericulture in areas where the mulberry could be easily cultivated.

Edo had a population of about half a million at the end of the seventeenth century and by the end of the eighteenth century it contained nearly a million people. This growth occurred despite the many disasters which struck the city. The houses, being built of wood, burned easily, and fires were a constant threat. Particularly disastrous fires destroyed much of the city in 1657, in 1772 and in 1806, but fires were an almost daily occurrence, and many of these were aggravated by the frequent earthquakes which are still a feature of life in Tokyo. Overcrowding made the city vulnerable to disease. Violence and disorder were rife in the city, especially in the early part of the period, when many lawless *rōnin* and other vagabonds roamed the streets. But later on the authorities ensured peace at least after dark by erecting barriers between the different parts of the city which were closed at night. This did not, however, prevent the inhabitants enjoying night life. Edo grew because it was the adminstrative centre of the country and because the daimyō all had to have large residences there. Temples and shrines proliferated. Every section of the city had its public bath-house, which with the barber's shop provided gossip and news at a time when there were no newspapers and when even news-sheets had to be produced surreptitiously and disguised as advertisements.

To supply the wants of the daimyō and their retainers craftsmen and shopkeepers congregated in the city. At first the shopkeepers in a particular trade had shops in the same street. Among the first merchants to develop a major stake in the retail trade were the Mitsui family. They came originally from Matsuzaka near Ise, where they were pawnbrokers and sake brewers. In 1627 one Mitsui Toshitsugu opened a small draper's shop in Edo. This was called the Echigoya. Members of the family also took up money exchange business and developed a system of promissory notes. From these small beginnings there energed in due course the great Mitsui trade and industrial empire. The Echigoya for its part became the prestigious department store chain called Mitsukoshi.

Edo naturally had its pleasure quarters. The Yoshiwara (meaning 'reed plain') was established in 1617. It moved to a location in the eastern outskirts of old Edo after the disastrous fire of 1657; it continued there in one form or another until prostitution was formally banned in 1958. The Yoshiwara was surrounded by walls, and there was only one gate to ensure that customers should not leave without paying for their pleasures and to prevent the prostitutes escaping. (Most of the girls had been sold into prostitution by poor parents.) The streets of the Yoshiwara were lined with willow trees in accordance with ancient Chinese tradition. The total number of licensed prostitutes in the gay quarters of Edo varied between two and three thousand. They were divided between some two hundred houses. There was a carefully devised hierarchy among these ladies of the town. The highest class were the *tayū*, who can be described as courtesans. Below these were various grades of prostitutes (*jorō*), but numerous other words such as *yūjo* ('play-girl') were used to describe these women. Assignations were made through intermediaries in 'tea-houses' in the quarter. The lower-class prostitutes were put on display behind wooden bars to entice potential customers. Geisha were entertainers and were not supposed to compete with the courtesans. The first geisha in the Edo period were in fact men, but the occupation was soon taken over by women, whose function was to provide entertainment primarily by singing and dancing. They did have patrons with whom they lived, but they were not (and are not) prostitutes.

The largest city after Edo was Kyoto, which had a population of about 400,000 at the end of the seventeenth century. Although the court was poor and of little account in the Edo period, Kyoto remained an important religious and educational centre throughout the period. Japan's most important commercial city was Osaka, with a population little less than that of Kyoto. It became the centre of the rice trade. Rice was brought by coastal ships from areas such as the present Niigata on the Japan Sea coast, which had a surplus over local requirements. Rice was also shipped to Osaka from other fiefs in need of money or other goods which were unobtainable locally. The Osaka rice brokers made a lucrative business lending money to indigent daimyō and samurai against their rice stipends. They soon developed a market in rice futures, and many merchants made large fortunes. But as Japan was totally dependent on rice grown in Japan and as Japanese harvests varied greatly according to the prevailing weather patterns the price of rice tended to fluctuate wildly. At times in the eighteenth century it was so low that the farmer and the landlord received very little for their surpluses. At other times after some natural disaster or crop failure prices rose so high that famine developed. The worst of these periods of fluctuating prices was from about 1735 to 1745 during the shōgunate of Yoshimune. In some parts of the country rice riots, called *uchikowashi*, occurred with increasing frequency; the first such riot took place in 1733.

Most of the main towns of the daimyō, the castle towns (*jōka-machi*), developed

144

apace in the Edo period. There were a number, including Kanazawa, Sendai and Kagoshima, which had populations of over 50,000. It is hardly surprising, therefore, that the townspeople (*chōnin*) came to form a distinct group within the society of the Edo period. They were the patrons of the popular arts of the time and the forerunners of the entrepreneurs of the new Japan which emerged after the restoration of 1868. They worked hard making money and developed their own ethics on the basis of their interpretation of Confucian teaching. The Edokko, or Edo 'cockney', was a freer spender than his Osaka counterpart, but both were equally despised for their plebeian ways (*chōninkonjō*, that is, 'townsman's way of thinking') by the snobbish and arrogant samurai who had lost their *raison d'être*.

The Japanese road system was greatly improved during the Edo period. The most important highways radiating from Edo were the Tōkaidō ('eastern sea road') and Nakasendō ('middle of the mountains road'), both of which led to Kyoto, the Kōshūkaidō, leading to the castle town of Kōfu by Mount Fuji, and the Tōhokudō, leading to the north-eastern provinces. The old routes from Kyoto to the west such as the Sanyōdō ('road on the sunny side of the mountains') along the southern coast of Honshū and the Sanindō ('road on the shadow side of the mountains') along the northern coast to the straits of Shimonoseki remained important for the local daimyō. However, as the land journey involved much hard travelling over mountain passes and rivers which in the rainy season could be impassable many travellers from Kyūshū preferred to travel by sea through the Inland Sea as far as Osaka.

The Tōkaidō has been immortalized in a famous series of wood-block prints by Utagawa Hiroshige (1797–1858) under the title of the 'Fifty-Three Stations of the Tōkaidō' (*Tōkaidō gojūsan-tsugi*). An amusing account of what it was like to travel on the Tōkaidō in the first half of the nineteenth century is contained in the novel *Hizakurige* by Jippensha Ikku (1765–1831).[2]

The various stations included inns,[3] 'tea-houses' and stables. At these stations coolies and horses could be hired for the next stage. There was no wheeled traffic on these highways. The roads were rough and crossed many mountain passes as well as wide rivers without bridges over which travellers had to be carried by men who waded through the water. People travelled either on horseback or on foot, or they were carried in palanquins. These were borne by two or four men. The simpler type were called *kago* (basket) and were little more than a bamboo frame. The more elaborate sort used by daimyō and senior officials were called *norimono* (riding thing). These had blinds and could be used by aristocratic ladies. Despite the slowness and discomforts of road journeys many Japanese were frequent travellers. Apart from business trips between cities many pilgrimages were made to important shrines and temples. Ise with the shrine of the sun goddess was the objective of many pilgrims, but famous temples such as Zenkōji (Nagano city) were also much visited.

The roads were not suitable for bulk freight traffic. Runners did, however, carry some supplies as well as messages. For instance, mackerel (*saba*) were brought to Kyoto by teams of fast coolies from the port of Obama in Wakasa province, now part of Fukui prefecture, over what came to be called the Sabakaidō ('mackerel road').

After the isolation of Japan from the outside world in 1639 the construction of large vessels capable of making long voyages across the seas was banned.

Owing to the precipitous nature of most of the Japanese islands few rivers are suited to goods traffic, although some such as the Yodo river between Lake Biwa and Osaka and some others in the Kantō plain, such as the Sumida, did carry a fair amount of traffic. In the main, however, goods in bulk had to be transported by small coastal ships or junks. These were fairly primitive affairs with a small cabin at the stern and a single hemp sail. They carried some thirty or more hands to row the boat if the winds failed. In order to bring rice supplies to Edo and Osaka from ports on the Japan Sea coast, two annual circuits of Honshū were arranged. One, called the eastern circuit, went through the Tsugaru straits between Honshū and Hokkaidō, while the other, or western circuit, went through the straits of Shimonoseki between Honshū and Kyūshū up the Inland Sea to Osaka. There were also regular sailings between Osaka and Edo. One line called the Higaki (diamond) was started in about 1620. Another line called the Taru (barrel) was started in about 1660. By paying 'thank' money to the authorities the two lines managed to fix a monopoly which was only abolished in 1830.

Because of the problem of predicting storms, many ships foundered. Some were blown off course, and a number of Japanese seamen were shipwrecked off the Kurile Islands or Kamchatka where the Russians were beginning to settle. Under the exclusion edicts Japanese who had been shipwrecked were not permitted to return to Japan. Some were thus forced to settle in Russia. One Japanese called Denbei who had been stranded in Kamchatka was sent to Moscow and in 1702 was received by Peter the Great. Another called Kōdaiyū in the time of Catherine the Great taught Japanese at Irkutsk. Some in the early part of the nineteenth century even drifted across the Pacific to the shores of North America. The first of these seems to have been one Jūkichi, whose ship sailed from its Japanese port in October 1813. His companions all died, but he was rescued by an American ship in March 1815. Two shipwrecked Japanese seamen who got to America, Joseph Heco and Dankichi, later served as interpreters to the American and the British legations after the reopening of Japan in the middle of the nineteenth century.[4]

Foreign Relations and Trade

Ezo, the modern Hokkaidō, was considered remote and inhospitable by the Japanese in pre-Edo times and had been largely left to the indigenous Ainu, whom the Japanese despised as hairy savages and whom they had forced out of northern Japan in earlier centuries. The only fief on the island was Matsumae on the north coast of the Tsugaru strait. Indeed, in early maps the whole island of Ezo is sometimes referred to as Matsumae. The lords of Matsumae were *tozama* daimyō with an assessed revenue of 30,000 *koku*; in fact the fief produced no rice, being too far north for rice growing until new strains of cold-resistant rice were developed in the twentieth century, but it had income from gold, timber and fisheries. The fief was run on independent lines, and at first the Tokgawa shōguns showed no interest in the area. For their part the Matsumae fief made little or no attempt to explore Ezo let alone the Kurile Islands. However, the Russian presence in the north forced the *bakufu* to pay some attention to their northern borders.

In 1792 Lieutenant Adam Laxman in a ship called *Ekaterina* from Okhotsk proceeded on an expedition sent by Catherine the Great down the Kurile Islands to Ezo. On his arrival in Nemuro on the north-east coast of Ezo he was kindly treated by Japanese officials and managed to repatriate a number of Japanese castaways including Kōdaiyu. After procrastinating in a way which became habitual for the *bakufu* when dealing with unwelcome foreigners, the authorities told Laxman that he would have to go to Nagasaki, which was the only port that could be visited by foreigners. Laxman sailed away, and it was not until 1804 that a Russian warship with Vasilii Rezanov as official ambassador arrived in Nagasaki. He was eventually turned away, but took his revenge by organizing raids on Ezo and the Kurile Islands where there were Japanese outposts. The Japanese then began to improve their defences, and the famous Japanese cartographer Inō Tadataka (1745–1818) was commissioned in 1800 to survey the island. When in 1811 a Russian ship, the *Diana*, called at places in the southern Kuriles, Vasilii Golovnin, the captain, was captured, cruelly treated and imprisoned for two years at Hakodate.

In 1808 HMS *Phaeton*, searching for Dutch prizes in the Napoleonic Wars, called at Nagasaki and only left after supplies were provided. In 1797 an American ship, the *Eliza*, had called at Nagasaki and returned annually until 1803. The Japanese seclusion policy was being challenged.

Despite the Draconian nature of Japan's seclusion laws, the country was not completely insulated from the outside world. Trade was limited to exchanges with China and Holland, but numerous Chinese junks visited Nagasaki every year, and there was a Chinese merchant colony in the port. The trade with China and Holland, however, caused some economic problems, because imports were generally paid for in silver and copper, and this led to a loss of specie. As a result trade was formally limited in the early part of the eighteenth century to thirty Chinese vessels and two Dutch vessels each year, and the amount of silver and copper permitted to be exported was controlled. The main Japanese imports from China were silk, skins, sugar, medicines, books and paintings. None of these items, except perhaps medicines, could be described as necessities. Japanese imports from Europe via Holland were even less necessary, but Dutch studies (*rangaku*) became of increasing importance as the Edo period wore on (see page 154).

The Dutch provided Japan's one window to the West. The official visits to Edo which were made almost annually by the Dutch *opperhoofd*, the head of the Dutch settlement on Deshima, also add interesting sidelights on Japanese life under the Tokugawa shōguns. Most of the Dutch merchants were dull fellows, but their life on Deshima was monotonous and boring. They were not allowed to leave the island except on rare occasions and under escort. They could not practise the Christian religion, and the only women allowed were selected Japanese mistresses. Fortunately some of their doctors were outstanding characters. Engelbert Kaempfer (1651–1716), Carl Peter Thunberg (1743–1822) and Philip Franz von Siebold (1796–1866) were exceptional men and good observers. Kaempfer and von Siebold came from Germany, Thunberg from Sweden. Kaempfer has described how the Dutch mission were received by the shōgun and his courtiers and presented their 'gifts'.[5] On the first occasion Kaempfer was asked all sorts of questions by inquisitive Japanese officials. When he went again in 1692 the Dutch visitors were forced to amuse the Japanese by play-acting, dancing and singing. The Japanese seemed to regard the Dutch as if they were monkeys in a zoo.

Trade was also conducted indirectly with China through the Ryūkyū (Loo Choo) Islands[6] to the south of Kyūshū. In the early Edo period the Satsuma fief asserted suzerainty over the islands and began to develop the sugar resources of the islands.

The Tokugawa Shōguns

One of the main reasons why the Tokugawa shōgunate continued for over two and a half centuries was because the regime provided the internal peace which Japan so badly needed after centuries of civil strife. Its survival owed little to the capabilities of the Tokugawa shōguns after the death in 1651 of Iemitsu, the third shōgun.

The second shōgun, Hidetada (1579–1632), had served as a general under his father. The dual regime from 1605, when Ieyasu handed over the post of shōgun to Hidetada until his death in 1616, did not always work smoothly. Ieyasu from Sunpu (Shizuoka) retained much of the real power in his own hands, but Hidetada had some of his father's patience, and this ensured that friction was kept within bounds. Hidetada's period as shōgun (he handed over the reins to his son Iemitsu in 1623) was one of consolidation.

Iemitsu (1604–51) was determined to ensure that his personal rule was not challenged. After his father's death in 1632 he forced his brother, who might have challenged him, to commit suicide. He made it clear to the daimyō that he intended to have effective control and, in addition to instituting the *sankinkōtai* system, he treated the daimyō in a high-handed manner and did not hesitate to confiscate lands wherever he saw an opportunity to do so. He was particularly zealous in his persecution of the remaining Christians and was a cruel and odious tyrant.

Iemitsu's successor, Ietsuna (1641–80), suffered from ill health and was weak and of no account. When he died there was some talk of reverting to the Kamakura pattern and appointing a shōgun from the imperial family; but one of Iemitsu's ladies, the daughter of a greengrocer in Kyoto, had a son, Tsunayoshi (1646–1709), and she intrigued effectively to get him appointed shōgun. She favoured Chinese studies and Buddhist practices including the protection of animals; Tsunayoshi followed her advice in these and other matters. But he was also determined to assert himself, and his behaviour tended to be arbitrary and excessive, suggesting that he was abnormal. A Buddhist monk thought that Tsunayoshi had no male heir because in a previous existence he must have taken life. As Tsunayoshi was born in the year of the dog, he was advised to pay special attention to the welfare of dogs. He insisted that the city of Edo should build special shelters for dogs, which were to be addressed only in honorific language. Not surprisingly he was known as 'the dog shōgun'. He appears to have liked pretty boys as much as girls. His successors, Ienobu (reigned 1709–13) and Ietsugu (reigned 1713–16), were of no importance.

The eighth shōgun, Yoshimune (1684–1751), on the other hand, did play a significant role during his time as shōgun from 1716 to 1745. Before being chosen to succeed Ietsugu he had been head of the Kii branch of the Tokugawa family. He created the three junior Tokugawa families, known as the *go-sankyō*. He was determined to exercise his personal authority and refused to be ruled by the bureaucrats. He was aware of public grievances and in 1721 he instituted a box, called a *meyasubako*, at the gates of Edo castle into which citizens could insert complaints and petitions. He recognized that there were serious problems in the economy and instituted the first of a series of reforms which the regime hoped would solve their problems. Unfortunately he and later reformers did not understand the real nature of the issues facing Japan or how to deal with them. One of the main problems of his time was the price of rice (he was given the popular name of 'the rice shōgun').

Yoshimune was succeeded by his son Ieshige, who ruled from 1745 to 1760. Ieshige suffered from ill health and had a speech defect. He was popularly known as *shōben kubō* ('the pissing prince'). His successor, Ieharu (reigned 1760–86) was little more than a puppet in the hands of Tanuma Okitsugu (1719–88), who became a byword for corruption.

The eleventh shōgun, Ienari (1773–1841), held the title for longer than any other Tokugawa shōgun. He came from the Hitotsubashi branch of the family and he had the help in his early years of one of the outstanding reformers and administrators of the Tokugawa regime, Matsudaira Sadanobu. After Sadanobu's retirement in 1793 Ienari had the good fortune to live in times when harvests were good. He produced some 55 children by 40 consorts who had 900 female attendants. He used his children to good effect by arranging marriages for them in a way which strengthened his regime. Ieyoshi (1792–1853), Iesada (1824–58) and Iemochi (1846–66), the twelfth, thirteenth and fourteenth shōguns, were not important in themselves. The last and fifteenth shōgun, Yoshinobu or Keiki (1837–1913), is mentioned in the next chapter.

Economic Problems and Attempts at Reform

Confucianism provided the Japanese leaders in the Edo period with their political philosophy, but the Confucianists had little understanding of economic issues and how to deal with them, although they did not hesitate to offer advice on such matters.

The issues were much the same throughout the period. The Japanese economy remained essentially agricultural; it had to support the heavy burden of a large unproductive class of samurai. Food production depended greatly on the vagaries of the climate. Prices fluctuated wildly. Producers and consumers suffered, and, although living standards in general improved during the period, economic unrest became endemic.

The solutions attempted tended to be variations on the themes of higher taxes, increased production, tinkering with the coinage, cuts in stipends and expenditure, and Draconian but ineffective sumptuary laws. Although there were many lesser attempts at reform, there were three main movements.

The first were the so-called Kyōhō reforms (named after Kyōhō era, 1716–36) instituted by the shōgun Yoshimune. He saw that the *bakufu*'s finances were in a serious state and he wanted to return to the spirit of Ieyasu's times. He called for retrenchment and a cut in living standards. He reduced the stipends of the *hatamoto* and the *gokenin*. He demanded a special contribution from all daimyō amounting to 100 *koku* for each 10,000 *koku* of their revenue. He gave orders for more land to be brought under cultivation and instituted various development schemes. His sumptuary rules were detailed. For instance, nightdresses, coverlets, mattresses and so forth were not to be of fine embroidered fabrics, and the number of palanquins at a wedding reception was not to exceed ten. Yoshimune also supported the revision of the currency which had been effected under his predecessor on the advice of the Confucian scholar Arai Hakuseki (1656–1725). The gold coin known as a *koban* had had a gold content at the beginning of the seventeenth century of 85.65 per cent. By 1695 it had been debased so far that it contained only 56.4 per cent gold. Confidence in the currency declined, and counterfeiting increased. New coins introduced in 1714 reverted to the old standard, and prices in gold and silver stabilized. Yoshimune's efforts were partially successful in restoring some stability to the economy, but he failed to tackle effectively the problem of the unproductive samurai and he took a restrictive attitude to foreign trade which might have been developed to achieve a better equilibrium between demand and supply. These failures inevitably meant that problems would recur.

The second major effort to reform the system came with the so-called Kansei reforms of 1787–93. These were proposed and carried out by Matsudaira Sadanobu (1758–1829), a grandson of the shōgun Yoshimune and chief of the *rōjū*. They followed a series of natural disasters, peasant uprisings and urban riots. Revenues had fallen, and inflation had risen, while corruption at the centre had become ever more scandalous during the period when Tanuma Okitsugu had been chamberlain to the shōgun (*sobayōnin*). In 1787 the Treasury was almost empty. Instructions were once again issued for a reduction in expenditure and for an increase in tax collecting. Sadanobu also ordered a reduction in the rate of interest charged by rice brokers lending money to the shōgun's retainers. This led to trouble between the samurai and the merchants and proved unenforceable. His efforts to control prices and limit commercial activities turned out to be equally unworkable. Gold coins were revalued and silver pieces recoined, while the rate of exchange was manipulated to the advantage of Edo over Osaka. Foreign trade was further curtailed, and a number of monopolies which had developed were abolished. Further sumptuary rules were declared. Peasants who had left the land and gone to the towns in search of work were sent back to their villages, and some of the worst abuses of the tax collection system were abolished. But the peasants continued to be squeezed, and rural disaffection remained. The reforms provided some temporary alleviation to Japan's economic problems, but in the main it was a series of good harvests which kept the economic problems from reaching crisis point.

The third major series of reforms were the Tempō reforms of 1830–44, carried out by Mizuno Tadakuni (1794–1851), daimyō of Hamamatsu. A series of poor harvests in the 1830s led to a renewal of unrest. In 1837 rioting in Osaka, organized by Oshio Heihachirō, led to bitter fighting. The riots were suppressed, but in the course of the struggle thousands of houses and store houses were destroyed by fire. Riots followed in other parts of Japan. In the same year Tadakuni, one of the senior *rōjū*, was made responsible for finance and became the effective head of the government. His policies were puritanical and reactionary. He repeated Sadanobu's orders that peasants were to be returned to their villages from the towns. He instituted further land reclamation. He tried to keep down prices by administrative fiat. He abolished merchant monopoly associations (such as the *kabunakama*)[7] and took other steps to discourage commercial activity, at the same time levying taxes on the merchant class. He aimed to improve the currency by reminting certain coins. He redefined the sumptuary rules, outlawed gambling and dealt sternly with corrupt officials. He ordered the samurai to practise the military arts and took other measures to strengthen Japanese defences including training in firearms and the casting of cannon. He also ordered improvements in Japan's coastal defences. His reforms were followed in many of the fiefs, including the Tokugawa Mito fief, where Tokugawa Nariaki had become the daimyō in 1829. Among other fiefs to adopt reforms were Saga and Satsuma (in Kyūshū) and Chōshū (western Honshū). The reforms were once again only partially and temporarily successful.[8]

The economic problems of the first half of the nineteenth century in Japan required much greater flexibility, imagination and initiative than was possible under the rigid Tokugawa system of government.

Intellectual Trends and Education

The comparative absence of civil strife and increased prosperity meant that more resources could be devoted to education, but the rigid system of the Tokugawa *bakufu* was inimical to freedom of thought. The authorities wanted only orthodox philosophers who would support the maintenance of the existing system. In these circumstances Confucianism with its emphasis on hierarchy and harmony and its conservative morality naturally found favour with the ruling class. Confucianists served as government advisers, but the meritocratic principles of Confucianism were never allowed to upset the Japanese hierarchical structure based on birth in a specific class. Confucian attitudes permeated ethical thinking among all classes of society. The samurai code (*bushidō*) drew on Confucian principles. Buddhism and Shintō were also made to conform to Confucian concepts. Education was essentially Confucian.

The predominant form of Confucianism in the Edo period was that developed by the Sung-dynasty philosopher Chu Hsi (Zhu Xi) (1130–1200) and his contemporaries, who produced a new version of Confucian thinking by amalgamating Confucian ideas with some elements of Mahayana Buddhism. Their ideas had first reached Japan during the Kamakura period, and their form of Confucianism is known as Neo-Confucianism. Chu Hsi's 'New Commentary on the Four Classics', entitled in Japanese *Shishō shinchū*, was the key work used by Japanese New-Confucian scholars. The Japanese, who had little interest in metaphysics and preferred the practical to the philosophical aspects of Confucian teachings, were primarily interested in the ethical aspects of Chu Hsi's interpretation. These centred on the five human relationships and their accompanying obligations. The five relationships were those between father and son, ruler and subject, husband and wife, older and younger brother, and between friends. For their part the Japanese put the main emphasis on the relationship between ruler

151

and subject and stressed the prime importance of loyalty, although they also emphasized the duties of children towards their parents and of reverence for ancestors. 'The Classic of Filial Piety' accordingly remained one of the major Confucian books to be studied.

Chu Hsi argued that man's true and original characteristics were innately disposed towards righteous conduct, but had become obscured by his involvement with material concerns. Nature was animated by beneficial principles. 'Evil' was 'disarrangement' or 'confusion' disrupting the essential harmony of man and nature. He argued that man and nature operate according to the same basic moral principles and in this way justified the Confucian ethical system. Chu Hsi's emphasis on mutual obligations within specific relationships was conducive to the development of disciplined and integrated groups but was inimical to concepts of individual responsibility. It lies behind the groupism and corporate culture which still mark current Japanese attitudes.

The first exponent of Chu Hsi's philosophy in Japan was a Buddhist priest, Fujiwara Seika (1561–1619). His disciple Hayashi Razan (1583–1657) became an adviser to Ieyasu and founded the Confucian academy in Edo in 1633. This became in 1690 the Shōhei-Kō (Shōhei was the Japanese name for Confucius's birthplace in China). Both Seika and Razan asserted that Confucianism (that is, Confucian ethics) and Shintō (that is, the Shintō myths) were essentially the same because both demanded loyalty to the sovereign. This view was echoed by other Neo-Confucian scholars such as Yamazaki Anzai (1618–82), who emphasized the importance of 'reverence' and loyalty to the ruler. Such views in due course undermined the position of the shōgun, as the sovereign in Japan, 'descended from the gods', was clearly the Emperor.

Particularly in the early part of the eighteenth century the *bakufu* employed a number of Confucian scholars as advisors, including Arai Hakuseki (1657–1725), Muro Kyūso (1658–1734) and Ogyū Sorai (1666–1728). Hakuseki believed that harmony in society was best achieved by 'rites and music'; by this he meant that etiquette, ceremony and ritual were of outstanding importance. Hakuseki was also an historian. His work *Dokushi Yoron* ('A Reading of History') outlines Japanese history from the ninth century to the end of the sixteenth century. The general tone is favourable to the development of feudalism as he points to the decline in imperial competence to rule Japan, but its interest lies not so much in its accuracy as a record (it is in fact inaccurate in parts) but in its attempts at interpreting historical events. Muro Kyūso was concerned by the commercialization of Japanese life and argued that the samurai should live a frugal life and have no thought for money matters. Ogyū Sorai, who belonged to a different philosophical school, was a faithful supporter of *bakufu* absolutism but he argued, contrary to Chu Hsi's views, that the institutions of government were created by man and were not part of the unchanging order of nature.

Despite the *bakufu*'s preference for orthodoxy some different interpretations of Confucian doctrines did appear. Nakae Tōju (1608–48) expounded the doctrines of Wang Yang Ming (1472–1529), known in Japanese as Ōyōmei, who took a more subjective approach to ethical questions than Chu Hsi. He argued that men had a faculty which should guide them in their conduct (that is, conscience). Tōju also advocated introspection and was thus supportive of meditation. Another school was that of the *kogakuha* ('ancient learning sect'). This was advocated by

Yamaga Sokō (1622–85), who argued that society should be regulated by rituals and formal codes of conduct. He was influential in formalizing the rules of *bushidō*.

In the final years of the Edo period the emphasis began to be placed more and more on a synthesis between Confucianism and Shintō. This led to increasing support for the view that the shōguns were usurpers of imperial power, which should be restored. The lead in this was taken by the Mito school where the loyalist tradition went back to Tokugawa Mitsukuni (1628–1700) under whose patronage the *Dainihonshi* ('History of Great Japan') had been started in 1657; it ran to 397 volumes and was written in *kanbun*.[9]

The identification of Confucianism with Shintō encouraged the study of classical Japanese literature and ancient texts. Such studies thus came to be called *kokugaku* ('national learning'). These began as a philological rather than a philosophical movement. Among the first *kokugakusha* (that is, *kokugaku* scholars) were Keichū (1640–1701) and Kada no Azumamaro (1669–1736). At the request of Tokugawa Mitsukuni of Mito, Keichū completed an annotated text of the *Manyōshū*. Kamo no Mabuchi (1697–1769) also studied the *Manyōshū*, which he praised for its 'lofty and honest spirit'. But the outstanding *kokugakusha* was Motoori Norinaga (1730–1801), who took thirty-four years to complete his annotated version of the *Kojiki*. In this he sharply criticized the Chinese way of thinking (*karayō*). He asserted that the *Kojiki* and other early Japanese writings represented the Way of the Ancients (*kodō*). Hirata Atsutane (1776–1843) transformed this into nationalist ideology by stressing that Japan followed the way of the gods – that is, Shintō – which was superior to any other system. He argued that the gods had created and procreated in a way which made Japan unique. Atsutane's thinking lies behind the growth of Japanese racialism, nationalism and imperialism in the first half of the twentieth century as well as the myth perpetuated by Japanese and some foreign scholars of Japanese uniqueness.

In the seventeenth century all western books and learning were suspect because they might promote either directly or indirectly Christian ideas, and even Chinese books were carefully and pedantically censored to remove any conceivable reference to Christianity.

At first there was little communication between the Japanese and the small Dutch merchant community in Deshima. The Japanese had had to have Portuguese interpreters to deal with the Portuguese merchants, and Portuguese had been the initial language used with the Dutch. However, after the expulsion of the Portuguese and the decline of Portuguese power in the East, there were few Dutchmen who understood any Portuguese. The Japanese in the second half of the seventeenth century, therefore, began to train some Dutch interpreters to enable them to cope with the Dutch merchants. The first interpreters do not seem to have been up to much; the Dutch complained that they could not understand even simple Dutch, and written communications were for a time accompanied by Chinese translations, but as these were word-for-word translations they must have been largely incomprehensible. In the eighteenth century the shōgun Yoshimune instructed two scholars to make a proper study of Dutch. They were Noro Genjō, who was given a brief to look into Dutch science, and Aoki Konyō, who had the task of compiling a Dutch–Japanese dictionary. Thereafter the Japanese had a staff of competent Dutch interpreters, and there were increasing numbers of Japanese scholars who were able to read and translate works from the Dutch.

153

However, even before any Japanese had a competent knowledge of Dutch and Dutch books could be imported and studied, some Japanese had begun to show an interest in certain aspects of western science. In 1650, for instance, the doctor to the Dutch colony, Caspar Schambergen, who accompanied the Dutch mission to Edo, was asked to stay on in the capital and instruct Japanese students in western medicine. A Dutch gunner, Juriaen Schaedel, was also employed for some months in 1650, with three companions, to give lessons in mathematics, gunnery and surveying.

Dutch studies (*rangaku*) did not, however, really develop until the eighteenth century. Arai Hakuseki, who was interested in what was going on outside Japan, interrogated Father Sidotti, an Italian Catholic missionary, who attempted to enter Japan in 1708 and was immediately imprisoned in the *Kirishitan yashiki* in Edo (where he was eventually sentenced to being buried alive for converting two servants to Christianity). Hakuseki also met Dutch visitors to Edo and advocated a relaxation on the import of Dutch books. For his part Yoshimune wanted to reform the Japanese calendar and was interested in western science. In particular he sought information on geography, astronomy, weapons, medical techniques, animals, plants and food. He accordingly relaxed the rules on book imports.

One prominent scholar of Dutch learning was Sugita Genpaku (1733–1817), who came across the *Tafel Anatomia*, produced in 1647 by J. A. Kulmus. He translated this work, and his translation became the first book on scientific anatomy in the Japanese language. Medicine indeed was one of the most important subjects of study by the *rangakusha*. Honda Toshiaki (1744–1821) and Hayashi Shihei (1738–93) advocated the development of Ezo, the modern Hokkaidō, in the light of their *rangaku* studies. Western painting and perspective were studied and used by painters such as Hiraga Gennai (1729–80) and Shiba Kōkan (1747?–1818), who was also interested in Dutch science. In 1811 a department was established by the *bakufu* for the study and translation of western books. In 1838 Ogata Kōan, a physician, set up a school in Osaka for young officials and others to study Dutch learning. The average number of students at any one time was said to have been one thousand. Among them were men like Fukuzawa Yukichi (1835–1901), who played a prominent part in the new Japan after the Meiji restoration. As a result of the work of the *rangakusha* Japan was not totally ignorant of the rest of the world when Commodore Perry's 'black ships' arrived off Uraga in 1853, and Japanese were able to communicate with the 'red-haired barbarians', as the Japanese termed the westerners, through the medium of Dutch.

The spread of Confucian ideas prompted many of the daimyō to establish their own schools. In the seventeenth century there were only a few fief schools, but the number increased in the eighteenth century, especially in the latter decades. By 1865, 73 per cent of the daimyō had their own fief schools. These were staffed by Confucian scholars, and the main emphasis was placed on learning by rote the Confucian classics, which were read as *kanbun*. A number of private Confucian schools were also established; these, like the fiefs' schools, were primarily for the sons of samurai. The ordinary people had to rely for such education as was available to them on village schools called *terakoya* (literally, temple huts, because the Buddhist temples were the main cultural establishments in the villages, not because they were run by Buddhist priests) or *tenaraisho* (writing schools). As the latter name implies their main function was to teach reading and writing, but the promotion of Confucian ethics was also a fundamental element in their curriculum. Many of these schools were established by charitable gifts. By 1870 there were 11,000 such schools throughout Japan, and it is estimated that about 40 per cent of Japanese boys and 10 per cent of Japanese girls were attending schools of some kind at the time of the 'restoration' of 1868.

The Performing Arts: *Bunraku* (*Jōruri*) and *Kabuki*

Nō plays continued to be written and performed in the Edo period and were the preferred medium for dramatic performances before the daimyō and members of the aristocracy. But the Nō had ceased to develop and it had lost the vital and imaginative force of the masters of the Muromachi period. The new middle classes in the city, on the rare occasions on which they were permitted to watch Nō, found the performances boring and long drawn out. They wanted something which appealed much more directly to their emotions and which would amuse and excite them without their having to make any great intellectual effort. They found this in the popular forms of theatre which developed in the Edo period. *Bunraku* and *kabuki* were entertainments designed to appeal to audiences in the cities of Edo, Osaka and Kyoto.

Bunraku is the popular Japanese term for the puppet theatre. There are comic scenes in Japanese puppet plays, but most Japanese puppet dramas still performed today are tragedies or at least deal with heroic episodes. *Bunraku* goes back to the sixteenth century, but the term dates from the beginning of the nineteenth century. A troupe of puppet performers, which came from the island of Awaji in the Inland Sea, was organized by one Uemura Bunrakuken (died 1810). This troupe managed to survive as a commercial enterprise and gave its name to the Japanese puppet theatre. The correct term for the Japanese puppet theartre is, however, *ayatsuri jōruri*, where *ayatsuri* means to manipulate a puppet and *jōruri* (literally, lapis lazuli) means the dramatic text used and the method of chanting this text.

According to Japanese legend the name Jōruri was that of a girl with whom the famous warrior Minamoto no Yoshitsune had a one-night love affair and who later nursed him back to health when he fell sick. The *Jōruri hime monogatari*, first mentioned in 1485, told her story. It became very popular and was frequently recited to an accompaniment on the *biwa*, a kind of Japanese lute, by *biwa-hōshi*, who were travelling minstrels and many of whom were blind. The *biwa* was replaced by the *samisen*, a kind of three-stringed Japanese guitar which was imported into Japan through Okinawa in the sixteenth century. The form of recitation used became stylized and was adapted to the puppet theatre in the seventeenth century. *Jōruri* at first developed on separate lines in Edo, Osaka and Kyoto. In Edo it became popular through its use of the tales of an imaginary hero called Kinpira who had exceptional strength and carried out many violent deeds. The rough style of Edo *jōruri* contrasted with the softer style developed in Osaka, where the most famous chanter in the history of the Japanese puppet drama made his name. He was Takemoto Gidayū (1651–1714), who in about 1686 established the *gidayū* tradition of *jōruri* chanting.

In *bunraku* the puppets are approximately one-half to two-thirds the size of human actors and are highly stylized so that one face will, for instance, represent any beautiful woman. They are normally manipulated by three operators. The main puppeteer, who is generally visible full face to the audience, operates the head, including the eyelids, eyeballs, eyebrows and mouth, with his left hand and the puppet's right arm with his own right hand. An assistant, who will be covered by a black cloth to make him seem invisible, operates the left arm, while another assistant is responsible for the puppet's legs. The story is told by the chanter. In most scenes he has to represent all the characters on the stage by different tones of voice. In particularly dramatic episodes, however, there may be separate chanters for each of the main characters. The chanting is accompanied by the *samisen* player, who sits next to the chanter on a separate elevated section of the stage. The movements of the puppets are highly stylized to give maximum dramatic effect.

The *kabuki* theatre began at much the same time as *bunraku*. The word *kabuki* is now written with three Chinese characters for 'song', 'dance' and 'skill', but the term seems to have derived from the verb *kabuku* meaning to flirt or disport oneself. In the early seventeenth century the population of Edo contained a number of people on the fringe of society who were known as *kabukimono* (which may be translated as 'eccentrics').

According to popular legend *kabuki* had its origins in performances by a woman dancer from the great shrine of Izumo called O-Kuni, who did a performance in 1586 in the dry bed of the Kamo river in Kyoto. She began with a prayer but apparently included a good deal of erotic gestures in her act. Her performances became popular and gradually more elaborate. Among her themes were the story of the Soga brothers (see pages 107/8) and of the life of Yoshitsune and his mistress Shizuka Gozen. O-Kuni, who probably died around 1610, had many imitators, and troupes of women actors were formed. These were called 'pleasure–women's *kabuki*' (*yūjo-kabuki*) and consisted largely of prostitutes. These duly attracted the attention of the puritanical *bakufu*, who in 1629 banned such performances; and for the rest of the Edo period women were not allowed to appear on the theatre stage. *Kabuki* was, however, by now too popular to be forced out of existence by a ban of this kind. Instead 'young men's *kabuki*' (*wakashū-kabuki*) was developed. The young men taking part in these performances were handsome youths; the term *wakashū* was at that time used to describe the young men who accompanied the samurai, carrying their swords, dancing at banquets and serving as catamites. The *wakashū-kabuki* became associated with homosexuality. Men began to play women's roles; actors specializing in such roles were known as *onnagata*. Eventually the *wakashū-kabuki* also attracted the disapproval of the authorities and in 1652 it too was banned. In its place men's *kabuki*, known as *yarō-kabuki* was developed. Performances henceforth had to depend not on the sex or the good looks of the actors, but rather on their dramatic abilities. Throughout the Edo period the authorities remained suspicious of the theatre, maintained a strict censorship of the plays performed and kept a watch on contacts with the actors.

Permanent *kabuki* theatres, which were established in Edo, Osaka and Kyoto in the second half of the seventeenth century, tended to develop on somewhat different lines, although because of their proximity there was more interchange between Kyoto and Osaka. In Edo the audiences wanted excitement and found this in violent scenes and melodramatic fantasies. The great actor of the Genroku era (1688–1704), which has come to symbolize the heyday of Edo prosperity and the life of the townspeople, the *chōnin*, was Ichikawa Danjūrō the first (1660–1717). His heroes tended to be superhuman beings who could lop off numerous heads in a single blow. He adopted many of the gestures and wild actions which marked *kimpira jōruri*. This style of acting came to be known as *aragoto* ('rough-house stuff') in contrast with the *nuregoto* ('tear-jerker material') which appealed to the Osaka audiences.

The *kabuki* stage soon developed certain special characteristics which have lasted to this day. Because the audiences demanded elaborate scenery the revolving stage was invented to enable quick changes of scenes to be made. To provide melodramatic effects the stage had various trapdoors. To give greater prominence to dramatic entrances and exits the *hanamichi*, which was a path through the audience to the stage, was created. Wigs, costumes and scenery were colourful, elaborate and stylized. Make-up tended to be exaggerated, and gestures, often based on those borrowed from the puppet theatre, were emphasized to bring out particular dramatic points, eyebrows for instance being used to particular effect.

In the Edo period *kabuki* performances lasted all day between sunrise and sunset. Evening performances were banned because of the fear that artificial lighting would lead to fires.[10]

Kabuki plays had various types of musical accompaniment. The main instruments used were the *samisen* and the hand drum. Chanters, on the lines of the *jōruri*, performed with pieces derived from those in the puppet theatre. Music was often used to provide dramatic effects and convey moods; it was also an accompaniment to dances, while chanters gave commentaries to explain and enhance the story. Dialogue in *kabuki* is spoken by the actors, but in a generally stylized way. Dramatic moments in a play would be marked by a shout from among the audience and by the sound of wooden clappers. These were also used to mark the end of a play or an act.

There are three main categories of *kabuki* plays. These are period pieces (*jidaimono*), everyday or contemporary pieces (*sewamono*) and dance plays (*shosagoto*). *Jidaimono* were not only historical pieces; they also included plays which covered contemporary events but where the events had been transposed to a different age and where the names had been changed in order to satisfy the censors. Typical of such plays was the story of the revenge of the forty-seven *rōnin* in *Chūshingura* (see page 000) where the names and the period were transposed. *Sewamono* tended to be plays about recent events. For instance, a double suicide which had created a local sensation might be re-enacted on the stage with famous actors playing the roles of the suicide couple. The double suicide theme was a popular one as it represented a typically Japanese conflict, that between duty or obligation and human feelings or the heart, that is, between *giri* and *ninjō*.

The success of *bunraku* and *kabuki* was due in great measure to the genius of the playwrights, who wrote for the Japanese stage in the late seventeenth and eighteenth centuries. Of these the most famous was Chikamatsu Monzaemon (1653–1724), who worked first in Kyoto and later in Osaka. He wrote the texts used by the chanters in puppet plays. These consisted of a narrative with dialogue and descriptions of scenes. Some 100 plays have been attributed to him. Many of his *jidaimono* include *michiyuki* (poetic accounts of journeys). But his *sewa-mono*

157

brought him special popularity and fame. In 1703 the double suicide of a shop clerk and a prostitute attracted much attention in Osaka. In three weeks Chikamatsu turned this story into the play called *Sonezaki shinjū* ('The Love Suicides at Sonezaki'). In 1712 he wrote *Shinjūten no Amijima* ('The Love Suicides at Amijima'). Professor C. J. Dunn says: 'Chikamatsu's successful portrayals caused such an increase in the frequency of these suicides that the authorities made them a crime, with a surviving partner decreed guilty of murder, and the corpses of the lovers exposed like those of common criminals.'[11] Chikamatsu's most famous *jidai-mono* was *Kokusenya kassen* ('The Battles of Coxinga'). This embroiders the story of Coxinga, a half-Chinese, half-Japanese pirate who drove the Dutch from Formosa (Taiwan) and went to China in an attempt to restore the Ming dynasty after its overthrow by the Manchus. Dunn describes it as 'a play of violent contrasts, with rough humour, comic comparisons between Chinese and Japanese, a famous fight with a tiger, scenes of bloodshed and eye-gouging, and a ripped open womb in a puppet Caesarian that would do credit to the goriest Elizabethan drama'.

Chikamatsu's plays are a mixture of verse, prose and dialogue. The *michiyuki* of the lovers in *Sonezaki shinjū* begins:[12]

> Farewell to this world, and to the night farewell.
> We who walk the road to death, to what should we be likened?
> To the frost that leads to the graveyard,
> Vanishing with each step we take ahead:
> How sad is this dream of a dream!

The Takemotoza, a puppet theatre established in Osaka in 1685, was managed by three successive men with the name Takeda Izumo. Takeda Izumo II (1691–1756) was encouraged by Chikamatsu Monzaemon to write for the puppet theatre. His most famous works, which were also adapted for the *kabuki* theatre, were written jointly with Namiki Sōsuke (1695–1751?) and Miyoshi Shōraku (1706?–72?). They include *Sugawara denju tenarai kagami* ('Sugawara and the Secrets of Calligraphy', (1746), *Yoshitsune senbonzakura* ('The Thousand Cherry Trees of Yoshitsune', (1747) and the famous *Kanadehon Chūshingura* of 1748.

One of the most famous and popular *kabuki* plays of the Edo period is *Kanjinchō* ('The Subscription List'). This was adapted from the Nō play *Ataka* by Ichikawa Danjuro VII in 1840. It covers an episode which is alleged to have occurred during Yoshitsune's flight to the north. Yoshitsune and his faithful follower Benkei are travelling in a group disguised as monks. When they are stopped at a barrier the loyal and courageous Benkei to prove their authenticity pretends to read a list of subscribers to a famous temple for which the monks claim to be making a collection. The officer in charge of the barrier guesses who they are, but admiring Benkei's loyalty is prepared to allow them to pass. At this point one of his men is doubtful about one of the young men in the party who seems too good looking and delicate. To disarm suspicion Benkei strikes the young man with his staff; he thus beats his master Yoshitsune. This ruse is allowed to work, and the party passes on. Benkei then apologizes profusely to Yoshitsune, who, however, praises his loyal retainer for his presence of mind. The party leave the stage quickly via the *hanamichi*, followed by Benkei who departs in a series of dramatic and triumphant bounds.

Two other dramatists of note were Tsuruya Namboku IV (1755–1829) and Kawatake Mokuami (1816–93).

Literature

In the seventeenth century books became more easily available as wood-block printing developed, and there was a vast output of stories and novels.

Stories written mainly in *kana* began to appear in large numbers. Such books, which were given the generic name of *kana-zōshi*, included moral tracts and guidebooks to places like Kyoto, Nara and Kamakura. Parodies of famous works were also to be found among the early *kana-zōshi*; the most famous of these was the *Nise monogatari* ('Fake Tales'), which was a parody of the famous Heian-period classic *Ise monogatari*. At first they were intended primarily for the samurai class, but they soon attracted the attention of the *chōnin*.

Stories written in earlier periods were also published, for example in the *Otogi-bunkō*[13] put out by an Osaka publisher called Shibukawa in about 1700. Most of the stories in this collection were on serious and tragic themes such as jealousy, insanity and murder, but they also included stories of heterosexual love and homosexual affairs between priests and their acolytes.

The most famous novelist of the Edo period was Ihara Saikaku (1642–93). He was at first known for his ability as a composer of linked verses (*haikai no renga*). His novels, which were hastily written, soon became immensely popular. His output covered three different types of subject; these were accounts of erotic life, of samurai behaviour and of merchant attitudes. His first important story was *Kōshoku ichidai otoko* ('The Life of an Amorous Man'), produced in 1682.[14] This is a picaresque account in fifty-four chapters (the same number as in the 'Tale of Genji') covering the annual erotic adventures of Yōnosuke from the precocious age of seven to sixty when he sets sail with some companions in a boat loaded with aphrodisiacs and other erotogenic items for the Island of Women. Yōnosuke boasts that by the age of fifty-four he had had affairs with 3,742 women and 725 young men. The story is episodic, the characterizaion one-dimensional and the style elliptical and colloquial.

In 1685 Saikaku wrote *Kōshoku gonin onna* ('Five Women Who Loved Love').[15] The stories are told with ironic humour and unsentimental realism. One story, based on a notorious episode in the history of Edo, deals with the affair of Oshichi, a greengrocer's daughter who in order to enable her to be with her lover starts a fire. She is convicted of arson and is punished by being burned alive. In a story translated as 'The Barrelmaker Brimful of Love' the 'heroine' Osen goes off on a pilgrimage to Ise with an old crone. They are joined by Kyūshichi, a manservant, and a barrelmaker or cooper; both have designs on Osen. Saikaku gives an amusing acccount of how at an inn

the two men stood in each other's way the whole night through. The upshot of their bedroom activities was only this: that Kyūshichi, who started the evening with his pillow to the west, wriggled around and wound up with his

159

head to the south and his underclothing missing – a shocking piece of care-
lessness for a pilgrim with money in his waistband; while the cooper slept with
a resentful scowl on his face, a wad of tissue paper in his hand, and a clamshell
of clove oil [used like toilet water] beside him.

Four months later Saikaku published *Kōshoku ichidai onna* ('The Life of an
Amorous Woman').[16] This purports to be the confessions of an old woman about
her descent through the ranks of prostitution. It is a cynical account of the life of
a nymphomaniac. *Nanshoku ōkagami* ('The Great Mirror of Manly Love') is a
collection of stories about homosexual relationships, which some samurai saw as
superior to heterosexual affairs.

Saikaku's most famous collections of stories about the *chōnin* were *Nippon
eitaigura* ('The Japanese Family Storehouse or The Millionaires' Gospel Modernized'),[17] published in 1688, and *Seken mune sanyō* ('This Scheming World'),[18]
published in 1692. In these works Saikaku gives cynical and ironic advice on how
to get on in the merchant world. Saikaku noted: 'Money is the townsman's
pedigree, whatever his birth and lineage. No matter how splendid a man's
ancestors, if he lacks money he is worse off than a monkey-showman.' Fujiichi,
in the story from the Eitaigura translated as 'The Foremost Lodger in the Land',
'never passed by anything which might be of use. Even if he stumbled he used
the opportunity to pick up stones for fire-lighters, and tucked them in his sleeve.
The head of a household, if he is to keep the smoke rising from his kitchen, must
pay attention to a thousand things like this.'

In the story from the same collection translated as 'A Dose of What the Doctor
Never Orders', a rich man tells a poor man of his nostrum called 'The Millionaire's
Pill'. The prescription consists of:

Early rising	5 parts
The family trade	20 parts
Work after hours	8 parts
Economy	10 parts
Sound health	7 parts

The rich man also warns that 'it is imperative to abstain from certain noxious
things'. In the list of sixteen things to avoid Saikaku pokes fun at contemporary
society. For instance, the aspirant must abstain from 'Kickball, minature archery,
perfume appreciation, and poetry gatherings... Flower-viewing, boating excursions, baths in the middle of the day ... Temple-going, and preoccupation with the
next world ... *Sake* with supper, excessive pipe-smoking, unnecessary journeys to
Kyoto ... Familiarity with kabuki actors, and with brothel quarters.' The story
concludes with these words of wisdom: 'The golden rule for men is to save in
youth and spend in old age. It is impossible to take your money to heaven, and
it is essential to have it on earth.'

Modern critics deny that Saikaku's erotic stories are pornographic. Certainly
he does not go into detailed accounts of the sex act. Saikaku had a good sense of
irony and he has left an amusing and realistic picture of life in the Genroku period
in Edo Japan, but his novels lack in–depth characterization.

The genre which Saikaku began came to be called *ukiyozōshi* ('stories about the floating world'). Saikaku's most famous successor in this genre was Ejima Kiseki, who wrote for the Hachimonjiya (Figure-of-Eight Shop).[19]

The most important writer of stories in Japanese in the century following Saikaku's death was Ueda Akinari (1734–1809). He is particularly famous for his collection of stories the *Ugetsu monogatari*, ('Tales of Moonlight and Rain').[20] These were first printed in 1776. They deal mainly with ghosts and other supernatural phenomena. There are nine stories, divided into five books. Akinari was much influenced by Chinese and Japanese classics, as well as by Shintō, Taoist, Confucian and Buddhist beliefs. He had an evocative style, as the following quotation from *Kikuka no Chigiri* ('The Chrysanthemum Tryst') suggests:

He stepped outside the door and looked about. The Milky Way shimmered with a pale light. The moon's icy wheel shed its glow on him, aggravating his loneliness. A watchdog's bark rang out through the clear air, and the sound of waves in the bay seemed as if surging round the very place where he stood. The moon presently disappeared behind the mountain peaks, and about to give up, Samon decided to go back in and close the door, when he happened to take a last look. Out of the dim shadows a man emerged, as if mysteriously borne on the wind.

The term *gesaku* ('stories written for amusement') is used to describe the various types of fiction which followed Ueda Akinari. *Gesaku* encompasses *sharebon* (punning or witty books), which were stories about the licensed quarters, *kibyōshi* ('yellow books'), which had numerous illustrations, *gokan* ('books bound together'), which also had lots of illustrations, *yomihon* ('reading books'), *kokkeibon* (humorous books) and *ninjōbon* (stories about human feelings).

Perhaps the most famous writer of *yomihon* was Takizawa Bakin (1767–1848). He is best known for his monumentally long novel *Nansō Satomi hakkenden* ('The Biography of Eight Dogs of the Satomi Family'). It describes how the fortunes of a fifteenth-century samurai family are revived with the help of eight warriors, all of whose surnames begin with the character read in Japanese as *inu* meaning 'dog' (the Chinese reading of the character is *ken*; thus *hakken* from *hachiken* or 'eight dogs'). It is an allegorical story written in classical Japanese with many Chinese constructions.[21]

The outstanding *kokkeibon* of the Edo period was the *Tōkaidōchū hizakurige* ('Shank's Mare'),[22] which was published in parts between 1802 and 1822 by Jippensha Ikku (1765–1831). It recounts the comic adventures on the Tōkaidō of the two plebeian heroes Kitahachi and Yajirōbei.

Shikitei Samba (1776–1822) was another writer of *kokkeibon*. His two most famous works were *Ukiyoburo* ('The Floating World of the Bath House', 1809–13) and *Ukiyodoko* ('The Floating World of the Barber's Shop', 1813–14).[23] These books recounted the gossip of the townsmen in the bath and the barber's chair and provide amusing sidelights on life in Edo in the first half of the nineteenth century. The following extract from *Ukiyoburo* gives some idea of the atmosphere:

The pungent smell of soap powder wafts over to prick the nose of the bath attendant, and someone raps the side of the wooden tub to wake the bucket-boy. Wailing voices, excited babble: 'Too hot!' 'Too cold!' 'And a little cold water!' 'No, don't!' Through the din and bustle cuts a voice singing *Makura tanzen*, and suddenly a naked figure appears, striking exaggerated theatrical poses in *roppō* style. Someone chants a *sumo* scene, and a bather makes his exit imitating a wrestler entering the ring.... One person holds his head and groans, while another slaps his buttocks as he talks. One man sings with a foot in the air, and another shouts with his feet planted wide apart on the floor. Some sit, some stand; and a bad imitation of a *samisen*, in a voice as artless as a monkey's, comes from a figure crouched in a corner of the bath.... This is the bath of the Floating World, overflowing with gods and Buddhas, moral lessons, love, and evanescence: the place could be anywhere, but the time is the middle of the month.

Linked verses (*haikai no renga*) and *waka* continued to be composed in the Edo period. While many of these poems were competent pieces they did not add any new dimensions to the art. Two new forms of poetry were, however, developed in the Edo period from the light-hearted *haikai no renga*. These were *haiku* and its witty counterpart *senryū*. Both forms and the *hokku*, which was the first part of a *renga*, consist of three lines of five, seven and five syllables as in the first three lines of a *waka*. The one essential characteristic of a *haiku*, at least in the Edo period, was a reference to the season. *Haiku* are the briefest of vignettes, designed to appeal to the reader's imagination. It is not so much what they say as what they suggest which matters. The words must, however, be carefully selected for euphony and rhythm as well as for their implications and allusions.

The greatest *haiku* poet in Japanese literature and the originator of *haiku* as an accepted and serious poetic form was Matsuo Bashō (1644–94). Bashō was the son of a low-ranking samurai of Ueno in Iga province (part of Mie prefecture). He studied Zen Buddhism, and his poems and prose writings were deeply influenced by Zen. In 1684 he set out on the first of a number of journeys which he recorded in poetic journals. The most important of these was a trip which he made to the north and the Japan Sea in 1689. This was the subject of his famous work *Oku no Hosomichi* ('The Narrow Road to the Deep North'),[24] which contains some of his finest poems. The basic theme is the quest for the ultimate in beauty and truth. It also epitomizes his concept of *sabi*, which implies elegance, restraint and simplicity.

Haiku, because of their brevity and allusiveness, are difficult to translate effectively into English. The following are a few representative poems by Bashō:

Furu ike ya	An old pond
Kawazu tobikomu	A frog jumps in
Mizu no oto	The sound of water.

(This is perhaps the most famous *haiku* ever written. It is considered to be a Zen poem, the splash caused by the frog perhaps bringing sudden enlightenment.) The following six *haiku* are from *Oku no hosomuchi*[25]:

Natsugusa ya	A mound of summer grass
Tsuwamonodomo ga	Are warriors heroic deeds
Yume no ato	Only dreams that pass?

Shizukesaya	In this hush profound
Iwa ni shimi-iru	Into the very rocks it seeps –
Semi no koe.	The cicada sound.

Samidare wo	Gathering as it goes
Atsumete hayashi	All the rains of June, how swiftly
Mogami-gawa.	The Mogami flows.

Atsuki hi wo	The river Mogami
Umi ni iretari	Has drowned the hot summer sun
Mogamigawa.	And sunk it in the sea.

Araumi ya	O'er the wild ocean spray
Sado ni yokotō	All the way to Sado isle
Ama no gawa.	Spreads the Milky Way.

Yo mo sugara	All through the night
Akikaze kiku ya	I listened to the autumn wind
Ura no yama.	In the lonely hills.

Meigetsu ya	The full moon
Ike wo megurite	I wandered round the pond
Yo mo sugara.	All night long.

Another famous *haiku* is:

Kare-eda ni	On the withered branch
Karasu no tomarikeri	A crow flies down
Aki no kure.	Autumn evening.

And his final verse:

Tabi ni yande	Becoming ill on a journey
Yume wa kareno wo	In my dreams I wander round
Kakemeguru.	The withered moorland.

Some of Bashō's disciples have left famous *haiku* such as this by Kikaku (1661–1707):

Meigestsu ya	The full moon
Tatami no ue ni	On the tatami mats
Matsu no kage.	Casts the shadow of a pine tree.

After Bashō the most famous *haiku* poet of the Edo period was Yosa or Taniguchi Buson (1716–84), who was also a famous painter. He is reputed to have written some three thousand *haiku*. Here are a few examples of *haiku* by Buson:

Tsurigane ni	On the temple bell
Tomarite nemuru	A butterfly has
Kochō ka na.	Stopped and gone to sleep.

Botan chitte	The peony flowers
Uchikasanarinu	Fall and lie on top of one another
Ni-san-pan.	In piles of two and three.

Harusame ya	In the spring rain
Monogatari-yuku	I see a straw raincoat and an umbrella
Mino to kasa.	Walking along in conversation.

Ochi kochi ni	Here and there
Taki no oto kiku	I hear the sound of a waterfall
Wakaba ka na.	Through the young leaves.

Yanagi chiri	The willows are bare
Shimizu kareishi	The water has dried up
Tokorodokoro.	And stones have appeared here and there.

Yūkaze ya	An evening breeze
Mizu aosagi no	Blows the water
Hagi wo utsu.	Against the heron's legs.

The third great *haiku* poet of the Edo period was Kobayashi Issa (1763–1827).[26] Issa was a more down-to-earth character than either Bashō or Buson, and this is reflected in his poems:

Yuki tokete	The snow thaws
Mura ippai no	And suddenly the whole village
Kodomo ka na.	Is full of children.

Suzume no ko	Fledgling sparrows
Jizō no sode ni	They are sheltering there
Kakurekeri.	In Jizō's sleeve.

Neko okite	Sleeping, waking,
O akubi shite	Giving such tremendous yawns –
Neko no koi.	The cat goes courting!

Inu no ko no	Under the willow
Kuwaete netaru	With a leaf stuck in his mouth
Yanagi ka na.	The puppy sleeps.

Utsukushi ya	What loveliness
Shōji no ana no	Seen through a crack in the wall
Ama-no-gawa.[27]	The River of Heaven!

(This last poem was written when Issa was ill.)

It is not always easy to say when a poem ceases to be a *haiku* and becomes a *senryū*. The origins of *senryū* lie in a technique called *maeku-tsuke*, which involved capping a previous verse, the *mae-ku*, written by someone else. The *tsuke-ku*, when they stood alone, became *senryū*. Donald Keene suggests that in general *haiku* deal with nature and *senryū* with human beings. *Haiku* try to capture both the eternal and the momentary, but *senryū* 'is content with a single sharp observation'.[28] The language of *senryū* is colloquial, even vulgar. Most of the older *senryū* are anonymous. Many *senryū* need to be explained to be understood by anyone unfamiliar with the circumstances which inspired the verse. Some *senryū* were parodies of famous *haiku*.

R. H. Blyth, quoting from a letter from R. L. Stevenson to W. E. Henley in 1884, concludes: '*Senryū* is 'beauty touched with sex and laughter'. It 'attends on all our steps in life', and of all the arts, 'embraces the greatest number of elements of fate and character', looking upon all things 'with pity and mirth'.'[29] This overestimates the value of *senryū*.

It is difficult to quote a representative selection of Edo-period *senryū*, but the following may give the flavour:[30]

Kome tsuki ni	If you ask directions
Tokoro wo kikeba	From a man pounding rice,
Ase wo fuki.	First he wipes the sweat.

Ofukuro wo	As a weapon
Odosu dōgu wa	To intimidate his Ma,
Toi kuni.	Distant employment.

Keisei wa	Even when the courtezan farts,
Toppa zushite mo	She does it
On ni kake.	As a favour.

Nyōbo wa	The chap
Osogaru yatsu wa	Who's afraid of his wife,
Kane ga dekiru.	Makes money.[31]

Art

The Edo period was the richest and most productive of all the different eras in Japanese art. The comparative peace and prosperity of the times provided a favourable climate for artists. The military aristocracy did much to promote artistic development by their demands for magnificent screens and lacquer ware.

The interests of the townspeople inspired new forms of art, in particular the wood-block print, and provided incentives for the development of Japanese craftsmanship. This was also the great age of Japanese ceramics. Some of Japan's most beautiful gardens were made in Kyoto despite the decline of the nobility. Only in sculpture and religious art was there a real falling off in artistic ability and inspiration.

The Kanō school of painting, which had had such success in the Momoyama period, continued to find patrons in the Tokugawa shōguns. In view of the interest of the military aristocracy in Confucianism there was a considerable demand for paintings of Chinese subjects, including portraits of Confucius, as well as of sacred or mythical Chinese animals such as lions, tigers, dragons and the *kirin*, a fabulous animal with affinities to the giraffe. The tiger was usually depicted among bamboo which was supposed to deter elephants. The lion was often shown among peony flowers. The Kanō artists particularly liked to paint pines, plum trees and bamboos, which were regarded as symbols of good luck and happiness. As landscape subjects they frequently chose the eight famous views of the Chinese lakes Hsiao and Hsiang (in Japanese, *Shōshō-hakkei*). In the seventeenth century three Kanō brothers dominated the work of the school. They were Tan-yū (1602–74), Naonobu (1607–50) and Yasunobu (1613–85). Of these the greatest was Tan-yū, who was asked to move to Edo in 1617 and was given a residence there by the shōgun. He received commissions to do paintings for Edo, Nijō, Nagoya and Osaka castles, as well as for the Tōshōgu mausoleum at Nikkō. In Kyoto he did many paintings for the great Zen temple of Nanzenji.

The Tosa school, which had evolved from the *yamato-e* style, continued to work primarily for the court aristocracy and to specialize in themes from classical literature, especially scenes from the 'Tale of Genji'. The most important representative of the Tosa school in the early Edo period was Mitsuoki (1617–91), who produced many paintings of flowers and birds. Tosa-school paintings became highly stylized. The Sumiyoshi school of painters, which was a subsidiary school in Edo, tried to revitalize Tosa-style painting. It also provided artistic advice to the shōgunate.

The most striking and significant painters of the seventeenth century were artists of the Rimpa school of decorative painting. The members of this school were influenced by Tosa, Kanō and Chinese styles. The three outstanding painters of the Rimpa style in the seventeenth century were Tawaraya Sōtatsu (?-1643?), Honami Kōetsu (1558–1637) and Ogata Kōrin (1658–1716). They must surely count among the world's greatest painters.

Little is known about the life of Sōtatsu, but he worked mainly in Kyoto. He was a master of colour with a deep appreciation of contrasts and intensity. He also understood how to mix hard and soft lines and in his depiction of flowers and grasses he showed a realistic and instinctive feeling for natural phenomena.

Honami Kōetsu was a designer who co-operated with potters, lacquer craftsmen and metalworkers, but he was above all a calligrapher. He particularly admired the graceful and delicate writing of the Heian period. He often collaborated with Sōtatsu.

Kōrin, who was probably the greatest of the three, came from a merchant family in Kyoto. He seems to have enjoyed a life of pleasure during which he

166

squandered his inheritance. This forced him to take up painting and to collaborate with his brother Kenzan, who had become a potter. He is particularly famous for a number of magnificent screens painted in gorgeous colours as well as in gold and silver. The earliest of these is thought to be the screen of irises (*kakitsubata*) in the Nezu Art Museum in Tokyo. His pair of screens, depicting red and white plum trees in blossom (*kōhakubai*), which dates from his final years, is in the MOA museum of art at Atami. It is a bold and unconventional composition. There is also a striking and memorable screen by Kōrin of rough waves in the Metropolitan Museum in New York.

One of Kōrin's able successors in the Rimpa school was Hōitsu (1761–1828). But of greater importance was Maruyama Okyō (1733–95), who learned western perspective through painters in Nagasaki and also studied Chinese bird and flower painting. He is particularly remembered for his fine paintings of birds and flowers. One of his students was Matsumura Goshun (1752–1811), who founded the Shijō school of painting, named after his studio on Shijō street in Kyoto. The Shijō school combined western perspective and realism with traditional Japanese techniques.

Itō Jakuchū (1716–1800) was a painter renowned for his detailed and realistic depictions of birds, although he also produced a number of unconventional *sumi-e* (ink paintings).

Chinese paintings of the so-called southern school of Sung painters with its softer lines, in contrast to the harder and bolder lines of the northern school which had influenced the Kanō artists, inspired the *nanga* (literally, 'southern painting') style painters of the *bunjin* (literati) who had some popularity in Japan in the eighteenth and nineteenth centuries. They concentrated on typical Chinese themes including landscapes and bird and flower paintings. One of the *bunjin* painters was Buson, the famous *haiku* poet (see page 164).

For many westerners Japanese art is almost synonymous with the colour print. Prints were cheap in the nineteenth century and were among the first examples of Japanese art to reach the West. With their bold colours, unconventional composition and striking lines they had an immediate impact on western artists and were a major influence on the Impressionists and Post-Impressionists. They began the vogue for *Japonisme*.

Ukiyo-e (literally, 'pictures of the floating world') has come to be used to describe Japanese wood-block prints; but many of the artists renowned for their prints also produced paintings in the form of hanging scrolls (*kakemono*) and screens (*byōbu*). The early prints were in black and white, as a technique for colour printing was developed only in about 1745.

The colour print required co-operation between the publisher, the artist or designer, the engraver of the wood-blocks and the printer. The artist supplied a drawing on transparent paper with an indication of the colours to be used. The engraver pasted the drawing face down on to a block of hard wood such as cherry, cut along the lines of the drawing and dug out the wood in between the lines so that they stood out in relief. Ink was then rubbed on to the raised lines, and a proof was taken. Separate blocks were thereafter prepared for each of the different colours to be used. Sometimes in complicated prints there might be as many as ten separate blocks. As the colours were mixed separately for each printing and as the blocks were used many times over, it is not surprising that prints varied greatly in colour. Until the nineteenth century the colours were mainly of vegetable origin and so have faded with time. Some collectors find these mellow colours particularly attractive.

The standard size of most wood-block prints (*hanga*) was about 38 x 25 cm (15 x 10 inches). This was the so-called *ōban* size. Half-size prints were known as *chūban*. *Surimono* were prints issued for specific occasions such as New Year's greetings. They are usually of small size. A touch of reddish colour was added to some of the early black-and-white prints; these became known as *tan-e*. Paintings to which black lacquer and colour were added were called *urushi-e*. *Ukiyo-e* are sometimes referred to as *nishiki-e*, literally brocade prints; this term arose in the eighteenth century as colour printing developed.

Iwasa Matabei (1578–1650) is traditionally regarded as the founder of *ukiyo-e*. He belonged to the Tosa school and moved to Edo from Kyoto in 1637. One famous screen believed to be by him is that of 'Ladies-in-Waiting Viewing Chrysanthemums' in the Yamatane Art Museum in Tokyo. But of greater importance for the development of *ukiyo-e* was Hishikawa Moronobu (died 1694). He began work as a book illustrator, and his illustrations for *kōshokubon* (erotic stories) made him famous. He later produced a number of single-sheet prints in sets of twelve. These were the first Japanese wood-block prints. His best-known works are the *Yoshiwara no tai*, a set of twelve black-and-white prints depicting scenes in the Yoshiwara gay quarter. He thus inaugurated the *bijin-e*, or paintings of beautiful women, which became one of the main themes of *ukiyo-e*. His style was bold and simple, and his prints were uncluttered with detail.

Some of the first *ukiyo-e* were sex manuals, called in Japanese *shunga* ('spring pictures'). The sex act was depicted explicitly, but naked figures were rarely shown, the participants being at least partly clothed. The first sex manuals were anonymous, but in due course the production of *shunga* became part of the stock-in-trade of the *ukiyo-e* artist.

Torii Kiyonobu (1664–1729), who founded the Torii school of *ukiyo-e* and who was much influenced by Hishikawa Moronobu, produced prints of famous beauties. But as the son of a *kabuki* actor he also took a close interest in the theatre and prepared designs depicting theatrical scenes and actors, thus inaugurating what became another popular theme in *ukiyo-e*.

Perhaps the greatest artist to specialize in depicting beauties was Suzuki Harunobu (1725–70), who is also credited with creating the *nishiki-e*. Harunobu's prints have a delicate romantic quality far removed from the earlier and more overtly erotic illustrations of *kōshokubon*. He concentrated on slim and graceful figures of boys, girls and mothers with children. His prints were mainly executed in the *chūban* size. In his most active five or six years, when his style had matured, he produced about a thousand different prints. Among his best-known works are a set of 'eight living-room scenes' (*zashiki hakkei*).

One of the most famous Japanese *ukiyo-e* artists who specialized in prints of beauties or courtesans was Kitagawa Utamaro (1753–1806). His women were more realistic than the idealized beauties favoured by Harunobu, and his prints have a strong element of eroticism in them. His portraits thus emphasize the sensual aspects of feminine beauty, but his figures remain graceful and charming. Torii Kiyonaga (1752–1815), a contemporary of Utamaro, produced *kabuki* prints as well as pictures of famous beauties. Like Utamaro he was more of a realist than an idealist in his depiction of women, but some critics have found the perfection of his compositions somewhat dull and lifeless.

Theatrical subjects were the speciality of Utagawa Toyokuni the first (1769–1825) and of Tōshūsai Sharaku (late eighteenth century). Toyokuni's realistic depictions of *kabuki* actors in dramatic stage poses were immediately popular. Toyokuni also produced prints of courtesans and did numerous book illustrations. Very little is known about Sharaku except that he produced 145 prints of *kabuki* actors in the two years 1794–5. Sharaku in his striking portraits of actors exaggerated elements of the dramatic art and brought out the more grotesque aspects of Japanese acting. His highly novel portraits were unpopular with the theatre fans of his time, and he was apparently forced to withdraw from his unrewarding task after making some unsuccessful attempts to attract buyers by modifying his style to meet popular taste. In so doing his artistic merits declined. Few original Sharaku prints survive; they are much sought after.

In the late eighteenth and nineteenth centuries artists began to produce prints of birds and flowers as well as of landscapes. The outstanding artist of the late Edo period, who was a master of such themes as well as of human figures, was Katsushika Hokusai (1760–1849). Hokusai, who was very much an Edokko, or townsman of Edo, had a good sense of humour and was a master of line and colour. He brought a fresh sense of observation and a bold imagination to his compositions. His *Manga* (literally, 'cartoons'), which were published in fifteen slim volumes between 1814 and 1834, were really notebooks containing sketches of people and things which interested him. Some are humorous and cast a light on contemporary life. Others demonstrate his understanding and observation of nature. His most famous series of colour prints were his 'Thirty-Six Views of Mount Fuji' (*Fugaku sanjūrokkei*), which began to appear in 1831 and with a supplement involved the production of forty-six separate prints. In 1834, inspired by or jealous of the success of Hiroshige's masterpiece, 'The Fifty-Three Stations of the Tōkaidō' (*Tōkaidō gojūsan-tsugi*), which appeared in 1831, he produced a set of three picture books containing 'One Hundred Views of Mount Fuji' (*Fugaku hyakkei*). He also did various sets of prints of waterfalls, bridges, birds and ghosts before he died at the age of eighty-nine. In old age he liked to use the pen name Gakyo-rōjin, which means 'old man mad with painting'. His output was indeed prolific. He is thought to have produced over thirty thousand designs or sketches in his long life. Some critics have condemned his lack of discrimination, but prints such as those of Mount Fuji at Dawn, Mount Fuji in Storm and Mount Fuji under the Wave at Kanagawa reflect not only Hokusai's artistry, but also the wonders of a mountain which has become a symbol of Japan.

After Hokusai the Japanese print artist whose name is most widely known among westerners is Hiroshige. Utagawa or Andō Hiroshige (1797–1858), like Hokusai, was born in Edo. Inspired by the works of the great master he began to concentrate on landscapes. The first of his famous series of prints were a set of ten entitled 'Famous Spots in the Eastern Capital' (that is, Edo, now Tokyo, which means eastern capital) (*Tōtō meisho*) and 'The Fifty-Three Stations of the Tōkaidō' (*Tōkaidō gojūsan-tsugi* – this set actually contained fifty-five prints). Among other famous sets by Hiroshige were 'Eight Views of Omi', that is, Lake Biwa (*Omi hakkei*), 'Sixty-Nine Stations on the Kiso-kaidō', that is, the *Nakasendō* (*Kisokaidō rokujūkyū tsugi*) and 'One Hundred Views of Famous Places in Edo'

169

(*Meisho Edo hyakukei*). He also produced a number of fine prints of birds and flowers. Hiroshige had a wonderful sense of colour, a keen and observant eye and a fertile imagination, which helped him to create new perspectives in composition.

Ceramics have long been recognized as a major art form in Japan. In the Edo period some of the finest ceramic works of art were produced. The four main kinds of ceramics made in Japan were unglazed earthenware (*doki*), glazed earthenware (*tōki*), stone ware (*sekki*) and porcelain (*jiki*). The popularity of the tea cult provided a major incentive to the development of ceramics in the Edo period. The Korean potters who arrived in Japan following Hideyoshi's abortive attempt to conquer Korea (see Chapter VII) brought new tehniques and provided artistic inspiration.

Kilns at Hagi (Yamaguchi prefecture) and various potteries in Kyūshū, including Karatsu in Saga prefecture, Takatori, Koishiwara and Agano (Fukuoka prefecture), produced glazed earthenware tea bowls and other tea ceremony wares. Their pots were without decoration or with only limited incised or painted designs. Hagi wares tend to have an off-white or pinkish glaze. There were two main types of Karatsu ware; these were the *e-garatsu* which have a brownish glaze and simple painted black designs and *chōsen-garatsu* which, as the name implies, were Korean in design and technique and generally distinguished by the use of two different colours of glaze and a somewhat rough texture. The leading family of exponents of *e-garatsu* ware was that of Nakasato Tarōemon; the present holder of that name is the thirteenth generation.

Other traditional kilns, such as those at Bizen (Okayama prefecture) and Seto near Nagoya, continued to develop throughout the Edo period, and new kilns were set up in various other parts of the country including Kyūshū, Shikoku and Honshū.

One of the most striking developments in ceramics in Japan during the Edo period was the growth in the production and variety of decorative wares. The main centres were Kyoto, Kanazawa, Arita in western Kyūshū and Satsuma in southern Kyūshū.

Two Kyoto potters of outstanding artistic ability were Ninsei and Kenzan. Ninsei (?1596–?1660),[32] at first known as Nonomura Seibei or Kiyoemon, appears to have learned how to use the potter's wheel at the Awata kiln in Kyoto. He later established his main kiln at Omuro near the Ninnaji temple in Kyoto. Ninsei had remarkable technical ability and a fine sense of design and colour. Thirteen famous tea-urns (*chatsubo*), with four ears for a string to secure a tight cover, have been identified as being by Ninsei.[33]

Ogata Kenzan (1663–1743) was the brother of the painter Ogata Kōrin. He studied with Ninsei and in 1699 set up his own kiln nearby. Kenzan experimented with a variety of techniques and types of ceramic wares and was much influenced by Kōrin, who did the underglaze paintings on his early works. He made good use of overglaze enamels as well as gold and silver. His designs were elegant and graceful although less immediately striking than those of Ninsei. He produced many *raku* pieces and used a full range of blacks, reds, greens, yellows and blues. His wares were widely imitated, and genuine works by him are difficult to find and identify with certainty. The problem is complicated by the fact that his four successors, also called Kenzan, imitated his style.[34]

Kyoto remained throughout the Edo period a major ceramic centre. At the kilns near the Kiyomizu temple, blue and white wares as well as porcelain decorated with red and green enamels were produced. In addition to *raku* wares produced by Chōjirō (see page 129), particularly fine tea bowls were made by Honami Kōetsu (1588–1637), the famous calligrapher.

Kutani wares were made in the province of Kaga near the modern city of Kanazawa. *Ko-kutani* (old *kutani*) wares[35] were made from 1655 to 1704 for the use of the Maeda, the daimyō of Kaga. Overglaze enamel *ko-kutani* dishes, mainly in dark greens with some yellow, purple and dark blue designs, vigorously executed, suggest late Ming (1368–1644) and early Ching (1644–1912) dynasty models. An attempt was made to revive the *ko-kutani* style in the nineteenth century when red and gold pieces of *kutani* ware, which became very popular in the West, also began to be produced.

In Kyūshū the town of Arita became the main centre for porcelian production. The wares produced there are normally given the generic name of Imari, which was the port nearby from which they were shipped. Some of the first products from Arita were blue and white wares based on Korean and Chinese models. When the Ming dynasty suddenly collapsed in 1644, Chinese exports of blue and white ware to Europe ceased for a time, and the Dutch turned to Japan for supplies to meet European requirements. This huge and unexpected demand inevitably led to an element of mass production and higher prices, but the quality of Japanese blue and white was high and even influenced Chinese wares when under the Ching dynasty Chinese exports of blue and white were resumed in about 1690. Japanese blue and white also had a considerable influence on European blue and white beginning with Delft.

But the Japanese porcelain style which had the gratest influence in Europe in the eighteenth century was *kakiemon*. The first potter to use the name Kakiemon lived from about 1596 to 1666. He is supposed to have succeeded in firing porcelain with a red overglaze decoration similar in colour to that of a persimmon, known in Japanese as *kaki*. *Kakiemon* wares as we know them today date from the time of Kakiemon V (1660–91). *Kakiemon* wares consist of a milky white porcelain with a delicate overglaze decoration in red, green, blue and black. Designs tend to be conventional, with birds and flowers predominating, but the execution is fine and graceful without any attempt to fill up the white background with unnecessary detail. *Kakiemon* wares were much appreciated in Europe and even in China. Copies and adaptions of *kakiemon* originals were made at Meissen, Chelsea and Bow, among other European ceramic factories.

Another important style of porcelain made at Arita was *nabeshima* ware. Nabeshima was the family name of the daimyō of Saga, and it was made for his family. The *nabeshima* kiln was founded in 1722 and flourished particularly during the eighteenth and early nineteenth centuries. The wares were primarily by a family of potters called Imaemon, who still continue to produce ceramics in Arita. The most important products of this family of potters were *iro-nabeshima* (coloured *nabeshima*) ware. The porcelain was of a very fine quality, pure white or with a slightly blueish tinge. The fine painted designs are thought to be similar to those used by dyers and weavers of the period. Designs used include fruit, vegetables and flowers, executed in a simple decorative manner.

Korean influences were dominant in the highly decorated wares produced in Satsuma and known as *satsuma-yaki*. Many different types of wares were produced in Satsuma including black wares (*kuro-satsuma*) which were primarily used in the tea ceremony. But the most famous type of *satsuma* is white *satsuma* (*shiro-satsuma*). This was produced by the Korean family Chin Jukan at Naeshirogawa in Kagoshima prefecture. The family came from Korea at the end of the sixteenth century and still use their old Korean name. White *satsuma* is a highly decorated and colourful style of porcelain with complicated shapes and designs, ranging from vases and plates to figures. The basic white glaze has a distinctive crackled effect. It was very popular in Europe in the late nineteenth century. Many of the wares exported to Europe now seem over-elaborate, but the best pieces must be admired for the high quality of the techniques used and the vast amount of work required to produce them. *Satsuma*-type pots were also made in Kyoto.

The demand for lacquer wares increased vastly in the Edo period. The daimyō used lacquer bowls, trays and small tables for their banquets. Their ladies had elaborate lacquer toilet sets. On their journeys to and from Edo under the *sankin kōtai* system they used lacquer chests and portable medicine holders, small oval boxes with generally three tiny compartments kept together with cords (*inrō*). For their writing they wanted ink stone boxes with space for their brushes (*suzuribako*). For the tea ceremony they looked for small and exquisitely decorated caddies (*natsume*). The rich merchants soon developed similar tastes and the money to support and encourage a growing body of specialist artisans.

The tehcnique of gold lacquer and *maki-e* was refined, and a vast range of designs was developed. These included not only the traditional birds, flowers and grasses, but also figures and subjects from Japanese and Chinese literature. Some of the great painters of the period also contributed designs. Among the most famous were Kōetsu and his brother Kōrin. While Kyoto remained the most important centre for the production of gold lacquer wares, craftsmen also congregated in other cities, in particular Kanazawa, the capital of Kaga province and the seat of the Maeda family. Less expensive lacquer wares, sometimes in red and using powdered charcoal and other decorative techniques, were produced at places such as Wajima (in Ishikawa prefecture), Echizen, (now Fukui prefecture) and Hirasawa on the Nakasendō.

The production of lacquer calls for great patience and skill. The basic material, usually wood, is painted with a coat of lacquer and is then covered with a piece of fine linen cloth over which many further separate coats of lacquer are painted. It is next polished repeatedly to achieve a glossy finish before the designs are applied by hand with meticulous care. Thin transparent lacquer is used to cover the design prior to final polishing.

Cloisonné (*shippō*), a type of enamelling involving the application of glass on a metal base, had been produced in Japan from very early times, but it became widely used only from the seventeenth century. Items such as door-pulls (*hikite*) for sliding screens and small pieces of sword furniture were then made in *cloisonné*. Some of these pieces are of fine workmanship and delicate design. In the early nineteenth century new techniques were developed as a result of the study of European enamelling. In the late nineteenth century European methods were introduced and the basis layed for the modern commercial manufacture of *cloisonné*.

Metalworking tehcniques were refined in the Edo period to meet the demand for architectural ornaments, sword furniture and armour. In the absence of civil strife or attempted invasion the vast majority of items in metal were made for decoration and display. Many sword guards or *tsuba* were produced with intricate designs involving meticulous and detailed workmanship of a very fine order.

Netsuke were used with *inrō* to fasten the medicine case to the holder's belt. The carving of *netsuke* was developed in the Edo period into a fine art. Delicate and minute figures of animals and people were carved in wood, ivory and walrus tusk. Craftsmen in the Edo period also developed the art of making beautiful and intricate baskets primarily for use in flower arrangement.

Silk production grew vastly in the seventeenth and eighteenth centuries, and weaving techniques, which were much influenced by Chinese models, were greatly improved. To meet the requirements of Nō actors various fabrics had to be made. These included *kara-ori* (a form of brocade), *nui-haku* (a fabric with an embroidered design) and *suri-haku* (a fabric with a gold leaf pattern). The daimyō's ladies, as well as the wives of rich merchants and the higher class of courtesans, needed silk for their *kimono* and *obi* (a kind of thick sash worn by ladies over and around their *kimono*). Materials used included satin (*shusu*), figured damask (*donsu*) and crêpe (*chirimen* or *yūzen*). Gorgeous and complicated patterns were decorated on these materials by dyeing, embroidery or weaving on the loom. Some of the designs were based on paintings or drawings by artists such as Kōetsu and Kōrin.

Numerous shrines, temples and palaces were built or rebuilt in the Edo period. Elaborate decoration in the form of carved and coloured lintels and beams was a particular feature of many of these buildings. The most exuberent and ornate was the Tōshōgu shrine and mausoleum of Ieyasu at Nikkō. The Japanese have a saying which means you cannot say 'superb' (*kekkō*) until you have seen Nikkō. Set among vast crypotmerias in the foothills of the mountains, Nikkō represents a kind of Japanese rococo; the Yōmeimon gateway is magnificent, gorgeous and popular. The carvings on the lintel above the shrine stable of the three monkeys representing the three Buddhist principles of 'Hear no evil, speak no evil, see no evil' (one monkey covers his ears, another his mouth, and the third his eyes), and another carving in the main precincts of the shrine representing a sleeping cat, attributed to the famous sculptor Hidari Jingoro, are famous.

If such shrines sometimes seem gaudy, the tea-houses (*cha-shitsu*) of the aristocrats represent the height of restrained or *shibui* (literally, 'astringent') taste. They were built in various sizes in simple materials. The ceilings were of unvarnished wood or bamboo, and the sliding panels (*fusuma*) were covered in simple papers. The roof would be thatched or covered in wooden shingles. The tea-room of four and a half mats (*yojōhan*) would be reached through a small entrance (*nijiriguchi*) which forced the participant to bend down and humble himself to get in. In the alcove (*toko-no-ma*) the hanging scroll (*kakemono*) might be a black-and-white sketch or a piece of calligraphy.

During the Edo period various tea ceremony schools developed. The Sen no Rikyū tradition was handed down to his grandson Sōtan (1578–1658), whose three sons founded their own schools. Sōshitsu (1622–97) established the Ura Senke, Sōsa the Omote Senke and Sōshu the Mushanokoji Senke school. The largest today is the Ura Senke, which is still headed by a Sen Sōshitsu and has branches abroad. The headquarters in Kyoto contains beautiful and refined *chash-itsu* and small gardens of evergreens, shrubs, ferns and moss. In the inner garden by a tea-house there is normally an arrangement of stones called the *tsukubai* or *chōzubachi*, a stone basin, from which the guests ladle water to wash their hands. The tea ceremony, the articles used in it and the rooms and gardens associated with it are a peculiarly Japanese art form of great refinement and delicate beauty.

In the Japanese art of flower arrangement the *nageire* (literally, 'to throw in') style developed in conjunction with the tea ceremony. Because of the character of the tea ceremony, the style was marked by an effort to conform to nature. There were thus no fixed rules, and the emphasis was on freedom and spontaneity. In the latter part of the seventeenth century a style called *shōka*, or 'living flowers' (the characters can also be read as *ikebana*), developed. This was an attempt to combine the formal *rikka* style (see page 119) with the simplicity of *nageire*.

Another art which matured in the Edo period was that of bonsai, literally 'tray planting', but meaning the growing of miniature trees. The art had originated in China and was first introduced into Japan in the Kamakura period, but it was not until the peaceful Edo years that it became popular. Some of the finest Japanese specimens of evergreen, maple, plum and cherry tree bonsai, planted in the Edo period, are still treasured by Japanese connoisseurs of the art.

Many of the most beautiful Japanese landscape gardens which have survived into the twentieth century were constructed in the Edo period. Some were very small, like the tea-house gardens. Others were as large as parks. In Kyoto the three great imperial gardens of the Sento palace and of the Katsura and Shūgakuin detached palaces date from the seventeenth century. They are perfect examples of the Japanese art of landscape gardening at its best. All three are of the stroll type (*kaiyū-shiki*). Lakes, bridges, streams, waterfalls and rocks are carefully arranged to blend harmoniously with evergreens and shrubs. At the Shūgakuin the mountains on the opposite side of the valley provide a natural view, called in Japanese a *shakkei* ('borrowed view'). The tea-houses and simple palace buildings in these gardens are made to harmonize in a natural way into the environment and form part of the charm and beauty of the gardens. The buildings of the Katsura are marvellous examples of the finest Japanese domestic architecture. They have been meticulously restored. Good examples of Edo-period gardens in Tokyo are the Kōrakuen. Rikugien and Hama-no-Rikyū (Hama Detached Palace) gardens. The three most famous gardens or formal parks outside Tokyo and Kyoto, the Kairakuen at Mito, the Kenrokuen at Kanazawa and the Kōrakuen at Okayama, also date from the Edo period, as does the Ritsurin park at Takamatsu on the island of Shikoku.

The perfection of the Japanese style of domestic architecture, which is exemplified in the few remaining genuine Edo-period buildings, was recorded in his book *Japanese Homes and their Surroundings*, published in 1886, by Edward S. Morse, the great American zoologist and director of the Peabody Museum in Salem, Massachusetts. He had the quality which the Japanese describe as *me-kiki*, literally 'the effective eye'.

IX

Japan Reopened: Modernization (1853–94)

By 1853 the *bakufu*[1] had lost its way. The daimyō, particularly the *tozama* diamyō, were discontented with their lack of power outside their own domains and the way they were treated by the shōgun's officials. Many of the samurai were bored and in debt. In some of the fiefs the more ambitious and intelligent junior samurai had come to recognize the need for change and were attracted by revolutionary ideas calling for an end of *bakufu* rule and the re-establishment of the central role of the Emperor. Their philosophy was based partly on Neo-Confucianism and partly on a nationalist belief in the uniqueness of Japan as the land of the gods. Some of these young samurai acquired influential positions and instituted reforms in their fiefs, but their efforts were frequently frustrated by conservative elements. The farmers were crushed by the burden of taxation and felt poor and oppressed. The merchants had difficulty in enforcing their claims against the samurai and resented bureaucratic interference, the ineffective sumpturary laws and the contemptuous way in which they were treated by the samurai. There was not yet a revolutionary situation in Japan, but criticism against the usurpation of imperial power by the shōguns was growing. The catalyst for change came from foreign pressure.

The Japanese achievement in the final decades of the nineteenth century was remarkable. In this period the new Japanese leaders managed to engineer a generally peaceful revolution which abolished the old feudal structure and established the basis of a modern state.

In the 1850s it seemed to some observers that Japan might, like most other oriental states, succumb to western pressures and become a colonial or semi-colonial dependency. Yet by 1894 equality of status with the western powers had been largely achieved. The samurai were quickly pensioned off. Compulsory education and conscription were enforced. The foundations of a modern industrial and commercial structure were built. New western-style legal codes were drawn up, and a constitution based on the German model was introduced. Western dress and practices were generally adopted, and western ideas and culture were studied with enthusiasm, although not always with discrimination. By 1894 Japan had undergone a major social and political revolution, and western liberal thinking was beginning to permeate. But the leaders of Meiji Japan regarded liberal doctrines with suspicion and hostility. Japan remained an autocracy. The old behaviour patterns, inculcated over the centuries by the Japanese interpreters of Confucian doctrines, continued. In 1894 Japan had not yet become an imperialist power, but nationalist sentiments were growing and were encouraged by the Meiji leaders, who saw them as an essential unifying force. Some Japanese now wanted to emulate the western powers and share in the spoils they thought might be gained in China.

The 'Unequal Treaties' (1853–60)

The Japanese authorities should not have been surprised by the arrival of Commodore Perry's 'black ships' of the US Navy in 1853. They had received various warnings. In 1837 the unarmed US ship *Morrison* had vainly tried to return Japanese castaways at Uraga, near Edo. In 1844 the Dutch King William II had written to the shōgun warning him of what was happening in China (the first opium war had begun in 1840), but his advice had been ignored. In 1845 the Royal Navy survey vessel HMS *Samarang* had called at Nagasaki and demanded stores. In 1846 Commodore Biddle of the US Navy had tried to establish contacts with the *bakufu*, but had been rebuffed. In 1849 HMS *Mariner* carried out a survey of the approaches to Edo, and the USS *Preble* called at Nagasaki to secure the release of some seamen wrecked from an American whaler. Whaling in the north Pacific had grown greatly, and the American interest in trade with China had increased with the opening up and development of the Pacific west coast of America. The European powers, following the Industrial Revolution, were looking for new outlets for their products and would have turned their attention more quickly to Japan if it had not been for their preoccupations in China or if they had foreseen more clearly the potential opportunities in Japan. It was becoming increasingly unacceptable in western countries that Japan not only should be unwilling to enter into trade relations, but should also refuse to provide stores and refuge for vessels in distress and should ill-treat and imprison shipwrecked seamen.

Commodore Matthew Galbraith Perry, the US naval commander who arrived off Uraga on 8 July 1853, had strict orders. He was to deliver a letter from President Fillmore and was to insist on a proper reception. President Fillmore's letter was firm but reasonable. It sought fair treatment of shipwrecked seamen, the opening of Japanese ports where US ships could obtain stores and coal and the establishment of trade relations. Commodore Perry added a letter of his own; this made it clear that, if these 'pacific overtures' were not accepted straight away, he would have to return in the spring of 1854 with a much larger force. The threat to use force was thus made explicit. Perry's arrival caused consternation in Edo. He demanded that he should be received at a high level and refused to discuss matters with any junior officials, who had to deal with the commodore's subordinates. In face of the real threat which Perry's arrival clearly posed, the shōgun's officials decided that they had to receive these missives with due solemnity. Appropriate arrangements were accordingly made for the handing over of the letters and the presents which the Americans had also brought with them, but the *bakufu* officials were in no position to give an immediate answer. So Perry sailed away towards China.

The senior councillor in the *gorōjū* was Abe Masahiro (1819–57), who had been appointed to the post in 1845. He vacillated and decided first to consult Tokugawa Nariaki of Mito and then, when Nariaki called for the expulsion of the 'barbarians', to seek the views of the daimyō. This move was a serious error of judgement as it demonstrated the weakness of the *bakufu*. Inevitably the majority of the daimyō favoured the maintenance of the policy of seclusion, but failed to recognize that the shōgunate did not have the power to enforce such a policy. One of the few to take a realistic view was Ii Naosuke (1815–60), the senior *fudai* daimyō of Hikone on Lake Biwa. He thought that Japan should build up her strength through overseas trade and create a modern navy which could deal on equal terms with the West. No agreement could be reached except that the Japanese should seek to persuade Perry to leave with only a vague response. This was basically a decision to procrastinate and was bound to fail.

When Perry returned in February 1854 with eight ships, he insisted on the early conclusion of a treaty between the USA and Japan. After a good deal of haggling on such questions as the ports which were to be opened to US ships, agreement was concluded and signed at Kanagawa near Edo on 31 March 1854. It was agreed that Shimoda, at the end of the Izu peninsula and in those days very remote from Edo, would be opened immediately and Hakodate in southern Ezo (Hokkaidō) in a year's time. Only on trade did Perry make any substantial concession to the Japanese point of view. As a naval officer he had no real interest in commerce, and no trade provisions were included in the treaty.

Perry's example was soon followed by other powers. For the British, Rear-Admiral Sir James Stirling of the China squadron reached Nagasaki in September 1854 and concluded a treaty similar to the American except that Nagasaki and Hakodate (not Shimoda) were to be the specified treaty ports. Article VII of this treaty was extraordinary and unrealistic: 'When this convention shall be ratified no high officer coming to Japan shall alter it.' The Russians led by Admiral Putiatin concluded an agreement in January 1855, and an agreement with the Dutch followed in November 1855.

The treaties concluded by Perry, Stirling and Putiatin were regarded by the merchants in the Far East as useless, and the governments were pressed to renegotiate to ensure that trading rights and extra-territorial privileges were obtained. The merchants wanted similar conditions in Japan to those they had obtained in the treaty ports in China as a result of war with China. It fell to the US Consul-General in Shimoda, Townsend Harris, to do much of the initial spade work for such treaties. He arrived in Shimoda in August 1856. The *bakufu* officials in Shimoda were generally obstructionist, and Harris and Henry Heusken, his Dutch interpreter, had a difficult and lonely time. The Japanese did not have any English interpreters at this stage, and all communications had to be translated first into Dutch and then into Japanese; this inevitably caused delays and misunderstandings.

Meanwhile in Edo, Abe Masahiro had resigned as senior *rōjū* in 1855 and had been replaced by Hotta Masayoshi (1810–64), who took a fairly realistic view about the need to allow foreign trade. Trading arrangements agreed with the Dutch and the Russians in Nagasaki in 1857 did not, however, satisfy Townsend Harris. He managed to get away from Shimoda and go to Edo in the late autumn of 1857. He saw Hotta on 12 December 1857 and demanded that the Japanese should agree to the appointment of an American minister in Edo, that there should be no official interference with trade and that there should be more treaty ports. When Hotta consulted the daimyō on these proposals, opinions were still divided, but the number of voices favouring trade with the foreigners had increased. Matsudaira Yoshinaga[2] wanted Japan to 'shatter the selfish designs of the brutish foreigners' by building a fleet and annexing nearby territories. Hotta determined to go ahead with a treaty, and in the early part of 1858 negotiations with Townsend Harris made progress. However, when the treaty was ready for signature he found such strong opposition from the daimyō that he decided to go in person to seek the Emperor Kōmei's approval. Hotta had assumed that this would be a routine matter, as the court traditionally did as they were told by the *bakufu*. The Emperor agreed under pressure, but let it be known that he had been forced to accept the treaty against his will. Hotta was then instructed to reconsider the whole policy. At this point the *bakufu* recognized the existence of a crisis and decided to appoint a *tairō*. They chose for this post Ii Naosuke, the foremost advocate of a positive policy towards the hated foreigners, and it was he who, despite the opposition of the imperial court, gave the orders for the signature of the commercial treaty between Japan and the USA signed on 29 July 1858. Harris threatened that, if the treaty were not signed, a British fleet would soon arrive and extort even tougher terms. The threat of force was always implicit and frequently explicit in western dealings with Japan in the middle of the nineteenth century.

The Dutch and the Russians concluded similar treaties in August 1858. Lord Elgin, who led a British mission to Japan, also signed a commercial treaty on 23 August 1858. An agreement was reached with the French in October of that year.

The treaties provided for extra-territoriality (that is, that foreigners were subject to their own consular courts and not subject to Japanese jurisdiction) and for the appointment of diplomatic agents with the right to reside in Edo. The ports of Hakodate, Kanagawa and Nagasaki were to be opened to trade from 1 July 1859, Niigata or another convenient port on the Japan Sea coast from January 1860, and Hyōgo (Kōbe) from 1 January 1863. In additon traders were to be permitted to reside at Edo from 1 January 1862 and at Osaka from 1 January 1863.

The political situation was complicated by a dispute about succession to the shōgunate. When the shōgun Iesada died in 1858 there were two rival candidates. Tokugawa Iemochi (1846–66) of the Kii branch had the support of Ii Naosuke. Tokugawa Yoshinobu, better known as Keiki or Hitotsubashi Keiki (1837–1913), had the backing of Tokugawa Nariaki of Mito, Matsudaira Yoshinaga of Echizen and Shimazu Nariakira of Satsuma. Ii Naosuke won. In the so-called Ansei purge conducted between 1858 and 1860 he did his best to neutralize his opponents. Tokugawa Nariaki of Mito was, for instance, imprisoned in his own fief, thus arousing fierce resentment among Mito samurai. But Ii Naosuke made no real attempt to strengthen the *bakufu* or to institute effective reforms. The last chance of saving the shōgunate was thus lost.

The imperial court now became the focus for opposition to the *bakufu*, which had ignored the court's instructions to Hotta to reconsider his policies towards the foreigners. The slogan was '*Sonnō Jōi*' ('Revere the Emperor and expel the barbarians'). The most famous exponent of this doctrine, which derived from both the nationalist philosophers (the *kokugakusha*) and Japanese interpretations of Neo-Confucian political theory evolved mainly by Mito scholars, was Yoshida Shōin (1830–59), a samurai of Hagi in Chōshū (now Yamaguchi prefecture). In 1854 he had tried to get to the USA as a stow-away on board Perry's flagship the USS *Powhattan* when it was anchored at Shimoda. For this he was imprisoned for a time, but on his release he did his best to enthuse with his own patriotic spirit the young samurai of Chōshū who studied in his school at Hagi, the Shōka Sonjuku. Among his pupils were some of the leaders of the Meiji restoration such as Itō Hirobumi (1841–1909) and Yamagata Aritomo (1838– 1922). Shōin urged his pupils to rise against the shōgunate, which, he declared, had betrayed Japan by its failure to tackle the foreign threat and had forfeited its right to rule. Following an attempt to assassinate a *bakufu* official, Shōin was arrested, sent to Edo and in 1859 executed.

The foreigners for their part were also critical of the *bakufu*. They found Japanese officials deceitful, vacillating and obstructionist. Having promised to open Kanagawa on 1 July 1859, the authorities developed instead Yokohama, a small fishing village across the bay. Kanagawa was on the Tōkaidō. Yokohama was off the main road and could be cut off from the mainland rather as Deshima was from Nagasaki. The powers protested but to no avail. The merchants found the facilities of Yokohama acceptable and did not care about the specific wording of the treaty. But Yokohama was not a safe or agreeable place; the merchants were mostly a ruthless and unscrupulous lot, and Yokohama seemed to many like a western frontier town. There were various murders. In November 1859 the British consul instructed British subjects to go about armed and gave permission for firearms to be used 'on any reasonable provocation'.

Edo, where the diplomatic representatives lived, was equally unsafe. Rutherford Alcock, the British Consul-General and first British Minister to Japan who was installed at the end of June 1859 in his Legation at Tōzenji, a temple near Shinagawa in Edo, felt cut off and insecure. He reported in August 1859 that it was a daily occurrence for members of the Legation to be insulted and pelted with stones. In January 1860 he noted that 'sinister rumours of a general massacre of foreigners were circulating' and 'the commonest sound in Edo is the musket and artillery practice of the soldier'. On 29 January 1860 his Japanese linguist was murdered.

On 24 March 1860 a band of anti-foreign samurai from Mito and Satsuma intercepted Ii Naosuke on his way to Edo castle and assassinated him outside Sakurada-mon. Following Ii Naosuke's death the *bakufu* tried to reach some understanding with the daimyō and with the court, while at the same time unwilling and unable to take the effective action against the foreigners which their opponents demanded. The end of the *bakufu* was now inevitable. The only questions were how long it would take and how it would be effected.

The Fall of the *Bakufu* (1860–8)

Before he was murdered Ii Naosuke had arranged for a mission to go to the USA to exchange ratifications of the commercial treaty of 1858. The mission left Yokohama on 13 February 1860. The three ambassadors and their suite[3] travelled on the USS *Powhattan* and on the *Kanrin-maru*, a Japanese ship of 300 tons which had been built in Holland.[4] The Japanese did not know what to expect and took masses of Japanese food and other supplies with them. They received a spectacular welcome wherever they went including a banquet given in their honour by President Buchanan and a pageant on Broadway. For the Japanese, who had been

179

cut off from the rest of the world for so long and who had not yet encountered the Industrial Revolution, the experience was unforgettable, if not always to their liking. For the Americans the Japanese with their traditional costumes were objects of curiosity.

In Japan the situation after Ii's murder deteriorated. The year 1861 began inauspiciously for the foreign community with further rumours of a general massacre. On 14 January 1861 Heusken, Townsend Harris's interpreter, was murdered. The British, French, Dutch and Prussian Legations withdrew for a time to Yokohama; Townsend Harris insisted on staying in Edo.

In July 1861 Rutherford Alcock, the British Minister, decided that as the security situation seemed to be improving he would return to Edo after a visit to Nagasaki. On the night of his return, 5 July 1861, the British Legation at Tōzenji was attacked by *rōnin*. Ten members of his guard were wounded and two were killed. One of the injured was Laurence Oliphant, who had accompanied Lord Elgin to Japan in 1858. Alcock exploded in anger when 'in token of amity' after the attack he was sent a basket of ducks and a jar of sugar by one of the commissioners of foreign affairs. The Legation was again withdrawn to Yokohama. All this helped to bring Alcock gradually round to the view that there would be real dangers if the British insisted on the dates in the treaty for the opening of additional ports. He arranged for a Japanese mission to travel to Europe early in 1862, when he would himself be on home leave. The mission of thirty-six men led by two of the commissioners for foreign affairs left Japan on 30 January 1862 in advance of Alcock's departure. Lord Russell, the British Foreign Secretary, insisted on waiting for Alcock's return before starting negotiations with the japanese mission. while awaiting the arrival of alcock the members of the mission did some sightseeing. They visited the arsenal at Woolwich, saw a series of manoevres and visited the International Exhibition, the House of Lords, the Tower, the Bank of England and the Mint. They were much impressed by all they saw.[5] Alcock was put in charge of the negotiations with the mission. On 6 June Lord Russell duly gave his approval to an agreement which came to be called the London Protocol. This accepted the postponement both of the opening of further ports and of permission to reside in Edo and Osaka until 1 January 1868.

During Alcock's absence there were further serious incidents involving foreigners in Japan. In June 1862 Lt-Col St John Neale, the British chargé d'affaires, decided that the Legation should return once more to Edo. Hardly had they taken up their old quarters, accampanied this time by a unit of British marines provided from HMS *Renard*, than they were once more set upon in a second night attack by *rōnin* (it was the anniversary by the lunar calendar of the previous attack). A British corporal was killed, and the Legation returned once more to Yokohama. On 14 September 1862 a party of three British riders from the foreign settlement in Yokohama encountered the train of Shimazu Hisamitsu (also known as Shimazu Saburō), the uncle of and power behind the daimyō of Satsuma. One of the party, Lennox Charles Richardson, a merchant from Shanghai, was cut down and killed by Satsuma samurai at Namamugi on the Tōkaidō. The foreign community in Yokohama called for armed protection; British and French garrisons were duly sent but did not arrive until 1864. The British government demanded an indemnity of £100,000 from the *bakufu* and £25,000 from Satsuma as well as the execution of the murderers.

In the meantime the *bakufu* continued to vacillate. It knew that Japan lacked the power to enforce the expulsion of the foreigners, but it could not persuade the daimyō and the court to accept the continued presence of the foreign communities. In Kyoto retainers from the *tozama* fiefs of Satsuma and Chōshū intrigued against the *bakufu*, and the court was persuaded to send an envoy to Edo to demand that the shōgun should visit Kyoto to discuss the steps necessary to enforce expulsion. The *bakufu* undertook to make changes. Tokugawa Keiki was appointed guardian to the shōgun, and Matsudaira Yoshinaga was given a senior position in the government. In October 1862 the *sankin-kōtai* system was modified, and the daimyō were no longer required to spend as much time in Edo as previously and did not have to leave hostages there. Shimazu Hisamitsu of Satsuma was satisfied, but the Chōshū samurai and other extremists in Kyoto were not. Shimazu Hisamitsu withdrew to Kagoshima, while a few able and daring samurai from Chōshū, Satsuma and Tosa (in Shikoku) controlled the policies of the court.

When Keiki and Matsudaira Yoshinaga visited Kyoto in early 1863 they had differing views about the policies to be adopted, but despite calls for caution from Satsuma they capitulated to the demands of the extremists. The Emperor was to assume the military command, an imperial army was to be formed, and the date of 25 June 1863 was set for the expulsion of the foreigners. The *bakufu*, however, had no intention of provoking hostilities or taking more than perfunctory steps to comply with the orders from Kyoto. When the first instalment of the indemnity to Britain was paid in June 1863, the *bakufu*'s officials tried to start negotiations for the closure of the ports. This proposal was naturally rejected, but on 25 June, the day stipulated for expulsion, Chōshū batteries fired on an American ship in the straits of Shimonoseki, and after further attacks on other foreign vessels it became clear that for the time being Chōshū controlled the straits.

The British had been unable to extract any compensation from Satsuma. So after various delays a British squadron entered the bay of Kagoshima in August 1863. Three Satsuma steamers were seized, firing ensured, Kagoshima was bombarded from the sea, and the town was set on fire. The British squadron suffered heavy damage and withdrew. Satsuma claimed a victory, but agreed to punish the murderers of Richardson, if they could be found, and to pay an indemnity, although in the event they got the *bakufu* to provide the money. Thereafter relations between Britain and Satsuma changed from hostility to friendship. The men of Satsuma were realists and knew that they could win only if they had modern weapons.

Satsuma now decided to act against the extremists in Kyoto and insisted on a reconciliation between the *bakufu* and the court. When the shōgun Iemochi visited Kyoto in February 1864, however, there were disagreements between the *bakufu* and Satsuma, which erupted in a personal quarrel between Keiki and Shimazu Hisamitsu.

In the absence of instructions, the representatives of the foreign powers had delayed taking action to reopen the straits of Shimonoseki. However, when Sir Rutherford Alcock returned from leave in 1864 he decided to take firm action. This decision was reinforced by the *bakufu* proposing, in response to a demand for the reopening of the straits, that Yokohama should be closed. Abortive discussions to persuade the Chōshū authorities to yield were held with two

181

Chōshū samurai, Itō Hirobumi and Inoue Kaoru (1836–1914) who had managed to get a passage on a British ship in June 1863 and had spent six months studying in England. Finally in September 1864 a joint force of seventeen ships[6] bombarded the Chōshū batteries, which were then dismantled. Chōshū was thus forced to agree to keep open the straits and to pay an indemnity. In Yokohama in October the *bakufu* finally accepted responsibility for the expedition and undertook to pay $3 million to the powers concerned.

The British had now taken the lead among the foreign powers. Much of the inspiration for a forward policy came from the new British Minister, Sir Harry Parkes (1828–85), who arrived in Japan in 1865 and was to stay until 1883. Parkes, with the able assistance of Ernest Satow (1843–1929) and A. B. Mitford (1837–1915), later Lord Redesdale, saw that the future lay with the anti-*bakufu* forces and began to develop contacts with the men of Satsuma and Chōshū.

Meanwhile new alliances had begun to be cemented between the fiefs and the young and ambitious samurai who increasingly seized the initiative and pushed the daimyō into the background. Kido Kōin (Takayoshi) (1833–77) and Takasugi Shinsaku (1839–67) had emerged as the main samurai leaders in Chōshū. Takasugi had organized a militia of Chōshū samurai in 1863, and he and Kido deployed Chōshū's army of samurai and farmers in resistance to *bakufu* attempts to punish Chōshū. Two other Chōshū samurai, Itō and Inoue, meanwhile were employed in buying arms through the British in Nagasaki. In Satsuma the lead had been taken by Saigō Takamori (1827–77).[7] In 1864 he was employed in leading Satsuma forces in an expedition against Chōshū on behalf of the *bakufu*. But a reconciliation between Satsuma and Chōshū was achieved, and in March 1866 Kido reached agreement with Saigō and Sakamoto Ryōma (1836–67) of Tosa (now Kōchi prefecture in Shikoku) on an alliance aimed at the overthrow of the *bakufu*. This was the origin of the Satchō oligarchy which exercised a controlling influence in the Meiji government.

In the same year 1866, following the appearance of a foreign squadron off Hyōgo and a threat from the shōgun that he would resign if the court were not amenable, the court eventually and reluctantly sanctioned the agreements of 1858. A further campaign against Chōshū was launched, but in the absence of help from Satsuma, which remained neutral on this occasion, the shōgun's forces were pushed back. Then in September of that year the shōgun Iemochi died, and a truce was called with Chōshū.

In January 1867 Keiki was persuaded to accept the post of shōgun. He thus became the fifteenth and, as it turned out, the last Tokugawa shōgun. Although he had been willing to reach an accommodation with the court, he was not yet ready to surrender the *bakufu*'s powers to the court and the other daimyō. British support for the anti-*bakufu* forces being now apparent, Keiki was tempted to turn to the French. They had already helped to establish a number of industrial enterprises, including a dockyard at Yokosuka, and had agreed in November 1866 to send a military mission to Japan. Léon Roches (1809–1901), the French Minister, whose relations with Parkes were distinctly frosty, recommended to the new shōgun a radical reorganization of the government, but this was too much for Keiki. Meanwhile the Emperor Kōmei had died and been succeeded by the boy Emperor Mutsuhito (1852–1912), better known by his reign name of Meiji. He came increasingly under the influence of Saigō Takamori, Okubo

Toshimichi (1830–78), another leading samurai from Satsuma, and the low-ranking but able and influential courtier Iwakura Tomomi (1825–83).

In June 1867 Keiki met with representatives of the daimyō and the court in Kyoto to consider the problem of the promised opening of Hyōgo on 1 January 1868 and further action against Chōshū. Keiki forced the court to accept a compromise decision accepting the opening of Hyōgo on the due date and agreeing that Chōshū would be teated 'leniently'. This annoyed the Satsuma representatives, and another confrontation seemed likely. To avoid this and to give the other fiefs a say in future policies Yamanouchi Yōdō (1827–72) of Tosa and his chief adviser Gotō Shōjirō (1838–97) in October 1867 urged that a council of daimyō should be formed with Keiki as chairman and that Keiki should resign to facilitate the formation of such a council. Keiki, who had only assumed the office of shōgun reluctantly, agreed and submitted his resignation to the court on 9 November 1867. But this was not enough to satisfy the young samurai. They objected to Keiki becoming chairman of the proposed council of daimyō and to the Tokugawa retaining their vast estates. On the morning of 3 January 1868 troops under the command of Saigō Takamori seized control of Kyoto, and a decree was issued depriving Keiki of his offices and lands. The first step had been taken in the Meiji restoration and what was to be a major social revolution.

Although the final outcome was never in real doubt, the overthrow of the *bakufu* was not a bloodless revolution. Following the decree of 3 January 1868 Keiki withdrew to Osaka, where he had substantial forces and where the representatives of the powers had gathered for the opening of the port of Hyōgo, later known as Kōbe. He was in no mood to fight, but the daimyō of Aizu and Kuwana were determined to resist and on 26 January marched their forces towards Kyoto. A clash took place at Toba-Fushimi on the outskirts of Kyoto between them and Satsuma and Chōshū forces; after some tough fighting they were forced to retire to Osaka.

Keiki, who then fled to Edo, was declared a rebel by the court. The castle of Osaka was set on fire, and the foreign representatives forced to retire to the newly opened port of Kōbe. An incident occurred when some soldiers from Bizen (now Okayama prefecture) fired on some foreigners at the port. The man alleged to be responsible for this incident, Taki Zensaburo,[8] was duly condemned to commit ritual suicide in front of foreign representatives.

Fortunately for Japan a major civil war was avoided as Keiki insisted on early surrender. Edo was occupied in April without much fighting, and the terms offered to the Tokugawa were generous. The Aizu fief, however, refused to submit, and the imperial forces, called the *kangun*, consisting mainly of soldiers from Satsuma and Chōsū, had to fight a tough campaign to capture the Aizu stronghold of Aizu-Wakamatsu castle (Fukushima prefecture).

The only other serious resistance was that of Enomoto Takeaki, who late in 1868 escaped from Edo bay with eight warships of the former Tokugawa navy and five French advisers. He seized control of Hakodate in December 1868 and on 27 January 1869 from his fortress at the Goryōkaku in Hakodate declared the independence of Ezo (Hokkaidō). The new government sent an expeditionary force to Ezo under the leadership of a Satsuma samurai, Kuroda Kiyotaka (1840–1900), to attack Enomoto and his forces. After heavy fighting Enomoto surrendered on 27 June 1869 on the understanding that he alone should be held responsible. He was sentenced to imprisonment but granted a special pardon in 1872 and later gave distinguished and loyal service to the government.

The foreign powers led by the British quickly recognized the new regime. Parkes visited Kyoto in March 1868 to pay his respects to the Emperor. While he was on his way to the Imperial Palace from the Chionin temple, where he was staying, his party were attacked by *rōnin*, and members of his escort were wounded. Mitford caught one of the terrorists, who was later executed. The audience eventually took place on 26 March. New credentials were duly presented on 22 May 1868 by Parkes to the Emperor Meiji at the Nishi Honganji temple in Osaka which the young Emperor was visiting at that time.

Modernization of the Political and Economic Structure (1868–77)

The new leaders faced formidable problems. The fiefs had been largely self-governing with a multiplicity of differing regulations and tax regimes. The limited central government structure of the *bakufu* was destroyed by the civil war of 1868–9, and there was no substitute organization ready to replace it. There was thus a grave danger that anarchy and chaos would result from the fall of the shōgunate. Anarchy would have jeopardized the lives of western traders in the treaty ports, and active intervention by the western powers would have become unavoidable. The Japanese had only to look at the situation in China to see the likely consequences of such intervention. To meet this danger Japan had to have a new and effective government as quickly as possible. Administration had to be centralized, an industrial base developed and a disciplined and united defence force, provided with modern equipment, established. Despite many setbacks these requirements were largely met during the first two and a half decades after the restoration. They represented a remarkable achievement by a small number of able, determined and far-sighted men of samurai descent who overcame the reactionary and fissiparous elements in the country.

There were in fact few major winners or losers in the civil war which came to be called the *Boshin* war. The main opposition to the new government had come from the central and northern fiefs, and this was firmly crushed. The remaining rivalries lay between the various western fiefs of the former *tozama* daimyō. There was general recognition of the need for quick and effective action to strengthen Japan against the potential western threat, but there were disagreements between conservative and reformist elements about the pace and extent of the changes needed. Inevitably there was also much jockeying for position and influence.

The fall of the *bakufu* was not a democratic upheaval designed to overthrow an oppressive autocracy. The initial aims of the daimyō and the court were the removal of the Tokugawa and the redistribution of their feudal lands, substituting the Emperor for the shōgun. The early euphoria following the restoration dissipated as the extent of the problems facing Japan became apparent and as the disagreements about how these should be tackled grew more acrimonious. In these circumstances it was inevitable that the determined and far-sighted younger and junior samurai, who had master-minded the restoration and who initially at least managed to maintain a relatively united front, should assume the leading role. Up to 1873 samurai from Satsuma, Chōshū, Tosa (in Shikoku) and Hizen (in western Kyūshū) took the lead; thereafter power lay primarily in the hands of men from Satsuma and Chōshū (the Satchō oligarchy).

The new leaders, having achieved power on the basis of the slogan '*Sonnō jōi*', had little difficulty in showing their respect for the sovereign, but they were in no position to expel the foreigners, although some samurai tried to force the regime to take action by continuing to attack foreigners. The slogan '*Fukoku kyōhei*' ('A rich country and a strong army') was gradually adopted as an alternative rallying cry. This slogan implied that for the moment the foreigners had to be tolerated, but once Japan had the strength a new relationship would be worked out. The 'unequal treaties' were shameful and must be revised as soon as possible. These attitudes were bolstered by the thinking of the Mito school of Neo-Confucian nationalists who feared that the West would destroy the true character of Japan. They termed this the *kokutai* and proclaimed Japan as 'the country of the gods' (*shinkoku*) with the Emperor as the head of Japan's hierarchy. This thinking was to lead in the twentieth century to extremist views of the 'divine' status of the Emperor.

In 1868 the Emperor was still a youth and had to be educated for the role which the leaders were designing for him. He listened to lectures on Confucianism and the Chinese classics, but he was also taught some French and German law. He studied calligraphy and the Japanese classics, where his preference was for the old military chronicles. He became an accomplished writer of Japanese verse. He was short of stature and unimpressive in appearance. In accordance with the theories of the Mito philosophers the young Emperor and the imperial house were projected by the new leaders as the symbol of the unity of Japan and the Japanese people. In theory the Emperor was to be supreme in all matters but, although he was strong-willed and interested in martial affairs, he never became in any sense a dictator. He generally seems to have followed the advice which he received from the leaders of his various governments and to have been content to play the largely symbolic role worked out for him.

One of the first attempts at defining the aims of the new regime was the drafting of the so-called Charter Oath. This was taken by the Emperor on 6 April 1868. It is a vague document which can be interpreted in various ways and of which differing English translations have been made. It demonstrated adherence to traditional Confucian principles but it also recognized the need to adapt Japanese customs to western attitudes. Article I called for the establishment of councils to discuss policy, that is, consensus should be sought. Article II called on all classes to devote themselves to the advancement of the national interest. Article III declared that the people should be allowed to realize their just aspirations. Article IV called for the abolition of uncivilized customs and the maintenance of justice and equity (torture was still an officially recognized element of Japanese 'justice'). Article V declared that knowledge should be sought throughout the world.

In June 1868 a new government was proclaimed. This was based on the old system derived from Chinese models. The supreme organ of government was the Dajōkan (council of state) which had legislative, executive and judicial authority. A number of senior councillors (*gijō*) and junior councillors (*sangi*) were appointed, and a deliberative council was established. The government was divided into departments of state. These covered religious affairs (that is, Shintō), the imperial household, finance, military questions, foreign affairs and civil affairs. The highest posts were filled by members of the imperial family and senior daimyō, but the real power was in the hands of the young samurai who acted as officials in the departments of state. The deliberative assembly had two chambers. One was composed of daimyō and the second and larger of samurai from the clans. It was given no real function, and its discussions were sterile, being usually on questions which had already in fact been decided by the government. It soon lapsed.

The structure of government was revised in 1871 when Sanjō Sanetomo (1837–91), who for most of the time was little more than a figurehead, was appointed chancellor (dajōdaijin), a post which he filled until 1885 when the cabinet system was introduced. Ministries of Justice and Education were created in 1871 and separate Army and Navy Ministries in 1872. The ministry of civil affairs became the Home Ministry in 1873. The Ministry of Agriculture and Commerce was only established in 1881.

One of the first decisions taken by the new government after the defeat of the Tokugawa forces was the removal of the capital from Kyoto to Edo, which in September 1868 was renamed Tokyo, that is, 'eastern capital'. The Emperor began to use the old Tokugawa castle as his residence from mid-1869, but it did not become the Imperial Palace until 1873. An important factor leading to the move from Kyoto was the stultifying atmosphere of the court, which was out of touch with the rest of Japan and knew nothing of the outside world.

The first significant step taken to change the social structure was the abolition of the traditional shi-nō-kō-shō division of classes. Instead in 1869 the people were divided into aristocrats (kazoku), gentry (shizoku), retainers (sotsu) and commoners (heimin). More important than this interim measure, however, was the abolition in the same year of the domain registers. This was the first major step towards the destruction of feudalism. It followed efforts by Kido Kōin to persuade Mōri, the daimyō of Chōshū, in 1868 to surrender his lands voluntarily to the Emperor. Okubo Toshimichi of Satsuma agreed to try to get the Shimazu to do the same. Eventually in March 1869 the daimyō of Chōshū, Satsuma, Tosa and Hizen submitted a memorial to the throne putting their lands and people at the disposal of the Emperor. The exact meaning of this offer was not clear, but other domains were ordered to follow this example, and the daimyō were then apponted governors of the provinces which they had nominally surrendered. This was soon followed by orders for the reapportionment of revenues from the domains and a 'review' of samurai stipends.

These measures alienated some of the more powerful of the restoration leaders such as Saigō Takamori who had led the imperial forces in the civil war. Further steps to destroy feudalism had to be delayed until adequate support had been secured. Saigō was eventually persuaded to withdraw his opposition and in August 1871, Okubo having become Minister of Finance, the abolition of the fiefs was announced. All land was declared to be imperial territory, the daimyō were to cease to exercise any local jurisdiction, and their armies were to be disbanded. In place of the old fiefs and provinces prefectures were established with governors appointed by the central government. In order to sweeten the pill the daimyō were allowed to keep one-tenth of the revenue of their former domains as private income; the samurai did less well.

In 1872 the feudal ban on the sale or transfer of land was abolished, and in 1873 a new land tax, worked out by Okuma Shigenobu, the vice-Minister of Finance, came into force. This was to be based on the capital value of the land rather than as hitherto on the annual crops. The rate was fixed at 3 per cent and was to be paid in money not produce as hitherto, irrespective of whether the harvest was a good one or not. The rate was supposed to be roughly in line with the old assessments, but there was less scope for evasion, and it inevitably led to the alienation of land from small peasant cultivators who found themselves unable to meet tax demands. Land accordingly came to be concentrated in the hands of landowners and money-lenders. The land tax was thus the cause of much rural unrest and poverty in years to come. The inequities which developed were only liquidated by the land reform carried out during the occupation of Japan after the Second World War.

In December 1871 a major diplomatic mission to the USA and to Europe left Yokohama. It was to seek knowledge of the world outside Japan and revision of the treaties. It was led by Iwakura Tomomi and included Kido Kōin, Itō Hirobumi and Okubo Toshimichi. The Iwakura mission, during its eighteen-month travels, was firmly told that talk of treaty revision was premature. The mission recognized how far Japan was behind western countries in science and technology and realized that Japan would have to acquire western learning and customs if it was to establish itself as an equal power with western countries. This process was euphemistically called *bunmei kaika* ('cultural enlightenment').

While the mission was away the caretaker government, dominated by Saigō Takamori, were incensed by alleged insults from Korea, which continued to maintain a policy of seclusion. Saigō advocated a policy of conquest (*seikanron*), which he saw as a way of employing the samurai. He proposed in 1873 that he should go to Korea in the expectation that he would be assassinated and war would become unavoidable. But the Emperor, on the advice of Sanjō Sanetomo, declared that the decision must await Iwakura's return. Iwakura in fact ruled against the proposal. Saigō in fury returned to Satsuma, refusing to co-operate further with the new government. A number of other important leaders of the new government also resigned, including Etō Shimpei (1834–74) from Hizen, Gotō Shōjiro (1838–97) and Itagaki Taisuke (1837–1919) from Tosa.

In 1874, however, the firebrands were allowed to mount an expedition to Taiwan (Formosa). This was a response to the murder two years previously of fifty-four shipwrecked seamen from the Ryūkyū Islands by Taiwanese natives. The expedition met fierce resistance and suffered badly from malaria. A settlement of the issue was obtained through the mediation of the British minister in Peking. China agreed to pay an indemnity, and the force was withdrawn.

The dismantling of feudalism continued apace. In 1871 the government issued an order encouraging men to dispense with their traditional topknot hair-style. Samurai were also permitted to go about without their swords and were forbidden to exercise their traditional privilege of trying out their swords on living people (*kirisute gomen*). Finally in 1876 the wearing of swords by samurai was totally forbidden. Meanwhile the status of the samurai class as the fighting men of Japan was undermined by the decree issued in December 1872 setting up a system of conscription, under which all men of whatever class reaching the age of twenty were liable for service in the forces. In January 1873 the western Gregorian calender was adopted instead of the old lunar calendar.

The government had a major financial problem. They had to find ways of financing a growing central government, a new army and navy and the modern industries required to make Japan strong. The land tax was the main source of revenue but it was insufficient to meet the needs of the new state and to pay the unproductive samurai. In 1873 the samurai had been offered the opportunity to commute their stipends into a capital sum, but the terms were unattractive and few accepted. In 1876 all stipends were compulsorily commuted into government bonds. Those receiving the larger stipends received bonds bearing 5 per cent interest capitalized at five to seven and a half years. Those on smaller stipends received bonds paying higher rates of interest and capitalized on the basis of longer periods, but as inflation was then running at high levels the daimyō and the samurai faced a huge cut in their standard of living. The daimyō were left with enough to enable them to remain in the aristocracy. Many samurai, however, had to seek work as officials, cultivators or policemen, or find posts in the army or navy. Some went into commerce, where their capital, however small, was of importance for the development of Japanese industry.

A rebellion in 1874 in Saga (the former Hizen province) led by Etō Shimpei was quickly suppressed. Etō was captured and executed. The Satsuma rebellion of 1877 was not so easily suppressed, although the rebels never really had a chance of success. Saigō Takamori, since his withdrawal from the central government in 1873, had set up a network of schools which put the emphasis on military training. His conservative supporters dominated the government in Kagoshima, the old capital of the Satsuma fief. These steps aroused suspicions in Tokyo, and when measures were taken by the central government to remove some munitions from Kagoshima fighting broke out. Saigō, who had taken no part in the action so far, now felt impelled to assume the leadership of what had become a rebellion. A motley force of some 40,000 men was organized, and Saigō proposed to march on Tokyo. The rebels, however, encountered stubborn resistance from government forces in Kumamoto castle. The Kumamoto garrison was relieved after some fifty days' fighting, and the rebels were then forced to retire to the mountains of southern Kyūshū. Finally Saigō with 400 men made a last stand at Kagoshima. On 24 September 1877 he committed suicide, and the rebellion was crushed. Saigō remained a popular tragic Japanese hero and was eventually granted a posthumous pardon in 1891.

The Satsuma rebellion (also known as the *seinan* or 'south-west' war) did not end Satsuma participation in the Meiji government, although for the next few years the people of Kagoshima had a rough time. But it ended the career of Okubo Toshimichi of Satsuma, who had been Home Minister during the war and was regarded as responsible for the measures taken against the former fief. He was assassinated by six ex-samurai from Satsuma on 14 May 1878. The war also marked the ascendancy of Chōshū men in the Japanese army; although Oyama Iwao (1842–1916) from Satsuma rose to the rank of field marshal and chief of the army staff, the leading figure in the build-up of the army was Yamagata Aritomo (1838–1922) from Chōshū. Satsuma men, however, took the lead in building up the Japanese navy with British advice and assistance.

By 1880 significant progress had been made in forming an effective central administration. The process was largely completed during the next decade.

188

Political Parties and the Meiji Constitution of 1889

There was no Japanese press before the restoration, and news was spread either by broadsheets or by word of mouth. The *bakufu* had neither interest in nor respect for public opinion and they had no intention of allowing it to maifest itself. However, after the establishment of the treaty ports they could not prevent the development in the ports of English-language newspapers for the use of the foreign community there. The first of these papers was the *Nagasaki Shipping List and Advertiser* which was produced from June 1861 by a Mr A. W. Hansard. In November 1861 Hansard moved to Yokohama, where he launched the *Japan Herald*. Other English-language papers were later published in Yokohama, Kōbe and other treaty ports. Selected articles from these papers were translated and published in Japanese. The first Japanese-language 'newspaper' seems to have been the *Bankokushinbunshi* ('All Countries Newspaper'), which was produced irregularly in Yokohama by an eccentric English clergyman, the Reverend Buckworth Bailey. The first number appeared in the winter of 1867, and eighteen issued in all were produced up to the spring of 1869. The first Japanese daily paper was the *Yokohama Mainichi Shinbun* which was launched in 1871. It was followed by many other Japanese-language newspapers. The early Japanese news-papers were limited in size and circulation and tended to seek popularity by sensational reporting and vitriolic criticism of the authorities. They soon irritated the Meiji authorities by their irresponsibility, and regulations to control them were made in 1873. In 1875 the first of many laws designed to limit the freedom of the Japanese press was enacted. Newspapers were regularly suspended and fined and editors imprisoned. One dodge, employed by some of the papers affected by the censorship rules, was to employ an editor whose main job was to go to prison when the paper was prosecuted.

The early Meiji press reflected the intellectual ferment of the age. Japanese intellectuals eagerly sought ideas from the West. Many of these were ill digested and sometimes misunderstood, but they were an important ingredient in the growing pressures for political and social change. The Meiji leaders recognized that Japan had to be modernized, but they were determined to ensure that the pace and nature of reform should be carefully controlled so that Japan would become strong under a unifed and central government. The imperial house 'descended from the sun goddess' provided the symbol needed to win the loyalty of the many potentially fissiparous elements in the new Japan which was emerging. But the Satchō oligarchy realized that traditional methods of autocratic rule could not ensure their athority in a period when society was changing so fast to meet the challenges of the second half of the nineteenth century. The Satsuma rebellion also clearly demonstrated the need for some kind of safety valve. Moreover, although the Charter Oath of 1868 had spoken of deliberative assemblies, the first council of daimyō and samurai had been allowed to lapse as it had had no real function. The new leaders were determined that, when another assembly was set up, it should not be in a position to threaten the basic policies of the new regime and their assessment of Japan's national interests.

As a first step prefectural assemblies were established in 1878. The franchise was narrowly based and the assemblies' powers strictly limited. but the government recognized that more concessions would have to be made to popular pressure for

189

a say in government; the demand for people's rights (*minken*) was growing. In 1881 Okuma Shigenobu, who had come from Hizen (Saga prefecture) and had been Finance Minister since 1873, but who felt himself isolated among the Satchō oligarchs in the government, submitted a memorandum to the throne in which he called for early action to promulgate a constitution. This should, in his view, provide for party governments and a cabinet responsible to parliament. Okuma's proposals were rejected, and he was forced out of the government. Meanwhile Itagaki Taysuke and Gotō Shōjirō had formed the Jiyūtō (Liberal Party). This example was soon followed by Okuma Shigenobu, who established the Kaishintō (Progressive Party). The Jiyūtō took its ideology from French radicalism and found its initial support in rural areas. The Kaishintō recieved backing from the cities and wealthy merchants and industrialists. It was also joined by disaffected bureaucrats. A third party, the Teiseitō (Imperial Government Party), was formed by conservatives, but it was of no real significance. The radical parties were unable to operate effectively as they were subject to constant harassment and police repression. Their existence coincided with a period of rioting and violence caused by economic grievances, and the parties began to become associated with these anti-government activities. The party leaders felt that they could not afford to be branded as violent extremists. The Jiyūtō was, therefore, disbanded in 1884, and Okuma left the Kaishintō, which then ceased to be of any importance. The government at the same time did all they could to lower the reputations of the party leaders.

Factionalism has always been a major problem in Japanese politics. It arose from the traditional Japanese attachment to personal loyalties and relative indifference to questions of ideology. Ozaki Yukio (1859–1954),[9] the grand old man of Japanese parliamentarianism, summed up this phenomenon in these words:

> Here in the Orient we have had the conception of a faction; but not of a public party ... when political parties are transplanted into the East, they at once partake of the nature of factions, pursuing private and personal interests instead of the interests of the State ... political parties ... are really affairs of personal connections and sentiments, the relations between the leaders and members of a party being similar to those which subsisted between a feudal lord and his liegemen.

In March 1882 Itō Hirobumi, who had assumed responsibility for the drafting of a constitution, left for Europe on an eighteen-month tour to study European models. He went first to Berlin and Vienna, believing that he would find there constitutions which would be more appropriate for Japan than those of France or Britain. He perceived similarities between the situation in Japan and in Germany, where he was attracted by the strong position of the German Emperor. Both countries had autocratic and militarist traditions and both had a powerful class of conservatives and nationalists who were determined to achieve for their country a major position of power in the world. In Bismarck, Itō thought he had found a kindred spirit; at least they shared a distaste for democratic institutions. Itō indeed tried in the future to model himself on Bismarck. In London he met the political philosopher Herbert Spencer, who tried to explain to him the theories of parliamentary government, but the German influence remained dominant.

Back in Japan, Itō joined with his colleagues in extensive preparations for the promulgation of a constitution. In 1884 a hereditary peerage on European lines was established so that a house of peers could form part of the legislative process. There were five ranks, namely prince (*kōshaku*), marquis (also *kōshaku*, but the character for *kō* was different), count (*hakushaku*), viscount (*shishaku*) and baron (*danshaku*); 508 titles were created in 1884. Court nobles and ex-daimyō were given appropriate ranks, and peerages were also conferred on the Meiji leaders as well as on some senior officers in the army and navy.

In 1885 the civil service was reformed, and competitive examinations for candidates were established. At the same time a cabinet on European lines was formed in place of the old Dajōkan. In 1888 a privy council (*sūmitsuin*) was appointed to act as the supreme advisory body in Japan. In 1889 two elder statesmen with the title of *genrō* were named as informal supreme advisors. They were Itō Hirobumi and Kuroda Kiyotaka (1840–1900), one of the Meiji leaders from Satsuma, who was Prime Minister in 1888. Five other leaders were later appointed as *genrō*; these were Matsukata Masayoshi (1835–1924), Oyama Iwao (1842–1916), Saigō Tsugumichi (1843–1913) (younger brother of Saigō Takamori), Yamagata Aritomo (1838–1922) and Inoue Kaoru (1836–1915). In 1912 Katsura Tarō (1847–1913) and Saionji Kinmochi (1849–1940) were also named *genrō*, but the number of members dwindled as the *genrō* died, and their influence declined after the end of the Meiji period in 1912.

The Meiji constitution was promulgated on 11 February 1889. It was clearly stated to be a gift from the Emperor to his people, and many powers were reserved to him, including declarations of war, conclusion of treaties and supreme command of the armed forces. The Emperor also kept extensive powers to issue ordinances and he could freely adjourn or prorogue the Diet. This was the name given, after the German model, to the house of peers and the house of representatives which were established by the constitution. The two houses had equal rights. The cabinet remained responsible to the Emperor, not to the Diet, whose powers were further restrictd by the provision that, if the budget were not passed, the government had the right to repeat the budget of the previous year. Initiatives to revise the constitution could only come from the Emperor. Articles 1 and 3 perpetuated the myth of the unique nature of the Japanese people and the divine ancestry of the imperial house. Article 1 read: 'The Empire of Japan shall be reigned over and governed by a line of Emperors unbroken for ages eternal.' Article 3 declared: 'The Emperor is sacred and inviolable.'

However, the courts were empowered to act in the Emperor's name independently of the executive. The Diet did have the power to initiate legislation, and in practice Japanese cabinets thereafter could not operate wholly without reference to the Diet. Just sufficient powers were granted to the Diet to buy off the politicians pressing for people's rights.

In December 1889 Yamagata Aritomo became Prime Minister, and in July 1890 the first elections to the house of representatives were held. The franchise was narrow. Men paying 15 yen or more each year in taxes were qualified to vote, but this meant that there were only 500,000 men with the right to vote out of a population at that time of some 40 million. There were 300 seats in the house of representatives. Gotō Shōjirō, Itagaki Taisuke and Okuma Shigenobu were among those elected and had sizeable factions of between 50 and 60 members each; they and the 140 independents all tended to be critical of the government. Inevitably, therefore, when the house met in November 1890 there was immediate trouble. The house demanded large cuts in the budget, and a compromise was only reached after bribery and threats had been used by the government. Yamagata then handed over to Matsukata Masayoshi, but despite his long experience as Minister of Finance (he had held the post since 1881) he failed to get the next budget through, and the house was dissolved in December 1891.

The elections in February 1892 were marked by intimidation and violence, and after the house had held stormy initial sessions Matsukata resigned and Itō took his place in August that year. An attempt was made to impeach the government in 1893, and the house was again dissolved. The next election in March 1894 failed to produce results any more satisfactory to the government, and the Diet was once more dissolved in June 1894. All this suggested that the constitution was unworkable, but elections were expensive and Itō was willing to try to work out a compromise with the politicians who wanted a share in the power. Factions and power-broking rather than expensive elections and ineffective parliamentary motions of no confidence accordingly came to dominate the political scene in Tokyo in the final years of the nineteenth century.

Treaty Revision

A fundamental aim of the Meiji leaders was the achievement of equality with the western powers. They wanted above all a revision of the treaties which had been concluded with the western powers in 1858. These were regarded as 'unequal' because of the powers granted under them to the consular courts of the treaty powers to try their own nationals for offences committed in Japan under extra-territorial provisions which were an infringement of Japanese sovereignty. There was also resentment over the limits placed on Japanese power to fix tariff rates.

Following the Iwakura mission, however, it became clear to the Japanese leaders that revision could not be achieved quickly and that significant changes in the way Japan was governed and in Japanese behaviour would be required before the western powers would agree to changes in the treaties. There was, for instance, no chance that the powers would agree to Japanese jurisdiction over their nationals so long as Japanese justice remained arbitrary and uncoded or while torture of suspects was accepted as normal. The Japanese also had to accept that they would be regarded as uncivilized and outlandish while their customs and habits were so different from those of western countries.

The authorities accordingly took early steps to reform criminal proceedings. In 1873 a new code was introduced which, however, merely incorporated the main lines of that operating in China under the Ch'ing (Qing) dynasty. This clearly did not meet western concerns, and a new code, based on French principles of law and on the advice of a French legal expert, Emile Gustave Boissonade de Fontarabie, was adopted in 1880 and came into force in 1882. It remains the basis of the criminal law operating in Japan today. Japanese prisons were also improved, and model prisons were shown to foreign visitors.

The adoption of a western-style civil code took longer. Boissonade de Fontarabie also produced a draft civil code for Japan in 1881; this was revised after lengthy arguments, adopted in 1888 and embodied in a law of 1890, but the code was further revised and was not enforced until 1898. The delays were caused by controversies between proponents of English and French law and over the adaption of western concepts of civil rights to Japanese traditional attitudes towards the family and the 'house'. The code finally enforced was a compromise incorporating some German elements but retaining the paternalist, male-dominated household system based on traditional Confucian values.[10]

In the first two decades of the Meiji period prior to the promulgation of the constitution the authorities did all they could be promote western customs. In response to Victorian sensibilities Japanese were forbidden to go about naked or inadequately clothed, and mixed bathing was banned. The court adopted western clothing, and all guests at imperial garden parties had to appear in frock coats. Japanese bureaucrats wore western clothing in their offices although they changed into more informal Japanese dress at home. Schools and universities adopted western-style uniforms, and the colourful costumes of the Edo period were replaced by a drab uniformity. Court ceremonies and protocol were made to conform to the prevailing European pattern. Japanese ministers and senior officials worked hard to learn European languages and regularly met members of the small foreign diplomatic community in Tokyo. They gave western-style garden parties, dinners and even balls and readily accepted invitations from the ministers in charge of the foreign legations. Indeed, in those years Japanese ministers were much more accessible to the foreigner than they are today. To provide a meeting place for social events, involving Japanese and foreigners, the Rokumeikan (literally, the Deer Cry Pavilion), a western-style building in brick, was built in Tokyo in 1883 on a site by the present Hibiya park.[11] In its heyday in the 1880s the Rokumeikan became the symbol of Japanese westernization and was the scene of many receptions, balls and musical events. Japanese men played cards and billiards with their western acquaintances there, and charitable bazaars brought the ladies together. In 1887 Itō, then Prime Minister, gave a fancy-dress party at his residence. He appeared as a Venetian nobleman, while Inoue Kaoru, the Foreign Minister, was dressed as a strolling musician. This display sadly shocked the conservatives, and a reaction set in against such 'decadent' western customs. In the 1890s there was a sharp swing back to traditional values based on nationalist interpretations of the Confucian ethical system.

In the late 1870s Terajima Munenori (1832–93), then Japanese Foreign Minister, offered to open additional ports in return for tariff autonomy. His proposal was acceptable to the United States but not to Britain. In the 1880s Inoue Kaoru, after he had taken over as Foreign Minister, made proposals for revision which would have increased Japanese tariff autonomy and provided for an element of Japanese jurisdiction over foreigners. Preliminary talks in Tokyo in 1882 were followed by more substantive discussions in 1886. Inoue's proposals envisaged the abolition of the extraterritorial provisions in the 1858 treaties and the opening of the country beyond the treaty ports to foreigners. The establishment of a system of 'mixed courts', with the participation of foreign judges and with primary jurisdiction in all cases involving foreigners, was an important element in the proposals. It was designed to win the agreement of the powers to the ending of their extraterritorial privileges. However, when these proposals leaked out in Japan in 1887, they aroused furious opposition on the grounds that the 'mixed courts' were an infringement of Japanese sovereignty. Negotiations had to be suspended. Inoue then resigned.

In 1888, when Okuma Shigenobu was Foreign Minister, another attempt was made to get agreement on revision. He managed to reach agreement with Germany and the USA and was in the course of negotiations with Britain, when a draft of the treaty was obtained by a Japanese newspaper. Although many of the more unpalatable features of the Inoue proposals had been removed, the appointment of foreign judges to Japanese courts trying foreign nationals remained in the draft. This aroused a public outcry in Japan, and Okuma was seriously injured in a bomb attack by an extremist. This was the era of the *sōshi*. They may be described as political bully boys who in a frenzy of Japanese chauvinism also attacked foreign diplomats in Tokyo.

A further attempt by Mutsu Munemitsu (1844–97), who became Foreign Minister in 1892, was at first no more successful. Public opinion as represented by the press and by members of the house of representatives was opposed to any concessions which might in their view lead to infringements of Japanese racial and cultural purity as a result of opening the country to foreigners. Eventually, however, in 1894 the British were persuaded that Japan had made sufficient social and legal progress to permit the abolition of extraterritoriality and a new Anglo–Japanese commercial treaty, based on the principle of reciprocity, was signed in 1894 to come into force in 1899 when the legal codes would be fully enforced. The other powers followed suit, and by 1897 the process of revision had been completed. The new treaties, however, provided that Japan would not gain full tariff autonomy for twelve years after the treaties came into force, that is, not until 1911. (Under the earlier treaties most Japanese tariffs had been fixed at 5 per cent.) This limitation on her freedom of action was a cause of continuing resentment in Japan. This apart, however, Japan could claim, following the revision of the treaties of 1858, to have acquired equal status with the western powers.

Economic Developments

When Perry's 'black ships' arrived off Uraga in 1853 Japan had very little industry, although in a number of fiefs some beginnings had been made. Commerce especially in Osaka and Edo, where relatively sophisticated markets and exchange facilities had developed, was an important element in the economy.

The first reverbatory furnace (used in the making of cannon) had been established in 1850 in Hizen (Saga prefecture). Similar furnaces were built in Satsuma (Kagoshima prefecture) and in Mito (Ibaragi prefecture) in 1853. Two iron smelters had been constructed in Satsuma in 1852, and by 1856 the fief had managed to produce six ships equipped with cannon. In Chōshū (Yamaguchi prefecture) an iron foundry was built in 1854, and a shipyard was opened in 1857. The *bakufu* arranged for a steamboat to be built in Japan in 1857, and in 1865, with French help, the Yokosuka iron foundry and dockyard were constructed.

The Satsuma fief bought various ships from Britain in the 1860s as well as sugar factories for the development of the Ryūkyū sugar industry. In about 1866 they also purchased a textile spinning and weaving factory from Britain and had the factory installed by English technicians.[13] The fiefs and the *bakufu* also operated at least ten important mines extracting minerals and coal.

The industrial base at the time of the restoration was, however, rudimentary, and Japan was in no position to compete effectively with western industrialized countries. Owing to miscalculations about the relative values of silver and gold, Japan lost considerable amounts of specie in the first years after the opening of the treaty prots, and there was little or no knowledge or understanding at this time of economics, nor appropriate Japanese words to describe the basic economic factors. Japan had also not got the basic infrastructure nor the capital resources on which a modern industry could be built. The initiative for industrial development inevitably had to be taken by the government. The era up to about 1880 was thus one of state capitalism. Industries, particularly strategic but also civil, were established and developed with funds provided through the state. Large numbers of foreign experts were employed by the government as engineers and teachers.[14] Almost half came from Britain, but experts from France, Germany, the USA, Holland and other countries were also employed by the Japanese government.

Some of the first foreigners to arrive were railway engineers. In November 1869, on the advice of Sir Harry Parkes, the British Minister, the Japanese government decided to build an extensive railway network. A loan was raised in London, and work began in 1870 on the first railway from Yokohama to Tokyo. This was completed in the autumn of 1872. The next line to be built was that between Kōbe and Osaka; this was then extended to Kyoto, and the whole line was opened by the Emperor in February 1877. Further lines were built in the course of the next few years, but for financial reasons the pace of development slowed down in the early 1880s. The line between Tokyo and Kyoto was only completed in 1889. Thereafter railways were built to connect all the main towns of Japan. A narrow gauge was chosen, because it was thought that this would simplify construction in a country as mountainous as most of Japan. In the first few years, in additon to British railway engineers, British train drivers operated the trains. At first the British engineers were critical of Japanese workmen and work practices, but the Japanese soon learned to build and operate the railways without foreign help.

In 1868 Richard Brunton arrived from Britain to establish a lighthouse service, and initially British and European lighthouse keepers were employed. Brunton was also involved in the construction of the first telegraph line between Yokohama and Tokyo. By 1872 a line had been constructed between Tokyo and Nagasaki, and telegraphic communication between London and Tokyo became possible via the Great Northern Telegraph. Brunton also advised on such subjects as drains and roads for Yokohama and made surveys of the ports of Osaka and Niigata. Not all his advice was followed, and he found working for the Japanese authorities a frustrating business, as he had to work under a Japanese official without engineering experience.

The first foreign bank to establish a branch in Japan was the Chartered Mercantile Bank of India, London and China, which opened an office in Yokohama in 1863. Other British banks soon followed, but only the Oriental and Mercantile banks survived an economic crisis which occurred in Yokohama in 1866.

In 1868 the new government arranged to purchase the Hong Kong mint, but before it could start operating the machinery was destroyed by fire. A new mint was completed in the autumn of 1870, and a British superviser was appointed. The new currency, denominated in yen, then replaced the Mexican dollar which had hitherto been the currency in general use in the treaty ports.

In 1869 eight exchange companies (*kawase kaisha*) were established in Japan to handle deposits, loans and remittances, but many of these were not soundly based. In December 1872 a National Bank Ordinance was issued establishing a banking system on US lines. By 1876 only four national banks had been established under this ordinance because of the onerous obligations which the banks had to meet. These regulations were then relaxed, and by 1879, when the rules were again tightened, there were 153 national banks. A central bank on European lines was needed, and the Bank of Japan was established in 1882 with the sole right to issue notes. In the meantime efforts to mobilize Japanese savings, which were required to finance industrial development, were made through the post offices and specialized savings banks. The commutation of samurai pensions injected much-needed funds into the system, but added to inflationary pressures in the economy. This led to a financial crisis which was only overcome when Matsukata Masayoshi became Finance Minister in 1881 and managed to bring the budget under control.

Foreign trade had grown quickly in the years immediately following the restoration, but the pace of growth declined in the latter part of the 1870s. In most years imports exceeded exports by a large margin, and the adverse balance of payments had to be covered by capital movements. Imports were mostly textiles, including cotton goods from Manchester, and capital goods such as machinery, ships, railway equipment and munitions, mainly from Britain. Japan's chief exports were raw silk (there was an outbreak of silkworm disease in Europe at this time) and tea. But rice, copper and traditional Japanese craft items were also exported. To deal with the requirements of foreign trade the Yokohama Specie Bank (now the Bank of Tokyo) was established in 1880.

In the initial stages of industrialization the emphasis is normally placed first on textiles and light industries, but in the Japanese case the need to build up Japanese defences meant that the defence industries were given priority. The Japanese government did, however, also set up model textile factories and established glass and cement factories. In 1880 the Japanese authorities decided that the time had come to privatize civil enterprises so that they could concentrate on those of a strictly military character. The Ministry of Agriculture and Commerce, formed in 1881, was given responsibility to put this policy into effect. Many of the government enterprises found their way into the hands of groups such as the Mitsui and Mitsubishi, which were to grow in later years into what came to be called the *zaibatsu* (financial groups). Mitsui, for instance, took over the Shinmachi spinning mill and the Miike coal mines, while Mitsubishi acquired the Nagasaki shipyards. Mitsubishi also benefited from government generosity when the thirteen ships used to transport the expedition of 1874 to Taiwan were handed over to Iwasaki Yatarō (1835–85), the founder of the Mitsubishi group, which in 1885 established Japan's premier shipping line, the Nippon Yūsen Kaisha (NYK). Most of Japan's famous industrial groups indeed had their origin in the Meiji period, including other top *zaibatsu* firms such as Sumitomo and Yasuda.

The Japanese authorities were able to dispense with most of their foreign advisers after about 1880, although a few experts and teachers stayed on through the 1880s. The Japanese learned quickly and had no inhibitions about copying foreign products. The role played by the government in building up Japanese industry and providing the necessary finance meant that from the beginning the relationship between the bureaucracy and industry, commerce and finance was very close. The bureaucrats, who were initially mainly of samurai stock, were very much the élite and expected to be obeyed. The foundations for the influence and prestige of the Ministry of Finance and the post-war Ministry of International Trade and Industry were thus laid in the Meiji era. The comparative lack of private funds available for industrial development meant that Japanese banks and financial institutions rather than private shareholders played a key role in the build-up of Japanese industry, and this facilitated the growth of the *zaibatsu* and Japanese-style capitalism.

Education

The new leaders recognized that, if Japan was to achieve equality with the western powers and become strong and prosperous, the country had to adopt western technology and industrial methods. This required an adaptable and well-trained work-force as well as an educated élite to provide the necessary leadership. The network of clan schools and *terakoya* which had been developed during the Edo period meant that there was a basis on which to build a new educational system. Moreover there was a tradition in Japan, arising from Confucian ethics, of respect for learning and for teachers. The term *sensei* (literally, 'former born' but meaning 'honoured teacher') is still a term of respect in Japan today, even if it has now been debased by its use in addressing members of the Diet as well as doctors and teachers.

As a first step a Ministry of Education was created in 1871, and a centralized educational system, incorporating the former *terakoya* as primary schools, was established by an order issued in 1872. Tanaka Fujimaro (1845–1909), who had been a member of the Iwakura mission and had been charged to look at foreign education, was appointed vice-Minister of Education in 1874. With advice from David Murray, an American educationist, he attempted to revise the system on American lines and make it less centralized. The emphasis was placed on western-style education rather than on Confucian moral teaching. This inevitably aroused the opposition of the old-style samurai who despised such practical subjects as arithmetic. From 1880 the government decreed that the key aim of education was to be moral training (*shūshin*). Nationalist indoctrination with particular stress on extreme respect for the Emperor and the imperial institution became important features of the Japanese educational system. These elements were further developed by Mori Arinori (1847–89), who became Minister of Education in 1886. He believed that the purpose of education was to train the Japanese people to serve the state. He imposed military-style discipline and training in secondary schools and reinforced central control of education. Ironically, he was seen by reactionary fanatics of his day as being too westernized and he was assassinated on 11 February 1889.

The reactionary educational philosophy of the Meiji leaders was reflected in the Imperial Rescript on Education published in 1890. It is more a high-sounding statement of moral principles than a declaration of educational policy. It called on all Japanese: 'should emergency arise, offer yourselves courageously to the State; and thus guard and maintain the prosperity of Our Imperial Throne coeval with heaven and earth'. Sansom sums it up as 'the culmination of a movement in favour of native traditions and away from that pragmatic, utilitarian view of life which (as the governing classes saw it) was destroying the ancient morality of Japan – what they called the National Essence – and putting in its place nothing but a dangerous utilitarianism and a subversive materialism'.[15] Fortunately in practice the Meiji leaders were generally pragmatic and utilitarian, and the educational system managed to produce practical men and competent leaders.

Tokyo University was founded in 1877 through an amalgamation of the Kaisei school of the Edo period and separate colleges of medicine and engineering.[16] It soon became the most prestigious of the government-sponsored universitites, and graduates of Tōdai, as the university of called in Japanese, have always regarded themselves as the *crème de la crème*. The university of Kyoto was not established until 1897, but some important private universities were founded in the first decades of the Meiji period. Keiō school, which had been set up in Edo in 1858 by Fukuzawa Yukichi (1835–1901) for the study of Dutch, became a university in 1890. Waseda school, founded in 1882 by Okuma Shigenobu, became Waseda University in 1902. Another famous university in Tokyo, Hitotsubashi, was originally a school for commercial law founded by Mori Arinori. Dōshisha University in Kyoto grew out of a college founded in 1875 by Niijima Jō in co-operation with American Congregational missionaries.

Intellectual Trends and Language Developments

The 1870s and 1880s were years of intellectual ferment. There was intense curiosity about the West and about western ideas as well as products. Western styles and fashions were slavishly copied and intitially at least native traditions despised. But in the second half of the 1880s nationalist sentiment forced a reversion to native traditions, although some of the foreign influence remained, and Japanese literature and language had changed significantly.

Inevitably there was a rush to translate foreign books into Japanese. This, however, presented real language problems, and the first attempts, which used Chinese read as if it was Japanese (a form of *kanbun*, called *kanbun chokuyaku*), were neither felicitous nor accurate. Among early translations into this form was one by Oda Junichirō, who had studied law at Edinburgh University. This was an attempted translation of *Ernest Maltravers*, a political novel by Bulwer Lytton (1803–73), a prolific English Victorian writer whose works, apart perhaps from *The Last Days of Pompeii*, are little read today. Lytton's novels, as well as those of Benjamin Disraeli (1804–81), were avidly perused by the young intellectuals. Among other English novels translated into Japanese in these years were works by Jules Verne such as *Around the World in Eighty Days*. Possibly the most influential and popular of these early translations was that of *Self Help* by Samuel Smiles (1812–1904). This piece of Victorian social philosophy appeared in a Japanese version in 1870. The traditional Japanese preference for political philosophy rather than metaphysics was demonstrated by an indiscriminate Japanese interest in works by Montesquieu (1689–1755), Jean-Jacques Rousseau (1712–78), John Stuart Mill (1806–73) and Herbert Spencer (1820–1903) among others. The resulting intellectual indigestion needed the antacid provided by the works of Charles Darwin (1809–82) and Thomas Huxley (1825–95). The concept of the survival of the fittest (*yūshō reppai* or 'the superior wins and the inferior loses') aroused a sympathetic response among Japanese politicians of the day. This was a useful 'argument for abolishing what you did not like or building up your strength against enemies'.[16]

Among the many western concepts for which there were no Japanese equivalents was that of the rights of the people. This was translated as *minken*. At first in the 1870s the ideas behind this word aroused an enthusiastic response among young intellectuals, but by the late 1880s many of them had seen the way the wind was blowing and had come to espouse more authoritarian, Germanic and conservative notions. Certainly any manifestations of interest in socialist thought were ruthlessly suppressed. Even the concept of 'free trade' began to be frowned on as inconsistent with putting Japan first in all things.

Men like Nishi Amane (1829–97)[17] and Fukuzawa Yukichi made significant contributions to Japanese thought and to Japanese vocabulary, adapting combinations of Chinese characters to convey such ideas as competition (*kyōsō*), nature (*shizen*) and liberty (*jiyū*).[18] The Japanese at this period had not yet adopted the modern practice of using foreign words transliterated into the *katakana* syllabary, sometimes abbreviated or mispronounced so that they are no longer intelligible to the native speaker of the language from which the word is borrowed. However, *kana* came to be used increasingly in Japanese writings, not least because of the clumsiness and complexity of *kanbun*. The use of *kana* was promoted by the writings of Kanagaki Robun (1829–94). Kanagaki, which means 'to write in *kana*', was a pseudonym of Nozaki Bunzō, a popular writer of humorous stories, who also made fun of the pompous and ultra-serious intellectuals of the time, including Fukuzawa Yukichi. But the most important linguistic development of these years was the introduction of more colloquial forms into the written language in what was called *genbun-itchi* ('unification of the spoken and written languages').

Fukuzawa Yukichi devoted his whole life to propagating western thought in Japan. His most famous work was his *Seiyō jijō* ('Conditions in the West'), which appeared in three volumes in 1866, 1868 and 1870. His *Gakumon no susume* ('An Encouragement of Learning'), which appeared between 1872 and 1876, was a major contribution to the promotion of 'cultural enlightenment' (*bunmei kaika*). Fukuwaza tried hard to promote practical studies and was one of the first and few early male champions of women's rights in Japan.

An interesting example of another Japanese intellectual who did not succumb to reactionary pressures was Baba Tatsui (1850–88), who had been a student at Fukuzawa's Keiō school. He spent two periods in England in the 1870s, where he was a nationalist in his criticisms of the 'unequal treaties', but on his return to Japan he did his best to promote popular rights. This led to his arrest in 1885. On his release in 1886 he went as a political exile to the United States, where he died in 1888.

Despite men like Fukuzawa, Baba and others, the reaction against western individualism and liberalism had set in by 1894. The establishment in Japan

199

remained firmly authoritarian. Nationalist sentiment was dominant, and the imperial myths, propagated by the Meiji leaders to justify their retention of power and build up Japanese unity and strength, were not effectively challenged. There was thus no firm basis for any powerful intellectual opposition to the growth of Japanese imperialism and expansionism in the first half of the twentieth century.

Religion

The fall of the *bakufu* had serious implications for Buddhism in Japan. Many of the loyalist supporters of the restoration favoured Shintō and disliked the synthesis which had been achieved between Shintō and Buddhism. The new government declared that it did not seek to eradicate Buddhism (*haibutsu kishaku*) but rather to separate Shintō from Buddhism (*shinbutsu bunri*). In practice, however, the new leaders were unsympathetic to Buddhism and in the process of eliminating Buddhist influences from Shintō shrines they adopted measures which were inimical to Buddhism. Temple lands and property were confiscated, and in many places Buddhist images and temples were destroyed by nationalist zealots.

A system of national shrines was established, and the office of Shintō rites (*jingikan*) became a part of the apparatus of government. Shintō was made into a national cult in support of imperial rule, and the concept of Japan and the Japanese as unique descendants of the gods was promoted. This 'state Shintō' was taught in schools and was increasingly used to give backing to nationalist ends.

Ryōbu-Shintō may have been officially suppressed, but most Japanese followed both Buddhist and Shintō rites. Many households had and some still have both a *kamidana* (a god shelf) to show their respect for the Shintō gods and a *Butsudan* (Buddhist altar), if only as a memorial to the souls of their ancestors.[19]

In the increasingly materialist society of Japan in the late nineteenth century religion came to matter less for many Japanese families. Those who sought spiritual comfort and could not find this in traditional forms of Buddhist and Shintō ceremonies were forced to look elsewhere. Of all the Buddhist sects Zen was more successful than most in maintaining its vitality. Largely through the writings of Suzuki Daisetsu (1870–1966) it succeeded in attracting foreigners and well as Japanese in search of enlightenment. But there has been little significant philosophical development in Japanese Buddhism and Shintō.

Some Japanese found an answer to their needs in the new religions which developed in Japan. These were generally derivations of Shintō or Buddhism, sometimes with Christian elements added. All were developed by charismatic figures who claimed divine inspiration.

Tenrikyō, one of the most influential of the new religious groups with its headquarters at Tenri city in Nara prefecture, was founded in the late Edo period by Nakayama Miki (1798–1887), a remarkable woman who claimed that she had received a revelation from God on 9 December 1838. She sought to deliver people from suffering and establish the perfect world united in a blissful life with God the parent. At first Tenrikyō semed to the authorities a subversive movement for social reform, and Miki's followers were persecuted for many years. Miki's teachings are far from clear.[20] One of the more important Tenrikyō scriptures is *Mikagura uta* ('Dancing Psalms'). Another is the *Ofude saki* ('Tip of the Writing-

Brush'), which contains 1,711 hymns said to have been revealed to Miki by God. Miki fixed the location of the *jiba* (sacred place) in the main temple at Tenri, where a monument (*kanrodai*) was built and where she departed this life in 1887. A year later the government permitted the legal incorporation of Tenrikyō. During the period up to 1945 Tenrikyō was regarded as a Shintō sect and forced to conform to Japanese nationalist policies, but in the post-war era it has become fully independent. Its head is the *shinbashira* ('true pillar'), who controls a large central organization at Tenri city, where in addition to the temple there is a university, a fine library, museum, hospital and radio station. A significant element of faith-healing is included in its doctrines. It also emphasizes the dignity of labour and of service to others. At Tenrikyō schools a part of the day is devoted to manual labour in which all take part. Tenrikyō schools and the university are also keen players of rugby football. The sect today claims over two and a half million followers and has significant funds at its disposal.

Another new religion or sect of Shintō which came into prominence in the Meiji period is the Konkōkyō. This was founded in 1859 by a farmer called Kawate Bunjirō (1814–83) who lived in what is now part of Okayama prefecture. He was struck down by illness but recovered after offering prayers of supplication and apologies to his guardian god Konjin. He claimed to have received divine revelation direct from the god. The basic doctrine is that people should live a life in harmony with nature and should be unselfish and kind to others. (In 1978 it claimed just under half a million adherents.)

Despite the vicious persecutions of the Edo period the old Christian teachings of the Jesuit missionaries in the sixteenth and early seventeenth centuries managed to survive in secret, if only in a debased form, in a few villages in Kyūshū. In 1865 a small group of villagers from Urakami professed their faith to French Catholic missionaries in the newly built cathedral at Nagasaki. But Christianity remained proscribed in Japan, and in 1867 nearly two hundred Japanese Christians were arrested and some sixty died as a result of the harsh conditions in which they were held. The Meiji authorities were equally intolerant, and after 1868 Christians were persecuted for refusing to conform to Shintō rites. Christians were also arrested in Nagasaki and the Gotō Islands. In January 1870 2,810 Christians in Urakami were exiled to other provinces. The diplomatic and consular representatives of the treaty powers in Japan urged the Japanese authorities to desist, but to no avail. These representations were reinforced to the Iwakura mission, who were told that there would be no prospect of negotiations on treaty revision until the persecutions ceased. Eventually on 14 March 1873 the authorities withdrew sanctions and allowed the exiles to return to their homes; 660 of the Urakami Christians had died in exile. But, although the notice boards banning Christianity were removed, the edicts against Christianity were retained, and the authorities remained hostile to the newly arrived missionaries. Freedom of religion was not officially granted until the promulgation of the Meiji constitution in 1889, but it was even then qualified by the words 'within limits not prejudicial to peace and not antagonistic to their duties as citizens'.

The missionaries' difficulties were compounded by the xenophobic atmosphere of opposition to the treaties. In 1875 a Confucian scholar produced a book entitled *Benmō* ('An Exposition of Falsehood') which had a preface written by Shimazu Hisamitsu, the arch-conservative of Satsuma. The prime objection of the Japanese authorities to Christianity was that by putting God above the Emperor it was contrary to the Confucian principles of loyalty to superiors and to the state. The book was reprinted in 1881 and continued for some years to be used to counter missionary efforts.

By 1883 there were 93 Protestant churches from 18 different sects and 145 foreign Protestant missionaries in Japan. But they had made relatively little headway in their efforts at conversion, as it is estimated that they only had some four thousand regular church-goers at that time. The multiplicity of sects was one cause of confusion. The difficulties of translating the Bible into Japanese was another. Many of the missionaries, despite their sincerity, were also narrow minded and lacking in a sense of humour and proportion. However, the Protestant missionaries do seem to have manged to arouse a revivalist fever among some Japanese converts. There were a number of outstanding figures among the Protestant missionaries. One of these was Dr James Hepburn (1815–1911) of the American Presbyterian mission in Yokohama, who in addition to his contributions to lexicography was the originator of the system of romanization (*romaji*) still mot generally used in Japan today. Another was Dr John Batchelor (1854–1944), who devoted his whole life to Ainu studies and to trying to convert the Ainu of Hokkaidō. (On the outbreak of war in 1941 all foreign missionaries were interned or repatriated, and in response to government pressure some thirty Protestant sects were amalgamated into a 'United Church of Christ in Japan'. After the war a number of Protestant sects, including the Anglicans, withdrew from the union.)

The Catholic mission activity in the nineteenth century was largely in the hands of French Catholics. They were somewhat more successful than the Protestants especially in Kyūshū and particularly around Nagasaki, where Christian practices had survived over two centuries of isolation and persecution. (In 1932, when some Christian university students refused to bow before the Yasukuni shrine to the Japanese war dead, Christians were accused of lack of loyalty and patriotism. Eventually in 1936 the Catholic authorities in Rome agreed that such ceremonies were civil rather then religious expressions, and Catholics were accordingly allowed to participate. As war approached, foreign Catholic bishops resigned, and the Catholic hierarchy in Japan was filled by Japanese.)

Today there are probably not much more than about one million Japanese Christians of all the different sects, but their influence, especially in social questions, has been greater in the post-war world than their numbers might suggest.

Christianity faced many obstacles in Japan over and above the hostility of the authorities and proscription for well over two centuries. Japanese polytheism had little difficulty in working out a synthesis with Buddhism; such a synthesis was not possible with Christian monotheism. Confucian ethics, as adapted by the Japanese with the emphasis on the group rather than the individual, and on the primacy of loyalty to temporal rulers and an Emperor allegedly descended from the gods and said to have divine qualities, could not be easily squared with Christian moral values.

Literature

The final years of the *bakufu* were a period of literary sterility.[21] But in the new era, Japanese literature, especially the novel, revived and began to attract western interest.

The first few years of Meiji were essentially a period of transition and experiment, during which the Japanese learned about western literature, and the Japanese language developed more colloquial and comprehensible forms. Many of the best works of Japanese fiction belong to the twentieth century rather than to the period covered by this chapter, but some historically important works of literature appeared in the final decades of the nineteenth century.

Tsubouchi Shōyō (1859–1935) is best known for his translation into Japanese of Shakespeare, but he was also a novelist and critic. His book *Shōsetsu shinzui* ('The Essence of the Novel'), published in 1885, was a landmark. In it and especially in the preface he rejected the old principles of the novel in Japan, as for instance in Takizawa Bakin's *Nansō satomi hakkenden*, which were based on *kanzen chōaku* ('encourage good, punish evil'). Tsubouchi Shōyō called for an artistic approach to novel writing and argued that Japanese writers should seek to be realistic, objective and serious in their writing. Characterization was also important, and the thoughts and emotions of modern individuals should be portrayed. Unfortunately his own attempts at novel writing in the 1880s were generally unsuccessful.

The first modern Japanese novel which reflected the ideas of Tsubouchi Shōyō was *Ukigumo* ('The Drifting Cloud') by Futabatei Shimei (1864–1909). *Ukigumo* was written between 1887 and 1889. Futabatei Shimei had studied Russian literature at what is now the Tokyo University of Foreign Studies and was greatly influenced not only by Tsubouchi Shōyō but also by Russian novelists, particularly Turgenev, a number of whose works he translated into Japanese. Donald Keene sums the novel up in the following words:

> The conversations capture with a marvelous exactness the speech of the day, and the character portrayals are brilliant.... A new kind of hero made his appearance in Japanese fiction. Unlike the all-conquering soldiers and lovers we find in earlier writings, the leading character of *The Drifting Cloud* is timid before the woman he loves, loses his job, becomes the object of the laughter and contempt of everyone, and finally exasperates the reader with his ineptitude.[22]

The most important woman writer of the Meiji period was Higuchi Ichiyō (1872–96). She was a poet and wrote many *tanka*, but she is mainly remembered for some twenty short and medium-length stories. One of these, *Takekurabe* ('Comparing Heights'), produced in 1895–6, tells the story of some young people growing up outside the Yoshiwara, the licensed pleasure quarters in Tokyo. It is a sad and beautifully written story.[23]

The Japanese were not only interested in foreign novels. They also tried to translate English poems into Japanese and began to seek new forms of verse. *Shintaishi-shō* ('A Selection of Verse in New Forms'), published in 1882, contained translations of poems such as the famous 'Elegy Written in a Country Churchyard' by Thomas Gray (1716–71) and 'The Charge of the Light Brigade' by Alfred

203

Lord Tennyson (1809–92). It also included some Japanese efforts at writing poems which did not conform to the basic *tanka* or *haiku* forms.

One outstanding poet of the period was Masaoka Shiki (1867–1902). He injected a new realism into *haiku* and *tanka*. He attacked the contemporary *haiku* as sterile and unimaginative and advocated the use of unconventional words and themes. He founded the famous *haiku* magazine *Hototogisu* (the name of a Japanese cuckoo). One of his disciples was Takahama Kyoshi (1874–1959), another famous modern *haiku* poet. Shiki advocated similar changes in the composition of *tanka*. He urged Japanese poets to return to the standards of the *Manyōshū* of the eighth century and adopt a new vigour and directness. One of his followers as a writer of *tanka* was Saitō Mokichi (1882–1953), who became one of the outstanding poets of the first half of the twentieth century.

It is hard to convey the nature of Shiki's contribution to the development of the *haiku* in a few brief verses, but the following indicate the range of his themes:

Kaki kueba	As I bite into a persimmon
Kane ga narunari	A bell responds
Hōryūji.	At Hōryūji [a famous temple outside Nara].

Yuki furu yo	Snow's falling!
Shōji no ana wo	Through a hole in the shutter
Mite areba	I see it . . .

Suzushisa no	From the cool
Hate yori detari	Edge of the skyline
Umi no tsuki.	The moon emerges from the sea.

(Perhaps reflecting Basho's famous *haiku* beginning 'Furu ike ya' (see page 162):

Furu ike no	On the old pond
Oshi ni yuki furu	Snow is falling on the mandarin ducks
Yūbe kana.	As evening sets in.

Hiru naka ya	It is midday
Kumo ni tomarite	Perched on the clouds
Naku hibari.	The nightingales are singing.

Hito iyashiki	Base men
Ran no atai wo	The price of orchids
Ronjikeri.	Are discussing.

In 1898 Shiki wrote the following *tanka* which shows how far he had departed from the old conventions:

Hisakata no	Far away
Amerikabito no	Americans
Hajime ni shi	Have begun

204

| *Besuboru wa* | To play baseball. |
| *Miredo akanu kamo.* | I should like to watch it for ever. |

The Japanese theatre, especially the *kabuki,* continued to be popular. The outstanding dramatist of the period was Kawatake Mokuami (1816–93). He became famous for his plays about the life of the people of the towns (the so-called *sewa-mono*) and in particular for his pieces about thieves and other criminals. After the restoration he presented plays in modern western dress and with *kabuki* actors who wore their hair cropped in the foreign fashion. Some of these plays included imports such as steam boats, trains and even hot air balloons. He is said to have written some 360 plays; many of them are still in the repertoire.

Meanwhile in a new theatre established in Osaka in 1888 attempts were made to put on modern plays with realistic acting. In 1891 Kawakami Otojirō (1864–1911) organized a theatrical group which put on political plays in a *kabuki* style. From 1893 he switched to melodrama but put on patriotic battle plays during the Sino-Japanese war of 1894–5. Between 1903 and 1905 he staged some of Japan's first professional productions of Shakespeare's plays.

A new and significant period of Japanese literature had begun.

Art

In the second half of the nineteenth century Japanese art had at least as much influence on western art as vice versa. But *le Japonisme* and its impact on the Impressionists and Post-Impressionists, fascinating though it is, lies outside the scope of this book.[24]

One of the western art critics who helped to promote the understanding of Japanese art abroad, especially in North America, was Ernest Fenellosa (1853–1908). He also made a significant contribution to the reassessment of Japanese art by Japanese in the Meiji period. He was invited to Japan by Edward Morse (1838–1925), a zoologist at Tokyo University, who through his work *Japanese Homes and their Surroundings* (1886) did so much to explain and depict to English readers the beauty and harmony of Japanese domestic architecture. Fenellosa worked at first as a teacher of philosophy and economics, but he resigned in 1886 and thereafter devoted himself to art. He was horrified by the decline and destruction of traditonal Japanese arts and supported the movement which led to the foundation in 1889 of the school which later became the Tokyo University of Fine Arts and Music (popularly known as Geidai, short for Geijutsu Daigaku). Fenellosa and Okakura Kakuzō (1862–1913) were members of the Japanese government's commission which investigated western art administration. From 1890 to 1897 he was head of the Oriental Department of the Boston Museum of Fine Arts. Okakura Kakuzō was *de facto* director of the School of Fine Arts from 1890 to 1898 and concurrently curator of the Imperial Household Museum, now the Tokyo National Museum. Okakura worked hard to explain the essence of Japanese taste to westerners. His most famous book in English is *The Book of Tea,* which appeared in 1906.

Some art critics regard the art of the Meiji period as decadent with its purity debased by vulgar western tastes and mass production methods. In some areas, particularly the plastic arts, the demands of western tourists for curios and souvenirs led to significant exports of ivory carvings, including *netsuke*, as well as of *cloisonné* and porcelain designed for the western markets. Many of these works were undistinguished and made in accordance with Victorian rather than traditional Japanese taste, but these export products often combined good Japanese workmanship with elements of artistry.

Japanese print artists of the *bakumatsu* and early Meiji period generally lack the finesse and fertile imagination of their predecessors, while the chemical-based colours used often seem crude compared with the natural colours of the old prints which have faded with time. However, many Meiji prints are well executed, colourful and amusing. Some of the most interesting Japanese prints of the period were what have come to be called *Yokohama-e*. These prints, which depict foreigners, their houses, manners and customs, were the successors of the *Nagasaki-e*, which protrayed the Dutch in Nagasaki during the Edo period. *Yokohama-e* were produced in large numbers and sold instead of photographs and postcards, in response to Japanese curiosity about the 'barbarians', whom many of them had never seen. The Japanese were fascinated by foreign-style buildings, steam-ships, railway trains and the rickshaw (*jinrikisha*, that is, 'man-power vehicle') which was first brought into use in Japan in the late 1860s.[25] After the first official missions had been sent abroad, artists produced prints of London, Washington and other foreign places, but, as they did not accompany the missions and had never been abroad, the scenes were far from being accurate depictions. The production of prints on topical themes such as the opening of the Diet and Japanese exploits in wartime continued up to the Russo-Japanese war of 1905. Artists in this genre incuded Hiroshige II and Hiroshige III, Sadahide, Yoshitora, Yoshikazu, Yoshiiku and many others.

Traditional Japanese painting survived the restoration, but there were few really outstanding Japanese-style painters in the first years of the Meija era. Kanō Hōgai (1828–88) began to paint during the Edo period as a member of the Kanō school. He became a friend of Fenellosa and adopted some western painting techniques in his later works. Hashimoto Gahō (1835–1908) was also a member of the Kanō school of painting and became the chief professor of painting at the Tokyo School of Fine Arts when it was founded in 1889. The last painter of merit in the Bunjinga style of painting was Tomioka Tessai (1837–1924), who specialized in Chinese subjects. Kōno Bairei (1844–95) was an accomplished painter of the Maruyama-Shijō school in Kyoto. Another famous painter of the same school was Kawabata Gyokushō (1812–1913), who briefly studied western-style painting in Yokohama. Shibata Zeshin (1807–91) was skilled in lacquer painting of nature scenes which won prizes in international exhibitions. The Tokyo School of Fine Arts provided in the 1890s a base for the development of a new form of Japanese-style painting, which maintained the old traditions, but developed new vigour and reflected some influence from western art forms. Painting in this form is called *Nihonga*. Among *Nihonga* painters who began to gain fame in this era were Takeuchi Seihō (1864–1942) and Yokoyama Taikan (1868–1958).

Interest in western-style painting, which was called *yōga* to distinguish it from the traditional *Nihonga*, began in 1857 when Kawakami Tōgai (1827–81) was ordered by the *bakufu* to study western techniques of drawing and painting. From

Left, Gomadō (main hall) of the Sanbōin, Daigoji temple, southern Kyoto. Momoyama period (late 16th century).
Centre and bottom, Garden of the Sanbōin, Daigoji temple, southern Kyoto (late 16th century).

Above, *Karamon* (Chinese-style gate) which was the *Chokushimon* − imperial gateway − to the Sanbōin, Kyoto (late 16th century.). *Below,* Engraving of Himeji castle, built in the late 16th century.

Left, Painted screen of ladies taking the air. Entitled the 'Hikone screen' (17th century). Anonymous. *Below*, Painting of bird and bamboo by Sakai Hōitsu (1761 – 1828). Seikadō.

Above, Painting of cranes over a poem by Tawaraya Sōtatsu (17th century). Kyo National Museum.
Left, Painting of ducks (par of a sliding screen) by Matsumura Keibun (1779–1843). Nezu Museum, Tokyo.

Left, Portrait or copy of a portrait of St Francis Xavier by an unknown Japanese artist (late 16th century). Kobe City Museum.

Right, Detail of a Nanban (Southern Barbarian) screen. Probably by Kanō Naizen (late 16th or early 17th century). Kobe City Museum.

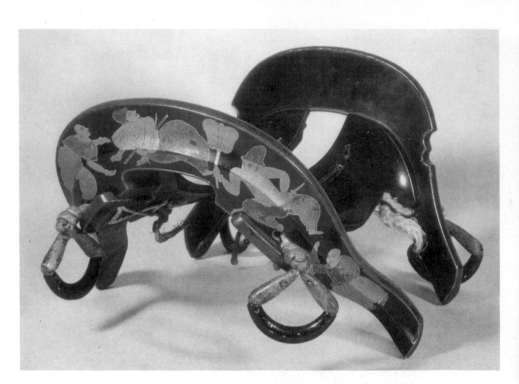

Above, Lacquer saddle with designs of foreigners (late 16th or early 17th century). Fuji Art Museum. *Below,* Nō mask (painted wood) — Muromachi period (14th – 16th century). Fuji Art Museum.

Left, Nō costume — Edo period
(17th – 19th century). Nezu
Museum.

Right, Ceramic tea jar by
Nonomura Ninsei (17th century).
Tokyo National Museum.

Above, Lacquer box with wheel design — Heian period (probably 12th century). Tokyo National Museum. *Below*, Lacquer writing box *(suzuribako)* attributed to Hon'ami Kōetsu (1588–1637). Tokyo National Museum.

Below, Lacquer writing box *(suzuribako)* with a design based on the Tale of Genji — Edo period (17th–19th century). Fuji Art Museum.

about 1860 he began to teach western-style painting in Japan. Some of his students were also taught by Charles Wirgman (1832–91), the correspondent in Yokohama of the *Illustrated London News*, who produced between 1862 and 1887 a satirical magazine entitled *The Japan Punch*. After the restoration a department of western art was set up to train art teachers. In 1876 Antonio Fontanesi, an Italian painter of the Barbizon school, and two other Italian artists were employed to teach western art at the Technological Art School (Kōbu Bijutsu Gakkō) in Tokyo. A number of the more promising pupils were later sent abroad to complete their training.

In 1882, however, a reaction set in, and opponents of western-style painting, supported by a faction in the Ministry of Education, barred any painting showing western influence from official exhibitions; when the Tokyo School of Fine Arts was established in 1889, no provision was made for the teaching of western-style painting. An exhibition of *yōga* in 1889 was nevertheless attended by the Empress and members of the court. The proponents of the two styles were now at loggerheads, and it was many years before harmony between the two could be established. However, in 1896 western-style painting, despite Okakura Kakuzō's opposition, became part of the curriculum at the Tokyo School of Fine Arts, and by the end of the century *yōga* had become an acceptable and established art form in Japan.

One of the western-style painters to study abroad was Kuroda Seiki (1866–1924), who went to Paris in 1884. In Paris he was attracted by the *plein air* artists, who depicted nature as they saw it in outdoor light. When he returned to Japan in 1892 he soon became the undisputed leader of *yōga*. One of his most famous paintings, entitled 'By the Lake', depicts a Japanese lady in traditional dress sitting by the side of a lake with mountains in the background. Asai Chū (1856–1907), who studied in France and came under the influence of the Impressionists, was a realist in his choice of subjects and became a rival of Kuroda. Aoki Shigeru (1882–1911) was a romantic, as was Fujishima Takeji (1867–1943). None of these artists achieved a position of eminence in the world of painting outside Japan, but Japanese artists in the western style were beginning to produce works of some distinction. They learned how to use colour effectively and to depict Japanese scenes and objects in a western style.

Soon after the restoration western methods of architecture began to be adopted. In 1876 Josiah Conder (1852–1920), a British architect, accepted a teaching post in Japan, and the first Meiji-period western-style buildings were built in wood or brick. Most of these old buildings have unfortunately been destroyed by fire, war or simply a desire for modernization, but a number have been preserved at Meiji Mura, a museum and park not far from Nagoya. They are a reminder of the Japanese capacity for adapting foreign styles and adding a Japanese dimension. Among Japanese architects in the western style were Tatsuno Kingo (1854–1919), who in 1895 designed the Bank of Japan building in Tokyo in Italian Renaissance style, and Katayama Tokuma (1854–1917), who between 1892 and 1895 designed the National Museums in Nara and Kyoto. The Heian shrine and garden in Kyoto were built in 1895 to commemorate the 1,100th anniversary of the founding of Kyoto. The buildings, which are supposed to be a replica on a smaller scale of the first palace of 794, show that traditional Japanese architects had not lost their skill.

Western-style sculpture was taught at the Kōbu Bijutsu Gakkō, opened in 1876, by Vincenzo Ragusa (1841–1928), an Italian classical sculptor, who stayed in Japan until 1882. A full course in western-style sculpture was eventually established in 1899 at the Tokyo School of Fine Arts.

Japanese artists were becoming competent in western art forms, but had not lost their traditional skills.

X

Imperialism (1894–1945)

By 1894 Japan had established a modern constitutional structure which enabled the oligarchy to maintain a generally autocratic control over policy. Agreement had been reached on the revision of the 'unequal treaties'. A significant army and navy, comparatively well equipped and trained, had been built up. Japan was now ready to join in the scramble for a stake in the dieing Chinese Empire with the assurance that her home base was reasonably strong and secure.

There was no premeditated plan of expansion aimed at hegemony in Asia. Imperialist ambitions grew as Japan became stronger and as the military increased their power in the Japanese hierarchy. The war of 1941–5 was only inevitable because it was the culmination of a series of steps on an imperialist course, during which the Japanese could have drawn back from the brink if the country had had wiser and more moderate leaders at crucial moments.

The key incidents in this sad and cruel story of aggression and ultimate defeat were the Sino-Japanese war of 1894–5, the Russo-Japanese war of 1904–5, the annexation of Korea in 1909, the twenty-one demands on China in 1915, the Manchurian 'incident' of 1931, the beginning of war with China in 1937 and finally the attack on the US fleet at Pearl Harbor on 7 December 1941 before the declaration of war had reached the American government. Japanese arms at first seemed invincible, and Japanese forces occupied South-east Asia and began to threaten India and Australia. But as the allied war effort developed the tide turned. The Japanese forces were overstretched, and their home base was gradually destroyed by American air attacks. US forces landed on the Japanese island of Okinawa and defeated the Japanese in a bloody and decisive manner. By mid-1945 most of Japanese industry and many Japanese cities had been destroyed in air-raids. The dropping of atomic bombs on Hiroshima and Nagasaki on 6 and 9 August 1945 and the entry of the Soviet Union into the war against Japan on 9 August finally made it clear that the only alternative to surrender was annihilation. The end of the war was signalled by a broadcast by the Emperor. Japanese forces obeyed the call to surrender despite the attitude of some of the more stubborn militarists.

Throughout the period the Japanese Diet continued to exist, and the Meiji constitution was maintained. In the 1920s it seemed to some observers that Japan might be able to move towards a more democratic system. But this was not to be.

The military took control with the backing of ultra-nationalist movements and opinion which had been deliberately fostered by the oligarchy. Opposition was ruthlessly suppressed, and a dictatorial system of thought control was established in the 1930s. But Japanese fascism was different from German Nazism and Italian fascism. There was no fascist revolution engineered by a mass party. As Maruyama Masao puts it: 'The process was rather the gradual maturing of a fascist structure within the State, effected by the established political forces of the military, the bureaucracy, and the political parties.'[1]

Ultra-nationalism was nourished by what many Japanese saw as European and North American racialist attitudes towards Japan and the Japanese people. The Japanese leaders noted the development of European colonialist expansion in East Asia and wanted their share in the spoils. The xenophobic and racialist attitudes of the Japanese military caste also grew as a reaction to the poverty of the farming class from which so many officers and soldiers came. The industrial and trading conglomerates, which formed the *zaibatsu* and whose profits and future were bound up with the success of Japanese arms, became increasingly concerned by signs of discontent among their work-forces caused by the world economic problems and by exploitation of labour by Japanese capitalists. These elements combined so that Japanese aggression in East Asia had the general backing of those in power. Popular support was ensured by manipulation of the educational system and the media.

The Empeor Meiji died in 1912. His successor, the Emperor Taishō, who was the son of a concubine of the Meiji Emperor, suffered from mental problems, and in 1921 the then Crown Prince Hirohito (1901–89) assumed the imperial functions as regent. He succeeded his father on the latter's death in December 1926 with the era name of Shōwa, which ironically means 'brilliant peace'. Despite the powers reserved to him under the Meiji constitution the Shōwa Emperor, like his father and grandfather, was forced by custom and tradition to play a largely symbolic role and to accept the advice of his entourage and his ministers. Only when at the end of the war, his advisers were divided and he was asked to make a decision was he in any position to exercise effective power.

Inevitably these were difficult years for literature and the arts, but Japanese literary and artistic abilities survived, and some significant developments took place which helped to provide a basis for the post-war flowering of the arts in the atmosphere of freedom made possible by the defeat of the military.

The Japanese Armed Forces in 1894

The French had supported the Tokugawa shōgunate, and in 1868 the image of the France of the Emperot Napoleon III had impressed the new Japanese leaders. They therefore looked initially to France for help in creating an army, but the participation of French officers in the Hakodate campaign and the defeat of the French in the Franco–Prussian war of 1870–1 caused disillusionment with the French. Instead some Japanese leaders began to think of Prussia as a model for Japan to follow in military matters. Yamagata Aritomo and Oyama Iwao, who were in Europe during the Franco–Prussian war, admired the discipline and competence of Prussian forces. Katsura Tarō (1847–1913), who had served as military attaché in Berlin, also advocated adoption of a German system in the Japanese army. In 1878 an independent general staff was created for the Japanese army. In 1884 a pupil of the Prussian Field Marshal von Moltke was invited to become an instructor at the Japanese defence college. In the same year a large-scale expansion of the Japanese army was started, although the budgetary burden on a developing country, such as Japan was in the second half of the nineteenth

210

century, was very heavy. By 1894 Japan had just under a quarter of a million trained soldiers, but about one-half were reservists; and if the members of the territorial forces and the gendarmerie are excluded, the actual permanent peace-time strength was less than 60,000 men.

The Japanese navy developed rather more slowly. The navy looked primarily to the Royal Navy as its model. Japanese naval officers, including Admiral Tōgō Heihachirō (1848–1938), studied in Britain, and some of the first Japanese naval ships made in steel were built in British yards. However, Japanese yards, under the guidance of a French expert, were quickly developed to produce ships of all types, and by 1894 Japan was in a position not only to build major warships but also to produce modern naval armaments such as torpedoes. In 1894 the Japanese navy had twenty-eight steam-powered warships totalling 57,000 tonnes. An independent naval general staff was established in 1893. Although much smaller and less influential than the army, by 1894 the Japanese navy was a significant force.

Conscription was introduced in 1873. It was not at first a popular measure. The samurai disliked it because it undermined their privileged position as the fighting men of Japan; the ordinary people were troubled by the removal of breadwinners for service in the forces, and initially various exemptions were allowed. At the time of the Satsuma rebellion of 1877 the conscript army proved its worth, and conscription became an accepted duty to the country and the sovereign.

Patriotism (*aikoku-shugi*) was inculcated in schools in line with the Imperial Rescript on Education, through state Shintō and through the hard training which conscripts had to undergo.

The Sino-Japanese War of 1894–5 and its Aftermath

Japan had nearly gone to war with Korea in 1873, but, by the treaty of Kanghwa of 1876, a *modus vivendi* between the two countries was reached. Under the treaty three Korean ports were opened to trade, and Korea was recognized as an independent state. Following this treaty the Japanese increased their presence and influence in Korea. These moves aroused Chinese hostility and suspicions, as China considered that it had suzerainty over Korea. A mutiny in Korea in 1882 was used by both China and Japan as an excuse to establish their own garrisons in the country. In August 1882 the Japanese right to keep 'some' soldiers in Korea was recognized by the treaty of Chemulp'o; but the Japanese suffered a setback when a Japanese-backed *coup d'état* in Seoul in 1884 failed. Japanese traders, however, managed to increase their share of trade with Korea at the expense of the Chinese merchants. The Formosa expedition of 1874 had earlier exacerbated relations with China, and, although a settlement had been reached, Sino-Japanese rivalry over Taiwan had continued.

Sino-Japanese friction resulted in war in 1894. The specific cause of the conflict was the Chinese decision to send an expeditionary force to Korea to suppress the so-called Tonghak rebellion. Itō Hirobumi's government, anxious to divert attention from their difficulties with the Diet, decided to send their own expeditionary force to Korea. The Japanese demanded reforms by the Korean authorities and occupied the Korean royal palace. They installed a puppet government which 'requested' the Japanese to expel Chinese forces from Korea. Japan then declared war on China.

One of the first episodes in the war was the sinking, on the orders of Captain (later Admiral) Tōgō, of a British merchant ship, the *Kowshing*, which was carrying Chinese troops. Although this action took place before the Chinese had received the declaration of war, it was accepted that the Japanese had acted within their rights under international law. The Japanese and Chinese fleets met in the battle of the Yalu, and although both sides claimed victory the Japanese fleet achieved control of the Yellow Sea. Japanese forces quickly took control of Korea. Two divisions, under General Yamagata Aritomo, moved into Manchuria, while another force, under General Oyama Iwao, attacked the Liaotung (Liaodong) peninsula, capturing first Port Arthur (Ryōjun in Japanese, Lüshun in Chinese) – where some Japanese soldiers appear to have inflicted 'vengeance' on Chinese in the city for the alleged torture of Japanese prisoners – and then Weihaiwei. The Japanese were now in a position to move on Peking. Chinese resistance had collapsed, and the Chinese government sued for peace. The Japanese terms were harsh. Under the treaty of Shimonoseki, which was concluded in April 1895, the Chinese had to agree to recognize the 'independence' of Korea, to cede Formosa (Taiwan) and the Liaotung peninsula, including Port Arthur, to open four more Chinese ports to foreign trade and to pay a large indemnity. Most foreign observers had thought that in a war between the two countries the Chinese would win easily. In fact the Chinese were badly led, and the Japanese did not encounter any serious problems in defeating the Chinese forces. Japanese self-confidence was high, and the spoils of victory seemed rich.

Japanese euphoria did not last long. On 23 April 1895 the Russian, French and German representatives in Tokyo told the Japanese authorities that the Liaotung peninsula should be returned to China on the grounds that Japanese control of the area would be a threat to China. In fact the Russians wanted scope for their own expansionist plans, and the French and Germans also sought to increase their areas of influence in China. The Japanese government were understandably reluctant to accept the demand of the three powers (subsequently called the triple intervention). They feared a public outcry at what would be seen as a humiliation. They were also concerned about the reaction of the victorious army. But the Ministers of the Army and Navy and their chiefs of staff declared that it was impossible for Japan to contemplate resistance against the forces of the three powers in the circumstances then prevailing. Although the Japanese had easily defeated the Chinese, the strain on Japanese resources had been severe. It was clear that neither the British nor the Americans were prepared to give effective support to the Japanese if they resisted. On 5 May the Japanese government reluctantly announced their agreement to return the Liaotung peninsula to China. Ratifications of the revised treaty (the Japanese had to be content with an increased indemnity) were exchanged three days later. On 10 May the Emperor issued a proclamation giving his endorsement of the decision, and Yamagata Aritomo was sent to explain the reasons to the officers of the Japanese expeditionary force. The Japanese deeply resented this loss of face and spoils. Extremist and ultra-nationalist influence grew as a result.

The government took advantage of the country's mood to increase the strength of the armed forces. In 1896 six new divisions were added to the regular army, and the front-line strength was doubled. Equipment was improved, and a major naval building programme was launched. This provided for four new battleships, sixteen cruisers and twenty-three destoyers as well as other ships. These measures involved a major increase in government expenditure which had to be met by new and higher taxes and by foreign and domestic loans. At the same time heavy industry was given priority. Engineering investment increased over fivefold in the ten years after 1893. In 1896 the Yawata steelworks were established. Coal production rose from 5 million tons in 1895 to 13 million tons in 1905. Ship-building and merchant shipping were also boosted by subsidies.

The triple intervention forced the Japanese to behave with a measure of caution both in Korea and towards China. Japanese ambitions in Korea and Manchuria inevitably clashed with Russian aims in these territories. The establishment of a Japanese protectorate over Korea had to be postponed, although Japanese commercial interests were promoted, and plans for railway building in the peninsula were developed. The Japanese noted with envy and concern the expansion of western influence in China, whose weakness had been demonstrated by the Japanese defeat of Chinese forces. In 1896 the Russians secured the right to build a railway across Manchuria to Vladivostock. In 1898 the Germans obtained a naval base at Kiaochow (Jiaozhou) and extensive rights in Shantung (Shandong). The Russians then won a lease on Port Arthur and recognition of their special rights in Manchuria. France gained a base at Kuang-chou (Guangzhou) bay and railway rights in Yunnan, while the British obtained the new territories opposite Hong Kong island and a lease on Weihaiwei.

The Boxer rebellion of 1900 gave the Japanese government, then led by Yamagata Aritomo, an opportunity to re-establish its influence in the Far East. When the foreign legations in Peking were besieged the Japanese were the only power with substantial troops readily available in the area. Japan in fact provided almost half the relieving force, and in the settlement reached in 1901 the Japanese received their share of the large indemnity which the Chinese were forced to pay.

One indirect consequence of the war was the issue of an ordinance which became effective in 1900 and which confirmed existing practices. This reserved the posts of War and Navy Ministers to officers on the active list.[2] It gave the armed forces an effective veto on the formation of future Japanese governments. It also gave them indirectly the power to compel acceptance of their demands as they could at any time of their choosing withdraw their ministers and force the resignation of the government. Yamagata probably saw this as a way of keeping the politicians in order and preventing them from interfering in the armed services. But it was to be a crucial factor in the development of Japanese imperialism.

The Anglo-Japanese Alliance

Many of the British and Japanese politicians who look back with nostalgia to the friendship between Britain and Japan, which they thought was brought about by the Anglo-Japanese alliance, have only the vaguest idea about the nature of the alliance. In fact there were three different 'alliances'. The original alliance of 1902 was revised during the Russo-Japanese war in 1905; it was again revised in 1911, and this treaty was renewed for one year in 1920. It was essentially, at first at least, an alliance between two powers, Britain and Japan, with imperialist interests against a third imperialist power, Russia, which posed a threat to Japanese ambitions in north-east Asia and British interests in the Far East and elsewhere. The existence of the alliance facilitated both the Japanese annexation of Korea in 1910 and the expansion of Japanese economic dominance in Manchuria. It thus helped to establish the base for Japanese military and economic expansion in Manchuria and China in later decades.

The conclusion of the alliance was a significant and unique step for both countries. Britain had not previously concluded alliances of this nature in an area as remote from Britian as the Far East; it was Japan's first alliance with a European power and confirmed her status as a world power. British neutrality during the triple intervention helped the Japanese to overcome their suspicions of the British which had been aroused by the difficulties encountered in getting British agreement to treaty revision. Japanese success in the Sino-Japanese war of 1894–5 helped the British to overcome their tendency to look down on the Japanese and to treat the Japanese as equals.

The negotiation of the alliance took time and was a complicated process. Skilled advocacy and careful diplomacy were required by individuals such as Viscount Hayashi Tadasu (1850–1913), the Japanese minister in London from 1900 and the first Japanese Ambassador to Britain after the conclusion of the alliance. The negotiations also called for some hard bargaining. The British wanted the treaty to cover their interests in India, while the Japanese sought a clear recognition by Britain of Japanese aims in Korea. The conclusion of the treaty was also held up while Itō Hirobumi tried to get some concessions from the Russians in the course of a private visit to St Petersburg. The treaty, as signed on 30 January 1902, was a compromise. The British agreed to drop their insistence on India being covered by the alliance; and the references to Korea in Article I were diplomatically vague, indicating that the British were primarily interested in China while Japan was 'interested in a peculiar degree politically as well as commercially and industrially' in Korea. The two parties agreed, under Article II, to maintain strict neutrality, if the other party was involved in war with a third power. Under Article III Britain and Japan committed themselves to armed intervention in support of their ally, if 'any other Power or Powers should join in hostilities against the Ally'. The treaty did not require ratification and came into force immediately.

The second alliance was concluded on 12 August 1905 before the end of the Russo-Japanese war. It was more far-reaching and specific. In negotiations formulas were found to cover British interests in India and Japanese ambitions in Korea. One of the main objectives of the treaty was declared to be 'the maintenance of the territorial rights of the High Contracting Parties in the regions of Eastern Asia and of India, and the defence of their special interests in the said regions'. Article II on this occasion called for mutual assistance in the event of 'unprovoked attack or aggressive action' against either contracting party by any other power. The two allies agreed, in such an event, to 'conduct war in common, and make peace in mutual agreement', but under Article VI, in the Russo-Japanese war then taking place, Britain merely agreed to maintain strict neutrality unless another power came to the assistance of Russia. Article II recognized Japan's 'paramount political, military and economic interests' in Korea and her right to 'take such measures of guidance, control and protection' in Korea as 'she may deem proper and necessary'. The only limitation imposed was that the 'principle of equal opportunities for the commerce and industry of all nations' should be observed.

The existence of the first alliance gave the Japanese the assurance which they wanted that, in the event of war with Russia, they would have an ally if the Russians tried to bring in the French and the Germans on their side, as they had done in the triple intervention. The importance of the alliance declined after the end of the Russo-Japanese war and when Russia was no longer clearly the mutual enemy.

The Russo-Japanese War of 1904–5

The Japanese hoped that the conclusion of the first Anglo-Japanese alliance would persuade the Russians to reach a settlement with Japan about their mutual interests in north-east Asia. It seemed at first that their hopes might be realized. The Russians agreed in 1902 to withdraw their forces from Manchuria in six-monthly stages. The first stage was carried out by transferring troops to other parts of the region, but the second stage due to take place in April 1903 failed to materialize. The Japanese decided to seek a general settlement with the Russians; they proposed mutual undertakings to respect the territorial integrity of China and Korea as well as recognition of Russian railway interests in Manchuria and Japanese political and economic interests in Korea. Russian counter-proposals were totally unacceptable to the Japanese; and although negotiations continued throughout 1903, no mutually acceptable basis could be found for a settlement. The basic problem was that, to quote Professor Ian Nish, 'there was in both countries an expansionist group tussling with a more moderate one which was equally determined to pursue national interests but in ways which would avoid confrontation or offence to other powers. The attainment of rational solutions was often lost because of the factional infighting.'[3] Itō Hirobumi worked hard for a compromise, but Yamagata Aritomo and his protégé Katsura Tarō, Prime Minister at the time of the conclusion of the Anglo-Japanese alliance, took a hard and uncompromising stance. They were supported by the jingoist attitude of the popular press. In Russia the Czar Nicholas II was weak and obstinate, and many Russian leaders thought that the Japanese were bluffing. In fact the Japanese military leaders were determined and had made their calculations and plans carefully.

On 6 February 1904 the Japanese broke off diplomatic relations with Russia. On 8 February the Japanese fleet, under Admiral Tōgō Heihachirō, attacked and trapped the Russian fleet in Port Arthur. On 10 February, two days after this act of war, war was declared.[4]

A Japanese expeditionary force landed in Korea and, quickly moving north, crossed the Yalu river into Manchuria. One of the main land battles of the war took place around Port Arthur. This finally fell to the Japanese third army, led by General Nogi Maresuke (1849–1912), in which Japanese forces displayed a total commitment to victory and willingness to sacrifice life to achieve it. The Japanese followed this by launching an attack on Russian forces at Mukden (Shenyang). After ten days of bitter fighting, costing the Japanese 70,000 casualties, they occupied the city in March 1905. The Japanese army had now lost a significant proportion of their officer corps and were running short of ammunition.

At sea the Japanese were at a numerical disadvantage, but the morale of their officers and men was high. Their main striking force consisted of six modern battleships, all built in British yards, including the *Mikasa*, Tōgō's flagship. The decisive naval battle of the war was the battle of Tsushima, known in Japan as the battle of the Japan Sea (*Nihonkai kaisen*). This took place on 27–28 May 1905 when the Russian Baltic fleet, under the command of Vice-Admiral Rozhestvenskii, was defeated by the Japanese fleet, commanded by Admiral Tōgō Heihachirō. Admiral Tōgō ordered his ships to cross in front of the approaching Russian vessels and subjected them to a withering fire. Only three Russian ships reached Vladivostock intact; Japanese losses were reported to be three torpedo boats and 110 men. The Russian fleet, on their long voyage from the Baltic to the Far East, almost brought Britain into the war. In an incident in fog in the North Sea, Russian ships fired at British fishing trawlers, sinking one boat and killing members of the crew. War was only avoided by Russian promises of compensation and punishment of those responsible.

The Japanese now decided to negotiate peace terms, and President Theodore Roosevelt of the United States was asked to mediate. Negotiations, which took place at Portsmouth, New Hampshire, resulted in the signature on 5 September 1905 of a treaty which provided for Russian recognition of Japanese predominance in Korea, transfer to Japan, subject to Chinese agreement, of Russian leases on Port Arthur and Dairen (Talian) on the Liaotung peninsula and Russian railway rights in south Manchuria and cession to Japan of the southern half of Sakhalin. The Japanese had sought the whole of Sakhalin, which they had occupied during the war, as well as payment of a large indemnity. They only agreed reluctantly to a compromise because of the increasingly serious burden which the war had imposed on the Japanese economy and on the armed forces, which despite their victories had suffered grievous losses. The Japanese were also subjected to pressure from countries such as France which feared the revolutionary effect the war had had on Russia. The treaty was, however, greeted with dismay by Japanese popular opinion, which remained chauvinist; a mass rally at Hibiya Park in Tokyo was followed by a march to the Imperial Palace with demands that the treaty should be rejected. This led to a clash with police and imperial guards; in the widespread disorders which followed many buildings, including police stations and Christian churches, were destroyed. Martial law was declared, but there were many casualties before law and order were restored.

Despite the popular discontent and the serious losses which the war had caused, Japan had in fact won a significant victory. The Japanese had revenged the humiliation of the triple intervention and had shown that an Asian country could defeat one of the great European powers. Japanese self-confidence was boosted, and the basis for further expansion had been laid.

Japan in Korea, 1904–5

On the outbreak of the Russo-Japanese war the Japanese had quickly gained effective control of Korea, and Japanese advisers were introduced into the administration. The treaty of Portsmouth, confirming Japanese predominance in Korea, gave Japan the right 'to direct, protect and supervise'. In November 1905 Itō Hirobumi, as special envoy to Korea, forced a reluctant and divided Korean government to agree to a Japanese protectorate. In February 1906 Itō was appointed the first Resident-General in Korea. In 1907 he replaced the then reigning Korean 'Emperor', who had sent a secret mission to the World Peace Conference at The Hague to plead Korea's case, by his son, who was a simpleton. Korean forces were disbanded, and Korean opposition to Japanese colonialism, particularly from a militant group calling themselves the 'righteous army', was ruthlessly suppressed. In addition to the Japanese garrison of two divisions a military police force (*kenpeitai*) was organized to ensure that Japanese orders were strictly obeyed. Korean villages were burned, and many thousands of Koreans were killed by the Japanese occupation forces in the years up to the formal annexation. The Japanese also took a firm hold on the Korean economy; they soon had full control of finance, banking, mining, transport and communications.

In 1909 the Japanese government, following agitation by ultra-nationalists such as members of the Kokuryūkai (the Amur River Society), decided that Korea should be annexed. Itō, who was opposed to immediate annexation, resigned as Resident-General, but a pretext for annexation was provided to the Japanese government when Itō was assassinated at Harbin on 26 October 1909 by Korean nationalists. In May 1910 Terauchi Masatake (1852–1919), the Japanese Minister of War, was appointed concurrently minister resident in Korea. The formalities of annexation were completed by a treaty signed on 22 August 1910. The western powers, including the United States, accepted without protest this colonialist and imperialist act.

Following the annexation the Japanese established a colonial administration for Korea under Terauchi, who became the first Governor-General. The Japanese administration took charge of all aspects of Korean life and economy. Koreans were forced to learn Japanese. Japanese immigrant farmers were brought in to replace Koreans who had been dispossessed. Demonstrations in 1919 caused the Japanese to introduce some modifications to their colonial policies in Korea, but after the beginning of the Manchurian incident in 1931 the Japanese authorities increased their efforts to assimilate Korea. The Korean economy was harnessed to support the Japanese war effort, and in 1942 Koreans were conscripted into the Japanese forces and into Japanese factories and mines.

Japan in Manchuria, 1904–31

By the treaty of Portsmouth in 1905 the Japanese had acquired Russian interests, concessions and territories in southern Manchuria. Before they could exploit their gains they had to get Chinese acquiescence in their assumption of Russian rights. After difficult negotiations a treaty was signed with the Chinese on 22 December 1905 which confirmed the Japanese take-over. The Chinese also agreed to make some reforms in Manchuria and to consult Japan before permitting the building of other railways in south Manchuria which might compete with the now Japanese-contolled South Manchuria Railway. The Chinese, however, refused various other demands including one that they should guarantee not to alienate Manchurian territory to any other power.

In 1909 the Japanese finally won from the Chinese mining rights in important coalfields in Manchuria as well as a number of concessions over railways in the area. In 1910 they reached a secret agreement with the Russians providing for recognition of the Russian position in the northern part and of Japanese hegemony in the southern part of Manchuria.

The Japanese immediately set out to exploit their position in Manchuria, and increasing numbers of Japanese were sent to the area as colonists. The Japanese made the South Manchuria Railway Company their key organization in the area. It took control of 'attached lands' and expanded into adjacent towns and villages. Japanese consular posts and consular police in Manchuria at the same time began to interfere in local affairs. The South Manchuria Railway was supported by railway guards and Japanese military garrisons at key centres, including Mukden. In 1919 these units came under the command of the Japanese Kwantung (Guandong), formerly Liaotung, army headquarters at Port Arthur. The Kwantung army were determined to consolidate Japanese control in southern Manchuria.

In the 1920s such Chinese authority as remained in Manchuria was exercised by the warlord Marshal Chang Tso-lin (Zhang Zuolin). He irritated the Japanese and was disposed of when his train was blown up at Mukden in 1928. His son Chang Hsueh-liang (Zhang Xueliang) acknowledged the authority of the Chinese Nationalist government, and friction between the Japanese and the Chinese in Manchuria grew. After the Russo-Japanese war the British and the Americans wanted the so-called 'open door' policy, which meant equal rights for all to exploit the Chinese market, to apply also in Manchuria. Their efforts to achieve this were frustrated by the Japanese, but the two powers were unable and unwilling to take effective action to enforce their wishes in relation to Manchuria.

Japan and China 1911–22 and the First World War

The Chinese revolution of 1911–12 in which the Manchu dynasty was overthrown presented Japanese leaders with problems and opportunities for the expansion of their interests in China.

Chinese students had come to Japan in the early years of the century and had there absorbed modern and revolutionary ideas for their country. Sun Yat-sen (1866–1925), the first provisional President of the Chinese republic and leader of the Kuomintang (Guomindang), had before the revolution spent six years in Japan and made many Japanese friends. But Sun Yat-sen was quickly induced to resign in favour of Yuan Shih-k'ai (Yuan Shikai), the Chinese general who had forced the last Ch'ing (Qing) Emperor to abdicate. The Japanese were divided over whom to support. They were also divided on whether to concentrate on defending and expanding their stake in Manchuria or extending their economic interests in the rest of China. Various plots were hatched, but little was achieved before the outbreak of the First World War provided the Japanese with an ideal opportunity to exploit the situation in the Far East to their own advantage.

The Japanese were not obliged by the Anglo-Japanese alliance, as revised in 1911, to join the war, as the alliance did not apply to Europe. Moreover the British were reluctant to see Japan use the war as an opportunity to expand her interests in China at the expense of the allies who were preoccupied in Europe. However, in August 1914 the British sought Japanese help in protecting Hong Kong and the British base at Weihaiwei. The Japanese government decided that it would be to their advantage to enter the war as a full belligerent. On 23 August 1914 Japan declared war on Germany following rejection of their demands for the withdrawal of German ships from the Far East and surrender of the German base at Kiaochow (Ziaozhou) on the Shantung (Shandong) peninsula. On 7 November 1914 Tsingtao (Qingdao) fell to the Japanese, and this concluded the campaign in Shantung. Meanwhile in October 1914 the Japanese had occupied the German-held islands in the Pacific north of the equator.

The Japanese now saw their chance to improve their position in China. A list of demands was drawn up, and in January 1915 the so-called Twenty-One demands were presented to Yuan Shih-k'ai in Peking (Beijing). The demands were in five groups. The first covered the transfer of German concessions in Shantung to Japan. The second were concerned with Japanese rights in Manchuria, including the extension of the Japanese lease on Kwantung to the end of the twentieth century, permission for Japanese to own or lease property outside the treaty ports and the extension of Japanese privileges in Manchuria to the eastern part of Inner Mongolia. The third demanded acceptance of Japanese participation in a mining and metal complex in central China. The fourth called on the Chinese not to make further cessions or leases other than to Japan and was intended to prevent any American move in Fukien (Fujian) opposite the Japanese-occupied island of Taiwan. The fifth, which were initially concealed from the British, called for the appointment of Japanese advisers to the Chinese government, Japanese participation in administering the Chinese police and extensive railway rights in the Yangtse (Yangzi) region where the British claimed a special interest. The demands aroused strong opposition in China and remonstrations from the Americans and British. The Japanese then revised their demands and agreed to drop the fifth group. The Japanese government issued an ultimatum to the Chinese on 7 May 1915, and after the British had urged the Chinese to accept the revised demands President Yuan acquiesced. A series of agreements were signed between Japan and China on 25 May 1915.

In January 1917 the British asked the Japanese for naval assistance in the Mediterranean and agreed in return to recognize Japan's right to German islands in the Pacific north of the equator. The American entry into the war in April 1917 was followed by an understanding between the Americans and the Japanese (the Lansing–Ishii agreement of 2 November 1917). The Americans recognized Japan's special interests in China, and both reaffirmed their support for the independence and territorial integrity of China and the principle of the 'open door'.

In 1918 the United States invited Japan to take part in a joint operation in Siberia to enable Czech troops, who had deserted from the Austrian forces, to reach the western front. The Japanese poured troops into northern Manchuria and Siberia. The allies supported Admiral Kolchak's counter-revolutionary forces, but in February 1920 Kolchak was captured and executed by the Bolsheviks, and allied troops, other than the Japanese, were withdrawn. The Japanese stayed on, claiming that their presence was necessary to protect their nationals and maintain peace and order in the region. Criticism in Japan of the costs and casualties of the operation and pressure from abroad eventually persuaded the Japanese to withdraw in October 1922.

At the Versailles Peace Conference in 1919, the Japanese delegation, led by Saionji Kinmochi (1849–1940), clashed with the Americans, who were opposed to the continuance of the Japanese take-over of the former German base and other rights in Shantung. The American President Woodrow Wilson only accepted the *fait accompli* in order to get Japanese participation in the League of Nations, which he regarded as the key to future peace in the world. The Japanese for their part had to accept that the former German islands in the Pacific which they had occupied during the war were to be administered by them as a League mandate. The Japanese, who deeply resented American discrimination against Japanese immigrants in California, proposed that the League charter should include a clause banning racial discrimination. As a result of opposition from America, Australia and Britain this proposal was not adopted. Its rejection aroused deep resentment in Japan and encouraged Japanese xenophobia. It did not augur well for the future of the League.

The British were alarmed that American–Japanese hostility might eventually lead to a conflict between Japan and the USA which, because of the Anglo-Japanese alliance, could embroil Britain. A conference was accordingly called in Washington in 1921 to consider the problems of the Far East and the Pacific. Agreement was reached in December 1921 on a Four-Power Pact between Britain, France, Japan and the United States, under which the powers agreed to respect their national rights in the area and to consult if a crisis arose. This was to replace the Anglo-Japanese alliance. An agreement was also eventually reached, after hard bargaining, providing that Britain, America and Japan would maintain a ratio for the tonnage of capital ships in their respective navies of 5 : 5 : 3. The sizes of battleships and aircraft carriers were also to be limited, and agreement was reached banning new fortifications at any base nearer to Japan than Hawaii or Singapore. This ensured Japanese naval predominance in the western Pacific. In addition a Nine-Power Treaty, including Belgium, China, Italy, the Netherlands and Portugal, concluded in February 1922, reiterated the general principles of the 'open door' to China as well as the integrity and independence of China. It also allowed the Chinese more control over their customs than they had had hitherto. The main result of the Washington conference was a temporary easing of tension in the Far East. The Japanese used this to expand their economic interests in the area.

The Japanese Political Scene, 1894–1924

The Japanese Diet ostensibly operated like a European parliament. It was elected and had political parties which adopted modern names such as the 'Liberal Party' and the 'Progressive Party'.[5] But in practice Japanese politics conformed to Japanese traditions rather than to foreign models. The parties in the Diet were distinguished more by factional and personal loyalties than by policy differences.

Itō Hirobumi in an essay entitled 'Some Reminiscences of the Grant of the New Constitution' described Japan of the days before the Meiji constitution in these words:

> Homogeneous in race, language, religion, and sentiments, so long secluded from the outside world, with centuries-long traditions and inertia of the feudal system, in which the family and quasi-family ties permeated and formed the essence of every social organization, and moreover with such moral and religious tenets as laid undue stress on duties of fraternal aid and mutual succour, we had during the course of our seclusion unconsciously become a vast village community where cold intellect and calculation of public events were always restrained and even often hindered by warm emotions between man and man.[6]

He thought that the 'moral and emotional factor' in Japanese attitudes would, 'in the future, form a healthy barrier against the threatening advance of socialistic ideas'. He also noted that 'in a village community, where feelings and emotions hold a higher place than intellect, free discussion is apt to be smothered, attainment and transfer of power liable to become a family question of a powerful oligarchy'.

Japanese governments before the outbreak of the Sino-Japanese war had had constant difficulties with fractious members of the Diet who tried to disrupt government business. The war, however, proved a unifying force. The government had no difficulty in getting the Diet to vote the necessary funds to prosecute the war and build up Japanese forces. Indeed, members of the Diet were more chauvinist than the government and were highly critical when the government were forced to give in to the triple intervention. This atmosphere and the desire of the politicians for political office enabled the oligarchs to enlist the support of the party leaders. Itō Hirobumi managed to come to an arrangement with Itagaki Taisuke, and Matsukata Masayoshi with Okuma Shigenobu. In 1898 Okuma and Itagaki even came together, merging their parties into a new 'Constitutional Party' (Kenseitō) and forming a party cabinet, but their government only lasted four months because of squabbles between party members over ministerial appointments and of intrigues against them led by Yamagata Aritomo. The Kenseitō then split. From one group Itō formed in 1900 the 'Friends of Constitutional Government Party' (Rikken Seiyūkai, more commonly known as the Seiyūkai). Okuma headed the other section, which was known as the 'True Constitutional Party' (Kensei Hontō).[7]

After the resignation of the first Okuma cabinet in 1898 Yamagata Aritomo, as Prime Minister, managed the Diet by a mixture of manipulation and bribery. Itō Hirobumi, however, resented Yamagata's ascendancy and the influence of the army which grew under his auspices. This was a major factor in the formation of the Seiyūkai in 1900. Itō managed to form a government in 1900, but this lasted less than a year. Thereafter Itō and Yamagata in their capacities as *genrō* preferred to manipulate power through their protégés. Katsura Tarō was Yamagata's man, and Saionji Kinmochi was Itō's. Governments headed by them alternated for the next twelve years.

Katsura Tarō, who had no formal party affiliation, was Prime Minister from June 1901 until he was forced out by opposition to the treaty of Portsmouth at the end of 1905. Saionji, the nominal leader of the Seiyūkai, headed the government from January 1906 until June 1908 when he fell out with the *genrō* over finance. Katsura had similar problems and handed power back to Saionji. Saionji held on until December 1912 when he had to go because the Army Minister resigned over retrenchment in the armed forces and no serving officer was allowed to replace him. Saionji's cabinet was thus the first victim of Yamagata Aritomo's rule of 1895 (see page 213).

Attempts to form a socialist party in Japan were frustrated by the government, which proscribed any such organizations almost as soon as they had been formed. Katayama Sen (1860–1933) was a moving force in these efforts (from 1921 until his death in 1933 he lived in Moscow). Another was Kōtoku Shūsui (1871–1911), who was indirectly involved in a plot to assassinate the Emperor Meiji in 1910. He was arrested, convicted and with twenty-three others executed. The 1910 incident provided the authorities with a further excuse for repression; it also encouraged patriotic fervour and expressions of nationalist loyalty to the sovereign.

The death of the Emperor Meiji in 1912 did not result in any change in the Japanese power structure. Even in his later years when he had gained much experience he rarely intervened in government except for occasional requests for the advice of the *genrō*, but he had been placed on such a pedestal by the Meiji leaders that his death inevitably resulted in an outpouring of respect for the throne and the further development of state Shintō involving the building of the great Meiji shrine in Tokyo. His death was also the occasion for an example of an outdated form of loyalty. General Nogi Maresuke, the hero of the siege of Port Arthur, committed ritual suicide on the eve of the Emperor Meiji's funeral in an act of *junshi*, which the Tokugawa had abolished as a practice in the seventeenth century (see page 141).[8]

The fall of Saionji's government at the end of 1912 caused the parties to come together to seek a way to end the stranglehold of the *genrō* on the formation of Japanese cabinets and the policies which they should adopt. In 1913 the government was headed by Admiral Yamamoto Gonnohyōe (1852–1933). In 1914 Okuma Shigenobu returned from retirement to head the government which brought Japan into the First World War and instituted the twenty-one demands on China. But in 1916 he had to give way to General Terauchi Masatake, whose government lasted until 1918 when he was replaced by Hara Takashi (1856–1921), the leader of the Seiyūkai and the first commoner to head a Japanese government. His government lasted until he was assassinated in 1921. The era of what Hugh Byas has called 'Government by Assassination'[9] had begun, but one result of Hara's murder was that the *genrō* were able to nominate the next three Prime Ministers, who covered the period until 1924. Then a coalition party cabinet under Katō Takaaki (1860–1926) was formed, and for a few years it seemed that 'normal constitutional government' might be possible in Japan

Hara Takashi has been called by some the first 'great commoner' in Japanese politics. He certainly seems to have had great force of character, but, according to Morgan Young, 'Exactly what political views he held it might not be easy to define....Hara had a gift...of attaching men to himself in bonds of personal loyalty....He was a party man first and last....He was, like most of his countrymen, patriotic, but he could hardly be called scrupulous....He gave countenance to the institution of the political bully.'[10] He was murdered by a railway employee on 4 November 1921 who denounced Hara as a corrupt and degenerate politician.

The Japanese Diet and the politicians in these years were far from popular. Economic unrest led to rice riots in 1918, and there were mass rallies in 1919 and 1920 in favour of universal manhood suffrage. Despite the repressive measures taken by the government there was a growing tendency for dissent to manifest itself.

Economic and Social Developments, 1894–1924

The Japanese population in 1872 was reported to be just over 33 million. It rose steadily during the next fifty years and according to the census of 1920 it had then reached just under 57 million. By 1940 it had risen to over 73 million, and Japanese leaders were speaking of a target of 100 million people. The increase in the population was due partly to lower death rates, as a result of improved hygiene and a reduction in infant mortality, but two-fifths of Japanese deaths in the years between 1920 and the outbreak of the Second World War were still due to preventable diseases such as tuberculosis, dysentery and typhoid.

The vast majority of the Japanese population continued to be employed directly or indirectly in agriculture, although this proportion steadily, if slowly, declined over the years. Some 84 per cent of the Japanese population lived in rural areas in 1893; in 1913 the proportion was 72 per cent. The increase in the population meant that Japanese food production had to grow quickly. This was achieved by bringing more land under cultivation, by improvements in farming methods and by ever more intensive farming. The average plots worked by Japanese farmers remained small; a holding of half a *chō* (about half a hectare) was a fair average for a Japanese peasant. Even such tiny holdings were generally split into small strips or consisted of little terraces on hillsides. The number of peasant proprietors steadily decreased so that by 1910 it has been estimated that 45 per cent of all arable land in Japan was being farmed by tenants. Standards of living remained low, and the life of the Japanese peasant was a hard one.

Rice remained the staple crop; rice production more than doubled between the 1880s and the 1930s. Wheat, barley and oats were produced in limited quantities, and some farmers diversified into vegetables and fruit to meet demands from the growing cities. The introduction of foreign seeds and the development of research into their adaptation to Japanese soils and climatic conditions led to improvements in quality and quantity. Labour being plentiful and cheap, little thought was given to labour-saving devices. Although more and better chemical fertilizers were used, the main manure for paddy fields and vegetable plots, in the absence of any large number of farm animals, was human excrement.

Industrial crops also grew in importance. In the latter part of the nineteenth century raw cotton had been produced in sufficient quantity to meet domestic demand, but the removal of the duty on imported raw cotton in 1896 made cotton growing uneconomic. The production of raw silk, however, continued up to the Second World War to be significant to farmers in areas where the mulberry, which provided food for the silkworms, could be grown easily. Many peasants in the years up to 1914 were engaged in silk reeling as well as raw silk production. Silk weaving was also concentrated into relatively small enterprises, although in the next decade the process of industrialization led to the concentration of the manufacturing process into larger firms. However, up to the 1930s the bulk of Japanese production of raw silk was exported as a raw material rather than as a manufactured product.

In the first decades after the restoration Japan was a net importer of cotton textiles, but the rise in prices in the 1890s, the availability of cheap Indian cotton and access to the Korean market after the Sino-Japanese war of 1894–5 acted as a spur to the development of the Japanese cotton textile industry. In 1893 Japan had only 382,000 spindles. By 1913 there were 2,415,000 spindles. A similar growth occurred in the production of woollens and worsteds for which there was no indigenous tradition. Thus on the outbreak of the First World War the textile industry was the most important part of the Japanese manufacturing sector.

The availability of cheap labour from the agricultural areas was an important factor in the growth of the industry. The textile firms employed agents who travelled around the country districts and concluded contracts with the heads of farming families. The farmers were induced to send their daughters to work for a few years in the mills where the owners provided accommodation and food. Wages were low, and conditions in the overcrowded factory dormitories were primitive. But the semi-annual bonuses and discharge allowances were a boon to the poor peasants. The system of employment reflected not only the needs of the industry but also Japanese paternalist traditions.

Coal mining, shipbuilding and engineering works, which had been established before or after the restoration, at first expanded relatively slowly, and up to the First World War much of Japan's requirements of equipment for railways, factories, mines and power stations was imported. But after the railways were nationalized in 1906 the government discriminated in favour of local manu-facturers. This discrimination together with subsidies, easy credit terms for indus-trial expansion projects, preferential tariff rates and government investment in infrastructure provided effective incentives for the development of a major indigenous engineering industry. In the first decade of the twentieth century greater use began to be made of electric power, and hydroelectricity schemes were promoted. This led to the appearance of major companies such as Hitachi. Light engineering, however, remained largely in the hands of small firms in back-street workshops. Foreign observers at this time remained sceptical of the Japanese capacity to develop an effective industrial base, but Japanese production of manufactured goods steadily increased. Raw materials formed a growing element in Japanese imports, while exports of finished products also grew.

The First World War provided a major boost to the Japanese economy. Japan moved from having a regular net imbalance in trade to being in significant surplus. The chemical industry was stimulated by the disruption of trade with Germany, and demand for Japanese products increased in the Chinese and other Asian markets as European exports declined. There was also a flood of military orders for Japanese industry. The boom brought increased prosperity especially for the growing middle classes. But it also caused serious social problems. There were large inflationary rises in prices; the wholesale price index rose from 100 in 1913 to 322 in 1920 when the boom collapsed. Inflation caused widespread economic discontent which culminated in numerous labour disputes and in serious rice riots in 1918, in which the premises of rice brokers, money-lenders and other merchants were looted by crowds of discontented labourers. The depression which hit Japan in 1920 caused major falls in prices. Workers had to be layed off; stock market prices fell, and there were many bankruptcies. Japan's overseas trade moved back into deficit. This was covered by using up the credits which had been piled up, especially in New York, after the Americans had banned the export of gold in 1917. One result was that Japan was left with an overvalued currency. The government and the Bank of Japan proved incapable of controlling the money supply or dealing with the exchange rate problem.

On 1 September 1923 disaster struck Japan. In what came to be called the Great Kantō Disaster (*Kantō daishinsai*) a major earthquake struck the area of Yokohama and Tokyo. Many buildings crumbled and communications were disrupted as fissures and upheavals occurred. The earthquake was followed by innumerable fires which turned parts of Tokyo into infernos and which could not be controlled as water supplies had been disrupted. The number of dead and missing was over 100,000, and more than 50,000 people were injured. Well over 3 million homes were destroyed or damaged. Rumours that Koreans were lighting fires and poisoning water sources led to many Koreans being murdered (the highest figure given is some 6,000, but this is probably an exaggeration). The military police (*kenpeitai*) also took advantage of the declaration of martial law to get rid of a number of radical dissidents.

Insurance policies excluded earthquake damage. The government were forced to declare a moratorium on loans and to advance special credits to firms affected by the disaster. This helped to fuel a mini-'reconstruction boom'. But the basic imbalances in the economy remained. The widespread discontent among peasants and workers, combined with the signs of incompetence and corruption in business and government, provided a fertile breeding ground for the growth of Japanese militarism.

Party Government, 1924–31

These years have sometimes been called the 'liberal' 1920s, because party governments alternated. It was certainly a more democratic period than any that had gone before, and Japanese governments during these years were more ready than their predecessors to seek peaceful solutions to the problems of achieving Japanese economic and political aspirations. But 'liberal' is hardly an appropriate adjective for these years.

In 1924 Katō Takaaki and his allies won the election, and Katō formed a government which from 1925 was made up of members of the Kenseikai (later renamed the Minseitō). Katō's government included Hamaguchi Yūkō (Osachi) (1870–1931) as Finance Minister, Wakatsuki Reijirō (1866–1949) as Home Minister and Shidehara Kijurō (1872–1951) as Foreign Minister. The first two were to serve in due course as Prime Minister before the war and the latter briefly as Prime Minister after the war. Katō, who had been Ambassador in London and Foreign Minister at the time of the twenty-one demands, had a forceful personality.

In May 1925 the vote was given to all males aged over twenty-five, and the electorate was thus expanded from 3 million to 13 million. Katō also instituted cuts in the bureaucracy and the army, which had to disband four divisions. These were significant steps, but the new electorate, which had been fed for so long a diet of propaganda about the divine origins of the Japanese, became enthusiastic supporters of military expansion abroad after the economic depression of the late 1920s and early 1930s. The bureaucracy and the army deeply resented the cuts imposed on them and sought ways of getting their revenge on the politicians.

Shidehara has been described as an advocate of international co-operation and as conciliatory towards China. A career diplomat, he had been Ambassador to the United States and wished to maintain friendly ties with the USA and Britain. Shidehara in his two periods as Foreign Minister between 1924 and 1927 and again between 1929 and 1931 did his best to achieve compromises which, while protecting Japanese national interests, would not lead to armed conflict, but he and the Foreign Ministry lacked the power and authority to prevent the Manchurian incident of 1931. At heart a traditionalist and conservative, Shidehara had neither the will nor the force of personality needed to lead an effective movement against the growing power of the military. Professor Beasley summed up Shidehara's attitude in these words: 'Shidehara believed that Japan's progress and stability depended on the growth of industry; that this in turn relied on foreign trade; and that it was therefore the task of diplomats to avoid any action, notably territorial expansion, likely to deprive Japan of international sympathy in pursuing its economic ends.'[11] Shidehara declared that it must be 'A priority for Japan to maintain the great market of China'. In the 1920s this form of economic imperialism was acceptable to Japanese industrialists.

The Katō government had no intention of allowing socialist or revolutionary parties to challenge its authority, and the first 'peace preservation law' (chian ijihō) was enacted in 1925. The inspiration came from Hiranuma Kiichirō (1867–1952), an influential official of the Ministry of Justice, who as an uncompromising nationalist disapproved of party politics and the 'internationalist' tendencies of Shidehara. He went on to become president of the privy council in 1936 and Prime Minister for eight months in 1939.[12] The law was amended in 1928, and its provisions were strengthened as Japan came nearer to war.

The law was approved by both houses of the Diet, the government having explained that it was aimed at extremists of the left. In 1928 some 1,600 suspected communists were arrested, and General Tanaka Giichi (1864–1929), then Prime Minister and leader of the Seiyūkai, had the law strengthened so that the death penalty could be applied to those found guilty of offences against the law. But in practice the death penalty was rarely exacted for such crimes in Japan.

The prestige of the Diet was lowered by the way in which corrupt and strong-arm tactics were used in elections and in the house of representatives. Morgan Young commented that the debates,

even when concerned with serious matters, were conducted with little dignity. Flushed gentlemen, clad without in frock coats but warmed within by too copious draughts of *sake*, roared and bellowed, and arguments frequently culminated in a rush for the rostrum, whence the speaker of the moment would be dragged into the midst of a free fight. At one sitting Bedlam was let loose when a live snake came flying down from the spectators' gallery and fell among the *Seiyūkai* benches.[13]

In fact the snake had been dropped by a hired bully from the Seiyūkai.

Japan suffered as much as other industrialized or industrializing countries as a result of the world's economic problems in the 1920s and 1930s. Rural poverty had been endemic in Japan, but it was exacerbated by the fall in the price of rice after 1927. The collapse of the American economy in 1929–31 caused a disastrous fall in silk prices. This added to the distress of the farmers who had augmented their meagre incomes by cultivating silkworms. The slump in international trade at the same time drastically reduced Japan's cotton exports, and many of the textile operatives were returned to their villages. Many went hungry. Rural destitution was quickly reflected in the army, whose main recruiting grounds were in rural areas. More and more of the junior officers in Japan's conscript army in these days came from farming districts and were no longer of samurai descent.

A Naval Conference was convened in 1930 to review the Washington agreement of 1922. The Japanese delegation sought, on instructions from Prime Minister Hamaguchi, to increase the ratio of naval ships which Japan might possess from 6 to 7 against the 10 allowed to the Americans and the British. The Japanese were granted the ratio they requested only in respect of vessels below eight-inch gun cruisers, but they were allowed parity in submarines. The treaty aroused fierce opposition in Tokyo. Admiral Katō Hiroharu, the Chief of the Naval Staff, protested that the government's acceptance of the terms of the treaty infringed the power of supreme command granted to the Emperor under Articles 11 and 12 of the Meiji constitution. Admiral Katō was forced to resign, and the treaty was eventually ratified by the privy council on the insistence of Prime Minister Hamaguchi; but in November 1930 he was shot by a nationalist and he died in August of the following year. Hamaguchi was succeeded as Prime Minister by Wakatsuki Reijirō, who only lasted until December 1931. His fall was engineered by Adachi Kenzō (1864–1948), a singularly unsavoury character, who was then Minister of Home Affairs and who had been implicated in the murder of the Queen of Korea in 1895. Following the start of the Manchurian incident in 1931 he decided to side with the military. He refused to resign when asked to do so and thus forced the resignation of Wakatsuki and his cabinet.

The Manchurian Incident

The incident on the night of 18–19 September 1931, which led to the take-over of Manchuria by the Japanese army, had been carefully planned in advance by Colonels Ishiwara Kanji and Itagaki Seishiro. It seems clear that they acted independently of the government in Tokyo, although members of the army general staff knew and approved of their plans. The Kwantung (Guandong) army launched a sudden attack on the Chinese garrison in Mukden on 18–19 September 1931. The attack was said to be a retribution for alleged attacks on the tracks of the South Manchurian Railway by the Chinese army, but the incidents had been fabricated by the Japanese army. Vain efforts were made from Tokyo to control subsequent events, but by December 1931 the Japanese army controlled most of southern Manchuria. The government in Tokyo refused to agree to the annexation of Manchuria. So the army set up a puppet government, which came to be called Manchukuo.[14] The forced resignation of the Japanese government in December 1931 and changes within the army staff in Tokyo facilitated the subsequent operations to complete Japanese conquest of Manchuria. By January 1933 Manchuria had been subjugated, and the neighbouring province of Jehol (Rehe) was then invaded.

The League of Nations was unable and unwilling to take effective steps to deal with Japanese aggression. In 1932 a League commission of inquiry, under the chairmanship of Lord Lytton, concluded that Japanese actions in Manchuria were unjustified; the Japanese responded by walking out of the League.

Hostilities were not, however, confined to Manchuria. In January 1932 an incident was provoked in Shanghai which led to extensive fighting throughout February and to bombing of densely populated parts of the city by Japanese naval aircraft. Many Chinese were also killed in the streets in ways which horrified the foreign residents of the Shanghai settlement.

As a result of the Manchurian incident Japan found herself increasingly isolated. The Soviet Union, fearing a threat to its position in Siberia, strengthened its forces in the Far East, and the Japanese responded by building up their forces in Manchuria and Kwantung. In China the Japanese action boosted anti-Japanese feeling and Chinese nationalism.

The Development of Japanese Fascism

Right-wing extremism and chauvinism were encouraged by the success of Japanese arms in Manchuria, by the impotence of the League and by the Chinese government's failure to take effective steps against Japan.

A number of Japanese 'patriotic' and ultra-nationalist societies had by this time gained a certain aura of respectability in Japan. Toyama Mitsuru (1855–1944), the leader of the Kokuryūkai (Amur River Society), was, for instance, an establishment figure in pre-war Japan. But the leadership of the movement for what was called a 'Shōwa restoration' was seized by right-wing fanatics who advocated violent revolution. One group which inspired the young turks in the army and navy was the Yuzonsha (Survivors' Society), founded in 1919 by among others Kita Ikki (1883–1937) and Okawa Shūmei (1886–1957). Kita Ikki and his friends advocated the establishment in Japan of an authoritarian regime which would rid the country of corrupt politicians and businessmen. Industries would be nationalized, private property limited, and a land reform would ensure that the farmers were equitably treated. The new regime which would be established at home would enable Japan to assume her rightful role as leader of Asia.

In the Japanese army at this time there were two main factions. One of these was given the name kōdōha ('imperial way') faction because of the emphasis it placed on 'spiritual' training, devotion to the Emperor and 'direct action'. It was led by Generals Araki Sadao (1877–1966) and Mazaki Jinzaburō (1876–1956). The other faction was the tōseiha ('control group'). It favoured mechanization of the Japanese army and practical measures to strengthen Japan including the economic integration of Manchuria. Its main leader was General Ugaki Kazushige (1868–1956) who had been Army Minister in the Hamaguchi cabinet at the time of the reduction in army divisions. The *kōdōha* were in the ascendant in Tokyo at the time of the outbreak of the Manchurian incident. In October 1931 members of the *kōdōha* planned a *coup d'état* in which Prime Minister Wakatsuki was to be murdered. The plans leaked, and the participants were arrested, but General Minami Jirō (1874–1955), the Army Minister at the time and sympathetic to the actions being taken in Manchuria, excused the participants on the grounds that they had acted with an excess of patriotic zeal. When Wakatsuki resigned in December 1931, the *kōdōha's* position was strengthened by the appointment of General Araki Sadao as Army Minister in the cabinet of Inukai Tsuyoshi.

The lenience of the authorities only encouraged the extremists, who drew up lists of politicians and businessmen who, they considered, should be eliminated. On 9 February 1932 Inoue Junnosuke (1869–1932), the Finance Minister in the governments of Hamaguchi and Wakatsuki, was assassinated. On 5 March 1932 Dan Takuma (1858–1932), then head of the Mitsui *zaibatsu* was murdered. These murders were the work of the so-called *ketsumeidan* ('league of blood') which had been formed by the ultra-nationalist Inoue Nisshō (1886–1967).

On 15 May 1932 a group of young naval officers plotted to overthrow the government of Inukai Tsuyoshi. They succeeded in murdering the Prime Minister, but failed in their other objectives. However, this spelt the end of party government. Saionji Kinmochi, the last of the *genrō*, recommended Admiral Saitō Makoto (1858–1936) to form a cabinet of national unity. General Araki, known to be sympathetic to the murderers, was retained as Army Minister. The perpetrators of the 15 May incident were leniently treated by the military and civilian courts which tried them, and the accused were allowed to use their trials as a forum to propagate their cause.

The jealousy between the *kōdōha* and the *tōseiha* was more a matter of personalities than of ideology. It led to the next assassination. Major-General Nagata Tetsuzan (1884–1935), who belonged to the *tōseiha* and had been appointed to the powerful post of Chief of the Military Affairs Bureau, was murdered in his office on 12 August 1935 by Lt-Col Aizawa Saburō (1889–1936).

The next incident in this sorry tale of murder, fanaticism, indiscipline and intrigue was the most serious of all. On 26 February 1936 (the so-called *ni-ni-roku jiken*) a group of about 1,400 troops under the leadership of junior army officers seized control of the central part of Tokyo. They killed the Finance Minister Takahashi Korekiyo, the Lord Keeper of the Privy Seal Admiral Saitō Makoto and the Inspector-General of Military Education General Watanabe Jōtarō (1874–1936). They also attacked the residences of the Prime Minister, the Grand Chamberlain and the former Lord Keeper, but were unsuccessful in these latter attempts. The rebels then approached the Army Minister General Kawashima Yoshiyuki (1878–1945) and demanded that a new cabinet be formed. But, although some high-ranking officers supported the rebels, the general staff were opposed to them, and the Emperor, in whose name the rebels pretended to be acting, was furious and demanded firm action. Negotiations with the rebels having failed, martial law was proclaimed on 27 February. The rebels were ordered back to barracks, and loyal troops surrounded them. The rebel soldiers, who had thought that they were acting on the orders of the Emperor, then surrendered. Two of their leaders committed suicide; the rest allowed themselves to be arrested in the expectation that, as in previous cases, they would be allowed to use their trials as a forum to propagate their ideas. They were disappointed, and following a secret tribunal nineteen, including Kita Ikki, were executed. The 'young officers' movement had been destroyed, but the army used the incident as an excuse to strengthen its hold on power and bolster its imperialist ambitions.

Japanese fascism had now established its hold on the military leadership. It was different both in its origins and in significant aspects of its development and philosophy from Nazism and Italian fascism. Its main base was among agrarian rather than industrial workers. It drew its strength from Japan's traditional beliefs in the supremacy of the Emperor, in the central role of the Japanese imperial state and in the overriding importance of the group. It was firmly opposed to any form of western individualism. It saw Japan as having a significant role in the emancipation of Asia.

The ideology of Japanese fascism can be traced back to the nationalist philosophers of the Mito school whose ideals had swayed the drafters of the Imperial Rescript on Education (see pages 197–8) and of the articles in the Meiji Constitution on the role of the Emperor. As Professor Maruyama Masao has explained, the rescript was 'an open declaration of the fact that the Japanese state being a moral entity monopolized the right to determine values'. Thus:

> the Empire of Japan came to be regarded *per se* as 'the culmination of the True, the Good and the Beautiful' and was by its very nature unable to do wrong; accordingly the most atrocious behaviour, the most treacherous acts, could all be condoned.... This point of view about the automatic righteousness of the nation's conduct can also be explained by the interfusion of ethics and power that occurred in Japan.[15]

This meant that the closer a Japanese felt to the 'mystic' or 'divine' power of the Emperor, as the military did in pre-war Japan, the less they had to worry about legality or western concepts of objective morality.

The prosecutors and interrogators in the post-war war crimes trials were astonished and perplexed by the fact that the perpetrators of atrocities were largely unconscious of the evil they had committed. Japanese leaders seem to have had an almost infinite capacity for self-deception and inability to perceive reality. These attitudes were nourished by the sense of racial superiority which was engendered by the inculcation of belief in the myths about Japan's divine origins and mission in the world, as well as in the 'unique' characteristics of the Japanese people. Japanese felt that they had been bullied by the West and had been made to feel inferior by the racialist attitudes of western people towards Japanese. In their turn they became the bullies of the East and treated other peoples with a racialist contempt based on their belief in their inherent superiority.

Central to Japanese fascist ideology was the concept of *kokutai*, which may be translated as 'the national polity' or 'national essence'. It meant the special character of Japan based on descent from the gods. The concept was refined into official doctrine in the *Kokutai no hongi* ('Cardinal Principles of the National Essence'), a political pamphlet put out by the Ministry of Education (Monbushō) in 1937. This gave prominence to phrases such as *hakkō ichiu* ('the whole world under one roof'). It asserted that Japan must 'eliminate the tyrannical policies of the powers in East Asia'. Japan was to 'provide leadership and guidance' to 'backward peoples'. This was intended as the justification for the 'Greater East Asia Co-prosperity Sphere' and provided propaganda cover for Japanese aggression in East Asia.

The absurd lengths to which Japanese ultra-nationalists went in defence of the *kokutai* can be seen in the notorious case involving the generally respected constitutional lawyer Minobe Tatsukichi (1873–1948) who became a member of the upper house of the Diet in 1932. In 1935 he was charged with *lèse-majesté* for suggesting that the Emperor was 'an organ of the state'. This was regarded as undermining the *kokutai*, and he was forced to resign from the upper house.

The 'peace preservation laws' were used to enforce conformity to the *kokutai*. A 'thought police' section and a 'special higher police' (*tokkō* or *tokubetsu kōtō keisatsu*) were set up within the Ministry of Justice. They were backed up by a special military police force (the notorious *kenpeitai*) which had some 7,500 members in Japan during the war.

The *kenpeitai* became the favourite instrument of General Tōjō Hideki (1884–1948), who was Prime Minister during the war from 1941 to 1944. Apart from terrorizing any Japanese suspected of being dissidents, the military police committed some of the worst Japanese atrocities in territories occupied by Japanese forces during the war. They also behaved with brutality towards any foreigners in Japan who came under suspicion. Anti-foreign feelings were fomented by the governments and their agencies in the 1930s and the first half of the 1940s. The Japanese developed a pathological suspicion of foreign spies, and no unauthorized person was allowed anywhere near a military base. Even innocent photography in coastal areas could lead to arrest and interrogation if not worse. Most foreigners found life in Japan in these years difficult and frequently unpleasant if they came into any kind of conflict with the authorities.

The main task of the special police forces was to try to ensure that offenders who had committed 'thought crimes' (*shisōhan*) were apprehended and 'converted' to orthodox views. The methods used to achieve conversions were more like those described by George Orwell than the cruder methods of the Gestapo in Germany. These methods could be singularly unpleasant for anyone brave or foolish enough to hold out, but they were generally pretty effective. Many former communists were 'converted' and subsequently 'rehabilitated' into society. Between 1928 and the outbreak of war in 1941 some 74,000 persons were arrested for violations of the 'peace preservation laws', but only 5,000 were prosecuted. At the end of the war approximately 2,500 political prisoners were discovered in Japan by the occupation authorities. Most Japanese had been so indoctrinated that they preferred silence to protest. The late Richard Storry has commented: 'Moral courage was displayed, it is true, by a few men in public life; and from this honorable category the Emperor himself is not excluded. But devotion to principle, to a rationally thought-out and accepted personal point of view, was a rare phenomenon.'[16]

War in China and Advance to the South, 1937–41

After the murder of Prime Minister Inukai in 1932 the Japanese government recognized the state of Manchukuo. Pu-i (Puyi), the last Emperor of the Ch'ing (Qing) dynasty, was brought out of retirement and in 1934 became 'Emperor' of Manchukuo, but his regime was a puppet body with no real power. In theory the Japanese were only responsible for internal security and defence, but in practice all matters of importance were decided by the Japanese Kwantung army and the Manchurian Affairs Board in Tokyo.

In withdrawing from the League of Nations in 1933, following the report of the Lytton commission which had condemned Japanese aggression in Manchuria, the Japanese had declared that China could not be regarded as 'an organized state'. This meant that Japan regarded China as a legitimate prey and intended to prevent any other power interfering against her interests. A Japanese memorandum of December 1934 declared that Japan must 'exploit internal strife' in China to her own advantage. Both the army and navy believed that the resources of north-east Asia must be mobilized for Japan's defence, but the navy, which was concerned about its requirements of oil, wanted to put increasing emphasis on penetration of South-east Asia.

A clash between Japanese and Chinese troops at the Marco Polo bridge on the outskirts of Peking (Beijing) on the night of 7 July 1937 provided the excuse for action against China. Tientsin (Tianjin) and Peking were soon occupied, and by September 1937 Japan had some 200,000 men in the newly formed North China Army. Japanese forces moved up the Yangtse (Yangzi) river and on 13 December 1937 Nanking (Nanjing), capital of Chiang Kai-shek's (Jiang Jiaeshi) Kuomintang (Guomindang) government, was occupied. According to estimates presented at the Tokyo War Crimes Trials after the war about 42,000 civilians, mostly women and children, as well as some 100,000 'prisoners of war', military and civilian, were killed by members of the Japanese forces in Nanking. There were also some 20,000 rapes in what were some of the most appalling atrocities committed in China by Japanese forces. No attempt was made by Japanese officers to prevent these crimes. The commander of Japanese forces in Nanking, Matsui Iwane (1878–1948), was executed in 1948.

The Japanese soon gained control of the main ports and strategic centres in China, including Hangchow (Hangzhou) and Canton (Guangzhou), and tried to cut China off from the rest of the world. But they never succeeded in conquering and controlling the Chinese mainland. In March 1940 the Japanese managed to establish Wang Ching-wei (Wang Jingwei) as head of a puppet government in Nanking; he never gained a proper following in China. The war continued with the Kuomintang and with the Chinese communists up to Japan's surrender in 1945. Sometimes it was a phoney war; at other times it was brutal and bloody, especially for the Chinese peasantry, over whose land the fighting took place.

Japan's aggression in China caused incidents on the Yangtse river involving the Americans and the British; it also undermined British and American trading interests in China, and there was much popular sympathy for the Chinese especially after the rape of Nanking. But neither Britain nor the USA was willing to do anything effective against the Japanese.

Border clashes occurred with the Soviet Union in July 1938 and again in May

1939 at Nomonhan on the border between north-western Manchuria and Outer Mongolia. The Japanese suffered reverses in fighting with mechanized Soviet forces and the Japanese 23rd Division is reported to have lost over 17,000 men dead or missing. A cease-fire was eventually agreed in Moscow on 15 September 1939.

In 1936 the Japanese had signed an anti-Comintern pact with Germany, and from 1938 negotiations for closer German–Japanese ties started in Berlin. The conclusion of the German–Soviet non-aggression treaty of August 1939 brought these negotiations to an end, but they were resumed in 1940 when Konoe Fumimaro (1891–1945) was Japanese Prime Minister and Matsuoka Yōsuke (1880–1946) was Foreign Minister. On 27 September 1940 a tripartite pact was signed with Germany and Italy. Matsuoka expected Britain to fall and did not foresee the German invasion of the Soviet Union in June 1941.

The British preoccupation with war in Europe, the German occupation of the Netherlands and the fall of France provided the Japanese with the opportunity to expand southwards. In September 1940 the French authorities in Indo-China agreed to the establishment of Japanese air bases in northern Indo-China and the right of passage of Japanese troops through French territory. In July 1941 substantial Japanese forces entered Indo-China. The Dutch were less amenable, and Japanese demands for the bulk of the oil production of the Netherlands East Indies were parried.

The main obstacle to a southward move by the Japanese was American opposition. The Americans had become increasingly concerned about the effects of Japanese aggression in China and in 1939 the US–Japan commercial treaty, due to expire in 1940, was not renewed. In 1940 the United States began to take a series of economic measures designed to increase pressure on the Japanese government to desist from further expansion and aggression. Licences were introduced for the export of oil and scrap metal, and later all steel and iron exports to Japan were embargoed. In 1941 following the entry of Japanese forces into southern Indo-China all Japanese assets in the USA were frozen, thus disrupting trade.

Negotiations for an understanding between Japan and the USA took place in 1941. The Americans sought an undertaking that Japan would respect the territorial integrity of her neighbours, including China and the Philippines, would use only peaceful means to support her policies and would guarantee equality of opportunity in territories under her control. The Japanese demanded American help in securing their needs for rubber and oil and in persuading the Chinese to accept Japanese terms for a settlement. The two sets of demands were irreconcilable, and the proposal for a personal meeting between Prime Minister Konoe Fumimaro and President Roosevelt in August 1941 was rejected by the Americans as a pointless gambit in the absence of any sign of movement on the Japanese side.

The Japanese military planners decided in September 1941 that, unless there were major concessions by the Americans, military action should be taken against the USA by December 1941, because in their view Japanese stockpiles of raw materials and likely weather conditions necessitated action by then. The civilian members of Konoe's government were unwilling to accept this ultimatum, and Konoe resigned on 16 October 1941. On 18 October he was replaced by General

Tōjō Hideki (1884–1948), the Army Minister. Nicknamed 'Razor', Tōjō was an uncompromising martinet.

A special envoy, Kurusu Saburō (1886–1954), was sent to Washington to support Ambassador Nomura Kichisaburō (1877–1964) in negotiations with the Americans. The Japanese continued to demand that the Americans cease to support China and make economic concessions to Japan; if the Americans agreed to these demands the Japanese undertook to halt their advance elsewhere. The Americans were unable to accept the Japanese terms, which would have meant a total reversal of their policies in East Asia. They also had reason to doubt whether the Japanese would fulfil any undertakings they might make. There had been too many Japanese promises in the past which had been broken. On 26 November 1941 the Americans rejected the Japanese proposals. An imperial conference in Tokyo on 1 December 1941 decided to launch an attack on the USA. The Emperor acquiesced as he had done at an earlier conference in September 1941. On that occasion he had expressed his disapproval indirectly by quoting a poem by his grandfather, the Emperor Meiji, which demonstrated his love of peace. Tradition dictated that the Emperor followed the advice of his entourage. The Japanese declaration of war was not delivered until after the Japanese had launched a devastating blow against the American fleet at Pearl Harbor on the morning of Sunday 7 December 1941. Eight battleships were sunk or damaged, and 90 per cent of the US air and surface forces in the area were immobilized. Once again, as in the Sino-Japanese and Russo-Japanese wars, the Japanese had struck without warning.

Did the Japanese have any reasonable grounds for attacking the Americans? The Japanese economy had encountered real difficulties as a result of the slump of the late 1920s and the early 1930s and of growing protectionism in the West combined with 'imperial preference', but Japan had secured major markets in north-east Asia. The Japanese argument that the growing population of Japan needed *Lebensraum* was specious when Hokkaidō remained vastly underpopulated; the argument is in any case discredited by the way in which a population of over 120 millions today against some 71 million in 1937 has had no difficulty in living in the Japanese islands. Japan's raw material requirements were certainly a problem, but if Japan had pursued a peaceful policy, as it has in the post-war world, there is no reason to suppose that she could not have bought what she required from America and South-east Asia. American immigration policies were discriminatory, and racialist attitudes in North America had aroused real resentment in Japan, but these did not justify Japanese aggression. The only 'justification' for war was the fact that the USA was an obstacle to Japanese imperialism.

Were Japanese claims that they were seeking to liberate the countries of Southeast Asia from colonial exploitation and establish an Asian 'co-prosperity sphere' mere hypocrisy? Certainly there were some people in Japan who were convinced by their own propaganda and who believed that Japan had a god-given role to lead Asian countries. But there was a considerable element of racial and nationist arrogance even among the idealists. Japanese actions certainly gave a boost to anti-colonial movements in the territories they occupied, but Japanese colonial policies were in practice more tyrannical as well as racialist and involved more direct economic exploitation than those of the colonial powers they displaced.

Could the war have been prevented? American concessions in 1941, even if these had been politically possible for President Roosevelt, would almost certainly have encouraged the Japanese to demand more and more. Military imperialist ambitions could at that late stage only be curbed by firm and determined resistance. If we look back over the history of Japanese imperialism, we can see a number of possible turning-points, when Japan might have moved in a different direction, but the indoctrination of the Japanese people by Japanese leaders since the Meiji restoration about the superiority of Japan and the pre-eminence of the imperial throne, as well as Japanese emphasis on group loyalties, meant that there was no effective opposition or advocacy of alternative policies. The Americans and the British by their acquiescence in the Japanese exercise of hegemony in Korea and by their failure to take effective action against Japanese expansion in Manchuria and China must share an element of responsibility for the tragic outcome of Japanese imperialism.

The Pacific War

At first Japanese forces achieved overwhelming victories. They were well led and well trained; Japanese soldiers, sailors and airmen fought with courage and determination, bolstered by patriotic and ultra-nationalist sentiments.

Bullying and hazing were part of the everyday training of recruits. They were taught to regard themselves as members of a superior race. The traditional Japanese emphasis on group loyalties and disregard of the individual, as well as the indoctrination which they received to induce a willingness to sacrifice their own lives for Japan and the Emperor, meant that to become a prisoner of war was regarded as being shameful in the highest degree. As a consequence the general attitude towards Japan's opponents and in particular towards Allied prisoners of war was at best one of contempt and frequently of brutality. Many members of the Japanese forces were equally contemptuous of the people of occupied territories, and indications of opposition were liable to be suppressed with ruthless cruelty. As a result the Japanese left behind in South-east Asia and among former Japanese prisoners of war a legacy of bitterness and hatred which erupted once again at the end of the Showa period in January 1989 with the death of the Emperor Hirohito. As a result of the hold which the military obtained on government, education and thought in Japan in the 1920s and 1930s Japanese behaviour deteriorated significantly in this period. Russian prisoners of war in the Russo-Japanese war of 1904–5 and German prisoners of war in the 1914–18 war seem to have been reasonably treated.

A few hours after the attack on Pearl Harbor the Japanese launched an offensive against American forces in the Philippines. Most American military aircraft at Clark Field north of Manila were destroyed on the ground, and Japanese forces soon pushed the American–Filipino army into the Bataan peninsula. These groups held out, longer than the Japanese expected, until 6 May 1942. After the surrender 75,000 prisoners, including 12,000 Americans, were forced to march under horrific conditions to a camp some 60 miles distant. Many thousands died as a result of what came to be called the Bataan death march. General Douglas MacArthur, the American commander, under orders, escaped to Australia to carry on the fight against Japan. After the American surrender the Japanese established a puppet regime in the Philippines.

At the same time the Japanese launched an attack on British positions in Malaya from bases in Thailand and Indo-China. The modern British battleship HMS *Prince of Wales* and the veteran HMS *Repulse*, which had no air cover, were sunk by Japanese naval aircraft on 10 December 1941. Hong Kong fell on 29 December 1941. The British forces in Malaya were ill prepared for the Japanese onslaught and retreated in a demoralized state to Singapore, the main British base in Southeast Asia. They surrendered on 15 February 1942. After the British surrender, the Japanese massacred considerable numbers of Chinese suspected of being communists or involved in anti-Japanese activities. Mass graves of those killed were discovered in 1962, and this led to an outburst of anti-Japanese feeling in Singapore. During the war Singapore was renamed Shōnantō. Malaya and Singapore were considered by the Japanese during the war as forming part of Japanese territory and were not thought suitable for puppet regimes, although in Malaya the Japanese tried to use the Malays and their traditional rulers against the Chinese.

After the fall of Singapore, Japanese forces had little difficulty in taking over the Netherlands East Indies from Sumatra, through Java, Borneo and the Celebes to New Guinea. At the same time their forces advanced as far as the Solomon Islands. Following an attack on Port Darwin in January 1942 Australia seemed threatened. In the Netherlands East Indies (now Indonesia), Japanese officials took over from the Dutch. The Dutch were interned and the Eurasians and Chinese harshly treated. At a Japanese imperial conference on 31 May 1943 it was decided to treat the area as Japanese territory but to allow the local inhabitants some say in the administration of the territories. The Indonesian independence movement was thus given limited scope to develop.

Japanese forces also advanced into Burma, and the British were forced out in humiliating circumstances. Ba Maw was set up to head a puppet government, and on 1 August 1943 a Burmese declaration of independence was promulgated, but the Burmese found that they had only exchanged one form of hegemony for another more autocratic and demanding.

In March 1942 the Japanese navy launched attacks in the Indian Ocean and on Ceylon (now Sri Lanka). The British feared that their position in India was threatened. No immediate attempt was made to invade India, but Indian prisoners of war were recruited into the so-called Indian National Army to fight alongside the Japanese, and in 1944 Japanese forces penetrated into Assam. The only remaining supply route to China (following the Japanese occupation of the Chinese coast and Japanese command of the sea in the area) was thus placed in increasing jeopardy. In order to ensure their lines of supply to Burma the Japanese decided in 1942 to build a railway from Siam. Work began on the railway in November 1942 and was completed on 17 October 1943. Allied prisoners of war and local forced labour, under the supervision of Japanese forces, were employed on this task in appalling conditions. Brutal treatment, disease and starvation led to the death of many thousands. One estimate puts the number of dead as 63,000 including 16,000 British and Australian prisoners of war.

But Japanese forces had become overstretched long before 1944. Moreover their commanders had failed to comprehend the reaction of the peoples allied against Japan to their initial defeat and humiliation as well as to what was seen as the treachery of the attack on Pearl Harbor and the cruelty and barbarity of Japanese behaviour in occupied territories and towards prisoners of war. The tide gradually began to turn against Japan.

A battle between Japanese and American naval forces in the Coral Sea in May 1942 was indecisive, but in the naval battle of Midway in June 1942 the Americans sank four Japanese carriers, and the Japanese navy were no longer in command of the Pacific.

On 18 April 1942 American carrier-based aircraft carried out their first raid on Tokyo. But the bombing of Japanese cities only became a major feature of the war against Japan after the Americans had obtained land bases within striking distance of the Japanese main islands.

The Japanese fought back stubbornly. After very fierce fighting the Japanese were forced out of the island of Guadalcanal in the Solomons in February 1943. Saipan was retaken by the Americans after a bloody battle in July 1944. In October 1944 American forces landed on Leyte island in the Philippines and inflicted a decisive defeat on Japanese naval forces. The Philippine island of Luzon was invaded in January 1945 and Manila recaptured in March.

Meanwhile in February 1945 US marines had landed on the Japanese island of Iwojima. On 1 April 1945 American forces invaded Okinawa, the main island in the Ryūkyū group and indisputably part of Japan. After three months of fierce fighting the Japanese garrison of some 110,000 men was wiped out, and more than 150,000 civilians were killed. Okinawa was devastated. American losses were severe, and many ships were lost as result of suicide attacks by so-called *kamikaze* ('divine wind') aircraft. These were any planes which could be made airworthy with a load of explosives; the pilot was to fly directly into his target and die in the explosion. The Japanese air forces were by now outnumbered and outarmed and were incapable of carrying out normal defensive actions.

The British too had launched an offensive in Burma. Mandalay was recaptured in March 1945 and Rangoon in early May. Landings in Malaya were planned for August 1945.

Japan itself was devastated by massive attacks by American aircraft loaded with incendiary bombs. These began in March 1945. In the first attack on Tokyo on the night of 10 March 1945 some 100,000 people died. As a result of this and subsequent raids over half the buildings in Tokyo were destroyed and most of the main cities of Japan devastated. Only Kyoto and Nara were spared. It has been estimated that by the end of May 1945 over 13 million Japanese had been made homeless.

There had been no co-ordination between Japan and Germany in the direction of the war, and relations with the Germans were distant. German surrender in May 1945, however, dealt a further blow to Japanese hopes of a compromise peace. It also raised the spectre of attack from the Soviet Union, which had not so far declared war on Japan.

When it must have been obvious that Japan was defeated and that further resistance could only lead to the total destruction of the Japanese way of life, why did not the Japanese make real efforts to seek peace? The basic problem was the obstinacy of Japan's military leaders. Japanese propaganda and indoctrination had induced blind self-delusion. Yet Japan was not during the war years a totalitarian dictatorship like Germany, although the Japanese were mobilized for war in a highly organized way, and all opposition was muzzled.

All the political parties had been absorbed in 1940 into the Imperial Rule Assistance Association (Taisei-Yokusankai) during the government of Konoe Fumimaro. The Association was used to enlist popular support for the war, but it never resembled the Nazi Party of Germany or the Communist Party in the Soviet Union and in a typically Japanese way was affected by factionalism. Wartime Japan was in practice dominated by the bureaucracy. Every ten households were forced to form a neighbourhood association (*tonarigumi*), and representatives of these associations formed local town or villages groups called *chōkai*. Membership of a *tonarigumi* was essential in order to obtain rations of food, which was in increasingly short supply. It was, however, only after the war had begun, and it was clear that it would not end as a result of a quick and decisive Japanese victory, that full mobilization of labour was enforced. In 1944 school education was reduced to an hour or two a day so that all older children could join in productive work. Life became increasingly hard for the Japanese people as shortages of all kinds of consumer goods developed and inflation became rampant. As the cities were destroyed, people moved to the countryside in large numbers. The family structure and patterns of group loyalty remained largely untouched.

The house of representatives, elected in April 1937, should have been dissolved in April 1941, but the Konoe cabinet decided that an election at a time of such international tension should not be held, and the Diet agreed to postponement. However, in 1942 Tōjō thought that an election would help to consolidate 'national strength' and an election was called in April 1942. The Imperial Rule Assistance Association put up a list of candidates, which the government hoped would be elected. There were no other official parties, although the Tōhōkai, a right-wing group led by Nakano Seigo, an admirer of Hitler and Mussolini, put up a list of forty-six candidates. Independents, including current Diet members not included in the official list, were also able to stand. All critical comments on the regime and the conduct of the war were suppressed, and a number of rallies were broken up. The veteran parliamentarian Ozaki Yukio was one of a number of candidates arrested during the campaign. But the government's attempts at intimidation were by no means wholly successful. Eighty-five independents were elected including Ozaki Yukio and Ashida Hitoshi (1857–1959), who held the post of Prime Minister for six months in 1948. Ozaki Yukio was charged with *lèse-majesté* during the campaign. He was found guilty in December 1942 and sentenced to eight months in prison; but as he was then eighty-four years old, the sentence was suspended for two years. Ozaki appealed to the Supreme Court, which in 1944 overturned the verdict, and he was acquitted. The Japanese courts thus showed that they could not be regarded as mere tools of the bureaucracy and the government.

Efforts were made during the war to eradicate western cultural influences. The press enthusiastically vilified the Americans and the British. English words which had been Japanized were banned for a time, and English lessons were made optional in Japanese middle schools. German and Nazi achievements were praised even by eminent men such as Professor Koizumi Shinzō (1888–1966) the president of Keio University, who was to play a part in the post-war world as tutor to the present Emperor Akihito. Some Japanese, including Shiratori Toshio, who had been Japanese Ambassador to Sweden and Italy, adopted the anti-semitic attitudes of the Nazis. In fact there were no Japanese Jews. Foreign Jews in Japan during the war were treated according to their nationality and were not persecuted for being Jews.

Although Tōjō, in addition to being Prime Minister and Army Minister, had himself appointed Chief of the Army Staff, he had to work within the Japanese system and was not a one-man dictator. Criticism of him grew as Japan's military position deteriorated. In 1944 the Emperor was known to want to bring the war to an end, but he did not know how to achieve this and feared a major clash with the army. When it was suggested to the Emperor that he should resign to make it easier to seek peace, he demurred; he believed that it was up to him to try to lead the Japanese people out of the current mess. In July 1944 Tōjō made proposals designed to strengthen his administration, but these aroused fears of another shōgunate. The seven *jūshin*, who were all the living former Prime Ministers, met, and Tōjō was forced to resign.

Unfortunately, however, the stranglehold of the army and the navy on government was such that the removal of Tōjō did little to facilitate progress towards peace. General Koiso Kuniaki (1880–1950), who became Prime Minister after Tōjō, was a retired officer with only a limited following and was unable to exercise any effective influence on events. On 5 April 1945, the day when the Soviet Union announced that it would not renew its non-aggression treaty with Japan when it expired in 1946, Koiso resigned. He was replaced by Admiral Suzuki Kantarō (1867–1948), the 78-year old president of the privy council, and Japan began a dangerously slow shuffle towards peace which culminated in surrender in August 1945.

The Japanese Surrender: August 1945

Admiral Suzuki chose Tōgō Shigenori (1882–1950) as Foreign Minister. Tōgō had been Ambassador to Germany and the Soviet Union and favoured an early peace. The hope was that he could be instrumental in getting the Soviet Union to mediate. As Army Minister, Suzuki chose General Anami Korechika (1887–1945). The army insisted that the government must continue to prosecute the war with vigour. The cabinet was thus divided from the outset. It was hardly surprising, therefore, that progress towards peace was at best hesitant.

On 8 June 1945 an imperial conference was told that public morale had declined. By the end of July over 188,000 Japanese had been killed in air-raids, and the economy was in chaos. Nevertheless the army insisted on the continuation of preparations for the final battle which would inevitably take place on Japanese soil and lead to the devastation of Japan on the model of what had happened in Okinawa. Even so martial law was not declared, although the Diet was required to pass an emergency measures law which made similar provisions. Those suspected of belonging to the 'peace group', including Yoshida Shigeru (1878–1967), former Ambassador to Britain and later Prime Minister of Japan, were arrested.

On 22 June the Emperor called on the members of the supreme council for the direction of the war 'to give immediate thought to the ways of ending the war, notwithstanding hitherto accepted concepts'. But despite the Emperor's prestige his advice seemed to be ignored, although Tōgō continued to put out various peace feelers through the Swedes and the Russians. On 26 July 1945 the Presidents of the United States and China (Presidents Truman and Chiang Kai Shek) and the Prime Minister of Great Britain[17] issued the so-called Potsdam declaration which demanded the destruction of Japan's potential for making war and the establishment in Japan of democratic freedom and human rights. To this end the Allies expressed their intention of occupying Japanese territory and called for 'the unconditional surrender of all Japanese armed forces'. Admiral Suzuki announced that Japan would 'ignore' the declaration.

In the face of this response and the continuing preparations to defend the Japanese main islands to the end, President Truman decided to use a new weapon against Japan, namely the atomic bombs which had been developed in secret. The first of these was dropped on the city of Hiroshima on 6 August 1945. Some 90 per cent of the city was destroyed, and about 200,000 people died as a direct result of the bomb. On 9 August a second bomb was dropped on the city of Nagasaki leading to the death of about 140,000 people.

On 9 August 1945 the Soviet Union declared war on Japan and launched attacks on the Japanese positions in Manchuria. The army still argued that the war should continue until Japan could obtain adequate assurances from the Allied powers. The civilian members of the government for their part prepared to accept the terms of the Potsdam declaration on the 'understanding' that the imperial institution would be preserved. At a meeting of the supreme council on 9 August 1945 there was an equal division of opinion, and the 'advice' of the Emperor was sought. He supported the 'peace party'.

The Americans responded to this conditional offer to surrender by stating on 11 August 1945 that the authority of the Emperor must be subject to the Supreme Commander of the Allied Powers and that the 'ultimate form of government of Japan shall . . . be established by the freely expressed will of the Japanese people'. This was not the sort of reply for which the Japanese were hoping but, equivocal though it was, it provided the Japanese with a straw on which to build their hopes. At the meeting of the supreme council on 14 August the army demanded further clarification, while the others recommended immediate surrender. The Emperor once again supported those in favour of accepting the Allied terms. On 15 August he broadcast to his people calling on them to 'endure what is difficult to endure, and to suffer what is difficult to suffer'.

On the night of 14 August the Commander of the Imperial Guards Division was murdered, and an attempt was made by mutineers to destroy the disc containing the Emperor's recorded broadcast and to attack the residences of the Prime Minister and the Lord Keeper of the Privy Seal. The mutiny was suppressed, and Japanese forces obeyed the Emperor's orders to surrender, although a few senior officers, including General Anami, the Army Minister, committed suicide. Admiral Suzuki, assuming responsibility for the surrender, resigned as Prime Minister.

General Prince Higashikuni Naruhiko, the Emperor's uncle, was appointed Prime Minister, and Shigemitsu Mamoru (1887–1957) became Foreign Minister. The surrender was formally signed on board the USS *Missouri* in Tokyo Bay on 2 September 1945 and accepted by General Douglas MacArthur, the Supreme

Commander Allied Powers (SCAP). The war was over, and the occupation of Japan had begun.

Was the decision to drop the two atomic bombs on Hiroshama and Nagasaki morally and strategically justified? The main arguments in favour of the decision were that the losses on both sides from an opposed landing of Allied forces on the Japanese mainland would have been far greater than the numbers killed by the bombs and that the Japanese authorities needed an excuse to justify surrender. It can also be argued that if the Japanese had discovered the bomb first they would not have hesitated to use it, but two wrongs do not make a right. It has been further suggested that the Americans could have offered to demonstrate the bomb to the Japanese in a deserted spot, but it is inconceivable that Japanese leaders would have accepted such an offer at that time and it would have meant unacceptable delays during which there would have been many casualties. But was it necessary to drop two bombs? Would not one have been enough? Was adequate time given to the Japanese to respond after the first bomb? These are not easy questions to answer. The bombing of Nagasaki was brought forward by two days because of weather conditions, and this reduced the time available for a Japanese response to the first bomb. But the Japanese authorities had not reported to the public the nature of the attack on Hiroshima and the extent of Japanese casualties. It seemed to the American authorities that the Japanese were continuing to prevaricate and that a response had to be forced from them. The Americans in particular had suffered grievous losses in the fighting, and the thought of a repeat of the Okinawa tragedy was a horrifying one.

Could the war have been ended earlier if the Allied powers had not insisted on unconditional surrender and had been willing to make a clearer statement about the position of the Emperor after surrender? The Potsdam declaration included fairly clear terms for surrender, and the American reply of 11 August 1945 contained as broad a hint as the Americans felt they could give at that stage of their intentions towards the imperial institution.

In the final analysis the responsibility for the bombing of Hiroshima and Nagasaki and the tragedy which war brought to Japan rests clearly with Japan's military leaders and those who in the earlier years indoctrinated the Japanese people with chauvinism, ultra-nationalism and ideas of Japanese racial and cultural superiority. In 1945 it looked as though Japanese civilization had received a self-inflicted deadly blow and that the Japanese achievement would perhaps be remembered as 'the flower that was Japan'. But Japan and Japanese culture revived in the second half of the twentieth century.

Literature

Japanese literature was inevitably affected by the currents of ultra-nationalism in Japan, but it was for most of the period able to develop on independent lines. Works began to be written in a generally colloquial style which can be understood by a well-educated Japanese without recourse to dictionaries and commentaries. Japanese authors in these years have left works which are not only significant in Japanese literary history but have a rightful place in the history of world literature.

The terms 'romantic', 'realist' and 'naturalist' are freely bandied about by the

241

critics and literary historians in their analysis of the literature of this period. In fact many of the major novelists cannot be easily categorized, or at least their works were so varied that at times they seemed realists, while at other times they wrote works which some might describe as romantic. Most of the novelists were, however, agreed on the importance of psychological analysis of the motives of the characters in their books, and introspection was a prime feature in the 'I novels' (*watakushi shōsetsu*) of the period.

One of the most influential novels of the end of the century was *Konjiki yasha* ('The Golden Demon') by Ozaki Kōyō (1867–1903), published between 1897 and 1902.[18] This was not a great novel, and its style is outdated, but it was very popular. It is the story of a girl who jilts her lover to marry a rich man. The jilted young man determines to make himself equally rich and becomes a dedicated and implacable usurer (hence the title of the novel).

Kunikida Doppo (1871–1908) started as a romantic poet. He also wrote romantic short stories, but gradually moved over to a more naturalist approach to writing. His story *Gen oji* ('Uncle Gen')[19] is one of his more famous romantic and lyrical stories. Shimazaki Tōson (1872–1943) also started as a romantic poet, but is better known as a novelist. His first novel *Hakai*[20] is the story of a Japanese teacher who was a member of the outcast class, the *eta*, who keeps his origin secret until after his father's death. He then emigrates to America. Another of his novels *Ie* ('House') is regarded as a classic of its kind. In this work Tōson maintains a strictly objective approach to his characters in line with Tsubouchi Shōyō's injunctions (see page 203).

Tayama Katai (1872–1930) started by associating with Ozaki Kōyō and Kunikida Doppo but later developed as a naturalist writer. His most famous novel was *Futon* ('The Quilt') which appeared in 1907.[21] One of his stories was *Ippeisotsu* ('One Soldier')[22] published in 1908, the story of a soldier in the Russo-Japanese war. It was based on his observations as a war correspondent. Its anti-militarist tone offended the authorities. Another representative of naturalism was Nagai Kafū (1879–1950). His novels centred on the life of Tokyo and its pleasure quarters.[23] One of his most famous stories was *Sumidagawa* ('The Sumida River'). *Bokutō kidan*, published in 1937 (translated as 'A Strange Tale from East of the River'), is regarded as his masterpiece.

The two outstanding Japanese novelists of the first two decades of the twentieth century were Natsume Sōseki and Mori Ogai. The works of Natsume Sōseki (1867–1916)[24] have been widely translated into English. He came under the influence of Masaoka Shiki and began by writing *haiku*. In 1900 he went as a government student to England, where he was influenced by the novels of George Meredith, but he became depressed as a result of loneliness and poverty. Perhaps as a result a strong element of melancholia and introspection can be traced in his novels. He could also be satirical and humorous. His novel *Wagahai wa neko de aru* ('I Am a Cat'), published in 1905 is a rather long-winded satire on human life in a so-called civilized society. His most popular novel was *Botchan* ('Boy'), published in 1906. It recounts the experiences of a young man born in Tokyo who is sent to teach at a country school on the island of Shikoku.

‧ Mori Ogai (1862–1922) was trained as a doctor and became an army medical officer. In 1884 he was sent to Germany, where he studied hygiene and diet. During his four years in Germany he read widely in European, especially German, literature and rejected the realist approach. He wrote three short stories in 1890–1, but his main literary period was between 1909 and 1912, when he produced a number of novels based on his personal experiences. He was much impressed by the ritual suicide of General Nogi Maresuke in 1912 and wrote various stories about suicide and patriotic sentiment. *Gan* ('The Wild Goose'),[25] tells the story of the mistress of a usurer who falls in love with a student. *Wita sekusuarisu* ('Vita Sexualis'), published in 1909, is a frank account of the role of sex in his life as a boy and a student and in later life. It shocked some of his contemporaries. Ogai also wrote a number of historical/biographical novels.

Shirakaba ('White Birch') was the name of a monthly journal which concentrated on literary and artistic themes and was published between 1910 and 1923. The writers who contributed to the journal are described as belonging to the *Shirakaba* school, but they lacked any common approach, and the term 'school' is an inappropriate one. The most prominent writer in this amorphous group was Shiga Naoya (1883–1971). Some of his early short stories such as *Kamisori* ('Razor') were not autobiographical, but his main works seem to have been based on his own life, and he is regarded as epitomizing the 'I novel' (*watakushi shōsetsu*). His most famous work, *An'ya kōro* ('A Dark Night's Journey'),[26] published between 1921 and 1937, traces the emotional experiences of the novel's main character until he comes to terms with nature, death and humanity. Although he lived into the post-war world he produced nothing of importance after *An'ya kōro*. Other famous writers in the *Shirakaba* group included Mushanokōji Saneatsu (1885–1923), Arishima Takeo (1878–1923) and his brother Satomi Ton (1888–1983).

Akutagawa Ryūnosuke (1892–1927) was one of the most remarkable writers of the first quarter of the twentieth century. He became fascinated by the works of European authors such as Ibsen, Edgar Allan Poe, Baudelaire and Oscar Wilde; he was also influenced by both Natsume Sōseki and Mori Ogai. He started to publish stories while he was still a student of English literature at Tokyo University. One of his most famous stories, *Hana* ('The Nose'),[27] recounts the embarrassments of a Buddhist priest who is disfigured by his enormous nose. *Jigokuhen* describes an eccentric artist who is commissioned to depict the agonies of hell on a screen. Akutagawa's story *Yabu no naka* ('In a Grove') provided the idea for the brilliant film *Rashōmon* made by Kurosawa Akira in 1950. Akutagawa, who committed suicide at the early age of thirty-five, was a master of the grotesque and the macabre. The Akutagawa Ryūnosuke prize for literature established in 1935 is one of the most important of Japanese literary prizes.

Kikuchi Kan (1888–1948), who was a friend of Akutagawa Ryūnosuke, began as a writer of plays. One of his first plays, *Chichi kaeru* ('The Father Returns'),[28] written in 1917, has become a classic of the modern Japanese theatre. Kikuchi Kan also wrote short stories and novels. In 1923 he founded the *Bungei Shunjū*, one of Japan's most influential monthly magazines.

Japanese writers were not generally political activists, although some writers in the 1920s and early 1930s contributed to efforts to improve the lot of workers who suffered poverty and exploitation especially in the years of economic depression. Their writings are referred to as 'proletarian literature'. In March 1928 the *Zen Nihon Musansha Geijutsu Renmei* (All-Japan Federation of Proletarian Arts) was formed and immediately came under communist control. It was banned in 1934. One writer of 'proletarian' works was Kobayashi Takiji (1903–33). His story *Kani kosen* ('Crab Factory Ship'),[29] published in 1929, describes the appalling conditions on a Japanese crab canning boat in the Okhotsk Sea and the attempts of the workers to organize and achieve improvements in their lot. His account of how the bank for which he worked had acted as an agent in the exploitation of farmers in Hokkaidō was published in 1929 under the title *Fuzai jinushi* ('The Absentee Landlord'). This led to his dismissal, and he went underground. He was arrested in February 1933 and apparently died in police custody as a result of torture during interrogation. The novel *Tsuchi* ('The Earth') by Nagatsuka Takashi, published in 1910, was the classic example of what came to be called 'peasant literature'. The novel revolves around the hard life and poverty of tenant farmers in Ibaragi prefecture. It was made into a famous film in 1939 by Uchida Tomu (1898–1970).

One novel about Japanese military involvement in China was *Mugi to heitai* ('Wheat and Soldiers'),[30] published in 1938, by Hino Ashihei (1907–1960), who started as a left-wing activist, was arrested in 1932, then recanted his views and finally committed suicide. *Mugi to heitai* was a realistic account of the war through the eyes of an ordinary soldier. Hino Ashihei was subject to military discipline and was not permitted to criticize the forces or to report on 'the kind of criminal acts that inevitably accompany warfare'.

The writers of the 1930s tended to be conformists, and many were prepared to give their support for the goals of Japanese imperialism. The Shōwa Research Society (*Shōwa Kenkyū-Kai*), which was an advisory organ to Konoe Fumimaro, attracted the support of intellectuals such as Royama Masamichi who favoured a controlled economy and a militant foreign policy. The society was inspired by fascist models and formulated a plan for a new political order to transform Japan into a semi-totalitarian state. The novelist Mushanokōji Saneatsu was enthusiastic in his denunciations of western imperialism, while Tokutomi Sōhō (1863–1957) heaped abuse on the Americans and British. In December 1942 the 'Great Japan Patriotic Writers' Association', was established to support the Japanese war effort; Tokutomi Sōhō became its president, and many of the writers of Japan greeted the war with enthusiasm. The writer Dazai Osamu (1909–1948), a former communist, felt uplifted by the attack on Pearl Harbor. The 'Japan Literary Patriotic Association' formed in May 1942 included novelists such as Shiga Naoya and Tanizaki Junichirō (see Chapter XI), as well as the ethnologist Yanagita Kunio (1875–1962). The Association's chairman was Kikuchi Kan, the playwright and founder of the *Bungei Shunjū* magazine. Monthlies such as the *Bungei Shunjū* and the *Chūkōron* gave their active support to Japan's war effort.

Some novelists such as Nagai Kafū continued to write but published nothing during the war. His diary published after the war was damning about Japan's militarists. As Japan entered the New Year of 1945 he noted that Japan had not faced as forlorn a New Year since the founding of the country: 'For this fact we may thank the militarists. Let their crimes be recorded for eternity.'

Tanka and *haiku* continued to be written. Some of the poets using these forms managed to produce poems of originality and artistry. Many also wrote *shi* (*shintaishi*), which are poems in a free style.

An outstanding poet of the early years of the twentieth century was Ishikawa

Takuboku (1886–1912). His first book of poems, *Akogare* ('Longing'), which was published in 1905, consisted of poems in free verse. His first collection of *tanka* was published in 1910 under the title *Ichiaku no Suna* ('A Handful of Sand').[31] In these poems he brought a new vitality to the *tanka* form by writing directly and frankly about aspects of daily life. He was shocked by the arrest of socialists charged with plotting to murder the Emperor Meiji in 1910 and began to study socialist thought, but he became ill in 1911 and died at the early age of twenty-six.

The following translation of some lines of free verse by Takuboku conveys the flavour of his writing:[32]

> There are some lives duller
> Than dusty glass
> Of windows, hot in the sun past noon.
> Emptied of thought, senseless,
> A young man sleeps, sweating, snoring.
> Yellowish teeth protrude from his mouth.
> The summer sun through the windowpane
> Shines on his hairy leg,
> And a flea crawls on it.

Here are three examples of Takuboku's *tanka*:

Ishi hitotsu
Saka wo kudaru ga
Gotoki ni mo
Ware kyō no hi ni
Itaritsukitaru.

Like a stone
That rolls down a hill,
I have come to this day.

Kyōshitsu no
Mado yori nigete
Tada hitori
Kano shiro-ato ni
Ne ni yukishi ka na.

Running away
From the window of a classroom,
Alone,
I lay down among the ruins of a castle.

Hotobashiru
Pompu no mizu no
Kokochi yosa yo
Shibashi wa wakaki
Koro mote miru.

How pleasant
Is the water gushing from a pump!
Awhile with the soul of a youth
I watch it.

Among Takuboku's friends were the poets Yosano Tekkan (1873–1935) and his wife Yosano Akiko (1878–1942). While he was a romantic and a patriot, she was critical of Japanese imperialism and was a better poet than her husband. Her first volume of poetry, *Midaregami* ('Tangled Hair'), was regarded as passionate and sensual. She was also a critic and literary historian. Her version of the 'Tale of Genji' in modern Japanese is famous.

Saitō Mokichi (1882–1953) is considered by critics to have also been instrumental in reviving the art of writing *tanka*. He trained as a doctor and was active as a psychiatrist. He was also a literary critic, and his work on Kakinomoto Hitomaro is considered to be a standard work. During the war he wrote poems backing the war effort. One of his *tanka* reads:[33]

Shimashi ware wa	As I close my eyes
Me wo tsumurinamu	The high sun falls ...
Mahi ochite	I hear crows cawing on their way
Karasu nemuri ni	to sleep.
Yuku koe kikoyu.	

One poet who became famous for his poems in free-verse style was Hagiwara Sakutarō (1886–1942). His first collection of poems, *Tsuki ni hoeru* ('Howling at the Moon'), was published in 1917. 'Sensuous', 'sceptical', 'pessimistic' and 'melancholic' are adjectives sometimes used to describe his verse. The following lines from a poem entitled 'Night Train'[34] give an idea of his ability as a poet:

> The pale light of daybreak –
> The fingerprints are cold on the glass door,
> And the barely whitening edges of the mountains
> Are still as quicksilver.
> As yet the passengers do not awaken;
> Only the electric light pants wearily.
> The sickening sweet odor of varnish,
> Even the indistinct smoke of my cigar,
> Strikes my throat harshly on the night train.

Another exponent of the free-verse form was Kaneko Mitsuharu (1895–1975). Kaneko was an individualist, a Japanese Bohemian eccentric, whose 'determined libertinism' brought him no satisfaction. He spent long periods in Belgium and France. A poem entitled 'Awa', or 'Foam', was 'an exposure of the Japanese Army's atrocities' in China.[35] The poem begins:

> The sky snivels green snot.
> There is war.
> But what is reflected in my glasses is the Yangtse River's water gleaming fitfully like a dull ache.
> That's all.
> Water thin as mucus from the womb ... water that sounds *slup-slup*.
> Upon the swell of curling waters,
> More senile than any shadow,
> The shadow of our ship advances.
> At the rail, lingering there
> And staring at the fret, my shadow.
> It is a loveless blue sky.
> The sun's orb is a dead coin.

The Arts

Industrialization and 'modernization' led to a deterioration in Japanese crafts-manship and artistic values. However, the 'folk-craft' (*mingei*) movement, which developed in the years between the end of the First World War and the beginning of the Second World War, contributed to a new appreciation of the beauty which can be found in everyday utensils.

The philosopher of the *mingei* movement was Yanagi Sōetsu (Muneyoshi) (1889–1961). While still a student Yanagi joined in the foundation of the *Shirakaba* magazine (see page 243) and began to develop a new approach to aesthetics. He became a friend of the English potter Bernard Leach, who was then studying in Japan, and was introduced by him to the works of William Blake and William Morris. He was also influenced by modern attitudes to Zen Buddhism, as expounded by Suzuki Daisetsu. During a trip to Korea in 1916 he became deeply impressed by Korean arts and crafts (he courageously supported the Korean independence movement). He was struck by the fine artistic qualities of everyday items produced in the Edo period by unknown craftsmen.

In his comments[36] on the tea ceremony, on pattern and on the beauty of irregularity, Yanagi displayed attitudes which have come to represent typically Japanese aesthetic values. He emphasized that appreciation of beauty is not a question of knowledge, but one of seeing.[37] Bernard Leach, who was one of the founders of the Japanese *mingei* movement, highlighted a basic problem:

> I have had a sense of doubt on one main issue – the relationship between the conscious artist and the comparatively unconscious craftsman. Yanagi's constantly reiterated theme concerns the exceeding difficulties experienced in attaining a like purity and wholeness by the artist. He says our arts and crafts are in a diseased condition – with that I agree – but he turns to the artist-craftsman to act as the pilot in this dilemma because of his greater awareness, thereby indicating the power that has come to conscious man through the evolution of intellect. The results are not the same.

The movement helped to revive many of the traditional crafts of Japan from Okinawan textiles to local potteries such as that at Onda in Oita prefecture in Kyūshū. But *mingei* is best known by the famous artists who worked with Yanagi. Apart from Bernard Leach these were the potters Hamada Shōji (1894–1978), Kawai Kanjirō (1890–1966) and Tomimoto Kenkichi (1886–1963), the woodcut artist Munakata Shikō (1903–75) and the textile designer Serizawa Keisuke (1895–). All worked in very different ways and media.

Hamada Shōji produced ceramics for a time with Leach at St Ives and was greatly impressed by old English slip-ware. He established his kiln at Mashiko in Tochigi prefecture.[38] Kawai Kanjirō lived mainly in Kyoto.[39] His earlier pieces were in line with Korean and Japanese traditions, but in the post-war period he branched out and produced some unconventional ceramic sculptures. Tomimoto Kenkichi is best known for his porcelain pieces, blue and white, overglazed enamels and plain white. His enamelled pieces were much influenced by his study of *kutani* wares from Ishikawa prefecture.

Munakata Shikō was born in the northern prefecture of Aomori.[40] He was

247

very short-sighted, but had boundless energy and imagination, working at great speed. He was much influenced by Shintō and Buddhism as well as by western artists like Van Gogh and Toulouse Lautrec. His themes were wide ranging, and his prints vary greatly in size and style, but the outstanding characteristic is boldness. Serizawa Keisuke was influenced by Okinawan designs, and his works use bright colours and traditional motifs.

Two distinct forms of painting continued to exist side by side in Japan. These were *Nihonga* (Japanese-style painting) and *yōga* (western-style painting). The two styles were not without mutual influence but they remained distinct from one another.

In *Nihonga* the artists Yokoyama Taikan (1868–1958) and Takeuchi Seihō (1864–1942) had begun to make their mark in the Meiji period, but some of their best works were produced in the first half of the twentieth century. Both artists experimented with colour and line and made use of western perspective. Some of Yokoyama Taikan's best pictures are, however, in Japanese traditional black and white. He was particularly successful with his paintings of mountains and seas.

Kawai Gyokudō (1873–1957) was more traditional in his approach, basing himself primarily on the Maruyama-Shijō and Kanō schools of painting in the Edo period. Hishida Shunsō (1874–1911), who worked with Yokoyama Taikan, experimented with the Rimpa style. He preferred to leave the outlines in his pictures soft and to bring out shapes through variations in the use of colour than by hard and distinct lines.

Other famous *Nihonga* artists of the first half of the twentieth century included Kobayashi Kōkei (1883–1957), Maeda Seison (1885–1977), Sakakibara Shihō (1887–1977), Kawabata Gyokushō (1842–1913) and Kawabata Ryūshi (1885–1966). All to varying extents were influenced by a mixture of Japanese and western styles of painting. Sometimes the results were beautiful; at other times some of the paintings tended to emphasize the pretty-pretty or seem to be merely seeking effect.

Painting in the *yōga* style was mainly influenced by Impressionism and Post-Impressionism. Paris became the mecca for all Japanese students of western painting. Two outstanding geniuses of *yōga* in these years were Yasui Sōtarō (1888–1955) and Umehara Ryūzaburō (1888–1986). They both studied in Paris and on their return promoted the styles of Pissarro, Cézanne and Renoir. Under their influence and that of other Japanese artists who went to France to study, Japanese connoisseurs began to build up collections of Impressionist and Post-Impressionist paintings.[41]

A few Japanese artists found the European art scene so attractive that they settled in Europe. One of these was Fujita Tsuguhara (1886–1968), who is better known by his European name of Leonard Foujita. He went to Paris in 1913, where he met Picasso, Modigliani and Soutine. He became a French citizen in 1955 and a Catholic in 1966. Like the Impressionists and Post-Impressionists he was inspired by Japanese *ukiyo-e*. He became famous for his nudes, self-portraits and depictions of cats. He is probably the best-known western-style artist of Japanese origin in the European art world.[42]

Another Japanese artist, who fell in love with England, was Makino Yoshio or, to use the English spelling of his name, Yoshio Markino. He wrote charming accounts of his life in London[43] in which he included many reproductions of his paintings combining Impressionism with Japanese style.

From 1940 there was only one theme which Japanese artists could tackle. That was war. Many famous Japanese artists seem to have taken to the task with enthusiasm. Some 17,000 war paintings were confiscated by the occupation authorities after the war ended. No artistic evaluation of these paintings seems to have been made.

One Japanese potter who attained world fame and was active in the first half of the twentieth century was Kitaōji Rosanjin (1883–1959). He began by studying *kutani* wares, but then established his own kiln at Kita-Kamakura. He was a gourmet, with his own Japanese-style restaurant in Tokyo. As a result he concentrated on producing ceramics to use with Japanese food. At first he concentrated on porcelains, being inspired by *imari* and *kutani* wares. Later he turned to producing stoneware, including pieces in *bizen* and *minō* styles. Hamada Shōji criticized Rosanjin as a mere decorator, but he was certainly an able one, and his pots fetch very high prices.

Japanese sculptors had begun in the Meiji period to study western-style sculpture. In the early twentieth century the Japanese became enthusiastic admirers of Rodin, and Rodin provided the initial inspiration of such modern Japanese sculptors as Ogiwara Morie (1879–1910) and Takamura Kōtarō (1883–1956), also known as a poet. They worked in bronze. However, traditional Japanese sculptors continued to produce works of competence in wood. In the 1920s and 1930s Japanese sculptors came under the influence of Antoine Bourdelle and Aristide Maillol.

XI

From Defeat to Riches
(1945–89)

In August 1945 Japan was defeated, impoverished and almost starving. The country was occupied by Allied forces, very largely American, between September 1945 and April 1952. The occupation, although traumatic for many, brought generally beneficial reforms to Japan. A new democratic 'peace' constitution was enacted, which described the Emperor as 'the symbol of the state and the unity of the people'. Inflation was brought under control. Japanese industry, which had slowly begun to recover, was given a major boost by the Korean War, which broke out in 1950.

The peace treaty which came into force in 1952 confirmed the ending of Japanese claims to Manchuria, Korea, Formosa (Taiwan) and territories to the north of Hokkaidō, but the treaty was not signed by the Soviet Union, and a dispute continued between Japan and the Soviet Union over islands in the southern part of the Kuriles.

Under a security treaty with the USA, concluded at the same time as the peace treaty, American forces remained in Japan to provide the main element of Japan's defence against a possible Soviet or Chinese threat. Much of the 1950s was dominated by proposals to revise the security treaty to make it a more equal instrument. The revised treaty which, despite strong left-wing opposition, came into force in 1961 eventually defused the issue. Since then Japanese self-defence forces have gradually assumed an increasing role.

Japanese industry was rebuilt behind protectionist walls and under government guidance. Japanese management learned much from the USA, and Japanese workers, after a brief period of turmoil, provided a highly disciplined and educated work-force. Exports were promoted, and productivity was expanded faster than wages. The Olympic Games in Tokyo in 1964 gave a boost to the development of infrastructure, but industrial development caused major environmental problems. The first oil shock brought serious inflation. The Japanese responded quickly. Inflation soon fell back, and great progress was made in energy conservation. Japan weathered the second oil shock better than most other countries.

As Japanese exports continued to grow, industries in western countries began to suffer from Japanese competition; and with the growing Japanese trade surplus, economic friction became a major problem in the latter part of the 1970s and the 1980s. Japanese standards of living rose quickly, and the fall in the value of the US dollar against the Japanese yen in the late 1980s meant that Japan was able to build up huge assets overseas.

Japanese culture, freed from the deadening effects of militarism, flourished

250

anew. American influence was at first all pervasive, but Europe also had an important cultural impact on Japan.

The death of the Showa Emperor on 7 January 1989 marked the end of an era which covered imperialist aggression, defeat and regeneration. But as Japan entered the 1990s, problems remained. Economic friction with the USA and Europe had not been solved. The Japanese sought a better quality of life, but the ageing society meant an increasing burden on the younger people at work. Corruption in political life had led to a growing disillusionment with the politicians of all parties, and public dissatisfaction with money politics and over the consumer tax introduced in April 1989 forced the resignation in June 1989 of Mr Takeshita Noboru as Japanese Prime Minister. The extremists of the right and the left had, however, no real popular support, and revolutionary change seemed unlikely.

Japanese economic succcess led to occasional displays of arrogance, and many Japanese continued to believe that they were racially and culturally unique. The buzz-word became 'internationalization', but the concept was illdefined. Riches had brought prosperity and diversity, but had Japan found a new cultural identity?

The Occupation (1945–52)

At the end of the war on 15 August 1945 the main Japanese islands had not been invaded, and the only major Japanese island devastated by fighting was Okinawa. But sixty-six Japanese cities had been largely destroyed in air attacks. Half of the housing in the cities had been lost; an even higher proportion of Japanese commercial and industrial property had been so heavily damaged that it was unusable. Japan's export trade had ceased to exist, and the Japanese merchant marine had been reduced to a few coastal ships. A year after the end of the war Japanese industrial production was barely 30 per cent of what it had been pre-war. The harvest in 1945 was disrupted and totally inadequate for Japanese needs. The Japanese people were demoralized and near starvation. Members of the armed forces had been so indoctrinated that they were reluctant to accept the facts of defeat, and some tried to prevent the Emperor's broadcast calling on the Japanese to surrender; in the event the Emperor's command was obeyed, and further fighting was avoided. Many Japanese feared rape and rapine from the occupation forces. But the American troops who arrived in Japan in the autumn of 1945, battle-seasoned though they were, did not follow the example of Japanese forces in China and South-east Asia and, with some exceptions, behaved well. The Americans did not seek revenge. They were, however, determined to do all they could to ensure that Japan would not in future menace the peace of Asia and the world.

The American occupation forces were joined in 1946 by forces from the British Commonwealth under an Australian Commander-in-chief.[1] The British Commonwealth Forces were allocated to the western part of Honshū and the island of Shikoku. They had no role in military government, and most of the forces were pulled out by the end of 1947.

Because Japan had not been a battlefield the Japanese government and bureaucracy were still able to operate. The situation in Japan was thus different from that in occupied Germany. From the beginning the military government operated indirectly through the Japanese authorities not directly as in Germany. This enabled the Japanese authorities to act both as a buffer between the occupation and the Japanese people and as a delayer and occasionally as a frustrator of occupation policies, but it also meant that policies could be adapted to suit Japanese conditions and circumstances.

In theory the occupation was subject to the decisions made by the Far Eastern Commission in Washington, which included representatives of the eleven Allied powers involved in the war against Japan. There was also an Allied council in Tokyo consisting of representatives of the USA, the British Commonwealth, China and the USSR. Neither body proved effective; this was partly due to the deliberately disruptive policies of Soviet representatives, but even the British Commonwealth representatives were far from united. The Americans were understandably irritated by the often irresponsible attempts of these two bodies to interfere and generally went their own way.

In practice occupation policies were largely decided by the American authorities and in particular by the Supreme Commander Allied Powers (SCAP), General Douglas MacArthur (1880–1964). General MacArthur, who had commanded the US forces in the Pacific during the war, was autocratic, inconsistent and vain, but he had vision, outstanding abilities as a leader and a crusading spirit. Firmly anti-communist and at heart a conservative, he nevertheless pushed through a series of democratic reforms which brought revolutionary changes in Japanese society. He firmly believed that democracy would only take root in Japan if the Japanese themselves were convinced that changes were in their own best interests. Many Japanese came to regard MacArthur as a 'father-figure' and substitute Emperor.

The two most important sections in MacArthur's headquarters were the government section, headed by Major General Courtney Whitney (1897–1969), and the intelligence section under Major General Charles Willoughby (1892–1972). Both men were arrogant and rude and cordially disliked one another. But they had access to SCAP and were loyal and hard-working. Whitney, a lawyer, was a liberal idealist. Willoughby was stridently anti-communist (MacArthur referred to him as 'my loveable fascist'). Whitney was supported by idealists, moralists and liberals such as Charles Kades and Alfred Hussey. Many of the reforms instituted by the government section, however well intentioned, were inadequately researched and had to be adapted in practice. Willoughby and Japanese conservatives took every opportunity to exploit the problems encountered to further their own interests.

The first task which SCAP and the Japanese authorities had to tackle was demilitarization. Some three and a half million members of the Japanese armed forces and about the same number of civilians had to be brought back to Japan from occupied territories. The armed forces had to be disbanded and if possible jobs and accommodation provided for them. Demobilization was at first carried out by the Ministries of the Army and Navy, but they were abolished on 1 December 1945 and turned into demobilization bureaux. Large numbers of ex-soldiers had, at least temporarily, to be absorbed into the villages in labour-intensive farming. Most of the Japanese in Manchuria and Korea were seized by the Russians, employed as slave labour and given communist indoctrination. Many never returned. Japanese stocks of arms and ammunition were traced and destroyed. All weapons in private hands were seized, and any activity which could be interpreted as having a militarist overtone, including fencing, was rigorously banned. Equipment in 394 Japanese factories, which might be used as reparations for countries conquered by the Japanese, was confiscated, and industries indirectly involved in the machinery of war were controlled and production limited. The Allies had great difficulty in allocating Japanese plant in reparations, and in practice little was shipped abroad. Japan needed everything it had left to maintain a bare self-sufficiency.

Another major early objective of the occupation was the removal from public life and positions of influence of all who could be regarded as in any way responsible for the war. The 'purge' was effected by a series of SCAP directives barring various categories of persons from holding public office. All Diet members who had been selected in 1942 as official candidates of the Imperial Rule Assistance Association were, for instance, purged. So were numerous others who in the judgement of the occupation authorities had 'by speech, writing, or action... shown themselves to be an active exponent of military nationalism and aggression'. Among those purged on these grounds were Hatoyama Ichirō (1883–1959), who organized the Japan Liberal Party (Jiyūtō) after the war, and Ishibibashi Tanzan (1884–1973), editor of the *Tōyō Keizai*, an economic journal. Both were later to become Prime Minister of Japan if only for brief periods. By May 1946, 210,288 Japanese had been purged, and all ultra-nationalist organizations had been dissolved. Thereafter, as the occupation was wound down, the purge was relaxed, and many were rehabilitated. The purge, if only because of its sweeping character, inevitably involved injustice to many who were little more than nominal members of banned organizations. But it did bring new men into responsible positions in politics and made it easier for other democratic reforms to be carried out.

Some six thousand Japanese, accused of war crimes in occupied territories and against Allied prisoners of war, were tried by Allied courts; 920 were sentenced to death and executed. An international Military Tribunal for the Far East was convened on 3 May 1946. Twenty eight military and political leaders were charged with conspiracy to commit aggression, with aggression and with war crimes. The trial, before eleven judges representing the Allied powers, lasted until November 1948. Seven of the accused were condemned to death. These included former Prime Ministers General Tōjō Hideki (1884–1948) and Hirota Kōki (1878–1948) as well as Generals Itagaki Seishirō (1885–1948) and Matsui Iwane (1878–1948). While there is ample evidence of crimes against humanity committed by members of the Japanese forces, the processes of justice were not always strictly observed and particularly in the Tokyo trial were without precedent. Aggression was not a crime defined in international law. Of the Allied judges only one, the Indian judge Radhabinod Pal, who found all the defendants not guilty, had any background in international law. There were also many procedural flaws in the trial. In particular the trial, conviction and sentence of seven years' imprisonment of Shigemitsu Mamoru (1887–1957) on charges of waging aggressive war and failing to prevent war crimes were considered by many to have been unjust.[2] The hatred which the Japanese behaviour during the war aroused, and which led to examples of Allied brutality in return, provides the background to these trials, but punishments inflicted by the victor often smack more of revenge than of justice.

In order to eradicate militarist and imperialist thinking from Japan SCAP *education* recognized that early reforms must be made in the Japanese educational system. The first requirement was to remove the teachers who had been particularly active in indoctrinating Japanese youth. Well over 100,000 were quickly forced to resign. Programmes to recruit new teachers and to 'reorient' the minds of those who remained were devised. In December 1945 history and geography courses were temporarily suspended while textbooks were revised. The teachings of morals (*shūshin*) was abolished; instead children were to be taught civics and social studies. The old élite high schools were replaced and an American system of six years' primary school followed by three years' middle school and, for those going on to further education, three years' high school was adopted. Many colleges were upgraded to university status, and higher education both public and private was encouraged. Conservative Japanese were worried by the influence of left-wing teachers belonging to the teachers' union (Nikkyōsō) and the probable replacement of old Japanese ethics of loyalty and hard work by western individualist thinking. As soon as they had the chance they tried to revise the system back to what it had been. They were only partly successful. The competitive element in the Japanese educational system remained very strong, and the pressures on the young to pass the necessary examinations to enter the best high schools and universities increased rather than diminished under the new system. Rote teaching continued to be a major element in the Japanese educational system.

Under a civil liberties directive, issued by SCAP on 4 October 1945, all laws restricting freedom of thought, speech and assembly were to be abolished, the secret police dissolved and political prisoners released. On 15 December 1945 orders were issued for the separation of the state from religion. Shintō thus ceased to have any official status. This decision undercut the notion that the Emperor, the land of Japan and the Japanese people were of 'divine' origin. On 1 January 1946 the Emperor issued a rescript which declared that the ties between him and the Japanese people were not 'predicated on the false conception that the Emperor is divine'. He did not deny his descent from the sungoddess, nor did he cut himself off from the performance of Shintō rites, but the rescript was a significant follow-up to the call which he made on General MacArthur, on his own initiative, on 27 September 1945. It also made possible the definition of the Emperor's position in the new constitution (see page 256) and made easier the preservation of the imperial institution in Japan.

trade *econ. powers* The basic initial post-surrender directive had called for the encouragement of 'wide distribution of income and of the ownership of the means of production and trade'. This was the basis for SCAP's attack on the pre-war *zaibatsu*, which had worked with the militarists and maintained semi-feudal relationships in Japanese industry. In October 1945 the four great combines – the Mitsui, Mitsubishi, Sumitomo and Yasuda – were invited to submit plans for the ending of their commercial empires. The Yasuda were the first to respond, the others quickly following suit. But, although these plans were at first accepted, they were declared in March 1946 to be mere cosmetic gestures, and a directive was issued for the destruction of excessive concentrations of economic power. In July 1947 SCAP ordered the dissolution of the Mitsui and Mitsubishi trading companies, the enactment of an anti-monopoly law and the establishment of a Fair Trade Commission to enforce the law. Some two thousand business leaders were purged and instructions issued to prevent relatives being brought in to replace those removed from office. These measures caused a great deal of business disruption at the time and, although they did succeed in loosening the ties between the companies in the big groups, they have not prevented the re-emergence of the groupings in new forms. The new groups (*keiretsu*) which have been formed are no longer autocratically controlled from the centre, but the large trading companies (the *sōgō-shōsha*) and their related banks still provide the core of most of the groups. Cross-shareholdings are limited by law, but as each company in the group may hold shares in all the other group companies, the web is closely knit.

In December 1945 Japanese workers were granted the right to organize unions, bargain collectively and strike. This was followed by other pieces of legislation providing for the establishment of a separate Ministry of Labour, of labour relations committees and of labour exchanges. The labour standards law of April 1947 set out a comprehensive set of rules covering safety, hygiene, working conditions, sick leave, holidays and accident compensation. Labour unions were quick to develop in the new climate and by June 1949 unions claimed a membership of over six and a half million. In the immediate post-war period strikes were frequent and disputes acrimonious. However, under the labour relations adjustment law of September 1946 strikes by public employees were prohibited. The left-wing unions responded by calling a general strike for 1 February 1947. This was banned, and the tide was turned against the left-wing agitators who had gained control of many of the unions.

In 1945 almost 50 per cent of Japan's population of 72 millions lived in rural areas. The farmers had provided the bulk of the old Japanese army. They had been exploited for centuries. They were generally poor, and their life was hard. Many were tenants who paid rents in kind and barely made a subsistence out of their small landholdings (27 per cent owned less than 10 per cent of the land they farmed, and a further 17 per cent less than 50 per cent of the land they cultivated). Under the land reform instituted by the occupation and enacted in October 1946 a large-scale redistribution of land was carried out. The government was enabled to buy all the land of absentee landlords and dispose of this to tenant farmers. As a result of a very complicated system, which because of inflation amounted in practice to expropriation of absentee landlords, the percentage of fields owned by the cultivator rose to some 90 per cent by 1949. Almost all farms remained tiny, and many small farmers were left with widely scattered plots of land. The law made it very difficult for the more efficient to build up larger and more economical holdings, but the reform encouraged the intense cultivation needed to provide rice for the growing Japanese population at a time of world shortage of foodstuffs. It also led to the development of agricultural co-operatives and strengthened village harmony. The small farmers were instinctively conservative and became firm supporters of the Liberal Democratic Party (LDP) which has dominated politics in Japan since its formation in 1955.

The New Constitution (1946–7)

The most significant reform achieved during the occupation was the drafting and enactment of a new constitution. This replaced the Meiji constitution of 1889. The Potsdam declaration had called for the removal of 'all obstacles to the revival and strengthening of democratic tendencies among the Japanese people. Freedom of speech, of religion, and of thought, as well as respect for the fundamental human rights, shall be established.' The declaration also called for the establishment 'in accordance with the freely expressed will of the Japanese people' of 'a peacefully inclined and responsible government'.

In October 1945 Prince Konoe Fumimaro, Lord Keeper of the Privy Seal in the government of Baron Shidehara Kijūrō, began to investigate the need for constitutional reforms, but in December 1945 Konoe committed suicide on the eve of his arrest as a major war criminal, and nothing came of his study of the problem. A group under Matsumoto Jōji (1887–1954) was separately commissioned to produce proposals for revision. These, however, proved totally unsatisfactory to SCAP. The government section were then instructed to prepare a draft constitution as a guide to the Shidehara cabinet. This draft was delivered to the Japanese cabinet on 13 February 1946. The Japanese were warned that, if its basic principles were not adopted, it might be difficult to prevent the Emperor from being tried as a war criminal. The Shidehara cabinet quickly complied and produced on 6 March 1946 a draft based on the SCAP model; the only basic change was the proposal that there should be a bi-cameral legislature rather than a uni-cameral one as in the American draft. This draft formed the basis for a constitutional revision bill which was approved by the privy council and submitted to the Diet for approval. The Emperor had indicated his acceptance of the suggested formula proposed to cover the imperial status, and the bill was passed almost unanimously by the two houses of the Diet as an amendment to the Meiji constitution. It was promulgated on 3 November 1946 and came into effect on 3 May 1947.

Chapter 1 dealt with the position of the Emperor. Under Article 1 the Emperor was declared to be 'the symbol of the State and of the unity of the people, deriving his position from the will of the people with whom resides sovereign power'. The Emperor was empowered to act in matters of state only 'on the advice and approval of the Cabinet' and as 'provided for in this Constitution and he shall not have powers related to government'. The Emperor's ten functions, as defined under Article 7, covered such acts as convoking the Diet and dissolving the house of representatives, awarding honours and receiving foreign ambassadors, but always 'with the advice and approval of the Cabinet'.

Chapter II consisted of only one article (Article 9) covering 'Renunciation of War'. It was particularly significant. It reads:

Aspiring sincerely to an international peace based on justice and order, the Japanese people forever renounce war as a sovereign right of the nation and the threat or use of force as a means of settling international disputes.
(2) In order to accomplish the aim of the preceding paragraph, land, sea, and air forces, as well as other war potential, will never be maintained. The right of belligerency of the state will not be recognized.

Chapter III (Articles 10 to 40) dealt with the rights and duties of the people. Article 13 declared that 'All of the people shall be respected as individuals. Their right to life, liberty, and the pursuit of happiness shall, to the extent that it does not interfere with the public welfare, be the supreme consideration in legislation and in other governmental affairs.' Equality under the law was guaranteed, and sexual and other discrimination was banned. The peerage was abolished. Freedom of thought and of religion was proclaimed. The rights of citizens to a fair trial were spelt out. The rights of workers to organize, bargain and act collectively were emphasized. Suffrage was to be universal. Education was to be compulsory and free. The right to own or to hold property was declared to be inviolable, and 'all people shall have the right to maintain the minimum standards of wholesome and cultured living'.

Chapter IV (Articles 41 to 64) was concerned with the Diet. Article 41 declared that 'The Diet shall be the highest organ of state power, and shall be the sole law-making organ of the State.' Other articles provided for an elected house of representatives and house of councillors. The term of office of members of the house of representatives was limited to four years. Members of the house of councillors were to be elected for six-year terms, but half the seats were to be contested every three years. If a bill passed by the house of representatives were rejected by the house of councillors the house of representatives could overrule the upper house by passing the bill again with a two-thirds majority. The powers of the upper house in relation to the budget were also limited by the constitution. Detailed provisions about elections and procedures were to be settled in separate legislation.

Chapter V (Articles 65 to 75) covered the cabinet and its powers. Article 65 declared firmly that 'Executive power shall be vested in the Cabinet'. Article 67 provided that the Prime Minister was to 'be designated from among the members of the Diet by a resolution of the Diet'. Chapter VI (Articles 70 to 82) dealt with the judiciary and affirmed the independence of the judges. It also covered the establishment of a supreme court with powers to determine whether laws and orders are constitutional. Chapter IX (Article 96) headed 'Amendments' provided that amendments to the constitution had be initiated in the Diet and required 'a concurring vote of two-thirds or more of all the members of each House'. Amendments would then have to be submitted to the people for ratification with 'the affirmative votes of a majority of all votes cast'.

There has been much discussion in the post-war era about amending the constitution, which some Japanese regard as being alien in tone and forced on the Japanese government against their will by the occupation authorities. Amendments have, however, never been formally proposed in the Diet, not least because there has been no chance of their being accepted by the necessary two-thirds majority.

Article 9 in particular has had widespread support, but the interpretation of the article in 1954 to permit the establishment of the Japanese self-defence forces has aroused much controversy. The Japanese government view has been that, while the constitution forbids war as a means of resolving international disputes, it does not negate the right of self-defence, and the ban on armaments in the second paragraph is qualified by the phrase 'in order to accomplish the aim of the preceding paragraph'. Yoshida Shigeru (1878–1967), who succeeded Shidehara Kijūrō as Prime Minister in May 1946 and was responsible for piloting the new constitution through the Diet, wrote in his memoirs that he was personally in favour of Article 9: 'Since it was an accepted idea among the Allied Powers that Japan was a militaristic nation, it was most necessary to take steps indicating that it was not.'[3] Yoshida added that it was his impression that the clause was suggested by General MacArthur to Shidehara. Yoshida, who was later responsible for the self-defence forces law, believed that the article did not need to be amended.

During the drafting of the constitution the position of the Emperor caused the Japanese government the greatest qualms. But, according to Yoshida, the Emperor let it be known that in his view 'it would be unwise to delay the revised Constitution more than was unavoidable, and that there seemed to be nothing wrong about the definition in it of the position of the Emperor'.[4] The Japanese people were generally realists; they recognized that pre-war concepts of a 'divine' Emperor and of Japan with a 'divine' mission had demonstrably failed and were no longer relevant. Outdated myths had to be cast aside if they stood in the way of the country's present top priority which had to be speedy economic recovery.

Economic Problems Following the War

The first years after the end of the war were a period of great economic hardship for the Japanese people. Food was very scarce and rations meagre and irregular. Many city dwellers had to scour the countryside to find enough food on the black market to keep their families from starving. Inflation wiped out most savings, and investments became largely valueless. To stay alive people sold their household possessions and family treasures. Many people had to exist in shacks and tents or under bridges. Fuel was in very short supply, and the few trains and buses (operating largely on charcoal) were dangerously crowded and slow. The farmers were a little better off, but they had to make do with human manure for fertilizers, improvise agricultural tools and absorb a large population of returnees and demobilized soldiers. Consumption was down to less than half of what it had been pre-war. While machinery was collected for reparations, workers struggled to find food and shelter. There were no resources to pay for imports of essential raw materials, and production recovered slowly.

SCAP realized that Japan's economic distress did not provide a fertile ground for the development of democracy and that the Japanese could not be allowed to starve. The Japanese Ministry of Agriculture calculated in the autumn of 1945 that some four and a half million tons of grain were needed to prevent starvation. In fact this was a gross overestimate, and only about 700,000 tons were required immediately. But at the end of the war even to find this amount, let alone to pay for it, was a major problem. President Truman in 1946 appealed for the help of the American people to alleviate world famine and sent Herbert Hoover as his special envoy to report on world food conditions. The government of Yoshida Shigeru in mid-1946 appealed to SCAP for assistance, and over 500,000 tons of rice belonging to the Australian forces in Japan were released to tide the Japanese over to the next harvest. But for the next three years the Japanese government had much difficulty in procuring foodstuffs from the Japanese farmers and had to rely on American aid; $392 million worth of American food aid was received in 1948 and $429 million in 1949. This enabled the Japanese to increase food imports to 1.7 million tons in 1948 and to 2.4 million tons in 1949. By 1949 the crisis was over, but rationing of staple foodstuffs continued until after the end of the occupation in 1952.

The steps initially taken to deal with inflation, Draconian though they were, were ineffective in the absence of goods for sale. The situation was exacerbated by the labour unrest which followed the granting of union rights and which developed in the face of economic unrest. Government attempts to deal with problems by subsidies added to the inflationary pressures. The Americans became increasingly irritated by the Japanese government's failure to take effective measures, and in 1948 they appointed a Detroit banker, Joseph M. Dodge (1890–1964), to make recommendations for a cure. He prescribed some harsh but necessary measures. These included a demand that the Japanese government should balance the national budget, should terminate the inflationary loans made by the Reconstruction Finance Bank, should decrease government intervention in the private economy through subsidies and price controls, should return foreign trade to private hands and should then establish a realistic exchange rate of 360 yen to the US dollar. Measures on the lines recommended by Dodge were instituted from March 1949. The central government dismissed some 140,000 employees. There was a minor recession and an increase in unemployment. This caused social unrest, but inflation was largely brought under control, and the Dodge Plan, as it came to be called, marked the turning-point in Japanese post-war economic recovery.

The Korean war which broke out in June 1950 provided a major stimulus to Japanese production, which was then still below pre-war levels; it exceeded pre-war levels for the first time in 1951. The Americans recognized their need for bases in Japan, and special procurements from Japan brought valuable orders to Japanese industry.

American aid was not restricted to food aid and to special procurements. Financial assistance was given to enable the Japanese to import essential raw materials. But in the long run perhaps the most significant American aid was education in management and quality control. In 1946 a quality control seminar was organized in Japan by the telecommunications industry. In 1950 Edward Deming, an American expert on statistical quality control, was invited to Japan to attend a seminar. In the following year the Deming prize for enterprise in developing and using effective quality control was introduced.

As soon as foreign exchange permitted, Japanese students were sent abroad to study and to learn about successful foreign methods of management and of technology. Japanese companies quickly adapted what they had learned, and imports of foreign technology, carefully controlled and vetted by the Ministry of International Trade and Industry (MITI), were rapidly absorbed by the quickly recovering Japanese industries.

Japanese Politics During the Occupation

As soon as the war ended the pre-war politicians began to reorganize political parties. In October 1945 the Japan Socialist Party (JSP) (Nihon Shakaitō) was launched. In November 1945 the Japan Liberal Party (Nihon Jiyūtō) was formed by Hatoyama Ichirō, mainly from former memebers of the Seiyūkai. At about the same time the Japan Progressive Party (Nihon Shimpōtō) was formed by politicians who had been active in the Imperial Rule Assistance Association. The Japan Communist Party (JCP) (Nihon Kyōsantō) was established soon after the release of political prisoners in October 1945. But the purge ordered by SCAP soon altered the picture; it almost wiped out the Progressive Party and prevented Hatoyama from remaining leader of the Liberals. The vacuum thus created was largely filled by the recruitment of new leaders from the bureaucracy, which was for the most part untouched by the purge. These included Yoshida Shigeru, a former diplomat, who was persuaded to take over the leadership of the Liberals from Hatoyama. Other recruits to the Liberal Party, who were to go on to become Prime Ministers of Japan, were Ikeda Hayato (1899–1965), who was the permanent vice-minister of Finance, and Satō Eisaku (1901–75), who was permanent vice-Minister of Transportation.

The Japanese government led by Prince Higashikuni Naruhiko, which signed the surrender on 2 September 1945, only lasted until October that year. His successor was Shidehara Kijūrō (1872–1951), who was regarded as pro-American. Shidehara's main aim seems to have been to ensure the preservation of the imperial system, and to this end he accepted the American proposals for a new constitution. At the time of the first post-war election in April 1946 Shidehara was nominally head of the Progressive Party. His party was defeated in the election. He accordingly resigned, and in May 1946 Yoshida Shigeru, who had served as Foreign Minister in Shidehara's government, took over as Prime Minister and head of the Liberal Party in place of Hatoyama. Yoshida's government saw the new constitution through the Diet and the enactment of a revised electoral system. This continued the old system of electoral districts, where three, four or five members were elected on the basis of each elector having one ballot. Victory went to the candidates who obtained the largest numbers of votes in each district. This system, which has remained largely unaltered, makes it very unlikely that there will be landslide victories, such as can occur under the first-past-the-post system in one-member constituencies. It has some of the advantages of a proportional representation system, but it also encourages pork-barrel-type politics.

In the election of April 1947 under the new constitution the JSP won a plurality of seats, but had no overall majority. Katayama Tetsu (1887–1978), a Christian socialist from the right wing of the JSP, formed the only post-war government of Japan to be led by other than a conservative leader, but his government was a coalition with the Democratic Party (Minshūtō), a conservative-inclined party organized by Ashida Hitoshi (1887–1959). Katayama was weak and ineffective, and his government fell in February 1948 when his budget was defeated by a combination of the left wing of the JSP and the communists. Katayama was succeeded by Ashida, who had been his Foreign Minister. Ashida was no more successful than Katayama in making the coalition work and after six months he was forced to resign following a scandal involving corruption on the part of the Shōwa Denkō company. Yoshida Shigeru then resumed the post of Prime Minister. The Diet was dissolved in January 1949, and Yoshida won an overwhelming victory; this ensured his control of the Japanese government through the negotiations leading to the peace treaty concluded in 1951 and the end of the occupation in 1952. The scene had now been set for the maintenance of conservative rule for many decades to come.

Yoshida was by nature a conservative autocrat. He was also a wily politician, who manipulated the occupation authorities to serve his own ends. He knew how to obfuscate and delay, playing effectively with misunderstandings based on language difficulties. He was strongly anti-communist at a time when the tide of anti-communism was rising in America and Europe. He disliked the encouragement which the occupation had given to unionism and abhorred the freedom given to the communists to disrupt the economy and the political scene. He welcomed the denunciation of the JCP by General MacArthur in May 1950 following the criticism of the party by the Cominform for not opposing the occupation sufficiently strongly. The subsequent purge of communist leaders included Tokuda Kyūichi (1894–1943) and Nosaka Sanzō (1892–). The subsequent adoption of violent revolutionary tactics by the JCP and terrorist acts committed by JCP members during the Korean War provided the basis for the subversive activities prevention law of 1952 which permitted the government to dissolve organizations engaged in terrorism. This law aroused fears of a reversion to the system operated under the 'peace preservation law' of 1925, but partly because of restrictions written into the law and because of the political opposition which its use arouses it has been rarely used. The JCP was a major disruptive force during the occupation, and to preserve the potentially fragile democratic atmosphere in post-war Japan effective action had to be taken against the JCP.

The San Francisco Peace Treaty and the US–Japan Security Treaty of 1951–2

Following the imposition of the Dodge Plan to reform the Japanese economy, SCAP began to grant the Japanese government the rights and privileges of an independent government. By 1949 MacArthur had concluded that, in view of the growing communist threat in Asia, Japan should be built up as a stabilizing force in the Far East and that a peace treaty should be concluded.

The outbreak of the Korean war in June 1950 underlined the need for an early peace treaty, but it also emphaiszed the importance to the Americans of having bases in Japan and greatly increased American hostility to the Chinese communists (the Chinese People's Republic had been proclaimed in Peking in October 1949). A peace treaty would, the Americans decided, have to be accompanied by a security treaty enabling their forces to stay in Japan. The Soviet Union would not accept this, and the Americans, who would not recognize the Chinese communists were not prepared to countenance any involvement by the Chinese communists in the peace treaty process. An impasse was thus created. The only way out seemed to be a separate peace treaty between America, Britain and other friendly Allies on the one hand and Japan on the other. However, the Japanese were at first reluctant to contemplate a peace treaty which was not a comprehensive one as well as a security treaty with America. Many Japanese feared that, if they committed themselves firmly in this way to the anti-communist nations, they would lose trade opportunities in communist Asia. They also had doubts about the extent of the American commitment to Asia. The US Secretary of War Kenneth Royall had made the unfortunate comment in an unofficial press conference in Tokyo in 1949 that in his view the armed forces had better pull out of Japan, as 'Japan had to be written off in the event of a war with Russia.'[5]

The Americans tried hard to overcome Japanese suspicions and to begin the build-up of a Japanese defence capability. A first step was taken in July 1950 just after the outbreak of the Korean war and the removal of US forces from Japan to defend Korea. SCAP then ordered the Japanese government to form a national police reserve of 75,000 men. This was the nucleus of what became in 1952 the national safety forces and in 1954 the self-defence forces. But these forces were insufficient to defend Japan. The Japanese people, however, to say nothing of the peoples of the Asian countries which had been overrun by the Japanese, would not accept any significant derogation from Article 9 of the constitution or any major Japanese rearmament.

In May 1951 John Foster Dulles (1888–1959), a special adviser to the US Secretary of State, was charged with the task of preparing a peace treaty and other arrangements which would protect American special interests, overcome Japanese doubts and provide for the future defence of Japan. Dulles visited Japan three times to discuss terms with the Japanese. He persuaded Yoshida Shigeru, the Japanese Prime Minister, that the terms proposed were fair and reasonable in the circumstances. The British, who had for long advocated the conclusion of a peace treaty, but who had wanted to include a number of commercial restrictions on Japan in the treaty, were also brought round and agreed to co-sponsor the draft. This was published on 12 July 1951, and the Allied powers were invited to attend a conference beginning on 4 September 1951 in San Francisco. The Soviet and other communist delegates attempted to raise procedural difficulties but were overruled by the American chairman, and the treaty was duly signed on 8 September by Japan and forty-eight Allied nations. The communist powers, as well as India and Burma, did not sign. The China problem was bypassed. Neither the Communist Chinese nor the Chinese Nationalists were invited to attend; but after a warning from Dulles that the US Senate might refuse to ratify the treaty if the Japanese had any dealings with the Communist Chinese, Yoshida Shigeru wrote a letter to Dulles on 24 December 1951 promising that the Japanese would deal only with the Nationalists.

On 28 April 1952, the day on which the San Francisco treaty came into force, the Japanese concluded a separate treaty on similar lines with the Nationalist Chinese in Taiwan. In June 1952 a separate treaty was also concluded with India, which had objected to the exclusion of Communist China from the San Francisco conference.

The terms of the peace treaty were moderate. The Japanese recognized the independence of Korea and renounced all claim to Formosa, the Kurile Islands and South Sakhalin as well as to the Pacific islands over which they had had a League of Nations mandate. Japan also agreed to the USA assuming a mandate over Okinawa, the Ryūkyū and Bonin islands. She undertook to abide by the obligations set out in the United Nations Charter and she renounced all special rights and interests in China. The Japanese government also accepted the judgements of the war crimes trials and undertook to enforce the sentences passed on Japanese nationals by these courts. The Japanese government agreed to negotiate promptly treaties on fisheries, civil aviation, trade and commerce with those powers seeking such agreements.

The Kurile Islands were not listed. The Japanese claimed that the islands of Kunashiri, Etorofu, Shikotan and Habomai at the southern end of the chain, which had been occupied by the Soviet Union at the end of the war, had always been Japanese and were not covered by this renunciation. The dispute over these northern islands has been a major issue ever since in Soviet–Japanese relations and has prevented the conclusion of a peace treaty between the two countries.

The articles on claims and property were generous to Japan. The Japanese agreed that Japanese property in neutral or other countries at war with the Allies should be transferred to the International Red Cross for the benefit of former prisoners of war and their families 'who suffered undue hardships while prisoners of war of Japan'. Unfortunately the amount available under this article was small, and the sums received by ex-POWs were considered by many to be derisory.

On reparations Article 14 declared that 'It recognized that Japan should pay reparations to the Allied powers for the damage and suffering caused by it during the war. Nevertheless it is also recognized that the resources of Japan are not presently sufficient, if it is to maintain a viable economy, to make complete reparations for all such damage and suffering and at the same time meet its other obligations.' The Japanese accordingly agreed to enter into negotiations with 'Allied Powers so desiring, whose present territories were occupied by Japanese forces and damaged by Japan, with a view to assisting to compensate for the cost of repairing the damage done'. Eventually reparations agreements were reached with the governments of the Philippines, Burma, Indonesia and South Vietnam. The payments mainly took the form of capital goods. They became in effect a form of aid to developing countries and assisted Japanese economic objectives in South-east Asia.

The peace treaty provided for the withdrawal of the occupation forces when the treaty came into force, but it left open the possibility of foreign forces remaining in Japan under any bilateral or multilateral agreement which might be concluded with one or more of the Allied powers and Japan.

The security treaty concluded with the United States at the same time as the peace treaty was a short document which permitted the retention of US forces in Japan and called on Japan to assume increasing responsibility for its own defence while avoiding any armaments which might be regarded as an offensive threat. Article 1 provided for the stationing of US forces in Japan to contribute to international peace and the security of Japan, including assistance, at the request of the Japanese government, against internal disturbances. Japan was also prohibited by the treaty from granting bases to other powers. The treaty did not include an explicit obligation on the United States to defend Japan if she were attacked, but did allow the United States to use US forces in Japan, without the prior agreement of the Japanese government. The treaty was accordingly criticized not only because of the lack of reciprocity in its provisions but also because of the implied derogation of Japanese rights.

The detailed implementation of the security treaty was to be regulated by an administrative agreement. This was concluded on 28 February 1952 and was also regarded as 'unequal'. The Japanese particularly objected to the article which provided for extraterritorial jurisdiction over members of the US forces. This article was, however, amended in September 1953, in conformity with the arrangement made for US forces in European countries under the North Atlantic

263

Treaty, and members of the US forces became subject to Japanese jurisdiction in criminal cases.

The Japanese were the first to ratify the peace treaty and the US–Japan security treaty. Their instrument of ratification was deposited on 28 November 1951. The Japanese socialists were split. Neither the left nor the right wing favoured the accompanying security treaty; the left wing were also opposed to the peace treaty not least because it had not been signed by the communist powers. But there was never any real doubt that the Japanese would accept what was after all a generous settlement. The British ratification of the peace treaty followed on 3 January 1952, and the Americans finally ratified on 28 April 1952, thus bringing the treaty into force.

On that day, therefore, Japan became once more an independant nation able to regulate its own internal and external policies, although it remained subject to US influence as a result of the security treaty. Japanese officials and politicians began to flex their muscles, and there was a recrudescence of anti-American and some anti-foreign feeling. The communists also thought they saw a chance, and on May Day 1952 demonstrations around the Imperial Palace in Tokyo led to outbreaks of violence. But the communists had no real following in the country.

The first priority for Japan in 1952 was economic recovery. This required infinite patience, ruthless determination, careful planning, hard work and a willingness to sacrifice individual well-being to the common good. The Japanese people who had suffered so much during the war showed themselves ready to display all these qualities. Progress in the next few years was uneven but significant. The Japanese had started along the fast track towards the goal which they then set themselves of catching up with the West. Consciously or unconsciously they had come to accept that they would become members of the 'western' world of advanced capitalist economies and, spurred by their defeat, they determined to reach the front rank.

Politics, foreign affairs, society, economics, and culture were inevitably inter-twined in the Japan of the second half of the twentieth century. It is artificial to consider them as wholly separate elements in the history of modern Japan, but a purely chronological treatment would be confusing.

The Bureaucracy

The civil bureaucracy had played a major role in the modernization of Japan in the nineteenth century and had remained a significant force, even when the power had shifted to the military in the first half of the twentieth century. The purging of so many politicians during the occupation gave the bureaucrats an advantage in post-war Japan, and many senior officials went into politics, where by their ability and experience they were able to achieve positions of real power. But those who remained in the civil service were not thereby deprived of influence. The prestige of the senior civil service has always been high.

The power of Japan's élite civil servants is based on a number of factors. First are their undoubted intellectual abilities, boosted by their education largely at the prestigious Tokyo University (known as Tōdai) and by the fierce competition to get into the policy-making grades in the civil service. Second is the determination with which they pursue their particular aims. Third are their contacts with politicians and senior businessmen who may well have been at the same university or high school as they have been and among whom they will eventually work. On reaching retirement in their early fifties they 'descend from heaven' (*amaku-dari*) and generally enter politics or the private sector.

Finally their power has been increased by the way in which ministers have come to be appointed in Japan's post-war governments; most ministers are appointed on the Buggins's turn principle, that is, on the basis of seniority in the government party (they need to have been elected six times to the Diet before they are generally regarded as eligible for a ministerial appointment) and the influence of their faction. The majority only stay in their post for about one year, from one cabinet reshuffle to the next. In each ministry there is only one full minister, who is kept exceedingly busy travelling and dealing with Diet matters as well as with the problems of his own constituency. It requires a minister of outstanding experience, drive and determination to ignore or overrule the advice given him by his able civil servants. Parliamentary vice-ministers have never been given any significant power. Japanese bureaucrats normally have little difficulty in manipulating most ministers so long as they work carefully with the relevant party committees. This inevitably leads some to become arrogant. Their single-mindedness sometimes also makes them seem blinkered and unable or unwilling to work for Japan's wider interests. At least until the end of the 1980s, when the Recruit/Cosmos scandal was uncovered and a number of senior bureaucrats were accused of accepting bribes, they have not been thought to be corrupt. The continuity of conservative governments should perhaps have led to their power being reduced, but in practice it consolidated the triumvirate of politicians, bureaucrats and senior businessmen who came to form the Japanese establishment and to monopolize power in the post-war years.

Politicians and the Japanese Party System

The Japanese party system remained relatively fluid until 1955. But some of the basic features of Japanese party politics have remained unaltered since parties were first formed in Japan. Personalities count for more than policies and ideology. 'Conservative' parties in particular have remained essentially groups of factions owing loyalty to a leading figure capable of collecting money and influencing the allocation of jobs and appropriations to suit the constituencies represented by the members of his faction. Despite stringent rules about election expenses, politics in a multi-member constituency, where a member may be dependent on gaining the votes of many tens of thousands of electors particularly in the under-represented urban constituencies, inevitably costs a lot of money. The member has to spend much of his time cultivating his supporters (his *jiban*) through supporters' associations (*kōenkai*) in each section of his constituency. This has meant attending weddings, funerals and parties of various kinds to all of which he will be expected to make a donation and a speech. The successful politician has to be accessible, have good intuition and be willing to be flexible. These are qualities much more highly prized in a Japanese politician than commitment to a fixed set of policies or an ideology. Indeed, few voters bother about the ideology of a politician so long as he is thought capable of getting generous allocations for his constituency from the national budget.

The Liberal Democratic Party (LDP)

The Liberal Democratic Party (LDP), which was formed in 1955 and has held power in Japan ever since, was the successor to the Liberal Party led from 1946 by Yoshida Shigeru. It was and still is a coalition of factions, whose strengths vary from year to year as the prestige of the factional leaders waxes and wanes. Such ideology as it has is conservative. In economic issues it supports the market economy so long as this does not go against the interests of its main supporters, but it has also promoted welfare programmes. It is in effect a coalition of generally conservatively inclined factions, whose members range from right-wing nationalists to middle-of-the-road liberal-minded people. Its supporters have been firstly the small farmers, who are dominant in the rural constituencies which are over-represented in the Diet. Secondly the party has been able to rely on the support of the large number of small businesses which are dominant in the retail sector and which provide the bulk of the subcontractors who remain the mainstay of manufacturing industry of Japan. Thirdly the party has been able to count on the backing of industry and commerce generally through such organizations as the Federation of Economic Organizations (Keidanren) (the equivalent of the Confederation of British Industry, the CBI, but with considerably more influence and prestige), the Federation of Employers' Associations (Nikkeiren), the Japan Committee for Economic Development (Keizaidōyukai) and the Japan Chambers of Commerce and Industry (Shōkōkaigisho).

After he had been depurged and the peace treaty had come into force, Hatoyama Ichirō (1883–1959) thought that Yoshida would cede the leadership of the Liberal Party to him. But Yoshida had no intention of giving up the power which he enjoyed exercising and only resigned when he was forced to do so by the defection of Hatoyama at the end of 1954 and after the formation by him of the so-called Japan Democratic Party (Nihon Minshūtō). Hatoyama won the support of the Reform Party (Kaishintō), which had replaced the Progressive Party (Shimpōtō). Following the general election of February 1955 the various conservative parties merged and became the Liberal Democratic Party (Jiyū-Minshūtō) under the leadership of Hatoyama.

Japanese Governments Since 1955

Hatoyama, the first LDP Prime Minister, wanted to revise the constitution, and despite strong opposition from the Japan Socialist Party (JSP) a law was passed in 1956 setting up a commission on the constitution. It deliberated until 1964; it was abolished in 1965 without any changes being formally proposed to the Diet. Hatoyama managed in 1956 to re-establish diplomatic relations with the Soviet Union, but the Soviet Union refused to make any concession over the four northern islands. As a result no peace treaty was concluded with the Soviet Union. However, following Hatoyama's agreement with the Soviet Union, the Russians withdrew their veto on Japanese membership of the United Nations (UN), and in December 1956 Japan became a member of the UN.

Hatoyama was briefly succeeded as Prime Minister in 1956 by Ishibashi Tanzan (1884–1973), but he had to resign owing to ill health after only two months in office. The next LDP leader and Prime Minister from 1957 was Kishi Nobusuke (1896–1987). He sought to improve US–Japan relations and achieve greater independence for Japan by putting the US–Japan security treaty on a more equal basis. A revised co-operation and security treaty between Japan and the United States was signed on 19 January 1960, and a new administrative agreement was also concluded. The new treaty reaffirmed the parties' adherence to the principles of the UN Charter and their determination 'to uphold the principles of democracy, individual liberty, and the rule of law'. No reference was made to intervention in the case of domestic violence in Japan. The United States undertook to 'act to meet the common danger' in the event of an attack on Japan. The treaty also committed the parties to consult from time to time whenever the security of Japan or the Far East was threatened. The Americans agreed to consult if Okinawa and the Ryūkyū Islands were threatened, but the Americans refused to end their continued occupation of these islands despite the strongly expressed request of the Japanese. A high-level consultative committee was established, and it was agreed that the treaty could be terminated after ten years, at one year's notice on either side.

The new treaty was undoubtedly more equal than the previous one and enhanced Japanese independence. But it aroused a furore of opposition in Japan. The left, who were joined by many moderates, argued that the treaty was likely to arouse the hostility of the communist powers and might lead to Japanese involvement in a nuclear war. Prior consultation, in their view, increased rather than decreased the risk to Japan, as Japan would thereby be identified as a voluntary supporter of the United States. The fear was also expressed that under American pressure Japan would rearm in contravention of Article 9 of the constitution. Kishi was determined to get the treaty ratified in time for the planned visit to Japan in June 1960 of President Eisenhower from the United States and attempted to use his majority in the Diet to achieve this. The Socialists for their part resorted to strong-arm tactics to prevent Diet approval being given, and the speaker eventually called in the police to restore order in the Diet building. On 29 May 1960 Kishi took advantage of his majority to 'ram' the agreement through the Diet. Kishi's behaviour was criticized as 'undemocratic'. (It is a peculiarity of the general Japanese view of democracy that the majority must not use its superior numbers to force measures through and should seek a consensus or, if one is not attainable, should make concessions to the minority.) Mass demonstrations against the treaty and the Prime Minister were held in Tokyo. The radical student group Zengakuren, in particular, organized noisy protests, and one person was trampled to death. The planned visit by President Eisenhower was called off, and an unsuccessful attempt was made to assassinate Kishi. After the instruments of ratification had been exchanged in Washington, Kishi felt obliged to resign, thus accepting responsibility for the disturbances and the cancellation of the President's visit.

Kishi was replaced in July 1960 by Ikeda Hayato (1899–1965), who had had long experience of economic affairs as Finance Minister and Minister of International Trade and Industry. He took a generally 'low posture', a favourite Japanese phrase meaning the avoidance of any measures likely to provoke the opposition. He concentrated on economic affairs and launched a 'double the income' policy which by a combination of increased public expenditure, lower taxes and low interest rates set Japan on the path to economic expansion. A highlight of his period of office was the holding of the Olympic Games in Tokyo in 1964. In the same year Japan became a member of the Organization for Economic Co-operation and Development (OECD). In November 1964 Ikeda was forced to resign because of ill health (he had terminal cancer).

Ikeda had been unsuccessfully challenged for the party leadership in 1964 by Satō Eisaku (1901–75), but when he resigned he nominated Satō as his successor. Satō, another ex-bureaucrat, had had a murky past, having been arrested in 1954 for accepting bribes, but in 1956 following a general amnesty he returned to politics and proved an astute politician in the Japanese mould of wheeling and dealing with the factions. He had a record run as Prime Minister, lasting until July 1972. He continued Ikeda's economic growth policies, and when he resigned Japan had succeeded in becoming the third largest economic power in the world. During his term in office relations with South Korea were normalized (1965). In 1970 he allowed the US–Japan security treaty to be automatically renewed and he worked hard to improve relations with the United States. In 1972 the USA finally agreed to the reversion of Okinawa and the Ryūkyū Islands to Japanese rule, while retaining bases on Okinawa. But US–Japan relations came under strain as a result of a serious dispute over Japanese exports of textiles to the USA and because of the shock caused by the sudden announcement in 1971 of President Nixon's visit to Communist China. The Japanese had hitherto loyally supported Taiwan in accordance with what they thought were American wishes. Satō agreed to Japan signing the nuclear non-proliferation agreement in 1970 but did not press for ratification. He did, however, pronounce three non-nuclear principles for Japan, which were eventually adopted by the Diet in a unanimous resolution in 1972. These were that Japan would not manufacture nuclear wepons, would not possess such weapons and would not allow their introduction into Japanese territory. These principles were cited as one of the main reasons for the award to him in 1974 of the Nobel Peace Prize.

Satō's successor, Tanaka Kakuei (born 1918), was a very different character, although equally astute as a politician. Unlike Ikeda and Satō he was not a former bureaucrat. He had had no higher education and had built up his own construction company. His company made a lot of money, and with his newly aquired wealth he won in 1947 a seat in the house of representatives and quickly built up a faction which became very powerful in the LDP. With its backing he was elected president of the party in 1972 and thus became Prime Minister. In foreign affairs his main achievement was the establishment of diplomatic relations with the People's Republic of China, following a visit which he made to Peking (Beijing) in September 1972. But he is best known for his concept of the 'remodelling' of the Japanese islands. By this he meant decentralization of industry from the overpopulated Tokyo and Osaka regions to areas such as Niigata on the Japan Sea coast where his own constituency was situated. The plan involved massive

268

public investment in roads, railways and other infrastructure projects As a result of his plans the Japanese network of motorways and new railways began to expand, but the recession of 1973 following the first oil crisis put a brake on these schemes.

Tanaka was forced to resign in December 1974 following allegations about financial dealings. He was arrested in 1976 after it was revealed that the Lockheed Aircraft Company of the United States had paid large sums to induce All Nippon Airways (ANA) to buy Tristar wide-bodied aircraft. Tanaka was in due course found guilty of accepting a bribe and was sentenced to imprisonment, but he appealed, and by the autumn of 1989 the Supreme Court had not yet passed judgement. Although he had to resign from the LDP, he suffered from a serious stroke and his faction split, he still retained influence into the late 1980s.

The LDP had difficulty in choosing a successor. The two main candidates, Fukuda Takeo (born 1905) and Ohira Masayoshi (1910–80), could not agree on who should have the job, and eventually Miki Takeo (1907–88), the leader of one of the smaller factions, was chosen as a compromise candidate. As a kind of 'Mr Clean' he set himself the task of trying to reform Japanese party politics. His government accomplished little, and he was forced to resign in 1976 following a setback for the LDP in the election that year. He was succeeded by Fukuda Takeo, a former bureaucrat from the Ministry of Finance. During Fukuda's term of office the factions were officially disbanded, but they were soon re-established and were as influential as before. Fukuda's government managed to conclude a peace treaty and a long-term trade agreement with the People's Republic of China, but he was ousted in 1978 by Ohira, another former Ministry of Finance official who won the position of president of the party in the first primary elections held under revised party rules governing the choice of party president. Ohira called for tax reforms designed to reduce the mounting budget deficit and proposed new indirect taxes. These were fiercely opposed by many members of the LDP, and in 1980 he lost an unprecendented vote of 'no confidence' in the house of representatives. He then called for new elections, but he died before they could be held.

The LDP gained a number of sympathy votes as a result of Ohira's untimely death and won an election victory. Suzuki Zenkō (born 1911), known as an emollient moderator, became Prime Minister. He had first been elected to the house of representatives as a socialist, but had soon moved over to the conservatives, where he thought he could be more effective. He resigned suddenly in 1982 and was replaced by Nakasone Yasuhiro (born 1918). Nakasone, nicknamed 'the weather-vane', was much more outward-going and PR conscious. He had in his early days as a politician urged that Prime Ministers should be directly elected by the voters. But he was better known as an advocate of revision of the constitution as well as of increased arms expenditure. He was generally regarded as a right-wing nationalist. However, once in power he determined to play a part on the international stage and advocated the 'internationalization' of Japan. It was never quite clear what he meant by this, but during his five years in the office of Prime Minister he became wellknown as the Japanese representative at the annual summits of the advanced countries and was highly regarded in western countries for the positive and generally helpful line which he took at international meetings. He managed marginally to break the barrier, which Japanese governments had created for themselves, limiting defence expenditure to one per cent of GNP. But his government did not succeed in making many significant changes in internal policies, and like Ohira he failed to achieve a tax reform involving a new indirect tax. Nevertheless, partly because agreement could not be reached on a successor, he managed to win two terms of two years as president of the party and was allowed an unprecedented extension of one further year, giving him five years in all as Prime Minister.

In November 1987 Nakasone nominated Takeshita Noboru (born 1924) as his successor. Takeshita was the leader of a major faction which had broken away from the old Tanaka faction. No one really knew what he stood for, but he had the reputation of being an effective manipulator of factional interests. He was also regarded as an astute politician who by the studious use of vague phrases avoided making commitments which might have awkward implications. His slogan was 'Furusato', literally 'the home village', but implying regional development. Takeshita succeeded in ramming tax reform measures through the Diet before the end of 1988. These provided for cuts in direct taxes as well as the introduction from 1 April 1989 of a 3 per cent consumption tax. The tax was unpopular, and the fear was that it would be increased at some later date.

In the first few months of 1989 Takeshita's government had lost credibility owing to a share scandal involving the Recruit-Cosmos employment company and senior politicians and bureaucrats. Politics seemed to be dominated by money. Nakasone who was deeply involved was forced to resign from the party and his faction and Takeshita in his turn had to take responsibility for the scandals which had caused a serious loss in popular support for the LDP. On 2 June 1989 Uno Sōsuke (born 1923) was nominated by Takeshita and appointed Prime Minister. He had been Foreign Minister in Takeshita's government and was a member of Nakasone's faction. He was regarded as 'clean', but he had no real power base in the party and his political obligations to Takeshita and Nakasone made him seem a puppet. Allegations about sexual relations between him and a woman who had once been a geisha combined with anti-feminist remarks by one of his ministers aroused the fury of women voters. Continuing popular dissatisfaction with the consumption tax and disillusionment with the LDP for failing to tackle political reform reduced popular support for the LDP to an unprecedentedly low level in July 1989 when elections for half the seats in the upper house had to be held. The LDP lost their majority in the upper house. Uno had to accept responsibility for this defeat and resigned. On 8 August 1989 Kaifu Toshiki, aged fifty-eight, a former minister of education and member of one of the smaller factions, was chosen as president of the LDP and subsequently elected prime minister by the house of representatives. He faced formidable problems. Political reform was the top priority if he was to win back the confidence of the electorate, but he also needed to woo the female vote and at least amend the consumption tax to make it more acceptable. The fear was that like Uno he would be controlled by the party bosses and made the scapegoat for the LDP's likely losses in the next general election for the house of representatives. In 1989 the LDP hold on power was threatened.

Above, Wood block print of two actors as samurai by Tōshūsai Sharaku (late 18th century).
Below, Wood block print of girls walking by the shore by Suzuki Harunobu (1725–1770).

Right, Wood block print of the actor Sawamura Gennosuke II at Yayoinosuke by Shunshi (circa 1828). Fuji Art Museum.

Left, Wood block print of the actor Sawamura Kunitarō as the geisha Kikuno by Jukōdō Toshikuni (mid-19th century). Fuji Art Museum.

Left, Photograph of a kabuki performance. *Onnagata* dancing. Japan National Tourist Organization.

Right, Photograph of a *gagaku* dance at the Itsukushima shrine (Miyajima). Japan National Tourist Organization.

Above and below, Wood block prints of Mount Fuji (two of thirty-six views) by Katsushika Hokusai (1760–1849).

Opposite page, top, Photograph of a Bunraku performance. Japan National Tourist Organization.
Centre, Photograph of a Nō performance. Japan National Tourist Organization.
Bottom, Photograph of courtiers playing a game of *kemari* (court football) to entertain Her Royal Highness Princess Alexandra of Kent on the first British Royal Visit to Japan after the Second World War (November 1961).

Above, Wood block print of Hara in the series fifty-three views of the Tōkaidō *(Tōkaidō gojūsan tsugi).*

Below, Wood block print of Inagawa ridge, Nojiri on the Kisokaidō (Nakasendō) by Eisen (about 1836).

Left, Painting of a crow on a winter tree by Hishida Shunsō (1874–1911). Kyoto National Museum.
Below, Painting of mountains and mist by Higashiyama Kaii. Wall painting in the Tōshō Daiji.

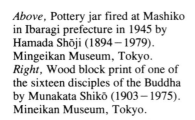

Above, Pottery jar fired at Mashiko
in Ibaragi prefecture in 1945 by
Hamada Shōji (1894–1979).
Mingeikan Museum, Tokyo.
Right, Wood block print of one of
the sixteen disciples of the Buddha
by Munakata Shikō (1903–1975).
Mineikan Museum, Tokyo.

The Opposition Parties

A peculiarity of post-war Japanese-style parliamentary democracy was the monopoly of power by the 'conservatives'. Since the socialist Katayama Tetsu headed a coalition government in 1947–8, the Socialists (still less any of the other opposition parties) had not succeeded in forming a government, but the opposition parties have together been able to muster enough votes to block any revision of the constitution. The opposition parties have remained divided on issues of policy and ideology and have been riven by factionalism. They had thus not been able to present a credible alternative to the LDP.

The main opposition party has remained the Japan Socialist Party (JSP) (Nihon-Shakaitō), but it has suffered from various splits and ideological and personality struggles. In 1951 the party was united in its opposition to the US–Japan security treaty but could not agree on whether to accept or reject the peace treaty. The moderates were prepared to, but the left were against doing so. The split between the two wings lasted until 1955 when they were reunited. Unity was, however, never more than superficial and did not last long. In 1960 the moderates defected and formed the Democratic Socialist Party (DSP, known since 1970 as Minshatō). The JSP took the lead in 1960 in opposing the revised security treaty; this aroused the ire of right-wing groups, and the party chairman Asanuma Inejiro (1898–1960) was assassinated in October 1960 during an election speech by a right-wing fanatic. In the early 1960s Eda Saburō (1907–77), who realized that the revolutionary Marxist ideology of the party was not acceptable to the Japanese electorate, propounded a theory of 'structural reform'; this called for worker participation in the existing capitalist system as a step towards socialist revolution. The left wing, however, denounced these ideas, and eventually in 1977 Eda seceded from the party. Party congresses have continued to be dominated by Marxist rhetoric, ideological strife and factional disputes. The main backing for the party came from Sōhyō, a left-wing group of largely public-sector unions. But privatization and a move towards greater unity in the labour union movement have reduced the effectiveness of union support. The JSP had its best election result in 1958, when it gained 166 seats and 32 per cent of the popular vote. In subsequent elections the party's fortunes varied; in 1986 the party only gained 85 seats and 17.2 per cent of the popular vote. However, in the upper house election in July 1989, the party's fortunes changed once again. Under the charismatic leadership of Miss Doi Takako the JSP managed to win more votes and seats than the LDP. But Miss Doi's pronouncements on the policies, which the JSP would adopt if they won power, were vague and the party's success in the upper house election was not necessarily an accurate forecast of how they would do in the next election for the house of representatives. Their cooperation with the other opposition parties remained fragile.

The DSP, since its formation in 1960 up to the 1986 election, never managed to gain more than 8.8 per cent of the popular vote; this it achieved in 1960. In the 1986 election it won 6.4 per cent of the popular vote and 26 seats. The party rejects Marxist revolutionary dogmas and has espoused policies similar to those of the Social Democrats in West Germany. It advocates establishment of a Japanese welfare state. Its main support came from Dōmei, a federation of mainly private-sector labour unions. But it has also been able to win the backing of some small businesses, disillusioned by the role of big business in the LDP.

The second largest opposition party in the 1970s and 1980s was Kōmeitō, the political wing of Sōka Gakkai, an offshoot of Nichiren-Shōshū Buddhism. It became independent in 1970, having won 47 seats and 10.9 per cent of the popular vote in the election in December 1969. In the 1979 elections it gained 57 seats, but suffered a setback in 1980 when it only won 33 seats. It recovered in 1983, winning 58 seats, and in the 1986 elections it largely maintained its position with 56 seats. Kōmeitō espouses 'humanitarian socialism', but supports the maintenance of the free enterprise system, while calling for business to be more socially responsible and for more equality of wealth. In foreign policy the party calls for strict neutrality by Japan. In general the party has been pragmatic and flexible in its approach. But, despite or perhaps because of the support of the powerful Sōka Gakkai organization, the party has been unable to win the general backing of the electorate.

The Japan Communist Party (JCP) (Nihon-Kyōsantō) was established as a legal party in October 1945. Despite the ban by SCAP on the proposed general strike in 1947, the JCP grew in strength during the occupation and in January 1949 won nearly 3 million votes and 35 seats in the house of representatives. The Cominform, the Soviet-dominated association of communist parties, criticized the JCP in 1950 for their supine attitude to the occupation. The JCP accepted the criticism and began openly to advocate violence. SCAP responded by the so-called 'red purge', banning communists from politics. JCP-inspired acts of terrorism during the Korean war led to a fall in popular support, and the JCP was listed in 1952 as a subversive group under the subversive activities law. In the 1952 election the party lost all its seats in the house of representatives, although it still won nearly 900,000 votes. In the 1950s the party gradually adopted more moderate policies, and a new programme, approved in 1961, spoke of the possibility of a peaceful transition to socialism. In 1976 the party began to advocate parliamentary democracy and denied the need for 'dictatorship' as practised in the Soviet Union. In the early 1980s it even modified its opposition to the existence of the self-defence forces and became more independent and nationalist in its outlook. It grew closer to the communist parties of Italy and France; it remained on bad terms with the Chinese Communist Party. In the 1980, 1983 and 1986 elections it gained between 5 and 6 million votes. In the 1986 election this gave the party 26 seats.

Extremist organizations on the far left and right, which have existed outside the Diet, have been a nuisance rather than a real threat to parliamentary democracy in Japan. But acts of terrorism by, for instance, the Red Army Faction (Seki-gunha), a radical student group formed in 1969, have given the authorities inside and outside Japan serious grounds for concern. In March 1971 an airliner of Japan Air Lines (JAL) was hijacked by members of the Red Army. In May 1972 a machine-gun and grenade attack at Tel Aviv airport caused the death of twenty-four people. Other acts of terrorism caused by the Red Army in the 1970s included another hijack of a JAL aircraft in 1973, the hijacking of a ferry in Singapore in 1974, the seizure of the French Embassy in The Hague in 1974, the seizure of the US Consulate in Kuala Lumpur in 1975 and another JAL hijacking in 1977. In 1972 two Japanese policemen were killed in a siege of a mountain lodge held by Red Army supporters. Subsequent interrogation of those arrested revealed that Red Army members had tortured and killed fourteen of their fellow-members on grounds of ideological deviation.

Student groups, which formed Zengakuren in 1948 under JCP auspices, and from which the Red Army Faction split, caused much trouble for the authorities especially in 1960 and subsequent years. After the security treaty struggles in that year Zengakuren split into various factions which organized anti-establishment movements in the universities. These began with a dispute at the private university of Waseda; this resulted in a student strike lasting five months. In January 1969 riot police intervened at Tokyo University where students had blockaded many of the university buildings. Students also initiated a series of armed confrontations with the police off the campuses. Many of these were anti-American in origin. The radical students also took the lead in opposing the construction of the new Tokyo international airport at Narita in Chiba prefecture. But by 1970 the student struggles had run out of momentum, and the 1980s were comparatively peaceful.

Ultra-nationalism and right-wing extremism have continued to have some support within the Japanese political system. Some members of the LDP have, for instance, made public remarks with racialist overtones and have attempted to exonerate Japanese behaviour in China, Korea and other occupied territories during and before the last war. Some members have also advocated official recognition of the Yasukuni shrine to the war dead in Tokyo despite the fact that the 'souls' of convicted war criminals are enshrined there. Such ultra-nationalists would like to see a revision of the Japanese constitution to give the Emperor a more central role, as well as a revival of nationalist-inspired holidays such as National Foundation Day (11 February, marking the mythological foundation of Japan by the first Emperor Jinmu). Fortunately they have not won a great deal of popular support for these ideas, and ministers who have made racialist remarks have had either to apologize or to resign.

Outside the Diet rightist parties such as the Japan Patriotic Party (Aikokutō), have been a noisy nuisance in the Tokyo streets with loudspeakers demanding the return of the northern islands held by the Soviet Union, criticizing the Chinese communists, supporting revision of the constitution and demanding Japanese rearmament. Some acts of terrorism have been perpetrated by rightists, including the murder of Asanuma (see page 271) and in 1987 of journalists on the *Asahi* newspaper which has been regarded by some as left inclined. Threats from rightist organizations are also thought to have caused Japanese business organizations to cancel company parties during the Shōwa Emperor's illness in the autumn of 1988. The sensational ritual suicide in November 1970 of the famous writer Mishima Yukio (1925–70) (see page 292) in support of Japanese rearmament has not been copied, and the Japanese self-defence forces have been careful to appear apolitical. But, in view of earlier Japanese history, right-wing extremism, as well as left-wing violence, in Japan needs to be carefully watched.

Defence

Article 9 of the constitution has not prevented Japan from building up forces for the defence of Japan, but it has inhibited the use of these forces overseas, even in support of United Nations operations, and has helped to ensure that Japanese rearmament has been curbed and civilian control of the defence forces maintained.

The national police reserve of 75,000 men, established in 1950 under orders from SCAP, became in 1952 the national safety forces. These in turn became in 1954 the self-defence forces. Under the self-defence forces law a Defence Agency (Bōeichō) was established, and the ground, sea and air self-defence forces (rikujō-, kaijō- and kōkū-jieitai) were formed. Supreme command of the forces rests with the Japanese Prime Minister, and the minister in charge of the Defence Agency acts under the Prime Minister's orders. The minister is assisted by civilian officials and the joint staff council of chiefs of staff of the three services. Under Article 3 of the law establishing the forces, their chief function is defined as being the preservation of the peace and independence of Japan and defending the country against direct and indirect aggression. 'When the need arises' the forces can also 'be employed to preserve public order'.

In the 1980s the self-defence forces were authorized to employ just under 300,000 men, but actual strengths rarely reached 90 per cent of this total; well over half were in the ground self-defence force. Members of the forces were all recruited as volunteers on initial two- to three-year terms of service. The defence budget was limited until the late 1980s to less than one per cent of GNP and in 1988 only marginally exceeded this sum. As some expenses such as retirement pensions are not counted under the defence budget, gross defence expenditure was somewhat higher. Owing to the size of Japan's GNP the budget ensured that net expenditure on defence by Japan was comparable to that of many NATO countries.

The Japanese were at first reluctant to admit that their most likely enemy was the Soviet Union and that the main threat to Japan came from Soviet forces in Soviet territories to the north of Hokkaidō, where by the 1980s the Sea of Okhotsk had become practically a Soviet-controlled lake. As a result a major part of Japan's ground self-defence force has been stationed in Hokkaidō. In the defence expansion plans in the 1980s the emphasis was placed on building up the Japanese capability to withstand a surprise attack. Particular attention has also been given to developing Japan's fighter strength against air atttack and maritime forces to defend Japan's sea lanes.

American pressure in the 1980s for an increase in defence expenditure evoked a cautious response from the Japanese authorities, who were conscious of likely repercussions to any significant Japanese rearmament from the peoples and governments of countries occupied by Japan before 1945. But by the late 1980s the self-defence forces had become generally accepted by the Japanese people; and with increasing doubts about American willingness and ability to defend Japan and maintain a nuclear umbrella, there was a growing recognition that defence expenditure would have to rise.

Japan's defence industry grew in the 1980s, but the continuation of a ban on exports of military equipment has prevented the industry from becoming a significant world force.

Foreign Affairs

In the 1980s Japan was frequently described as an economic giant but a political dwarf. This was an exaggeration. However, Japanese governments, following the traumatic experiences of defeat, have generally since the war been reluctant to take political initiatives on foreign policy issues. They have feared that such initiatives might force them to accept responsibilities which the Japanese people would be unwilling to accept or which might be regarded as provocative by the governments and peoples of other Asian countries which have suffered from Japanese aggression. They realized that their limited self-defence forces did not provide them with any real muscle in international disputes and they were unwilling to re-arm to the extent needed to give them effective forces other than to provide a response to a surprise attack.

In world political issues such as the Arab–Israeli conflict or the Soviet invasion of Afghanistan the Japanese have preferred to assume a low profile. The Iran–Iraq war in the 1980s posed a serious threat to Japanese energy supplies, but the Japanese government could not, under Japanese law, send maritime self-defence force ships to the Persian Gulf on convoy duty and had to limit their intervention to a half-hearted effort at a diplomatic mediation.

Since Japan was admitted to the United Nations (UN) on 18 December 1956, Japanese governments have constantly underlined the importance they attach to the UN. The three principles of Japanese foreign policy have been declared as being 'the centrality' of the UN, co-operation with the economically advanced western nations and Japan's identity as an Asian country. Japan has accordingly tried within the UN to act as a bridge between the advanced western countries and Asian countries. It has also been an active member of UN bodies, including the Security Council, to which it has been elected six times as a non-permanent member. Some Japanese think that Japan's economic power gives it a greater claim to a permanent seat on the council than either Britain or France, but the Japanese government recognize that there is no chance in present circumstances of getting agreement to the necessary revision to the UN Charter.

Despite the human rights provisions in the Japanese constitution, Japanese support for human rights in South Africa has seemed to many foreign observers more a matter of lip-service than of enthusiasm, perhaps because Japanese trade with South Africa has been significant.

Because of the importance to Japan of trade and financial issues Japan has attached great significance to her membership of such organizations as the International Monetary Fund (IMF), which she joined in 1952, the General Agreement on Tariffs and Trade (GATT), which she joined in 1955, and the Organization for Economic Co-operation and Development (OECD), which admitted Japan to membership in 1964. Having begun her membership as a major borrower, by the early 1980s Japan had become one of the five largest investors in the IMF. When Japan joined the GATT, fourteen other members invoked Article XXXV of the agreement against Japan; this article allows member countries to withhold most-favoured-nation (MFN) treatment from new members at the time of their accession. Governments invoking this article, such as Britain, feared that Japan would take advantage of MFN treatment to swamp their markets with goods produced by Japanese 'cheap labour'. Most GATT members, including Britain, agreed to grant Japan MFN treatment when they concluded with Japan new treaties of commerce and navigation in the 1960s. The Japanese government, for its part, maintained high tariffs and quota restrictions against imports until it was forced by international pressures in the 1960s, 1970s and 1980s to liberalize its markets. The Japanese government came to recognize that freeing trade was very much a Japanese interest, but producer lobbies, especially for agricultural products, have delayed the process of liberalization and increased economic friction with foreign countries.

The key bilateral relationship for Japan since the war has been that with the United States. This is not only because of Japan's dependence for its ultimate defence on the American nuclear umbrella and US forces based in Japan and the Far East. The USA has also been the most important single market for Japanese exports as well as a significant source of supply of energy, food, raw materials and manufacturing technology. In the 1980s the USA became a major debtor to Japan as the US budget deficit grew. Japanese industry increasingly developed its own plants in the USA in response to signs of a rise in US protectionism. At the same time Japanese banks bought US banks, especially in California, and Japanese insurance companies purchased large hunks of US real estate. The occupation, followed by controversies over the revised US–Japan security treaty, over US bases in Japan, over nuclear weapons on US warships and over the reversion of Okinawa, had left some underlying resentments in Japan. When these were combined with increasing Japanese self-confidence as a result of their economic success, they led some Japanese politicians and businessmen in the 1980s to become condescending and somewhat arrogant towards the USA. Responsible people in both countries, however, recognized the importance of the relationship and tried to keep the temperature down.

Japan's relations with the Soviet Union have remained cool since relations were resumed in 1955. The Japanese have reason to fear the large Soviet forces in the territories to the north of the Japanese islands. Resentment over the continued Soviet occupation of the northern islands (see page 263) has been exacerbated by the difficulties which Japanese fishermen have had in northern waters, in which they have traditionally made large catches. The large Soviet Embassy in Tokyo and Soviet contacts with the JCP also made the Japanese fear Soviet interference in internal Japanese affairs. But some Japanese businessmen would welcome economic concessions in Siberia. If the Soviet government were willing to agree to some move over the northern islands, this would bring a thaw in relations.

Relations with the People's Republic of China (PRC) were bedevilled by the existence of Japanese ties with the Chinese Nationalists in Taiwan until the 'Nixon shock' in 1971, when, without any warning to the Japanese government, US President Nixon announced that he would be visiting Peking (Beijing). Diplomatic relations were established by Japan with the PRC in September 1972, and negotiations on a treaty of peace and friendship were started. But the negotiations were not completed until 1978. One of the main points of controversy was over the anti-hegemony clauses which the Chinese demanded and which the Japanese feared would be regarded by the Soviet Union as provocative and might restrict their ability to maintain an independent foreign policy. Eventually agreement was reached on an article which provided that neither party would seek hegemony in the Asia Pacific region or any other region. Since then Japan–China trade has expanded, and the Japanese have tried to develop their investments in China, but the imbalance in trade in Japan's favour began to cause problems in the late 1980s. Japanese tend to see themselves as having a special relationship with China, if only for reasons of race and Japan's cultural borrowings from China, but this view is not generally shared in the PRC.

Post-war relations with the Republic of Korea (ROK or South Korea) were fraught with difficulties from the opening of preliminary negotiations in 1951 before the peace treaty with Japan came into force. Fishery and property claims caused problems, and in 1955 the ROK even prohibited trade with Japan for a time. Another problem was that of the status of Koreans resident in Japan (many of these people had been brought to Japan during and before the war to work in Japanese mines and factories) and the repatriation by the Japanese of some Koreans to North Korea. Korean resentment against Japan and the Japanese was deep, and Japanese negotiators were not always as tactful as they should have been. As a result it was not until 1965 that negotiations were successfully concluded. Thereafter trade between the two countries expanded quickly, and Japan began to exercise an increasingly important influence on the Korean economy. But problems continued to affect official relations. The abduction by Korean intelligence agents of the Korean opposition leader Kim Tae-Jung in August 1973 from a Tokyo hotel understandably enfuriated the Japanese authorities. However, in the late 1980s following the establishment of a more democratic regime in the ROK relations have improved.

Japanese relations with other countries in Asia in the post-war period have not always been easy. Resentment against Japan, because of the behaviour of Japanese forces during the war, was slow to disappear. Japanese investment and aid were welcomed but revived fears of a new type of Japanese economic imperialism. In the late 1980s the Japanese realized that the newly industrialized countries (NICs) in South-east Asia, as well as Korea and Taiwan, were becoming major competitors in the North American and West European markets, although many of the exports from these countries came from Japanese-owned factories. Japanese governments quickly recognized the importance of the Association of South East Asian Nations (ASEAN–Indonesia, Malaysia, the Philippines, Singapore and Thailand) and have tried to establish a special relationship with ASEAN.

The Japanese government's attitude to Europe in the post-war years has been ambivalent. The Japanese have recognized the importance of European markets and the position of Britain, France, West Germany and Italy as members of the conclave of heads of governments of advanced countries (the summit countries), as well as Japan's cultural debt to Europe. But Japanese governments were for long sceptical about the reality of the European Community, and many politicians and businessmen were openly contemptuous about European economic failings. The imbalance in trade betwen Japan and the European Community countries and trade grievances on both sides tended in the 1980s to dominate relations, but increasing Japanese investment in Europe, especially Britain, together with a growing recognition in Europe of the importance of Japan and in Japan a realization that the European Community was becoming a more closely integrated economic bloc, underlined the need to seek a closer relationship and a better understanding.

As the 1980s wore on, the question of Japanese aid to developing countries began to assume much greater importance. Some people in North America and in Europe saw increased Japanese aid not only as a means of recycling Japan's vast trade surpluses, but also as a way in which Japan, precluded for historical and constitutional reasons from increasing her defence expenditure, could share some of the burdens of the advanced countries. When in the second half of the 1980s almost all other parts of the Japanese public expenditure budget were being cut, only aid and defence were allowed increases. The Japanese were, however, criticized for tying too much of their aid to purchases from Japan and not giving enough to the poorest countries. Official development assistance from Japan in 1987 amounted to about 7.45 billion US dollars and was 0.31 per cent of GNP, against the average in that year for Development Assistance Countries (DAC) of 0.34 per cent.

Economic Growth and Success

Japan's post-war economic 'miracle' has turned Japan into an economic super-power and made her one of the richest nations in the world.

The first Japanese industries to revive were naturally those which had become important in pre-war Japan and which were not directly tied to the military machine. These were textiles, pottery, cutlery, toys and other everyday consumer goods. Labour was cheap and plentiful. In 1960, 29 per cent of the labour force was still employed on the land, and it was only after 1964 that more Japanese worked in manufacturing than in agriculture. Textiles accounted for half of Japanese exports in 1950, but represented only 5 per cent of Japanese exports in 1975.

The Japanese authorities recognized that prosperity could not be achieved without the development of heavy industry and engineering. The Ministry of International Trade and Industry (MITI), which was one of the key organizations in the planning and execution of the Japanese economic miracle, worked out, in co-operation with industrial leaders, a strategy for investment in steel, ship-building and heavy engineering. They also recognized the central role which the motor-car industry had played in America and Europe and gave priority to its development. The potential of the electronics industry was quickly appreciated. These key industries were granted access to capital and were protected by high tariffs and quotas against imports from abroad, but as a spur to increased pro-ductivity competition within Japan was encouraged.

The first problem was shortage of capital. Japanese savings had been wiped out by war and inflation, and capital resources, as in the early Meiji period, had to be provided under government auspices. This ensured that the Ministry of Finance (MOF) and the Bank of Japan played a significant role from the outset. The Bank of Japan acted as lender of last resort and especially in the early days was able to dole out credits to meet government-determined priorities.

Under the occupation the organization of Japanese banks and the securities industry was reformed on American lines, ensuring, under Article 65 of the securities exchange law of 1948, that banks could not undertake securities business and that securities companies were forbidden from taking part in banking activities. The banks were regulated by the Banking Bureau of MOF and the securities industry by the Securities Bureau. Banks were also divided into separate categories with differing roles. There were in 1989 thirteen city banks, the top six being Daiichi Kangyō, Sumitomo, Fuji, Mitsubishi, Sanwa and Mitsui with the Bank of Tokyo, the former Yokohama Specie Bank, acting as the main foreign exchange bank. There were three specialist banks for long-term financing of industry – the Industrial Bank of Japan, the Long Term Credit Bank and Nippon Credit Bank. Trust business was confined to the seven trust banks – Sumitomo, Yasuda, Mitsubishi, Mitsui, Chūō, Tōyō and Nippon Trust and Banking Corporations. There were also over 100 regional banks, specialist banks such as Nōrinchūkin, which served the agricultural co-operatives, and numerous credit associations designed to serve small and medium-scale businesses. The postal savings system was given special privileges in order to mobilize small savings. The securities companies, which were headed by the big four (Nomura, Daiwa, Nikkō and Yamaichi), came into their own in the 1960s when Japanese individuals began to show greater interest in equity investments through the Tokyo and Osaka stock exchanges.

In the rush for growth in the late 1950s and the 1960s living standards and the environment were neglected. By 1970 Tokyo was one of the most overcrowded and polluted cities in the world. Smog got so bad at times that those with bronchial weaknesses had to remain indoors. In 1979 Sir Roy Denman, then director-general responsible for external trade in the European Commission, offended the Japanese by describing them as 'workaholics living in rabbit-hutches'. Many Japanese later came to accept the phrase as a compliment to their dedication to economic growth. Low living standards were generally accepted by the Japanese work-force; disparities in wealth were limited, and the Japanese saw themselves as living in an egalitarian society. Private-sector unions tended to be company unions which were induced to recognize that the prosperity of their members depended on the success or failure of their company.

Japanese GNP grew between 1955 and 1970 at an average annual rate of 10.3 per cent. Between 1960 and 1973 manufacturing output increased by more than four and a half times, and GNP per head in real terms nearly quintupled. This growth was achieved largely through investment in plant and equipment and by soaring exports (in 1967 Japanese exports amounted to 10 per cent of GNP). In the early years Japanese growth had come in surges; these had caused balance of payments difficulties and had in turn resulted in temporary setbacks. But aided by an undervalued yen (at a then fixed rate of 360 to the US dollar) and by the dedication of Japanese manufacturers to expanding world market share, Japan had by 1970 achieved a balance of payments surplus. Between 1967 and 1971 Japanese exports increased from 10 billion US dollars to 24 billion, an average increase of more than 20 per cent. Vehicle exports grew from 370,000 vehicles in 1967 to 2.4 million in 1971. There were similar increases in exports of consumer electronic items such as television sets and tape recorders. Industries in North America and Europe affected by the flood of Japanese exports demanded protection, and so-called 'voluntary' restraint agreements were negotiated, with discreet government support, by industrial and trade organizations. These arrangements enabled the European industries involved and the US car industry to remain afloat, but cushioned them from the competition needed to improve their efficiency. These measures also harmed the interests of consumers in Europe and

North America. Nevertheless some industries, such as the British motor-cycle industry, were overwhelmed, as Japanese manufacturers of motor cycles competed vigorously against one another and foreign producers for control of foreign markets.

Apart from American assistance, foreign technology and Japanese determination, there were other important factors which made possible Japan's outstanding economic success. Some of these were only partly peculiar to Japan. Management methods adopted by large Japanese firms, such as quality control and just-in-time stock arrangement, had been advocated by American management consultants. The peculiarity about their application in Japan was the enthusiasm with which they were adopted and developed.

Good man-management and the creation of company loyalty should be features of successful companies anywhere, but the Japanese took these further than their opposite numbers in North America and Europe. Confucian concepts of loyalty and obligation and a paternalist tradition helped to make Japanese companies strong and closely integrated. Most Japanese had been taught that loyalty to the group came even before family loyalty, and it was certainly more highly regarded than individual happiness or success. In all walks of life in Japan the relationship between the boss (*oyabun*) and his followers (*kobun*), implying a parent–child relationship, has been prized. The relationship was strengthened by egalitarian arrangements at work. Management and workers used the same canteens and lavatories and wore the same company overalls. All sang the same company songs, recited the same company mottoes and took part together in daily exercises.

These methods helped to win the support of Japanese unions and their members, but the traditional Japanese preference for consensus over confrontation has also been an important factor for successful management and the reduction of labour disputes in Japan. Consensus is sought by seemingly endless meetings and by the so-called *ringi* system whereby all managers are expected to consent to a decision by placing their 'chop' (that is, their individual seal) on any proposal of importance.

Jealousies over promotions and salary differentials were generally avoided by the Japanese tradition of respect for age and seniority. So up to middle management at least all tended to progress together, and bonuses depended on the overall success of the company not on a subjective assessment of an individual's contribution. Starting salaries could be kept relatively low because recruits knew that with time and loyalty to the company they would gradually earn more. The difference between minimum and maximum salaries was also kept down to avoid envy, and rewards have often taken the form of perks, such as chauffeur-driven cars and lavish company expenses accounts, enabling senior managers to enjoy golf at prestigious and expensive clubs or extravagant parties in exclusive Japanese restaurants with high-class geisha in attendance. Expenditure on company entertainment was estimated in the 1980s as exceeding that on public education.

Another important factor has been the relative unimportance of the shareholder. This was partly the result of the way in which in the early years of postwar economic growth most capital had to be borrowed from the banks. The banks did not want repayment of loans so long as the company to which they had lent money was making a profit and growing. This enabled companies to take a long-term view and put the emphasis on gaining market share. In the late

1970s and the 1980s companies became much less dependent on bank loans, and many were able to finance expansion out of retained profits. Japanese companies belonging to one of the large groupings (*keiretsu*) have also had a stable shareholder base and have not therefore been too concerned if their share priced is volatile, as only a relatively small part of their equity is ever bought or sold on the stock exchanges. This has also meant that they have been almost entirely exempt from take-overs by predators.

In the immediate post-war period there was no shortage of labour in Japan; and, Japanese educational standards having been comparatively high since before the Meiji restoration, Japanese companies had easy access to an intelligent and educated work-force. Engineering and technology were highly regarded as qualifications in industry, and in many large manufacturing companies it was common for a majority of the members of the board to be technically qualified people. Nevertheless Japanese companies have taken seriously their responsibility to train and improve the quality of their work-force. In doing so they have known that, because of the tradition of staying all one's basic working life with one company, the value of in-house training will not be lost by an employee who has been trained in one company going to work in another. As labour became more costly and better machines were developed, Japanese companies did not hesitate to invest in sophisticated machinery and robots. They realized that in many cases a robot was more reliable than a human being and that quality, to which they attached so much importance, would be improved by using such machines.

The Japanese have sometimes been accused of being mere imitators who have contented themselves with improving what they have copied. In fact Japanese companies have invested huge amounts in research and development. In 1986 nearly 50 billion US dollars was spent on research in Japan, representing 3.18 per cent of GNP. Of this only 19.6 per cent was financed out of public funds. Nevertheless in the 1980s the Japanese feared that they might be falling behind in basic research, and major efforts were made by the government to promote such research. In particular the Japanese intensified their efforts to develop a fifth-generation computer, and Prime Minister Nakasone launched his 'human frontiers' research programme. Innovation has been greatly prized by the successful Japanese companies which have competed fiercely with one another to bring out new products and exploit gaps in the market.

Japan has been a free market economy with fierce competition between Japanese companies. But free enterprise has been guided by the government. The 'old boy' network remained strong, and government relations with industry were based on co-operation rather than confrontation. When difficult times occurred for particular industries, the Japanese authorities did not hesitate to organize recession cartels. The Japanese sense of identity also ensured that almost all Japanese companies were prepared to work together against foreign competition.

Small and medium-scale companies with limited resources have played a vital role in Japanese economic growth. They have supplied parts and services to the larger companies and with less bureaucratically controlled work-forces have often been better able to adapt in times of recession. Bankruptcies have been frequent, but help from larger firms with which they have been connected and from central and local governments has ensured the survival and growth of the better firms. Their entrepreneurial and innovative skills have been valuable to the Japanese economy.

281

lack of defence spending

The fact that Japan did not have to spend anything like as high a proportion of her GNP on defence was a factor peculiar to Japan among advanced countries, but the importance of savings on defence should not be exaggerated. This was a contributory rather than a fundamental factor in Japan's economic success.

savings habit

More important was the Japanese personal savings habit. This was partly the result of traditional attitudes, but it was also given a major boost by the poverty which was such a dominant feature of the immediate post-war years, and by the absence in those years of an adequate social security system in Japan. Japanese savings were encouraged by tax incentives especially through the postal savings system and by the Japanese tradition of paying two bonuses at the middle of the year and at New Year. These have often amounted to a third or more of annual salaries and, as consumption tends to be based on net monthly earnings, have either been saved or used to pay for large consumer items.

econ. weaknesses

Not all sectors of Japanese commerce and industry were equally successful. The weaknesses in the Japanese economic structure began to become more apparent in the 1970s and 1980s. Japanese agriculture, based on small farms, grossly over-subsidized and protected, was a glaring example long before the Americans turned the spotlight on it in the 1980s. Service industries were mostly overmanned, and the inefficiency of the small retail sector, which was protected by bureaucratic rules against competition from the large department store and supermarket chains, became still clearer when the yen began to rise in the 1980s and the prices of imported goods failed to go down. The Japanese economy achieved remarkable successes, but we should not exaggerate these or assume that the Japanese have a special secret for success which no one else can emulate.

energy crisis in 70s

In 1971 the decision by President Nixon to float the US dollar forced a rise in the yen, but this was insufficient to alter the fundamentals. The huge rise in oil prices engineered by the oil-producing countries in OPEC in 1973, however, caused major economic problems for the Japanese, who were still aiming to achieve annual growth of over 10 per cent. As a result Japan faced massive inflation, a balance of payments crisis and then a major recession. The Japanese authorities gave priority to the fight against inflation and applied strict controls on the money supply. Dearer oil forced Japanese firms to make great efforts to conserve energy, and investment in new technologies was stepped up while excess capacity and inventories were ruthlessly cut. Real wages fell, but unemployment only rose marginally. Redundancies, in accordance with traditional Japanese practices, were covered by early retirements and transfers to different jobs within groups of companies. Labour productivity continued to expand, increasing by one-fifth between 1974 and 1980. Heavy industries, which were large consumers of imported energy, were cut back, and Japanese companies moved up-market, placing greater emphasis on higher-value-added products. During the late 1970s and 1980s there was a major expansion of tertiary industries, including commerce and services. Between 1970 and 1979 the proportion of GNP provided by commerce and services rose from 50 to 59 per cent. Nevertheless manufacturing industry remained strong.

The second oil crisis of 1979 once more caused some inflation and a recession in Japan, but the Japanese economy weathered the crisis better than most. Japanese energy conservation measures had significantly reduced Japanese oil imports. By 1980 Japan was using only 73 per cent as much energy per unit of output as it

282

had used in 1973. By 1982 the proportion had declined to 63 per cent. To cover the cost of imported energy Japanese exports had increased to 17 per cent of GNP by 1984, but then, with the decline in the oil price, Japan began to achieve a huge balance of payments surplus. The surplus came to over 80 billion US dollars in 1986 and 1987 and showed little decline in 1988.

The yen, which had remained at about 240 yen to the dollar for many years, was allowed to appreciate in the second half of the 1980s and had reached almost 120 yen to the dollar in early 1988, but weakened somewhat in 1989. This, together with a significant rise in internal demand, partly stimulated by government actions as a result of foreign pressure and by low interest rates, led to a welcome increase in manufactured imports. But Japanese exports continued to be buoyant, partly as a result of lower import prices of raw materials and energy, but also because Japanese manufacturing industry displayed great resilience. Productivity continued to expand. Japanese industries moved still further up-market to higher-value-added products. As Japanese wages and general living standards were now higher than in North America or Europe, Japanese companies expanded manufacturing investment abroad. Japanese consumer products were increasingly made abroad, and Japanese exports consisted more and more of sophisticated parts and luxury goods.

Economic friction with other advanced countries, which had been endemic since the late 1960s, became increasingly acrimonious in the second half of the 1980s. Accusations that the Japanese market was closed continued to be levelled against the Japanese, although Japanese tariffs had become generally lower than those of other advanced countries, and much had been done to reduce non-tariff barriers against imports.

The Europeans took tough measures against Japanese imports which they claimed were being dumped. The Americans became ever more critical of Japanese agricultural protectionism. In 1988 an understanding was reached about the eventual liberalization of imports of oranges and beef from the USA despite vociferous protests from Japanese beef farmers and growers of *mikan* (Japanese mandarin oranges). The Americans then turned their attention to rice, imports of which were banned by the Japanese to protect Japan's small farmers, who by this time were mainly part-time or 'Sunday farmers'. The LDP, fearing that liberalization, although very much in the interests of the Japanese consumer, might jeopardize their support in rural constituencies, fought back, arguing that Japan needed to protect its rice farmers in order to maintain some form of security of food supplies. As there was no way that Japan's population of over 120 million could possibly be fed without imports this was a questionable argument. In 1989 the American action in naming Japan and certain specific Japanese trade practices as 'unfair' under Article 301 of the latest American Trade Act was strongly resented by the Japanese authorities, who had failed to realize the extent of American frustration with Japan.

Japanese investment overseas, although welcomed by many people abroad because it brought jobs to countries suffering from high unemployment rates, also attracted some criticism. Some governments accused the Japanese companies of only investing in 'screwdriver operations'. The large number of Japanese trading companies, banks and financial institutions in places like London and New York also caused some people to object to the 'over-presence' of Japanese

283

firms. Even the large numbers of Japanese tourists going abroad were not always regarded kindly.

The Japanese government in the early 1980s faced a huge budget deficit partly caused by large issues of government bonds made to cover deficits after the first oil crisis. This formed the basis for the initial Japanese reluctance to increase internal demand. It also, however, focussed the attention of government and business leaders on the need for 'administrative reform', which was a euphemism for cutting down the civil service and reducing subsidies. This led to the privatization of Japan Air Lines (JAL), Nippon Telegraph and Telephone (NTT) and Japan National Railways (JNR). JNR had made huge losses and was grossly overmanned.

The extent of the deficit and the growing burden of social security costs, caused by the decline in the death and birth rates and the consequent ageing population of the country, made tax reforms in Japan essential. There were also strong pressures from abroad to reduce tax incentives for savings and to alter the liquor tax system, which discriminated against imported liquors. The Dodge Plan had put the emphasis in Japan on direct taxes; the main burden of income tax fell on salary earners, as collection from them was easy. Farmers, small businessmen and professional people, who could charge expenses against tax, faced a lesser burden. There was clearly a need for a broad-based indirect tax and for reductions in direct taxes. But small businesses were firmly opposed to any new tax and fought hard against reform. Prime Ministers Ohira and Nakasone tried to get reforms through the Diet. The Takeshita government finally succeeded in getting a tax reform bill through at the end of 1988. This provided for cuts in direct taxes and for the introduction from 1 April 1989 of a 3 per cent consumption tax. This latter measure was highly unpopular among LDP supporters.

Japan achieved remarkable economic success in the years after the end of the occupation, but in 1989 the Japanese people did not feel as wealthy as GNP per capita suggested they were. In dollar terms per capita income was higher than in the USA, but in purchasing-power-parity terms the yen was overvalued. Tokyo, where property prices had grown enormously in the 1980s, had become the world's most expensive city for foreigners. It was overcrowded, and the infrastructure was inadequate.

Life and Social Change in Post-War Japan

Defeat brought major changes to the fabric of Japanese life, but many of the fundamental principles of Japanese society were modified rather than transformed by it and by the occupation. Defeat showed that militarism had failed. Failure was a cause for shame, which has held a much more important position in Japanese beliefs than the concept of guilt, which is not part of the Confucian ethical system as developed in Japan. There was little recognition in Japan of the evil which the Japanese military had done to Japanese and non-Japanese people. Defeat, however, demonstrated that military imperialism had been unsuccessful and should be discarded. The atomic bombs dropped on Hiroshima and Nagasaki, which were considered by many Japanese as more reprehensible than anything the Japanese had done in occupied territories, underlined the futility of war. The Japanese people generally accepted Article 9 of the new constitution with relief. Most also found little difficulty in admitting that the Emperor did not have 'divine' status and that state support for Shintō should be ended. They were ready to give western ideas of parliamentary democracy a try, but they added a Japanese dimension. They were not prepared to discard all their traditions and their own set of values. They were Japanese, and many still mistakenly believed that Japan and the Japanese were unique. The *Nihonjinron*, which may be translated as discussion about what it means to be Japanese, has been a growth industry among Japanese intellectuals in the post-war years.

uniqueness

The poverty and hardships of the first two decades after the war brought out the traditional Japanese virtues of patience and endurance. The labour troubles and communist-inspired violence during the occupation turned many against left-wing politicians. If the group and hence Japan were to survive, revive and rival the victors, the Japanese had to work together. Loyalty to the group was still of paramount importance. The new leaders had mostly been civil servants, who were known to be members of the élite; they were regarded as able, intelligent and generally honest.

The absence of effective social security systems and the shortage of housing meant that the old family system of three generations under one roof had to be maintained. The new constitution called for sexual equality, but the small number of feminists in Japan were regarded by many Japanese women in the aftermath of the war as irrelevant. Many older Japanese women had ruled their families and kept the purse strings. It was still the job of the majority of Japanese women to stay at home, look after the children and mother-in-law and await the return of the 'lord and master', ready to produce tea and slippers however late he came home. Many marriages continued to be arranged, and few married women went out to work. They shopped daily for their food from small neighbourhood stores and lived simple lives in Japanese-style houses, with little furniture or other amenities such as washing machines or flush toilets. The staple food remained rice, and most of the meals were Japanese style, with fish rather than meat providing protein. The web of obligation, counter-obligation and duties (*on, on-kaeshi* and *giri*) ensured that society operated smoothly.

The real changes in Japanese life, society and attitudes which became increasingly apparent in the 1970s and 1980s were brought about more by physical alterations in the Japanese way of life than by modifications in attitudes as a result of American or European ideas imported into Japan by the occupation.

One of these changes was the decline in the rural population and the urbanization of Japan. In a mountainous country like Japan space was at a premium, and industry had priority over housing. More and more Japanese in the 1950s and 1960s, who moved to the cities in search of employment, had to live in barrack-like apartment blocks in which there was no room for the three generations. The old people had to remain in the villages, look after themselves in the towns or go to old people's homes – something which would have been unthinkable in the past. The problems of looking after the older members of the family was exacerbated by the significant increase in life expectancy achieved in post-war Japan as a result of better hygiene, nutrition and health care. By 1987 a Japanese male had a life expectancy at birth of 75.6 years and a female of 81.4 (this compared with 71.3 for men in America and 71.8 for men in Britain). As soon *old age burden*

as Japanese economic growth allowed, social security systems were introduced or improved, and investment in hospitals increased. By 1989 one of the main problems facing Japanese society was the ageing population. By 1990, 11.4 per cent of Japan's population will be over 65, and demographers predict that the proportion could rise in 2025 to 20.3 per cent (in the USA the figure then could be 17.2 per cent and in Britain 18.7 per cent). The burden on the working population which this implies became a major factor in Japanese political and economic thinking in the late 1980s.

Urbanization and improved living standards also brought down the Japanese birth rate. Smaller families and the competition to get into the better schools meant that many mothers gave more attention to their children. A phenomenon of the post-war period has been the 'education mother' (kyōiku-mama) who will not go out in the evening if one of her children is preparing for a crucial examination. But the declining birthrate has also meant that there has been an increasing demand for married women to work in offices and shops. More Japanese women have found that they have time to go out to work, welcomed the companionship which work provided and wanted the money they earned to pay for consumer goods or meet the huge and growing cost of buying housing, if only in one of the numerous blocks of apartments, called 'mansions', which have been built in and around the Japanese cities. But, while the status of women had improved by the 1980s and there were some women in the Diet and in the professions, industry and commerce remained largely male preserves.

Many marriages were still arranged in 1989 at least nominally by an *omiai* (literally, 'see and meet'), and a go-between (nakōdo) was generally chosen to officiate even in love matches, as he had become part of the tradition of Japanese marriage ceremonies. Weddings became increasingly expensive and ostentatious affairs. Ceremonies were generally Shintō in form, although Christian weddings were also held even by non-Christians. Brides sometimes wore first a white western-style wedding dress and then a formal Japanese wedding kimono; the men mostly wore formal western clothes. Divorce rates in Japan, according to 1986 statistics, were less than half the UK rate and less than a quarter of the US rate.

Japanese housing remained compact, although the 'rabbit hutch' image of Sir Roy Denman (see page 278) was unfair. The average Japanese dwelling was certainly much smaller than the average American, but not all that much smaller than those in Western Europe. Amenities greatly improved, especially in the 1980s. In the first decades after the war most Japanese had to do without effective heating or air-conditioning, but in the later years Japanese homes became over-heated in winter and over-cooled in summer. Kitchens had all modern con-veniences, and western-style rooms with western-style furniture became more general, although most apartments or houses, space permitting, would have at least one Japanese-style room with *tatami* mats. The old-style Japanese wooden house had not entirely disappeared by the late 1980s, but it was becoming a rarity especially in the cities. Japanese houses were being built to withstand earthquakes and to be more resistant to the fires which had decimated Japanese cities in the past. They had, however, lost much of the charm of the old-style Japanese dwelling, although they were undoubtedly much more comfortable to live in.

The tradition of travel in Japan may have originated in the Japanese love of pilgrimages. Even the appalling conditions of travel by train or bus in the immediate post-war era did not extinguish the Japanese travel habit. Many roads during the occupation were little more than unpaved tracks, and trains were slow and grossly overcrowded. As living standards improved and the Japanese motor-car industry developed, the ambition of vast numbers in Japan was to own 'my car'. Roads had to be improved to sustain the communications needed by Japanese industry; and in addition to the paving and improving of main and side roads, a network of motorways and so-called 'high-speed' elevated roads was built in major cities such as Tokyo and Osaka. But Japanese traffic expanded faster than Japanese roads, and traffic congestion became endemic. 'High-speed' elevated roads became at best 'slow-speed' tracks, and one of the first words every foreigner learned on coming to Japan was *jūtai*, meaning 'traffic jam'. As jams were constant on some roads, Japanese signs began to read '*shizen-jūtai*', meaning 'Natural traffic jam'.

Japanese railways had been built with a small gauge in order to reduce the costs of building lines through the mountainous countryside, but they were too slow and small to carry the traffic of a modern industrial country. The first new broad-gauge fast-track railway between Tokyo and Osaka was built in 1964, in time for the Tokyo Olympics. These new lines were called in Japanese *shinkansen*, although foreigners called them 'bullet trains', because they travelled at speeds of over 200 km per hour. In the 1970s the first of the new lines was extended to Fukuoka in Kyūshū; by the 1980s other new lines had been built as far as Morioka in the north and Niigata on the Japan Sea cost. In 1988 further extensions were planned. In the same year a rail tunnel between Honshū and Hokkaidō and the first bridge between Honshū and the island of Shikoku were opened.

Internal and foreign air travel developed quickly especially in the 1980s, and many new airports, including Tokyo international airport at Narita in Chiba prefecture, were opened. Construction was also proceeding in the second half of the 1980s on an entirely new international airport for Osaka; this was being built on an island constructed in Osaka bay.

As living standards improved, Japanese people demanded better and more recreational facilities. *Pachinko* parlours, which were shops with serried ranks of pin-tables/fruit machines and which had become very popular in the dull days after the war, continued to be popular with working men who had got hooked on this mild form of gambling. Mah-jong was a favourite game of many businessmen who went to mah-jong parlours after work and a round of the numerous bars to be found in Japanese cities. Baseball, which had been imported from America and Japanized, attracted vast crowds of enthusiastic supporters. Some Japanese teams even imported American stars on huge salaries to boost their performance. Traditional Japanese sports such as *sumo* (Japanese-style wrestling), which the Shōwa Emperor greatly enjoyed watching, became big business. Golf was the favourite sport of Japanese businessmen. Golf ranges were put up in the suburbs so that learners could practise in the evenings. Huge sums had to be paid for membership of the top clubs. Even the more distant and less exclusive clubs charged large sums for a single round. Rugby football and rowing were played by students of Keiō and Waseda private universities in Tokyo and by some clubs. Tennis and badminton were also becoming popular where space could be found for courts. Swimming pools were full in the summer, as were skiing resorts in the winter.

287

Space being at a premium, Japanese cities had few and smaller public parks than cities in Europe (4 square metres per head of population compared with 30 square metres in London). Japan had, however, numerous fine national parks and innumerable hot-spring resorts, although unfortunately developers have been allowed to disfigure many beauty spots with ugly and vulgar resort buildings and amusement facilities.

As more people had money to spare, bars and restaurants grew up in profusion in every city. Restaurants varied from McDonalds and Mr Donut franchises to the most exclusive Japanese-style restaurants where an introduction and a fat expense account were prerequisites. Japanese specialities, such as *sushi* (raw fish on rice), *tempura* (fried fish and vegetables), *sukiyaki* (meat cooked with vegetables in a soyabean (*shoyu*) sauce with sugar), *yakitori* (barbecued chicken) and *soba* (buckwheat noodles) were popular with Japanese families. The Japanese diet had, however, become more westernized. Many families found it easier to prepare a western-style breakfast or evening meal than a Japanese one, which requires more courses and more dishes to wash up. Meat, bread and milk were being consumed in increasing quantities in the 1980s, but the prices of meat and dairy products, because of the protection and subsidies given to Japanese farmers, meant that these products were regarded more as luxuries than as necessities.

Japanese, who have few inhibitions about getting tipsy and whose physical make-up seems to give them weak heads when drinking alcohol, have always enjoyed merry drinking parties; they were able to indulge themselves more as their income rose. Japanese sake (rice wine) has always been popular, but in the 1980s many Japanese took to drinking *shōchū* (a white spirit especially popular in southern Kyūshū, where it is often made from sweet potatoes, but it can also be made from various kinds of grain). Whisky, normally taken with water and ice, was drunk by many men. The better grades of Japanese whisky had Scotch malt added.[6]

Japanese business entertaining, supposed to oil the workings of business relationships, absorbed huge sums of money, especially in the 1970s and 1980s. Almost all of this entertaining was for men only, with geisha provided for the more exclusive parties in Japanese-style restaurants and hostesses for entertaining in bars and on other occasions, for example at the vast receptions held in western-style hotels to mark important company events such as the appointment of a new president. A popular evening pastime among Japanese businessmen was *karaoke* singing, when men could let go their inhibitions, while roaring out their favourite songs to canned music.

Many businessmen rarely came home on weekday evenings for supper with their wives and children; some were regular *gozen-sama* (meaning someone who comes home after midnight). Many Japanese businessmen were indeed so devoted to their jobs that they would readily go abroad on posting or to another part of Japan for a year or more without their wives. This practice was called *tanshin funin*. Hardly surprisingly pornography became increasingly popular. Apart from films and videos, pornographic strip cartoon books were sold in large quantities.

Yet Japanese crime rates have remained astonishingly low. The London *Economist* in December 1988 noted that a resident of New York was six times likelier to be murdered, 25 times likelier to be raped and 140 times likelier to be robbed than a resident in Tokyo. Among the reasons for the comparatively low crime rate in Japan were the Japanese sense of discipline and their communal spirit. Another was the Japanese police systtem with the local police boxes from which the policemen got to know all the people in the neighbourhood for which their box was responsible. The Japanese police, especially the military police (the *kenpeitai*), had a bad reputation before the war for arrogance and cruelty. Although complaints were still made about police behaviour towards suspects to induce confessions, the reputation of the Japanese police had vastly improved.

An important factor influencing patterns of behaviour in Japan has been that of education. In 1986, 93.8 per cent of all children in Japan completing middle school, and therefore compulsory education, went on to high school; and over 35 per cent went on to some form of tertiary education. Standards, of course, varied enormously. The best universities, such as the national universities of Tokyo, Kyoto and Osaka, were some of the best higher-education establishments in the world. Some of the private universities, such as Keiō and Waseda, had enviable reputations. On the other hand, some of the short-term universities (*tanki-daigaku*) were little more than girls' finishing schools.

Japanese attitudes have also been greatly influenced by the media. Apart from some sporting papers, daily newspapers in Japan were mostly serious journals covering much the same news in ways which did not differ greatly in substance. They had huge circulations. The largest was the *Yomiuri* with a circulation for the morning edition in 1986 of over 8.8 million and for the evening edition of over 4.8 million. The *Asahi* had a circulation of not much less. The *Nihon Keizai*, a daily economic journal, had a circulation for the morning edition of nearly 2.4 million. There were English-language newspapers such as the *Japan Times*, but it had only a circulation of some 54,000. Japan also had numerous popular weeklies as well as some influential monthlies. The most important of these latter were the *Bungei Shunjū* and the *Chūkōron*. Television developed enormously in post-war Japan. NHK (*Nihon Hoso Kyokai*), the Japanese equivalent of the BBC, with two channels, faced competition from commercial channels allied to the big newspapers; NTV was part of the *Yomiuri* network, and *Fuji* was part of the *Sankei* newspaper group.

One feature of the post-war has been the development of Japanese museums and art galleries. Almost every prefecture has one or more, and there are many outstanding galleries and museums in Tokyo. Many of these are private foundations such as the Gotō, Nezu, Suntory, Idemitsu and Yamatane museums in Tokyo or the Tokugawa museum at Nagoya. The National Museums of Tokyo, Kyoto and Nara have superb collections particularly of Japanese art. In the post-war era, especially since the yen became so strong, Japanese collectors and galleries have built up their collections of western art. The Japanese have had a particular liking for Impressionism and Post-Impressionism, perhaps because of the influence of Japanese art on these movements.

Religion has played only a limited role in the formation of Japanese ethics, and appearances suggested that few Japanese people had deeply held religious convictions. Japanese traditional behaviour patterns have been pragmatic, and the outward signs indicate an increasingly materialist culture. But most Japanese would still claim, if questioned, that they had some belief in Buddhist and Shintō practices. The big shrines and temples, especially those in Japan's beauty spots, still attract many Japanese sightseers, particularly at festival times and at New

Year. Japanese people enjoy 'all the fun of the fair' and the colour which festivals in Japan attract.

Not all Japanese, however, have found the conventional and traditional religious practices adequate, and in the post-war era there has been a significant growth in adherents of some sects and 'new religions'. Mention has already been made of Sōka Gakkai, which developed from Nichiren-Shōshū Buddhism. In 1980 it claimed over 6 million followers. Another popular Buddhist sect in post-war Japan has been Risshō Kōseikai, which in 1980 claimed just over 5 million adherents. It was founded in 1938 by Niwano Nikkyō (born 1906) and Naganuma Myōkō (1889–1957). It too was inspired by Nichiren Buddhism and the Lotus Sutra. The sect, and Niwano in particular, have been enthusiastic advocates of world peace. A number of sects which have emphasized faith healing, also developed. One of these is Sekai Kyūseikyō, founded by Okada Mokichi (1882–1955). It claimed some 800,000 followers in 1977 and emphasized the value of fine art in uplifting the spirit. The sect, often referred to as MOA, has two good museums at Atami and Gora near Hakone, which contain some of Japan's greatest art treasures. Sōko Gakkai too has art museums, which contain some fine screens, lacquer and other art objects.

In the 1970s and 1980s a new generation, who had been born and brought up after the war and who had not known the hardships of earlier years, joined the work-force. To members of the older generation they seemed more selfish, less dedicated to work and to their company and altogether more interested in leisure and pleasure. They were called the *shinjinrui*. Those who liked to ride noisy motor cycles in gangs, causing a nuisance on the roads and streets, were called *bōsōzoku*. The richer ones preferred to drive around in fast cars and flout Japanese conventions.

In the 1960s it was said that any young person of character would support the student agitators, but as soon as he joined a company and got his first job, he would conform once again, as he had been forced to do at school. Observers, however, were beginning in the latter part of the 1980s to wonder whether the new generation would be quite so ready to conform. Many more Japanese had lived abroad, and some had been brought up in foreign societies. They had begun to savour a new freedom, and many, when forced to go home again to Japan, found it difficult to settle down in the more constrained atmosphere of their own country. They disliked being treated as 'outsiders' or as renegades.

Language

Since the war attempts have been made to simplify and modernize the Japanese language. All documents are now written in a semi-colloquial style using straight-forward verb endings; this is a style generally referred to as *de aru* to distinguish it from the polite forms ending in -*masu*. The old literary style called *bungotai* and the epistolatory *sōrōbun* are practically never used in modern Japanese.

The orthography used in writing in the Japanese sylllabaries (*hiragana* and *katakana*) has also been standardized and simplified. The new orthography was explained in a cabinet order of November 1946. It was intended to be as near as possible to modern Japanese pronunciation, but the particles *wa*, *o* and *e* are still written *ha*, *wo* and *he*, and there are a few other exceptions.

In 1946 the Ministry of Education also selected 1,850 Chinese characters, out of the 40,000 to 50,000 found in the larger dictionaries, for general use. These were termed the *tōyō kanji*. In 1981 this list was superseded by a slightly larger list of 1,945 characters, called the *jōyō kanji*. Japanese schoolchildren are supposed to master 881 essential *kanji*, the *kyōiku kanji*, during their six years in primary school and the *jōyōkanji* by the time they leave middle school. Newspaper articles normally use only the 1,945 *jōyō kanji* and if they need to use other characters will explain how these are read by attaching to the characters in question the correct reading in the *kana* syllabary in small print called *furigana*. A number of the more complicated characters have been simplified for everyday use. Unfortunately these simplifications are not always the same as those used in modern China.

In 1946 the US Education Mission to Japan recommended that the Japanese should romanize their script as one way of achieving democratization. This recommendation did not find favour, not least because of the implications for Japanese art and literature. There were also strong practical objections because of the large number of Japanese words using combinations of Chinese characters (*kango*) which have the same pronunciation and can only be distinguished by the context or the way in which they are written. Most dictionaries use the standard system of romanization based on that pioneered by the American missionary and lexicographer Dr J. C. Hepburn (1815–1911); but some Japanese authorities prefer the so-called *kunrei* system based on Japanese orthography but reflecting less directly the sounds used in modern Japanese. (The Hepburn system has been used throughout this book.)

Since the war the vocabulary of modern Japanese has been expanded, or some would say adulterated, by a massive import of foreign words mostly of English or American origin, but including some of French and German origin. In many cases, such as for technical terms or for modern items for which there is no natural Japanese word, the use of a foreign word is sensible. But in some cases it seems that foreign words have been adopted without any good reason. For instance, it is odd to find words like *supiido* for 'speed' when there is an adequate word of Japanese origin with basically the same meaning (*sokudo*). Modern 'Japlish' or Japanized English is far more common than 'Franglais' is in France and even more damaging to the Japanese language. Still foreigners studying Japanese may be able to get by in Japan if they know how to pronounce English words in the Japanese way. But most foreigners have particular difficulty with the Japanese habit of abbreviating foreign words when adopting them. Thus *suto* is the shortened form of *sutoraiku* ('strike') and is used for a withdrawal of labour by employees. *Geba* from the German *Gewalt* means 'violence', and *uchi-geba* means 'a violent struggle inside an organization'. Interestingly, in view of the history of Japanese nationalism, there have been no public campaigns to clear away these foreign imports. In any case it is now too late to produce a purified form of Japanese.

Literacy rates are not measured in modern Japan, but probably nearly 100 per cent of all who are not mentally or physically handicapped are able to read a newspaper and write at least simple Japanese.

Post-War Literature

Japanese literature, which was little known outside Japan before the war, became much more widely appreciated as a result of the large number of works which were translated into English in the post-war years. Most of the early translations were done by scholars, such as Professors Edward Seidensticker and Donald Keene, who had taken up the study of Japanese during the war. Many of the writers who became prominent in the immediate post-war years had been active before the war and provided a bridge between the pre-war and post-war periods and attitudes. Three modern Japanese writers, Tanizaki Junichirō, Kawabata Yasunari and Mishima Yukio, achieved world reputations which did much to enhance the popularity of the Japanese novel among readers of English.

Tanizaki Junichirō (1886–1965)[7] published his first story in 1910. It was entitled *Shisei* ('The Tattooer'). This is the story of a tattoo artist who inscribes a giant spider, representing evil, onto the flesh of a beautiful young woman. The erotic and masochistic elements in the story were to be reflected in many of Tanizaki's later works. One of his more famous pre-war novels was *Tade kuu mushi* ('Some Prefer Nettles'), published in 1928–9. During the war Tanizaki occupied himself by putting the 'Tale of Genji' into modern Japanese. In 1942 he also began work on perhaps his greatest novel *Sasameyuki* ('The Makioka Sisters'). This novel, which describes the decline of a family that had once been proud and rich, gives an elegant account of middle-class life before the war. Publication began in 1943 but was halted as it was regarded with disfavour by Japan's military rulers. The story was completed in 1948.

Tanizaki was married three times, and sex was a dominant theme in many of his novels. Indeed, as he grew older he seemed to become obsessed with sex. *Kagi* ('The Key'), published in 1956, was written in diary form and describes the sexual problems of an ageing professor and his wife. His last novel, *Futen rōjin nikki* ('The Diary of a Mad Old Man'), which was published in 1961–2, is an account of the infatuation of an old man for his daughter-in-law and his fascination with her feet. Tanizaki was an outstanding novelist, and *Sasameyuki* 'The Makioka Sisters' is one of the finest novels to come out of post-war Japan. But it requires a special kind of eclectic taste to enjoy his later novels, though we may admire his style and his ability to describe the sordid sexual feelings of old men.

Kawabata Yasunari (1899–1972)[8] was awarded the Nobel Prize for literature in 1968, his novels having become known to English readers largely through the translations of Edward Seidensticker. Melancholy and nostalgia are dominant notes in Kawabata's novels, but he was also absorbed by sensuality. One of his first was *Izu no odoriko* ('The Izu Dancer'), which was published in 1926. It tells the story of a young student who, on a trip to the Izu peninsula, falls for a young dancer. *Yukiguni* ('Snow Country') appeared in book form in 1937. It describes an affair between a dilettante from Tokyo and a geisha in a town in the mountains on the Japan Sea side of the country. These works contain lyrical evocations of scenes and atmosphere. Kawabata is content to suggest and he frequently leaves episodes hanging inconclusively.

During the war Kawabata began to write *Meijin* ('The Master of Go'). This is a fictionalized account of a famous match played in 1938. (*Go* is a complicated form of chequers.) His two most important post-war works were *Senbazuru*

('Thousand Cranes') and *Yama no Oto* ('The Sound of the Mountain'). Both began to appear in serialized form in 1949. Both end uncertainly. *Senbazuru* is concerned with the tea ceremony. *Yama no oto* is another story of an old man's love for his daughter-in-law. *Nemururu bijo* ('The House of the Sleeping Beauties'), published in 1960–1, describes how an old man frequents a brothel which purveys drugged girls to old men no longer capable of having sex with them, but who enjoy fondling them. *Koto* ('The Old Citadel') was published in 1961–2. It is a nostalgic, lyrical and melancholy story about Kyoto without the sordidness of *Nemurur bijo*; but the plot, such as it is, is unconvincing, and the Kyoto dialect used cannot be reflected in translation. Kawabata was found dead in a gas-filled room in Kamakura in April 1972; he probably committed suicide.

The ritual suicide of Mishima Yukio (1925–70)[9] on 25 November 1970 in a military headquarters in Tokyo made him a world-famous figure and aroused fears of a revival of Japanese ultra-nationalism and militarism which have fortunately so far proved unjustified. Mishima had undoubted ability as a writer – some would say genius. He had a wide knowledge of Japanese and foreign literature and became a master of Japanese style. He also had a vivid imagination and was an effective story-teller. But, as his melodramatic death showed, he lacked balance. He was egotistical and arrogant, with a liking for publicity. He was fascinated by sex and by death, and some would describe his works as *malsain*. Mishima claimed to have great admiration for Kawabata Yasunari; but while Kawabata was deeply influenced by Japanese traditional culture and the softer, more feminine aspects of old Japan, Mishima was more interested in western culture, especially that of classical Greece, and in the masculine and warrior traditions of Japan.

Mishima began to write during the war. He managed to escape call-up on grounds of ill health. His first work of major significance was *Kamen no kokuhaku* ('The Confessions of a Mask'). This appeared in 1949. Disguised as fiction, it was in fact a revelation of his own personality and sexual instincts. Homosexual and sado-masochistic, Mishima liked to identify himself with St Sebastian. *Kinjiki* ('Forbidden Colours'), which appeared in 1951, described the world of Tokyo's homosexuals.

Shiosai ('The Sound of Waves'), which was published in 1954, was a very different book. This story of a fisherboy and fishergirl on an island off the coast near Ise was inspired by the Greek romance *Daphnis and Chloe*. It was an immediate success rather to Mishima's chagrin as, according to Donald Keene, he probably thought of it 'essentially as an exercise in stylistics'.[10] *Kinkakuji* ('The Temple of the Golden Pavilion'), which was published in 1956, is generally regarded as Mishima's most successful work. It was based on the fire which destroyed the temple in Kyoto in 1950, and recounts the reasons why the monk in the story decided to commit arson. This was not the only novel of Mishima's based on contemporary events. *Utage no ato* ('After the Banquet'), which appeared in 1960, was inspired by the case of a former conservative politician, Arita Hachirō (1884–1965), who was an unsuccessful candidate, with socialist support, for election as governor of Tokyo in 1955 and 1959. He married the proprietor of a famous Tokyo restaurant, the Hannyaen. She threw her financial resources into his campaign in 1959, but when the source of her funds became known this helped to ensure Arita's defeat. Arita sued Mishima for invasion of his privacy through the novel, which was too close to the truth for his liking. The case was eventually settled out of court.

Mishima's final work, *Hōjō no umi* ('The Sea of Fertility'), began to appear in 1965. There were four volumes, entitled *Haru no yuki* ('Spring Snow'), *Homba* ('Runaway Horses'), *Akatsuki no tera* ('The Temple of Dawn') and *Tennin gosui* ('The Decay of the Angel'). One theme of these volumes is the illusory nature of life. Donald Keene has commented on 'Spring Snow' that it 'is the supreme product of the skill that Mishima had aquired as a storyteller. It contains a most moving evocation of romantic love... As Japanese prose, *Spring Snow* is remarkably beautiful, and as a nostalgic evocation of the Meiji era it is one of Mishima's most successful re-creations of the past.'[11] The subsequent volumes are less easy to appreciate, and his xenophobia may be hard for some foreign readers to take. Donald Keene believes that 'Mishima was the most gifted and achieved the most of all the writers who appeared after the war.'[12]

Shortly after the end of the war a group of writers, known as the *burai-ha*, or 'decadents', began to publish novels. The leader of the group was a young man of aristocratic family called Tsushima Shūji, but better known by his pen name of Dazai Osamu (1909–48).[13] He began to write in the 1930s as a disciple of Ibuse Masuji (born 1898), who is best known for his novel *Kuroi ame* ('Black Rain'),[14] which is a story about the atomic bomb attack on Hiroshima and its aftermath. Dazai Osamu became famous as a result of two first-person novels (*watakushi shōsetsu*), *Shayō* ('The Setting Sun'), published in 1946, and *Ningen shikkaku* ('No longer Human'), which appeared in 1948. He committed suicide that year by jumping into a river swollen by the summer rains. *Shayō* recounts the decline of an aristocratic family, largely seen through the eyes of the daughter Kazuko. It also includes the last long letter which her brother wrote to her before his suicide.

Ooka Shōhei (1909–88) is another of Japan's post-war pessimists. His novel *Nobi* ('Fire on the Plains'),[15] is a depressing account of how Japanese soldiers in the Philippines at the end of the war took to cannibalism in order to survive. Abe Kōbō (born 1924) is an 'avant-garde' novelist and playwright who has been preoccupied by the stifling effect of urbanization. His most famous novel has been *Suna no onna* ('The Woman in the Dunes').[16] This describes how a schoolteacher goes to some remote sand dunes to collect insects. He is trapped in a deep pit, where a woman is living, and is forced to spend his days shovelling away at the encroaching sand. Another gloomy writer much influenced by Sartre is Oe Kenzaburō (born 1935).

A noteworthy modern novelist was Osaragi Jirō (1897–1973), who wrote both historical and contemporary novels and was a major exponent of popular fiction. His best known post-war work was *Kikyō* ('Homecoming')[17] which tells of the return home of a Japanese naval officer from South-east Asia and his disillusionment with the society he finds in Japan. Ariyoshi Sawako (born 1931) is one of the better-known and popular women novelists in modern Japan.[18] Inoue Yasushi (born 1907) has had a prolific output of historical and autobiographical stories.[19] Endō Shūsaku (born 1923), a Catholic writer, became famous as a result of the publication in 1966 of *Chinmoku* ('Silence').[20] This is a powerful and moving account of the persecution of Christians in seventeenth-century Japan. Endō Shūsaku studied in France and was much influenced by French literature. Some of his other novels such as *Obaka-san* ('Wonderful Fool') contain a welcome dash of humour. Unfortunately most Japanese writers in a comic or satirical vein, such as Genji Keita,[21] Inoue Hisashi, Shiroyama Saburō and Maruya Seiichi,[22] tend to be regarded by Japanese and foreign critics as too popular to be worthy of much serious attention, and few humorous Japanese novels have therefore been translated into English.

A number of novelists such as Mishima Yukio and Abe Kōbō have written for the modern Japanese theatre. Other dramatists who have written effective plays in post-war Japan include Kinoshita Junji (born 1914), Tanaka Chikao (born 1905) and Yamazaki Masakazu (born 1934), but few of their plays have been translated into English.

In the post-war period Japanese poets have continued to write *haiku* and *tanka* as well as free verse. Ogiwara Seisensui (1884–1976) was an exponent of free-style *haiku*. Takahashi Shinkichi (1901–87) is a Zen poet who began as a Dadaist. But it is too soon to judge what modern Japanese poetry will survive into the twenty-first century.

Performing Arts

The performing arts boomed in post-war Japan. Tokyo was not only the centre of traditional Japanese arts but also became a major world centre for western culture.

Modern western-style theatre became something of a cult among groups of intellectuals, but it has not so far won the sort of wide audience that there is for the theatre in London or New York. Western musicals such as *Oliver, Cats* and *Les Misérables*, however, attracted huge audiences, when they were performed in Japanese with Japanese actors. Japanese theatre groups such as the Ninagawa *gekidan* became famous abroad.[23]

The *kabuki* was subject to censorship during the occupation. The occupation authorities disapproved of the 'militaristic' tendencies of samurai dramas, and swords were banned. But the *kabuki* soon revived and became increasingly popular as people had more money and leisure. The Kabukiza theatre in Tokyo was rebuilt, and a National Theatre with two auditoriums was built in the 1960s in a style based on the Shōsōin at Nara next to the Supreme Court building at Miyakezaka in Tokyo. The great actors of the *kabuki* theatre, such as Ichikawa Danjūrō XI (1909–65), Nakamura Utaemon (born 1917) and the *onnagata* Onoe Baikō VII (born 1915), attracted huge audiences and commanded large fees. Younger actors such as Ichikawa Ennosuke (born 1939), Matsumoto Kōshirō (born 1942) and Ichikawa Ebizō X (born 1951) were making names for themselves in the 1970s and 1980s. The classical repertoire was revamped, and scenery and effects became more elaborate and colourful, as modern machinery made possible quick changes of elaborate sets and lighting effects were developed.

The *bunraku* was neglected in the immediate post-war years when some Japanese at least turned away from their traditional culture towards western culture. In 1949 two rival troupes were organized as a result of a dispute over unionization, but neither group had the necessary resources for development, and *bunraku* was in decline. However, following the merger of the two troupes in 1963 the puppet theatre has revived, and *bunraku* has come to be recognized as a major Japanese art form.

295

Japanese had been making films since the beginning of the twentieth century, and avant-garde silent films had been made in the 1920s. In the 1930s sentimental love stories became popular. But these were soon replaced by war films, and the cinema was used by the military to promote Japanese imperialist ambitions. After the war the cinema quickly revived. The television age had not yet begun, and the Japanese were starved of entertainment. The Japanese film was established as an art form by a number of brilliant and imaginative directors, such as Kurosawa Akira (born 1910), Mizoguchi Kenji (1898–1956) and Ozu Yasujirō (1903–63).

Kurosawa became internationally famous with *Rashōmon*, made in 1950, which won many awards. In this historical film Kurosawa moved away from the conventional Japanese depiction of the fighting man. The film examines the nature of illusion and reality. *Ikiru* ('To Live'), made in 1952, relates the story of a petty bureaucrat who discovers that he has terminal cancer and seeks a purpose in life for his remaining months. *Shichinin no samurai* ('The Seven Samurai'), made in 1954, was an action-packed film which became very popular abroad. Another film which became famous outside Japan was *Kumon-sujō*, made in 1957 and given the English title *Throne of Blood*. The bandit in *Rashōmon* was played by Mifune Toshiro (born 1920), who has achieved world fame as a film star.

Mizoguchi Kenji is probably best known outside Japan for his film *Ugetsu monogatari*, made in 1953. One of Ozu Yasujirō's masterpieces was *Tokyo monogatari*, which recounts a visit to their married children in Tokyo by an elderly couple from the country. Other Japanese films to win foreign awards include *Jigokumon* ('Gate of Hell'), directed by Kinugasa Teinosuke and *Muhō matsu no isshō*, which was shown abroad under the title *Rickshaw Man*, directed by Inagaki Hiroshi.

The Japanese cinema reached a peak of poularity in 1958, when there were reported to have been 1.3 billion cinema visits in one year. In 1960, 547 films were produced by the industry. As television developed and almost every Japanese home had at least one colour TV set, the number of cinema-goers began to decline rapidly. In 1987 the number of cinema visits had dropped to 144 million or 13 per cent of what it had been in 1958, and the number of cinemas had fallen from over 7,000 in 1960 to about 2,000 in 1986. The number of new films produced in 1980 was down to 320; since then the figure has varied little. The number of Japanese films shown on television reched 440 in 1986.

In the 1960s Japanese film makers turned to sex and violence as their main themes, and the Japanese film began to decline. But the art of the film in Japan was far from dead, and good new films were still being made in the 1980s. *Tampopo* ('Dandelion'), directed by Itami Jūzō, was, for instance, well received in London when it was shown there in 1988. The photography in the best Japanese films was brilliant and imaginative. Ozu in particular developed new camera techniques, for instance low-angle shots.

Traditional Japanese dancing has been maintained by a number of schools. Fujikage Shizue (1880–1966), who established the *shinbuyō* ('new dance') movement, encouraged women to perform *kabuki* dances, hitherto the preserve of men. Geisha, of course, continued to perform traditional Japanese dances as part of the entertainments they gave at parties. There has also been a revival of regional folk-dancing. Dancing remained a popular element in the *o-bon* ceremonies in midsummer in honour of the dead.

Western-style ballroom dancing was introduced into Japan in the Meiji period, but was frowned upon by the military and was little practised in the years leading up to the war. It revived in the post-war era, but never achieved the sort of popularity with younger Japanese that it had in western countries.

Giovanni V. Rossi, an Italian, began to teach classical dance to pupils in Tokyo in 1912. The great ballerina Anna Pavlova gave performances in Tokyo in 1920 and 1922, and ballets were performed in Tokyo by Japanese groups of dancers during the 1920 and early 1930s. Classical ballet was revived soon after the war and became popular with visits by famous ballet groups including the Bolshoi from the Soviet Union and the Royal Ballet from Britain. Japanese ballet companies, such as the Maki, Asami and Matsuyama, achieved increasingly high standards from the 1960s onwards. Some companies, such as the Tchaikovsky memorial Tokyo ballet company, made tours abroad and were well received by the critics. The Japanese ballerina Morishita Yōkō (born 1948), who began with the Matsuyama ballet company, was widely acclaimed, particularly for her performances in *Swan Lake*, which has been a favourite ballet with Japanese audiences.

Traditional Japanese music was nurtured by the imperial court musicians, by shrines and by the theatre. Young ladies still learned to play the *koto*; some also learned to play the *samisen*, which remains the instrument most favoured by geisha and is much used in the traditional theatre.

The development of western music in post-war Japan has been striking. Interest in western-style music had begun in the Meiji period, and concerts of western music by Japanese musicians were given in the final years of the nineteenth century. In 1914 the Tokyo Philharmonic Society gave its first orchestral concert, and in 1922 the Tokyo Symphony Orchestra was formed. In 1934 the Japanese tenor Fujiwara Yoshie (1898–1976) established his own opera company, the Fujiwara *geikidan*. A number of foreign artists visited Japan in the 1920s and 1930s to give concerts. By 1937 Japan had become the largest market in the world for records of western classical music. Despite the disapproval of the military, western classical music was kept alive in Japan during the war by the Japan Symphony Orchestra, which gave concerts even in 1945 in Hibiya Hall in Tokyo.

After the war Japanese interest in western music grew quickly. Major symphony orchestras, such as the NHK Symphony Orchestra, were formed. By the mid-1980s Tokyo had six symphony orchestras, and most music played on radio and television was western. Yamaha had become the world's largest maker of pianos and other musical instruments.

Foreign performers began to visit Japan from about 1950 and foreign orchestras from about 1955. In the 1950s there were few suitable concert halls, and it was not until the Ueno Bunka Kaikan was constructed in 1961 that Tokyo had a good concert hall. Since then many other concert halls have been constructed up and down Japan. One of the latest was the fine Suntory Hall at Ark Hills in Tokyo, which was built in the mid-1980s. Since the 1960s, Japanese audiences have been able to hear all the best orchestras in the world and to see performances by all the major opera companies.

Japanese orchestras toured abroad and were enthusiastically received, while Japanese conductors came to be increasingly employed by foreign orchestras. Ozawa Seiji (born 1935), for instance, became music director of the San Francisco

Symphony Orchestra in 1970; in 1973 he was appointed music director of the Boston Symphony Orchestra. Japanese soloists, such as the pianist Uchida Mitsuko, also became world famous.

Great interest has been shown abroad in the Suzuki violin method. This is a method developed by Suzuki Shinichi (born 1898) for teaching very young children how to play the instrument. Suzuki founded his school at Matsumoto in Nagano prefecture; over 100 schools were affiliated to it.

Japanese composers of western music have been encouraged by these developments and by the growth in musical education in Japan. Dan Ikuma (born 1924) wrote a number of operas and symphonies as well as chamber and choral pieces. His best-known opera, *Yūzuru* ('The Twilight Crane'), had its première in 1952. It is based on a Japanese folk tale; the libretto was written by the playwright Kinoshita Junji. Mayuzumi Toshirō (born 1929) introduced electronic music to Japan. In 1958 he composed a symphony, entitled *Nehan* ('Nirvana'), which was influenced by Buddhist music. In 1976 he produced an opera based on Mishima Yukio's novel *Kinkakuji*. Takemitsu Tōru (born 1930) established an international reputation particularly through performances of his works conducted by Ozawa Seiji. He tried in his compositions to combine western and Japanese traditional music and wrote works for Japanese musical instruments such as the *shakuhachi*, a kind of flute, and the *biwa*, a kind of lute. Fukushima Kazuo (born 1930), a professor at Ueno Gakuen College, became known for his works for the flute, which were influenced by the Japanese Nō drama, Buddhism and Celtic myth.

Japanese sales of classical records continued at record levels, and in 1988 Sony bought out CBS records in the USA. But Japanese interest in western music was not confined to classical works. Jazz had many admirers in Japan, and pop music concerts by western and Japanese groups played to packed stadia. Japanese audiences proved just as enthusiastic as British or American, and stars like David Bowie had a huge following in Japan. One of the most famous Japanese pop stars in the 1980s was Sakamoto Kyū.

The 'walkman', invented by Sony, was first tried out in Japan. It was so popular that soon all the other Japanese producers of electronic equipment had produced similar devices. The thump of pop music was just as pervasive in Japan as elsewhere in the world.

The tea ceremony remained a popular art in Japan. In the 1980s it was estimated that over 10 million people were studying the tea ceremony in Japan, some 90 per cent of the students being women. Large numbers of tea utensils were made in Japan every year, and practically all Japanese kilns produced tea bowls, many of a very high quality. Several of the schools had classes for foreigners, and some, such as the Urasenke, had branches overseas.

The art of flower arrangement (*ikebana*) also developed rapidly after the war and became popular among foreign ladies who came to live in Japan. Ikebana International was established in 1956 and has over 100 branches in foreign countries with some 12,000 members from the different schools of flower arrangement. It was particularly strong in the USA.

The Ohara school of *ikebana* was established by Ohara Unshin (1861–1914) in 1912. He had been the first to use in traditional *ikenobō* arrangements some of the new flowers which had been brought to Japan after the Meiji restoration. He had also been the first to develop the *moribana* ('piled-up flowers') style, stressing colour and natural growth and using shallow containers.

Teshigahara Sōfū (1900–79) founded the Sōgetsu school in 1926. He and his followers sought to free the art from past traditions and aimed to produce *zeneibana*, which may be translated as 'avant-garde flower arrangements'.

The three main schools in the 1980s were Ikenobō, Ohara and Sōgetsu, which are all incorporated as foundations with one to three million students each.

Bonsai, the Japanese art of growing miniature trees, which originally came to Japan from China, has continued to be popular in Japan, especially among older men. Bonsai competitions and exhibitions are held regularly up and down Japan. Foreign interest in bonsai began before the war, but it developed greatly in the post-war period.[24]

Visual and Plastic Arts

Painting in both western and Japanese styles (*yōga* and *Nihonga*) grew in popularity after the war. As income increased, Japanese companies and individuals purchased or commissioned more paintings for their offices and homes. The annual Nitten exhibitions, first under the auspices of the Japan Art Academy and later under the control of an independent body, provided opportunities for artists to exhibit their work, although the establishment character of these exhibitions aroused some criticism.

Soon after the war a new 'creative art' group of painters was formed; this came to be called the Sōgakai (Creative Painting Group). They wanted to establish a new style of painting which reflected the nature of post-war Japan and the world in which Japan found herself. This involved bringing the *Nihonga* style closer to that of western painting. *Yōga* painters for their part were increasingly influenced by the Japanese view of nature, and *Nihonga* painters, who had hitherto tended to stick to traditional Japanese themes and styles, began to depict such *yōga* subjects as the nude and to use colours and styles which would in earlier times have been regarded as essentially western.

Some of the greatest post-war artists began to paint before the war. In *yōga* for instance, Umehara Ryūzaburō (1888–1986) remained active; and in *Nihonga* Yokoyama Taikan (1868–1958) continued to produce paintings in his old age.

Among *Nihonga* artists who achieved fame after the war, Maeda Seison (1885–1978) was inspired in some of his works by cave paintings which he saw in China. It was appropriate, therefore, that he should have been appointed in 1949 to lead a team of experts in the restoration of the ancient wall paintings at the Hōryūji in Nara after they had been damaged by fire.

Ikeda Yōson (1895–1988) spent some time in Paris where he was influenced by Munch and Goya. He determined to introduce western painting techniques into his own work, but on his return to Japan he found himkself once more attracted by traditional methods and by *ukiyo-e* and applied himself to depicting landscapes in the Japanese style.

One outstanding *Nihonga* artist was Higashiyama Kaii (born 1908). Higahiyama Kaii had a remarkable ability to capture the feel of mountains, trees and waves; he knew how to suggest as well as to depict with accuracy. He was commissioned to produce the 'Landscapes of the Four Seasons with the Sun and the Moon' in the Crown Prince's palace (Tōgu-gosho) in Tokyo. He also painted the 'Morntide' mural in the entrance hall to the new Imperial Palace. But perhaps his greatest set of works were the murals which adorn the sliding screens in the Mi-Eidō in the Tōshōdaiji in Nara. He undertook this commission at the request of Morimoto Chōrō, the abbot of the Tōshōdaiji. He began in 1972 to do research into the life of Ganjin, the T'ang priest who founded the temple in the seventh century. He decided that Ganjin would best be commemorated by paintings of Japanese mountains, which represented the loftiness of his teachings, and of the sea, which reflected the depth of his philosophy. Higashiyama Kaii travelled all over Japan sketching mountains and sea. He then depicted on sliding screens misty mountains for the *jōdan-no-ma* (upper room) and the rolling waves of the sea in the *shinden-no-ma* (main room). He entitled the works 'Mountains in Mist' and 'Sound of Waves' and to use his own words he 'used subdued colours to achieve an effect of quiet reflection. I have always thought that to paint is to pray, and this time I was even more conscious of a deep sense of humility.'[25] He later painted scenes from China on the screens in the inner hall. He regarded his efforts at Tōshōdaiji as his lifework.

The Yamatane Museum located in the stock exchange district of Tokyo is devoted to *Nihonga* and contains fine examples of most of the best post-war artists. Among particularly noteworthy examples are ten views of Koshiji, painted in 1968 by Yokoyama Misao (1920–73); these views convey largely in blacks, browns and white the loneliness and bleakness of winter landscapes on the western side of the mountains of Honshū. Sugiyama Yasushi's nude on a rock in a waterfall (1970) is very different from other *Nihonga* paintings. Two paintings by Morita Kōhei (born 1916) are reminiscent of both *ukiyo-e* and colourful seventeenth-century screens of beauties and court ladies. Iwahashi Eien (born 1903) painted 'Aspects of the Sea in the North' in 1980. One of these shows the sun going down over a red sea with a red sky behind and birds flying across the rays of the sun. Another depicts white drifting ice with birds flying across, with a dark grey sky and a strip of yellow along the horizon.

Japanese artists took up with enthusiasm all the latest art trends such as abstract painting, art informel and action painting. It is not yet clear how far Japanese artists have succeeded in establishing a world reputation for themselves in these genres, but the Japanese traditions of asymmetry and the willingness of modern museums in Japan to feature avant-garde works should help.

The art of the print in Japan revived, with a number of able modern print artists bringing new concepts and perspectives to the art.[26] One great print artist was Munakata Shikō (1903–75) of the folk-craft (*mingei*) movement. Another artist who brought a new eye to traditional Japanese scenes and has had a prolific output was Saitō Kiyoshi (born 1907). Saitō described himself as a frustrated oil painter and names Redon, Munch and Gauguin as the strongest influences on his art.

Photography had developed as a Japanese art form during the Meiji period. In the twentieth century it became increasingly popular. Many amateur groups were formed and exhibitions held. During the war photography was made to serve the war effort. In the post-war period Japanese photographers have had the benefit of an advanced camera industry which has been innovative and highly productive.

Mount Fuji must be the most photographed mountain in the world. Okada Kōyō (born 1895) produced books consisting solely of photographs of the mountain. Hayashida Tsuneo (born 1935) devoted almost his whole life to photographing the red crested crane (*tanchō-zuru*) in its natural habitat.[27]

Japanese sculptors after the war began to send pieces to international exhibitions and to make items for display out of doors in sculpture parks. They also took up abstract sculpture. Funakoshi Yasutake from Iwate prefecture was acclaimed as one of Japan's best modern sculptors, and his head of the poet Hagiwara Sakutarō (1886–1942) as one of his masterpieces. Among the avant-garde sculptors Okamoto Tarō has established a considerable reputation in Japan with his startling mosaics and an extraordinarty bronze bell which he made for a temple in Nagoya. (The top of the bell is covered with protuberances which resemble water-buffalo horns.)

Japanese potters found that affluence increased the demand for good pots, especially those made by traditional kilns. Famous Japanese potters such as Arakawa Toyozō (1894–1985) in the Shino-Oribe tradition, Fujiwara Kei in Bizen, Miwa Kyūwa (1895–1981) in Hagi and Hamada Shōji (1894–1978), one of the founders of the folk-craft or *mingei* movement in Mashiko were designated 'living national treasures' (*ningen-kokuhō*). Some kiln sites, such as Hagi in western Honshū and Karatsu in northern Kyūshū, make mainly tea ceremony ware. Mashiko near Utsunomiya in Tochigi prefecture, where the finest living exponent of the *mingei* tradition, Shimaoka Tatsuzō, has his kiln, produces wares of all kinds, as does Koishiwara in Kyūshū. Onda, across the mountains from Koishiwara, was until recently a small unsophisticated pottery village. Okinawa is famous for its colourful wares. Satsuma in southern Kyūshū is the home of highly decorated crackled-glaze pots. Arita in northern Kyūshū contains many famous kilns including those of the Kakiemon and Imaemon families. The art of ceramics is very much alive in Japan; and even if some wares might seem derivative, there are many potters with imagination and artistic feeling actively producing fine and interesting pots in an infinite variety of designs, shapes and glazes.

Japanese traditional craftsmen in lacquer, basketware and various kinds of wood and metal received encouragement from competitions such as the annual 'traditional industrial craft exhibition' (*dentō kōgeiten*) held at the main Mitsukoshi department store in Tokyo. Education and training in Japanese crafts developed, and much effort was put into the teaching and perfection of good design.

Architecture

The visitor to modern Japanese cities such as Tokyo and Osaka might think that he had come to just another concrete jungle, a hodgepodge of ugly skyscrapers mixed up with jerry-built apartment houses and shops. Tokyo suburbs seem to be a conglomeration of villages without anyone having given a thought to practical town planning. Kyoto, the old capital, should be a wonderful city of gardens and temples, but the visitor has to look for them among a jumble of ugly western-style buildings which seem to have been put up irrespective of their environment. As seen from the *shinkansen* train between Tokyo and Kyoto the main island looks like an urban nightmare of factories and workshops. Yet in post-war Japan some of the world's best modern architects have designed buildings which are exciting and beautiful. They are both innovative and faithful to tradition.

Probably the Japanese architect who has achieved the greatest fame outside Japan is Tange Kenzō (born 1913). Tange has designed many municipal buildings, including the Kagawa prefectural offices with their balconies reminiscent of the double eaves of the five-storeyed pagoda of Daigoji in Kyoto. He has also been active in town planning. One of his first designs to attract public attention was that for the Hiroshima Peace Centre in 1949. For the Tokyo Olympic Games in 1964 he designed the Yoyogi National Gymnasia, which, with their sweeping curved roofs and steel suspension roofing, created a sensation. One of his most striking and effective designs was that for the Catholic Cathedral of St Mary in Tokyo.

Taniguchi Yoshirō (1904–79) was responsible for the design of the Okura Hotel in Tokyo and the Tokyo National Museum of Modern Art. He has also played a key role in the preservation of older Japanese buildings in his capacity as head of the Meiji Mura foundation outside Nagoya, where buildings from the Meiji and Taishō periods have been reconstructed and preserved.

Kikutake Kiyonori (born 1928) was responsible for designing the futuristic 'Aquapolis' for the marine exposition on Okinawa in 1975. His design for the treasure house of the Izumo Taisha shrine in Shimane prefecture in 1963 effectively combined modern and traditional elements.

One of Tange's pupils, Isozaki Arata (born 1931), has designed a number of striking municipal buildings and museums. One of Kikutake's associates was Kurokawa Kishō (born 1934), who was responsible for the design of the Great Japan Exhibition held at the Royal Academy in London in 1981–2. Another able Japanese architect who has produced aesthetically pleasing modern buildings is Maki Fumihiko (born 1928)

Domestic architecture has not been overlooked by modern Japanese architects, but shortages of space have made it difficult for them to spread themselves. The emphasis placed on simple austere lines has sometimes made the houses they design seem cold and uncomfortable.

Postscript

The Japanese achievement in the post-war years has been a truly remarkable one. In 1945 Japan had been totally defeated, her industry was destroyed, and her people were cowed and near starvation. Some forty-five years later Japan had not only made an astounding economic recovery. She had a colossal balance of trade surplus. Japanese companies had established factories in developed and developing countries. Japanese investment in property, bonds and equities in foreign countries, especially in North America, was growing fast. Japanese were travelling abroad in vast numbers, and there were large communities of Japanese businessmen in all major countries, but especially in the English-speaking world. Japanese influence in international economic organizations was significant. Japan had indeed become an economic superpower.

Japan had also built up significant defence forces and the views expressed by Japanese delegates at the United Nations, where Japan sought to be a bridge between the developed countries of the West and Asia, deserved attention. But she was still ultimately dependent for her defence on the United States' nuclear umbrella and her laws did not allow her to send military observers abroad in support of United Nations operations. Japan could not be counted as a world superpower in the same league as the United States and the Soviet Union, but nor could any other power, even China, and it is hard to see why any Japanese should want Japan to have political superpower status. The Japanese suffered greatly as a result of the Second World War and were the only country to experience directly the devastation caused by nuclear weapons. The 'peace constitution' and Article 9 in particular represented the post-war feelings of the Japanese people. It has served Japan well.

The basic aim of the Japanese government and people in the post-war years was to catch up with the West. In the late 1980s some people in Japan were asking what should be her next objective. If the Japanese could not reach a consensus on where they were going, they would, so the argument went, enter the 1990s rudderless. It is easy to understand why the question is put, but do a country and a people need any objective other than to live in peace in the world and maintain and develop their living standards? Does Japan really need more than its present armed forces for its defence? Can she not contribute to world peace just as well through economic aid to and trade with developing countries as by assuming defence responsibilities abroad? It is sometimes argued that Japan is shirking and not carrying a fair burden of the costs of defence of the 'free world'. But Japanese aid has begun to increase significantly, and the burden sharing argument will carry less weight in the future. In any case those who argue for a greater Japanese defence contribution need to consider carefully the implications. No country in Asia would be happy, after their experiences in the Second World War, to see a revival of Japanese militarism, to which a major increase in Japanese defence expenditure could lead.

Where a balance exists, as it does at present, between the two main superpowers

303

and there is no likely military threat in the foreseeable future from the only other potential superpower (China), the pressure on Japan to assume a larger political role should be containable. But the Japanese do have reasons to feel uneasy.

They note the strong Soviet forces to the north of the Japanese islands and have doubts about the stability of the Gorbachev regime in the Soviet Union. They also wonder how China will develop. Will Chinese economic reforms succeed? If they do, what will this mean ultimately for Japan's own dominant economic position in Asia? If they do not succeed and chaos were to recur in China, what would this imply for Japan? The brutal suppression of the efforts of Chinese students and workers in June 1989 to achieve a more democratic regime in China came as a shock to the Japanese, although because of Japanese trading interests in China the Japanese reaction was more muted than that of the Americans and the Europeans.

The Japanese are worried by the huge US trade and budget deficits. Some doubt how long the United States will be able and willing to maintain its position as one of the two superpowers. US-Japan friction over trade and investment grew increasingly acrimonious in the late 1980s and posed a serious threat to the stability of the US-Japan relationship.

Major world political issues will increasingly impinge on Japan in the 1990s, and it will require sound leadership if Japan is to maintain balanced progress and solve the problems of economic friction with North America and Europe. Unfortunately in 1989 it seemed doubtful whether Japan would find wise and effective leaders who will ensure the survival of a real parliamentary democracy and the substantial and significant changes required to improve the quality of life for the ordinary Japanese. There are many question marks over Japan's future, and predictions are inevitably superficial and tentative.

A recrudescence of ultra-nationalism seems unlikely but cannot be ruled out, particularly if the prestige of parliamentary institutions continues to fall. Any attempt to amend the present constitution would be strongly opposed and could lead to violent disturbances if pressed. It is therefore unlikely to be proposed unless attitudes and circumstances change radically.

Factionalism and attachment to money politics have been problems for the Japanese electorate and politicians at least since the first Meiji constitution and in 1989 it seemed unlikely that effective political reforms which would change the pattern could be enforced but the LDP had lost its majority in the upper house because of money scandals and the unpopular consumption tax. Japanese politics which had been stable for decades under a conservative-led coalition of factions had become much more fluid. In 1989, the JSP had achieved significant gains. But there were real doubts about whether the JSP could stop its ideological bickering and put forward policies which would present the electorate with a reasonable and acceptable alternative. The LDP have hoped that if they were to lose their majority in the lower house they could get the support of one or more of the centre parties (Komeito or DSP) for an LDP dominated coalition in return for a share in power and some modification of LDP policies. But in 1989 the LDP position seemed threatened. The LDP will need to adapt significantly to the changing political and economic environment if they are to regain popular support and retain power.

The present constituency system with its inequalities beween rural and urban voters should be reformed, but many in the LDP and the opposition parties would lose if radical changes were made such as the adoption of one member constituencies on the British model. The power of interest groups such as farmers and small shopkeepers ought to be reduced to the benefit of the consumers, but such groups are well-organized and vocal while consumers seem to lack the power to exert effective pressure on politicians.

Japanese society will alter as the new post-war generation assumes greater power in the civil service, politics and business, but changes are unlikely to be more than gradual. The status of women has improved, but despite Miss Doi Takako's efforts it will be difficult for Japanese women to achieve real equality with men. There is no obvious reason why crime should soar in Japan. Barring natural disasters such as a major earthquake, Japan should continue to be a safe place in which to live. Japanese will want to work fewer hours and have more leisure. But competition and peer group opinion are likely to militate against any very significant alteration in Japanese attitudes to work. Japanese savings rates will probably continue to fall, but will remain high by the standards of other developed countries. The cost of land and housing will be one factor. Another will be the salary system with two annual bonuses. But the most significant will be the ageing society. Indeed, this is likely to be Japan's biggest social and economic problem in the early years of the twenty-first century. Another significant issue will be education. The Japanese problem is not that of standards, as in Britain and North America, but rather how to maintain standards while reducing the 'examination hell' and developing personality and originality.

Despite, or perhaps because of, Japan's economic successes Japan will encounter major economic problems in the 1990s. Japan's continuing trade surplus and protectionism, especially in agriculture, are likely to mean that trade friction with developed countries will remain a major issue in Japanese foreign relations. Japanese investment abroad in developing countries will probably lead to increasing accusations of economic imperialism. At home the Japanese economy has so far managed to avoid major unemployment and the hollowing out of industry as production moves abroad. This has been achieved by great flexibility in industry and a conscious move up-market to greater value-added products. This move has been made possible by the high standards of education in Japan, especially technical education, and by the willingness of the work force to adapt to new requirements. It will not necessarily be as easy to maintain this process, especially if the value of the Japanese yen is forced up under pressure from Japan's favourable trade balance and as a result of economic friction with developed countries. Other continuing economic problems will include the need for further tax reform and further liberalization of distribution and financial services. There will also be difficulties for Japanese companies in expanding abroad by mergers and acquisitions unless ways can be found to make it easier for foreign companies to acquire Japanese companies. The pace of Japanese investment in infrastructure, including roads and drains, will have to be maintained, but even at present high growth rates it will be difficult to keep the expanding traffic of modern Japan moving. Protection of the environment and of the natural beauty of the Japanese islands should be a major issue for the Japanese, but it is by no means certain that it will be given the priority it deserves.

The intermingling of Japanese and western culture will continue. Japanese culture will be increasingly internationalized in the sense that Japanese literature and Japanese art will become better known abroad. Western culture will become still more an integral part of modern Japanese life. Japan is unlikely to lose its cultural identity in the process. Japanese culture over the centuries has been eclectic and has managed to make something essentially Japanese of what it has absorbed from abroad. Japanese introspection about the nature of Japan and the Japanese heritage could harm the process of development and of internationalization. Japanese uniqueness needs to be seen as the myth which it is.

Perhaps the most important requirement for the future healthy development of Japan and her culture is for the Japanese people not to take themselves too seriously. No student of Japan can fail to see the great achievements of Japanese civilization and Japanese people, but these achievements need to be seen in context and with a sense of both proportion and humour.

Notes

Chapter 1

1. See Ryūnosuke Tsunoda, *Japan in the Chinese Dynastic Histories*, South Pasadene, P. D. and Ione Perkins, 1951.
2. The *Kojiki* was written in Chinese characters generally used phonetically to reproduce early Japanese words (see Chapter II), but it also used various Chinese words and constructions. The translation by Basil Hall Chamberlain was first published by the Asiatic Society of Japan, in Tokyo in 1883, reprinted in 1973. A new translation by Donald L. Philippi was published in Tokyo in 1968.
3. The *Nihonshoki* was written in Chinese, although Japanese names had to be written phonetically as in the *Kojiki*.
4. The eighteenth-century Japanese nationalist scholar Motoori Norinaga argued that *matsuigoto* originally meant 'to offer services to the Emperor'.

Chapter 2

1. Quotation from Sir Charles Eliot, *Japanese Buddhism* London, 1935, p. 34.
2. Prince Naka no Oe (626–72) became Crown Prince and later Emperor, assuming the name of Tenchi or Tenji, and reigned from 661 to 672, although his formal enthronement did not take place until 668. Between 661 and 668 he preferred to exercise power in his capacity as regent.

Chapter 3

1. Donald L. Philippi has produced a new translation of the *norito*, *Norito, A New Translation of the Ancient Japanese Ritual Prayers*, Tokyo, 1959.
2. R. H. Brower and E. Miner, *Japanese Court Poetry*, London, 1962, p. 149.
3. Cf. W. G. Aston, *Japanese Literature*, London, 1899, p. 31.
4. R. H. Brower and E. Miner, *Japanese Court Poetry*, pp. 136 and 508.
5. Ibid., p. 88.
6. Ibid., p. 103.
7. Ibid., p. 112.
8. Ibid., p. 150.
9. The *Manyōshū* (published with roman-script Japanese text) Tokyo, 1940, p. 296.

Chapter 4

1. The Genpei wars (i.e. the rivalry between the Minamoto and the Taira clans), which lasted between 1156 and 1185, were the precursor of the subsequent Kamakura period and are covered in Chapter V.
2. Sir George Sansom, *A History of Japan to 1334*, Vol. I of a 3 volume work, London, 1958, p. 136.
3. Ibid., p. 146.
4. Translated by Ivan Morris under the title *As I Crossed a Bridge of Dreams*, London, 1971, p. 41. The reference to Mount Fuji is on p. 48.
5. Translated by Uwano Zendo in *Kodansha Encyclopedia of Japan*, Tokyo, 1983, Vol. 3, p. 332.

6. Sir Charles Eliot, *Japanese Buddhism*, London, 1935, p. 340.
7. Ibid., p. 344.
8. Ivan Morris, *The World of the Shining Prince*, London, 1964, p. 93.
9. Ibid., p. 130.
10. Ibid., p. 127.
11. Ibid., p. 198.
12. Ibid., p. 195.
13. James Murdoch, *A History of Japan*, Vol. I, 2nd impression, London, 1925, p. 230.
14. *The Pillow Book of Sei Shōnogon*, translated and edited by Ivan Morris, London, 1967, p. 196.
15. Ivan Morris, *The World of the Shining Prince*, p. 18.
16. Ibid., p. 197.
17. R. H. Brower and E. Miner, *Japanese Court Poetry*, London, 1962, p. 3.
18. Donald Keene, *Anthology of Japanese Literature*, London, 1956, p. 76.
19. Cf. R. H. Brower and E. Miner, *Japanese Court Poetry*.
20. Translated by Donald Keene, *Anthology of Japanese Literature*, pp. 77, 78, 79 and 81.
21. Translated by Donald Keene under the title 'The Tale of the Bamboo Cutter', *Monumenta Nipponica* (Tokyo), 11 April 1956.
22. Translated as *Tales of Ise: Lyrical Episodes from Tenth-Century Japan*, by Helen Craig McCullough, Stanford, 1968.
23. Translated by Wilfrid Whitehouse as *The Tale of the Lady Ochikubo*, London, 1934.
24. Arthur Waley's translation of *The Tale of Genji*, 2 volumes, Boston and New York, 1935.
25. Edward Seidensticker's translation of *The Tale of Genji*, 2 volumes, New York, 1976.
26. A translation of sixty-two stories from the *Konjaku monogatari* by Marion Ury was published under the title *Tales of Times Now Past*, Berkeley, Calif., 1979.
27. Douglas Mills, *A Collection of Tales from Uji: A Study and Translation of 'Uji shūi monogatari'*, Cambridge, 1970.
28. *The Okagami*, translated by Joseph K. Yamagiwa, London, 1967.
29. *The Tosa Diary*, translated by William N. Porter, 1912, and by Earl Miner in *Japanese Poetic Diaries*, 1969.
30. Ivan Morris, *As I Crossed a Bridge of Dreams*.
31. Translated by Edward Seidensticker under the title *The Gossamer Years*, Tokyo, 1964.
32. Translated by Richard Bowring, *Murasaki Shikibu: Her Diary and Poetic Memoirs*, Princeton, 1982.
33. Translated by Edwin A. Cranston under the title *The Izumi Shikibu Diary: A Romance of the Heian Court*, Cambridge, Massachusetts, 1969; and by Earl Miner in *Japanese Poetic Diaries*.
34. Ivan Morris, '*The Pillow Book of Sei Shōnagon*', with quotations from pp. 50, 51, 56, 57, 64, 93, 186. Selections from the diary were translated by Arthur Waley under the same title, London, 1928.
35. William Watson, *Sculpture of Japan (From the Fifth to the Fifteenth Century)*, London, 1959, p. 32.
36. Sir Francis Piggot, *The Music and Musical Instruments of Japan*, London, 1893, p. 5.
37. Ivan Morris, *The World of the Shining Prince*, p. 190.
38. Richard Bowring, *Murasaki Shikibu: Her Diary and Poetic Memoirs*, p. 51.

Chapter 5

1. *Heike monogatari*, as translated by A. L. Sadler as *The Tales of the Heike*, Sydney, 1928, pp. 106–9.
2. Quoted by Sir George Sansom in *A History of Japan to 1334*, London, 1958, p. 397.
3. Ibid., p. 368.

4. Inazo Nitobe, *Bushido, The Soul of Japan*, Tokyo, 1900, p. 7.
5. Sir George Sansom, *A History of Japan to 1334*, p. 367.
6. Louis Frederic, *Daily Life in Japan at the Time of the Samurai, 1185–1603*, London, 1972, p. 199.
7. Sir George Sansom on Nichiren in Sir Charles Eliot's *Japanese Buddhism*, London, 1935, p. 431.
8. Ibid., p. 417.
9. E. Dale Saunders, *Buddhism in Japan*, Philadelphia, 1964; reprinted Tokyo, 1980, p. 206.
10. Suzuki Daisetsu, *An Introduction to Zen Buddhism*, London, 1948, p. 108.
11. Ibid., pp. 104 and 105.
12. E. Dale Saunders, *Buddhism in Japan*, p. 213.
13. Sir George Sansom, *Japan: A Short Cultural History*, revised edn, London, 1946, p. 339.
14. Donald Keene, *Anthology of Japanese Literature*, London, 1956, pp. 195 and 196. See also *Mirror for the Moon*, a selection of poems by Saigyō translated with an introduction by William R. Lafleur, New York, 1978.
15. Ibid., p. 192.
16. R. H. Brower and E. Miner, *Japanese Court Poetry*, London, 1962, p. 261.
17. Ibid., pp. 266 and 293.
18. *Tsutsumi Chūnagon monogatari*, translated by Umeyo Hirano, Tokyo, 1963. *Mushi mezuru himegimi*, translated as *The Lady Who Loved Insects* by Arthur Waley, London, 1929.
19. Jetavana was the monastery park at Savatthi.
20. A. L. Sadler, *The Ten Foot Square Hut and Tales of the Heike*, Sydney, 1928, p. 22. A new translation of the whole of the *Heike monogatari*, by Professor Helen Craig McCullough, appears under the title *The Tale of the Heike*, Stanford, Calif. 1988. McCullough's translation of this passage reads as follows: 'The sound of the Gion Shoja bells echoes the impermanence of all things; the colour of the *sala* flowers reveals the truth that the prosperous must decline. The proud do not endure, they are like a dream on a spring night; the mighty fall at last, they are as dust before the wind.' (p. 23)
21. A. L. Sadler, *The Ten Foot Square Hut and Tales of the Heike*, pp. 1–21.
22. As translated by Donald Keene in *Anthology of Japanese Literature*.

Chapter 6

1. The *Jinnō Shōtōki* has been translated by H. Paul Varley under the title *A Chronicle of Gods and Sovereigns*, New York, 1980.
2. Quoted by Sir George Sansom, *History of Japan, 1334–1615*, London, 1961, p. 41.
3. Firearms in Japan were at first called *tanegashima* after the island.
4. Coins cast in the Hung-wu era (1368–98) were called *kōbusen*, and those cast in the Yung-le era (1403–24) were called *eirakusen*.
5. Towns which sprang up at the gates of temples were called *monzenmachi*, and those around castles were called *jōkamachi*.
6. Yokkaichi, for instance, is the name of a city where there was a market on the 4th day of the month.
7. *Za* came to be used for other groups such as actors. Hence the name Kabukiza for the Kabuki theatre in Tokyo. The Ginza shopping area in Tokyo comes from a combination of the words *gin* and *za* where *gin* means silver, i.e. the area of the silversmiths.
8. See article on 'Population' in Kōdansha's *Encyclopedia of Japan*, Tokyo, 1983, Vol. 6, p. 222.

9. P. G. O'Neill, 'A *Michiyuki* Passage from the *Taiheiki*', *Bulletin of the School of Oriental and African Studies, University of London*, vol. XXXVI, part 2, (1973), pp. 360–1. The *Taiheiki* has been translated into English by Helen Craig McCullough, New York, 1959.

10. Douglas Mills has commented: 'As literature, the *Soga monogatari* is rather tedious, being overloaded with religious propaganda, but its evolution in various literary genres well repays study': Kōdansha's *Encyclopedia of Japan*, Vol. 7, p. 221; *The Tale of the Soga Brothers*, translated by Thomas J. Cogan, Tokyo, 1987.

11. Extracts taken from Donald Keene's translation published under the title *Essays in Idleness*, New York, 1967, (see sections 43, 72, 82 and 211 of translation). There have also been translations by William Porter and Sir George Sansom.

12. Translated by Donald Keene, *Anthology of Japanese Literature*, London, 1956, pp. 315–16.

13. Katō Shūichi, *A History of Japanese Literature, the First Thousand Years*, London, 1979, p. 296, quotes the following statement about *renga* by Nijō Yoshimoto: '*Renga* does not join one idea with the next. Success and failure, joy and sorrow, succeed one after another as often happens in this world. Even as one thinks of yesterday, today is gone; when one thinks of spring, autumn has come and cherry blossoms have become *momiji* [maple leaves]'.

14. P. G. O'Neill, *A Guide to Nō*, Tokyo, 1954, p. 1.

15. Arthur Waley, *The Nō Plays of Japan*, London, 1921, p. 50, commented of Zeami (Seami): 'He was not a profound or systematic thinker. More of a courtier than a philosopher, he was apt in moments of cynicism to regard the applause of his audience as the sole end of his art, and even to be indifferent whence that applause came.'

16. Translated by Arthur Waley in *The Nō Plays of Japan*, p. 224. Words spoken by the Chorus.

17. P. G. O'Neill, 'The Nō Plays *Koi no Omoni* and *Yuya*', *Monumenta Nipponica*, vol. X, 1–2 (1954), pp. 218–19. The 'Burning House' is a reference to a 'well-known Buddhist parable of the rich man's house catching fire with his children inside absorbed in their play. They are only persuaded to leave by being told that waiting outside are three carriages drawn by sheep, deer and oxen. The rich man represents the Buddha, the burning house the present world and the carriages the *sanjōkyō*, the Three Vehicles of Buddhist doctrine.'

18. Dr Richard N. McKinnon, *Selected Plays of Kyōgen*, Tokyo, 1968, as quoted in a lecture by Dr McKinnon to the Asiatic Society of Japan in May 1984, *Asiatic Society Bulletin*, no. 6 (June 1984), p. 3.

19. James T. Araki, *The Ballad-Drama of Medieval Japan*, Berkeley, Calif., 1964; p. 9 in the edition published by Charles E. Tuttle, Rutland, Vt, and Tokyo, 1978.

20. Saihōji is open only to visitors applying in advance, paying a hefty fee, listening to a Buddhist sermon and copying part of a Buddhist sutra.

21. Ryōanji attracts almost endless groups of tourists, and to find tranquillity it is necessary to visit the temple at an unpopular time out of the tourist season.

Chapter 7

1. The Momoyama period is also known as the Azuchi-Momoyama period. Azuchi was the name of the castle which Oda Nobunaga built on the shores of Lake Biwa near Kyoto. Momoyama was the name of Toyotomi Hideyoshi's castle at Fushimi on the outskirts of Kyoto. The period could be said to have ended with the battle of Sekigahara in 1600 as a result of which Tokugawa Ieyasu ensured the supremacy of his house or in 1603 when he had himself appointed shōgun. But it is convenient to end this chapter with the death of Ieyasu in 1616 following the final defeat of Toyotomi Hideyori, Hideyoshi's only son, and the fall of Osaka castle.

2. Professor C. R. Boxer entitled his masterly study of the first Christians in Japan *The Christian Century in Japan 1549–1650*. It was published in London in 1951.
3. The size of fiefs was measured by the number of *koku* of rice which the land in the fief was supposed to provide as determined by the census which began in 1590. A *koku* of rice was equivalent to about 182 litres (just over 5 bushels) and was supposed to provide enough cereals to feed one man for a year.
4. The central keep of Nijō castle was transferred from Hideyoshi's castle at Fushimi.
5. The Hiunkaku is normally closed to the public, but other parts of the Nishihonganji are open to applicants.
6. Fernao Mendes Pinto was born between 1509 and 1514. He probably visited Japan for the first time in about 1544. He wrote a book entitled *Peregrinacum* about his travels. A draft seems to have been available about 1569 but it was not published until 1614 (see Professor C. R. Boxer's *The Christian Century in Japan*, pp. 18 ff.).
7. Sir George Sansom, *A History of Japan 1334–1615*, London, 1961, p. 374.
8. *Anjin* was a word used to denote a ship's pilot. William Adams (1564–1620) has been the subject of various works in English including James Clavell's novel *Shōgun*, London, 1976.
9. During the Keichō period (1596–1614) eighty-two ship-owners are recorded as having received permits, and 182 voyages were authorized. Among the ship-owners receiving permits were fourteen Europeans.
10. Professor C. R. Boxer, *The Christian Century in Japan*, p. 361.
11. *Nanban* means 'southern barbarian'. The Portuguese coming from Macao were approaching Japan from the south. The word was used generally for art inspired by the Europeans as well as for works of art produced by the missionaries.
12. It has also been suggested that the word *tempura* may come from the Spanish word *templo*, meaning a temple, the implication being that it derived from the Christian practice of not eating meat on Fridays or during Lent.
13. The best collection of paintings by Catholic artists is in the Kobe City Museum.
14. Fine examples of Nanban screens can be seen in the Kobe City Museum and the Osaka Nanban Museum (a private foundation). There are also some very fine examples in the Museo Nacional de Arte Antiga in Lisbon.
15. One of the most celebrated pairs of map screens is held by Jōtokuji temple in Fukui city. It dates from the 1590s. It has been ascribed to Kanō Eitoku, but this seems doubtful. Kanō-school artists, however, certainly produced some fine map screens.

Chapter 8

1. The period is called Edo or Tokugawa, because the Tokugawa shōguns had their capital in Edo. It can be said to date from 1600, the year in which the battle of Sekigahara was fought, or from 1603, when Tokugawa Ieyasu had himself declared shōgun. But the death of Ieyasu following the fall of Osaka catle and the death of Toyotomi Hideyori mark a significant turning-point in Japanese history, hence the selection of 1616 as the date for the beginning of this chapter. The period ended either in 1867 when the last Tokugawa shōgun resigned or in 1868 when the 'restoration' of the Emperor was proclaimed and Edo, renamed Tokyo, became the imperial capital instead of Kyoto. But the arrival of the 'black ships' of the US Navy commanded by Commodore Perry in 1853 were a turning-point for Japan and marked the beginning of the end of the shōgunate.
2. The *Hizakurige* by Jippensha Ikku was translated under the title *Shank's Mare* by Thomas Satchell and published in Kobe in 1929.
3. Oliver Statler in his book *Japanese Inn*, New York, 1961, has described the history of one of the Tōkaidō inns, the Minaguchiya.
4. Jūkichi was returned to Hokkaidō despite the *bakufu*'s ban on returnees. Katherine

Plummer in her book *The Shōgun's Reluctant Ambassadors*, Tokyo, 1984, has described the story of these 'sea drifters'.

5. Engelbert Kaempfer's *History of Japan* was first published in English in 1727. It contains careful accounts of Japanese flora and fauna as well as many other facts which he had gleaned about Japan. He also gives accounts of the journeys of two Dutch missions to Edo in 1691 and 1692.

6. Okinawa and the Ryūkyū Islands still have Chinese elements in their culture.

7. The *kabunakama* were monopolistic trade associations which restricted access to trade and set prices (see Kōdansha's *Encyclopedia of Japan*, Tokyo, 1983, Vol. 4, p. 100).

8. Historians consider the Tempō reforms the least successful of the three major reform movements in the Edo period.

9. The *Dainihonshi* was only completed in 1906.

10. *Kabuki* performances today may last as long as five hours and usually consist of a number of contrasting pieces including acts or extracts from full-length plays.

11. See Professor C. J. Dunn's article on Chikamatsu Monzaemon in Kōdansha's *Encyclopedia of Japan*, Vol. 1, pp. 275–6.

12. Translated by Donald Keene in *Anthology of Japanese Literature*, London, 1956, p. 404.

13. The writing of short stories had begun in the Kamakura period and continued in the Muromachi period. In the Edo period these stories were called *otogi-zōshi* ('companion stories'). They should not be confused with *otogi-banashi* ('fairy tales') such as *Urashima-tarō* and *Issun-bōshi* ('Tom Thumb') which were, however, among the stories published in the *Otogi-bunkō*.

14. *Kōshoku ichidai otoko* was translated as *The Life of an Amorous Man* by Hamada Kengi, Tokyo, 1964.

15. *Kōshoku gonin onna* was translated as *Five Women Who Loved Love* by Wm Theodore de Bary, Tokyo, 1956.

16. *Kōshoku ichidai onna* was translated as *The Life of an Amorous Woman* by Ivan Morris, London, 1963.

17. *Nippon eitaigura* was translated as *The Japanese Family Storehouse or The Millionaires' Gospel Modernized* by G. W. Sargent, Cambridge, 1959. The passages quoted are from this translation.

18. *Seken nune sanyō* was translated as *This Scheming World* by Takatsuka Masanori and David C. Stubbs, Tokyo, 1965.

19. One of the stories from *Seken musume katagi* ('Characters of Worldly Young Women') and five stories from *Seken musuko katagi* ('Characters of Worldly Young Men') have been translated by Howard Hibbett in *The Floating World in Japanese Fiction*, Oxford, 1959.

20. *Ugetsu monogatari* has been translated as *Tales of Moonlight and Rain* by Leon Zolbrod, London, 1974.

21. *Nansō Satomi hakkenden* has not so far been translated into English; it would probably not find a wide readership.

22. See note 2.

23. See Robert Leutner, *Shikitei Sanba and the Comic Tradition in Edo Fiction*, London, 1985. The passage quoted is on pp. 142–3.

24. *Oku no Hosomichi* has been translated as *The Narrow Road to the Deep North* by Professor Yuasa Noriyuki, London, 1966; and as *A Haiku Journey: Bashō's Narrow Road to a Far Province* by Dorothy Britton, revised edn, Tokyo, 1980.

25. The *haiku* quoted from *Oku no Hosomichi* are as translated by Dorothy Britton. See pp. 57, 62, 63, 68, 72, 79.

26. A selection of *haiku* by Issa have been translated by Duncan Macfarlane under the pseudonym Lewis Mackenzie in *The Autumn Wind*, London, 1957.

27. *Shōji* are sliding windows made of paper. The Ama-no-gawa is the Milky Way.

28. Donald Keene in *World within Walls*, New York, 1976, p. 527.

29. R. H. Blyth in *Senryū: Japanese Satirical Verses*, Tokyo, 1949, p. 57.
30. The first two *senryū* are as quoted and translated by Donald Keene in *World within Walls*, p. 528. *Ofukuro*, literally 'the honorable bag', is a vulgar way of referring to a person's mother. By threatening to go a long way away to work the young man won his mother's agreement to what he wanted.
31. The second two *senryū* are as quoted and translated by R. H. Blyth, *Senryū: Japanese Satirical Verses*, pp. 17, 29.
32. Koyama Fujio, a famous Japanese art critic, considered Ninsei 'a potter of matchless fame' and 'possibly Japan's most admired individual ceramic artist'. Soames Jenyns, after quoting the above comments in *Japanese Pottery*, London, 1971, declares (p. 200) that 'Ninsei's wares seem to Europeans fussy, meticulous and over ornate.'
33. One of Ninsei's *chatsubo* with a plum blossom design is held by the National Museum at Ueno, another with a decoration of wisteria flowers is in the MOA Museum at Atami, and a third with a design of Mount Yoshino is in the Fukuoka Municipal Museum.
34. The English potter Bernard Leach made a study of Kenzan and his successors and wrote *Kenzan and his Tradition*, London, 1966.
35. There is a fine collection of *ko-kutani* wares in the prefectural art gallery by the Kenrokuen park in Kanazawa.

Chapter 9

1. The period from 1853 to 1868 is called *bakumatsu* ('*end of the bakufu*'). The year 1868 marks the nominal restoration of power to the Emperor. After the era-name of the Emperor Mutsuhito, it is called the Meiji period. This lasted until the death of the Emperor Mutsuhito in 1912. 1894 was the year in which agreement was reached on the revision of the 'unequal' treaties and the beginning of the Sino-Japanese war. It was accordingly a turning-point in Japanese history.
2. Matsudaira Yoshinaga of Echizen (Fukui prefecture) was also known as Keiei or Shungaku.
3. One member of the suite was Fukuzawa Yukichi (1835–1901), who later founded Keiō University in Tokyo.
4. The captain of the *Kanrin-maru* was Katsu Kaishū (1823–99), the dean of the naval academy which had been established in Nagasaki. He became the leading figure in the build-up of the *bakufu*'s naval forces.
5. The mission seemed exotic to the eyes of the inhabitants of Victorian London, and they were widely fêted. Fukuzawa Yukichi was their official interpreter. He was astonished and gratified when a member of parliament showed him a draft resolution criticizing Rutherford Alcock for his high-handed attitude towards the Japanese (see Grace Fox, *Britain and Japan 1858–1883*, Oxford, 1969, p. 94).
6. Nine of the ships were British. The remainder except for one US ship came from Holland and France.
7. Saigō Takamori had originally worked for Shimazu Nariakira, but had been twice banished for his part in anti-*bakufu* activities. He had also had various differences with Shimazu Hisamitsu (also called Saburō).
8. A. B. Mitford (later Lord Redesdale) has left a vivid account of this ritual suicide in his *Tales of Old Japan*, London, 1871. See also *Mitford's Japan*, edited by Hugh Cortazzi, London, 1985.
9. Ozaki Yukio, *The Voice of Japanese Democracy*, Yokohama, 1918; quoted by E. H. Norman in *Japan's Emergence as a Modern State*, New York, 1946, p. 86.
10. Cf. Sir George Sansom, *The Western World and Japan*, London, 1950, pp. 470–6.
11. The Rokumeikan was renamed the Peers' Hall in 1890. It was knocked down in 1941.
12. Under the 1858 treaties foreigners wishing to travel outside the areas of the treaty

ports had to seek permission from the Japanese authorities through their consular representatives and obtain special passports.

13. The factory consisted of 3,640 spindles and was supplied by Pratt and Company of Manchester. After the restoration the factory was moved to Sakai, part of Osaka, and was designated as official factory No. 1.
14. These foreign experts were referred to as *o-yatoi gaijin*. For a detailed account of these foreign experts see H. J. Jones, *Live Machines, Hired Foreigners and Meiji Japan*, Vancouver, 1980.
15. Sir George Sansom, *The Western World and Japan*, London, 1950, p. 491.
16. Ibid., p. 457.
17. Nishi Amane, despite his interest in western modes of thought, was a strong supporter of military discipline and obedience to authority.
18. Fukuzawa did not think that *jiyū* was a particularly appropriate word to express the meaning of 'liberty' but he could not think of a better word.
19. Children are still taken to be blessed at local shrines; prayers for examination success continue to be made at shrines dedicated to Sugawara Michizane (*Tenjin-sama*). Marriage ceremonies, including the drinking of sake in the *san-san-kudō* ('three-three-nine-times') rite, are held at Shintō shrines. Many Japanese today visit famous shrines at New Year, and ceremonies connected with the planting and harvesting of rice are observed by the Emperor. But funerals are almost always conducted in accordance with Buddhist rites.
20. Dr D. C. Holtom, *The National Faith of Japan*, London, 1936, p. 273, described the *Doro-umi Koki* ('Ancient Chronicle of the Mud-Sea') as a highly imaginative and mythological book of allegories' which impressed him vividly with its 'muddy incomprehensibility'.
21. Donald Keene, *Modern Japanese Literature*, New York, 1956, p. 13, has commented that in 1868 'Japanese Literature had dropped to one of its lowest levels. The popular authors of the time specialized in books of formless, almost meaningless gossip. The country ... seemed to have exhausted its own resources.'
22. Ibid., pp. 59–69, for an extract in translation. See also Marleigh Grayer Ryan, *Japan's First Modern Novel: 'Ukigumo' of Futabatei Shimei*, New York, 1967.
23. Ibid., pp. 70–110, translation by Edward Seidensticker under the title *Growing Up*.
24. See Sigfrid Wichman, *Japonisme*, London, 1981.
25. According to Basil Hall Chamberlain in *Things Japanese*, Tokyo, 1890, the popular theory was that the *jinrikisha* was suggested by an American named Goble, half-cobbler and half-missionary, in about 1867.

Chapter 10

1. Maruyama Masao, *Thought and Behaviour in Modern Japanese Politics*, London, 1963, p. 65.
2. This rule was modified in the 1920s to allow retired officers to fill these posts. It was restated in its original form in 1936 during the government of Hirota Kōki (1878–1948), who was eventually executed as a major war criminal.
3. Professor Ian Nish, *The Origins of the Russo-Japanese War*, London and New York, 1985, p. viii.
4. As in 1894 the Japanese leaders showed their contempt for the niceties of diplomacy and international law. The precedent had been clearly set for the attack on Pearl Harbour in December 1941 before the Americans had received Japan's declaration of war.
5. The Liberal Party was called in Japanese the Jiyūtō. It had been established in 1881 by Itagaki Taisuke, was disbanded in 1884 and reformed in 1890 and 1891. The Constitutional Reform Party was called in Japanese the Rikken Kaishintō. It was

established in 1882 by Okuma Shigenobu and renamed the Progressive Party (Shimpōtō in 1896.

6. An English version of this essay was included in *Fifty Years of New Japan* by Count Okuma Shigenobu, published in London, 1909, Vol. I, pp. 122–32. The quotation is from pp. 128–9.

7. The Kensei Hontō changed its name in 1910, 1913 and 1916, when it became known as the Constitutional Association (Kenseikai). Finally it was called the Constitutional Democratic Party (Rikken Minseitō or Minseitō for short). This name lasted until 1940 when the old political parties were disbanded.

8. A shrine to General Nogi Maresuke was built in Tokyo near Roppongi where his house has been preserved.

9. Hugh Byas, *Government by Assassination*, London, 1943.

10. Morgan Young, *Japan under Taishō Tennō*, London, 1928, p. 120.

11. Professor W. J. Beasley, *Japanese Imperialism*, London, 1987, pp. 168–9.

12. Hiranuma Kiichirō was tried as a major war criminal after the war and sentenced to life imprisonment. He died in prison.

13. Morgan Young, *Japan under Taishō Tennō*, p. 280.

14. Manchukuo (Manshūkoku) comprised all of Manchuria and a part of Inner Mongolia. When it was established it consisted of China's three north-eastern provinces – Liaoning. Kirin (Jilin) and Heilungkiang (Heilongjiang). The province of Jehol (Rihe) was annexed to Manchukuo in 1933. Manchukuo was largely populated by Manchurian Chinese and Mongols.

15. Maruyama Masao, *Thought and Behaviour in Japanese Politics*, pp. 5 and 9.

16. Richard Storry, *The Double Patriots*, London, 1957, p. 300.

17. Winston Churchill, who was Prime Minister at the opening of the conference, which lasted from 17 July to 2 August 1945, returned to London on 25 July 1945. Following the Conservative defeat in the British general election and the victory of the Labour Party, Churchill's place at the conference was taken by Clement Attlee, the Labour leader.

18. *Konjiki yasha* was translated by Arthur Lloyd into English as *The Golden Demon*, Tokyo, 1917.

19. *Gen oji* was translated by Houston Brock as *Old Gen*; see Donald Keene, *Modern Japanese Literature*, New York, 1956.

20. *Hakai* was translated by Kenneth Strong as *The Broken Commandment*, Tokyo, 1975. *Ie* was translated by Cecilia Segawa Seigle as *The Family*, Tokyo, 1976.

21. *Futon* was translated by Kenneth G. Henshall as *The Quilt*, Tokyo, 1981.

22. *Ippeisotsu* was translated by G. W. Sargent as *One Soldier* in Donald Keene's *Modern Japanese Literature*, Stanford, California, 1956.

23. Professor Edward Seidensticker, *Kafu the Scribbler*, 1965, found much in Kafu's writings to inspire his own interest in the city of Tokyo; see his *Low City High City: Tokyo 1867–1923*, New York, 1983. *Sumidagawa* was translated by Donald Keene in *Modern Japanese Literature*. *Bokutō kidan* was translated by Edward Seidensticker as *A Strange Tale from East of the River* in *Kafu the Scribbler* reprinted separately in Tokyo, 1972.

24. Many of Natsume Soseki's novels have been translated into English, including *Wagahai wa neko de aru* – translated as *I Am a Cat*, London, 1961; *Botchan*, Rutland, Vermont and Tokyo, 1972; *Kusamakura* – *The Three-Cornered World*, London, 1963; *Sanshiro*, Seattle, 1977; *Sorekara* – *And Then*, 1978; *Mon* – *The Gate*, London, 1972; *Kokoro*, Chicago, 1957; *Michikusa Grass in the Wayside*, Chicago, 1969.

25. Excerpts from *Gan* were translated by Burton Watson under the title *The Wild Goose*; in Donald Keene, *Modern Japanese Literature*.

26. *Anya Kōro* was translated by Edwin McClellan as *A Dark Night's Passing*, London, 1976.

27. Many of Akutagawa Ryunosuke's stories have been translated into English, e.g. in *Tales Grotesque and Curious* by Glen W. Shaw, Tokyo, 1930; *'Rashōmon' and other Stories* by Kojima Takashi and John McVittie, New York, 1964; two stories including *Jigokuhen*, translated by W. H. H. Norman, in Donald Keene, *Modern Japanese Literature*.
28. A translation of *Chichi Kaeru* under the title *The Father Returns* appeared in Glenn W. Shaw's *Tōjūrō's Love and Four Other Plays*, Tokyo, 1925. A translation of Kikuchi Kan's *Okujō no kyōjin* by Iwasaki Yōzan and Glenn Hughes under the title *The Madman on the Roof* appeared in Donald Keene's *Modern Japanese Literature*.
29. *Kani kosen* was translated by Frank Motofuji as *The Factory Ship*, Tokyo, 1973. *Jizai jinushi* was translated by Frank Motofuji as *The Absentee Landlord*, Tokyo, 1973.
30. See Donald Keene, *Dawn to the West*, New York, 1984, pp. 916–26; and extract in Donald Keene's *Modern Japanese Literature*.
31. *Ichiaku no Suna*, translated by Sakanishi Shio as *A Handful of Sand*, Boston, 1934.
32. Translated by Shio Sakanishi and quoted in Donald Keene, *Modern Japanese Literature*.
33. Translated by Howard Hibbett and quoted in ibid.
34. Translated by Donald Keene and quoted in ibid.
35. Kaneko Mitsuharu, *Shijin* ('Poet'), translated by A. R. Davies, Sydney, 1988.
36. See Bernard Leach, *The Unknown Craftsman: A Japanese Insight into Beauty*, New York, 1972, p. 98.
37. In Japanese a person with an intuitive appreciation of the beautiful is said to be *mekiki*, which may be translated as having an effective eye.
38. Hamada Shōji collected many things including traditional Japanese farmhouses (*minka*). His collection has been preserved in Mashiko, where there is a small Hamada museum.
39. Kawai Kanjirō's house and kiln in Kyoto are preserved as a museum.
40. There are collections of Munakata's works in Aomori and Kamakura.
41. Japanese collections of Impressionist and Post-Impressionist paintings include the Matsukata collection in the Museum of Modern Art at Ueno in Tokyo, the Ohara Museum at Kurashiki and the Hiroshima Art Gallery owned by the Hiroshima Bank.
42. A gallery devoted to the work of Fujita is at Akita in northern Honshu.
43. Books by Markino include *A Japanese Artist in London*, London, 1911, and *My Recollections and Impressions*, London, 1913.

Chapter 11

1. Lt-General Sir Horace Robertson was appointed C-in-C British Commonwealth Occupation Forces (BCOF) in April 1946 in succession to General Sir John Northcott.
2. Shigemitsu Mamoru was a career diplomat who served in Europe and in China. He was a member of the Japanese delegation to the Versailles Peace Conference in 1919. After negotiating a settlement of the Shanghai incident in 1932 he was seriously injured by a bomb. He favoured an aggressive policy in China. In 1936 he was appointed Japanese Ambassador to the USSR and in 1938 to London. In 1939 he opposed an alliance with Germany and in 1941 he was against war with the USA. From April 1943 to April 1945 he was Foreign Minister. He resumed the post of Foreign Minister in August 1945 and was present at the Japanese surrender.
3. Yoshida Shigeru, *The Yoshida Memoirs*, Cambridge, Mass, 1962, p. 137.
4. Ibid., p. 135.
5. Baron E. J. Lewe van Aduard, *Japan from Surrender to Peace*, The Hague, 1953, p. 103.
6. The protection afforded to Japanese whisky distillers was a major bone of contention between the British and Japanese governments especially in the 1970s and 1980s. It was supposed to have been finally phased out by the tax reform measures which came into force from 1 April 1989.

7. Many of the stories and novels of Tanizaki Junichiro have been translated into English: e.g. Howard Hibbett, *Seven Japanese Tales*, 1963; 'The Key' (*Kagi*), New York, 1961; 'Diary of a Mad Old Man' (*Futen rojin nikki*), New York, 1965; Edward Seidensticker, *Some Prefer Nettles* (*Tade kuu mushi*), New York, 1955, and *The Makioka Sisters* (*Sasameyuki*), New York, 1957.

8. Edward Seidensticker produced translations of many of Kawabata Yasunari's novels, e.g. *Snow Country* (*Yukiguni*), New York, 1956; *The Master of Go* (*Meijin*), New York, 1972; *Thousand Cranes* (*Senbazuru*), New York, 1959; *The Sound of the Mountain*, (*Yama no oto*), New York, 1970; *The House of the Sleeping Beauties*, (*Nemureru bijo*), Tokyo, 1969; *The Tzu Dancer* (*Izu no odoriko*), Tokyo, 1974.

9. Translations of novels by Mishima Yukio include: Meredith Weatherby, *The Sound of Waves* (*Shiosai*), New York, 1956, and *Confessions of a Mask* (*Kamen no kokuhaku*), New York, 1958; Ivan Morris, *The Temple of the Golden Pavilion* (*Kinkakuji*), New York, 1959; Donald Keene, *After the Banquet* (*Utage no ato*), New York, 1963; Edward Seidensticker, *The Decay of the Angel* (*Tennin gosui*), New York, 1974; Alfred H. Marks, *Forbidden Colours* (*Kinjiki*), London, 1968.

10. Donald Keene, *Dawn to the West, Japanese Literature in the Modern Era: Fiction*, New York, 1984, p. 1195.

11. Ibid., p. 1208.

12. Ibid., p. 1216.

13. Donald Keene, *No Longer Human* (*Ningen shikkaku*), New York, 1958, and *The Setting Sun* (*Shayō*), New York, 1956.

14. John Bester, *Black Rain* (*Kuroi ame*), London, 1971.

15. Ivan Morris, *Fires on the Plain* (*Nobi*), London, 1957.

16. E. Dale Saunders, *The Woman in the Dunes* (*Suna no onna*), New York, 1964.

17. Brewster Horwitz, *Homecoming* (*Kikyō*), New York, 1954.

18. Wakako Hironaka and Ann Siller Kostant, *The Doctor's Wife* (*Hanaoka Seishū no tsuma*) by Ariyoshi Sawako, Tokyo, 1978.

19. Leon Picon, *The Counterfeiter* ('*Aru gisakka no shōgai*') *and Other Stories* by Inoue Yasushi, Tokyo, 1965.

20. William Johnston, *Silence* (*Chinmoku*) by Endō Shūsaku, Tokyo, 1969.

21. Hugh Corazzi, '*The Lucky One' and Other Humorous Stories* by Genji Keita, Tokyo, 1980.

22. Dennis Keene, *Singular Rebellion* (*Tatta hitori no hanran*) by Maruya Seiichi, London, 1988.

23. The Ninagawa *gekidan* have played before audiences in Edinburgh and London. Their performances of *Macbeth* and *Medea* in Japanese in 1988 were widely acclaimed.

24. There is an active bonsai association in London which puts on displays at e.g. the Chelsea Flower Show.

25. Higashiyama Kaii, *Screen Painting of the Tōshōdaiji* (*Tōshōdaiji mieidō shōhekiga*), Tokyo, 1975, penultimate page.

26. See e.g. Oliver Statler, *Modern Japanese Prints: An Art Reborn*, Rutland, Vt, and Tokyo, 1956.

27. Dorothy Britton and T. Hayashida, *The Japanese Crane, Bird of Happiness*, Tokyo, 1981.

Glossary

agemai – a special tax levied in the early part of the eighteenth century on the daimyō to meet a deficit in the shōgun's finances.

aikokoshugi – patriotism.

Amabe – fishermen in ancient Japan.

amakudari – literally 'descending from heaven'; phrase used to describe civil servants going into the private sector on retiring from government departments.

aragoto – literally 'rough-house stuff', a style of *kabuki* acting.

ashigaru – foot soldiers of low rank.

ayatsuri-jōruri – correct term for the Japanese puppet theatre; *ayatsuri* means to manipulate a puppet and *jōruri* means the dramatic text used and the method of chanting.

aware – pity, compassion; favourite term of Heian poets.

azuma-uta – songs from the eastern part of Japan recorded in the *Manyōshū*.

bakufu – literally 'tent government'; alternative word for shōgunate.

bakumatsu – the period when the shōgunate was coming to its end in the nineteenth century.

be – hereditary corporations or guilds in ancient Japan.

bijin-e – pictures of beauties in Japanese wood-block prints.

biwa – Japanese lute.

biwa-hōshi – itinerant lute-playing priests, usually blind, reciting famous stories.

Bizen – fief in what is now Okayama prefecture; unglazed pottery made there.

Bōeichō – Self-Defence Agency.

bonsai – miniature tree in a pot.

Bosatsu – Boddhisattva; Buddhist saint.

Boshin war – civil war of 1868–9 which confirmed the downfall of the Tokugawa shōgunate and the Meiji restoration.

bōsōzoku – groups of young people who revel in making loud noises.

botan – button, from the Portuguese.

bugaku – traditional Japanese court music and dancing.

buke-shōhattō – laws for military houses; rules set out by Tokugawa Ieyasu.

buke-yashiki – samurai dwelling.

buke-zukuri – austere form of building as a samurai dwelling.

bundai – writing desk.

bungotai – classical Japanese.

bunjin – literati.

bunmei kaika – cultural enlightenment; a favourite phrase in early Meiji times.

Bunraku – the Japanese puppet theatre.

bushi – warrior.

bushidō – way of the warrior.

Butsudan – Buddhist altar in a house.

Butsuden – Buddha hall in a temple.

byōbu – Japanese folding screen.

chajin – a devotee of the cult of tea.

cha-no-yu – the tea ceremony.

cha-shitsu – a room or house for the tea ceremony.

cha-tsubo – urn for the storage of tea.

chian-ijihō – peace preservation law.

chigaidana – shelves beside the *tokonoma*.

chika-renga – literally 'underground linked verses', meaning *renga* composed by people of inferior class.

chirimen – crêpe.

chō – a surface measure equal to 10 *tan* or 3,000 *tsubo*, about one hectare.

chōdai – curtained platform about three metres square providing a kind of bed-chamber in an aristocratic dwelling in Heian times.

chōka – long poem as in the *Manyōshū*.

chōkai – town block association.

chōnin – townsman.

chōnin-konjō – mercenary spirit.

chūban – half-size print.

chūnagon – middle counsellor.

chūyō – the middle way or mean.

daibusshi – great Buddha master-sculptor.

Daibutsu – large statue of the Buddha.

daigakuryō – university for the teaching of the Chinese classics.

daigokuden – great hall of state in the imperial palace.

daimyō – feudal lord.

daishinsai – the great earthquake of 1923 which destroyed much of Yokohama and Tokyo.

dajōdaijin – chancellor.

Dajōkan – office of the chancellor.

danshaku – baron.

dentōkōgeiten – exhibition of traditional crafts.

dō – a group of provinces, e.g. Hokkaidō, or a major road such as the Tokaidō (eastern sea road).

doki – unglazed earthenware.

Dōmei – confederation of moderate unions in the private sector.

donsu – figured damask.

dōtaku – ancient bronze bell-shaped object.

e-awase – painting contest.

eboshi – court head-dress.

Edokko – inhabitant of Edo (Tokyo).

eirakusen – Chinese coins cast in the Yung-le era (1403–24).

emaki – a picture scroll.

emishi – early inhabitants of northern Honshū and Hokkaidō (Ezo).

enryō – reserve, deference.

erizeni – selecting out good coins.

enza – traditional Japanese doctrine of joint family responsibility.

eta – outcast; often employed as butchers, tanners.

Ezo – the old name for Hokkaidō and its indigenous inhabitants.

Fidalgo – Portuguese merchant adventurer.

fudai – hereditary vassal; fiefs of daimyō related to or consistently loyal to the Tokugawa.

fude – writing brush.

Fukoku kyōhei – nineteenth century slogan meaning 'a rich country and a strong army'.

fumi-e – a copper tablet with a crucifix on which Japanese were forced to tread to prove that they were not Christians.

fune – ship.

furigana – *kana* set alongside a character to show its reading.

furo – Japanese bath.

fusuma – sliding screen, partition.

gagaku – court music.

gagakuryō – court music office.

gakusho – court music school.

gakyō-rōjin – 'old man mad about painting', pen-name of Katsushika Hokusai.

geba – violence, from the German *Gewait*.

Geidai – short for Geijutsudagaku; Tokyo University of Fine Arts and Music.

geisha – female entertainer.

gekokujō – the low oppress the high.

genbun-itchi – unification of the written and spoken languages.

genrō – elder statesman.

gesaku – stories written for amusement.

gidaiyū – a tradition of *jōruri* chanting.

gigaku – ancient form of music.

gijō – senior councillor.

giri – duty, obligation.

giri-shirazu – someone who does not know his duty.

go – a district, also a game.

gohei – wands with strips of paper attached, used in Shintō shrines.

gojūsan-tsugi – fifty-three stages (of the Tokaido).

gokan – books bound together.

gokenin – house-men, vassals.

Gongen-sama – posthumous title given to Tokugawa Ieyasu showing that he had been canonized as a manifestation of the Buddha.

goningumi – groups of five households.

go-on – reading of a Chinese character according to the pronunciation thought to prevail in the province of Wu.

Gorōjū – elders.

gosanke – the three main houses of the Tokugawa: Owari (Nagoya), Kii (Wakayama) and Mito.

gosankyō – three additional Tokugawa families.

go-shūin-sen – august red-seal ships.

go-tairō – council of five elders.

gozen-sama – a husband who returns home after midnight.

gun – district comprising a number of *go*.

gunshi – governor of a *gun*.

gyōshō – a cursive style of writing.

haboku – broken ink style of painting.
haibutsu-kishaku – anti-Buddhist movement of the early Meiji period.
haikai-renga – humorous linked verses.
haiku – short poem of three lines of five, seven and five syllables.
Hajibe – guild of potters.
hakkō-ichiu – eight directions (i.e. the whole world) under one roof.
hakushaku – count.
hanamichi – elevated passageway from the back of a *kabuki* theatre to the stage.
hanga – wood-block print.
Haniwa – literally clay rings; clay statues in prehistoric Japan.
hanka – 'envoy' to a poem in the *Manyōshū*.
hanzei – 'half taxes' instituted by Ashikaga Takauji.
harakiri – vulgar term for ritual suicide by cutting open the belly; the correct
   term is *seppuku*.
Hasebe – potters in ancient Japan.
hatamoto – samurai with revenues of less than 10,000 *koku*.
hatsuboku – splashed ink style of painting.
hattō – preaching hall.
heimin – commoners.
hentaigana – cursive-style *kana* syllabary.
hichiriki – a kind of oboe.
hikite – a handle or puller on a sliding screen.
himeko – princess.
hinin – non-person, outcast.
hinoki – a kind of Japanese cypress tree.
hiragana – cursive *kana* syllabary.
hira-sansui – literally 'flat mountain water'; a dry garden.
hōjō – residential quarters of a Buddhist temple.
hokku – first part of a linked verse (*renga*).
honbyakushō – leading farmers.
hondō – main hall of a temple.
honji-suijaku – the manifestation of the prime noumenon, syncretism.
honke – main family.
Hō-ō – a retired Emperor who had taken the tonsure, also used for the Pope.
hototogisu – a Japanese cuckoo.
hyakushō – literally 'man with a hundred names'; a farmer.
hyōjōsho – a council of elders in Tokugawa times.
hyōrōmai – commissariat tax in the Kamakura period.
hyōshi – beat, rhythm.
ichiboku-zukuri – statue carved from a single piece of wood.
ie – house, household, family.
ikebana – flower arrangement.
ikki – riot, uprising.
ikkō-ikki – armed league.
Imbe/Imibe – guild of abstainers.
in – retired Emperor.
inga – cause and effect.
inkyō – to go into retirement.

insei – government by a retired Emperor.

inrō – small lacquer medicine box.

jiba – sacred place.

jiban – electoral base, supporters' groups.

jidaimono – period or historical *kabuki* play.

jieitai – self-defence forces.

jiki – porcelain.

jin – benevolence.

jingikan – council of religious practices in ancient Japan.

jinja – Shintō shrine.

jinrikisha – rickshaw, man–powered vehicle.

jiriki – one's own strength or exertions.

ji-samurai – samurai holders of small estates.

jisha-bugyō – commissioner for shrines and monasteries.

jitō – steward.

Jiyū-minshūtō – Liberal Democratic Party.

Jiyūtō – Liberal Party.

jōdan-no-ma – part of a room on a higher level.

Jōdo – 'Pure Land' Buddhism.

jōka-machi – castle town.

Jōmon – stone age; pots with a rope pattern of the Jōmon era.

jorō – prostitute.

jōruri – dramatic text and method of chanting used in Japanese classical puppet drama.

jōyō-kanji – list of 1,945 characters in common use.

jūichimen – eleven faces or heads.

junshi – suicide by a retainer following the death of his lord.

jūshin – senior statesmen, former Prime Ministers.

jūtai – traffic jam.

kabane – title in ancient Japan.

kabuki – classical Japanese theatre.

kabuki-mono – eccentrics.

kabunakama – monopolostic trade associations.

kageyushi – audit officers.

kago – palanquin.

kagura – dance accompanied by singing.

kagura-bue – a type of flute.

kagura-uta – songs performed at Shintō ceremonies.

kaidan – Buddhist ordination platform.

kaijō-jieitai – maritime self-defence force.

Kaishintō – Progressive or Reform Party.

kaiyūshiki – stroll-type (garden).

kaji – grace of the Buddha.

kakekotoba – pivot word in a poem.

kakemono – hanging scroll.

Kakiemon – family of Arita potters.

kakko – a type of drum.

kakun – family precepts.

kama – a broad knife.

Kamakura-bori – carved lacquer wares made in Kamakura.

kami – god, spirit.

kamidana – god-shelf, small Shintō shrine in a house.

kamikaze – wind of the gods, the wind which dispersed the Mongol invading forces; name given to Japanese suicide pilots in the Second World War.

kami-no-ku – first three lines of a linked verse.

kana – Japanese syllabary.

kana-bungaku – literature written in *kana*.

kana-majiri – writing combining *kana* and Chinese characters.

kana-zōshi – stories written mainly in *kana* during the Edo period.

kanbun – classical Chinese read in a Japanese way.

kanbunchokuyaku – direct translation into *kanbun*.

kango – words of Chinese origin.

kanji – Chinese characters.

kanjō – form of Buddhist baptism.

kanjō-bugyō – financial controller.

kan-on – reading of Chinese character in line with what the Japanese thought the pronunciation was in Shensi or Kansu province when the characters were imported into Japan.

kanpaku – regent, chief adviser to the Emperor.

kanrei – shōgun's deputy.

kanrodai – monument to the founder of Tenrikyō.

kanzen-chōaku – encourage the good and punish evil.

kara-e – Chinese-style painting.

kara-mon – Chinese-style gateway.

karaoke – singing to juke-box music.

kara-ori – a form of Chinese brocade.

kara-yō – Chinese style.

kare-sansui – literally 'dry mountain water', a dry garden.

kasutera – sponge cake (from the Portuguese, orginated in Castille).

katakana – square form of *kana*.

kataki-uchi – vendetta.

katana-gari – sword hunt.

katsu – shout used by Zen monks to induce enlightenment in novices.

kazoku – nobles.

kebiishi – imperial police in Heian times.

kebiishi-chō – office of the imperial police.

kega – injury, wound, defilement.

Keidanren – Federation of Economic Organizations.

keiretsu – economic grouping.

Keizaidōyūkai – Japan Committee for Economic Development.

kekkō – superb, excellent.

kemari – a kind of football played by courtiers.

kenpeitai – military police.

kengyō – the apparent (in Shingon Buddhism).

kenin – vassals.

Kenseihontō – the True Constitutional Party.

Kenseitō – Constitutional Party.

323

kenyōgen – pivot word.

ketsumeidan – 'league of blood'.

Kibe – woodcutters in ancient Japan.

kibyōshi – yellow books.

kichō – portable screen.

kimono – Japanese costume.

kinai – the home provinces.

kirin – a fabulous animal with affinities to the giraffe.

kirishitan-yashiki – prison in Edo for persons suspected of being Christians.

kirisute-gomen – permission to kill, a privilege granted to the samurai during the Edo period whereby they were permitted to kill members of the lower orders if seriously provoked.

kirokujo – public record office.

kōan – Zen problem or illogical proposition.

koban – a gold coin.

Kōbu bijutsu gakkō – technological art school.

kobun – junior partner, child, follower.

kōbusen – coins cast in China in the Hung-wu era (1368–98).

kodō – way of the ancients.

kōdōha – imperial way faction.

kōenkai – supporters' association.

Kofun jidai – burial mound period.

kogakuha – ancient learning sect.

kōhai – junior(s).

kokkeibon – humorous book(s).

koku – a measurement of rice equivalent to about 182 litres.

kokubunji – provincial temples.

kokugaku(sha) – national learning (scholars).

kōkū-jieitai – air self-defence force.

kokujin – holder of small estate; cf. *ji-samurai*.

Kokuryūkai – Amur River Society.

kokushi – governor of a province.

kokutai – national polity or essence.

kokutai no hongi – cardinal principles of the national polity.

koma-bue – type of flute.

Kōmeitō – 'Clean Government' Party.

kondō – golden (main) hall of a Buddhist temple.

kongōkai – the 'diamond' element.

kōshaku – prince or marquis.

kōshokubon – erotic stories.

kotoba – words, prose.

kouta – popular songs.

kowaka – ballad drama.

ku-bun-den – literally 'mouth–division–rice field', a system of dividing up land.

kumaso – indigenous tribes in Kyūshū.

kumonjo – document office.

kun – Japanese pronunciation (way of reading) of Chinese characters.

kundoku – Japanese way of reading a Chinese text.

kuni – province.

kunigae – province change, i.e. swapping of fiefs among diamyō.

kuni no hakase – 'teacher of the nation', title for a scholar.

kunrei(shiki) – method of romanization following Japanese orthography.

kuri – residential quarters in a Buddhist temple.

kurōdo (-dokoro) – bureau of archivists.

kurofune – 'black ships', term used for foreign ships (Portuguese and later American ships).

Kuroshio – literally 'black tide', a warm current.

Kutani – literally 'nine valleys', name given to pottery made in Kaga province, hence *ko-kutani* is old Kutani ware.

kyaku – regulations.

kyōgen – literally 'mad words', farces accompanying Nō plays.

kyōiku kanji – 881 essential *kanji* (Chinese characters) to be learned in primary school.

kyōiku mama – literally an 'education mother', i.e. a mother who becomes totally absorbed in the education of her children.

Kyōsantō – Communist Party.

kyōsō – competition.

machi-bugyō – city magistrate, administrator.

machishū – district association in a city.

magatama – curved jewel.

mai – dancing.

maki-e – sprinkle painting, method of making lacquer.

makimono – scroll.

makoto – sincerity; attribute of poems in the Manyōshū.

makura-kotoba – literally 'pillow word', a conventional phrase attached to particular words in poetry.

mandara – from the Sanscrit *mandala*, 'a circle or assemblage of persons in a limited space, and thence a picture, round or more often quadrilangular, divided into several compartments in which are arranged a number, often very considerable, of deities'.

mandokoro – family administrative office.

Manyōgana – *kana* syllabary developed for use in writing poems in the *Manyōshū*.

mappō – latter days of the law.

matsurigoto – celebrating, worshipping, also used to mean government.

Meiji ishin – Meiji restoration.

mekiki – literally 'an effective eye', used to mean someone who has natural good taste.

men – mask.

metsuke – inspector, spy.

meyasubako – box for complaints/petitions.

michi – way.

michiyuki – literally 'going along the road', a poetic description of a journey.

mikan – a Japanese mandarin-type orange.

mingei – folk-craft.

minken – people's rights.

Mino – a type of Japanese pottery.

Minseitō – Popular Government Party.

325

Minshatō – Democratic Socialist Party.

Minshūtō – Democratic Party.

miso – paste made from fermented bean sprouts.

mitsuda-e – painting in lacquer and lead colours.

mitsukyō/mikkyō – secret doctrine.

miya – shrine, prince.

Miyatsuko – title for someone close to the ruling family in ancient Japan.

momiji – maples.

mon – crest, gateway.

Monbushō – Ministry of Education.

monogatari – tale.

mono mane – mime.

mono no aware – sense of pathos, melancholy.

Mononobe – armourers in ancient Japan.

monzenmachi – towns before the gates of temples.

muga – non-self; denial of the existence of self.

mujō(kan) – (feeling) of the impermanence of all things.

Muraji – title for a lesser grandee in ancient Japan.

Nagasaki-e – pictures of foreigners at Nagasaki.

nairan – examiner of imperial documents.

Nakatomi – Shintō priests in ancient Japan.

nakōdo – go-between.

Nanban – southern barbarian, i.e. Portuguese or Spaniards.

nanbokuchō – period of the Southern and Northern Courts.

nanga – southern paintings, school of Sung painting using soft lines.

nao – a Portuguese ship.

natsume – lacquer tea caddy.

nehan – nirvana.

nenbutsu – invocation of the Buddha.

netsuke – carved toggle.

Nihonga – Japanese-style painting.

Nihon-hōsō-kyōkai – NHK, Japanese Broadcasting Corporation.

Nihonjinron – theories about the nature of Japan and the Japanese.

Nihonkai-kaisen – battle of the Japan Sea (1905).

Nihon-musansha-geijutsu-renmei – Japan Federation of Proletarian Arts.

nijiriguchi – entrance to a tea-house requiring the person entering to bend down and humble himself.

Nikkeiren – Japan Federation of Employers' Associations.

Nikkyōso – Japan Teachers' Union.

ningenkokuhō – living national treasure.

niniroku-jiken – 26 February (1936) incident.

ninjō – human feelings.

ninjōbon – stories about human feelings.

nishijin-ori – brocade silk.

nishiki-e – literally 'brocade picture', another word for *ukiyo-e*.

Nitten – annual art exhibitions.

Nō – classical Japanese drama.

norimono – a palanquin.

Nōrin-chūkin – Agricultural Co-operatives Bank.
norito – ancient Japanese Shintō prayers.
nuihaku – fabric with an embroidered design.
nuregoto – tear-jerker passages in a *kabuki* play.
ōban – large or standard-size print about 38 x 25 cm. (15 x 10 inches).
obi – sash for kimono.
o-ie-sōdō – succession quarrels.
Okurashō – Treasury.
ometsuke – chief inspector/spy.
Omi – title of a grandee in ancient Japan.
omiai – arranged marriage.
on – obligation.
onando-buppō – 'back-room Buddhism', euphemism for Christianity.
onnagata – a male actor who specializes in female roles.
on-shirazu – someone who does not recognize his obligations.
onyōdō – cult of divination.
onyōryō – bureau of divination.
opperhoofd – head of the Dutch settlement at Deshima.
Oribe – a type of Japanese pottery.
oyabun – boss.
o-yoroi – form of grand body armour.
pachinko – pin-ball games(s).
raku-yaki – earthenware made in Kyoto; the character *raku* means enjoyment.
ran – uprising, rebellion.
rangaku – Dutch studies (learning).
ranma – frieze above a sliding screen.
rekishi-monogatari – historical story.
renga – linked verses.
rikka – standing flowers (*tatebana*).
rikujō-jieitai – ground self-defence forces.
ringi – the process of obtaining sanction for a project by circulating a draft to those in positions of responsibility.
Risshō-kōseikai – modern Buddhist sect.
ritsu – penal code, a heptatonic mode.
ritsuryō – system of government based on Chinese models.
rōjū – elders.
rokkasen – the six poetic sages.
Rokumeikan – literally the Deer Cry Pavilion, a meeting place for social events involving foreigners and Japanese in the Meiji period.
romaji – Japanese written in Roman letters.
rōnin – literally 'wave men', masterless samurai.
ryō – a civil and administrative code, a heptatonic mode, a coin.
ryōbu-shintō – dual Shintō (syncretized with Buddhism).
sabi – literally rust, but used to mean elegant and restrained.
sadaijin – 'minister of the left'.
saiin – western temple.
Sakabe – sake brewers in ancient Japan.
sake – rice wine.

samisen – three-stringed musical instrument like a guitar.

sangaku – Chinese term for variety acts.

sangi – junior councillor.

sankin-kōtai – alternate attendance system instituted by Tokugawa Iemitsu, under which the daimyō were required to spend alternate periods in residence in Edo and their fiefs and to leave their wives and children in Edo as hostages while they were in their fiefs.

san-no tsuzumi – a side drum.

saru – monkey.

sarugaku – probably derived from *sangaku*, used to mean the Nō theatre.

Satsuma-yaki – Satsuma pottery.

sedōka – six line poem of 5, 7, 7, 5, 7 and 7 syllables found in the *Manyōshū*.

Seii-tai-shōgun – literally barbarian-quelling great general, usually shortened to shōgun.

seiji – celadon, also with different characters means government.

seikanron – argument advocating the conquest of Korea.

Seinan war – south-west war or Satsuma rebellion of 1877.

seiryōden – Emperor's living quarters in the imperial palace.

Seiyūkai – short for Rikken Seiyūkai, friends of the Constitutional Government Party.

Sekai-kyūseikyō – World Salvation teaching, modern faith-healing sect.

Sekigunha – Red Army Faction.

sekisho – barrier.

sekki – stoneware.

senbutsu – Buddhist images stamped in relief on brick tiles.

sengoku – the country at war.

senju – thousand hands.

senpai – senior(s).

senryū – a comic *haiku*.

seppuku – ritual suicide by cutting open the belly.

sesshō – regent.

setomono – pottery, Seto ware.

sewamono – contemporary plays in *kabuki*.

Shakaitō – Socialist Party.

shakkei – borrowed view.

shakuhachi – a kind of flute.

sharebon – punning or witty books.

shi – poems, modern poems.

shibui – astringent, restrained.

shiki – regulations.

shikimoku – a set of rules.

shikken – regent for a shōgun in the Kamakura period.

shimo-no-ku – second part of a linked verse (*renga*).

Shimpōtō – Progressive Party.

shin/shinshō – characters written in an accurate or angular form.

shinbutsu-bunri – separation of Shintō shrines from Buddhist temples.

shinbutsu-konkō – syncretism between Shintō and Buddhism.

shinbuyō – new dance.

shinden – master's quarter or main hall.

shinden-no-ma – main room.

shinden-zukuri – palace construction in Heian times.

shinjinrui – new generation.

shinjū – double suicide of lovers.

shinkansen – new broad-gauge railway.

shinkoku – country of the gods.

Shino – a type of Japanese pottery.

shi-nō-kō-shō – samurai, farmers, artisans, merchants: division of society into four classes in the Edo period.

shintai – literally 'god body', the symbol of the god.

shintai – real truth.

shintaishi – new forms of poetry.

Shintō – way of the gods.

shippō – *cloisonné*.

shiro – castle.

shishaku – viscount.

shishinden – ceremonial pavilion in the Emperor's palace.

shisōhan – thought crimes.

shite – lead part in a Nō play.

shizen – nature.

shizen-jūtai – natural (regular) traffic jam.

shizoku – gentry.

shōben-kubō – the pissing prince, Tokugawa Ieshige.

shōchū – distilled spirits made from sweet potatoes or cereals.

shōen – manors, estates.

Shōheikō – Confucian academy in Edo.

shōin-zukuri – Muromachi style of architecture.

shōka – living flowers, *ikebana*.

Shōka-sonjuku – school in Hagi in Chōshū established by Yoshida Shōin.

shōko – kind of kettle drum.

shōkōkaigisho – Chamber of Commerce and Industry.

shōnagon – junior counsellor.

shōnin – holy man, Buddhist saint.

shosagoto – kabuki dance play.

shoshidai – commissioner appointed to keep order in the capital of Kyoto.

Shōwa-kenkyūkai – Showa research society.

shoyu – soya sauce.

shūgenya – monks who lead an ascetic life.

shugo – constables.

shūji – writing of Chinese characters.

shunga – erotic pictures.

shūshin – ethics.

shusu – satin.

soba – buckwheat.

soba-yōnin – chamberlain to the shōgun.

Sōgakai – creative painting group.

sōgana – cursive *kana*.

sōgō-shōsha – Japanese trading company.

sōhyō – grouping of public-sector (left-wing) unions.

sokudo – speed.

sōmon – main gate.

Sonnō-jōi – respect the Emperor, expel the barbarian.

sōrō/sōrōbun – prose style used in the Nō.

sōshi – political bully boys.

sōshō – 'grass' or cursive style of writing.

sotoba – stupa.

sotsu – retainers.

sō-tsuibushi – constable.

sue ware – type of early Japanese pottery.

Suebe – makers of Sue pottery in ancient Japan.

suiboku – water and black ink painting.

sukiyaki – meat cooked with vegetables in a soya-bean sauce with sugar.

sukuse – destiny or fate.

sumi-e – painting with black ink.

sūmitsuin – privy council.

sumo – Japanese-style wrestling.

suihaku – fabric with a gold-leaf pattern.

surimono – prints for specific occasions.

sushi – raw fish on rice.

suto – strike.

suzuri-bako – ink-stone box.

tahōtō – pagoda of the treasures, Shingon sect pagoda.

taiko – a kind of kettle drum.

taikō – title of a retired regent, used by Toyotomi Hideyoshi.

tairō – elders, senior counsellor.

Taisei-yokusankai – Imperial Rule Assistance Association.

taizōkai – the womb in Shingon, emphasizing the element of living, growth and change.

taketakakiyo – lofty, elevated tone.

tan – area measurement, 993 square metres.

Tanabe – rice-field workers in ancient Japan.

tandai – shōgun's deputy in Kyoto during the Kamakura period.

Tanegashima – island off southern Kyūshū on which the Portuguese first made landfall in Japan; as they brought the first guns to Japan the term *tanegashima* was for a time used to mean a gun.

tanka – short poem of 5, 7, 5, 7 and 7 syllables, also called a *waka*.

tanki-daigaku – short-period university, a kind of polytechnic.

tanshin-funin – taking up an appointment unaccompanied by spouse.

tariki – other power, a Buddhist term.

tatami – Japanese straw mat.

tate – a shield.

tatebana – standing flowers (in the art of flower arrangement).

tayū – high-class courtesan.

Teiseitō – Imperial Government Party.

tempura – Japanese dish in which fish and vegetables are fried in batter.

tenaraisho − writing schools of the Edo period.

tendoku − skipping, i.e. reading sutras by reading out only a few phrases at the beginning, in the middle and at the end.

tengu − demon with a long nose.

tenjikuyō − Hindu style.

Tennō − Emperor.

Tenryūji-bune − ship sent to trade with China by Ashikaga Takauji at the prompting of the priest Musō Kokushi.

tenshūkaku − keep of a castle.

terakoya − village school(s) during the Edo period.

tōcha − tea contest.

Tōdai − Tokyo Daigaku, i.e. Tokyo University.

Tōgu-gosho − Crown Prince's palace.

tokkō/tokubetsu-kōtō-keisatsu−special higher police (for investigating thought crimes).

tōhōkai − a right-wing group during the Second World War.

to-in − T'ang dynasty pronunciations of Chinese characters.

Tō-in − eastern temple.

tōki − glazed earthenware.

toko-no-ma − alcove in a Japanese room.

tokusei − act of grace wiping out debts.

tomo − occupational group in ancient Japan.

tonarigumi − group of neighbours in wartime.

tonya/toiya − wholesaler.

torii − gateway before a Shintō shrine.

tōseiha − control group.

tōyō-kanji − the 1850 Chinese characters in most general use.

tozama daimyō − outer lords, i.e. daimyō not owing traditional loyalty to the Tokugawa.

tsuba − sword guard.

tsuchi-ikki − peasant uprising.

tsumi − 'sin', shame, defilement.

uchigeba − violent struggle inside an organization.

uchi-kowashi − rice riots.

udaijin − 'minister of the right'.

uji − 'clan'.

uji-gami/uji-kami − tutelary deity of a 'clan'.

uji-no-kami − chieftain, chief priest of a 'clan'.

ukiyo-e − pictures of the 'floating world', a generic name for Japanese wood-block prints.

ukiyo-zōshi − stories about the 'floating world'.

ukon − honary rank in the imperial bodyguard.

Urabe − guild of diviners in ancient Japan.

urushi-e − paintings to which black lacquer and colour had been added.

usucha − thin powdered tea.

uta-awase − poetry competition.

utai − verse in the texts of Nō plays.

utaibon − texts of Nō plays.

uta-monogatari − stories built round poems.

wa – harmony.

waka – Japanese poem, also called *tanka*, consisting of 5, 7, 5, 7 and 7 syllables.

wakadoshiyori – junior elders.

wakashū-kabuki – young men's *kabuki*.

wakō – Japanese pirates.

wari-hagi – split-and-fit technique of sculpture.

watakushi-shōsetsu – 'I novels', i.e. novels written in the first person.

wayō – Japanese style.

yagura – turret on a castle.

yakitori – grilled chicken.

yakko/yatsuko – slaves.

yakuza – gangster.

yamabushi – mountain priest.

yamakujira – literally mountain whale, euphemism for a wild boar.

yamato-e – Japanese style of painting.

yamato kotoba – words of native Japanese origin.

yang (yō) – positive or male principle.

yarō-kabuki – men's *kabuki*.

Yayoi – the Bronze Age in Japan.

yin (in) – negative or female principle.

yō – see *yang*.

yobai – literally night crawl.

yōen – ideal of ethereal beauty.

yōga – western-style painting.

yojōhan – four and a half mats in size (of a room in a tea-house).

yoki hito – the 'good' people, i.e. the aristocrats in Heian times.

Yokohama-e – prints of foreigners in the treaty ports especially Yokohama in the nineteenth century.

yomihon – 'reading books', a type of fiction in the Edo period.

yosegi – method of sculpture in which blocks or panels were put together and glued.

Yoshiwara – pleasure quarter in Edo/Tokyo, hence pleasure quarters.

yu – hot water, bath.

yūgen – mystery and depth.

yūjo – play-girl, courtesan.

yūjo-kabuki – pleasure-women's *kabuki*.

Yumedono – Hall of Dreams, famous building at the Hōryūji near Nara.

yūshō-reppai – the superior wins and the inferior loses, i.e. the survival of the fittest.

yuzen – crêpe.

yuzonsha – survivors' society.

yūzū – circulating (*nenbutsu*).

za – literally a seat, used to mean a guild.

zaibatsu – financial/industrial grouping.

zazen – Zen meditation.

Zengakuren – association of students' organizations.

zenpōkōen – square front, round back: term used to describe keyhole-type tombs.

zokutai – common truth, morality.

zuihitsu – jottings.

zusa – follower, attendant to a samurai.

zushi – portable shrine.

Suggestions for Further Reading

General Reference Works

Biographical Dictionary of Japanese Art, Tokyo Kodansha, 1981.
Biographical Dictionary of Japanese History, Tokyo Kodansha, 1978.
Biographical Dictionary of Japanese Literature, Tokyo Kodansha, 1976.
Chronology of Japan, edited by Toshiya Torao and Delmer M. Brown, Tokyo, Hitoshi Haga, 1987.
A Cultural Atlas of Japan, by Martin Colcutt, Marius Jansen and Isao Kumakura, Oxford, Phaidon, 1988.
Dictionary, History and Geography of Japan, compiled by E. Papinot, Tokyo and Yokohama, Kelly & Walsh, 1909.
A Dictionary of Japanese History, compiled by Joseph M. Goerdeter, New York and Tokyo, Weatherhill, 1968.
Encyclopedia of Japan, 9 volumes including index, Tokyo, Kodansha, 1983.
An Historical Grammar of Japanese, by George Sansom, Oxford, Clarendon Press, 1928.

General Histories

Beasley, W. G., *The Modern History of Japan*, London, Weidenfeld & Nicolson, 1963.
Hall, John Whitney, *Japan from Prehistory to Modern Times*, Rutland, Vt, and Tokyo, Tuttle, 1971.
Mason, R. H. P. and Caiger, J. G., *A History of Japan*, Rutland, Vt, and Tokyo, Tuttle, 1973.
Morris, Ivan, *The Nobility of Failure: Tragic Heroes in the History of Japan*, New York, Holt, Rinehart & Winston, 1975.
Murdoch, James, *A History of Japan*, 3 volumes (to 1542; 1542–1651; 1652–1868), London, Kegan Paul, 1925.
Reischauer, Edward, *Japan, the Story of a Nation*, 3rd edn, Rutland, Vt, and Tokyo, Tuttle, edn 1987.
Reischauer, Edwin, 0. and Craig, Albert, M., *Japan, Tradition and Transformation*, Rutland, Vt, and Tokyo, 1987.
Sansom, George B., *Japan: A Short Cultural History*, revised edn, London, Cresset Press, 1946.
Sansom, George B., *The Western World and Japan*, London, Cresset Press, 1950.
Sansom, George B., *A History of Japan*, 3 volumes (to 1334; 1334–1625; 1625–1867), London, Cresset Press, 1958, 1961, 1964.
Storry, Richard, *A History of Modern Japan*, Harmandsworth, Penguin, 1960.
Varley, H. Paul, *Japanese Culture*, Rutland, Vt, and Tokyo, Tuttle, 1986.
The Cambridge History of Japan in 6 volumes was being published by the Cam-

bridge University Press from May 1989 and should provide a comprehensive picture of Japanese history from the earliest times to the twentieth century. Volume 6, *The Twentieth Century*, appeared in May 1989. Volume 5, *The Nineteenth Century*, was published in October 1989.

Religion

Anesaki, Masaharu, *History of Japanese Religion*, London, Kegan Paul, 1930.
Aston, W. G., *Shintō: The Way of the Gods*, London, New York and Bombay, Longmans Green, 1905.
Blacker, Carmen, *The Catalpa Bow: A Study of Shamanistic Practices in Japan*, London, Allen & Unwin, 1975.
Eliot, Sir Charles, *Japanese Buddhism*, London, Edward Arnold, 1935.
Herbert, Jean, *Shintō: The Fountainhead of Japan*, London, Allen & Unwin, 1967.
Holtom, D. C., *The National Faith of the Japanese: A Study in Modern Shintō*, London, Kegan Paul, 1938.
Nukariya, Kaiten, *The Religion of the Samurai*, London, Luzac, 1973.
Ryūsaku Tsunoda, de Bary, Wm Theoore and Keene, Donald, *Sources of Japanese Tradition*, New York, Columbia University Press, 1960.
Saunders, E. Dale, *Buddhism in Japan with an Outline of its Origins in India*, Rutland, Vt, Tuttle, 1980.
Suzuki, Daisetsu, *An Introduction to Zen Buddhism*, London, New York, Melbourne, Sydney and Cape Town, 1948.
Tenrikyō Overseas Missions, *An Introduction to Tenrikyō, its History and Teachings*, Tenri City, Japan, 1978.
Wheeler, Post, *The Sacred Scriptures of the Japanese*, London, Allen & Unwin, 1952.

General Literature

Aston, W. G., *Japanese Literature*, London, Heinemann, 1909.
Blyth, R. H., *Senryū: Japanese Satirical Verses Translated and Explained*, Tokyo, Hokuseido Press, 1949.
Brower, R. H. and Miner E., *Japanese Court Poetry*, London, Cresset Press, 1961.
Kato Shūichi, *A History of Japanese Literature*, 3 volumes, London, Macmillan and Paul Norbury: Vol. 1, *The First Thousand Years*, 1979; Vol. 2, *The Years of Isolation*, 1983; Vol. 3, *The Modern Years*, 1983.
Keene, Donald, *Anthology of Japanese Literature. From the Earliest Era to the Nineteenth Century*, London, Allen & Unwin, 1956.
Keene, Donald, *Modern Japanese Literature from 1868 to the Present Day*, Rutland, Vt, and Tokyo, Tuttle, 1963.
Keene, Donald, *Landscapes and Portraits: Appreciations of Japanese Culture*, London, Secker & Warburg, 1972.
Keene, Donald, *World Within Walls: Japanese Literature of the Pre-Modern Era, 1600–1867*, New York, Grove Press, 1978.
Keene, Donald, *Some Japanese Portraits*, Tokyo, Kodansha, 1983.

Keene, Donald, *Dawn to the West: Japanese Literture in the Modern Era*, New York, Henry Holt, Owl Book Edition, 1987.

Miyamori Asataro, *An Anthology of Haiku, Ancient and Modern*, Tokyo, Maruzen, 1932.

Miyamori Asataro, *Masterpieces of Japanese Poetry, Ancient and Modern*, 2 volumes, Tokyo, Maruzen, 1936.

Miner, Earl, Hiroko Odagiri and Morrell, Robert E., *The Princeton Companion to Japanese Literature*, Princeton University Press, 1985.

A Reader's Guide to Japanese Literature from the Eighth Century to the Present, Tokyo, Kodansha, 1988.

Translations as listed in the text and footnotes.

Drama and Music

Adachi, Barbara C., *Backstage at Bunraku*, New York and Tokyo, Weatherhill, 1985.

Araki, James T., *The Ballad-Drama of Medieval Japan*, Rutland, Vt, and Tokyo, Tuttle, 1978.

Bowers, Faubion, *Japanese Theatre*, New York, Hermitage House, 1952.

Dunn, Charles J. and Torigoe Bunzo, *The Actors' Analects*, University of Tokyo, 1969.

Halford, Aubrey and Halford, Giovanna, *The Kabuki Handbook*, Rutland, Vt, and Tokyo, Tuttle, 1956.

Harich-Schneider, Eta Music, *A History of Japanese Music*, London, Oxford University Press, 1973.

Hironaga, Shuzaburo, *The Bunraku Handbook*, Tokyo, Maison des Arts, 1976.

Jones, Stanleigh H., *Sugawara and the Secrets of Calligraphy by Takeda Izumo*, New York, Columbia University Press, 1985.

Keene, Donald, *Major Plays of Chikamatsu*, New York and London, Columbia University Press, 1961.

Kenny, Don, *A Guide to Kyōgen*, Tokyo and Kyoto, Hinoki Shōten, 1968.

Malon, William T., *Japanese Music and Musical Instruments*, Rutland, Vt, Tokyo, Tuttle, 1959.

Miyamori Asataro, *Masterpieces of Chikamatsu*, London, Kegan Paul, 1926.

O'Neill, P. G., *Early Nō Drama*, London, Lund Humphries, 1958.

O'Neill, P. G., *A Guide to Nō*, Tokyo and Kyoto, Hinoki Shōten, 1954.

The Nōh Drama: Ten Plays from the Japanese, translated by the Special Noh Committee, Rutland, Vt, and Tokyo, Tuttle, 1985.

Piggott, [Sir] Francis T., *The Music and Musical Instruments of Japan*, London, Batsford, 1893.

Scott, A. C., *The Puppet Theatre of Japan*, Rutland, Vt, and Tokyo, Tuttle, 1984.

Waley, Arthur, *The Nō Plays of Japan*, London, Allen & Unwin, 1921.

The Arts

Akiyama, Terukazu, *Japanese Painting*, London, Skira and Macmillan, 1977.
Bushell, Raymond, *Netsuke Familiar and Unfamiliar*, New York and Tokyo, Weatherhill, 1975.
Feddersen, Martin, *Japanese Decorative Art: A Handbook for Collectors*, London, Faber, 1962.
Fennollosa, Ernest, F., *Epochs of Chinese and Japanese Art*, London, Heinemann, 1912.
Frederic, Louis, *Japan Art and Civilization*, London, Thames & Hudson, 1971.
Great Japan Exhibition, Art of the Edo Period, Royal Academy of Arts, London, 1981–2.
Grilli, Elise, *The Art of the Japanese Screen*, New York and Tokyo, Weatherhill, 1970.
Heibonsha Survey of Japanese Art (series), New York and Tokyo, Weatherhill, .
Hickman, B. (ed), *Japanese Crafts, Materials and their Applications*, London, East West Publications, 1978.
Hiller, J., *Japanese Masters of the Colour Print*, Oxford, Phaidon, 1954.
Hiller, J., *Hokusai, Paintings, Drawings and Woodcuts*, 3rd edn, Oxford, Phaidon, 1985.
Jenyns, Soame, *Japanese Pottery*, London, Faber, 1971.
Kidder, J. Edward Jnr, *Japanese Temples, Sculptures, Paintings, Gardens and Architecture*, Tokyo, Bijutsu Shuppansha, 1964.
Kidder, J. Edward, *The Birth of Japanese Art*, London, Allen & Unwin, 1965.
Kuck, Loraine, *The World of Japanese Gardens: From Chinese Origins to Modern Landscape Art*, New York and Tokyo, Weatherhill, 1982.
Lane, Richard, *Images from the Floating World; the Japanese Print*, New Jersey, Chartwell Books, 1978.
Library of Japanese Arts (series), Tokyo, Kodansha, 1977.
Masterpieces of the Ukiyo-e, 11 volumes by Muneshige Narazaki and others, Tokyo, Kodansha, 1968–70.
Michener, James, *The Floating World: The Story of Japanese Colour Prints*, London, Secker & Warburg, 1954.
Mody, N. H. N., *A Collection of Nagasaki Colour Prints and Paintings*, Rutland, Vt, and Tokyo, Tuttle, 1969.
Munsterberg, Hugo, *The Arts of Japan, An Illustrated History*, Rutland, Vt, and Tokyo, Tuttle, 1963.
Munsterberg, Hugo, *The Ceramic Art of Japan*, Rutland, Vt, and Tokyo, Tuttle, 1964.
Noma, Seiroku, *The Arts of Japan*, 2 volumes, 2nd edition, Tokyo, Kodansha, 1968.
Pageant of Japanese Art, 6 volumes, Tokyo, Toto Bunka, 1952–3.
Paine, R. T. and Soper, A., *The Art and Architecture of Japan*, Middlesex, Penguin, 1960.
Sanders, Herbert H., *The World of Japanese Ceramics*, Tokyo, Kodansha, 1967.
Smith, Bradley, *Japan: A History in Art*, New York and Tokyo, Weatherhill, 1970.

Smith, Lawrence, *The Japanese Print since 1900: Old Dreams and New Visions*, London, British Museum, 1981.
Smith, Lawrence, *Contemporary Japanese Prints: Symbols of a Society in Transition*, London, British Museum, 1965.
Statler, Oliver, *Modern Japanese Prints*, Rutland, Vt, and Tokyo, Tuttle, 1960.
Swann, Peter C., *An Introduction to the Arts of Japan*, Oxford, Bruno Cassirer, 1958.
Swann, Peter C., *The Art of Japan from the Jōmon to the Tokugawa Period*, New York, Crown, 1966.
Tsuda Noritake, *Handbook of Japanese Art*, Tokyo, Sanseido, 1935.
Warner, Langdon, *The Art of the Japanese Sculptor*, New York, Japan Society, 1936.
Watson, William, *Sculpture of Japan from the Fifth to the Fifteenth Century*, London, The Studio, 1959.
Wichmann, Siegfried, *Japonisme*, London, Thames & Hudson, 1981.
Yashiro, Yukio, *Art Treasures of Japan*, 2 volumes, Tokyo, Kokusai Bunka Shinkokai, 1960.

Early History

Elisseef, Vadime, *The Ancient Civilization of Japan*, London, Barris & Jenkins, 1974.
Frederic, Louis, *Daily Life in Japan at the Time of the Samurai, 1185–1603*, Rutland, Vt, Tuttle, 1984.
Hempel, Rose, *The Heian Civilization of Japan*, Oxford, Phaidon, 1983.
Kidder, J. E. Jnr, *Japan before Buddhism*, London, Thames & Hudson, 1963.
Kidder, J. E. Jnr, *Early Buddhist Japan*, London, Thames & Hudson, 1972.
Kidder, J. E. Jnr, *Ancient Japan*, Oxford, Elsevier/Phaidon, 1977.
Morris, Ivan, *The World of the Shining Prince*, London, Oxford University Press, 1964.

Pre-Modern History

Boxer, Charles, *Jan Compagnie in Japan*, The Hague, Martinus Nijhoff, 1950.
Boxer, Charles, *The Christian Century in Japan*, Cambridge University Press, 1951.
Boxer, Charles, *The Great Ship from Amacon: Annals of Macao and the Old Japan Trade, 1555–1640*, Lisbon, Centro de Estudos Historicos Ultramarinos, 1963.
Cooper, Martin (ed.), *They Came to Japan, 1543–1640*, Berkeley, University of California Press, 1965.
Cooper, Martin (ed.), *Southern Barbarians: The First Europeans in Japan*, Tokyo, Kodansha, 1971.
Cooper, Martin, *Rodrigues the Interpreter*, New York and Tokyo, Weatherhill, 1974.
Dunn, C. J., *Everyday Life in Traditional Japan*, London, Batsford, 1969.
Goodman, Grant K., *The Dutch Experience*, London, Athlone Press, 1986.
Keene, Donald, *The Japanese Discovery of Europe: Honda Toshiaki and Other*

Discoveries, London, Routledge & Kegan Paul, 1952.

Kirkwood, Kenneth F., *Renaissance in Japan; A Cultural Survey of the Seventeenth Century*, Rutland, Vt, and Tokyo, Tuttle, 1970.

Paske-Smith, M., *Western Barbarians in Japan and Formosa in Tokugawa Days, 1603–1868*, New York, Paragon, 1968.

Varley, H. Paul with Ivan and Nobuko Morris, *Samurai*, New York, Dell, 1972.

Modern History and Society

Abbeglen, James and Stalk, George Jnr, *Kaisha: The Japanese Corporation*, New York, Basic Books, 1985.

Akamatsu, Paul, *Meiji 1868; Revolution and Counter-Revolution in Japan*, London, Allen & Unwin, 1972.

Alcock, Rutherford, *The Capital of the Tycoon: Narrative of a Three Years Residence in Japan*, 2 volumes, London, Longman Green, 1863.

Allen, G. C., *A Short Economic History of Modern Japan, 1867–1937*, London, Allen & Unwin, 1946.

Allen, G. C., *Japan's Economic Expansion*, London, Oxford University Press, 1965.

Barr, Pat, *The Coming of the Barbarians: A Story of Western Settlement in Japan, 1853–1870*, London, Macmillan, 1967.

Barr, Pat, *The Deer Cry Pavilion*, London, Macmillan, 1968.

Beasley, W. G., *Great Britain and the Opening of Japan, 1834–1858*, London, Luzac, 1951.

Beasley, W. G., *The Meiji Restoration*, Stanford University Press, 1972.

Beasley, W. G., *Japanese Imperialism, 1894–1945*, Oxford, Clarendon Press, 1987.

Benedict, Ruth, *The Chrysanthemum and the Sword: Patterns of Japanese Culture*, London, Secker & Warburg, 1947.

Bingman, Charles F., *Japanese Government, Leadership and Management*, London, Macmillan, 1989.

Blacker, Carmen, *The Japanese Enlightenment: A Study of the Writings of Fukuzawa Yukichi*, Cambridge University Press, 1964.

Buckley, Roger, *Occupation Diplomacy: Britain, the United States and Japan, 1945–1952*, Cambridge University Press, 1982.

Buruma, Ian, *A Japanese Mirror: Heroes and Villains of Japanese Culture*, Harmandsworth, Penguin, 1988.

Byas, Hugh, *Government by Assassination*, London, Allen & Unwin, 1943.

Chamberlain, Basil Hall, *Things Japanese*, 1st edn, Kegan Paul, Trench Trübner & Co Ltd, London, 1890.

Christopher, Robert C., *The Japanese Mind: The Goliath Explained*, New York, Linda Press/Simon & Shuster, 1983.

Cortazzi, Hugh, *Mitford's Japan*, London, Athlone Press, 1985.

Cortazzi, Hugh, *Victorians in Japan, in and around the Treaty Ports*, London, Athlone Press, 1987.

Craig, William, *The Fall of Japan*, London, History Book Club, 1968.

Curtis, Gerald L., *The Japanese Way of Politics*, New York, Columbia University Press, 1988.

Doi, Takeo, *The Anatomy of Dependence*, Tokyo, Kodansha, 1981.

Dore, R. P., *Shinohata; A Portrai of a Japanese Village*, London, Allen Lane, 1978.

Dore, R. P., *Education in Tokugawa Japan*, London, Athlone Press, 1981.

Dore, R. P., *Land Reform in Japan*, London, Athlone Press, 1984.

Dore, R. P., *Flexible Rigidities: Industrial Policy and Structural Adjustment in the Japanese Economy, 1970–80*, London, Athlone Press, 1986.

Dore, R. P., *Taking Japan Seriously: A Confucian Perspective on Leading Economic Issues*, London, Athlone Press, 1987.

Fox, Grace, *Britain and Japan, 1858–1883*, Oxford, Clarendon Press, 1969.

Gow, Ian, *Okinawa: Gateway to Japan*, London, Grub Street, 1986.

Grew, Joseph, *Ten Years in Japan*, London, Hammond & Co., 1944.

Harries, Meirion and Harries, Susie, *Sheathing the Sword: The Demilitarization of Japan*, London, Hamish Hamilton, 1987.

Hendry, Joy, *Understanding Japanese Society*, London, New York and Sidney, Croom Helm, 1987.

Howarth, Stephen, *Morning Glory: A History of the Imperial Japanese Navy*, London, Hamish Hamilton, 1983.

Iriye, Akira, *The Origins of the Second World War in Asia and the Pacific*, London and New York, Longman, 1987.

Jansen, Marius B., Rozman, Gilbert (eds), *Japan in Transition from Tokugawa to Meiji*, Princeton University Press, 1986.

Johnson, Chalmers, *MITI and the Japanese Miracle: The Growth of Industrial Policy, 1925–1975*, Stanford University Press, 1982.

Jones, F. C., *Japan's New Order in Asia, 1937–45*, London, Oxford University Press, 1954.

Jones, H. J., *Live Machines, Hired Foreigners and Meiji Japan*, University of British Columbia, 1980.

Lehmann, Jean-Pierre, *The Image of Japan from Feudal Isolation to World Power, 1850–1905*, London, Allen & Unwin, 1978.

Lewe van Aduard, Baron E. J., *Japan from Surrender to Peace*, The Hague, Martinus Nijhoff, 1953.

Maruyama Masao, *Thought and Behaviour in Modern Japanese Politics*, London, Oxford University Press, 1963.

Morita, Akio, *Made in Japan: Akio Morita and Sony*, New York and Tokyo, Weatherhill, 1987.

Morris, Ivan, *Nationalism and the Right Wing in Japan: A Study of Post-War Trends*, London, Royal Institute of International Affairs, 1960.

Nakane, Chie, *Japanese Society*, Berkeley, University of California Press, 1970.

Nish, Ian, *Alliance in Decline: A Study in Anglo-Japanese Realtions, 1908–1923*, London, Athlone Press, 1972.

Nish, Ian, *The Anglo-Japanese Alliance*, London, Athlone Press, 1985.

Nish, Ian, *The Origins of the Russo-Japanese War*, London, Longman, 1985.

Norman, E. Herbert, *Japan's Emergence as a Modern State*, New York, Institute of Pacific Relations, 1946.

Okuma, Count Shigenobu, *Fifty Years of New Japan*, 2 volumes, London, Smith Elder, 1909.

Pacific War Society, *Japan's Longest Day*, Tokyo, Kodansha, 1968.

Passin, Herbert, *Japanese and the Japanese*, Tokyo, Kinseido, 1980.

Passin, Herbert, *Society and Education in Japan*, Tokyo, Kodansha, 1982.

Satow, Ernest, *A Diplomat in Japan*, London and Tokyo, Oxford University Press, reprint 1968.

Seidensticker, Edward, *This Country Japan*, Tokyo and New York, 1979.

Seidensticker, Edward, *Low City, High City: Tokyo 1867–1923*, New York, Knopf, 1983.

Shillony, Ben-Ami, *Politics and Culture in Wartime Japan*, Oxford, Clarendon Press, 1981.

Singer, Kurt, *Mirror, Sword and Jewel: The Geometry of Japanese Life*, Tokyo, Kodansha, 1951.

Statler, Oliver, *Shimoda Story*, New York, Random House, 1969.

Storry, Richard, *The Double Patriots: A Study of Japanese Nationalism*, London, Chatto & Windus, 1957.

Toland, John, *The Rising Sun: The Decline and Fall of the Japanese Empire, 1936–45*, New York, Random House, 1970.

Totman, Conrad, *The Collapse of the Tokugawa Bakufu 1862–68*, University of Hawaii, 1980.

Vogel, Ezra F., *Japan's New Middle Class*, Berkeley, University of California Press, 1971.

Vogel, Ezra F., *Japan as No. 1: Lessons for America*, Rutland, Vt, and Tokyo, Tuttle, 1979.

Vogel, Ezra F. (ed.), *Modern Japanese Organization and Decision Making*, Rutland, Vt, and Tokyo, Tuttle, 1979.

Waller, David, *The Short Victorious War: The Russo-Japanese Conflict 1904/5*, New York, Harper & Row, 1973.

Wilkinson, Endymion, *Misunderstanding: Europe vs Japan*, Tokyo, Chūōkōronsha, 1981.

Woronoff, Jan, *Japan: The Coming Social Crisis*, Tokyo, Lotus Press, 1980.

Woronoff, Jan, *Japan: The Coming Economic Crisis*, Tokyo, Lotus Press, 1981.

Woronoff, Jan, *Japan's Wasted Workers*, Tokyo, Lotus Press, 1982.

Woronoff, Jan, *Politics, the Japanese Way*, London, Macmillan, 1988.

Yoshida, Kenichi, *Japan Is a Circle*, Tenterden, Kent, Paul Norbury, 1975.

Yoshida, Shigeru, *The Yoshida Memoirs*, Cambridge, Massachusetts, Riverside Press, 1962.

Young, Alexander K., *The Sōgō Shōsa, Japan; Multinational Trading Companies*, 1982.

Young, Morgan, *Japan under Taisho Tenno, 1912–26*, London, Allen & Unwin, 1928.

Young, Morgan, *Imperial Japan, 1926–38*, London, Allen & Unwin, 1938.

Index

Abe Masahiro 176, 177
Adams, William (Anjin-san) 134
agriculture 1, 3–4, 102–3, 142–3, 223–4,
 255, 278, 282–3; yields 96, 102, 142 *see
 also* land reclamation
Ainu 2, 146, 202
Akamatsu Mitsuzuka 99
Akechi Mitsuhide 122, 123
Akutagawa Ryūnosuke 243
Alcock, Rutherford 179, 180, 181
Ama shōgun 75
Amaterasu-o'mikami 8, 9, 11
Amidism 53–4, 77, 85–6, 94
Anglo-Japanese alliance 213–15, 219
Ankokuji 106
Ansei purge 178
Arai Hakuseki 150, 152, 154
Araki Sadao 228, 229
architecture 3, 7, 26–7, 35–6, 55, 63–5, 95,
 117, 128–9, 173–4, 207, 301–2
Ariyoshi Sawako 294
armed forces (modern) 187, 188, 210–11,
 213, 222, 226, 228–30; self-defence
 forces 257, 262, 270, 272–5, 281–2, 303
armour 68, 83, 95, 117, 129, 172
Asanuma Inejiro 271, 273
Ashida Hitoshi 260
ashigaru 83, 102
Ashikaga *bakufu*: established 97;
 Nanbokuchō 97–9; shōguns 98–9; court
 100; Onin war 100; *sengoku* 100–2;
 economy and society 102–4; foreign
 relations 105–6; religion 106; culture
 107–20; fall 99, 122
Ashikaga family 74; Tadayoshi 97, 98;
 Takauji 76, 96–9, 101, 105–7, 118;
 Tomiko 100; Yoshiaki 96, 122, 132;
 Yoshiakira 98, 99; Yoshihisa 99;
 Yoshikazu 99; Yoshimasa 99, 100, 117,
 119, 126; Yoshimi 100, Yoshimitsu 98–
 100, 105, 112, 117; Yoshimochi 99, 105;
 Yoshinori 99, 105; Yoshiteru 131
assassination, 'government by' 222, 229–30
Asuka 26, 27
atomic bombings of Hiroshima and
 Nagasaki 240, 241

ayatsuri jōruri see bunraku
Azuchi (castle) 122, 132

balance of payments 224, 277, 279, 282, 283
bandits 101
banks 195–6, 197
Bashō *see* Matsuo Bashō
battle tactics 102
be (tomo) 10
Biddle, Commodore, USN 176
Boissonade de Fontarabie 192
bonsai 174, 299
Boshin war 184
Botchan, Natsume Soseki 242
Boxer rebellion 213
Britain 177, 178, 180–2, 194, 196, 211, 212–
 5, 219–20, 227, 232, 236–7, 240
bronze casting 36, 68, 95
Buddha *see* Siddhartha Gautama
Buddhism 18–24, 26, 29, 32–5, 43, 49–54,
 65, 77, 84–8, 94, 106, 122, 200–2, 289
buke-shōhattō 127
Bungei Shunjū 243, 244
bunmei kaika 187, 199
bunraku (*jōruri*) 155–7, 295–6
bureaucracy 191, 264–5
burial customs 3, 4, 5, 6–7
Burma 236, 237, 262, 263
bushi (*dō*) 81, 102, 140–1, 151, 153
Byōdōin 64, 65, 72

calligraphy (shūji) 16, 57, 66–7, 116
capital 195, 278–9 *see also* banks; investment
carpenters 35, 63, 84
ceramics 3–7, 68, 95, 103, 120, 125, 129,
 170–2, 247, 249, 301
Chang Tso-lin (Zhang Zuolin) 219
Chang-an (Sian) 29, 41, 42
Charter Oath 185, 189
Chiang Kai Shek 240
Chiba family 74
Chikamatsu Monzaemon 141, 157–8
China: early contacts 3–5, 7, 16, 24;
 language 13–16; Heian 41–3; Kamakura
 79; Muromachi 99, 103, 105;
 Momoyama 129–30, 135; Edo 147–8;

341